LEISURE: AN INTRODUCTION

Visit the *Leisure: An Introduction,* Companion Website at **www.pearsoned.co.uk/page** to find valuable **student** learning material including:

- **Extra case studies**

D1379999

PEARSON

We work with leading authors to develop the strongest
educational materials in leisure and tourism,
bringing cutting-edge thinking and best learning
practice to a global market.

Under a range of well-known imprints, including
Financial Times Prentice Hall we craft high quality
print and electronic publications which help readers to
understand and apply their content, whether studying
or at work.

To find out more about the complete range of our
publishing, please visit us on the World Wide Web at:
www.pearsoned.co.uk

Leisure: An Introduction

Stephen J. Page
London Metropolitan University

Joanne Connell
University of Stirling

Financial Times
Prentice Hall
is an imprint of

Harlow, England • London • New York • Boston • San Francisco • Toronto • Sydney • Singapore • Hong Kong
Tokyo • Seoul • Taipei • New Delhi • Cape Town • Madrid • Mexico City • Amsterdam • Munich • Paris • Milan

Pearson Education Limited
Edinburgh Gate
Harlow
Essex CM20 2JE
England

and Associated Companies throughout the world

Visit us on the World Wide Web at:
www.pearsoned.co.uk

First published 2010

© Pearson Education Limited 2010

ISBN: 978-0-273-72649-4

British Library Cataloguing-in-Publication Data
A catalogue record for this book is available from the British Library

Library of Congress Cataloging-in-Publication Data
Page, Stephen, 1963–
 Leisure: an introduction / Stephen J. Page.
  p. cm.
 ISBN 978-0-273-72649-4 (pbk.)
 1. Leisure. I. Title.
 GV14.P34 2010
 790'.0135—dc22

                                                            2009048616

ARP impression 98

Typeset in 10pt Book Antiqua by 73
Printed by Ashford Colour Press Ltd., Gosport

The Publisher's policy is to use paper manufactured from sustainable forests.

Contents

List of figures

List of tables

List of plates

Preface

This book has been developed as replacement for the former Pearson *Introduction to Leisure Studies* (Bull, Hoose and Weed 2003) as an introductory level text which examines the phenomenon of leisure, but with a wider-ranging global focus. We have deliberately avoided the use of the term 'studies' in the title because we do not wish to limit the readership or audience, since it is a wide-ranging review of leisure that will appeal to more than just the conventional leisure studies market. We have tried to provide a fresh, thought provoking, clear and reflective look at one of the most widely discussed phenomenon in the social sciences. Sometimes the phenomenon is examined very explicitly as leisure studies, but more often than not, it has become a theme explored as the setting for analyses of specific leisure-related themes in the social sciences. This transformation in the study and analysis of leisure over the last two decades has created a considerable degree of turbulence and flux within what was broadly defined and delimited as leisure studies. This was very much the subject of the main journals published around 20 years ago – *Leisure Studies*, *Leisure Sciences* and the *Journal of Leisure Research* (that dates to the 1960s) and more recent subject-specific journals such as *Managing Leisure* and the proliferation of other leisure-related journals.

These boundaries, however they were loosely defined 20 years ago, are shifting rapidly, in line with how social science has been evolving, where the domain of study is no longer the unique focus of a set of disciplines or scholars. These shifting boundaries are what make the subject so interesting. Equally, these shifting boundaries make it one of the most significant challenges in writing a book: this is because the immediate question you have to face is: where do you draw the line around the subject, to try and establish an agenda for writing an introductory book on such a broad theme as *Leisure*? This may explain why there is a comparative dearth of accessible, innovative, fresh and wide ranging texts on the market that do not adopt a specific disciplinary perspective. Most books on leisure are usually informed or require a detailed understanding of sociology, geography or economics to really understand the arguments and content. We argue that this is no longer a suitable starting point for the analysis of leisure as a subject, since there are many students who now study this as a one semester elective or optional module as part of an interdisciplinary approach to education, which does not flow into a specific disciplinary informed degree programme. This means that their educational needs (alongside the more specialist study of leisure) need to be recognised and accommodated where the origins and development of the subject is explained with no prior knowledge of the area.

This makes writing a compressed text a challenge that has a degree of *breadth* in what it covers and some degree of *depth* to fulfil the needs to the other major audience (often overlooked in academic texts) – the adopter who uses it as a text to support their teaching and student's learning. We have been fortunate that this book was subject to many different reviews from a wide range of teachers and researchers who made extremely useful and poignant comments on the proposal to help shape it so it meets the needs of the student and adopter of today and tomorrow.

This is certainly not the only book on leisure available on the market and not the shortest or longest text. But with nearly 40 years of teaching and writing experience between the authors, we feel that this is a reflective and balanced attempt to create a wide-ranging review that adopts a global perspective of leisure so that it is not introspective, parochial or inward looking. It examines the main principles and concepts in a fluent and thought provoking manner, and so deliberately avoids developing very narrow themes that take the reader down a dark tunnel. We also avoid over complicated text with theoretical jargon and literature that would frankly switch off the majority of readers. This is a major criticism which many lecturers and students make of the current books they use, and so addressing these shortcomings has been a primary objective in this case. We felt the book had to be accessible, self-contained and interconnected so that the themes flow together and provide a cohesive analysis of the broad phenomenon we call leisure. Clearly, books will never please all their readers, and if we stimulate a debate or provoke a healthy discussion on the subject among students and other readers, then we will have achieved our goal.

What we do not set out to do is to list every single leisure trend or activity there is. We intend to focus on the broad principles and concepts which any reader will need to know at an introductory level. We also add an extra level of discussion for the adopter or more advanced reader which traces the origins of the study of leisure or each major theme in the various chapters so there is a wider context to the subject. This is to draw attention to seminal studies, along with a wide range of contemporary studies and debates that now dominate the study of leisure. The subject matter of leisure always looks easy and unchallenging to the uninitiated, but anyone who teaches or researches in the area will know that leisure is not a simplistic subject to study: this is because it is a microcosm of society at large, since the trends affecting it and nature of leisure is as fluid as society – it is constantly in a state of flux and changing. For this reason, we seek to explain the principal concepts and ideas surrounding the study and analysis of leisure using diagrams and tables where they add value to the explanation, helping to simplify and exemplify the scope and nature of the issues which surround the concept.

We hope that the additional resources available on the Publisher website will also help to develop a more tailored solution to the precise nature of the course you are studying or teaching, so that additional cases are available to enrich the learning experience. Clearly in a book of this size, the number of cases has had to be limited and balanced against the need for breadth. We hope you will like reading this and that it helps you with your academic endeavours. We have enjoyed writing it, despite the challenge of trying to compress a rapidly changing and evolving subject into a concise and simple style that engages the reader without losing their attention. If you have any comments on the book, feel free to feed them back to the Publisher as we will happily consider them for subsequent editions.

Stephen J. Page
London Metropolitan University
and Joanne Connell
University of Stirling

Acknowledgements

Stephen Williams for permission to reproduce two figures from his book – *Urban Recreation*; Cengage Learning for Tables 5.5, 8.1, 9.1, 9.4 and 9.6 and Figure 1.7, 5.4 and 11.2 from *Tourism: A Modern Synthesis*; Natural England for Figure 11.8 and Taylor and Francis for Figure 4.2 from J. Pigram (1983); Pearson Education for Tables 7.2 and 7.3 from Kotler *et al.* (2005).

The authors would also like to thank Andrew Taylor for his professional treatment of the book through the commissioning stage, and help and advice. It is always a great pleasure to work with you, and of course, the Publishing Director – Matthew Smith who has supported the development of the title as a major text at Pearson. Also to Neil McLaren for preparing the tables and figures which greatly helped with the writing process.

We would also like to thank our co-authors on a number of case studies: Marjory Brewster and Alastair Durie at the University of Stirling and Michael Hall at the University of Canterbury, New Zealand. Lastly, Stephen would like to thank Paul Fidgeon at Thames Valley University who first got him interested in teaching and researching leisure, recreation and tourism all those years ago.

Publisher's acknowledgements

We are grateful to the following for permission to reproduce copyright material:

Figures

Figure 1.6 adapted from *The Geography of Tourism and Recreation: Environment, Place and Space*, 3rd ed., Routledge (Hall, C.M. and Page, S.J. 2006) figure 1.1. Copyright © Routledge, 2006; Figure 1.8 adapted from *Individual's Use of Leisure Time in EU Countries*, World Tourism Organisation (1983). Copyright © World Tourism Organisation; Figure 1.10 adapted from *Countryside for Health and Well-Being: The Physical and Mental Health Benefits of Green Exercise*, Countryside Recreation Network (Pretty, J., Griffin, M., Peacock, J., Hine, R., Sellens, M. and South, N. 2005). Copyright © Countryside Recreation

Network (CRN); Figure 3.1 adapted from *Leisure and Recreation Management*, 3rd ed., Routledge (Torkildsen, G. 1999) Table 5.1, p. 114. Copyright © Routledge, 1999; Figure 3.2 adapted from Harper, R. and Kelly, M. (2003) *Measuring social capital in the United Kingdom*, Table 1, www.statistics.gov.uk/ socialcapital, Crown Copyright material is reproduced under terms of the Click-Use Licence; Figure 4.2 adapted from *Outdoor Recreation Management* Routledge (Pigram 1983). Copyright © Routledge, 1983; Figure 4.3 adapted from "Motivations for Leisure", *Journal of Leisure Research*, 12, 45–54 (Crandall, R. 1980), copyright © National Recreation and Park Association; Figure 4.7 adapted from *The Social Psychology of Leisure and Recreation*, WM. C. Brown Publishers (Iso-Ahola, S. 1980). Copyright © Professor Seppo Iso-Ahola, Ph.D; Figure 4.8 adapted from *Recreation and Resources: Leisure Patterns and Leisure Places* Wiley Blackwell (Patmore, J.A. 1983). Copyright © Wiley-Blackwell; Figure 5.2 adapted from *The Leisure Industries*, Palgrave Macmillan (Roberts, K. 2004). Reproduced by permission of Palgrave Macmillan; Figure 5.5 adapted from *Outdoor Recreation Management* (Pigram 1983). Copyright © Routledge, 1983; Figure 5.8 adapted from "The dimensions of the home as a leisure space: Key attributes and issues after no place like home", *Leisure Studies*, Vol 1(3), pp. 247–62 (Glyptis, S. and Chambers, D. 1982). Reprinted by permission of the publisher Taylor & Francis Ltd, http://www.informaworld.com; Figure 5.9 adapted from *The Geography of International Tourism, Resource Paper No. 76-1*, Association of American Geographers (Matley, I. 1976). Copyright © the Association of American Geographers; Figure 6.4 adapted from *A Handbook of Leisure Studies*, Palgrave Macmillan (edited by Rojek. C, Shaw, S.M., and Veal, A.J. 2006). Reproduced by permission of Palgrave Macmillan; Figure 7.10 from *Principles of Marketing*, Pearson Education Ltd (Kotler, P. 2005). Copyright © Pearson Education Ltd; Figure 7.11 adapted from *The Marketing of Services*, Heinemann (Cowell, D.W. 1986). Copyright Elsevier © 1986; Figure 8.3 'Hierarchy of public open space in London – key characteristics' adapted from *Advice on Strategic Planning Guidance for London* (London Planning Advisory Committee 1994). Copyright © Greater London Authority; Figure 10.7 adapted from US National Park Service, www.nature.nps.gov/stats; Figure 11.11 adapted from 'Leisure Landscapes: Understanding the role of forests and woodlands in the tourism sector', in *Forest Research Annual Report and Accounts 2003–2004* (Martin 2004), pp. 54–65. With permission of Forest Research; Figure 12.2 adapted from *Futuring: The Exploration of Tomorrow*, World Future Society (Cornish, E. 2004). Copyright © World Future Society; Figure 12.6 adapted from Growth of World Tourism 1950–2020, www.unwto.org. Copyright © World Tourism Organisation.

Tables
Table 2.5 adapted from "Cultural Awakening to Post-Industrialism: The History of Leisure, Recreation and Tourism in Australia" by Hamilton-Smith, E., in *Time Out? Leisure, Recreation and Tourism in New Zealand and Australia*, pp. 34–50 (Perkins, H. and Cushman, G. (eds) 1998). Copyright © Pearson Education, Auckland; Table 2.6 adapted from "Frontier to Cyberspace: a History of Leisure, Recreation and Tourism in New Zealand" by J. Watson, in *Time Out? Leisure, Recreation and Tourism in New Zealand and Australia*, pp. 16–33

(Perkins, H. and Cushman, G. (eds) 1998). Copyright © Pearson Education, Auckland; Table 3.1 adapted from *A Handbook of Leisure Studies*, Palgrave Macmillan (edited by Rojek. C, Shaw, S.M., and Veal, A.J. 2006). Reproduced by permission of Palgrave Macmillan; Table 5.2 adapted from *The Leisure Industries*, Palgrave Macmillan (Roberts, K. 2004). Reproduced by permission of Palgrave Macmillan; Tables 7.2, 7.3 adapted from *Principles of Marketing*, Pearson Education Ltd (Kotler, P. 2005). Copyright © Pearson Education Ltd; Table 9.6 adapted from *Toursim: A Modern Synthesis*, Cengage (Page, S.J. and Connell, J. 2009). Copyright © Cengage Learning, 2009; Table 12.3 from *The Tourism and Leisure Industry: Shaping the Future*. Routledge (Weiermair, K. and Mathies, C. 2004). Copyright © Taylor & Francis Books. Permission conveyed through Copyright Clearance Center.

Text
General Displayed Texts on pages 58–60 from *The Classic Slum: Salford Life in the First Quarter of the Century* (Roberts, R. 1986). Copyright © Manchester University Press, Manchester, UK.

In some instances we have been unable to trace the owners of copyright material, and we would appreciate any information that would enable us to do so.

1 Introduction to leisure

Learning outcomes

After reading this chapter, you should be able to:

- Identify the different approaches used to define the term 'leisure'

- Distinguish between leisure, recreation and tourism

- Understand the different subjects which have contributed to the
  study of leisure

Introduction

In advanced industrial societies, leisure has now become a defining feature of
the way we live, work and spend our free time. Leisure has evolved into a complex phenomenon which has many meanings for different people and groups.
It is increasingly being associated with notions of well-being, so that enjoying
the activities we pursue in our leisure time gives us personal enjoyment, relaxation, personal fulfilment and a sense of pleasure to make us satisfied and complete human beings. In other words, leisure is vital to provide an outlet and
opportunity to do different things from the routine, daily activities and, for

those who work, a break from the mental and physical requirements of employment. Even in non-industrialised and primitive societies, leisure has a major role to play, creating opportunities for social and community interaction, reinforcing tightly knit relationships that exist among family and other social groups. Therefore, leisure is a ubiquitous notion or concept, occurring globally, but also a complex phenomenon because it means different things to different people, including children. Herein lies the challenge of this book – to provide a broad understanding of the meaning, significance and scope of leisure in modern-day society. The book does this by gradually exploring some of the concepts (i.e. the ideas and ways of looking at something) and theories (i.e. the complex explanations and methods of studying a subject), along with examples and case studies to illustrate the complexity of leisure.

Understanding what leisure is, why it is important in modern-day society and why it has become a key sector of the economy of many developed and developing countries helps us to recognise the type of society we live in and why people value leisure time and activities in different ways, along with its growth as a major area of personal and group expenditure. At a global scale, the continued growth in the way people seek to consume their leisure time and spend their financial resources on leisure pursuits provides an important starting point for this book. This is because it raises key questions about the processes and factors responsible for the increasing significance of leisure in society reflected in the following considerations:

- Leisure is a discretionary activity (people are not required to undertake it as a basic need to survive such as consuming food and water).

- Leisure activities are now key economic drivers for the global economy as well as in national and local economies, as advanced and developing economies see continued growth in service sector activities (of which leisure is one such area) to generate new employment opportunities.

- Leisure spending and activities have been embraced by many governments as a growth area to help develop, diversify and regenerate local economies dependent upon declining industries.

- Governments and international agencies (e.g. the United Nations World Health Organisation) are increasingly associating leisure activities and the enjoyment of our leisure time with quality of life issues because it offers the opportunity to escape the stresses, strains and perceived monotony of everyday routines, by doing something else we are not obliged to do. With the increase in sedentary lifestyles in developed countries, there are also important political objectives to be pursued by encouraging physical activity in leisure time to address the rise in obesity (see an interesting study by Olfert 2003 based on a city in Canada looking at developing a series of quality of life leisure indicators).

- Leisure time, expressed through employment and non-work time (e.g. annual holidays), is now seen as a basic right for all employees in advanced developed countries, and provides a block of time notionally dedicated to leisure activities. Yet there are worrying trends, as many employment surveys show that in advanced economies the corporate culture and employee perception of work expectations lead a proportion of staff not to take this entitlement. This illustrates one of the new terms being used to explain the growing dominance of work in people's everyday lives – being *time poor* but *cash rich* (i.e. people work long hours to earn money but do not have the leisure time to enjoy their increased income).

- Leisure activities, and leisure time in particular, are now a defining feature of non-work for those who are employed, while for those not employed, leisure time presents new opportunities and challenges (e.g. for those who have retired – how to fill a sudden increase in non-work time).

- Leisure for some social groups (e.g. the middle classes) has assumed a role in defining their differences from other social groups by seeking to imitate the leisure habits of higher social groups. This has typically involved spending their disposable income (i.e. that income available after basic necessities and household expenses have been budgeted for) to exhibit their affluence in terms of what they do in their leisure time and the physical symbols of that affluence displayed while at leisure (e.g. four-wheel-drive vehicles for largely urban use, despite the costs of urban motoring, as status symbols, dubbed in London 'Chelsea Tractors').

- In many advanced industrial societies, many leisure goods have become more widely available, so that they become everyday rather than luxury items (e.g. colour televisions). The result is that the notion of luxury has changed, and holidays previously associated with luxury (e.g. world cruises) are now widely accessible to a more affluent population.

- Leisure activities in the home have seen a major transformation over the past two decades; the home is viewed as a site for passive pursuits (e.g. watching television) as new technology has created home cinema and high-quality computer games with realistic graphics and media. Again, the diffusion of new innovations like the Xbox and Wii have made new technology commonplace in many homes.

- Leisure activities outside of the home, especially in the post-war period, are associated with greater access to personal mobility and a growth in leisure travel. Rising car ownership in the post-war period created many new leisure opportunities, removing restrictions imposed by pre-planning to use public transport. The car has allowed more flexibility and spontaneity in leisure travel along with changes to the destinations visited.

- Rapid global communications and media popularisation of leisure and sport brands together with the transmission of leisure habits and aspirations across cultures have created a demand for similar experiences globally. For example, the global expansion of the Disney company and the creation of a homogenous theme park experience irrespective of culture and location is one illustration of the process of serial reproduction (i.e. the copying and reproducing of the same experience/product) in leisure experiences.

- With the changing dimensions of luxury in leisure consumption (i.e. how different people consume leisure income to create specific experiences), there is a greater emphasis on the quality of the experience gained. Researchers have highlighted this growing pursuit of experiences as the acquisition of *cultural capital*, to enrich one's own status and position in relation to one's peers and friends. This explains why many young people take a gap year to travel the world before going to University, benefiting from the acquisition of greater life skills and the experience of new places and cultures.

- One specific form of leisure consumption that has seen an unprecedented growth in every developed country since the 1950s is tourism, initially as a domestic experience (i.e. taking a holiday or trip in one's own country) and latterly, international travel. In terms of leisure habits and experiences, international travel has also become more accessible to the general population owing to the rise of low-cost (also called budget) carriers like Southwest Airlines in the USA, Ryanair and easyJet in Europe and Air Asia and Tiger Airways in Southeast Asia.

- The type and nature of leisure experiences have also changed in the past two decades as new social processes emerge, such as the breakdown of the nuclear family, the rise of one-parent families and an ageing population in developed countries. Each of these processes has created constraints on the use of leisure time (e.g. shared custody of children splitting family leisure time) and major opportunities (e.g. the growth of entertainment complexes and eating-out venues for parents to enjoy leisure experiences with children).

This list, though not exhaustive, does provide a series of insights into why leisure is becoming a powerful and influential phenomenon, from the global scale right down to the family and individual. Although spending on leisure is a discretionary activity, much greater proportions of household expenditure are being directed towards home-based and out-of-home leisure. The rise in disposable income spent on leisure experiences reflects post-war trends in consumer spending on goods and services, starting with the pursuit of home ownership, then car ownership and then the greater expenditure on leisure (of which tourism and holiday-taking are a component). Therefore, leisure in developed countries has followed this pattern of development and it is now being mirrored in developing countries.

In the twenty-first century, leisure is without a doubt a key element shaping many of the lives of the population in every country worldwide irrespective of their development status, although most attention in research studies on leisure is given over to the developed world (often overlooking those marginalised people living in squatter settlements, as Chapter 12 will show). It is often an invisible activity, since a great deal of research attention has been given to one or two high-profile activities such as tourism. But leisure spending and activities occur much more frequently (typically every day for most people) than tourism and so leisure deserves much greater attention because how we spend and enjoy our free time is part of what gives us our identity and personal traits and influences many other aspects of our lives.

Leisure in a changing world – what is leisure?

In simple terms, leisure is usually associated with what we do in our non-work or free time. While this is a simplification for leisure researchers and analysts, it is important to commence with this fundamental analogy: *leisure is not work*. Against this simple relationship, we need to recognise, as the previous section discussed, that we live in a rapidly changing world where historically two features emerge:

- Society, the population and its pursuit of leisure have continued through history, albeit in different forms.

- The pursuit of leisure through history has seen changes in the way different social groups have gained greater access to leisure opportunities (e.g. in ancient times, only the affluent had the time and financial resources to pursue leisure activities without major constraints).

In other words, the evolution of leisure in different societies through time has seen the pursuit of leisure activities shaped by processes of *continuity* and *change* and the meaning of leisure has constantly developed through time. Whatever time period one examines, the notion of leisure has to be judged against how that society constructs its meaning of leisure. For example, hunting as an activity may be a vital necessity for a hunter-gatherer society, whereas in an advanced industrial society hunting may be a luxury experience where it is combined with a holiday and a wilderness environment. Therefore, attaching labels to what is and what is not leisure has to be thought about carefully. As Bull *et al.* (2003: xiv) concur, 'leisure . . . is a contentious term with a variety of meanings . . . leisure might be regarded as time free from obligations, as a collection of specific activities (embracing sport, recreation, tourism, arts and entertainment) or simply as a state of mind, it could be defined as whatever people perceive it to be'.

Most academic studies of leisure always begin by examining Ancient Greek society to trace the roots of the notion of leisure, where it emerged as a cultural ideal, since the Greeks established a leisure ethic by despising work. A reassessment of this leisure ethic by Sylvester (1999), examining the work of the Greek philosophers Aristotle and Plato, made associations between leisure and freedom, while Aristotle claimed that individual happiness depended upon leisure. Yet Sylvester (1999) also found evidence to suggest that work and leisure were compatible for the common citizen in Ancient Greece. This begins to question the assumption widely held by leisure researchers that leisure was the complete antithesis of work.

More common interpretations of leisure and its role in society are that it is conditioned by the Ancient Greek notion of leisure time being determined by wealth, privilege and an absence of barriers to participation. This approach is a useful starting point to the analysis of what we mean by the idea of leisure because the ancient civilisations and subsequent pre-industrial societies are characterised by leisure as a function of privilege. Yet there are also many examples of pagan festivals and leisure activities undertaken by entire communities, irrespective of privilege, to celebrate the close links between society and its dependence upon the earth.

One of the most widely recognised historical studies of leisure was by Clark and Critcher (1985) which charts the evolution of leisure in society as it developed from pre-industrial through industrial and post-industrial stages, where leisure is transformed in each stage. While the next chapter will explore these transformations in more detail, new forms of leisure were developed while others waned or were lost. One of the most telling changes in these transformations, which had a direct impact on the way leisure was constructed by each society, was the change from the pre-industrial to industrial stage and the introduction of a time-based work discipline. In a pre-industrial society, work and rural society, in particular, were organised around seasonal and daily rhythms. As a result, leisure time was less regimented and measured in terms of hours and minutes.

Consequently, in a pre-industrial society, leisure was a more fluid, flexible and spontaneous occurrence and male/female and family-based leisure was less segregated and routinised. In contrast, the onset of industrialisation and the shift from domestic to factory production completely transformed the lives of the working population and instituted a time-discipline. With employment and remuneration determined by the hours worked, an accompanying time-based regime developed that regulated the start and finish times of workers, often on a 65–70 hour, six-day working week. This clearly demarcated work and non-work time and is a basis for the identification of leisure as something that occurs in non-work time. This rigid distinction between work and non-work time did not change to any degree until the introduction of the late Victorian Bank Holiday and subsequent legislation that reduced Saturday working. Clarke and Critcher (1985) called this period of separation of work and leisure time part of the industrialisation process and the Victorians' desire to create a rational place for everything, with time being used to manage and regulate the population's use of their leisure. For example, leisure spaces in the industrialised cities, such as parks and gardens, were bound by time-based rules and codes of behaviour, and often enclosed by metal railings to prevent non-authorised use out of hours.

The late Victorians also provided much of the intellectual foundations to enable us to understand what leisure meant in a period of rapid industrialisation, through the work of early social observers such as Henry Mayhew, Charles Booth and Seebohm Rowntree with their focus on social conditions. Indirectly, these observers, who contributed to the evolution of sociology and other areas of study, such as leisure, noted the leisure habits of the diverse social mix of population in Victorian and Edwardian cities (see Chapter 2). The concern with 'the social condition' of the population, including poverty and deprivation among the labouring classes, recorded the routinised leisure activities of factory workers as well as the creation of an underclass based on the casual labour market where leisure activities were less dependent upon financial resources.

Among the contributions the Victorians made to modern-day leisure was the creation of mass organised and commercialised forms of rational recreation, such as spectator sports (e.g. football, rugby and horse racing), as well as mass entertainment (e.g. the cinema, theatre and music hall). The continuity of these mass forms of leisure was further observed in the Mass Observation Studies of the 1930s (Madge and Harrison 1939). Indeed, in the 1930s a range of early academic studies emerged which began to recognise the importance of understanding what leisure meant and its role in society (e.g. Burns 1932; Durant 1938).

Some of the interest in leisure in the 1930s was stimulated by mass unemployment, which created forced time available for leisure, some of which was perceived by governments as undesirable and a social problem. Yet this again illustrates the problem of creating an all-embracing definition of leisure. Nevertheless, what the discussion so far has highlighted is the importance of leisure in society in the past and today, which begins to show that there are a range of reasons why we should study leisure.

Reasons for studying leisure

There are many important reasons underpinning the analysis of leisure which are interrelated and provide a cohesive argument to justify the study of an area of activity often loosely termed 'fun', 'entertainment', 'enjoyment' and 'pleasure'. These stereotypes, sometimes bandied around in the popular media, fail to recognise the four parameters of leisure (Figure 1.1).

What Figure 1.1 shows is that to understand the domain of leisure (i.e. its scope and nature), four key perspectives provide a rationale for studying the leisure phenomenon:

- *Economic reasons*, where leisure has emerged as a key sector of many countries' burgeoning service sector economies, as consumer spending on leisure as a form of consumption creates a key economic activity. Given the globalisation processes now affecting many countries (see Chapter 3), leading to economic restructuring and relocation of industries to low cost-of-production

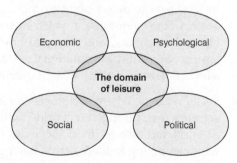

Figure 1.1   The four parameters of leisure

economies (e.g. Eastern Europe and Asia), the leisure economy has created an alternative form of employment and activity to replace that lost through globalisation. In addition, globalisation has seen global capital locate to areas where leisure development is part of a mixture of investment projects to regenerate areas of potential (e.g. former waterfront and dock areas). This reflects the high levels of leisure expenditure in many households in developed countries, which amounts to up to 25–30% of disposable income (when holidays and leisure travel are included). The knock-on effect for employment generation in the UK is that around 9% of the workforce is now working in this sector, an increase from around 6% in 1971. However, the precise economic contribution of leisure spending in many countries is based upon very incomplete data, usually derived from sample surveys by government statistical agencies. Data on the economic contribution made by different sub-sectors of the leisure economy (e.g. hotels, museums and leisure centres) remains difficult to quantify and measure. Nevertheless, the leisure economy has made a major contribution to national economies, helping to offset trade deficits. Leisure spending counteracts some of the revenue lost by importing manufactured goods and services produced in other countries.

- *Psychological reasons*, which emphasises the positive benefits for individual and family well-being through what psychologists call its contribution to life-satisfaction. What this means, as Aristotle acknowledged, is that personal happiness, contentment and being satisfied with one's life are enhanced by one vital ingredient – *leisure*. In particular, life-satisfaction is enhanced by the ability to rest and relax through leisure pursuits as well as being able to express one's desires and to meet one's expectations. Leisure can also have an educational role, where people pursue hobbies, learn new skills or seek to gain new knowledge or experiences in their leisure time. Yet probably the most widely cited reason for understanding leisure and its psychological effects on human beings relates to the health benefits of leisure. Nowhere was this more evident than in the late Victorian period in Scotland where hydropathic (abbreviated to hydro) hotels were built to provide water-based leisure therapies to aid one's health (Durie 2006). These health benefits of physical leisure activities are also associated with positive health benefits, where daily physical exercise of at least 30 minutes in one's leisure time is associated with positive physical and psychological benefits. In fact, psychologists point to the cognitive (i.e. how individuals become aware of the environment which surrounds them. Cognition involves thinking and reasoning, and refers to how humans process information about leisure opportunities), emotional and social development benefits of play as a form of leisure activity which contributes to life-satisfaction.

- *Social reasons*, where sociologists point to the potential of leisure to unite societies (e.g. through civic pride, with community events such as festivals or fairs) and also to divide societies (e.g. the divide which exists in cities with competing football teams having the potential to set one community against another). In other words, understanding the social dimensions of leisure helps us to recognise how major events such as the Olympic Games may bind a nation together through national pride while also encouraging interactions between different individuals, families and communities.

● *Political reasons*, where governments have an interest in how the public sector can assist in developing and implementing policies to manage public leisure provision, as the state is a major provider and manager of leisure services (e.g. outdoor resources such as parks and gardens, leisure centres, playing fields, arts centres and museums). The political perspectives of leisure, as discussed under the economic reasons, have been concerned with the value and economic significance of the leisure economy. One key concern in public policy settings is for the government to understand how public investment will affect the sector as well as how it can get best value for money from its expenditure on leisure. One organisation which governments rely upon to ensure best value for money is the audit commission or audit committee. Governments also have underlying political objectives for their public investment in leisure provision, such as encouraging national solidarity along with promoting desirable behaviour among the population (e.g. exercise and the reintegration of the homeless into society – see Karlis 2004) to improve well-being. These objectives also have obvious benefits for governments if the behaviour encouraged occurs, as increased physical activity and reductions in damaging activity (e.g. less sedentary lifestyles and banning smoking in public places) may lead to reductions in heart disease and reduce the cost of treatment under health budgets. The state also has an active interest in seeking to manage the impacts of individuals' and groups' leisure behaviour, by preserving and conserving vulnerable environments such as National Parks through planning policies and measures to manage leisure impacts through general taxation.

These reasons have a clear bearing on how we begin to understand what leisure is, how we can define it and why it is an integral part of everyday life and society. In studying leisure, one needs to be aware of two broad considerations prior to examining any definitions:

● *First*, an understanding of leisure enables us to appreciate how modern society is structured and operates. It is possible to understand these issues, as studying leisure helps us to:

   ● consider how people use their time, particularly when not working;

   ● evaluate who does what and why in relation to their leisure time as well as examining the activity patterns (i.e. where they spend their leisure in time and space[1]);

   ● examine the constraints and attitudes of different social groups in leisure settings.

---

[1]Space is a concept used by geographers to study where leisure occurs in relation to the home/out-of-home activities and the impact of these activities on leisure resources.

● *Second*, the origin of the term 'leisure' is derived from the Latin 'licere' which means to be permitted or to be free. This has an important bearing on the derivation of different elements which comprise any working definition of leisure.

Defining leisure

Many definitions of and approaches to the study of leisure exist, usually informed by the nature of the subject area from which people approach the study of leisure, which is illustrated in Figure 1.2. Yet each approach to leisure has been characterised by a number of key elements, as outlined in Figure 1.3, which illustrates that leisure may mean different things to different researchers depending upon the underlying approach, focus and concepts used by their subject area such as sociology (see Best 2010; Rojek 2010).

This means that leisure studies is not an academic discipline in its own right, but a subject area that has arisen from other disciplines which have approached it from different perspectives. Stockdale's (1985) review of the meaning of leisure, which looked at the concept of leisure, used many of the

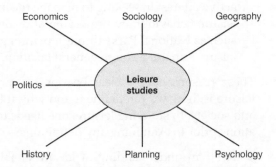

Figure 1.2   Subject areas which contribute to the study of leisure

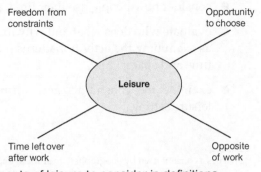

Figure 1.3   Elements of leisure to consider in definitions

elements listed in Figure 1.3 that have arisen in our discussion of the subject area so far. Stockdale (1985) listed three approaches to leisure:

- As *a period of time*, or focused on an activity or a 'state of mind' in which choice is the dominant feature. Therefore, leisure may be a form of free time for an individual.

- In *an objective sense*, where leisure is perceived as *the opposite of work* and so leisure time is construed as non-work or residual time (i.e. that time left after all of the normal obligations have been fulfilled).

- In a *subjective manner*, where leisure is viewed as a qualitative notion, so that leisure activities only take on a meaning in relation to the perceptions and belief systems of individuals, but these activities can occur at any time and in any context rather than being bound by time and work issues.

In fact, Herbert (1988) extended these three perspectives, arguing that leisure is related to the time when an individual exercises choice and is able to undertake activities in a voluntary manner, free from other constraints. A further refinement of this perspective of leisure was provided by Glyptis' (1981) concept of leisure lifestyles, which highlighted the key role of individual perceptions of leisure which will be discussed in Chapter 3.

Therefore, the precise definition that leisure researchers adopt will inevitably reflect their interest and bias, but as Figure 1.3 illustrates, combined with Stockdale's (1985) and Herbert's (1988) observations, a range of key issues need to be taken into account in defining leisure:

- the role of time;

- freedom from constraints or obligations;

- an individual's state of mind and perception of leisure;

- the significance of work and non-work (or for those with domestic responsibilities, the importance of the domestic routine), since Durant (1938: 31) recognised that the work ethic was the foundation of society, but 'Only when this division ceases, where leisure is complementary and not opposed to work' will the balance between leisure and work be better understood;

- the lifestyle of individuals;

along with the diversity of activities and interests which individuals pursue in that leisure time. Objective definitions of leisure which are time-based may help at a rudimentary level to identify the availability of time for leisure, but the desire for and use of that time require more detailed criteria to assess the subjective reasons for using leisure time in different ways. For example, Rowntree's seminal study of leisure in York in the inter-war period adopted a very prescriptive view of leisure demand that was described thus:

> When we talk about available leisure what we usually mean, in the case of people who work for a living, is the week-end and that time between getting home from work and bed-time . . . For wives of working men, it is the time left over after necessary household duties are performed. *(Rowntree 1941: 332)*

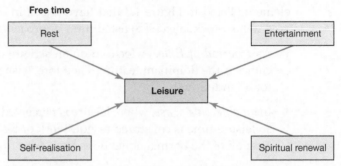

Figure 1.4 The relationship between free time and leisure

In fact, Csikszentmihalyi (1980) pointed to the interconnections between free time, attitudes and the activities of individuals and groups. Zuzanek (2006) examined the complexity of trying to define leisure 'as time would empty it of its contents' (Zuzanek 2006: 185) while 'anybody can have free time. Not everybody can have leisure'. Free time refers to 'a special way of calculating a special kind of time. Leisure refers to a state of being, a condition of man' (de Grazia 1962: 5). Yet the problem from a practical perspective, as Zuzanek (2006: 185) recognised, is that 'for most people, leisure remains time free of obligations'. Even so, free time may be a prerequisite to engage in leisure but it is not the same. As Meyersohn (1972) noted and as shown in Figure 1.4, for leisure to occur, free time is needed to fulfil a few key functions.

However, as the section on leisure and well-being will discuss later, a certain amount of free time is necessary to protect our emotional well-being. Yet in advanced industrial societies there is a growing recognition that many middle-class workers are seeing their leisure time constrained by lengthening hours of work so that they are 'time poor' and 'cash rich'. What the discussion of time and its use in leisure studies research shows is that 'From a research and measurement perspective it is easier to operationalise leisure as either discretionary time, or a socially defined activity, or an experience, *one at a time*, rather than opt for the conceptually appealing but methodologically elusive combination thereof' (Zuzanek 2006: 200), meaning that:

● Each distinct approach to trying to define leisure as *discretionary time* available is one possible approach.

● Looking at *people's participation in leisure* activities is another approach to help define leisure.

● People's behaviour and *experience of leisure* (i.e. the social psychology of leisure which is discussed in Chapters 3 and 4) is another valid approach.

These three perspectives are shown in Figure 1.5, which highlights the problem of trying to mesh all these approaches into one universal concept that can incorporate the role of leisure in our everyday lives and behaviours, which largely remains elusive.

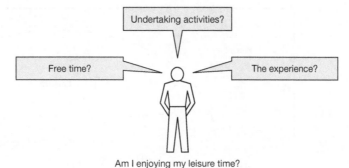

Am I enjoying my leisure time?

Figure 1.5 Understanding the complexity of conceptualising three perspectives on leisure simultaneously

Distinguishing between leisure, recreation and tourism

While definitions and the criteria used to construct those definitions are a starting point to derive a better understanding of leisure, leisure also embraces a diverse use of time and activities where tourism and recreation are also leisure-based activities. Parker (1999) summarised this relationship between leisure, recreation and tourism thus:

> It is through studying leisure as a whole that the most powerful explanations are developed. This is because society is not divided into sports players, television viewers, tourists and so on. It is the same people who do all these things. *(Parker 1999: 21)*

Hall and Page (2006) argue that there is considerable merit in viewing recreation[2] and tourism[3] as elements of a broader definition and concept of leisure. Figure 1.6 depicts these relationships and shows that the boundaries are somewhat blurred, as shown by the dotted lines.

Hall and Page (2006) show that while work is distinct from leisure, there is a degree of overlap when business-related travel is examined because it is a work-related form of travel, distinct from leisure-related travel. Furthermore, these boundaries between business and leisure travel led Stebbins (1982) to note the blurring where people pursue 'serious leisure' in which leisure and work activities overlap. To explain this emergence of 'serious leisure', Stebbins argued that:

> Leisure in post-industrial society is no longer seen as chiefly a means of recuperating from the travail of the job . . . if leisure is to become, for many, an improvement

---

[2]The term literally means re-creation, where physical pursuits, play, renewing one's spirits and improving well-being are key attributes of recreation. In capitalist societies, it is associated with ensuring that workers are more productive, usually involving physical pursuits.

[3]Tourism is travel away from one's home area for at least 24 hours, within one's own country, or travel to another country for less than one year.

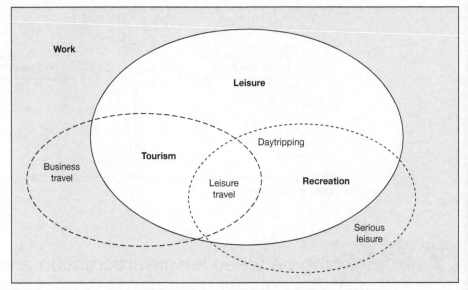

Figure 1.6 The relationships between leisure, recreation and tourism

Source: Adapted from Hall and Page (2006: 5). Copyright © Routledge 2006

over work as a way of finding personal fulfilment, identify enhancement, self-expression, and the like, then people must be careful to adopt those forms with the greatest payoff. The theme here is that we reach this goal through engaging in serious rather than casual or unserious leisure. *(Stebbins 1982: 253)*

This is epitomised, perhaps, by the executive who feels obliged to engage in golf matches in their leisure time to advance their career in a company. Another example would be those people who volunteer, serve on committees or pursue their hobby/interest via their work.

What Hall and Page's (2006) examination of the leisure–recreation–tourism relationship shows is that a leisure spectrum exists, with travel helping to differentiate between each activity, although the boundaries are still artificial, as Figure 1.7 shows.

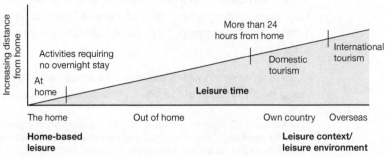

Figure 1.7 The leisure spectrum

Source: Page and Connell (2009)

It is not surprising, as Figure 1.7 shows, that many researchers and organisations blur the distinction between leisure, recreation and tourism. Many traditional definitions viewed leisure as a non-commercialised pursuit, in contrast to tourism with its costs of travel and accommodation (excluding those who stay with friends and families). There was also a notable distinction between the commercialised tourism industry being predominantly private sector and profit oriented, whereas many leisure activities did not generate the visitor spending of tourism, although these distinctions are changing as the impact of leisure shopping (i.e. conspicuous shopping for non-food items in one's leisure time) suggests. Many of these boundaries are increasingly blurring as leisure has become commercialised, and involves travel (often by car). Therefore, as Hall and Page (2006) argue, useful definitions are as follows:

- Leisure is viewed as the time, activities and experience derived, characterised by freedom.

- Recreation is about the activities undertaken in one's leisure time leading to renewal.

- Tourism is travel to a destination (involving an overnight stay and 24 hours away from home) which incorporates leisure and recreation activities.

With these issues in mind, attention now turns to approaches to defining leisure.

Approaches to defining leisure

According to Bull *et al.* (2003), there are four main ways of seeking to define leisure, expanding upon the discussion of defining the scope and nature of leisure, which are:

A time-based approach

As mentioned previously, leisure may be viewed as the time when you are not at work. It comprises the 'free time' or 'unoccupied time' which occurs when the daily obligations have been met. These obligations were examined by the United Nations World Tourism Organisation's (1983) *Individuals Use of Leisure time in EU Countries* where the daily use of time was comprised of the categories in Figure 1.8 where:

- Biological needs dominate the use of time, with sleep, meals and other necessities (43.3%).

- Work-related activities take up almost as much time as biological needs (34%).

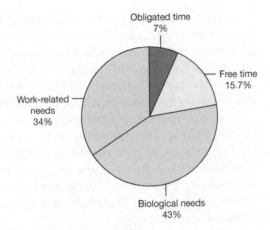

Figure 1.8   Individual's use of leisure time

Source: Based on data from UN-WTO (1983). Copyright © World Tourism Organization

- Free time, including weekends, holidays and day time freedom, accounted for around 16% of the time available.

- Obligated time, including daily travel and commitments, accounted for 7% of time.

In the UK, the Office for National Statistics (ONS) produced a Time Use Survey in 2003 (ONS 2003) which shed more light on the use of time as well as the times at which most people sleep and engage in leisure activities (see http:/www.ons.gov.uk for more detail). These time-based definitions of leisure suffer numerous problems as an all-embracing approach, as indicated earlier, and a number of difficulties emerge:

- If we assume that leisure as defined by time implies 'freedom from', it does not necessarily follow that this is the same as 'freedom to', as one's obligations may impact upon this time. In other words, just because someone is not at work, other responsibilities may fill the time deemed to be leisure. The stereotypical image of the working mother highlights the absence of dedicated leisure time, where child-care responsibilities (even where responsibilities are notionally shared) infringe upon that 'free time' when not working.

- The amount of time an individual has available varies according to the stage in the family life cycle (i.e. children or no children), or other caring responsibilities (i.e. relatives/friends) (see Chapter 3 for more detail). Qualitative judgements also exist, as it is not necessarily the amount of time, but the quality of the time and how it is spent that are important (i.e. the meaning and values attached to the time).

- Individuals face many structured determinants which affect the amount of time available for leisure, typically affected by gender, age, ethnicity, social class and many other variables (i.e. access to opportunities to spend leisure time on commercial activities).

- Leisure time is, for many people, confined to certain times of the day (i.e. after work hours have ended, which traditionally was 5 p.m. but this has changed with flexible working practices and working from home). In many countries, such as Japan and the USA, the dedicated block of time available for leisure is two weeks' annual leave, although in Europe the holiday entitlement varies from around 14 to over 35 days a year. One other block of time where leisure is concentrated is the weekend, but the liberalisation of weekend trading in many countries has eroded the weekend as the weekly leisure outlet, depending upon the groups and individuals involved.

- There is also a well-developed notion of 'enforced leisure', where unemployment or illness removed the work element. But is this really leisure time? Probably not, but if one uses a time-based approach it will give only a partial understanding of leisure amongst individuals and groups.

Activity-based approaches

Leisure is implicitly about the opportunity to pursue an activity, typically on a daily basis, selected by free will. Among such activities are those associated with:

- rest (e.g. watching television or reading a book);

- amusement (e.g. watching a comedy);

- education (e.g. undertaking adult education);

- participation (e.g. in sporting activities).

Yet there is an important qualifying statement to add in relation to the selection of activities by free choice, as it may sometimes reflect what other family members or friends want to do. Alternatively, the free choice may be conditioned by obligations such as visiting a family member or friend. Nevertheless, the ONS (2008) Lifestyles and Social Participation chapter in the annual publication *Social Trends* (www.statistics.gov.uk) provides a snapshot of the British population 'at leisure' as the following summary shows (also see Chapter 4) (also see Karlis 2004 for a similar review of Canada):

- Technological change has seen the proportion of households owning a mobile phone increase from 17% in 1996/97 to 71% in 2005/06, with 65% of children aged 8 to 15 years of age owning a mobile phone. Among the 12- to 15-year age group, the main reason for owning a phone was leisure related: for social networking with friends, typically by text message.

- In 2007, the UK resident population took 45 million holiday trips abroad, a 65% increase since 1996, which is also an exponential growth from the 6.7 million overseas trips made in 1971.

- In 2005, the number of domestic tourist trips taken (including at least one overnight stay) was 86.6 million, 62% for leisure and 38% for business and to visit friends and relatives.

- In terms of entertainment, 12.3 million visits in 2005 were made to West End theatres in London, with 165 million cinema admissions in the same year (41.3 million of which were in London).

These statistical insights provide a number of illustrations of the rest, amusement, educational and participative functions of leisure.

Attitude-based approaches

Attitude-based approaches to leisure have been very influential as 'The significance and meaning of a particular set of leisure choices. . . . can only be made intelligible by inscribing them on a map of the class-defined social field of leisure and lifestyle practices in which their meaning and significance is relationally defined with reference to structured oppositions and differences' (Featherstone 1987: 115). What this means is that individual attitudes and lifestyles condition how we view, understand and engage in leisure, often to set ourselves apart from others or to identify with others. In fact, the significance of leisure as an attitude of mind transcends narrow conceptualisations of what is and is not leisure.

The attitude-based approaches have been developed by researchers with an interest in the social psychology of leisure,[4] recognising that leisure is a complex, spiritual concept based on the motivation of the participant. In other words, leisure is more an attitude of mind or state of being, where the individual gives meaning to chosen activities or places (i.e. what does it mean to the participant or individual at leisure when undertaking their favourite activity?). This approach does not subscribe to simplistic notions that leisure is a result of spare time or a day off. Indeed, leisure as an attitude of mind can occur anytime, being less time-dependent. Therefore an individual's perception defines what leisure is, meaning that different people will feel a sense of pleasure from different contexts and activities. So leisure is not focused on time or activity (i.e. you could be at leisure in your office in your lunch hour if you adopt this approach), which means that leisure is intrinsic[5] to the person.

Quality-based approaches

These are derived from the work of psychologists, which emphasises the importance of the quality of free time and embodies many of the aspects of the previous approaches. This approach focuses on the individual and how they regard an activity

---

[4]Social psychology looks at the leisure behaviour of individuals, focusing on issues such as their motivation and attitudes to leisure, how their identities are influenced by leisure as well as perceptions of leisure. There is a long history of studying leisure in social psychology, as outlined by Argyle (1996).

[5]Intrinsic refers to a form of motivation where someone undertakes a specific activity because they want to as opposed to being paid to undertake it, such as in the case of work where the motivation is extrinsic.

and whether they perceive it as leisure or not. In this respect, the approach focuses on whether the time deemed to be leisure matches their attitude or not. Above all, this approach emphasises the quality of the free time and the opportunity this quality time offers for recuperation from the stresses of everyday life. For the psychologist, this means that the quality time is valued because it provides an opportunity for play and for personal and social development. This approach will also help us to understand the work–leisure relationship (which will be discussed in more detail in Chapter 3). Therefore, leisure in relation to quality-based approaches is about personal pleasure rather than just a time-filler, as the following analogy suggests: there are those people who live to work, and do not acknowledge leisure needs, and those who work to live, with personal satisfaction derived from leisure as opposed to being simply work and career focused. In the work to live analogy, individuals see work, in part, as a means to support their leisure lifestyles. To Bull *et al.*'s (2003) four approaches, we can also add a fifth approach – *leisure as a way of living*.

Leisure as a way of living

This is based on a growing body of research literature that suggests there is a perception that a particular form of employment or career may create a leisure-based lifestyle. In this approach, leisure is not so much a commodity, or based on time or a state of mind. It is a way of life where the productive activities of the lifestyle may pursue a personal interest or hobby as a career (e.g. an artist). For example, recent research on adventure tourism operators in the Highlands of Scotland identified that lifestyle and the opportunity to be one's own boss, to vary their daily activities and to work on an area of interest were influential in setting up their business. In other words, leisure as a way of life may provide the freedom for the type of life we want, by choosing our own direction where we are more in control of what we do. Interestingly, this lifestyle approach also typifies many of the motives associated with people who decide to purchase a bed-and-breakfast establishment prior to winding down for retirement, often in the mistaken belief that it may offer that leisure lifestyle.

Therefore, in seeking to *make sense* of leisure, Kelly (1982) provides a meaningful insight: if leisure is defined by the use of time, rather than the time itself, then leisure is defined by its meaning (in the attitude and quality-based approach), implying that there is far more complexity to leisure than time and activities. Ultimately, any definition of leisure must also remember that leisure is about enjoyment and personal satisfaction and is freely entered into (in the main).

The leisure society

Theoretical explanations of leisure have been advanced to try to explain why it is such a pervasive element in society. Leisure is now widely acknowledged as a social phenomenon, as the nature of society in most advanced developed countries has now changed from one that has traditionally had an economy based on manufacturing and production, to one where the dominant form of employment is services and consumer industries (i.e. those based on producing consumer goods and services). At the same time, many countries have seen the amount of leisure time and paid holiday entitlement for their workers increase in the post-war period so that workers now have the opportunity to engage in new forms of leisure consumption. There are even elements of this interest in the commercialisation of leisure dating to the turn of the twentieth century (e.g. Sizer 1917), where Durant (1938: 24) argued that

> in a world where relationships are in the main reduced to a cash nexus, the exploitation of leisure for profit is only to be expected. Nevertheless, it is often denied. We are told that the amusement industries . . . continued to flourish only because they supply what is wanted . . . In the relationship of demand and supply the producer is a significant, determining factor, particularly in the sphere of amusements. *(Durant 1938: 24)*

Changes since 1945, and particularly in the 1970s, have been described as being part of what has been termed as the *leisure society*, a term coined in the 1970s by sociologists. Sociologists were examining the future of work and the way in which society was changing; as traditional forms of employment were disappearing and new service-related employment emerged, increased leisure time and new working habits were observed (e.g. flexi-time and part-time work). Some commentators in the 1980s described this as a 'leisure shock', as many workers were still not prepared for the rise in leisure time and how to use it. Historically, late nineteenth-century studies such as Veblen's (1899) *The Theory of the Leisure Class* suggested that society was ruled by a leisure class, who were wealthy, undertook little labour and engaged in conspicuous consumption (akin to the Greeks). But changes in the work ethic and studies such as Schor's (1991) *The Overworked American* show that in post-1945 culture, work and not leisure has begun to define affluence, with the richest working the longest hours according to Rojek (2000). This is an interesting observation which begins to question how leisure, society and affluence have combined since 1945 to define new attitudes and styles of leisure consumption.

As society has passed from the stage of industrialisation to one now described as post-industrial (or the more widely used term postmodern), where new technologies and ways of communicating and working have evolved, sociologists such as Baudrillard (1998) in *The Consumer Society: Myths and Structures* argued that we have moved from a society where work and production were the norm to one in which leisure and consumption now dominate our consciousness and use of free time. This has been reflected in social changes, such as the worldwide rise in the new middle class in many developed and developing countries: one of the defining features is the concern with leisure lifestyles and consumption. A new-found wealth among the growing middle class has been reflected in increased spending on leisure items as well as a demand for tourism as an element of this (e.g. in 1911, 1% of the population had 70% of wealth, which dropped to 40% in 1960 and 23% in 2002 in the UK). In the UK, in the 1980s and 1990s sociologists observed the making of a new middle class, much of which was derived from the rapid expansion in the service economy (especially financial services and demand for managers), and similar trends have been observed in other countries. The international growth in leisure consumption is directly related to this new middle class. The increasing mobility of this group has been reflected in a six-fold rise in air passengers travelling in the UK between 1971 and 2003 and one-car-owning households rising from 52% in 1971 to 74% in 2004. But the greatest growth has been in two-car households, rising from 8% in 1971 to 29% in 2003. If the UK is fairly representative of changes occurring in other countries, then recent facets of consumer expenditure illustrate the growth of this leisure consuming society:

● Cheaper air fares and changing patterns of personal expenditure recorded in *The Family Spending Survey 2005–2006* by the Office for National Statistics found that household spending in the UK included £57.50 a week on recreation and culture, ranked second to transport. This included £12.50 a week spent on overseas package holidays and £1 on UK-based package holidays. In contrast, £5.50 a week was spent on sport fees, and £1.90 a week on cinema, theatre and museum admissions.

● This spending varied by age group: where the main respondent was aged 30–49 years they spent £65.59 a week on recreation and culture, equivalent to 12% of their budget; those aged 50–65 spent 14% of their household budget on leisure and those aged 65–74 spent 16% of their budget on leisure.

● The amount spent on overseas holidays has increased seven-fold since 1971, from 6.7 million trips to 41 million trips worth £26.7 billion in 2004, with those in managerial and professional employment (the new middle classes) spending double that of other employed classes.

● In the period 1993–2003, there was a 79% growth in domestic air passengers at UK airports, as low-cost air travel expanded alongside an expansion of outbound trips to 15 EU countries, with 30% of trips (30 million) to Spain and 18% to France.

But these approaches and definitions have led researchers to begin to try to seek more theoretical explanations of leisure in society, to which our attention now turns.

Leisure, recreation and play

One area often overlooked in the discussion of leisure is the relationship with recreation (physical activity) and play. Play may seem to be a simple notion, often associated with children, since it is one way in which children develop awareness of their environment as well as physical development (e.g. muscle development). These physiological and cognitive benefits follow through into adulthood, where playing as a child inevitably involves risk taking that continues through life. This relationship was observed as early as the 1930s by Burns (1932: 155) as 'play is no longer regarded as a waste of time' but as an important activity which helps to shape the character and personality of future adults. Burns also argued that in a democratic society, the less organised tradition of play had evolved, supported by the growth in facilities such as playgrounds in the last 50 years. In modern-day Western society there has been a substantial backlash against seeking to manage out the risk taking for children in play, reflected in the bureaucratic measures now confronting organisations involved in play. Some commentators have called this the risk averse society, where litigation is an inevitable outcome of accidents and injuries in play that can be attributed to a third party. Other commentators have argued that this also reflects a growing intrusion into, and regulation by the state of, our everyday life, including our leisure time, described as the 'nanny state', where paper trails and an audit culture are used to deflect blame and liability for the risk associated with play and leisure.

In a leisure setting, play is important for the development of children through to their adulthood, particularly their emotional development, because it can help foster greater self-confidence, discipline and self-worth, according to Bull *et al.* (2003). It may also instil an understanding of competitiveness and how the real world functions in adulthood, illustrating many of the rules and norms in society. The personal interaction derived from play may also help build teamwork ideas and the exploration of feelings, relationships with others and future managerial traits (e.g. leadership, teamwork, empathy, understanding, an ability to plan and coordinate the activities of others).

Above all, play is about the ability to express oneself spontaneously while gaining personal enjoyment, usually in leisure time. The capacity for play and gaining pleasure from play has a non-serious element, which is distinct from the work ethic in industrialised society. Participation in play is different from work since it is seen as non-productive, but for mental and psychological reasons, play can enhance the value and benefit gained from leisure time since it is freely chosen as an activity. There is also an element of chance in some forms of play (e.g. gambling and competitive games) along with the use of rules. Above all, play enables individuals and groups to pursue their fantasies, to become distant from work and everyday obligations while seeking pleasure in their leisure time. It can also help individuals to deal with new situations as well as developing one's physical, emotional and social abilities. As Torkildsen (1999) observed, play helps to shape human behaviour and can pervade all areas of our life (at home, work and school) and for children it can stimulate their early learning (e.g. developing imagination and creativity) through to later school attainment: it helps children to have fun and appreciate the importance of leisure time. From a psychological perspective it can: help improve our ability to socialise; increase our spontaneity, joy and humour; increase our learning; act as a source of therapy; and act as a form of arousal and stimulation which is an element of leisure enjoyment.

This focus on play may help to explain the levels of participation in sport discussed earlier, given its underlying importance in explaining sporting activity (e.g. playing games competitively and for fun). The notion of enjoyment as a means of fulfilling one's own desires in leisure time also manifests itself in many other ways, and one facet linked to conspicuous consumption is entertainment.

Entertainment as leisure

Throughout history, those with leisure time have not only pursued home-based and out-of-home leisure activities with friends and family, but have also undertaken a range of social-related pursuits which are passive (and active) (Figure 1.9). These pursuits have been spectator-based, from the Romans' gladiatorial events in purpose-built venues such as the Coliseum through to more modern mass spectator activities such as the rise of the Victorian music hall, theatre and the cinema. These out-of-home mass forms of entertainment provided a key outlet for working-class leisure and were dominant pursuits in each era. In fact, despite the rapid rise of in-home media and entertainment systems in many households, the cinema remains an enduring form of entertainment and a leisure pursuit, with attendances more than doubling in the UK since 1984. In India, it remains a massive social activity, with its own equivalent of filmmaking – the Bollywood phenomenon; there is a similar expansion in Africa based in Nigeria. The advent of television provided a major challenge to public media such as cinema, and it remains a key leisure activity in most industrialised societies, being a dominant daily and weekly leisure pursuit as will be shown in later chapters.

Similarly, home-based music technology saw over 200 million CDs a year purchased in the UK, and new technology such as iPods and MP3 players have provided increased flexibility for the social settings (e.g. commuting and

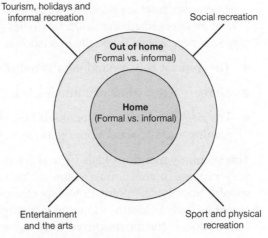

Figure 1.9   The social setting of leisure

travel) for consuming music in one's leisure or non-work time. Yet entertainment as a leisure experience is not necessarily confined to spectator events or media events such as listening to music, attending a music concert or visiting a club. Other social forms have evolved linked to the growth of different forms of socialisation, which may involve the consumption of food and drink as the focus for the experience.

Again, this is not a new phenomenon, as historically food and drink for the leisured classes were an important form of hospitality and entertainment, reflecting one's status and wealth. The venues and locations for consuming food and drink through history have expanded from the intimacy of the home to more commercial forms such as inns and hostelries through to the evolution of the café and restaurant. In the UK, as in many other developed countries, the most common non-home-based leisure activity is visiting the pub. In Australia, prior to the liberalisation of licensing laws, this was often associated with the hour after work between 5 and 6 p.m. when hostelries were open for social drinking as a cultural activity.

What is clear is that entertainment in its commercialised form is increasingly being viewed as a form of consumption, as discussed earlier in relation to Veblen's (1899) *The Theory of the Leisure Class*. This suggested that one's wealth and social position could be signified by the forms of leisure one engaged in, and distinguished one from the non-leisure classes. While the modern-day evidence to support Veblen's thesis is less clear, with the absence of a definite leisure class, conspicuous consumption and leisure practices remain important elements of this rise of modern-day leisure consumption. While consumption still defines one's position in society, it is a more complex sociological construct with specific behaviours, consumption and habits, as our identities and inner self are formed through our leisure encounters. These complex sociological constructs have provided many new directions for leisure researchers. As Cook (2006: 310) argues, 'it is not so much the question of whether leisure has been commodified – that much is evident. It is recognising that many leisure forms, contexts, practices and cultural arenas have arisen in and as commercial activity from their inception'.

Sociologists have analysed trends in leisure activities and point to some of the current areas of growth that illustrate Cook's (2006) arguments on commodification of leisure experiences, especially in relation to entertainment:

● The contrast between indoor and out-of-doors leisure consumption.

● The search for nature in outdoor leisure.

● The rise of in-home, personalised leisure epitomised by Internet browsing, gaming and social networking as forms of consumption.

This seeminly merging of leisure and consumption has seen critics point to the very process of consuming leisure, which may destroy the experience being sought. Sociologists point to the spectacle and extravaganza associated with activities such as leisure shopping (although it is not a new phenomenon as it has its roots in the nineteenth century and earlier): what is new is the spectacle, something which is also associated with attending sporting events where leisure becomes consumption. Nowhere is this more apparent than in the case of children's parties, as the following case study suggests. This shows that the commodification of leisure now stretches even into childhood, as Cook's (2004: 2) *The Commodification of Childhood* argues:

> The market culture of childhood represents a monumental accomplishment of twentieth-century capitalism. The rise and expansion of a child-world of goods, spaces and media over the last century signifies a development above and beyond the opening of merely one more market similar to others. The child market stands apart form others because childhood is a generative cultural site unlike any other.

These arguments emerge in McKendrick *et al.*'s (2000a) analysis of the 'kid customer' and the rise of distinct geographies of children's play (McKendrick *et al.* 2000b) as well as the commercialisation of that play experience, most apparent in the case of children's parties (Case Study 1.1).

Case Study 1.1	Children's parties and the consumption of leisure

The birthday party, as McKendrick *et al.* (2000b: 88) point out, is 'a major calendar event in the year of many children, and it is one that transforms domestic or commercial playspace for a fixed and limited time', being a very personal annual celebration. What has commodified this leisure experience is the way many parents' irrational fears about public play space have seen commercial, indoor soft play areas emerge as venues for children's parties. These commercial playgrounds are also a reflection of the consumer power of children, especially among more affluent and aspiring families, with pre-school and early years children. These playgrounds used for parties also fulfil a key need for adults about how they want their children to play and, in some cases, who they want them to play with.

From a commercial perspective, operators of these leisure spaces view parties as a way of introducing their venue to a wide range of potential clients, almost using a pyramid-selling concept. But these venues are also facing stiff competition in countries where the range of venues now offering to host children's parties has mushroomed (e.g. museums, theme parks, restaurants, aquariums and other entertainment venues offer party packages). For the over 10-year-old age group, activity-based parties are also popular. In some instances, cases of extreme extravagance have been reported, such as a children's party at a UK stately home for 30 children that cost £20,000 in 2007, with other parties topping £50,000. The cost of such consumptive experiences ranges from just over £100 to over £250,000, illustrated in 2007 by a BBC Television series, *The Madness of Modern Parenting*. In cultural terms, a major illustration of the expectations of children as consumers is the way they judge the ultimate success of the experience: the *quality of the party bag* which the party-goers take home. This is the benchmark by which the child as a consumer evaluates the nature of the experience they have consumed and how they have engaged with the party giver.

The impact of these cultural trends has seen a response by some groups because it can cause stress on families' budgets and the demand for experiences by children for each party to be bigger and better (the supersize culture). This also plays into the competitive habits of parents who try to outdo other parents, choosing bigger and better venues with the experiences being highly managed. The parties are also a spectacle for parents and party-goers, leading them to associate parties with materialism and accumulating things rather than enjoyment. Consequently, instead of the focus on happiness, play and fun in this leisure experience, the focus is on consumption and the material aspects of the event. This creates envy, resentment and an escalating demand for enhanced standards of party-giving. One movement, birthdayswithoutpressure.org, traces the origins of the party to nineteenth-century Germany where the individual was special, prior to the trend spreading to the USA. It was not until the 1920s that children began to have more input to parties in the USA, while the 1950s saw parties emerge as age-appropriate events for one's peers rather than mixed age-groups focused on family members. Initially, the mother retained all organisation of the party in the 1950s, whereas in the 1980s these parties moved outside the home in the USA. The American Greetings organisation undertook research that indicated that in the late 1990s, 95% of under-10-year-olds had some type of celebration for their birthdays.

Concerns over the children's parties market as 'out of control' is reflected in estimates of the size of the UK market at £1.25 billion by Virgin Credit Card and £1.4 billion by American Express. In the USA, the pressure group formed to combat excesses associated with children's parties, *Birthdays without Pressure*, epitomised these excesses with the use of stretched limousines to pick up and drop off children at parties and as treats. What is clear from this case study is that birthday party celebrations have assumed a ritualistic status, as Rook (1985) described, with these leisure pursuits now a highly commoditised experience. This spread to China in the late 1980s, as McDonald's and other fast food venues provided a new experience and venue for parties. For researchers, the whole ethos of children's parties as a leisure pursuit raises many sociological questions, particularly the psychological effect on those children *not* invited to such events, which has led some schools in certain countries to ban the distribution of party invitations in school so as not to create a culture of exclusion.

In spite of the problems associated with leisure experiences such as the children's party, leisure can perform an important social and mental role in relation to an individual's well-being. As Argyle (1996: 1) argued, 'leisure can be a major source of happiness and of mental and physical health'. For this reason, the link between leisure and well-being is an important relationship to examine.

Leisure, well-being and society

To understand the importance of leisure and the link with well-being, it is useful to consider the types of everyday lives, working experiences and trends in modern-day society that are concerning governments and policy-makers. According to Pretty *et al*. (2005), in the UK around 80% of the population live in urban areas, with hectic daily lives compounded by the stresses of commuting, work and in some cases their living environment. Pretty *et al*. pointed to the importance of two key factors that affect our emotional health and well-being (a term often used interchangeably with quality of life, which refers to indicators that affect one's standard of living and ability to enjoy one's life to a standard one aspires to). For example, indexes which try to calculate and quantify measures such as quality of life look at a wide range of statistical and non-statistical measures such as the cost of living, cultural and leisure provision, the level of employment available, the quality of the environment, health service provision, level of transport and infrastructure, and the level of personal safety in relation to crime and perception of crime. Pretty *et al*. argued that the quality of the home environment and the place where you work was an important determinant of your emotional health. Running alongside these measures of what might be construed as *quality of life* are a number of prevailing health problems confronting modern-day Western society, as illustrated in Figure 1.10. According to the World Health Organisation, by 2026, stress and mental illness will be the two greatest causes of ill-health alongside the other problems apparent in Figure 1.10.

Therefore, against this background, leisure assumes an even greater role in modern society, with evidence to suggest that viewing green spaces can reduce one's blood pressure and stress levels, illustrating the importance of building leisure spaces into crowded urban environments. Leisure is also acknowledged as an important weapon in the armoury to fight this scourge of modern-day society – *stress*. As the Barclays (2000) report *Leisure in the New Millennium* highlighted,

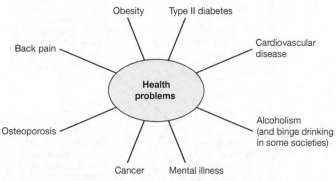

Figure 1.10 Health problems in modern society

Source: Adapted from Pretty *et al*. (2005). Copyright © Countryside Recreation Network (CRN)

we have very unhealthy modern lifestyles and the following observations illustrate the link between leisure and our well-being:

- Consumers have very high expectations of their leisure time, even if they are more likely to have 'shallow' and 'fleeting' interests in leisure activities.

- The discrepancy between rich and poor is accelerating in the UK (and other countries), creating different expectations on the value they attach to how and where they spend their leisure time (reflected in the boom in in-home entertainment and facilities).

- Working hours and working lives are shaping how leisure has to fit around the modern-day forms of employment, with a greater emphasis on spontaneity due to technology and social networking.

- Greater attention to *leisure nibbling* (i.e. bite-sized chunks of leisure time, such as the rise of micro breaks which are one-night stays) alongside more planned and routined annual leisure activities such as holidays and short breaks as well as day trips.

As the Barclays (2000) report highlighted, 69% of adults interviewed stated that a holiday could improve their quality of life, and 91% of General Practitioners questioned concurred with this statement. As Figure 1.11 shows, leisure can have many positive effects as Driver *et al.* (1991) identify, some of which are reproduced in relation to health and well-being, although there are examples of sedentary and individualised leisure activities which are not seen

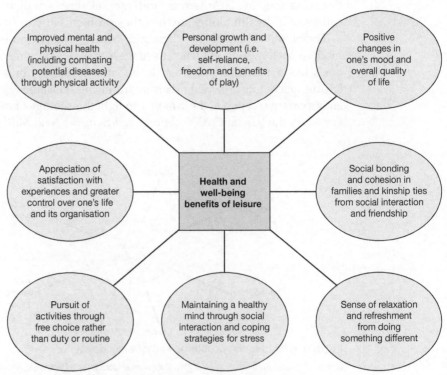

Figure 1.11 Health and well-being benefits of leisure

as contributing to health and well-being (e.g. smoking, drug-taking and excessive alcohol consumption) as they are health jeopardising and may involve personal risk. What is also worth stressing in Figure 1.11 is that in any leisure–well-being relationship, one or more benefits may be occurring simultaneously, or one positive benefit may be counteracted by negative leisure events through individualised or sedentary leisure.

Leisure and well-being

According to Coleman (2003: 548), 'well-being is the multi-dimensional capacity of an individual to function optimally and the extent of satisfaction with that functioning. Dimensions of well-being include physical health, mental health, social well-being and spiritual well-being and evaluative experiences such as the quality of life'. What this means is that well-being can be looked at objectively or subjectively, and psychologists have looked at the different facets of well-being (i.e. social, physical and mental) and focused on a number of key concepts:

- The psychology of leisure and well-being based on the concept of hedonism (i.e. well-being as happiness, enjoyment and pleasure and positive benefits).

- The psychology of leisure focused on self-growth and well-being, based on the idea of self-actualisation (the ability of an individual to fulfil their potential through leisure).

Yet a key element which shapes the relationship between leisure and well-being is the way it is consumed by individuals and groups, particularly the social context in which this occurs (i.e. with family, friends, groups or alone).

Leisure as a defining element of the individual, family and group

Sociology, which, broadly defined, focuses on human behaviour and the wider society we live in, has made major contributions to the study of leisure (which will be explored in more detail in subsequent chapters). One notable area of social inquiry by sociologists has been their analysis of family, community and other social elements of leisure such as its meaning to families and groups. For example, with the majority of leisure being home based (Patmore 1983), sociologists have looked at important gender differences in the use of leisure time between men and women, adults and children. The environment of the home has also become a defining feature of modern-day leisure (see Chapter 3 for more detail), as many houses in the developed world have been built with home-based leisure in mind (i.e. areas for media consumption such as sitting rooms, gardens, and individual bedrooms for children with televisions and computers). This reflects the changing living standards and socioeconomic status of families, with at-home entertainment a key feature of such trends in leisure consumption.

Sociologists have also examined how leisure can now be viewed as a defining feature of the individual, family and group in society. The arguments put forward by sociologists are that leisure choices and our leisure behaviour are influenced by society. Bull *et al.* (2003) point to early sociological studies of leisure which suggested that our leisure choices were influenced by:

- social institutions (e.g. the state, workplace, the family and other groups);

- class, gender and race;

which shaped our participation in leisure activities (this will be explored in more detail in Chapters 3 and 4). Table 1.1 summarises the debates by sociologists and presents the different theoretical perspectives they have adopted to explain how leisure choices are defined and structured, depending upon their specific position in relation to different theories of society.

Ultimately, Bull *et al.* (2003) simplify the social theory debates in leisure as falling into two broad areas which are not mutually exclusive:

- leisure as freedom;

- leisure as control;

and the ability of individuals to engage in leisure as a result of these competing explanations. Researchers try to generalise from these theoretical explanations to understand the underlying reasons why leisure is such a dominant element of our lives and social relationships with others, as well as how it helps to define these relationships. Irrespective of the sociological position one adopts from these prevailing interpretations of leisure, it is the norms, roles and values of individuals and groups which influence and shape the prevailing participation and experiences of leisure. As Bull *et al.* (2003) rightly point out,

> leisure choices are exercised, but are done so within constraints imposed by the structure of society. Individuals are integrated into society through learned norms, values and roles appropriate to the social group to which they belong and consequently, leisure behaviour tends to be that which is seen as appropriate for a member of such social groups. *(Bull* et al. *2003: 40)*

The key challenge here is assessing the extent to which the individual has choice and freedom to engage in leisure, as the debates in Table 1.1 highlight. There is clearly no consensus among sociologists who study leisure behaviour, but it is clear that the individual, family and group are defining elements of how leisure is viewed, consumed and experienced as well as constructed by the other social institutions. Add to this the recognition that time for and perception of leisure varies from one society to another, and the tendency to focus on leisure and the work ethic in Western society means that the predominant theoretical explanations of leisure suggest it is seen as a separate activity and the antithesis of work. But as this book will show, other trends such as serious leisure are impacting upon the Victorian notion of the weekend as a part of the week when people traditionally do not work. These developments and others, such as the rise of sub-cultures (i.e. social networks and groups that interact to create mini-societies), provide another outlet for leisure which does not necessarily conform to the norms or rules in society, being deliberately

Table 1.1 Sociological theory and leisure

- *Functional sociologists*
  This views society as a system, where different social institutions work in harmony to integrate individuals into society. Acceptable behaviours in society are set out and leisure is seen as an autonomous area of social behaviour. In other words, social theories developed by this group of researchers try to explain leisure in relation to its function within society, as a way of providing freedom from work. Some researchers have described functional sociology as conservative administrative sociology (van Moorst 1982) where leisure patterns in society can be improved through better planning to help keep the status quo in society. This approach does not challenge the institutions in society or their role as a potential source of societal problems. These functionalist approaches accept the status quo and separate leisure from society's structure, so it is an independent element.

- *Marxist sociologists: structuralists*
  Such proponents see conflict rather than consensus in society, focused around the ideas of Karl Marx and class conflict, which is a major determinant of society's structure. This creates a range of power relationships and social divisions, with one group dominating others. One argument advanced is that the capitalist society creates false leisure needs, where marketing and commodification mean that subordinate groups desire leisure goods, services or experiences which create an illusion of happiness or satisfaction. This may also deflect attention from the rural societal problems of inequality. It is argued that the dominant elites repress subordinate groups through leisure. These sociological interpretations argue that it is the structure of society which shape our leisure and constrain us.

- *Max Weber*
  Sociologists such as Max Weber focused on the effect of society's structures (which are unknown to individual(s)) but it can constrain our freedom of choice in leisure. The concept of an individual's choice was a key contribution to leisure theory because Weber observed that in spite of how constrained an individual is by the structures in society, there is always an element of individual choice. This feature was also argued by other sociological schools of thought such as interactionists.

- *Interactionist sociologists*
  Such sociologists argue that in spite of social constraints, there is always scope for creative action, with individuals interpreting the social world around them through the meaning they derive from the interactions with others. This has a significant value for leisure studies, as it goes a stage further than Weber's belief because it also influences the social setting they are involved in, shaping the context of leisure. They may be reflected in studies such as those on the rise of a creative class, as explored in Chapter 3. However, it does not give adequate weight to the broader structures in society (i.e. the state) which constrain behaviour.

Sources: Adapted and developed from Bull *et al.* (2003); Other sources

different and not constrained by societal structures. Examples such as the cult activity of wall jumping, which is leaping over walls as a sport, has spread as a global activity. This raises the issue of how another current theme in leisure – globalisation – has shaped what we do and consume as leisure experiences. This is introduced here and explored in more detail in Chapter 3.

Leisure and globalisation

According to Pigram (2003: 209), 'globalisation describes the process of integrating economic activities and decision-making beyond national and regional boundaries towards a borderless and interconnected world. A central feature of globalisation is the notion that many features of contemporary society can no longer be undertaken in relative isolation at the level of an individual nation or political unit. The focus is on the concept of a global system, reflecting centralisation and concentration of power and influence within private multinational firms and close-knit transnational groupings'. For leisure studies, this raises the spectre of the control of leisure choices, particularly electronic media (including television) and leisure practices, by large international organisations. Globalisation as a process is not new, as Friedman (2005) describes three eras of globalisation, the first dating to 1492 and lasting to the 1800s to 1900s. But it is the process dating to the 1990s which has affected our lives and leisure most profoundly. In the 1990s, it was the pace of change brought about by globalisation and increasing global interconnectedness that influenced leisure. As Jarvie and Maguire (1994: 230) suggest, it is difficult to understand local or national experiences of leisure without some reference to globalisation processes, especially the global flows of leisure styles and practices from one part of the world to another. Likewise, other increasingly dominant signs of globalisation (e.g. long-haul tourism and global events such as the Olympic Games) epitomise this international spread and a time–space compression. Jarvie and Maguire (1994) cited two examples. First, the consumption of sports events, such as the US National Hockey League which is broadcast globally by satellite and draws upon players from different countries. It also creates sporting ware which is then merchandised globally. This links to the second example of leisure ware which now represents cultural goods with internationally recognisable brands which are an integral element of consumer culture. However, these global brands have produced the leisure ware in low-cost countries in Asia, with local adaptation to consumer markets and international marketing campaigns. Part of that marketing process is endorsement by sporting stars and sponsorship of events and festivals to increase brand awareness.

Branding, as the chapter on marketing will show, is also a key development in this globalisation process. Theorists have argued that globalisation is also occurring alongside other macro and micro processes of change such as the role of government, commodification and other social, economic and cultural changes. Even so, in 1998, concerns about globalisation were raised at a leisure conference in Brazil, the 5th World Congress of the World Leisure and Recreation Association, which resulted in the São Paolo Declaration. From this Declaration it was evident that concerns were associated with the impact of globalisation on freedom and access to leisure opportunities, including the impact on local, national and international experiences of leisure. As Rojek (2005) observed, the rise of the person-to-person communication technology known as file sharing (P2P) may be one example of a new global leisure form that fosters social inclusion, empowerment and distributive justice in relation to the São Paolo Declaration. This is because of the low-cost and wide-ranging access which P2P now permits, combined with problems of weak policing and persistent downloading. While globalisation may be associated with one of the most obvious forms of modernity, the effect of global systems of production and exchange of goods and services, it is now affecting everyday leisure lives as a global consumer culture has emerged, and many developing countries' leisure time is given over to consumptive leisure habits, replicating the process from Western nations. However, researchers are increasingly focusing on the global and local inequalities of leisure which globalisation may be engendering, particularly in terms of tourism as a form of leisure. Tourism is one example where some global companies exploit less developed countries' labour and resources to fulfil tourists' needs and expropriate profits back to the company's country base.

Summary

It is evident from the discussion of 'what is leisure' in this chapter that there are no universally agreed definitions of leisure. Indeed, throughout the book, different interpretations and views of what constitutes leisure are introduced. If we adopt a seemingly simple notion of leisure as the antithesis (i.e. opposite) of work, it poses many questions for those groups who do not work (e.g. children, the unemployed, the elderly and home-based parents looking after children) and may be challenged by those with subsistence lifestyles, as will be shown in Chapter 3. It also poses many problems for researchers concerned about other interconnected notions such as play. A simple acknowledgement that we cannot easily segment our lives into leisure and non-leisure means that our experiences of leisure are extremely subjective, focused on the individual, and in some cases really removes the need for a precise and tightly defined notion of leisure. The chapter has explored some of the different approaches developed by leisure researchers to try to define what we mean by leisure, given its significance to our individual lives and the wider development of society. To understand leisure, we need first to understand the parameters of leisure as contributing to what is termed the domain of leisure. This provides an introduction to the basis of those elements which help us to begin to see what subjects have contributed to the development of leisure studies and their contribution to defining the subject, structured around four distinctive elements:

- leisure as freedom from constraints;

- leisure as time left after work;

- leisure as the opportunity to choose;

- leisure as the opposite of work;

along with the key role of time as a variable in seeking to understand what free time means for leisure as a construct. This then links to the four distinct approaches to defining leisure that characterise its study and analysis:

- time-based approaches;
- activity-based approaches;
- attitude-based approaches;
- quality-based approaches.

These four approaches each look at different facets of how we experience and enjoy leisure which need to be integrated to give a greater coherence to how we understand what seems a simple construct, which is actually very complex. This complexity is more than apparent from the different ways in which sociologists have approached the study of leisure using theoretical constructs. These lack a common focus or purpose due to the philosophical stance adopted by each school of sociological thought that informs their approach to leisure. However, what the social theorists do demonstrate, albeit in a sometimes abstract and complex manner, is that the leisure experiences we consume may be constructed, controlled or influenced (depending on your theoretical standpoint) and these social structures and institutions need to be understood. Ultimately leisure takes place in a social setting – the society we live in, which does shape how we view and perceive leisure (which also varies between different cultural groups) and this influences the leisure behaviour and choices we make (as Chapters 3 and 4 will demonstrate). And you probably thought that leisure was just a simple matter of fun, enjoyment and relaxation! To illustrate how leisure has developed as societies have changed, the next chapter focuses on the history of leisure, because it is only through such an approach that you can appreciate the antecedents of modern-day leisure.

Discussion questions

1. How would you go about developing a definition of leisure?
2. Why is time so important to the understanding of leisure?
3. How does the consumer society affect modern-day leisure patterns?
4. What is the significance of studying leisure for modern-day society?

References

Argyle, M. (1996) *The Social Psychology of Leisure*, Penguin: London.

Barclays (2000) *Leisure in the New Millennium*, Barclays: London.

Baudrillard, J. (1998) *The Consumer Society: Myths and Structures*, Sage: London.

Best S. (2010) *Leisure Studies: Themes and Perspectives*, Sage: London.

Bull, C., Hoose, J. and Weed, M. (2003) *An Introduction to Leisure Studies*, Pearson: Harlow.

Burns, C. (1932) *Leisure in the Modern World*, The Century Company: New York.

Clark, J. and Crichter, C. (1985) *The Devil Makes Work: Leisure in Capitalist Britain*, Macmillan: Basingstoke.

Coleman, D. (2003) 'Well-being', in J. Jenkins and J. Pigram (eds) *Encyclopaedia of Leisure and Outdoor Recreation*, Routledge: London, p. 548.

Cook, D. (2004) *The Commodification of Childhood*, Duke University Press: Durham, NC.

Cook, D. (2006) 'Leisure and consumption', in C. Rojek, S. Shaw, A. Veal (eds) *A Handbook of Leisure Studies*, Palgrave: Basingstoke, pp. 304–16.

Csikszentmihalyi, M. (1980) 'Subject elimination of the proposed leisure information network', in L. Bollaert *et al.* (eds) *The First International Leisure Information Network Conference*, VUB : Brussels.

De Grazia, S. (1962) *Of Time, Work and Leisure*, Doubleday & Company: Garden City, NY.

Driver, B.L. *et al.* (eds) (1991) *Benefits of Leisure*, Sagamore: Champaign, IL.

Durant, H. (1938) *The Problem of Leisure*, George Routledge & Sons Ltd: London.

Durie, A. (2006) *Scotland for the Holidays*, Tuckwell Press: Edinburgh.

Featherstone, M. (1987) 'Lifestyle and consumer culture', *Theory, Culture, and Society* 4 (1): 53–70.

Friedman, T. (2005) *The World is Flat: A Brief History of the Globalised World in the 21st Century*, Allen Lane: London.

Glyptis, S. (1981) 'Leisure life-styles', *Regional Studies* 15: 311–26.

Hall, C.M. and Page, S.J. (2006) *The Geography of Tourism and Recreation: Environment, Place and Space*, 3rd edn, Routledge: London.

Herbert, D.T. (1988) 'Work and leisure: exploring a relationship', *Area* 20 (3): 241–52.

Jarvie, G. and Maguire, J. (1994) *Sport and Leisure Social Thought*, Routledge: London.

Karlis, G. (2004) *Leisure and Recreation in Canadian Society: An Introduction*, Thompson Education: Toronto.

Kelly, J. (1982) *Leisure*, Prentice Hall: Englewood Cliffs, NJ.

Madge, C. and Harrison, T. (1939) *Britain by Mass Observation*, Penguin: Harmondsworth.

McKendrick, J., Bradford, M. and Fielder, A. (2000a) 'Kid customer? Commercialization of playspace and the commodification of childhood', *Childhood* 7 (3): 295–314.

McKendrick, J., Bradford, M. and Fielder, A. (2000b) 'Time for a party: making sense of the commercialisation of leisure space for children', in S. Holloway and G. Valentine (eds) *Children's Geographies*, Verso: London.

Meyersohn, R. (1972) 'Leisure', in A. Campbell and P.E. Converse (eds) *The Human Meaning of Social Change*, Russell Sage: New York, pp. 205–28.

Olfert, S. (2003) *Quality of Life Leisure Indicators*, Community-University Institute for Social Research: University of Saskatchewan, www.usask.ca/cuisr/docs/pub_doc/quality/OlfertFINAL.pdf

ONS (2008) *Social Trends*, The Stationery Office: London, www.statistics.gov.uk.

Page, S. J. and Connell, J. (2009) *Tourism: A Modern Synthesis*, 3 edn, Cengage Learning: London.

Parker, S. (1999) *Leisure in Contemporary Society*, CABI: Wallingford.

Patmore, J.A. (1983) *Recreation and Resources: Leisure Patterns and Leisure Places*, Blackwell: Oxford.

Pigram, J. (2003) 'Globalization', in J. Jenkins and J. Pigram (eds) *Encyclopaedia of Leisure and Outdoor Recreation*, Routledge: London, pp. 208–9.

Pretty, J., Griffin, M., Peacock, J., Hine, R., Sellens, M. and South, N. (2005) *Countryside for Health and Well-Being: The Physical and Mental Health Benefits of Green Exercise*, Countryside Recreation Network: Sheffield.

Rojek, C. (2000) *Leisure and Culture*, Palgrave: Basingstoke.

Rojek, C. (2010) *The Labour of Leisure*, Sage: London.

Rook, D. (1985) 'The ritual dimension of consumer behaviour', *Journal of Consumer Research* 12 (3): 251–64.

Rowntree, S. (1941) *Poverty and Progress: A Second Social Survey of York*, Longmans, Green & Co: London.

Schor, J. (1991) *The Overworked American: The Unexpected Decline of Leisure*. Basic Books: Durham, NC.

Sizer, J. (1917) *Commercialization of Leisure*, Four Seas Company: Boston.

Stebbins, R.A. (1982) 'Serious leisure: a conceptual statement', *Pacific Sociological Review* 25: 251–72.

Stockdale, J.E. (1985) *What is Leisure? An Empirical Analysis of the Concept of Leisure and the Role of Leisure in People's Lives*, Sports Council: London.

Sylvester, C. (1999) 'The classical idea of leisure: cultural ideal or class prejudice?', *Leisure Sciences* 21 (1): 3–16.

Torkildsen, G. (1999) *Leisure Management*, 3rd edn, Routledge: London.

Van Moorst, H. (1982) 'Leisure and social theory', *Leisure Studies* 1 (2): 157–69.

Veblen, T. (1899) *The Theory of the Leisure Class*, Allen & Unwin: London.

World Tourism Organisation (1983) *Individuals' Use of Leisure time in EU Countries*, World Tourism Organisation: Madrid.

Zuzanek, J. (2006) 'Leisure and time', in C. Rojek, S. Shaw and A. Veal (eds) *A Handbook of Leisure Studies*, Palgrave: Basingstoke, pp. 185–202.

2 The historical analysis of leisure

Learning outcomes

After reading this chapter you should be able to:

• Identify different approaches used by historians to analyse the history of leisure

• Trace the critical transformations that occurred in leisure from a pre-industrial through to an industrial and postmodern society

• Recognise the significance of understanding past trends and developments in leisure, and how they have contributed to present-day patterns of leisure

Introduction

This chapter seeks to explore the evolution of leisure as a phenomenon and social practice and how it developed as a key element of our everyday lives. The historical evolution is a complex and enormous subject for anyone to broach, and it is impossible in one chapter to provide more than a cursory overview of the subject area and material commonly addressed in leisure history. Instead of providing a comprehensive review, this chapter sets out to address a number of key questions so that the reader can appreciate why the subject material is coherent, relevant and able to demonstrate a clear evolution:

1. How did the current interest in leisure studies as a subject area emerge and what are its roots? This will help us to understand how the contemporary history of leisure over the past hundred or so years has been shaped by certain subjects, most notably sociology.

2. How did this evolving interest in leisure studies generate a range of research techniques and data which have helped historians to measure and analyse contemporary leisure?

3. How have historians embraced such data in their debates and analysis of leisure in past times?

4. What distinct eras exist in terms of leisure activity and what debates exist among historians over the categorisation and analysis of these eras?

As the discussion in this chapter is necessarily selective, it is important to identify a rationale for where to end the analysis of modern leisure as a historical form. The analysis of leisure will end in the 1980s, not least because this was a turning point in modern leisure as we experience it today, as will become clear later, but also because to progress any further will lead to potential duplication of discussion of leisure issues in different chapters throughout the book, when looking at trends and themes in recent years. The chapter does not seek to be a definitive history of leisure, but a review of the main issues and themes that influenced how leisure has changed through the ages as a context for other chapters that follow.

The history of the study of leisure studies

The comparative usefulness of modern-day leisure studies as a domain of study in universities, colleges and schools has been a frequent claim of many writers, often cited as an excuse for why leisure studies remains a largely underdeveloped area of study. This claim is one that this book would dispute, since a rich history of research and study of leisure (often as an adjunct to work or as non-work) exists. Beckers and Mommas (1996: 210) rightly acknowledge that 'Leisure exists as one of the oldest topics of social scientific research' which can be traced back to the nineteenth century, as Table 2.1 shows. This illustrates the rich sociological tradition of leisure research that emerged in three countries (although Mommas et al. (1996) can demonstrate a similar pattern of development across Europe and North American where similar examples also exist (e.g. Meyersohn 1969)); in other words, as nation states developed and political philosophies based on the welfare of the population (initially in Scandinavia in

Table 2.1 Evolution of leisure research traditions and contributions in selected European countries to 1970

United Kingdom

- Evolution was based on the collection of facts to categorise and measure 'the facts of leisure' and how it fitted into people's lives
- Origins lay in the UK empirical tradition in sociology such as Royal Commissions, social reformers and social commentators in the nineteenth century exemplified by:
  - Mayhew (1851) *London Labour and London Poor*
  - Booth (1881) *London's Poor*
  - Rowntree (1901) *Poverty* (based on York)
  - Rowntree and Lavers (1951) *English Life and Leisure*
  - Mass observation surveys of the 1930s by Charles Madge and Tom Harrison examining working-class culture in a work town (Bolton) and holiday making in Blackpool in Wakes Week, creating the first community studies
  - Community studies, examining leisure lives via ethnography and description
  - 1970s studies by Roberts (1970) and Parker (1971) establishing leisure as an area of academic endeavour alongside Patmore (1970)

France

- Nineteenth-century interest in social science research in the universities
- Collection of leading sociologists interested in employment and society (e.g. Durkheim) and slow evolution of sociology
- 1936   G. Friedman, *La Crise du Progrés*, where leisure could counterbalance the negative effects of work but part of the sociology of work
- 1950s   sociological importance of leisure recognised as part of daily life (e.g. Marxist sociologist Lefebvre)
- Evolution of anthropological study of leisure in the 1950s, recognising leisure time as a basis for games
- Sociologist Dumazedier establishes the Sociology of Leisure Committee in 1961 as part of the International Association of Sociology and publishes *Towards a Sociology of Leisure* in 1967.

The Netherlands

- No equivalent word for the concept of leisure. The word *Vrijetijd* can have several meanings depending on the context
- 1784 onwards   Dutch towns with societies for Public Welfare with middle-class membership seeking to civilise and educate people via clubs and societies
- 1924   International Labour Organisation conference on 'The Problem of Free Time' highlighted Dutch labourers' use of free time and impact of a decrease in working hours, following regulation of hours by law after 1919
- 1927   Committee concerning Folk Pleasures examined people's behaviour at dances and fairs, looking at moral behaviour, followed in 1931 by three government committees looking at such behaviour in parks, dance halls and cinemas
- 1934   J. Kruijt publishes an article in the journal 'Popular Education' (*Volksontwikkeling*) on sociology and free time

(continued)

Table 2.1 (*continued*)

- 1936   First nationwide survey of free time (Society for Public Welfare based on 621 questionnaires and 226 time budget surveys)
- Mass youth studies by the state in 1948 leading to 160 regional reports of free time behaviour
- 1945–66   180 observational studies undertaken by the state, aimed at those sections of society not adhering to middle-class family standards
- Rise of the consumer market in the 1950s, with a five-day week and paid holidays
- 1950s   Central Bureau for Statistics project to study the free-time activities of the Dutch population, led by sociologists, examining 7200 people, 3300 further interviews and 250 in-depth interviews
- 1968   Ph.D. by R. Wippler, 'The Social Determinants of Free Time Behaviour', using factor analysis to determine the free-time activities of different groups

Source: Adapted from Mommas *et al.* (1996)

the 1920s) emerged across many other Western countries. This was shaped by an interest by the state in leisure as a subject of research to inform policy choices and decisions (i.e. what governments do to use public resources to influence the choices they wish to make on how to treat their population and economy) on how to use leisure to assist the well-being of the population. Beckers and Mommas (1996) focus on a number of trends in the twentieth century which characterised interest in leisure at a public policy level:

- 1919–1935, termed the Quest for Leisure, with workers seeking an 8-hour day and a permutation of the $3 \times 8 - 8$ hours of sleep, 8 hours of work and 8 hours of leisure, which affected many countries' discussions on labour and working conditions in the 1920s and 1930s.

- The 1950s to 1960s and the gradual democratisation of leisure, with a greater state provision and involvement in leisure as a feature of government (although there is evidence of this pre-1950).

- The 1960s and 1970s, when a period of affluence and the rise of the consumer society saw state welfare policies on leisure at their zenith.

- The 1980s and 1990s, when we can discern a greater restructuring of the role of the state in leisure provision and a growing individualisation of leisure.

Bramham and Henry (1996) suggested that in the UK, since the nineteenth century, the purpose of leisure studies was to 'categorise and measure the facts of leisure in people's lives', epitomised by the great social explorers (Table 2.1) such as Booth and Rowntree. For example, Rowntree and Lavers' (1951) impressive analysis of leisure in the UK, with European examples, was based on extensive social investigation and empirical research (i.e. compiling factual and numerical evidence), with 975 case histories compiled in their study. Many of the early studies of leisure helped to pioneer many of the modern-day research techniques and tools which social science researchers use in leisure research, to yield empirical data of both a quantitative and qualitative nature (subsequently reappraised by many historians).

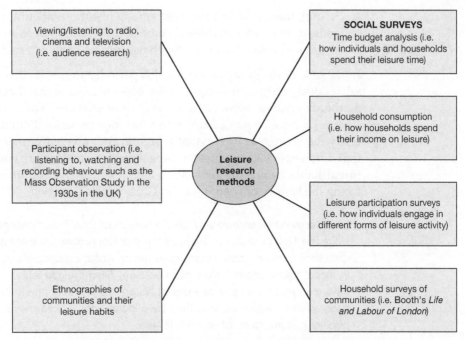

Figure 2.1 Research methods used by pioneering studies of leisure

Sources: Adapted from Mommas *et al.* (1996); Page (1988)

As Figure 2.1 shows, these methods of social inquiry have helped shape modern-day sociology, which expanded rapidly as a university-level subject in the 1960s. It may be argued that this is a partial explanation of why sociology has such a dominant influence over the subject's development and analysis today. It is often traced back to the late 1960s when the sociological teaching of the subject in universities developed as a distinct curriculum (although outdoor education as an element of education can be traced back much further when specific colleges were established to pursue this issue). With these issues in mind, attention now turns to the historical analysis of leisure.

Historical analysis of leisure

There are many debates among historians over the significance of leisure as a phenomenon that has evolved through the ages, much of which is based on two interrelated viewpoints:

● First, that leisure as a concept may have changed through time and so 'a central problem in characterising leisure is whether the concept has a historically stable meaning' (Borsay 2006: 8).

- Second, there is little agreement among historians about the problem of periodisation of leisure through time and its allocation to distinct epochs or distinguishable timeframes that have common characteristics.

In the case of the study of leisure, this periodisation is further complicated by what Borsay (2006: 20) suggests is the effect of leisure: that it evolved in society as the distinction between work and domestic life. 'For a historian . . . it [leisure] cannot be pinned down to a neat one sentence definition, for it is precisely the change in its use that is significant', given arguments by historians that differences between the time spent on work and leisure were largely indistinguishable before the nineteenth century in many countries. The problem facing the history of leisure was, as Cross (1990: 2) argued,

> to understand when and why leisure behaviour took major changes of course . . .
> since the 16th century . . . Perhaps the greatest problem is that historians have seldom shown much interest in the question of explaining people's use of free time . . .
> In recent years, social history has frequently filled the gap left . . . social historians
> have explored those private sides of history, family, community, and work that had
> been so long neglected; and they have increasingly linked these social spheres to
> popular culture, much of which is leisure.

This highlights the importance of the neglect by historians as well as the link to popular culture. This is related to the types of activities, attitudes and values people have towards popular culture in a society at a given time. *So how should we approach the history and evolution of leisure?*

Reconstructing past histories of leisure: interpretation, focus and sources

According to Watson (1998: 16), the art of the leisure historian is 'primarily concerned with explaining the causes and effects of historical developments rather than writing a narrative' (i.e. writing a story about the past histories of leisure for specific periods and themes). Much of the current interest in this area of history has largely been a product of the late 1960s and 1970s, with many impressive historical overviews of the subject (e.g. Walton and Walvin 1983; Cunningham 1980) and overviews of the progress in leisure history (Bailey 1989). To pursue this interest in leisure history, there are broadly two approaches used in historical research to examine a social phenomenon such as leisure:

- The analysis of how changes have come about and the formative influences on the contemporary era; and

- The in-depth study of specific eras and leisure phenomena in past times, described as a cross-section of a specific era. Historical researchers focus on specific themes and issues dependent upon their interest or specialism (i.e. economic, social, cultural and political dimensions).

While this chapter cannot present a comprehensive review of leisure through history, nor the separate leisure histories of the world's regions, it is hoped that some of these principal features of the historical analysis of leisure will be outlined. For example, historical analysis of leisure is being better understood through the use of oral history and a living tradition of leisure, which is the recording of past histories of how people remembered the past to understand the cultural meaning of leisure. However, prior to the eighteenth century only limited evidence survives to reconstruct leisure. One of the largely underexplored sources which historians of leisure have not fully embraced is diaries and autobiographies which typify the experiences of the masses, which often go unrecorded as we tend to rely on the written documents from those who were educated and able to record experiences. One notable autobiography which will highlight the depth and understanding which this source of information can bring to leisure research is R. Roberts' (1974) *The Classic Slum: Salford Life in the First Quarter of the Century*, as the following extract illustrates:

> Among women in shop talk the confinement of daily life was often a subject for bitter complaint. Some did manage an occasional visit to the cemetery, or an hour in a balding park on the edge of the village, but many were denied even this. One, I recall, spoke wearily of never having been more than five minutes' walk from her home in eighteen years of married life. Husbands were luckier: at least once a year a beer-house picnic would take them for a long boozing day in the country. Children too got intense pleasure from the outings that charity or the Sunday school provided. Our top people paid annual visits to Blackpool, New Brighton and Southport and made sure that everybody knew, especially about their first ride in a motor car. At Southport quite early in the century an enterprising young man was doing excellent business with his Daimler open saloon, taking half a dozen passengers a time for five-minute trips round the lake. *(Roberts 1974: 49)*

This quotation illustrates:

- the restricted nature of women's leisure patterns and activities and the differences with male leisure;

- the role of annual outings (days out);

- the emergence of annual holidays, the novelty of new technology and its use among the working class;

which are experiences that cannot easily be captured through other historical records.

Woody's (1957) early attempt to depict leisure in history characterises many of the subsequent studies which highlight this as a worthy area of research, focusing on the Greek tradition, the Ascetic persuasion (i.e. the evolution of the Christian ideal of leisure through the Middle Ages and the impact of monasteries and Christian learning), followed by the further development of Christian ideals of leisure through the Puritans and the Victorians, a model which was emulated in many subsequent historical overviews of leisure. But continued tensions exist in how historians seek to trace the history of leisure, largely focused on its periodisation through time.

Approaches and debates in the periodisation of leisure

In any historical overview of leisure, two underlying themes are important: *continuity* and *change*. Continuity means that leisure has continued to be an important process, which remained influential in the lifestyles of certain social classes. Change, on the other hand, characterises the evolution of leisure through the ages, since leisure is a dynamic, ever-changing phenomenon. Much of the change is based upon the interaction between the demand for, and supply of, leisure opportunities through time. In terms of supply, key factors promoting the development of leisure can be explained by the role of innovation (i.e. new ideas), which has generated new products, experiences, destinations and released a latent or pent-up demand for leisure. In other words, it is the factors that led to the enabling of a greater capacity for the individual and social groups to engage in leisure through time, often described by early studies of leisure as the rise of *mass leisure* (Larrabee and Meyersohn 1958).

This notion of mass leisure is often related to a greater commercialisation of leisure to meet the consumption needs of these masses with increased disposable income that is often dated to the late nineteenth century in many developed economies. As Borsay (2006: 79) argues, 'leisure was . . . an important arena in which to play out the social order', which is apparent as far back as one wishes to look in history. Even so, Thomas (1964: 138) argued that 'the greatest danger facing historians of our topic [leisure] is surely to assume continuity and to work with the modern concepts of leisure and sport, projecting them back on to the past without asking about the meanings which contemporaries gave to their activities'. This firmly establishes the case for the historical analysis of leisure to appreciate how it has evolved and developed through time.

Periods in the history of leisure

Historians and sociologists adopt a blend of periodisation and theoretical explanations to trace the evolution of leisure (see Figure 2.1 and Table 2.2), but there is no clear consensus on this. Much of the debate over periodisation hinges upon a historical debate, which can be traced to the 1960s, over the importance of the great divide in social history and its formative influence on leisure – the Industrial Revolution, and its antecedents. This debate largely follows the division of leisure into pre-industrial, industrial and post-industrial society and the impact on the social organisation and structure of society, and how this influenced the pursuit of and engagement with leisure in the lives of the population. This is depicted more clearly by Roberts (2006) in relation to the changes in society which shaped leisure

Table 2.2   Leisure in the UK through history

Era	Characteristics of leisure with selected illustrations and trends
1350–1530 Medieval (Merry England)	• Christian calendar as a determinant of leisure • Festivals, ale houses, summer games • Jousting, games, circuses, tennis and hunting as activities for elites • Agricultural activities and blurring of work and leisure, with labour task-oriented and leisure integrated into these tasks • 30% of UK country land area under Royal Forests
1530–1660 (Reformation)	• Rise of the Christian work ethic in the Reformation, with leisure associated with idleness (Calvinist ideals) • Attack on 'Merry England' and pleasure • Expansion of ale houses from 25,000 in the 1570s to 50,000 in the 1630s (1 ale house to 300 population) • 1580s onwards – the rise of clubs and societies associated with the Glorious Revolution • J. Stow (1603), *A Survey of London*, observed pastimes and sports among the youth on holy days such as 'leaping, dauncing, shooting, wrestling, casting of the stone or ball and cockfighting' (Coulton 1918)
1660–1780	• Emergence of newspapers and journals for elites and rise of reading rooms • Restoration of Charles II, the Enlightenment and the beginning of the commercialisation of leisure (e.g. horse racing and spa towns and theatre) • Royal patronage of elite leisure activities and the emergence of coastal tourism from the 1730s • Gradual narrowing of leisure activities for common people, as popular customs and activities are under threat
1780–1870 (Industrial Revolution)	• Continued commercialisation of leisure as entrepreneurs such as Thomas Cook promote travel for holidays in the mid-nineteenth century, involving increased use of capital and technology for leisure (e.g. the stagecoach and railway) which begin to extend leisure to a wider audience • Popular leisure survives until the 1840s as more state-sponsored cultural forms of leisure emerge (e.g. museums and libraries, parks and gardens) • Rise of mass leisure forms from 1850s reflecting the increasing urban industrialisation
1870–1960s	• Greater commercialisation, professionalisation and rise of leisure cartels (e.g. public house chains) • In the late nineteenth century 100,000 public houses with a ratio of 1 public house:300 population (dropping to 1:600 by the 1960s) • Rising incomes in towns and cities 1899–1936, by 30% • Greater disposable income for leisure consumption and new forms of spending (e.g. the rise of the fish and chip shop) • Expanding economy (domestic and international) and the development of mass spectator sports • Increasing state regulation of leisure habits and behaviour to address 'undesirable' activities (e.g. street gambling)

(continued)

Table 2.2 (*continued*)

Era	Characteristics of leisure with selected illustrations and trends
	• Emergence of a sport culture in the late Victorian period through the Edwardian years as well as other forms of mass culture (e.g. the music hall) and the bicycle • 1914–1918 continued expansion of leisure, and new forms of leisure expenditure by working women in munitions factories • 1920s and 1930s, the continued expansion of pre-war leisure (e.g. coastal tourism) and growing regional differentiation despite a depressed economy • Growing individualisation of leisure in the 1920s and 1930s (rise of the motorcar/motorcycle, cinema and radio) • Massive commercialisation of leisure by big business, including the use of marketing and promotion to attract the masses • Labour government post-1945 and collectivisation of state interest in leisure and well-being through active interventions • Post-1945, rise of new social groups and classes with greater wealth and more diverse leisure needs (e.g. children, women and housewives, the elderly and ethnic groups in the 1950s) • Greater access to finance for leisure (e.g. hire purchase) • Pressure groups rediscover and promote heritage and the past as leisure interests
1960s–	• Emergence of social and cultural revolution often described as dating to the 1960s and arguably the high point of 'modernity' • Commercialised youth culture develops (e.g. pop music and the 45 rpm 'single') • Growing internationalisation and globalisation of leisure owing to developments in communications and transport technology (e.g. aircraft, package holidays and long-haul travel) • Rise of late modernity/postmodernity • Growth of mega-events as a form of spectacle and celebration of culture • Expansion of in-home and personalised leisure through new media and technology (e.g. satellite television) • Growing consumer culture and application of more sophisticated marketing principles to leisure consumers • Blurring of work and leisure as integrated activities in many people's lives • Emergence of concerns over leisure, quality of life and work–life balance as progressively more women with family responsibilities enter the workforce • Commercialisation of leisure trends affects public sector leisure provision (e.g. rise of Compulsory Competitive Tendering and *Best Value* concerns for public spending) as the state withdraws from a former collectivist approach to state-sponsored leisure • Leisure and tourism are harnessed by the state to assist with regeneration of local economies as deindustrialisation accelerated by a state ideology wedded to a market economy and the focus on the private sector • Leisure and cultural industries are recognised as major economic activities, with a recognition of the value of 'leisure shopping' to promote service sector employment.

Sources: Borsay (2006); *Social Trends*; Page (2009); Hall and Page (2006); Coulton (1918); Burke (1994); Other sources

Key contributions by historian	Classification					
Borsay	Pre-industrial	1530–1660	1660–1780	1780–1870	1870–1960	1960–
Rojek			Roots of capitalism	Modernity	Postmodernity	
Marx	Feudalism			Capitalism	Communism	
Other historians	Pre-industrial//**Great Divide** (or different variants)		Industrial		Modernity	

Figure 2.2   Eras of leisure – interpretations by historians of leisure

Sources: Adapted from Borsay (2006); Burke (1994); Other sources

(Figure 2.2) but it does not give adequate attention to the period prior to the fourteenth century, simply assuming that work/non-work was intertwined and work was determined by the task and not by time. Bailey (1989: 108) traced the depiction of the evolution of leisure and its periodisation to Malcolmson (1973), who divided the history of leisure into the pre-industrial and traditional period (1700 to 1850) and then into the Victorian era, particularly the 1875–1900 period with the rise of the working class in the UK and the evolution of many of the features of modern-day leisure (e.g. the seaside resort and mass leisure). For this reason, this chapter seeks to provide a concise overview of the evolution of leisure through time, emphasising the way it continued with some of its traditions and antecedents and also changed. We draw upon experiences from across the world, as many histories of leisure are almost entirely Euro-centric or based on North American experiences, with only a limited number of comparative studies across countries (e.g. Cross 1990). There is also a predominant Western ethos in much of the published forms of leisure research.

Ultimately, much of the attention of researchers, especially historians, has been on the transformation of leisure, particularly in Western countries, even though rich histories exist for non-Western societies (e.g. India, see Bhattacharya 2006 where Western concepts may not necessarily apply and illustrated by Table 2.3). It is still the case, as Bailey (1989: 118) argued, that while 'leisure history is still locked into conventional periodisation, it has made few inroads beyond 1914, and its connection to the present has been slight. Its concern with the classic phenomena of industrialisation also narrowed its early attentions to typical manufacturing communities and larger cities', epitomised by large monographs and case studies of leisure in specific cities such as Rozenzweig's (1985) *Eight Hours for What we Will: Workers and Leisure in an Industrial City, 1870–1920*' based on Boston, USA. Bailey (1989) recognised that some of these deficiencies were under repair, particularly the neglect of gender and women's experiences through history as outlined above by Roberts (1974). Yet even the most up-to-date review of the field by Borsay (2006) does still highlight the absence of a 'comparative engagement with the history of leisure in cultures outside Britain, the USA and Europe with some notable exceptions in Australia and New Zealand', as will be illustrated later in the chapter.

Table 2.3   Recent examples of studies of non-Western histories of leisure

Study	Location and period of study	Characteristics of leisure
Bhattacharya (2006)	History of leisure in India	• Rich history of Indian cultures and diverse social and religious groups • Role of social and religious festivals in leisure activities • Role of religious pilgrimages • No dominant culture, which creates a unique set of leisure experiences
Weikin (2007)	Women's festivities in late Imperial China	• Examines the activities of elite and ordinary women in leisure festivals • Such festivals brought women to the outer world and relief from domestic drudgery
Hubertus (2005)	Fun, leisure and entertainment in Russia 1710–2000	• Review of Russian studies of leisure activities • Role of play, leisure and entertainment are reviewed, including football, horse racing, theatre and play • History of summer homes for elites are also reviewed
Akyeampong and Ambler (2002)	Leisure in African history	• Evolution of leisure activities in Africa, Including soccer, popular music and indigenisation of Western sport and leisure habits • Reviews of many of the key studies published on African leisure history • Identification of African concepts of leisure and leisure time through history, including during colonisation and post-colonialisation • Use of leisure time by colonial governments and employers as a means of social control, particularly in mining areas • Role of children's and women's leisure in Africa and the changes in indigenous and cultural forms of leisure through time
Walvin (1995)	Slaves in the seventeenth to nineteenth centuries in the USA	• Slaves and their availability of free time • Role of the Christian calendar • Role of rational recreation in slave leisure time

Leisure in primitive societies

The study of primitive societies has largely been within the remit of *archaeology*, which looks at the remnants and remains of previous societies to reconstruct the lifestyles and patterns of living in past societies, and *anthropology*, which is the study of man and civilisation. In the case of anthropology, the study of how others live (ethnography) helps to explain how play and the use of leisure fitted into primitive society and the lives of individuals and groups. The study of anthropology as an intellectual pursuit can be dated to the 1880s, and Tylor's (1881) publication, *Anthropology: An Introduction*, had a chapter on the art of pleasure which highlighted the significance of leisure as a feature of anthropological research. Other studies in the 1940s and 1950s examined the role of games in prehistory and throughout history (Roberts 1970), demonstrating that leisure had an important role in shaping the cultural evolution of society (Pieper 1958). Chick (2006) highlighted the importance of culture, which is a fundamental underpinning of society's leisure.

Anthropologists examine the way in which societies have communicated their activities and experiences through material objects, using symbols, as well as through dress, language, religion, rituals, games and human behaviour. In this context, leisure is a way in which culture has been expressed by primitive and modern-day society, also playing a key role in the transmission of rituals and activities from one generation to another. One of the key debates which Chick (2006) highlights is that we often assume that leisure did not exist in these primitive societies because nomadic people did not separate work (seeking food, shelter and water as basic human needs) from leisure. But there is evidence in many ancient civilisations that pre-date the Greek and Roman period that leisure existed, as games and play were a feature of such societies. Storytelling in aboriginal society, with its rich cultural history, was highlighted by Veal and Lynch (2001) in their analysis of leisure. Argyle (1996) also pointed to the informal nature of leisure in such hunter-gatherer groups, where talking, joking, music and storytelling were cultural forms of leisure as other studies of Aboriginal societies show (e.g. see Atkinson 1991; Blainey 1975). Chick (2006) also argues that simply to date leisure to a time when humans developed more sedentary activities, to increase food production and to form into permanent larger settlements and social groups, thereby creating leisure time, overlooks the important elements of leisure activity in primitive society. This questions simple assumptions that leisure can only be defined as a feature associated with work and that primitive societies were completely preoccupied with time for the equivalent of work.

Leisure in classical times

According to Toner (1995), the 'history of the pre-industrial world is an underdeveloped field'. The ancient civilisation of Greece was important for its major development of leisure as a concept, based on the Greek philosopher's recognition, endorsement and promotion of the concept of leisure. De Grazia's

(1962) influential study, *Of Time, Work and Leisure*, pointed to the Creto-Mycenaean period (i.e. when the Bronze Age Minoan civilisation emerged from Crete from 2700 to 1450 BC), which was followed by the Mycenaean civilisation which emerged between 1600 BC and ca. 1100 BC. It was followed by the ancient Greek civilisation which developed from 1100 to 146 BC. In ancient Greece, leisure was formally discovered and constructed as a key element of their society. Aristotle considered leisure to be a key element of the Greek lifestyle, where slaves and other people should do the work and the Greek freemen should put their leisure time to good use. This was based on the notion of freedom (i.e. freedom from work to engage in leisure), and a social and economic system with slaves doing the work and leisure as a minority activity. As Argyle (1996: 14) indicated:

> Most of the work was done by slaves, and it was believed that work was not suitable for freemen. Aristotle thought that the life of leisure was the only fit life for a Greek. The main purpose of life was the proper use of leisure, by self-development through education and contemplation, the pursuit of virtue through knowledge, and the practice of music, philosophy, ritual and athletics . . . The Greeks were the first people to have a positive doctrine of leisure, and a very interesting one – if there were someone else to do the work. Greek cities were well equipped for leisure, with parks. *(Argyle 1996: 14)*

What is important, as Hunnicutt (2006) argues, is that many of the philosophical debates on how to understand and conceptualise leisure, highlighted in Chapter 1, can be dated to the Greek philosophers and focus on:

● Work and leisure.

● Leisure and freedom (i.e. having the free time to engage in leisure).

● The role of leisure in society and its link to culture, establishing it as a social activity and way of life that involves activities, the arts and social interaction.

Even so, more recent evaluations of the role of leisure in Greek society questioned some of the interpretations of Aristotle, highlighting that leisure was purely an aristocratic notion. Sylvester (1999) questioned leisure as the antithesis of work, as something which was mutually compatible for the common citizen in Greece. What is apparent from the Greek philosophical basis of leisure was that it was based on wealth, privilege and an absence of barriers to participation. For the historian, the key debates are how these barriers were gradually removed to allow greater social participation in leisure through time, as society evolved from a pre-industrial to modern and then on to a postmodern or post-industrial society (see Clarke and Critcher 1985).

This positive leisure doctrine may well have been the original 'leisure lifestyle', where the pursuit of music, philosophy, non-work and measures of self-development were elements of Greek society. The development of the Olympic Games, after 776 BC, did provide a vital stimulus for leisure, based upon a major sporting event. There are also elements of tourism discernible in ancient Greece as Greeks travelled to the site of the Olympic Games and were housed in tented encampments, creating a tourism event.

In contrast, the rise of Rome (from the tenth century BC to the fifth century AD) and the Roman Empire (27 BC to AD 476) was based upon the twin elements of military conquest and administration. Toner (1995: 1) argues that 'the central themes of Roman life were connected to leisure on account that Rome was felt to be characterised by its abundant leisure', which represented the good life. The state and private individuals created leisure facilities (i.e. spas, baths (*thermae*) and resorts) and enjoyed similar leisure lifestyles to the Greeks. The construction of coliseums for events and spectator sports, as epitomised in the recent film, *Gladiator*, created the supply of leisure-related facilities. This featured gladiatorial combat, horse racing and chariot contests as well as athletic competitions. Above all, it was designed to be a spectacle for the masses which featured in everyday conversation and had cruelty, bravery, high levels of excitement and competitiveness at its heart. Therefore, two elements of leisure can be discerned in Roman society:

- First, leisure was focused on urban places where the resorts and facilities/events existed, so that the middle classes in Roman society had opportunity to spend their 200 holidays a year. In the case of Roman baths, they were a daily meeting place and performed many functions, not least as a place for relaxation, bathing, business and talking for the elites.

- Second, popular culture existed, comprising gambling, drinking in bars and taverns, the theatre and festivals related to religious events. Rome also emerged as an important urban tourism destination, with its capital city function. To service tourist needs, inns, bars and tour guides as well as souvenir sellers developed. In this respect, many elements of modern-day tourism were established in Roman times, mainly made possible by political stability and the provision of infrastructure and facilities, stimulated by prosperity among the middle classes who enjoyed travel for leisure and business.

The Middle Ages

Following the demise of the Roman Empire, historians have described the years from AD 500 through to the end of feudalism and the Black Death in 1381 as the Middle Ages. The early part of this period has also been described as the Dark Ages, a time when the civilisation and progress of the Roman era declined. In place of the pleasure-seeking society of the Roman era, the rise of Christianity and the development of monastic orders saw the evolution of a society based on landed estates, a feudal system of peasants and nobility. Yet even in these seemingly dark times leisure can be discerned, with the emergence of festival and event-based activities of the nobility and knights. Jousting tournaments and spectatorship by peasants and other nobility saw a demand for temporary accommodation and travel to these events. According to Hardwick (2008: 460), 'the term leisure first came into use in the late medieval centuries, and 500 years ago the term already had the same conceptual connotations as it does today: time free from work or other duties to pursue activities of personal choice'.

Interestingly, Hunnicutt (2006) traced the evolution of the concept of leisure from Greek times to the medieval period, noting that, in religious orders, for the first time work was separated from other activities amongst the monastic orders and clergy. Public duties and monastic activities were separated from contemplation, which involved activities of the mind directed to God. This provided the roots of the later Christian transformation of leisure as a distinct concept. What Hardwick (2008) identifies from a historian's perspective is the need for a longer history of leisure that is not simply based on the past 200 years. Indeed, Hardwick characterises the debate on the need for longer histories of leisure to understand how the history of leisure was transformed from the medieval period where a

> 'festival culture' existed (informal and irregular breaks from work primarily embedded in a liturgical [customary public worship by groups] calendar, no matter how often expressed in secular dancing, feasting and other pleasures of the flesh) versus a 'leisure culture' (weekends and vacations free from paid work and devoted in part to participation in organised activities that were clearly differentiated from those of the workplace. *(Hardwick 2008: 460)*

Hardwick also points to some of the influential studies of leisure in the Middle Ages (i.e. 1450 to 1750) (also see Burke 1995; Marfany 1997) which fail to discuss gender as a key feature of leisure in this period as gendered leisure (i.e. male drinking and gambling which grew in this period) and the socialising role among women arose as leisure pursuits. From the later part of the Middle Ages, pilgrimage to the Holy Land emerged. Travel was difficult due to the poor quality of access, although poor access created a demand for accommodation and hospitality services (e.g. food, drink and entertainment) en route. The amounts of business travel to centres of commerce across Europe and farther afield were modest. Yet around the notion of travel and hospitality and leisure grew the English alehouse, which was to evolve into the public house in the Victorian period that became the modern-day basis of the public house (pub), as Case Study 2.1 shows.

| Case Study 2.1 | The historical evolution of the alehouse as a site for leisure |

The alehouse has been a popular feature of many medieval analyses of leisure, not least in its role as a social and leisure institution. The most widely cited study of the subject by Clark (1983) traces its evolution from 1200 to 1830 when the public house began to replace the traditional alehouse. The term alehouse in the medieval period is often merged into three distinct though interconnected places in which drinking and hospitality and lodgings occurred: the inn, tavern and alehouse. Clark distinguishes between each category, with the inn and tavern aimed at a higher class of person who could afford drink in the Middle

Ages, offering lodgings for wealthy travellers and serving brewed ale and imported wine. These were settings for the
affluent, although by the 1800s they had
been eroded by competition with the
Georgian growth of coffee houses as
places to meet and do business, with
around 2000 in London in the 1700s. In
contrast, the taverns were more suited to
the drinking needs of the upper and
middle ranks of society from the twelfth
century, serving many of the functions of
inns but often smaller in size. The alehouse, in contrast, was a more widespread institution which met the needs of
the masses and can be dated to the
Roman period when ale selling was evident, further developing in the Anglo-
Saxon period. By 1309, London had 354
taverns and 1350 brew shops serving a
population of 30,000 to 40,000, and while

**Plate 2.1   Popularised in the
novel of the same name by
Daphne du Maurier, set on the
North Cornwall coast and
associated with smuggling.**

ale remained an expensive luxury for many, alternatives such as whey and
cider were also popular. Ale was consumed at communal festivals outside the
alehouse as well as at Wakes and holidays such as Whitsun. In the Tudor and
Stuart periods, the state began a process of trying to regulate these places
owing to the Puritans' concerns with drunkenness, though one underlying
reason was to levy taxation on drinking.

After 1660, Clark points to the rise of larger alehouses seeking to meet the
changing demands of consumers, with food and a more welcoming and hos-
pitable approach to serving drinkers and travellers. There is evidence of attention to the interiors of such premises, with a warm welcoming fire, a
feature of many rustic public houses even today. Signage for alehouses also
began to be displayed, leading to the ubiquitous public house sign in the
Victorian period (Plate 2.1).

The period from 1750 to 1830 saw the evolution of many of the traits of the
modern-day public house, with purpose-built premises and beer drawn from
the cellar. The heyday of the English public house was the Victorian period,
with 71,814 operating in 1881 dropping to 56,538 in 1935; today, around
57,000 exist, with about 15 million people in the UK enjoying a weekly drink
in such premises. The alehouse saw its new rival in the public house, and
competition permitted by the 1830 Beer Act, which allowed a lower level of
small premises to supply beer (46,000 existed in 1838), began to erode its function, as many evolved into public houses. The Beer Act saw several licensing
law changes in the Victorian period to tighten up the original 1830 Act, and
this gradually removed the smaller (in some cases domestic) premises.

The Renaissance and Reformation

The Renaissance originated in Italy after 1350 and reached its zenith in England during Elizabethan times. According to Cross (1990: 25), 'Between 1500 and 1660, many Europeans and (later in this period) American colonists began to question the traditional balance of work and play in daily life . . . In England and America these reformers, who embraced a work ethic, were usually radical Protestants or Puritans. Their gospel of labour was not merely a way of earning time and money for leisure; for them, work was an end in itself'. The earlier trends in festivals and fairs continued, again forming a nucleus of domestic tourism activity. The rise of travelling theatres and the patronage of the arts created opportunities for travel and a more enlightened era. The Reformation, in contrast, emerged after 1500 with the ideas of Luther and Calvin, their religious zeal creating what has been termed the Protestant work ethic. This is a notable turning point in the history of leisure and thereby tourism, as these Lutheran and Calvinistic ideas questioned the value of leisure, portraying it as idleness, when individuals should devote themselves to a life of good work rather than leisure and enjoyment of pleasure. These ideas can be seen more clearly in the rise of the industrial society, where leisure was denigrated by the needs of capitalists and entrepreneurs to create a more profitable economy. Although Puritanism was a minority movement, it established the work ethic which was later promulgated during the Industrial Revolution. Yet as Daniels' (1995) study of Puritans' leisure in New England shows, the grim and melancholy attitude of this group is challenged through an analysis of their appreciation of music, dinner parties, dancing and sports. Arcangeli (2003) also examined recreation in the Renaissance, illustrating how some medical writing in the period emphasised physical activities as a route to improved health along with a range of pastimes, demonstrating that leisure was fully established before the Industrial Revolution.

However, throughout the history of tourism, women remain generally hidden as tourists despite the way that, in Europe, the leisure and tourism activities of different social classes began to be separated. In one of the most influential studies of the history of tourism, Towner (1996) explains how the upper classes withdrew from popular culture (i.e. popular activities, pastimes and travel). Likewise, the affluent also began to move from town to country for tourism purposes (rest and relaxation) on both a short-term and long-term basis. The building of rural villas from the Roman period to the Renaissance and again in the eighteenth and nineteenth centuries epitomised this town to country shift for leisure. In Italy, this process of withdrawing to a country villa was called *villeggiatura* during the Renaissance. In England, the sale of Church lands after the dissolution of the monasteries by Henry VIII created vast areas which provided the basis for country estates as places for recreation and tourism.

In terms of the social organisation of the pre-modern family, all family members shared and played the same games and leisure activities, which are described as a *collective* outlook on leisure. This was reinforced by a lack of private living space, where communal activities dominated leisure. The distinction between rich and poor also dictated the types of activities individuals and families could engage in. This distinguished between elite and popular culture for the common people. Much of this dates to Aristotle and the Ancient Greeks and the construction of a leisure class based on freedom from the need to labour, with servants.

In the pre-modern world, 'a work ethic made little sense. Long days of work were often punctuated by moments of refreshment . . ., games or play. From the 16th century, English merchants tried to tap into this underutilised rural labour' (Cross 1990: 19), with the putting-out system using winter periods for spinning yarns or cloth making as in Leicestershire. But life also had periods punctuated by holidays; France had 84 holidays a year in 1700, and seventeenth-century Paris had 103 holidays, with 95 in Northern Italy in the sixteenth century (Cross 1990). Work-free days were tied to the religious calendar and rural working year, with specific customs and rituals. English parishes had Wakes Weeks, which were parish festivals celebrating the founding of the parish church, though by the seventeenth century, Cross (1990) argues that they had lost their initial religious meaning and were a period of sporting activity, drinking and revelry. Such holidays also had a clear link to annual fairs, where goods were traded alongside entertainment provided by travelling carnivals. Leisure and play were integrated into the rhythms of the agricultural seasons and year. Leisure customs survived for many centuries owing to the slow pace of economic and social change, with some French bakers enjoying 141 days of holiday a year in the seventeenth century (Cross 1990). In the USA on the eve of industrialisation, Cross (1990) indicated that popular pastimes were pursued among all classes, including blood sports and hunting for the elites. In the growing urban centres, arts and amusement such as theatre developed alongside the rise of urban and rural leisure, with rural retreats for the elites as well as the rise of travel and the use of spas and resorts. Among American colonists, Cross (1990) points to common traditions with Europe, especially the new-found wealth of elites and the universal consumption of alcohol and gambling.

As Cross (1990: 16) argues, 'In the Middle Ages, the aristocratic leisure class was materially based on ownership of land and control of peasant labour' reinforced by serfdom. For elite males, combat training and hunting were key activities, with hunting the exclusive right of the French aristocracy until the French Revolution of 1789. The Renaissance in Northern Italy and France in the late fourteenth and fifteenth centuries transformed elite leisure in urban centres such as Florence and Paris, with philosophy and the arts emerging in elite leisure. The invention of fashion at this time in history, as Cross (1990: 17) argues, was influential 'in the filling of hours of leisure. Even more important was the development and partial rediscovery of the ideals of self-cultivation' as the status-laden society emerged, based on etiquette and the social skills to engage in the elite aristocratic society of the time. For popular culture and leisure, less is documented and known, with many of the pleasures resisting industrialising processes and individualisation.

In pre-industrial Europe, breaks from work and popular leisure culture were based on the 'principle of *saturnalia*, which derives its name from the ancient Roman custom of a week of drink in early December. At its base was a "binge" – the unrestrained indulgence in food and drink, so often noted by anthropologists studying primitive village culture' (Cross 1990: 19).

In rural areas life had scarcely changed much since the Middle Ages even in the early 1800s, as it was not until the mid-Victorian period that the countryside was significantly transformed, as historians such as Mingay (1981) and Malcolmson (1981) show in their reviews of rural leisure. The situation was very different in towns. As Stobart and Schwarz (2008) show, in the eighteenth century towns specialising in resort and leisure activities emerged, representing a particular form of conspicuous leisure consumption with specific leisure facilities such as assembly rooms, theatres, libraries, horse racing walking and urban gardens. These were termed eighteenth-century leisure towns with access to luxury goods and services, such as Bath, with clothing outfitters for genteel society along with craftsmen able to meet the need for goods as well as professionals and those servicing the arts (e.g. booksellers, music sellers and portrait painters). The eighteenth century did see the evolution of a material culture based on consumption for elites, and shopping and leisure evolved as a key element of the social and cultural life of such groups as observed by Stobart (2005) in the Georgian period.

Industrialisation, leisure and the rise of organised leisure

According to Clark and Critcher (1985), during the evolution of a capitalist society such as Britain, the analysis of leisure and recreation has traditionally emphasised institutional forms of provision, while each social class has its own history of organised and informal leisure and recreation. The predominant histories are those of male leisure; female leisure and recreation were structured around the family, with free-time activities associated with the family, the street and neighbourhood in working-class society. Within historical analyses of urban recreation during the evolution of mass urban society in Victorian and Edwardian Britain, distinctive forms of recreation and leisure developed in different social areas of cities, associated with a number of concepts, the most notable being 'popular culture' (see Williams 1976 for a discussion of popular culture). As Clark and Critcher (1985: 55) argue, 'the early nineteenth century was to bring a dramatic transformation to the form . . . and context of popular culture, imposing very different parameters of time and space, rhythms and routines, behaviour and attitude, control and commerce'. Bull et al. (2003) distinguish between a number of key changes induced by industrialisation:

● The population migrated to cities from the countryside, splitting the population from its rural recreation activities.

● New urban pastimes developed in the crowded urban industrial environments of the early industrial period (1780 to 1830) as work regimes associated with the factory system transformed the population's lives and leisure.

● Leisure became a counter to work, with long hours of work of up to 12 hours a day in early industrialisation. This is where the current-day value of precious leisure time separate from work emerges among the masses. It was a stark contrast with not-working in an industrial and productive manner.

● A large working class emerged, with its own urban leisure needs, while a middle class populated by professionals also emerged and provided much of the later paternalistic and charitable interventions in working-class life to improve social conditions (e.g. sanitation improvements and reform of the penal system and measures for the poor). This resulted in the middle-class moralisation of desirable and undesirable leisure activities and the rational recreation movement (see Bailey 1987), with campaigns to ban blood sports. The middle classes sought to impose their values for education, outdoor recreation and the countryside and organised sport on the masses as a civilising influence. This was enshrined in Samuel Smiles' concept of self-help and self-improvement, which saw state intervention to establish institutions to promote local self-improvement such as libraries (1850 Libraries Act) and urban parks.

● The rise of mass leisure and organised commercial leisure, as leisure time expanded in the late Victorian years (after middle-class reformers campaigned alongside workers to develop the 1871 Bank Holiday Act).

● Technological change such as the railways, which saw large numbers able to travel to the 1851 Great Exhibition, as well as day trips to enjoy horse racing at emerging race courses, while urban tramways expanded in the later Victorian years, providing opportunities for urban leisure.

However, the resulting changes cannot simply be conceptualised as a straightforward linear progression, since different influences and cross-currents meant that this transformation affected different people and areas at different rates and in varying degrees. This is reflected in the way different local government bodies embraced the permissive legislation for public leisure provision (i.e. it was not a statutory requirement but permitted local councils to use the legislation to justify local improvements to local ratepayers).

According to Bailey (1989), it is widely accepted that by 1850, what we generally recognise as many of the forms of leisure and recreation that are seen as 'modern' had emerged. Among the key processes that mark the development of modern leisure, which eroded custom and community from the traditional period, were

a variety of attendant developments, notably a general increase in real earnings, new technologies (railways and the steam press) and a new range of leisure forms, sites and services (from croquet to skating rinks to travel agencies) combined to give shape and growth to what historians have labelled a 'virtual leisure revolution', a 'new leisure world'. *(Bailey 1989: 108)*

The impact of reduced working hours to allow more leisure time after the 1850s and technology and its impact on working-class leisure were apparent in Roberts' autobiography:

Before 1914 most working men put in not less than a 54-hour week, starting at six in the morning, with a break of half an hour and one hour for breakfast and dinner. The day's work usually finished at 5.30 p.m. People generally lived closer to their work than they do now but most were too tired at the end of it to take part in leisure activities outside the home except at weekends, when factories closed on Saturday at mid-day or one o'clock. The many looked for amusement, the few for education. And all suddenly found at hand a new mobility.

The introduction of all-electric tramcars in British provincial cities during the first years of the century profoundly influenced the lives of the common people. As early as 1903 horse-drawn trams vanished from the streets of Manchester. Having spent no less than £1.5 million the city had 140 miles of line and 400 tramcars of four different kinds. Salford was equally prompt in electrification, and city and borough possessed together a tramway network that remained for a decade the envy of the country. For the first time in history the underclass enjoyed the benefits of cheap urban travel. Municipal electric trams would now take passengers three-quarters of a mile for ½d; and more than two miles for 1d. *(Roberts 1974: 146)*

This illustrates the fact that even though Victorian cities expanded in the late nineteenth and early twentieth centuries, the major beneficiaries of that growth were the more affluent upper working classes and middle classes. But the slums persisted and many workers still lived within walking distance of their work.

One of the defining features of the mid-nineteenth century was the impact of middle-class reformers seeking to suppress traditional forms of leisure and impose counter-attractions to drinking, through the temperance movement and other commercial forms of recreation such as the music hall. Yet as Roberts (1974: 148) depicted, there were social divisions in working-class consumption of such leisure where a social hierarchy existed:

Nowhere, of course, stood class division more marked than in a full house at the theatre, with shopkeepers and publicans in the orchestra stalls and dress circle, artisans and regular workers in the pit stalls, and the low class and no class on the 'top shelf' or balcony. There in the gods hung a permanent smell of smoke from 'thick twist', oranges and unwashed humanity.

As Bailey (1989) argues, by the 1880s much of the leisure we can observe today (e.g. seaside resort trips, amusements parks, football and other sporting activities for mass consumption) was well established. Equally, drink and the public house remained enduring themes through industrialisation, as 'staple pleasures (consumption peaked in the 1870s yet remained high) but there were now competing alternatives as leisure commodities – fish and chips, ice cream, cigarettes, mineral waters and teashop fare' (Bailey 1989: 109), with many activities undertaken in a group manner, although home-based pursuits began to emerge in the late nineteenth century. The focus on the home was symbolised by the introduction of the piano as a form of home entertainment and, much later in the early Edwardian period, the gramophone. Again, as Roberts (1974: 153) described:

> Well before 1914 the piano and gramophone, two status-symbols of the highest sig-nificance, had already penetrated deep into top working-class homes. The gramo-phone, however, was one of the few objects valued which had not previously established itself among the bourgeoisie. Upper- and middle-class people tended to look down on the instrument and thought it 'all right for servants'. Children of the better-off workers now paid trips to the suburbs, where cards in bay windows an-nounced piano lessons at a shilling an hour. Mr W. A. N., for instance, gave instruc-tion there, advertising himself as 'Pianist, accompanist and experienced vamper. Terms moderate'. Nor were other art forms quite neglected. Miss M. in the same dis-trict provided facilities for 'painting, decorative art and Chrystoleum painting at 1s 6d for 10 lessons. Payable in advance'.

Clark and Critcher (1985) provide a useful historical analysis of leisure and recreational forms in Britain during the nineteenth and twentieth centuries, with the emphasis on the urban forms and political factors, forms of social control (Donajgrodski 1978) and the underlying development and functioning of an urban capitalist society; leisure and recreational forms emerged as a civilising and diversionary process to maintain the productive capacity of the working classes as central to the continued development of capitalism. At the same time, one indisputable feature of the period before 1914 was the much greater proportionate expansion of leisure among the wealthier classes epito-mised by the opulence and luxury of holidays by transatlantic liners. The Edwardian years were ones of new wealth and conspicuous consumption. Therefore, the geographical patterns and manifestation of urban recreation and leisure for all social classes in the British city in the nineteenth and twen-tieth centuries have to be viewed against the background of social, economic and political processes which conditioned the demand and supply of leisure and recreation for each social class. In Montreal, Dagenais (2002) highlighted the role of local government in park provision. Yet in more liminal locations away from the home (e.g. the seaside and the racecourse), less respectable and 'sinful' pleasures were consumed by the same middle class, where less re-spectable behaviour occurred.

According to Billinge (1996: 450), 'Perhaps the single newest element in the townscape after the general regulation of the street, was the park, and more specifically the recreation ground . . . [since] the urban park, as distinct from the garden square, was essentially a nineteenth century phenomenon' and a symbol of civic pride. In the case of the street, Roberts (1974: 153) also high-lighted the street's importance as a site for children's leisure:

> In the first quarter of the present century children's singing games in the streets reached their hey-day. This form of self-entertainment provided a ritual that gave young Edwardians pleasure unalloyed. Home duties done, children came together at some accepted place in the street, by a lamp or along a blank wall, and quite

spontaneously a performance would begin, while parents, sitting on doorsteps, watched indulgently. Certain unwritten rules existed. The choice and order of the games were usually decided upon by the eldest girl present, infants being excluded, while all boys above about the age of eight and all girls who had left school for work excluded themselves. It seems likely that many of these games were learnt first in school and then passed on to succeeding generations.

Billinge (1996: 444) recognised the way in which the Victorians engineered the term 'recreation' 'to perfection, they gave it a role and a geography. Confined by time, defined by place and regulated by content, recreation and the time it occupied ceased to be possessions freely enjoyed and became instead, obligations dutifully discharged.' The Victorians established a system of approved leisure activities and, as Billinge (1996) recognised, these were allocated to appropriate times and places. As Billinge (1996: 447) argued, it was 'the provision of set aside resorts for the masses at the scale of the whole township: the seaside resort where behaviour inappropriate in any other occasion could be loosed to burn itself out'. This can be viewed as a further example of the way in which Victorian society sought to exercise a degree of social control of recreational spaces and activities among its populace. This created a social necessity for recreation as freedom from work: a non-work activity to re-create body and soul, to be refreshed for the capitalist economic system, with its regulated time discipline of a place for everything, and everything in its place. In this context it is useful to consider the key features of Clark and Critcher's (1985) cross-section approach to analyse key periods in nineteenth- and twentieth-century British leisure pursuits in a little more detail.

The early Victorian period: the 1800s

As emphasised earlier in this chapter, Britain was in the process of emerging from a pre-industrial state. While cities were not a new phenomenon (Clark 1981), the movement of the rural population to nascent cities meant that the traditional boundary between work and non-work among the labouring classes was increasingly dictated by the needs of factory or mechanised production. Therefore, pre-industrial flexibility in the work–non-work relationship associated with cottage industries and labouring on the land changed. This led to a clearer distinction between work and non-work time, as time discipline emerged as a potent force during the Industrial Revolution (Pred 1981). In the pre-industrial, non-urbanised society, leisure and recreational forms were associated with market days, fairs, wakes, holidays and religious and pagan festivals which provided opportunities for sport. It is evident that 'The factory institutionalised the Puritan's work ethic . . . industrialisation substituted an ethic of economic accumulation for leisure. The factory imposed a new division in the lives of ordinary people: work time (for income) became separated from family time' (Cross 1990: 57). Factories disrupted the natural rhythms of leisure, the family and work as the invention of the clock provided a means to precisely quantify time, its use and output. The clock in factories became a tool of work-time discipline.

The factory initially led to longer working hours under industrialisation, up to 14 hours a day, six or seven days a week. This clearly separated home and work, splitting work and leisure time very distinctly, as the antithesis of each other, turning the home into a privatised place of non-work and differentiating the male/female split of work and leisure, developed in the Victorian period as home as the women's sphere of influence. Initially there was a drop in the time available for leisure during early industrialisation, and drink was an obvious escape from urban industrial lifestyles, poverty and deprivation. However, as industrialisation proceeded it led to a reduction in working times and an increase again in time for leisure.

While the 1800s are often characterised by brutish behaviour and ribaldry, civilising influences emerged in the form of Puritanism to engender moral sobriety and spatial changes associated with the enclosure movement, which removed many strategic sites of customary activity. In contrast, the geographical patterns of recreation of the ruling classes eschewed contact with lower orders. Its forms were as yet disparate. Shooting, hunting and horse racing: 'the major flat race classics date from the 1770s onwards. . . . For the increasingly influential urban bourgeoisie, the theatre, literature, seaside holidays and music hall denoted more rational forms of leisure which depended for their decorum on the exclusion of the mass of the population' (Clark and Critcher 1985: 55). Parratt (1999) points to the 1830s and 1840s which Cunningham (1980) depicted as the heyday of rational recreation for men.

The mid-Victorian period: the 1840s

In historical analysis, this period is often characterised as a period of deprivation for the urban working classes. Endemic poverty, associated with rapid urbanisation and inadequate housing, poor living standards and limited infrastructure, culminated in high rates of mortality, disease and exploitation of the labouring classes through long hours of work (12-hour day, 6-day weeks). In terms of urban leisure and recreation, the pre-industrial opportunities for pursuits decreased as did the legal outlets, with many customary pastimes suppressed so that popular culture was conditioned through legislative changes. For example, the 1834 *New Poor Law Act* (Rose 1985) aimed to control the movement of 'travelling balladeers', 'entertainers' and 'itinerant salesmen', all of whom were deemed as vagabonds and returned to their parish of origin. Similarly, the 1835 *Highways Act* was intended to remove street nuisances such as street entertainers and traders, while the 1835

Cruelty to Animals Act sought to suppress working-class pastimes involving animals, thereby driving many activities underground and leading to the emergence of a hybrid range of recreational activities including popular theatre, pantomime and circuses.

In the late 1840s, railway excursions pioneered by Thomas Cook also developed. In addition, a range of rational recreation pursuits emerged in purpose-built facilities made possible by Parliamentary Acts, including the *Museums Act* (1845), the *Baths and Wash Houses Act* (1846) and the *Libraries Act* (1850). These interventions are shown in Table 2.4 (which illustrates a longer history of state intervention in leisure than is acknowledged in most studies that can be pre-dated to before the Victorian period). Social theorists argue that such legislation may have acted as a form of social control (Donajgrodski 1978), to tame a new industrial workforce while demarcating recreation and work. Furthermore, the 1840s saw the emergence of the Victorian concept of domesticity and a bourgeois culture, with the use of a gender separation of male and female work.

Table 2.4   Examples of state intervention in leisure in the UK

- 1400–1700, demise of 'Merry England' with orders banning football in the medieval years
- Henry VIII and 1640s and 1650s examples of attempts to control public drama
- Laws to protect leisure for the privileged:
  - 1671 Game Act
  - 1770 Game Act (making poaching an offence punishable by six months' detention in prison)
- Nineteenth- and twentieth-century control of the consumption of alcohol (licensing laws)
- 1850s and 1870s gambling legislation and the 1906 Street Betting Act (with gambling legalised in 1960 with a Gaming Act setting up Betting Shops)
- Permissive legislation for local government (i.e. not obligatory due to the effect on local rates) such as the 1845 Museum Act and 1850 Museum and Libraries Act
- Rise of state-sponsored quasi-autonomous non-governmental bodies (QUANGOS) including
  - 1912 British Board of Film Censors
  - BBC (1922)
  - Central Council of Physical Recreation (1935)
  - Arts Council (1946)
  - National Parks Commission (1949)
  - Sports Council (1965)
  - National Tourism Organisations after 1945 and the 1969 Development of Tourism Act.

Sources: Adapted from Borsay (2006); Authors

The late Victorian years: the 1880s

While the mid-Victorian period saw the establishment of urban recreational fa-cilities, improved working conditions and living standards, in the mid- to late Victorian period a greater municipal provision emerged (Briggs 1969). As Clark and Critcher (1985) argue, four processes which were at work in the 1850s and 1860s led to significant changes in the 1880s:

1. A rise of middle-class urban recreation which excluded the working classes.

2. The expansion of local government's role in leisure and recreational provision.

3. An increasing commercialisation and greater capitalisation of urban rec-reation, relying upon mass audiences and licensing (e.g. the rise of football), which also required large areas of land.

4. Attempts by the working classes to organise urban recreation according to their own aspirations.

By the 1880s, the pattern of urban conurbations had emerged in England, focusing on London, the West Midlands, West Yorkshire, Merseyside and Tyneside (Lawton 1978). In addition to these trends in urban recreation, the rise of urban middle-class recreational pursuits, centred on religion, reading, music and annual holidays, reflected a more rational form of recreational activity. Nevertheless, the 1870s saw the growth in public parks and by 1885, nearly 25% of the urban population had access to public libraries.

Yet informal urban recreation based on street- and neighbourhood-based activities largely remains invisible in documentary sources and official records, although limited evidence exists in the form of autobiographies and oral history. For example, Roberts' (1974) *The Classic Slum* observed that the public house played a major role in informal recreation in Victorian and Ed-wardian Salford where a community of 3000 people had 15 beer houses. Through sexual segregation it was possible to observe the rise of male-only urban recreational pursuits in the 1880s. Yet the street life and neighbourhood forms of recreation remained unorganised and informal despite the institu-tionalisation, segmentation and emergence of a customer–provider relation-ship in Victorian urban recreational pursuits. Parratt (1999) acknowledged the rise of middle-class women pursuing philanthropy to help working-class women and the poor. Yet as Parratt (1999: 478) argues, 'the main leisure fare of working-class women [at the end of the nineteenth century] included gossip-ing, drinking, attending cheap theatres and music halls, meeting and prome-nading with friends, shopping, celebrating holidays, birthdays, weddings and a modest consumerism'.

Alongside these trends, one also has to acknowledge that in the Victorian period, a number of overseas colonies had been established and were devel-oping in Australia (see Table 2.5) and New Zealand (see Table 2.6) each with

Table 2.5   A historical overview of leisure in Australia to the 1920s

- Aboriginal culture dating back 60–80,000 years with a society rich in art, song, dance and ritual with over 700 languages and a hunter-gatherer lifestyle, with leisure a key element of their daily life (e.g. storytelling, games, music and dance)
- First settlers in 1779 and no recognition of the coast as a recreational resource
- Pioneer settlers brought colonial pastimes with an initial male dominance and a two-class society emerged 1810–21 (upper class and settlers)
- Emergence of Sydney as a settlement, with sports as key pastimes along with music, the arts and more genteel pursuits for the upper classes and alcohol, gambling and violence amongst other settlers at the turn of the nineteenth century
- Up to the 1850s, the discovery of gold generated affluence and new recreation and cultural development (e.g. Sydney's first Opera House is established in 1863)
- In the 1850–1900 period, rise of 'serious leisure' and naturalists; emergence of tourism, with excursions and holidays from Sydney to the Blue Mountains and coastal areas in New South Wales and Victoria
- Rise of socially improving leisure pursuits for the working classes (e.g. establishment of mechanics' institutes and free libraries to further education and training)
- Rise of a new middle class with interest in hunting, racing, concerts, art, dining and balls; under-classes frequent the 'pub' and sporting venues where drinking was available
- Rise of the eight-hour working day among trades from the 1850s, with public holidays and high value placed upon leisure time
- Distance and access to transport remain barriers to rural communities
- Innovations in the twentieth century in sport such as surfing and lifesaving and distinctive events such as the country show and idiosyncratic events such as log chopping
- Wildland reserves are the first established anywhere in the world and the rise of the car aiding personal mobility in the 1920s

Source: Adapted from Hamilton-Smith (1998). Copyright © Pearson Education, Auckland

their own leisure histories that have characteristics which are similar and yet different from the UK experience. The initial similarity with the imported culture of the colonialists soon diverged as distinctive antipodean cultural forms of leisure developed, as are evident in Tables 2.5 and 2.6. Indeed, the evolution of leisure trends and practices in each of these two countries illustrates how a wider understanding of the changing leisure phenomenon needs to accommodate the importance of place, space and the social and economic context of leisure. One important period omitted from Clarke and Critcher's analysis is the Great War (the First World War, 1914–1918) which is the focus of the following case study.

Table 2.6   Characteristics of the evolution of leisure in New Zealand

Eras in New Zealand leisure

Frontier recreation (1840s–1920s)

- Dominance of extractive industries, including agriculture, logging, flax growing, whaling, gold mining and gum digging
- Predominantly male population and drinking culture along with smoking/chewing tobacco as leisure activities
- Storytelling (yarning), contests of strength and other male sporting activities such as boxing and wrestling
- Social isolation and frequenting of prostitutes in male leisure time among some workers
- More respectable leisure pursuits among pioneers were reading, home-focused activities and amusements and in frontier towns, touring theatre companies existed.

Settler recreation (mid-nineteenth century–1920s)

- Rise of civilising process as nuclear families developed from settler communities and the associated institutions (e.g. the church)
- Drop in alcohol consumption and rise of Victorian 'rules and norms' as time-based work and family life evolved
- Rise of an urban industrialised society as immigration continued to fuel urban growth
- By 1890s, concerns over frontier fecklessness (i.e. larrikinism) led to a focus by the state and family on more rational and disciplined forms of recreation
- Emergence of a sport culture as a disciplinary influence (e.g. rugby)
- Clear class-based differences apparent in leisure behaviour by the late nineteenth century, with a 'landed gentry', the development of gentlemen's clubs in the towns and overseas travel
- Key sports developed (e.g. cricket, horse racing and rowing) and communal recreation such as going to church and employer/trade union outings around 1900
- In working-class communities, group activities were popular and mass recreation emerged at races, fairs, agricultural shows and events
- Domestic travel limited due to time available, cost and long distances to travel, with a reliance on public transport.

Modern society

- From the 1920s, a growing diversity of leisure choices emerges, focused on the individual consumer, commercialisation and role for women's and children's leisure
- The state plays a more active role in the 1930s with the building of leisure infrastructure (swimming pools, parks, museums and libraries) and discouraging undesirable activities (e.g. gambling was tightly restricted)
- Rise of the motor car giving greater personal leisure freedom from the 1920s
- Greater individual consumption of sports and leisure.

Source: Adapted from Watson (1998). Copyright © Pearson Education, Auckland

Case Study 2.2   The First World War and leisure in the UK

Bailey (1989: 110) argued that the war 'brought some disruption and curtailment, notably from tighter state controls, some of which, as in the regulation of the drink trade', persisted after the war (in the UK). But this is probably a gross simplification. As Page and Durie (2009) argue, the value of newspapers, national, regional or local, has been widely recognised by historical researchers as a vital source of information about issues and events. While they may inevitably be a source of bias over what was covered, as an elite activity, the use of a leading newspaper tracks general leisure in some degree of detail (as well as leisure). *The Times* newspaper, typically a 16-page broadsheet during wartime Britain, which was produced six days a week, carried reports on everyday matters as well as political and military affairs, on music, sport and travel as well as battlefield news. There were pages of advertising for hotels, resorts, excursions and sailings, as well as specific articles gauging the state of the holiday industry, travel to resorts and the impact of specific events on the sector. In the tourism sector, shelling of east coast resorts saw its trade decline sharply. In a letter to *The Times*, 13 July 1916, 'East Coast Resorts: Holiday visitors wanted', the writer noted 'the hotel keepers on the brink of despair' as visitors deserted the resorts after shelling. This led the government, via its fund for wartime activities affected by war, to compensate Scarborough with a £10,700 grant for the loss of rates due to unoccupied houses and the loss of rate income after the shelling of the resort. This simply shifted demand to other resorts despite government attempts in the First World War to restrict domestic travel, especially day trips.

As Page and Durie (2009) observed, evidence from *The Times* newspaper for 1915 to 1918 confirms this impact, as an article entitled 'Holidays at Home: Heavy traffic to South Coast resorts' (2 April 1915) noted the addition of relief trains to cope with Easter demand and the impact on 'Brighton, Folkestone, Eastbourne, Bournemouth and Torquay [which] attracted the bulk of holidaymakers', with hotels and accommodation establishments having 'full houses'. Similarly, the Isle of Wight, Matlock and Buxton 'attracted thousands', while 'Blackpool and other resorts' were busier with a 'greater use of bicycles and special omnibuses' to reach the destinations. This was reiterated in an article 'Holiday Prospects: Busy season expected at chief resorts' (31 July 1915). A similar article for Easter 1916, 'Seaside Resorts Crowded' (22 April 1916), commented on Brighton being a 'town full to eclipse all records' and on 25 April 1916 noted crowding in London at Easter ('Holiday Sightseeing: Crowds in London'), especially at key visitor attractions.

One group of workers with new-found money and leisure time were the emancipated workers – women working in munitions factories (munitionettes). The government was split between wishing to increase war output and recognising their need for leisure time. As Jones (1986: 89) argued, 'In official circles, leisure was linked directly to war aims and objectives; so the provision of spare time facilities for munitions workers was perceived as a way of increasing labour productivity by providing relief from monotony, a change of environment and a factor in recovery from industrial fatigue . . . Rational recreation was therefore stressed as a contribution to the war effort, indeed controlled leisure . . . [was] . . . eventually recognised as important in retaining workers at the huge armament factories' (Jones 1986: 89). This marked the beginning of a collectivist approach to state leisure provision in the 1920s and 1930s. The example of the munitionettes is an exception to the problem of a 'leisure history [which] has, on the whole, tended to concern itself with working class men, within a periodisation that has often ended with the First World War' (Langhamer 2001). The Prime Minister Lloyd George's speech reported in *The Times* (27 May 1916) criticised the impacts of Easter holidays on munitions output which dropped by 50%, described in 'The Deplorable Effect of Easter', and sought to cancel the Whitsun Holiday to help the war effort. At the same time, in the summer of 1917, the government appealed to the population to forgo the summer holidays of 7 and 14 days.

Plate 2.2 In the early 1920s, Thomas Cook began offering private chauffeur-driven tours by car in France. © Thomas Cook.

But as the following extract from *The Railway and Travel Monthly* shows, pleasure travel expanded in wartime alongside military traffic rather than contracting as military travel grew, which led to government restrictions and price increases on travel. As the article explained:

> Pleasure travel has also increased as a result of the war. So many hundreds of thousands of people who are earning wages largely in excess of those obtaining in normal times spend a proportion of their income in pleasure trips, that the trains are crowded with unnecessary passengers. From January 1st new restrictions [apply] – an increase in fares (50% for long-distance) with exceptional consideration in cases of travelling on business of national importance. *(Anon 1917: 33,* The Railway and Travel Monthly, *June)*

The munitions workers proved to be a powerful driver of leisure demand, with *The Times* carrying a one-page advertising sheet on 18 May 1917 entitled 'Resorts for War Workers', with a diverse range of English resorts and establishments promoting their wares. These promotions probably led to a further growth in resort tourism, even in the austere conditions of 1917, as *The Times* reported on 4 August 1917 that 'August Holiday: Holiday resorts crowded', commenting on the shift from east coast to south and south-west coast resorts. One indication of the new-found wealth of the munitions worker was the government's provision of bonuses of 7.5% to 12% (depending on the type of work/grade and method of payment) in January 1918, reported on 24 January 1918 by *The Times* ('Munitions Workers Bonus'). After the First World War, any decline in leisure and tourism activity quickly recovered in 1919 alongside the growth in the use of the motor car and charabanc (Plate 2.2) as a means of day trips and outings. The First World War was a turning point in leisure, as new trends developed and expanded in the 1920s.

Source: Page and Durie (2009)

The 1920s and 1930s

In Britain, the 1920s are frequently viewed as an era of mass unemployment, with social class more geographically defined in the urban environment. While the 1900s saw rising patronage of the cinema, with 3000 cinemas operating in Britain by 1926 and audiences of 20 million, and many people visiting the cinemas up to twice a week, this pursuit increasingly met the recreational needs of women as it displaced the Victorian music-hall, being more heavily capitalised and more accessible in terms of price and social acceptability. The ideological separation of work and home was firmly enshrined in the 1920s, with a greater physical separation and the rise of annual holidays and day trips expanded using charabancs and the car (Plate 2.3). For example, the number of workers receiving paid holidays rose from 1 million in the UK in 1920 to 1.5 million in the mid- to late 1920s and then doubled in 1938 when the UK Holidays with Pay Act was passed, based on the Amulree Report. The number of passenger miles travelled by buses and coach rose from 3.5 million in 1920 to 19 million in 1938 (Jones 1986). The charabanc provided the poorer classes with new opportunities to engage in leisure travel, linking rural areas with towns and cities for leisure and entertainment. Car ownership in the UK also rose (as it did in other countries) as prices declined, from 314,000 in 1922 to 1.8 million in 1937 (Jones 1986). As Jones (1986) shows, the 1930s were far from a period of Great Depression for the emerging leisure industries such as music, the cinema, tobacco consumption, children's toys and sport, which, while dropping from 1920 levels, were still high compared to pre-1914 levels of consumption.

Plate 2.3 The 1920s saw the rise of the modern-day coach excursion, in charabancs (extended vehicles), such as this example in Austria. © Thomas Cook.

Buoyant leisure demand in the inter-war years was enshrined in the commercialised provision of leisure and activities, as non-commercial activities (hiking and rambling and camping in the countryside) expanded. In fact, much of the expansion of leisure in the 1930s was directed to the 16–24-year age group. These non-commercial activities were supported by voluntary organisations and much of the activity was informal as 'the leisure time of ordinary people was not confined to a particular club or society. Many of the working class spent little time in organised leisure; they found the home or street more conducive to relaxation' (Jones 1986: 62). Even so, during the period 1920–39, Jones observed that consumer expenditure on admissions to theatres, cinemas and sporting events expanded by 15%. In 1934, Jones identified that there were 963 million UK admissions to cinemas and the number of cinema houses rose from 4305 in 1934 to 5300 by 1939 as newer establishments were able to seat up to 3000 people (or more) and had organs, such as Wurlitzers, which were played in the interval (which continued on a regular basis in many cinemas right up to the early 1970s). Likewise, between 1918 and 1924, some 11,000 dance halls opened in the UK. Spectator sports also retained large audiences, although social segregation based on social class, mass markets and institutional provision characterised this era. For example, Jones (1986) noted that greyhound racing attendance in London grew from 6.5 million in 1928 to 9 million in 1932, and football league attendance rose to around 31 million in 1937/38. It was estimated that employment in entertainment and leisure in the UK rose from 101,700 in entertainment and sport and 415,500 in catering and hotels in 1920 to 247,900 in entertainment and sports in 1938 and 494,000 in catering and hotels in 1938. Employment increased over 48% in these leisure industries (Jones, 1986). The late 1930s also saw the expansion of organised holiday camps with the Butlin's experience. An interesting development in leisure studies in the 1930s in the UK was the Mass Observation movement which used participant observation and listening to conversations (as well as written evidence) to report on contemporary leisure (see Madge and Harrison 1939 and details of the project and archives at www.massobs.org.uk).

Leisure was a highly commercialised experience in many Western countries by the late 1930s, reinforcing trends that developed in the 1920s as women enjoyed greater emancipation in wealthier situations, especially in industrial cities where they worked, but 'the working-class mother with a large family, more than any other group, had little time or money for leisure, especially if her situation was compounded by unemployment of her spouse' (Jones 1986: 59). The 1920s did, however, see the development of a wider 'range of municipal services and amenities for recreation . . . through access to a larger number of amenities such as parks, swimming pools and libraries' (Jones 1986: 87–88) following on from the high degree of state intervention in the economy and society during the First World War, most notably in the field of recreation with the Physical Training and Recreation Act of 1937 in the UK. This was vaguely disguised as improving the population's physical well-being on the run-up to a second war, by offering better opportunities for sport and recreation, implemented at the local authority level with large grants for capital and recurrent expenditure on swimming pools, gyms, campsites and playing fields, as per capita expenditure grew in the 1920s and 1930s. In London alone, by 1933 there were

733 council-provided tennis courts and 420 football pitches, and in 1935 the London County Council announced its intention to preserve London's green belt at a cost of £2 million. However, as Jones (1986: 195) acknowledged, 'the middle classes . . . were the backbone of a number of sports, such as tennis, golf and yachting . . .' but a degree of social mixing did occur and

> British pastimes were modified in a number of crucial aspects in the 1920s and 1930s. The main trend was the expansion of leisure. Most important of all was the unprecedented commercialisation of leisure, fed by rising real incomes and falling hours of work . . . Also, State spending on and regulation of recreation and culture appears to have increased despite financial conservatism and attempts at retrenchment. *(Jones 1986: 197–8)*

In fact, Bailey (1989: 111) argued that 'Against the odds, leisure continued its remarkable expansion during the Second World War and the austerities of its immediate aftermath' and the radio as a form of leisure entertainment was enhanced during the Second World War as the main medium of communicating with the population (alongside newspapers). In the post-war period, holidays grew in popularity alongside other forms of popular leisure consumption such as the cinema and sport spectating, culminating in a leisure explosion in the 1960s

The 1950s and 1960s

The late 1950s were marked by UK Prime Minister Harold Macmillan's oft-quoted speech in 1958 when he mentioned that '. . . most of our people have never had it so good', demonstrating a perception of increasing standards of living associated with rising economic activity (even though the statistical data upon which this statement was made is questionable). But this set the tone of the subsequent decade for many commentators as the 1960s were associated with increased levels of affluence. Clark and Critcher (1985) identified six distinct trends occurring from the 1960s affecting leisure:

1. Rising standards of domestic consumption.

2. Family-centred leisure.

3. The decline of public forms of urban leisure and recreation.

4. Emergence of a youth culture.

5. The establishment of an ethnic leisure and recreation culture.

6. Increased state activity in prescribed spheres of urban recreation and a growing commercial domination of leisure institutions and services.

These trends have been reviewed in the sociological literature but it is useful to highlight some of the changes and how they impacted upon leisure. In terms of recreation, various debates exist in relation to the changes induced by the shift from a modern society in the 1950s and 1960s to a post-industrial society in the 1970s. Social theorists point to the concomitant changes induced by economic, occupational and technological change, associated with the demise of manufacturing and the rise of the service sector in towns and cities, affecting the pattern of life and recreational activities of urban populations, associated with a growing polarisation of wealth and opportunity.

Even so, systemic problems of poverty and inequality remained in many Western societies, most evident in major cities in North America with the rise of ghettos replacing the notion of the Victorian and Edwardian slum as a focus for deprivation, as well as levels of rural poverty and deprivation which were often hidden from public view. At the same time, the 1960s in the USA (and other Western countries) saw a demand for greater personal freedoms from different social groups, culminating in the popular growth of the civil rights movement in the USA. This developed from a more liberal political environment with the election of President Kennedy, even though the decade ended in civil riots and urban unrest in many countries as anti-government demonstrations and riots affected many countries associated with the Vietnam War. Social theorists point to this as a symbol of counterculture revolution alongside the growth of other freedoms, such as sexual freedom in films. For women, one major personal freedom emerged in the wider availability of contraception (the pill), allowing greater choice in family size, reflected in declining fertility such as in Australia where the average number of babies born per woman dropped to 2.9 between 1966 and 1971. This is seen as a mark of the greater liberation of women as well as their ability to plan careers and family and integrate greater elements of leisure alongside smaller family size. As Prime Minister Macmillan announced in a tour of Africa, 'a wind of change' was sweeping across the continent as the UK (and other colonial powers) continued to accelerate its plans for decolonisation, providing a context for African nations to develop their own culture and models of leisure.

Part of the consumer age in the 1960s intensified notions of relative deprivation, as levels of absolute poverty were addressed by welfare reforms post-1945. Even so, increased affluence for many was accompanied by relative levels of poverty among others (i.e. access to the necessities of daily living taken for granted by many people, like washing machines, television and personal transport). As Patmore (1983: 11) argued, 'In 1956, for example, only 8% of British households had fridges, but this had increased to 33% in 1962' and changes in household labour through labour-saving devices saw more women enter the workforce in the 1960s; in 1961, 29.7% of married women were in employment and by 1979, 49.6% were (Patmore 1983). Similarly, holiday entitlement grew as the basic manual worker's holiday entitlement of 2 weeks in the 1960s in the UK rose to almost 4 weeks in the 1970s. The culmination of changes in the nature of the economy in the 1960s, as it expanded its manufacturing and productive capacity and also shifted from processing and transforming materials into manufactured goods to the provision of services (i.e. the tertiary sector), was part of the shift from a modern to a postmodern society in the 1970s. In a postmodern society, the economy becomes more dependent upon higher-level services (producer and consumer services) where information and knowledge are increasingly important to the economic wealth generated by these services. One manifestation of the changes in the 1960s and their impact on leisure was epitomised by the Dower report of 1965 in the UK (Dower 1965). This study depicted a *Fourth Wave* being unleashed as the combination of affluence, growing personal mobility and freedom to travel emerged. As Dower (1965: 5) described:

> Three great waves have broken across the face of Britain since 1800. First, the sudden growth of dark industrial towns. Second, the thrusting movement along far flung railways. Third, the sprawl of car-based suburbs. Now we see, under the guise of a modest word, the surge of a fourth wave which could be more powerful than all the others. The modest word is leisure.

The swinging sixties, as they have euphemistically been described, also saw alternative forms of leisure emerge, the flower power movement emanating from the USA with its own anti-war protest movement against the US war in Vietnam and a dropout culture with its own music and symbols. This generated a hippy culture and also incorporated a growing feminist movement which rebelled against middle-class life, with its focus on the norms and status quo of suburban life. This dropout counterculture allowed the more affluent to experiment with new forms of leisure and lifestyle, emanating from the coffee house culture of dissent in San Francisco in the early 1960s which then grew nationwide. As Cross (1990) points out, by 1970 there were 2000 communes in the USA, attracting hippies and a bohemian lifestyle, as an alternative to suburban lifestyles, with the rise of illegal use of narcotic substances such as marijuana. One very important element dating from this movement is the rise of large outdoor pop concerts such as Woodstock that have been reinvented in the new millennium as live music festivals for mass audiences. This was a direct result of changes dating from the 1950s when a youth culture emerged, as greater disposable income became available to this group as household incomes rose and less dependence was made upon children's income.

Cross (1990), in his discussion of 1950s and 1960s leisure in the USA, describes the growth of the youth entertainment market with rock and roll and pop music in the 1960s, as the importance of mass media and television helped grow audiences and the market for youth entertainment. One example was the Beatles' global success, which was heralded by the rise of the inexpensive 45 RPM (single) record which met a demand for cheap and accessible pop music. The 1960s were without doubt the era in which popular culture entered the leisure domain of most working-class families in some way. Interestingly, both Patmore (1983) and Cross (1990), looking at the 1960s and early 1970s, depict the sheer growth in leisure time, although other changes were running as cross-currents: 'From the 1960s, time available for recreation has declined in many families. Since then the dual-job family has increasingly become the norm . . . [And] . . . a drastic reduction of disposable time available per couple' (Cross 1990: 219). The natural speeding up of family life saw many new leisure habits emerge as short-cuts to less leisure time, including the growth of eating out (which expanded rapidly in 1990s Britain), day care for children, fewer children and more 'harried lives', epitomised by Linder's (1978) *The Harried*

SUMMER HOLIDAYS IN '65

SPAIN AND
PORTUGAL

THE BALEARIC ISLES · MADEIRA · CANARY ISLANDS

BOOK AT ANY BRANCH OF COOKS, DEAN & DAWSON, PICKFORDS OR ANY APPOINTED BOOKING AGENT

Plate 2.4 Spanish coastal resorts became popular with package tour companies in the 1960s. © Thomas Cook.

Leisure Class. In consequence, many traditional forms of leisure, such as going to the seaside, were replaced by other cultural forms such as overseas holidays and day trips replacing traditional domestic holiday trips as the car permeated more working-class families. By 1971, there were 4.2 million overseas holidays being taken by UK residents, the majority destined for Spain and a lesser proportion to France, stimulated by cheap air travel and package holidays. In the UK, the number of package holidays sold rose from 6900 in 1963–64 to 600,000 in 1970–71 (Patmore 1983) (Plate 2.4). This reflects the growth in the UK of increased paid holiday entitlement, from 40% of employees with paid holidays in 1938 and 91% by the 1950s.

The impact of the car and Dower's fourth wave led to the UK government recognising the growing pressure on countryside resources through unplanned and uncontrolled recreation and leisure. One consequence was the establishment of the Countryside Commission in 1968 and the formation of Country Parks near large urban areas to act as a conduit for urban recreation and leisure, as Chapter 8 will discuss. The 1960s saw a greater need for state intervention in the management of leisure resources as participation in a wider range of activities and opportunities occurred. Patmore (1983: 34) described the period since the mid-1950s where the 'growing ubiquity of the car for personal transport has been the underlying theme of the majority of recreational patterns' as the percentage of car-owning households in the UK rose from 31% in 1961 to 51% in 1968 to 58% in 1980. This was accompanied by major road-building programmes in many countries, making the countryside more accessible.

In the UK, a decline in state regulation of certain leisure activities such as gambling, embodied in the 1960 Betting and Gaming Act, led to an upsurge in activity, according to Dixey (1987). What is notable is how big business began to dominate commercial leisure provision in the 1960s, as the bingo craze developed. For example, the number of cinemas in the UK dropped from 1396 in 1950 to 510 in 1960 and 327 in 1965 and 193 in 1970. This was a direct result of many being closed due to falling attendances, presenting commercial opportunities to convert them to bingo halls after the 1960 Act. The 1960 Act also led to 8800 betting-shop licences being issued in 1961 and by 1962 this had risen to 13,340. This greater commercial exploitation of leisure opportunities, combined with the control and influence which large leisure conglomerates had over the population and government, led Williams (1981: 117) to describe it as the 'capitalisation, marketing and integration of the conglomerate, within which ownership and control over the means of cultural production has become a sector within the wider ownership and control of a much wider (non-cultural) productive and financial area'. Even by the 1980s, bingo was still enjoying audiences of 424,000 people playing every day, equivalent to 6 million playing a year in 1600 clubs, and, of course, with changes to UK Gaming Laws, this has also become an online phenomenon in the new millennium.

Yet, with the 1960s, there is a tendency to assume that many of the trends affecting Western leisure were homogenous, being a universal process of social change. This was certainly not the case in Eastern Europe, particularly if one considers the state command economies such as Russia. While Boutenko and Razlogov (1997) point to a general increase in workers' leisure time from the mid-1960s, in line with the West, there were few commercial leisure opportunities such as clubs, stadia and public houses in which leisure time could be spent. This led to a ratio of 1:21 in the way leisure time was spent between public and private leisure spaces, with nightclubs only developing in the 1990s and patronised by the wealthy in large cities. Similarly, while holiday entitlement rose during the 1960s from a minimum of 15 days' paid holiday to 20 in the 1970s, most of the free time was spent at home or visiting family/friends. This was due to restrictions on, and the cost of, overseas travel, while domestic travel was normally by train due to the cost of internal flights and inadequate roads and low car ownership.

The 1970s and 1980s

If the 1960s were the swinging period, the 1970s saw many trends continue at a slower pace, as economies went through a period of economic recession and decline. Williams (1995: 213) outlines the impact of such changes for post-industrial towns and cities, as older central areas of towns decayed as they lost their economic rationale. In some cases this has led to the creation of space for recreation, as high-density housing and industry have been removed and urban regeneration results. New trends emerged, such as a reversal of suburbanisation and the increase of gentrification in many old areas of North American cities and waterfront areas. New commercial forms of leisure also developed, emanating from the USA, such as the shopping mall and the growth of leisure shopping as a use of leisure time. Home ownership also rose sharply in the

USA, from 47% in 1900 to 55% in 1950 to 65% in 1976. In the UK the trend was slower as in 1976 only 50% of the population were owner-occupiers. Even so, continued suburban growth in many countries and a gradual growth of cities, with large house builders building on greenfield sites alongside the continued growth of new towns such as Harlow and Milton Keynes, created new communities which defined and developed their own leisure forms.

Some of these leisure practices were continued from former communities where the population had moved from, as Young and Wilmott's (1957: 126) *Family and Kinship in East London* observed in the move from Bethnal Green to a new housing estate in Essex: 'instead of the street for the children to play in, fields, trees and open country' existed, although this social relocation saw a decline in traditional patterns of kinship in urban areas in the period after the 1950s. As Dicken and Lloyd (1981: 340) argued, in such 1950s close-knit communities such as Bethnal Green in East London, 'the meeting points are the doorstep, the street, the local pub or the church hall. Interactions tend to be short distance; neighbouring is a prominent feature of social life' which shapes the localised forms of leisure and recreation in those communities. Some of these patterns broke down in the late 1960s, as social dislocation and changes to the relationship between home and work, with commuters travelling greater distances between home and work, reduced some of the traditional time spent on leisure despite the rise of the car. In the new town movement of the post-war period, a new genre of leisure habits and activities developed in these new social experiments of creating new communities on greenfield sites, with nearby employment and a higher standard of built and natural environment for leisure (see Roberts 1966; Willmott 1967; Heraud 1968; Schaeffer 1970). Indeed, reverse commuting from city centres to the suburbs and lateral commuting from the suburb to outlying industrial estates and clusters of employment changed the relationships between household, leisure and work.

Issues of crime and personal safety in the 1970s also began to define the social differentiation of the city and the desirability of residential areas and their proximity to leisure opportunities. For example, racial divides intensified in the 1970s with ghettoisation, with 45% of Chicago's black population having no access to a car in 1971 and suburban car ownership in London being much higher than in inner city households in the 1970s. This directly affects the ability to engage in different forms of leisure and personal travel, while public transport provision in 1970s US ghettos was equally poor.

With a post-industrial society and industrial restructuring came mass unemployment in the late 1970s, a phenomenon not experienced since the 1930s. As Patmore (1983) observed: in 1972 a sixth of the unemployed had been out of work for a year and by 1981 this had risen to one-fifth, focused on the young, unskilled, ethnic minorities and older workers. Such unemployment did not suddenly unleash a wave of free leisure time, as the unemployed did not see a lack of work as a rise in leisure time. The 1970s also saw a rise in one-person households, with implications for leisure provision, as noted in Chapter 1. Despite rising unemployment and inflation in many countries in the 1970s, the UK saw real disposable income for households rise 28% between 1970 and 1980, some of which was spent on leisure.

In Australia, like many other countries, the 1980s saw a new public sector culture enter into the ethos of leisure service provision by the state, particularly at a local level, to reduce state subsidies as a result of the political ideology of the new right – the user pays. This saw the emergence of the notion of leisure industries for the population as more commercial propositions, shifting the emphasis from a collectivist post-war welfare provision to a more commercialised one in the 1980s (Hamilton-Smith 1998). This accompanied a shift in emphasis from the collective to the individual, further eroding past attempts at social levelling and poverty reduction, with leisure being construed as a market product rather than a public good. The result has been a growing globalisation of leisure and new trends and fads in leisure aimed at individualised leisure, such as skateboards, roller blades and house-based technological leisure such as video recorders. A shift from a deliberate provision for the disadvantaged in the 1980s, as local authority budget cuts were imposed by central government ideology, led to massive restructuring of the public and private sector provision of leisure as the two areas began to blur. As Blacksell (1991) also observed, demographic changes affected leisure demand, as population growth and an ageing population began to shift attention to the retired and over-50 age group as new leisure consumers, with second home ownership growing in the 1970s and around 350,000 static caravans used for holiday-making. Martin and Mason estimated that in 1977 leisure spending in the UK was worth around £23 billion, comprising 27% of all consumer spending. Even excluding domestic travel and spending on clothing from these statistics, leisure spending was still equivalent to £17.25 billion or 20% of consumer spending (Martin and Mason 1979).

At a conceptual level, Stebbins (1997) observed that since the 1980s, there had been evidence of the development of casual leisure (as a contrast to serious leisure discussed in Chapter 1). This was associated with a postmodern society which was not synonymous with mass leisure or popular culture. Moreover, it was associated with more specialised forms of leisure or the activities of distinct 'tribes', groups of individuals with common characteristics and interests (which have also assumed an electronic form in the new millennium with social networking and e-tribes – see Chapter 7). Whereas mass leisure is undifferentiated and does not appeal to specific segments, casual leisure is more differentiated and targeted at niches. Stebbins (1997) defined this as an activity which is intrinsically rewarding, short-lived and pleasurable, with no or little training needed to enjoy it. Examples of casual leisure include social conversations, active forms of entertainment, activities involving play for adults where people can dabble in activities such as white water rafting and which tends to include an element of sensory stimulation. All of these are hedonistic activities (i.e. they produce pleasure for the participants). This is associated with the growth in many adventurous activities in the late 1980s, such as bungee jumping, and challenging activities as well as a diverse range of new passive activities. This is seen as a natural state of development in a postmodern society.

Despite studies like Schor's (1991) *The Overworked American*, the 1970s did not see any dramatic increase in working hours in the USA, as average hours have remained constant, although long and short working weeks have become more common, but this varies by occupational group and by country. Even so, Jacobs and Gerson (2001) have argued that there is a debate on this issue, with some authors pointing to a rise in leisure time while others dispute it. What they suggest is the need to look at the diversity of the population as opposed to simply classifying all workers, owing to the divergent experiences of occupational groups, individuals and countries. They also point to problems in Schor's (1991) arguments where the supposed increase in hours worked per week has not occurred: it is more the case that the number of weeks worked per year has dropped. Indeed, Robinson and Godbey (1997) suggest that between 1965 and 1997 Americans enjoyed more leisure time, although their results are based on time-diary data. Jacobs and Gerson (2001) conclude that certain groups, such as dual-income earners (whose numbers increased in the 1980s) and single-parent families, are squeezed between work and family and so leisure time is at a premium. Dual-income earners, especially those in professions in the USA, have seen their leisure time drop, but this is often a choice they have made by focusing on their careers. This has often led to family time deficits, with many working women seeking to balance home and family life and leisure time increasingly elusive.

So the period up to the 1980s saw major transformations, not only in the nature of society and the way it was governed as well as the political ideology that shaped state provision of leisure, but also in the debates over whether the population in general was enjoying more or less leisure time. The 1980s were probably a turning point in terms of leisure in many countries, given the end of a purely collectivist approach to leisure by the state and the focus on individualism, consumerism and the private sector to meet many of society's growing leisure needs. Some of the trends and fads of the 1980s, such as keep fit and jogging from the USA, have become global phenomena. At the same time, a continued decline in church attendance in the twentieth century was not reversed in the 1980s, although other religions expanded in many countries with a growing in-migration and changing ethnic composition. Certainly, as home ownership expanded a stage further in many countries in the 1980s (not least in the UK with the sale of state housing to sitting tenants), the home has been developed as a site for leisure even further, with an inward-looking approach as other forms of leisure have seen comparative declines (e.g. going to the local pub). The growing commercialisation of leisure in the 1980s is almost reminiscent of the mass recreation era of the late nineteenth century but with a subtle difference: the state withdrawal from its high degree of regulated involvement in public leisure provision owing to its high capital cost and competing demands from central government to spend resources on other areas of local service provision. This sea-change in the 1980s has not been reversed to any great degree in subsequent years.

Summary

As Argyle (1996: 31) aptly concludes: 'Leisure has shown extraordinary variations from one historical period to another, in the amount of leisure people had, what they did with it, and what they believed they should'. Argyle (1996: 31) summarised the main philosophical influences on the evolution of leisure:

● Aristotle saw leisure as important to moral and spiritual education and for the growth of virtue and wisdom.

- The Romans saw leisure as a means to promote fitness for health and military purposes.

- Many Christian groups viewed leisure as a means to prepare for the afterlife

- The Middle Ages and subsequent periods saw leisured classes able to spend leisure time because they had the means to do so (time and income)

- The Victorian middle classes pursued the idea of rational recreation both to improve themselves and for paternalistic reasons (i.e. to improve others) via education, exercise and commercial recreation as approved entertainment that was socially acceptable and as a riposte to drink. The Victorian social problem of drink was seen as a dominant working-class problem.

Technological changes, such as those identified by Dower (1965) in his four waves, and transport as well as other technologies such as the gramophone, radio, television, cinema, the car and air travel, have also shaped leisure activities and behaviour since the late nineteenth century, particularly since 1945 in the case of transport. Throughout the history of leisure, a variety of processes of change as well as continuity can be observed in the way that leisure activity has developed in different societies and communities. Leisure is as old as society itself, although there are debates on the actual emergence of this phenomenon. Hunziger (1939) argued that play was the origin of culture, and this can be traced back through time to most ancient civilisations. This is certainly discernible in ancient societies once the population began to live in permanent settlements where games and sport evolved. If music is also accepted as a form of leisure, then leisure can be dated back to many existing aboriginal groups. We should also not forget that even in the historical analysis of leisure, it is often assumed that work was the dominant focus of lives, which it may well have been for those involved in a daily struggle for survival. Even so, as Argyle (1996: 1) acknowledges: 'Leisure is a very important topic . . . many find their leisure more satisfying than their work; leisure can be a major source of happiness and of mental and physical health' and this is equally important for past societies as it is today.

Discussion questions

1. Why is the study of the history of leisure important to understanding modern-day leisure?

2. How do historians approach the study of leisure?

3. What are the main debates associated with the way historians periodise the history of leisure?

4. With reference to a selected period in history, outline the main themes which changed and those which remained constant.

References

Akyeampong, E. and Ambler, C. (2002) 'Leisure in African history: an introduction', *International Journal of African Historical Studies* 35 (1): 1–16.

Arcangeli, A. (2003) *Recreation in the Renaissance: Attitudes towards Leisure and Pastimes in European Culture, c.1425–1675*, Palgrave: Basingstoke.

Argyle, M. (1996) *The Social Psychology of Leisure*, Penguin: London.

Atkinson, J. (1991) *Recreation in the Aboriginal Community*, AGBS: Canberra.

Bailey, P. (1989) 'Leisure, culture and the historian: reviewing the first generation of leisure historiography in Britain', *Leisure Studies* 8 (2): 107–27.

Bailey, P. (1987) *Leisure and Class in Victorian England. Rational Recreation and the Contest for Control 1830–1885*, Routledge and Kegan Paul: London.

Beckers, T. and Mommas, H. (1996) 'The international perspective in leisure research: Cross-national contacts and comparisons', in H. Mommas, H. van der Poel, P. Bramham and I. Henry (eds) *Leisure Research in Europe: Methods and Traditions*, CAB International: Wallingford, pp. 209–44.

Bhattacharya, K. (2006) 'Non-western traditions: Leisure in India', in C. Rojek, S. Shaw and A. Veal (eds) *A Handbook of Leisure Studies*, Palgrave: Basingstoke, pp. 75–92.

Billinge, M. (1996) 'A time and place for everything: An essay on recreation, re-creation and the Victorians', *Journal of Historical Geography* 22 (4): 443–59.

Blacksell, M. (1991) 'Leisure, recreation and the environment', in R. Johnston and V. Gardiner (eds) *The Changing Geography of the UK*, 2nd edn, Routledge: London, pp. 362–81.

Blainey, G. (1975) *The Triumph of the Nomads: A History of Ancient Australia*, Macmillan: South Melbourne.

Booth, C. (1881) *Labour and Life of the People of London*, Macmillan and Co.: London.

Borsay, P. (2006) *A History of Leisure: The British Experience since 1500*, Palgrave: Basingstoke.

Boutenko, I. and Razlogov, K. (1997) *Recent Social Trends in Russia 1960–1995*, McGill-Queens University Press: Montreal.

Bramham, P. and Henry, I. (1996) 'Leisure research in the UK', in H. Mommas, H. van der Poel, P. Bramham and I. Henry (eds) *Leisure Research in Europe: Methods and Traditions*, CAB International: Wallingford, pp. 179–208.

Briggs, A. (1969) *Victorian Cities*, Pelham: Middlesex.

Bull, C., Hoose, J. and Weed, M. (2003) *An Introduction to Leisure Studies*, Prentice Hall: Harlow.

Burke, P. (1994) 'The invention of leisure in early modern Europe', *Past and Present* 146 (1): 136–50.

Chick, G. (2006) 'Anthropology/pre-history of leisure', in C. Rojek, S. Shaw and A. Veal (eds) *A Handbook of Leisure Studies*, Palgrave: Basingstoke, pp. 41–54.

Clark, P. (ed.) (1981) *Country Towns in Pre-industrial England*, Leicester University Press: Leicester.

Clark, P. (1983) The *English Alehouse: A Social History 1200–1830*, Longman: Harlow.

Clarke, J. and Critcher, C. (1985) *The Devil Makes Work: Leisure in Capitalist Society.* Macmillan: London.

Coulton, G. (1918) *Social Life in Britain from the Conquest to the Reformation*, Cambridge University Press: Cambridge.

Cross, G. (1990) *A Social History of Leisure since 1600*. Venture Publishing: State College, PA.

Cunningham, H. (1980) *Leisure in the Industrial Revolution, c1786–c1880*, Croom Helm: London.

Dagenais, M. (2002) 'Inscribing municipal power in urban space: the formation of a network of urban parks at Montreal and Toronto 1880–1940', *Canadian Geographer* 46 (4): 347–64.

Daniels, B. (1995) *Puritans at Play: Leisure and Recreation in Colonial New England*, Macmillan: Basingstoke.

De Grazia, S. (1962) *Of Time, Work and Leisure*, Anchor Books: Garden City, NY.

Dicken, P. and Lloyd, P. (1981) *Modern Western Society: A Geographical Perspective of Work, Home and Well-Being*, Harper Row: London.

Dixey, R. (1987) 'Bingo, the 1960 Betting and Gaming Act, the culture industry and . . . revolution', *Leisure Studies* 6 (3): 301–13.

Donajgrodski, A. (ed.) (1978) *Social Control in 19th Century Britain*, Croom Helm: London.

Dower, M. (1965) *The Challenge of Leisure*, Civic Trust: London.

Dumazedir, J. (1964) *Towards a Sociology of Leisure*, Free Press: New York.

Hall, C.M. and Page, S.J. (2006) *Geography of Tourism and Recreation*, 3rd edn, Routledge: London.

Hamilton-Smith, E. (1998) 'From cultural awakening to post-industrialism: the history of leisure, recreation and tourism in Australia', in H. Perkins and G. Cushman (eds) *Time Out? Leisure, Recreation and Tourism in New Zealand and Australia*, Addison Wesley Longman: Auckland, pp. 34–50.

Hardwick, J. (2008) 'Sex and the (seventeenth century) city: a research note towards a long history of leisure', *Leisure Studies* 27 (4): 459–66.

Heraud, J. (1968) 'Social class and the new town', *Urban Studies* 5 (1): 33–55.

Hubertus, J. (2005) 'Fun, leisure and entertainment in Russian history', *Kritika* 6 (4): 863–72.

Hunnicutt, B. (2006) 'The history of western leisure', in C. Rojek, S. Shaw and A. Veal (eds) *A Handbook of Leisure Studies*, Palgrave: Basingstoke, pp. 55–74.

Hunziger, J. (1939) *Homo Ludens*. Beacon Press: Boston.

Jacobs, J. and Gerson, K. (2001) 'Overworked individuals or overworked families? Explaining trends in work, leisure and family time', *Work and Occupations* 28 (1): 40–63.

Jones, S.G. (1986) *Workers at Play: A Social and Economic History of Leisure 1918–1939*, Routledge: London.

Langhamer, C. (2001) *Women's Leisure in England 1920–1960*, Manchester University Press: Manchester.

Larrabee, E. and Meyersohn, R. (1958) *Mass Leisure*, Free Press: New York.

Lawton, R. (1978) 'Population and society 1730–1900', in R. Dodgson and R. Butlin (eds) *An Historical Geography of England and Wales*, Academic Press: London, pp. 291–366.

Linder, S. (1978) *The Harried Leisure Class*, Columbia University Press: New York.

Madge, C. and Harrison, T. (1939) *Britain by Mass Observation*, Penguin: Harmondsworth.

Malcolmson, R. (1981) 'Leisure', in G.E. Mingay (ed.) *The Victorian Countryside*, vol. 2, Routledge and Kegan Paul: London.

Malcolmson, R. (1973) *Popular Recreations in English Society, 1700–1850*, Cambridge University Press: Cambridge.

Marfany, J. (1997) 'Debate: the invention of leisure in early modern leisure', *Past and Present* 148 (2): 174–97.

Martin, B. and Mason, S. (1979) *Broad Patterns of Leisure Expenditure*, Sports Council: London.

Mayhew, H. (1851) *London Labour and the London Poor*, 4 vols, Charles Griffin and Co.: London.

Meyersohn, R. (1969) 'The sociology of leisure in the USA, introduction and bibliography, 1945–1965', *Journal of Leisure Research* 1 (1): 53–68.

Mingay, G. (ed.) (1981) *The Victorian Countryside*, Routledge and Kegan Paul: London.

Mommas, H., van der Poel, H., Bramham, P. and Henry, I. (eds) (1996) *Leisure Research in Europe: Methods and Traditions*, CAB International: Wallingford.

Page, S. J. (1988) *Poverty in Leicester 1881–1911: A Geographical Perspective*, Unpublished Ph.D. thesis, University of Leicester, Leicester.

Page, S. J. (2009) *Tourism Management: Managing for Change*, 3rd edn, Elsevier: Oxford.

Page, S. J. and Durie, A. (2009) 'Tourism in wartime Britain 1914–1918: adaptation, innovation and the role of Thomas Cook & Sons', in J. Ateljevic and S. J. Page (eds) *Tourism and Entrepreneurship: International Perspectives*, Elsevier: Oxford, pp. 347–86.

Parratt, C. (1999) 'Making leisure work: women's rational recreation in late Victorian and Edwardian England', *Journal of Sport History* 26: 471–8.

Patmore, J.A. (1970) *Land and Leisure*, Penguin: Harmondsworth.

Patmore, J.A. (1983) *Recreation and Resources: Leisure Patterns and Leisure Places*, Blackwell: Oxford.

Pieper, J. (1958) *Leisure: The Basis of Culture*, Faber and Faber: London.

Pred, A. (1981) 'Production, family and free-time projects: A time-geographic perspective on the individual and societal changes in nineteenth century US cities', *Journal of Historical Geography* 7: 3–86.

Roberts, K. (1970) *Leisure*, Longman: London.

Roberts, K. (1976) *A Ragged Childhood*, Penguin: Harmondsworth.

Roberts, K. (2006) *Leisure in Contemporary Society*, 2nd edn, CABI: Wallingford.

Roberts, M. (1966) *Leisure in New Towns*, Department of Transportation and Environmental Planning: University of Birmingham.

Roberts, R. (1974) *The Classic Slum: Salford Life in the First Quarter of the Century*, Penguin: London.

Robinson, J. and Godbey, G. (1997) *Time for Life. The Surprising Ways Americans Use their Time*, Pennsylvania State University Press: University Park, PA.

Roca, E., Villares, M. and Ortego, M.I. (2009) 'Assessing public perceptions on beach quality according to beach users' profile: A case study in the Costa Brava (Spain)', *Tourism Management* 30 (4), 598–607.

Rose, M. (ed.) (1985) *The Poor and the City: The English Poor Law in its Urban Context 1834–1914*, Leicester University Press: Leicester.

Rowntree, S. (1901) *Poverty: A Study of Town Life*, Longmans, Green & Co.: London.

Rowntree, S. and Lavers, I. (1951) *English Life and Leisure*, Longman Green and Co: London.

Rozenzweig, R. (1985) *Eight Hours for What We Will: Workers and Leisure in an Industrial City, 1870–1920,* Cambridge University Press: Cambridge.

Schaeffer, F. (1970) *The New Town Story,* HarperCollins: London.

Schor, J. (1991) *The Overworked American,* Basic Books: New York.

Stebbins, R. (1997) 'Casual leisure: a conceptual statement', *Leisure Studies* 16 (1) 17–25.

Stobart, J. and Schwarz, L. (2008) 'Leisure, luxury and urban specialisation in the eighteenth century', *Urban History* 35 (2): 216–36.

Stobart, J. (2005) 'Leisure and shopping in the small towns of Georgian England', *Journal of Urban History* 31 (6): 918–21.

Sylvester, C. (1999) 'The classical idea of leisure: cultural ideal or class prejudice?' *Leisure Sciences* 21 (1): 3–16.

Thomas, K. (1964) 'Work and leisure in pre-industrial society', *Past and Present* 29 (1) 50–62.

Toner, J. (1995) *Leisure and Ancient Rome,* Polity Press: Cambridge.

Towner, J. (1996) *An Historical Geography of Recreation and Tourism in the Western World 1540–1940,* Chichester: Wiley.

Tylor, E. (1881) *Anthropology: An Introduction to the Study of Man and Civilisation,* D. Appleton: New York.

Veal, A. and Lynch, R. (2001) *Australian Leisure,* 2nd edn, Longman: Sydney.

Walton, J. and Walvin, J. (eds) (1983) *Leisure in Britain, 1780–1850,* Cambridge University Press: Cambridge.

Watson, J. (1998) 'From frontier to cyberspace: a history of leisure, recreation and tourism in New Zealand', in H. Perkins and G. Cushman (eds) *Time Out? Leisure, Recreation and Tourism in New Zealand and Australia,* Addison Wesley Longman: Auckland, pp. 16–33.

Weikin, C. (2007) 'In search of leisure: women's festivities in late Imperial Beijing', *Chinese Historical Review* 14 (1): 1–28.

Williams, R. (1976) *Keywords,* Collins: London.

Williams, R. (1981) *Culture,* Fontana: London.

Williams, S. (1995) *Recreation in the Urban Environment,* Routledge: London.

Willmott, P. (1967) 'Social research and new communities', *Journal of the American Planning Association* 33 (6): 387–98.

Wippler, R. (1968) *Sociale Determinanten van het Vrijetijdsgedrag (Social Determinants of Leisure Behaviour),* Van Gorcum: Assen.

Woody, T. (1957) 'Leisure in the light of history', *Annals of the American Academy of Political and Social Science* 313 (1): 470.

Young, M. and Willmott, P. (1957) *Family and Kinship in East London,* Routledge and Kegan Paul: London.

3 Leisure – the social context

Learning outcomes

After reading this chapter, you should be able to:

- Understand the importance of different social factors in shaping leisure

- Distinguish between different types of setting for leisure, such as the home and out-of-home environments

- Recognise the wide range of influences that shape leisure participation and some of the barriers that exist

Introduction

Leisure is an inherently social phenomenon and 'leisure encompasses the goals and activities people choose freely to fill their least obligated time' (van der Poel 2006: 9). Yet the notion of unobligated time does not necessarily mean that we have a free choice to engage in whatever forms of leisure we wish. To the sociologist we are not merely free: freedom to engage in leisure is socially conditioned and this really means that opportunities are determined by our circumstances, the society we live in and our position in that society. In other words, our ability to engage in leisure is a constant tension between our social conditions and our ability to believe we are free to engage in leisure. This chapter seeks to explore some of these issues in more detail, focusing on the social factors which researchers have identified as influential in shaping contemporary leisure. One of the early sociological studies of leisure by Parker (1976) explained that leisure is a form of social relationship. To understand this, more advanced explanations of leisure have been developed by researchers who point to the importance of social theory in which to embed our analysis of leisure (Chapter 1). This is so we can understand how it has evolved in a specific setting, as several advanced studies of leisure (e.g. Rojek's 1985 study *Leisure and Capitalism* and 1995 study *Decentring Leisure*) explore in detail.

At a more practical level, van der Poel (2006) poses an important question: What conditions need to be met to enjoy leisure? A feature directly shaped by the social context. According to Torkildsen (1999), there are a range of factors which influence our ability to participate in and enjoyment of leisure activities. As Figure 3.1 shows, these factors can be broken down into three interrelated groups:

● The *first* group are inherently personal factors, and focus on the individual, including some of the psychological aspects of leisure.

● The *second* group, labelled social and circumstantial factors, are also focused on the individual and some of the social aspects of the individual, structured around a number of economic issues such as work, income and wealth.

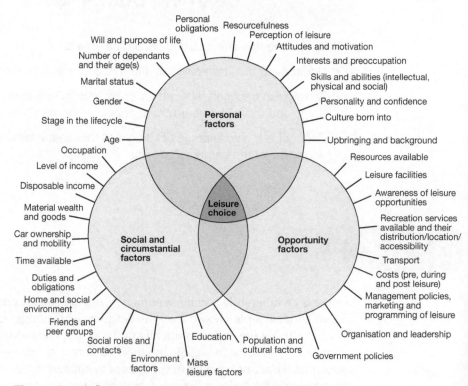

Figure 3.1 Influences upon leisure choices and participation

Source: Adapted from Torkildsen (1999), Table 5.1, p. 114. Copyright © Routledge, 1999

- *Third*, there are opportunity factors, which are largely structured around the notion that we need opportunities to engage in leisure. Many of these opportunities will be explored in more detail in Chapter 4 in relation to the demand for leisure, particularly the barriers which act as obstacles to participation. Figure 3.1 shows that these groups of factors are interrelated and coalesce into a common area which helps to create the *opportunity* for leisure. Yet above all, these key factors condition how we perceive, participate in and enjoy our free time.

As Chapter 2 illustrated, there have been major processes of social change occurring since the pre-industrial years. From a leisure perspective, it is possible to view these processes of change at two interrelated levels: on the one hand there are *macro* processes leading to profound shifts in the way society is organised and its composition. For example, one driver of these social changes which affects leisure is secularisation. In simple terms, secularisation is a term used to describe how the development of a modern-day Western society has been accompanied by a growing separation of the role of religion and religious organisations and their influence on society's norms and standards of behaviour. A visible sign is the drop in the number of church attendances in the UK, from its heyday in the Victorian period to its present-day role and status. Other key social changes which have occurred in leisure have resulted from a growing trend towards a greater focus on individualism (as opposed to community and collective interests). But one of the most profound social changes affecting leisure (including its worldwide commodification and analysis as a form of consumption) is the process of *globalisation* (see Table 3.1 for a summary of the main changes and impacts). There has also been a progressive increase in the level of education that people now enjoy (even though a critical debate has arisen over the standard of the attainment and whether this produces more able citizens compared to the immediate post-war period), opening up knowledge and interest in a wider range of opportunities for leisure. Overall, the post-war period in most countries has seen a shift and growth in the range of leisure preferences among the population as a result of these macro processes of change which have shaped the way we view and consume leisure in today's society.

Running in parallel to these macro processes of change are a range of *micro* processes of change. These, in part, result from the macro processes but also include changes occurring at the level of the *individual* and *family*. For example, there have been changes in the nature of social relationships between people and how they now spend their leisure time (e.g. social networking has certainly led to major changes in the way people communicate, plan, organise and spend their leisure time with technology using media such as Facebook). Leisure lifestyles now characterise the importance of leisure in individuals' identities and patterns of consumption. In other words, this means that leisure is a key element of how we organise and live our everyday lives. Yet leisure is not a ubiquitous and homogenous phenomenon (i.e. it does not occur in the same way everywhere at a global scale). Moreover, the type of society we live in determines how leisure is viewed from a philosophical standpoint (as

Table 3.1 Major impacts upon leisure as a result of globalisation

Impact	Effects
1. Globalisation of the economy	• Goods, services, labour and capital investment now move around the world more freely in a 'borderless world'. Leisure goods are available on a global rather than regional basis.
2. Dematerialisation and digitisation of the economy	• In material terms, goods are produced in low-cost locations to be sold globally (e.g. Nike Sportswear). • Companies produce for global markets and innovation/cost reduction and distribution chains distribute leisure goods globally. • The rise of 'entertainment' or an 'experience economy' in leisure, where time, experiences and the value added in the experience consumed are key.
3. Transnational corporations dominate leisure production	• Large corporations operating globally (e.g. BSkyB, Disney and McDonald's) now have a major impact on our consumption of leisure time.
4. Global organisations such as the UN, World Trade Organisation and EU policies have a major impact on the nation-state	• Many nation-states have lost control over the direction of development of their leisure economies and now compete with each other to attract global capital investment to develop leisure industries.
5. Time–space compression in our daily lives	• The rise of the virtual and non-virtual 24-hour society, cheap transport (low-cost carriers) and expansion of the internet has meant everything is readily available or easily accessible via transport and personal forms of mobility.
6. The rise of a network society	• Our lives are now more connected than ever before, with global events, through media, work, better education and technology. A defining feature of leisure consumption is the amassing of 'cultural capital' (i.e. the cultural value we derive from social and leisure experiences) which is now highly individualised.
7. Labour (work) and leisure have become blurred and de-differentiated	• The rise of 'serious leisure', the blurring of holiday making with work and working at home have eroded the distinction between work and leisure.
8. An abundance of 'leisure choices'	• Our participation in a 'connected world' opens up boundless opportunities for leisure which are limited by our ability to fit them into our lives. Daily life is not a simple concept, with defined roles in a household and traditional distinctions. Instead, accommodating leisure choices is a complex process for many households, especially those who perceive they are time poor but cash rich.

Source: Adapted from van der Poel (2006: 99–101). Reproduced by permission of Palgrave Macmillan

Chapter 2 illustrated) as well as its role in everyday lives: different types of leisure are permitted and encouraged by the state and by other organisations such as religious groups, as well as the culture and norms of that society. It is easy for a student of Western leisure to overlook, as Chapter 2 indicated, a rich and sometimes different set of leisure experiences in non-Western societies even if they are somewhat silent in the English literature on leisure, as Case Study 3.2 will show later.

A useful starting point to Chapter 3 is to summarise briefly some of the principal changes in modern societies in the post-war period, recapping some of the points from Chapter 2 that have affected the social setting in which leisure occurs:

- Homes have become more leisurely and private, reflected in the development of home-based entertainment: as Kynaston (2007a: 295) indicated, '. . . the radio remained in the early 1950s the mass media and capable of commanding huge loyalty', which was gradually replaced by the introduction of television in the 1960s. As many households became connected to mains electricity after 1945, it enabled consumers to buy *whiteware* goods (e.g. washing machines, vacuum cleaners and refrigerators) to reduce some of the monotony of everyday life. Yet as Kynaston (2007a: 293) argued, 'whether she enjoyed it or loathed it, housework was now an inescapable part of life for the servantless and as yet relatively gadgetless average middle class woman' in the immediate post-war period. Therefore it was not until the period after the 1950s that these labour-saving devices really came into their own. They were designed to increase the domestic leisure time of housewives, which, in some cases, was accompanied by their greater participation in the workforce. However, Roberts (1999: 41) maintains that 'since 1945 leisure has not become more home-based'. Instead, leisure has become focused upon outdoor activities, reflected in the growth of the car for leisure in most Western countries. This contributed to a greater propensity to undertake *out-of-home* leisure as well as a growth in holiday-taking, sports and other recreational activities (see Page 2009 for more detail on these trends in the twentieth century, particularly the impact of the package holiday).

- Personal entertainment in homes has increased, focused on home cinemas and other electronic gadgets such as Wii and Nintendo as the newer generation of computer games and entertainment for all ages.

- Mobile technology, such as mobile phones, iPods and MP3 players, provides flexible and on-demand personal entertainment that can be personalised to one's own tastes *in home* and *out of home*.

- A rise of a youth culture and new forms of leisure for the growth of a new leisure class – the *teenager*.

- The continued commercialisation of leisure by the private sector and emergence of large conglomerates and national organisations controlling leisure (see Chapter 2 for a discussion of the bingo hall in the UK), while the role of voluntary societies in leisure provision declined.

- A sharp increase in public sector involvement in leisure provision from 1945 until the late 1970s and then a sharp decrease in public sector involvement, termed the *decoupling of the state*.

- A de-standardisation of work and work time, and a greater focus on individualism, creating more flexibility in the way leisure is planned and consumed.

- The rise of an *experience economy* for some social groups (which will be discussed later in the chapter), shaping their consumption of leisure time.

Against this background of social changes affecting leisure, it is useful to focus on the implications of these macro trends and the implications at the micro level (i.e. the individual and family) for leisure consumption. To do this, we need to understand the social value of leisure. In other words, *why is leisure important to individuals and groups?*

What is the social value of leisure?

Social psychologists have a long tradition of studying leisure, epitomised by the famous book by Argyle (1996) on the *Social Psychology of Leisure*. Their interest in leisure largely emerges from a North American tradition of studying leisure, by looking at the psychological constructs which apply to leisure (e.g. see the classic studies by Neulinger 1974, Iso-Ahola 1980 and the review by Mannell *et al.* 2006). As Mannell *et al.* (2006) argue, one of the main reasons why the social psychologist has been interested in leisure is because of the highly individualised nature of many leisure experiences, as well as its link to the psychological health of individuals. As Mannell *et al.* (2006: 111) explain, the focus of psychology is on providing an understanding of the human being as an individual because

> Psychology is the science of mental processes and behaviour and their interaction with the environment, and psychologists study the processes of sense perception, thinking, learning, cognition, emotions and motivations, personality, abnormal behaviour, interactions between individuals, and interactions with the environment. *(Mannell* et al. *2006: 11)*

This quotation helps to explain why leisure is important to individuals. In other words, social psychologists are interested in leisure and the focus on the individual in terms of their feelings, behaviour, values and experiences. A central feature of this research has been a concern with motivation and satisfaction which will be addressed in Chapter 4. It is this focus on the individual that helps to probe *why we do what we do in our leisure time* and some of the theoretical explanations of how we spend our leisure time.

A principal consideration of the social psychologist, as Argyle (1996) argues, is to understand why people need social relationships and how these are expressed in terms of leisure behaviour, attitudes and activities. Argyle identified *three* main reasons why people seek social relationships in their leisure time:

- *To seek material and instrumental health*, which means that we seek out relationships which can be of benefit to us and also provide reciprocal benefits.

- *To gain emotional support*, which is often expressed in conversations between individuals and in groups, to reduce a sense of alienation or exclusion in social situations, particularly where there may be difficult personal circumstances.

- *To fulfil a desire for companionship*, which may be a function of the first two points above, but it is often seen as a basic human need in terms of assisting with happiness and personal fulfilment. At a rudimentary level, companionship can help reduce a sense of isolation and loneliness which may impact upon people with a weak social network. Companionship occurs where family and friends meet on a regular basis to reduce the sense of isolation.

Studies by social psychologists illustrate the *social benefits* of leisure, such as how it makes people happy, improves their mood and also increases their satisfaction with life. The social benefits can be examined at two levels.

- *First*, there is the benefit for the community in terms of cohesion. Social cohesion has seen a great deal of research interest generated by sociologists who are interested in the ways in which leisure can help maintain and enhance community identity. This is the case where there is an ethnic population who may comprise a significant section of society.

- *Secondly*, there are other benefits which accrue to the individual and individual groups within society, such as the elderly, children, the disabled, the unemployed, families and single-parent families.

The sociologist also has a long tradition of studying communities and the individuals within them (see Chapter 2), and especially the structure of the community, which may affect the nature and opportunity for leisure which takes place within it. For example, work by Tönnies (1964) on *Community and Society* explored the contrasting structure of the *gemeinschaft* and *gesellschaft* community (i.e. the former is a community which is closed and closely knit; the latter is based on individualism, independence and an absence of a meaningful community). In the former, social relationships are the basis of daily life in a close-knit community which can shape many interactions that occur in citizens' leisure time. Clearly this distinction is quite a simplified one, although it highlights the importance of community structure to leisure, echoed in concerns in the 1960s over the decline of a sense of community in urban studies. For example, Mumford (1961) observed the rapid effect of suburbanisation and corresponding decline in community connectedness with the shift to greater individualism.

At a community level, there is also growing evidence that support and investment in leisure, particularly where it has a physical or active recreation component, which may contribute to wider social benefits such as longer lives, disease-free lives and an overall increase in one's quality of life. While some of the evidence to support these assertions is sometimes scarce or contradictory (van der Poel 2006), there is a recognition that leisure is a necessity to improve the well-being of society. This is demonstrated by comments in a government memorandum by the UK Labour government in 1946/47 on the need for a socialist policy for leisure, which

> lamented the 'failure of the majority of British citizens to enjoy a full life through their leisure pursuits'; labelled the cinema and gambling as two prime examples of regrettably 'passive' and superficial leisure pursuits; and drew the rather defeatist conclusion that 'all forms of escapist entertainment or recreation are encouraged by the drabness, insecurity and hopelessness of daily life'. *(Kynaston 2007b: 175)*

Therefore, it is not surprising that many governments, seeking to harness the social benefits of leisure as a means to improve the physical and mental well-being of members of society, argue the case; the following quotation typifies many public sector attitudes to the social need for leisure:

> Leisure and recreation are both crucial components of a balanced and healthy lifestyle. Leisure time is a time when people can do what they want to do, away from work and other commitments. Recreation and leisure play an important role in social wellbeing by providing people with a sense of identity and personal autonomy. Involvement in leisure-time activities adds meaning to individual and community life and contributes to people's overall quality of life. Recreation can encourage personal growth and self-expression and provide increased learning opportunities, satisfying needs not met in people's non-leisure time. *(Ministry of Social Development 2008: np)*

The implications of this quotation are that:

- Leisure has a clear relationship with our social well-being.
- Recreation and leisure contribute to our sense of identity.
- Leisure has a direct effect on both the individual and community, especially in relation to their quality of life.
- Leisure can contribute to people's personal growth and self-expression as well as meeting their under-fulfilled needs.

These benefits illustrate some of the social as well as psychological benefits which accrue from leisure. For example, leisure may give us a sense of independence or freedom which is expressed as a high degree of autonomy, perhaps compensating for a lack of these attributes in daily work. At an individual level, leisure may also help improve our self-esteem, by building self-confidence and a sense of belonging. In other words, leisure may help individual members of society to fit in with other people, the community and the wider society (i.e. it has a *socialising* role).

Argyle (1996) provides one of the best overviews of the social benefits of leisure from a psychologist's perspective. He identifies a number of broad issues which we need to take into account when looking at the social aspects of leisure. The *first* is *social integration,* which relates to the way individuals and groups (particularly minorities or 'outsiders' in communities) are socialised into the local community and society as a whole. Argyle suggested that individuals engage in groups as a form of leisure to derive social rewards, develop a social identity (e.g. 'I am a member of . . .') and improve their self-esteem. Argyle lists a number of key features of social integration in leisure, including:

- Health and physical benefits related to the way individuals spend their leisure time, particularly where there is physical activity involved.

- In the workplace and in non-work time, individuals and working groups may play games, joke and gossip, which is a form of leisure activity that helps build closer working relationships. In some cases, where employers seek to build stronger teams of workers, they may use team-building exercises, such as outdoor adventure centres or military assault courses, to foster a team-building culture so the group leaves the event with a closer bonding and functioning team spirit. In other words, bonding may lead to improved personal and greater job satisfaction. But there are negative aspects to this, such as creating a clear distinction between 'in' groups and 'out' groups in the workplace and in the community. Such a distinction in leisure activity generates feelings of *involvement* for some and *exclusion* for others, generating negative attitudes and feelings of marginalisation among the 'out' group.

- It is often argued that sport generates improved social integration through team-based cooperation as well as cohesion among groups of supporters of teams, although antagonisms and violence may also arise from the anti-social aspects of attitudes to rival teams, such as with football hooligans.

- Leisure certainly aids individuals in forming closer social bonds such as friendships, and in nurturing a social network of acquaintances and virtual friends with the rise of social networking technology.

- Leisure may also help to give individuals a sense of social acceptance through membership of groups.

- In terms of families, leisure performs a *social bonding* role where there are parallel leisure interests that generate a sense of group enjoyment. For example, an entire family may watch a television programme together or take a holiday, and this shared leisure time may enhance family relationships. Conversely, leisure may also be a focal point for *conflict* within the family, such as a disagreement over what television programme to watch or where to go on holiday.

- Sociologists also examine the relationship between religion and leisure and its role in social integration, and how it may generate a socially cohesive group of people focused on a common set of beliefs, forming an 'in' group and, by association, creating an 'out' group. Religious worship and association with religious groups is an important leisure activity for many sections of society in many countries and needs to be recognised and acknowledged accordingly. Religion also provides a basis for social interaction among members of the same religion in their daily and weekly leisure. This is because religion may well be a basis upon which individuals build meaningful friendships, social relationships and networks in their leisure time.

Therefore, to summarise, some of these key points on social integration are that leisure time spent in groups may help to forge meaningful social relationships, which are cohesive and supportive. Individuals may become members of groups when undertaking leisure where they share similar ideals and common beliefs on the norms and standards of behaviour as well as a specific view of the world. The ongoing difficulty relates to the issue of in/out groups and whether this generates feelings of alienation, exclusion, marginalisation and a lack of power. This is because every group usually has its own 'social niche', according to Argyle, which is apparent or becomes apparent to group members. This is one reason why many governments have pursued strategies of social inclusion, as will be discussed later in Chapter 4, to try to overcome the broader social issues of inclusion and exclusion. This represents a major historical leap forward, as Gershuny and Fisher (1999) indicated: leisure started the century (i.e. in 1900) as a name of a *class* but is now a form of *consumption*. Governments are now seeking ways to introduce equality in provision, by addressing prejudice, racism, discrimination and ingrained cultural views on leisure, sometimes with the sanction of legislation (as in the case of racism and disability). As this chapter shows, different social groups have different experiences of leisure and Chapter 4 will certainly highlight some of the barriers experienced by different groups; which may lead to exclusion from certain forms of leisure.

The *second* area which Argyle focused on was the contribution of leisure to enhancing an individual's or community's social life. Our social lives overlap with all kinds of leisure, and it is certainly a principal motivator associated with how we use our leisure time. As this chapter demonstrates, leisure is a key feature of our social lives in relation to our family and our friends. These social lives have different meanings depending upon how we spend our leisure time, with whom it is spent and what we do in that leisure time. For example, there is a clear difference between leisure time that we spend in the home, with our family, and that time we spend outside the home with friends. As Argyle argues, one of the reasons we engage in leisure is to pursue the notion of sociability or a social environment where we can engage in conversation with others, as a form of social interaction, thereby creating socially enriching contexts in which to spend our non-work time. One important concept developed to try to measure how socially connected our society is, based on social networks and our involvement in local communities in our leisure time, is the notion of *social capital*. Social capital has been developed to try to understand the level of cohesion that exists in society, which may influence the social experience of leisure as the following discussion shows.

Social capital and leisure

Social capital is concerned with the ways in which individuals can work together to pursue shared objectives, to nurture reciprocal relationships and feelings with others (Putnam 1993). Putnam, when examining the USA, argued that social capital had declined in recent years. This conclusion resulted from looking at different measures and social indicators associated with individuals, groups and the wider society and the activities that occur in their leisure time. As Figure 3.2 shows, in any attempt to measure social capital, social interaction and membership of groups have a significant role to play. One of the underlying premises of social capital is the ability of individuals to associate together on a regular basis (Hall 1999; Glover and Hemingway 2005), and it has significant implications for leisure because participation in different groups in one's leisure time is one aspect of the way in which social capital is measured. In other words, how individuals spend their leisure time and the types of social interaction and involvement they have with the community and others can be conceptualised and measured. As Figure 3.2 shows, such measurement has many leisure-related dimensions which can be influenced by leisure (e.g. satisfaction with life, enjoyment of the living environment, social participation in groups and social networks). Research by Hall (1999) found no evidence of a decline in the UK population's involvement in voluntary associations, committees and other activities in the post-war period as one measure of social capital.

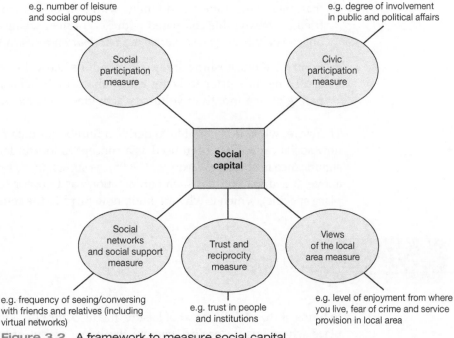

Figure 3.2   A framework to measure social capital

Source: Adapted from Harper and Kelly (2003: 1), Table 1. Crown Copyright material is reproduced under terms of the Click-Use Licence.

More informal activities, such as visiting friends, and leisure time spent outside the home have seen a significant increase since the post-war period, supporting the comments made earlier by Roberts. But these assertions need to be qualified, as Hall (1999) argues, given the disproportionate impact of the middle classes in post-war Britain in sustaining social capital. This is because the middle classes have the widest networks of friends, involvement in voluntary activities and groups. It is an important measure given the major expansion of the middle class in the UK since 1945, promoted by the rise of the service industries and a professional class. However, one major change observed since 1945 in studies of social capital is a decline in the public's trust of others. This also tells us something about the type of leisure now being undertaken in communities and how it has shifted from the collective focus (as discussed in Chapter 2) to a more individualised mode of consumption, often focused on immediate family and friends rather than extended family and local community. Social capital provides an important measure of the sociability of the population, their recreational endeavours and how far these are built around social networks and group membership. For example, data from the UK's *Social Trends* contains a number of leisure-related measures related to social capital, as the following points illustrate:

- The UK Social Attitudes Survey in 2006 found that 48% of the population aged 18 years or over saw friends and close ties as important; 13% valued close friends more importantly than close family ties (*social participation measures*).

- The Social Attitudes Survey in 2005 found that women spent more time than men with friends and family, with 65% of women seeing family and friends weekly; this compared with 57% of men seeing friends and family on a weekly basis (*social network participation measure*).

- From a UK citizenship survey, 73% of adults had volunteered in England in the 12 months prior to being asked about their habits, with 48% participating once a month in voluntary activities (*civic participation measures*).

Therefore, while it is possible to derive a number of data sources to illustrate how social capital has been used as a concept to look at leisure and its wider significance in society (Warde *et al.* 2005), as shown in each measure examined above, it is apparent that such participation has to occur somewhere (i.e. it is place specific), which is why attention now turns to the setting of leisure.

The leisure setting

In terms of the social context of leisure, it is also important to recognise that the place where leisure occurs, namely the home or out-of-home location, will have a major effect on the nature and timing of leisure activities. The home has been a traditional focus for leisure, with use expanding in the 1920s and 1930s

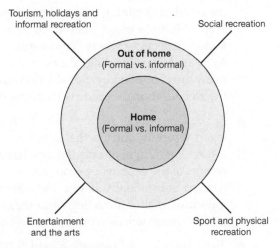

Figure 3.3 The social setting of leisure

as home-based leisure developed with typical activities such as listening to radio, reading and, more latterly, watching television (the most popular home leisure activity in most countries) and now the playing of computer games. Near-to-home activities such as gardening (as well as the enduring interest in allotments) are also very popular leisure pursuits, while the garden is also an important social context for other forms of leisure such as socialising and children's play. Figure 3.3 highlights the distinction between home-based leisure and out-of-home leisure, particularly the distinction between formal and informal forms of leisure.

Glyptis and Chambers (1982: 247) outlined the complexity of the home as a focus for leisure, illustrating why it is such an important setting:

> The home accommodates a variety of leisure demands which are both complex and dynamic. It must accommodate individual and communal activity, and perhaps several activities simultaneously for different members of the household, each with their own requirements for space.

According to Bull *et al.* (2003), citing research by Torkildsen, the commercial sector performs a major role in the provision of leisure opportunities in and around the home. Four categories of commercial provision are also identified, including:

● *Social recreation*, as one of the most popular forms of leisure which includes activities such as going to public houses for social drinking (as well as the rise of binge drinking among some age groups), a feature highlighted in Chapters 1 and 2. Since the 1960s, drinking habits in the UK have changed, from visiting community-based local public houses towards patronising larger, in-town drinking establishments as part of the 24-hour society and night-time economy which will be discussed below. Other forms of social recreation include eating out (i.e. going to restaurants and the rise of fast food chains). A growing number of multiplex cinemas have also reversed the trend of declining cinema attendance in many countries since the mid-1980s. Multiplexes typically have been located on leisure parks (or in converted cinemas) where commercial leisure premises have also been co-located (e.g. bowling alleys and restaurants) at out-of-town sites and many are controlled by global leisure chains. This is a very good example of the globalisation of leisure consumption and how it affects our leisure lives.

- *Entertainment and the arts*, which are commercial leisure activities undertaken typically outside the home in a wide range of locations. Since the 1980s, entertainment and the arts have been recognised as very major elements of the experience economy (see the discussion below) which has expanded substantially if one includes other elements of the arts such as museums, visitor attractions and theatres through to small local entertainment venues such as working men's clubs.

- *Sport and physical recreation*, which is a very diverse category with a large presence controlled by the commercial sector, with recent growth in fitness centres, health and leisure clubs, gyms and sports clubs.

- *Tourism, holidays and informal recreation*, which now account for large elements of our leisure spending on an annual basis, where leisure time is spent in a concentrated period as a holiday. This is a key element of our annual leisure time, especially for families.

Thus, an important social unit, which affects how, where and the types of leisure undertaken, is the *family*.

The family and leisure

The family unit has been a major focal point for leisure researchers as it usually comprises a household with a number of individuals whose activities give rise to a diversity of leisure experiences (see Harrington 2006 for an excellent overview of the subject). There is an ongoing argument amongst researchers over the importance of family-based leisure, with some arguing that it is the most important form of leisure that we can study because it is based on a family unit, which brings with it acceptance and trust. As Harrington (2006) highlights,

> Researchers in leisure studies know that for most people, most of the time leisure takes place within and around the home and usually occurs with members of their family and close friends ... This has come to be known as the privatisation thesis and has been stated in various ways, some of which emphasised home centredness more so than family centredness, but all capture the idea that in contemporary society, family and friendship-based home-life has taken precedence over leisure in the public sphere. *(Harrington 2006: 417)*

This is an interesting contrast to Roberts' (1999) view on post-1945 changes in leisure, which emphasised out-of-home leisure as the main catalyst of change.

Therefore, the home provides a comfortable and familiar environment where positive leisure experiences can be developed (Bull *et al.* 2003). On the other hand, as a family is comprised of a group of individuals, the

> individual's leisure lifestyle is heavily dependent on the expectations, duties and obligations placed on them by the family and on the way in which the family unit allocates its resources, including material, financial and time resource allocation. The family unit, on the other hand, may provide the necessary companionship, safety, finance and freedom to facilitate a fulfilling leisure experience. *(Bull* et al. *2003: 73)*

The result is that the family may offer a familiar environment for leisure experiences, but conversely, the experiences which emerge are often based on a tension between the individual's need for freedom and their own identity versus the collective need of the family group.

Probably the most important and influential study published on leisure and the family was Rapoport and Rapoport's (1975) *Leisure and the Family*. Even so, the major work of Rowntree and Lavers in the inter-war period, culminating in *English Life and Leisure* (Rowntree and Lavers 1951), certainly predates interest in family-based leisure and its social significance. Subsequent studies also highlighted the important role of the family as a social unit which conditioned individuals' leisure, particularly the socialisation role which the family plays as children grow, and the parents' values and behaviour are transmitted to them. What the Rapoport and Rapoport study identified was the notion of a family life-cycle model and the interrelationship between stage in the life cycle, work and leisure. This notion of a family life cycle was not new, even though most leisure researchers attribute this to the 1970s: the life-cycle concept can be dated to the influential work of Rowntree (1901) on poverty in York in the late Victorian period. Rowntree's life-cycle model was devised to identify periods in the family life cycle when there was a greater likelihood of experiencing poverty. If we take that basic model and apply it to leisure, we see that our interest in leisure will change as we go through different stages of the life cycle: this is the basis of the Rapoport and Rapoport model. This is important in conditioning the type of leisure in which we have opportunities to participate, which results from the interplay of factors in the family life cycle. In this sense the family is a very important social unit in terms of understanding the importance of leisure and changing uses through time. While this model is quite straightforward to understand, the original notions of life cycle and poverty have obviously changed since the late Victorian period as many countries now have a welfare state and we have a much longer life expectancy.

As Table 3.2 shows, the Rapoport and Rapoport study identified four stages in the family life cycle of significance to the study of leisure:

1. Youth

2. Young adulthood

3. Establishment

4. Later years

Table 3.2   The Rapoport and Rapoport model of the family life cycle and leisure

Stages

1. Youth/Young people	Those aged 15–19 form the basis of the first stage in the life-cycle model, where individuals explore leisure and their own personal identity. The choice of leisure activities is very fashion led, with enough opportunity for experimentation. It is also expressed in terms of youth culture and interest in music, particularly popular music. This stage of the life cycle also offers an opportunity for developing youth self-identity. Key influences upon the forms of leisure which young people engage in are at school, in the family and the wider community as well as an ability to access money to pursue one's interests. Towards the end of this stage in the life cycle, adolescents develop their own identity, interests and leisure lifestyles.
2. Young adults	This phase commences with the period when adolescents leave school and then enter the job market, leading up to the early period of marriage when two people meet and establish a family. This leads up to the next stage which is called establishment. The model argues that at this stage, the main interests in terms of leisure are related to occupation, intimate relationships, family interests and friendships. When the individual enters the workplace, at the early stage of this cycle there is a high degree of disposable income and few financial and family responsibilities. This is one explanation as to why the mass consumption of pop music and other forms of entertainment rose significantly from the late 1950s onwards, with their increased disposable income for leisure. In some senses, the forms of leisure which individuals pursue at this stage in the cycle may even be relationship seeking, such as going to nightclubs and other social settings to meet one's peers. The model also argued that at this stage, there is a rebuilding of relationships with parents and siblings reflecting the establishment of the child as an independent adult.
3. Establishment	The model suggests that this is the largest stage in the life cycle, where important social events occur. These key events include marriage, childbirth and rearing children, and establishing and maintaining friendships. Unlike stage 2, the emphasis is on the family couple rather than groups of friends as the main focus for leisure, although individuals will still pursue their own interests outside the home. Towards the middle of this stage, careers become established. It is not surprising, therefore, that leisure is a family-centred activity which is shared amongst family members in the middle stages. This is most typically described as family-based leisure, with more substantial events being family holidays and shorter events being day trips or eating out as a family. As this stage develops, and the role of the mother in terms of the required parenting declines, there may be an increased amount of time for leisure or opportunities to develop new interests. Towards the latter stages of this establishment phase, children become adolescents and increasingly

become more independent as they enter full-time education and potentially leave home. This can see considerable change in the family's leisure lifestyles as they need to adjust to the concept of empty nesting. There may be some opportunities for enjoyment of grandchildren, but this stage is certainly one of readjustment.

4. Later years	In this stage of the model, a dominant feature is retirement, which is a difficult stage for individuals, with the potential for elderly citizens to be alienated from society into which they have previously been integrated through their involvement in work. It was characterised as a stage where less physically active pursuits dominated the leisure habits of this group. Key concerns are financial resources to live meaningful lives, particularly the importance of pensions and state support in old age. This stage in the life cycle is characterised by a wide range of relationships for those entering older age, which could be the continuation of previous patterns of leisure, new leisure interests or withdrawal from previous leisure lives depending upon one's personal circumstances.

Sources: Rapoport and Rapoport (1975) developed from Bull *et al.* (2003: 74–9)

While this model is useful in helping us to understand different stages in a life cycle and the importance of leisure in each, Bull *et al.* (2003: 80) rightly argue that one major stage is missing, namely childhood leisure (also see Case Study 1.1 and Chapter 8). They also level other criticisms at this model, arguing that the model suggested that the family controlled many of the leisure activities in which young adults engage. This tends to ignore the importance of the individual in building their own leisure relationships and making friendships and other social networks (with some notable exceptions, as we explore in Chapter 12 on the consequences of over-parenting and childhood leisure). We also have to recognise that the model was developed in the 1970s, and there have been many changes since then, particularly the focus on how individuals make decisions in relation to the leisure they may choose to pursue. Other notable changes are that there has been an increase in divorce and remarriage, which has certainly changed the social dynamics of family-based leisure. There has also been a rise in single and separated parents, with new leisure patterns emerging from the impact of these relationship changes (i.e. separated family leisure and split weekend leisure time for parents and children – see Jenkins 2009). More women have also entered the workplace, as Bull *et al.* (2003) show, which produces a revision to the point at which certain aspects of the family leisure occur in their life-cycle model.

The relationship between leisure, occupation and family as set out in the model has seen major changes since the 1970s, with the breakdown (or as some commentators suggest, a redefining) of the nuclear family and the emergence of other family structures such as same-sex marriages which do not fit this conventional model. Similarly, the rise of single-parent households and divorcees does not fit this model, along with the impact of unemployment. Equally, the model is not able to recognise differences which are emerging from reduced pension values, which will mean that many people have to work for longer periods of time, extending the working age well into their late sixties or beyond, returning to the situation pre-dating the welfare state. As Haywood *et al.* (1989) argue, this model is also problematic because it is based on the biological evolution of individuals (growth to degeneration) and less concerned with life-phases or paths, where age is no longer a simple description of people's propensity to engage in leisure (also see Chapter 12 on trends which challenge these conventional models). But as Harrington (2006: 429) argues, the role of leisure within the family remains an important focus, particularly where children are present, because:

- Developing family leisure time is recognised as important to children who have memories of past, present and potentially future leisure time spent within the family.

- Children's perceptions of leisure show that *quality time* with parents helps to build more intimate social relationships between the child and the family unit.

- Leisure may help to build in parenting goals. This is described as *purposive leisure*, where the leisure has a purpose in terms of what it seeks to achieve (i.e. improved cohesion and greater functioning of the family unit via better communication and bonding).

However, an enduring concept that helps us understand how individuals engage in leisure as a social phenomenon is the term *leisure lifestyle*.

Leisure lifestyles

According to Veal (2000: 8), 'lifestyle is the pattern of individual and social behaviour characteristic of an individual or group'. The study of lifestyles can be dated to the 1920s but its application in the study of leisure largely dates to the late 1950s, with an expansion of interest in this concept in the 1970s and 1980s (Veal 2000). Much of the research activity emanates from sociology and there is a lack of agreement over the precise meaning and application of the term lifestyle. In Veal's analysis of lifestyle and its application to leisure, he highlights that it is associated with the mode of living and a number of key characteristics:

- Our activities and behaviour.
- Our values and attitudes.

- The nature of group-based or individual behaviour and how people interact.

- The extent to which coherent groups of activities can be identified and used to create a distinct lifestyle based on choice.

In other words, leisure is just one part of an individual's lifestyle associated with other aspects of their behaviour and life such as health, forms of consumption and other measures such as income and employment that affect the type of lifestyle pursued. One of the most influential studies on lifestyle and leisure was undertaken by Glyptis (1981). She argued for the adoption of the concept of leisure lifestyles in leisure research because of the focus on, and importance of, individual perceptions of leisure. 'This allows the totality of an individual's leisure experiences to be considered and is a subjective approach which shifts the emphasis from activity to people, from aggregate to individual and from expressed activities to the functions which these fulfil for the participant and the social and locational circumstances in which he or she undertakes them' (Herbert 1988: 243). What Herbert argues is that:

- The use of lifestyles as a concept to understand the type of leisure an individual undertakes can best be understood through this micro scale of analysis (which may involve measurement of quantitative measures and more qualitative aspects of leisure) based on the individual.

- A greater focus on the subjective aspects of leisure such as lifestyles and individual perceptions, which helps us to understand leisure, its social setting and meaning compared to general measures such as social class.

- The notion of lifestyle allows us to situate the leisure activities of an individual in their wider life course and social circumstances to understand how leisure interacts with other aspects of an individual's life.

In other words, leisure lifestyles help us to begin to understand how the individual's leisure is based on a certain way of life and how it is shaped by many of the factors identified by Torkildsen (1999) in Figure 3.1. This focus on the individual also has a salience given new ideas developed within the sociological research literature on consumption, namely the concept of the experience economy.

Leisure, lifestyles and *The Experience Economy*

Pine and Gilmore's (1999) *The Experience Economy* makes an interesting contribution to the study of the individual and their leisure experience as part of a wider lifestyle. They argue that the experience economy is the next stage in the evolution of society from a service economy. Pine and Gilmore argue that businesses need to create experiences which are memorable for consumers given the increased levels of education of many consumers, and their pursuit of value-added elements within the experience they purchase. While there is a great deal of debate over the value of the concept of the experience economy, given that research in tourism and leisure on the visitor experience has highlighted many of these qualitative attributes, their research focuses upon a number of key elements of individual consumption:

- the need to create a sensation;
- the need to personalise the experience, to develop trust and a bond with the consumer, which has been embodied in the use of brands.

The experience economy concept suggests that we need to focus on four areas of experience:

- entertainment;
- education;
- aesthetic (i.e. an ability to immerse oneself in something); and
- escapism in what is consumed.

In other words, we need to provide leisure experiences which allow the consumer to engage in a number of ways, ranging from absorption through to immersion in the experience, and at the same time through passive through to more active participation in the form of leisure. Above all, the experiences need to be able to engage all five of our senses (i.e. hearing, seeing, touching, smell and taste). This is one of the ways in which the National Tourism Organisation for Scotland, VisitScotland, has developed its brand wheel of products to appeal to consumers to encourage them to visit Scotland.

Above all, the experiences need to be inspirational and able to add value so that they are highly memorable. Clearly this has major implications for leisure, as it implies that certain social groups, particularly the middle classes, are now seeking high levels of experience from their leisure activities, as discussed in Chapter 2 in relation to adventure sports and the pursuit of cultural capital in terms of visiting places and taking holidays. While this theoretical approach to leisure consumption has been widely debated, it does illustrate that if we approach the analysis of leisure from a lifestyle perspective focused on the individual, we have a much better understanding of what people are looking for from experiences. If we start to think about the ideas of the experience economy concept, it may not apply in every case, particularly as many forms of leisure activity are passive, routine and not necessarily focused on commercial forms of consumption. Nevertheless, this does give us an opportunity to think about what is happening among certain groups of people and individuals in terms of how they are viewing leisure and what they seek from the experience. For this reason it is useful to focus on a case study of the types of experiences which are associated with youth culture and leisure, namely the role of music as a form of leisure activity.

Case Study 3.1   Youth culture, music and leisure

Music is one of the key parts of the fabric of our culture and we often celebrate events with music, so it is a major component of how we spend our leisure time. Music is an integral part of daily life, which we enjoy through listening to the radio at home, in the car and at work. Yet music is not just about listening, as it has a much more profound role in our lives, helping with learning, play and in performing. For example, about 49% of children in the UK have participated in some form of instrumental music lessons and about 25% of adults can play an instrument. Music is also a key social activity, particularly with the rise of karaoke in different settings as a form of entertainment. This is in stark contrast to the role of music as a home-based form of entertainment in the Victorian and Edwardian periods, associated with formal and polite entertaining, which filtered down to informal working-class entertainment epitomised by the piano in the local public house.

The UK is particularly significant in terms of music as it is about the third largest market in the world for the sale of music and the second largest source of musicians, and has a major contribution to make to British exports which are estimated to be around about £435 million a year (also see Chapter 8). On average, we each purchase about four music items a year in the UK. There are two ways in which we can enjoy music: through *live performances* and *recordings*. But how do we consume it? We typically consume recorded music in three ways: by buying recordings, through the radio and increasingly through personal compilations and downloads so we can listen to them on MP3 players and iPods. Recorded music now generates over £2 billion in sales a year in the UK, and an important trend is that as sales have increased, the price of recorded music has continued to decline.

An interesting trend observed by the record industry is that consumption of pop music has been decreasing in recent years while the consumption of rock music has increased, owing to the impact of contemporary groups such as Coldplay, the Stereophonics and REM. In other words, the consumption of recorded music is highly transitory and in a constant state of evolution, reflecting the very fickle nature and tastes of consumers. Music performs a number of different roles as it can mean anything to anyone, being used to pass time, to break up silence or to entertain. Music is important to young people's experiences, which have been increasingly individualised since the 1970s (Roberts 1997). Music also has an important bearing on how young people feel about themselves. Equally, music may be used to mark and control an individual space and identity, such as the teenager's bedroom. As Lincoln's (2005: 41) study of teenagers' bedrooms and music found, 'music is one of the primary cultural forms through which young people are able to transform the mundane space of the bedroom'. Youth typically judge their peers according to their musical tastes and they are an important group to focus on in terms of leisure, because they are major music consumers. As Chapter 2 indicated, they developed as a distinct segment of the market after the 1950s. In terms of popular culture, music helps young people to develop socially, politically and culturally to determine their attitudes, appearance and friendships. There are clearly different patterns of music consumption based on age and gender preferences as well as links between deviant behaviour and specific types of music. For example, there are stereotypes which associate heavy rock with working-class delinquent activity. Music is important to youth as their tastes tend to become more open and more fixated on commercial music as they grow older.

Research from the 1950s, which is still current today, highlighted the evolution of music consumers and observed two groups among youth. The first group, which characterised the *majority* of teenagers, had very undiscriminating tastes in music, liking mainstream commercial music and following the pop charts as well as music stars. This suggested that they were fairly uncritical fans. In contrast, the *minority* group comprised very active listeners, who had a very rebellious attitude to music and insisted on very rigorous standards of taste. This group preferred less commercial and small bands, and this formed the basis for the formation of sub-cultures associated with youth music. The sub-cultures use music as a mode of expression or lifestyle, and in some cases it may even create a whole genre of teenage groups, such as the skinhead movement in the 1970s: this was characterised by hardness, masculinity and working-class music combined with dress such as the 'bovver boots' (Dr Martens) and braces as well as other forms of dress such as the Ben Sherman shirt and bomber jacket which defined this subgroup.

Since the 1980s, there have been significant changes in terms of musical tastes, with one of the biggest impacts on youth culture being dance music, the role of nightclubs and youth culture. This created distinct leisure lifestyles associated with music, drink, fashion, relaxation and fun with the rise of the rave and other musical developments and trends. In some cases, it led to experimentation with drugs, just as the link between music and the hippy movement did in the 1960s (see Chapter 2). Northcote (2006) found that nightclubs were important to youth culture because they helped in the transition from childhood to adulthood. In some cases, tour operators like Club 18-30 seized upon the marketing potential of dance music, creating holidays in destinations such as Ibiza marketed as a fortnight full of Saturdays! Even so, music defines moments in time and, for some people, it has the ability to rekindle memories, nostalgia and help them to relive past events. What this case study shows is that music is particularly important as a defining feature of youth culture and their leisure habits. There are also clear links between music and social class to which attention now turns.

Social class and leisure

Social class is an awkward concept in that there are numerous dimensions associated with power, money, prestige, culture and background. According to Critcher (2006: 271):

> Class is one form of social division. Others include gender, age and ethnicity. All of these
>
> - are perceived as being substantially different materially or culturally;
> - are long-lasting and sustained by dominant cultural beliefs, the organisation of social institutions and individual interactions;
> - confer unequal access to resources – and thus different life chances and lifestyles;
> - engender shared identities in terms of perceived differences from those being an alternative category of the same division. *(Braham and Janes 2002: xiii cited in Critcher 2006: 271)*

This quotation illustrates the wide-ranging importance of social class as well as the wider implications for the study of leisure. Social class is used throughout social research as a means of segmenting the population (along with gender and age) for the purposes of surveys and opinion polls. Critcher (2006: 271) argues that a useful definition may be 'social classes as groups of people, more strictly speaking families or households, who can be ranked in terms of their access to income and wealth'.

So what is social class and how might it be an influence in terms of leisure? Social class was defined for the UK population census in 1911 to facilitate the analysis of the population by arranging the large number of occupational groups within a small number of categories. Hence individuals were assigned to a social class category where:

Class

I: Professional occupations
II: Intermediate occupations
IIIN: Skilled occupations non-manual
IIIM: Skilled occupations manual
IV: Partly skilled occupations
V: Unskilled occupations
VI: Armed forces and inadequately described

This initial system took no account of differences between individuals in the same occupation groups (e.g. in terms of remuneration) and over the years other systems have been introduced. For example, in 1951 (amended 1961) the seven social class groups were replaced by 17 socioeconomic classes for the UK census. Here the aim was to bring together people with jobs of similar social and economic status. Further, in common use is a system devised by the Market Research Society where:

Class

A   Professional/senior managerial
B   Middle managers/executives
C1   Junior managers/non-manual
C2   Skilled manual
D   Semi-skilled/unskilled
E   Unemployed/state dependants

The statistical data suggests that higher social class groups enjoy a more active and varied range of leisure activities. This led Roberts (1999) to identify a number of key relationships between leisure and social class. As Roberts argues, income is a key determinant of leisure participation, and income inequality is a direct cause of leisure, in part reflected in the notion of social class. This led Roberts to make the following generalisations about the relationship between social class and leisure:

● Income is significantly related to occupation and employment, and this relationship helps determine the remuneration one receives from employment. Consequently, this will influence the disposable household income available to spend on leisure.

● Within the social hierarchy that exists within society, as you move from the bottom to the top of the hierarchy, participation in leisure increases progressively. In addition, people spend more on leisure the higher they move up the hierarchy.

● Among lower social groups, leisure activities are typically dominated by television-watching, home-based activities and other things that do not cost money to participate in.

● Social class differences which persisted after the 1950s across much of rural Europe, especially in villages and communal leisure activities, have been transformed by affluence and the rise of consumerism.

● Prosperity has created a greater range of options for leisure, although some traditional leisure lifestyles still exist among certain social groups.

● Mass affluence has led to a spreading down the social hierarchy of leisure opportunities which were traditionally the preserve of elites, such as ballet and opera which are traditionally viewed as *highbrow* and in fact can now be enjoyed by a much wider range of the population.

● Roberts describes the economically privileged as *cultural omnivores* who want to consume or mimic the leisure lifestyles of the more affluent classes, consuming everything that will add to their cultural capital (as discussed in Chapter 1, these are the experiences that bring kudos and prestige among their peers, family and friends).

- One outcome of these changes in relation to social class is what Roberts terms a *leisure democracy*, where all members of a social stratum have relative access to all things. There are some exceptions to this, for example where the unemployed do not have access to leisure opportunities, which remains a constant concern for policy-makers.

- Our social experiences of leisure have become more individualised, meaning that it is much more difficult to segment or characterise specific groups of people consuming leisure in relation to very general terms such as social class. This is why notions of lifestyle are a more useful approach to leisure as part of an individual's wider life.

While it is fair to accept that aspects of social class do influence leisure, such assumptions should be approached with caution. Most class categories do not relate to life cycle: hence a young professional worker with four children may be in a higher class, but may have less disposable income than a working couple in the lower manual class who have no dependants.

It is also pertinent to note that social class has other, more subjective dimensions, more associated with class imagery. Here, an individual's accent, style of speech, residence, social network, job, educational background, dress, car, income, race, family background and leisure activities may be more influential. Above all, class is a measure of material inequality and focuses almost entirely on quantitative measures of the household and the accumulated income of the household. Even so, Critcher (2006: 285) argues that 'Class is the only or even the primary way in which contemporary leisure should be understood. A range of factors influence, we might say sociologically structure, leisure choices and practices', reinforcing its importance in the social aspects of leisure. With these general issues in mind it is important to focus on the role of work and leisure, as affluence and disposable income are largely determined by the ability of individuals and families to obtain money to further their leisure ambitions. The income from work is also one measure which influences social stratification in society and determines leisure habits.

Work and leisure

If social class was an important determinant of leisure participation, the link between work and leisure is an important one to examine, particularly when the growing importance of consumption as a central element of leisure is included, as:

> Those who submit to the rigours of industrial work are promised time and money. These are the central scarcities of life with which we create leisure and buy things . . . The accumulation of a material wealth has reduced time to money; potential leisure is often sacrificed to work in order to earn the wherewithal to pile up still more goods. This consumerism has been acquired in a long historical process. *(Cross 1993: viii)*

This is an interesting relationship because, as Chapter 2 highlighted, research on the sociology of work was largely responsible for the development of early research interest in leisure (e.g. Bouthoul 1924; Hanser 1928). Leisure was deemed to be the polar opposite of work: a form of non-work. At a more rudimentary level, this focus was developed in response to changing patterns of work, as the hours which people worked were reduced and conversely the amount of time for leisure increased, embodied in the development of the concept of the weekend (week-end).

According to Zuzanek and Mannell (1983: 327), research on the work–leisure relationship revolves around seven themes:

- Statistical reviews and time budget analysis (i.e. how we spend our time each day on different activities) to examine how people balance work, leisure and other obligations.

- The socioeconomic aspects of work and leisure, and the trade-off of income verses more leisure time.

- The socio-organisational and planning dimension, focusing on how people scheduled time due to busy working lives, especially with the impact of shift work.

- The sociological and socio-historical aspects, epitomised by Riesman's (1950) *The Lonely Crowd* which looked at the societal shift in belief from inner-directed values based on the work ethic to other directed values of interpersonal communication, leisure and society.

- The effect of work on socio-occupational status and social stratification and leisure; the direct effects of work on leisure and how it affects leisure behaviour.

- Socio-psychological aspects of leisure, discussed below in terms of the spillover, compensation and neutrality hypotheses on the relationship between work and leisure.

As Rybczynski (1991: 20) argues, 'universal leisure did not come to pass . . . For one thing the workday appears to have stabilised at about 8 hours' (see Cross 1986 on the origins of the eight-hour day) and an important focal point in the relationship between work and leisure is how leisure time has evolved as a result of the leisure–work relationship. Rybczynski (1991) traces the evolution of the modern-day working *week* and the rise of the *weekend* as a leisure setting from ancient times, especially the origin of the seven-day week.

The current seven-day week and five-day working week (which dominated industrial society but is now changing) resulted from the routinised working week and evolution of a defined weekend, as working hours were reduced from six days to five and a half and then to a five-day working week. Even so, for the working population 'there may not be more leisure, but there is no doubt the development of the weekend has caused a redistribution of leisure time which for many people has shortened and the work week . . . throughout the year' (Rybcyznski 1991: 21). Stalin restructured the Soviet calendar in 1929 into 12 months of 30 days, abolishing the distinction between the working week and weekend, creating extra days as public holidays so that factories could operate continuously with no breaks. This abolished the universal rest day, with four days working and a fifth day off. This was abandoned in 1940 because it was shown that it did not improve productivity. There are other extreme examples, such as the Khmer Rouge in Cambodia which created the *leisureless* society in the 1970s. Today, when looking at holidays and weekends, the number of days off we have varies between countries, from around 130 days off in the USA to 70 in China where working on a Saturday is commonplace.

As Schor (2006: 203) argues,

> the optimistic predictions of social scientists about the coming of a leisurely future are increasingly being discredited . . . As early as the 1960s, the optimists expected that by the 21st century, citizens of the advanced industrialized nations would be living lives of leisure, perhaps suffering from a crisis of leisure time, brought on by boredom and a failure to know how to spend time. And instead of boredom, time poverty and high levels of daily life stress appeared to be widespread . . . The trends and the subjective measures are readily explainable by developments in actual hours of work, and in particular a break from earlier patterns of rapid decline in work-time. For example, in the OECD, over the last 20 years average hours per working age person fell a meagre 2%, not per year, but for the entire two decades.

This is in sharp contrast to the drop in working time between 1950 and 1980 of 18% according to Schor (2006). Schor also argues that there is evidence of working time increasing in some countries, such as Australia, Canada and the Netherlands as well as the USA and UK, since 1980 for some groups, as discussed in Chapter 2. In fact Fuess (2006) observed that in Japan, even with initiatives to reduce working hours, leisure time did not noticeably increase between 1986 and 2001. This challenges much of the conventional thinking since the 1960s on the development of a 'leisure society', on the supposed rise of a surplus of leisure time as debated in Chapter 2 (see Schor 2006 for an in-depth analysis of changes to annual hours worked among workers in OECD countries between 1973 and 2000 and debates on whether we are living lives of increased leisure).

Some of the key concepts which help to explain the relationship between work and leisure date to the 1960s and 1970s. These emerged from the study of the social psychology of work which focused on a key relationship: work determined leisure time, which was associated with our state of mind, social relationships, our social identity and other social characteristics. As Roberts (1999) points out, two principal relationships emerge from this research:

- A spillover relationship which may exist between work and leisure, where work-based relationships and interests spread into one's leisure.

- A compensation relationship which may exist, when individuals use their free time to seek experiences which they could not get at work.

However, critics such as Parker (1971, 1983) argued that this distinction between these two approaches was inadequate and that we needed a more holistic view of the relationship between work and leisure. This holistic view needed to recognise that leisure not only depended upon our employment, but also on our experience and feelings of work. As a result, Parker identified three possible positions within a holistic framework of work and leisure. *First*, there is the opposition pattern, where work does not provide enough fulfilment and so we pursue leisure opportunities to meet that unmet need. *Second*, there is a clear link between some people who view leisure as an opportunity to extend their interest in work. *Third*, there is the midway point between the opposition and extension patterns, a *neutrality* position, where people pursue leisure, as neither of the explanations adequately fit the experiences of the participants. In other words, Parker was highlighting the problem of trying to make very broad generalisations about the relationship between work and leisure because there are just too many exceptions when looking at empirical evidence on the work–leisure relationship (see Evans 1969 for a review of 1919–1969).

What Parker was arguing was that under each condition of the work–leisure relationship, we need to consider the variables that have an impact upon how the relationship operates. For example, we need to consider the nature of the employment that the individual undertakes, how well this is demarcated from leisure, the individual's central interest in life and how far leisure impacts upon their work and vice versa. In terms of work variables, Parker also argued that we need to look at the level of autonomy people have in their work setting, how far they can use their work abilities in the workplace and whether leisure is needed to extend and develop their abilities. Other key variables to consider are the role of work colleagues, how far work encroaches upon leisure, and the typical occupations that people undertake. Other non-work variables which Parker identified as having a bearing upon the work–leisure relationship were the level of education, the duration of the leisure experience and the main function of leisure (i.e. is it a continuation of work as a form of work extension, recuperation from work, the polar opposite of work or part of a more neutral position where leisure may just be harmless entertainment?).

We also need to recognise that there have been significant changes in the way in which work and society are related. For example, Hutton (1995) pointed to the 40:30:30 principle, in the UK, where 40% of the population were in full-time work, 30% had no paid employment and 30% were in non-standard jobs or conditions of employment such as homeworking. This is a function of the de-standardisation of work time. One consequence of these changes in a post-modern society is that leisure and work are not so clearly demarcated. In other words, the traditional seven-day cycle in which two days at the weekend created a clear block of leisure time is no longer a simple truism which can be applied to all of the population. How people use their time and how their work is organised have had a major impact upon the social organisation of leisure.

One key issue which has perplexed many researchers is the leisure–work–unemployment relationship. As we have entered a post-industrial society, and the workplace has gone through many changes, unemployment has become a predictable outcome of the restructuring of many workplaces. Despite cycles in the economy where employment rises and falls, there have been many concerns within post-industrial society that a long-term unemployed underclass has developed. This underclass has not been able to adapt to the new demands of the society and employment opportunities. In the social setting, there has also been a great debate over the issue of whether unemployment is a form of leisure. According to Haywood *et al.* (1989), unemployment is not leisure on a number of grounds:

- Spare time which has arisen through unemployment is not the same as time free from work.

- As many forms of leisure pursuit are related to, or may even complement work, unemployment is not a form of leisure.

- With a growing trend towards commercialised forms of leisure as consumption, those who are unemployed cannot afford the cost of these types of leisure through lack of income. Hence they are excluded because of unemployment.

Notable studies of the unemployed and leisure (e.g. Glyptis 1985, 1989) have shown that unemployment does not necessarily mean that extra spare time leads to an increase in participation in leisure. In some cases unemployment leads to a decline, particularly in the quality of leisure, through a lack of enjoyment and reduced opportunities, particularly for youth. In other words, employment has an important role to play in a capitalist society in terms of leisure. It provides the means by which one lives, through earnings and other forms of income, and work has a very strong psychological role in helping to influence leisure.

For many people employment helps to define their social identity, status and role in society as well as providing a structure and routine to their day, week and year. Work also provides a degree of social contact, group experiences and routinised daily activity perceived as an obligation. While leisure may be able to meet some of these needs, it will never be a substitute for work, although in some instances leisure may provide new social contacts. But it is unlikely to be a substitute for structuring our daily activities. Work has a powerful influence upon individuals and it is not surprising that when many people are faced with retirement or unemployment, leisure is one of the last things on their minds because of the changes that this introduces to their life. What we can conclude is that the relationship between work and leisure is highly interconnected, but deriving generalisations about the relationship in a fast-changing post-industrial society, where the leisure lifestyles of the population are now complex, is far from easy. In fact, de Botton's (2009) *The Pleasures and Sorrows of Work* suggests that work is at the heart of most societies and that it may even provide pleasure, since people seek it even when there is no financial reward (e.g. volunteering). It provides a meaningful experience which helps individuals to define themselves. What this perspective on work suggests is that we need to recognise the wider social changes occurring alongside trends affecting leisure, such as changes in the nature of work and a greater focus on individualism and social networking, time-squeezing and the much more hectic pace of life in Western societies. The population has, in some cases, become much more gregarious and relationships have become far more temporary in leisure, as have the relationships between the home and family. One notable change which has occurred is the rise of 24-hour society, as briefly mentioned in Chapter 2.

The 24-hour society: implications for leisure?

Society has been transforming over the past decade, with the rise of a 24-hour society which has changed many of the relationships between work and the pursuit of leisure (Haworth and Lewis 2005). According to the Parliamentary Office of Science and Technology (2005), the 24-hour society has arisen because of a shift towards longer and non-standard business hours. Three of the key reasons behind this are:

- The pursuit of greater competitiveness, leading to extended opening hours, to increase productivity within businesses because of the impact of globalisation and technologies such as the Internet which require businesses to be available 24 hours a day.

- A growing consumer demand for what was traditionally termed *out-of-hours services*, which was led by the retail sector, particularly supermarkets who decided to open outside of the traditional 9.00 a.m. to 6.00 p.m. timeframe. As people now work longer and less routine hours, they now expect services to be available to fit around their new patterns of work. Equally, consumers expect leisure services to be available on the same basis.

- Governments have also promoted the 24-hour society through extending the opening hours for leisure consumption in bars and restaurants, as one example. A notable example of this has been a shift in student leisure habits in the UK in the past 20 years, which were dictated by the opening hours of bars and nightclubs that traditionally shut around about midnight. Since new licensing laws were introduced in the UK, a new evening and night-time economy based around leisure consumption has developed in many cities, with many students now starting their socialising at around 11 p.m. at night and going right through to the very early hours of the morning or later off-campus.

These new leisure practices also have an impact on what are called our circadian rhythms. Circadian rhythms, more commonly called our *body clock*, govern how we sleep and wake and fit in our daily activities such as work, leisure and necessities such as sleep. With the 24-hour society, undertaking leisure at different times of the day will significantly affect our circadian rhythms and, in the long term, this can also affect our health and well-being. While it is possible for the body to adapt and adjust to changes to our circadian rhythms over time, we need to be aware of the impact of leisure activities and a 24-hour society which conflict with our daily necessities such as sleep and work.

Gender and leisure

Gender is one of the key determinants of leisure choice and opportunity. However, researchers argue that dividing people on the basis of gender is a simplistic notion with respect to leisure activity. There is also an important social class dimension which has to be recognised in any discussion of gender. It is widely recognised that women have a tendency to spend more of their leisure time in and around the home and family. Traditional analyses of women and leisure highlight the time for leisure as restricted along with the opportunities and choice of activities they could engage in. Much of the research on leisure and women can be traced to the 1970s and 1980s (e.g. see Deem 1986). As Henderson and Shaw (2006) show, there are three key areas we need to think about when looking at the relationship between gender and leisure (especially the role of women):

- how their leisure is organised and their daily lives;
- their leisure behaviour and activities;
- the experiences and the meanings which they attach to their leisure time and activities.

Traditionally, male leisure was stereotyped into a simplistic distinction between work and non-work, with fewer constraints on their leisure time. In contrast, there are societal expectations upon women in terms of child rearing and caring for family that create a much more complex relationship between the factors they have to balance on a daily basis. Researchers also point to the ways in which these expectations have been socially constructed in different societies, examining notions of femininity, the role of women and motherhood and the role of women and familism (i.e. their focus on the family and looking after its members).

Theoretical explanations of gender and leisure point to power relations that have dominated the way women are perceived in society and their role. For example, in extreme situations such as Nazi Germany and the Third Reich, women's role and responsibility was to produce Aryan children and to further the aims of the state. Their leisure time was portrayed in Nazi propaganda as associated with the pursuit of healthy living, physical exercise and personal well-being to ensure healthy child bearing, rearing and caring. While this is an extreme example, there are other examples in society where women are not viewed with the same degree of equality as men. Research by Aitchison (2000) argued that leisure research on women was *inferiorised* in leisure studies (i.e. it has a low position in the scheme of research) and typically focused on the activities of white middle-class women. But since 2000, examples of research on other groups of women have emerged, as Case Study 3.2 which follows later will show.

Other trends which have challenged traditional stereotypes associated with women's leisure have been the increasing participation of women in the workforce and the rise of single parents. One consequence of the changes within families since the 1970s has been a greater balancing of child-caring responsibilities and shared decision making about family leisure. The greater participation of women in the workforce has also meant that this has intensified the factors to balance, resulting in legitimate concerns associated with *work–life balance*.

This term from the field of human resource management (which studies the workforce and the practices and behaviour of employers and employees) has seen a growing concern about such work–life balance issues. The arguments are quite simple to understand: with women entering the workforce, this has intensified the pressure to balance their career against the needs of family and home life. Add to this the growing pressures for a de-standardisation of working hours combined with the growth in working hours in some countries, and this balance between home and work becomes a key issue for women (and also for some men). The terminology, work–life balance, is very much the new mantra of the harried working family seeking to address issues of time pressure. Some employers seek to retain working women employees by offering flexible working practices to reduce a work–life imbalance in order to promote healthier lifestyles.

Even so, domestic responsibilities make it very difficult for women to delineate work from leisure (Haywood *et al.* 1989), as well as the fact that many women also have a major role to play in supporting children's leisure. There are also distinct differences in the way in which women's opportunities for out-of-home leisure, such as visiting parks and gardens, are constrained. There is adequate research now that demonstrates that women, particularly those from ethnic groups, feel there is a real danger of sexual harassment in outdoor leisure spaces, which restricts their use of such spaces. In other words, women's leisure is not a simple relationship between work/non-work: there are a wide range of factors that coalesce to affect the types and range of leisure women undertake, traditionally focused on the home and near to home. This is compounded in the case of single-parent households, where time to engage in leisure is even more constrained. There are also constraints when the relationship between gender and stage in the family life cycle is considered, because child rearing often limits the opportunity to engage in physical activities where child-care facilities are not available. This is one reason why many leisure providers seeking to tap into the growing market for women with preschool-age children, offering crèches for those women who are able to afford these commercial forms of leisure provision, as a break from family caring responsibilities.

The stage in the life cycle clearly has a very major impact upon women, particularly when looking at the balancing of family, work and children in the childbearing years of the family life cycle. One additional trend which is being noted in many Western countries is that women are also delaying having children, which is creating new problems and opportunities for leisure, particularly given the additional cost of rearing children and the impact on family budgets. Therefore, it is clear that the relationship between gender and leisure is blurring, particularly with the rise of greater female participation in the workforce and the impact upon family leisure time. The case study which follows examines a little-documented area of gender and leisure among the hill-farming women in Bangladesh, highlighting leisure issues in a non-Western society.

Case Study 3.2	Leisure lifestyles of Bangladeshi hill-farming women

In a study by Khan (1997), a number of hill-farming families in south-eastern Bangladesh were studied in order to understand the leisure experiences of rural women. As this case study will show, despite high levels of poverty and a subsistence lifestyle, women still have their own leisure experiences, some of which are linked into very routine forms of work which transform the experience into what is perceived as a more leisure-based activity. The research focus of the study was on more qualitative experiences of leisure, where the researcher interviewed different hill-farming women in villages to understand individual and group experiences of leisure, particularly the focus within the family and the link with work. As Khan found, there are two major forms of female labour: one was household chores and the other was working on agriculture/forestry. This is one of the very few studies of leisure experiences of women in the developing world and it highlights that many women do not have access to formal leisure opportunities in these rural areas: male and female leisure is very distinct in terms of the barriers and opportunities available to each group. Owing to religious and societal attitudes, formal forms of leisure such as going to the cinema or theatre have been viewed as places of men's recreation, according to Khan. Instead, many women build leisure into their routine work, by introducing elements of relaxation and enjoyment. Even so, in rural areas there were four distinct areas where leisure opportunities existed for women: through handicrafts, through dressing and food preparation, through meetings, and through social visits and festivals.

In the case of meetings, women gathered firewood through their daily activities of fuel collection (i.e. leaves, bark and shrubs for firewood) and fetching water, allowing social interaction through communal activities. These communal meetings provided informal opportunities for conversation, discussions about family and other matters as well as gossiping. In terms as social visits and festivals, this involved visiting other family members in their houses, which provided a break from the daily routine while also renewing social links with other kin. In particular, celebration of religious festivals also provides an opportunity for leisure time to be spent with other people. The issue of handicrafts illustrates how some women were involved in different household activities such as sewing and bamboo work as an economic activity, although the latter was seen as an opportunity for relaxation and recreation. Typically, Khan found that these handicraft activities took up around two hours each day. Dressing and food preparation provided opportunities for recreational interaction outside of the family, particularly with vendors selling goods. What Kahn shows is that for many women, our traditional definitions of leisure do not fit their use and perception of leisure time.

We might argue that much of their activity is work related and therefore they have no free time. However, when you start to understand what the leisure experience means to the individual women, you start to see how a break from a daily routine, even when it overlaps with domestic activities, is viewed as a leisure and recreational opportunity. In other words, this challenges the distinction of obligatory work-related activity and free activity time as a defining feature of what constitutes leisure. In these communities, leisure is not easily located on a work to non-work continuum because the subsistence lifestyle of these hill farmers means that much of their daily life is devoted to some form of productive activity just to survive. So what this case study shows is that women are able to enjoy leisure in their own unique way. As Khan (1997: 18) argued, 'leisure and recreation among the hill women seem to be an integral part of the day to day strategies for survival. Women have developed a skill to carve out pleasure from the everyday forms of struggle which surround their life and living'.

Ageing and leisure

According to Harahouson (2006), most Western societies, and indeed many developing countries, are now facing the problem of an ageing population. It is projected that by 2025, there will be one billion people globally who are aged 60 years or more. This is sometimes described as a demographic time bomb. That time bomb is an ageing population, which will need to be supported by a declining number of people of working age paying taxes to fund the services to meet the needs of the ageing population, given that they have increased expectations for leisure provision. For example, Harahouson (2006) highlighted that in the developing world alone, there will be 816 million people aged 60 or more, which is a major change in the demographic structure for many of these countries. This is a result of increased longevity in life expectancy, lower levels of fertility and improved health provision.

The process of ageing does not occur in the same way for everyone. It occurs in different ways for individuals and is not just associated with biological ageing, as there is also social and psychological ageing. Gerontologists, who study issues associated with ageing, observe that while some people may feel old at 55 years of age, others who are 80 years of age may still feel comparatively young. This illustrates the distinction between physical and psychological ageing. Research on ageing and leisure has tended to focus on six key themes: participation patterns, leisure needs, leisure preferences, leisure constraints, the role of active leisure in preventing disease in later life, and the ability of leisure to enhance one's life in later years (Harahouson 2006). Changing trends in employment have also created new groups, such as those who are part of the *third age*, namely those in late middle age who no longer are employed in the workforce and are typically over 50 years old.

Such changes have meant that the role of the family and leisure has changed significantly in the post-war period. For example, among many working-class families even in the 1960s, extended families lived in the same house where elderly relatives were often cared for by the family. This changed during the 1970s and through the 1980s, combined with the greater longevity of the elderly and their greater financial independence. New concepts in leisure research have also begun to emerge from gerontology, such as active ageing, which recognises that one can enjoy a higher quality of life in older age through the pursuit of leisure, particularly in the case of tourism. Since the 1980s, there has been a significant increase in the over-50 age group in Western countries taking domestic and overseas holidays, as the number of early retirees has also increased. Even so, socioeconomic differences have a key role to play: those who are retired from professional and managerial jobs are more likely to take a holiday each year than those who have retired from unskilled jobs.

It is clear that many of the traditional stereotypes of ageing that associate passive behaviour with leisure are no longer valid. Indeed, a global leisure industry and the media have seized upon the rise of the third age and changed many of the negative images, so that the aged are seen as a major market segment to target as consumers. Some researchers have viewed the relationship between ageing and leisure as one of growing disengagement, with a move away from traditional areas of activity to more passive forms of leisure and the general decline in participation levels. While there is evidence that some groups, in particular those with disabilities in older age, see their leisure opportunities constrained, there is also evidence that leisure is important to increase people's intellectual, physical and social activity in retirement. It is argued that this improves their satisfaction with life. Other theories also exist, which examine the link between leisure and later life, characterising participation in terms of withdrawal, continuity after work during retirement, as well as a growing involvement in leisure through adaptation to one's new circumstances after retirement. Research by Kleiber *et al.* (2008) provides an alternative assessment that leisure constraints in later life may not necessarily be negative – but may be beneficial. This may be part of adaptation to ageing, making participation in the remaining activities which are accessible more meaningful.

In most Western countries, leisure participation among those over 60 years of age has increased, although it does vary by gender, race, social status and other factors. Surveys such as the UK's General Household Survey show that there is a trend towards a decline in active leisure participation with age. Notable exceptions to this are China and Japan, where participation increases in later life. In the USA, for example, the growth of Elderhost, with its international and national programme of leisure activities for those over 50 years of age, illustrates a wide range of leisure activities in which these groups now participate, including long-haul travel. Marketers describe this group as empty nesters who no longer have children to support, with no mortgage and with financial stability which enables them to participate in a greater range of leisure activities. One important distinction, however, is the transition from middle to older age where our declining physical and mental abilities become more pronounced.

In later life, research shows that those over 65 suffer declining levels of health, reduced mobility and in some cases reduced income. These types of constraint on leisure participation can be split into two categories:

- *Societal constraints*, due to a lack of information, absence of facilities, lack of transport and opportunities. This is one reason why social support networks, such as those offered by churches and community groups, provide such an important lifeline in ensuring that elderly citizens are not excluded from leisure because of such constraints.

- *Individual constraints*, due to a growing fear of one's personal safety in local neighbourhoods and cities, a growing sense of social isolation and a lack of a partner or widowhood, depriving them of a partner with whom to enjoy leisure time. This is often exacerbated where ageing relatives live some distance away from their siblings and other family members and so do not have the same access to social networks or an extended family.

So, leisure can provide significant benefits for the elderly in later life, which Harahouson (2006) categorised into:

- *Physiological benefits*, such as maintaining or improving one's health.
- *Psychological benefits,* such as maintaining one's emotional health.
- *Social benefits*, derived from socialising, social interaction and a sense of reduced social isolation.

It is also the case, with ageing women, that many of the traditional stereotypes, such as performing a caring role for grandchildren, have been replaced by a more active pursuit of leisure. This has involved a focus on the grandparent(s)' own needs and pursuit of new leisure interests. What is clear is that the population in most countries is living longer, although there is clear evidence that women as opposed to males may be more likely to experience poverty in later life, due to their earlier role as family carers and to part-time working which has led to reduced pension benefits. Older women may also be more concerned about fear of violence owing to their greater reliance on public transport in later life, and there is a very clear emphasis away from the family as the focal point for elderly leisure. This may indicate a growing future role for community-based leisure, which is likely to be significantly different, as those of younger age today, with higher education levels, greater health consciousness, and awareness of leisure opportunities, will demand more facilities and services in the future.

What this illustrates is the need for greater provision for the transition between work and retirement, as Bull *et al.* (2003: 104) argue:

> where an individual's identity has been strongly tied in with their work role, leisure activities can replace a work sphere as a focus for social status and positive self esteem. Leisure can provide a replacement structured to the day or week that is lost through retirement and can provide a focus for a new timetable. It can also be an important means whereby the social contacts lost through retirement can be replaced.
> *(Bull* et al. *2003: 104)*

However, there is still considerable debate over the general validity of this assumption.

Race and leisure

According to Kraus (1994: 86, cited in Freysinger and Harris 2006), 'race is a statistical aggregate of people who share a composite of genetically transmissible physical traits', which illustrates one way of looking at race as a biological construct. But race and ethnicity have multiple definitions which are not simply related to skin colour. Beliefs, attitudes and behaviour distinguish one group from another, based on cultural elements (e.g. race, religion and language) which also help to define the basis of ethnicity. In many countries there is great ethnic diversity, largely because of global migration (see Holland 2002 on the contribution of African American recreation to American culture). Government policies focus upon ethnic groups because of issues of social inclusion, where power structures in society and prejudice can lead to racism. For example, Washburne (1978) identified the under-representation of African Americans in wildland recreation in the USA and Li *et al.* (2007) review many of the subsequent studies undertaken on ethnicity in leisure. Such research shows that ethnic groups have restricted access to leisure and services. In leisure research, we can identify three principal types of racism which may impact upon the ability of ethnic minorities to engage in leisure activities:

- *Structural racism*, which is firmly embedded in society and expressed through employment, education and housing and results in high levels of unemployment by some groups. This means that ethnic minorities contain the disproportionate share of disadvantaged people in terms of their ability to participate in the labour market. It affects the level of income they can earn, thereby impacting upon their leisure opportunities. This can lead to notions of marginalisation and an inward focusing of these groups, so that distinct leisure cultures develop at a tangent from the main forms of societal leisure.

- *Institutional racism*, where institutions, such as the arts, sports and leisure facilities, do not favour ethnic communities and thereby perpetuate discrimination. For example, the funding for certain forms of leisure favours those from more vocal, middle-class, white, male-dominated groups to the detriment of ethnic minorities in many developed countries. This is why some local authorities have employed outreach workers to try to forge links with ethnic minorities to increase the diversity of leisure activities available, addressing issues of social exclusion (also see Case Study 6.2).

Table 3.3 Characteristics of ethnic leisure habits in the USA: The African-American and Asian-American groups

Characteristics	
African-American	**Asian-American**
<ul><li>The patterns of leisure participation have been a key element which makes US leisure distinctive in relation to sport, the evolution of cultural practices and its rich history</li><li>The historical evolution of African-American leisure is a function of over 300 years of social, economic and political inequality which can be traced to slavery/forced migration and imported culture</li><li>The nineteenth century saw major changes due to emancipation, education, and the role of the church in leisure practices as well as the growing leisure mobilisation of such groups in the cities</li><li>Nineteenth-century migration from the south to the north, and particularly after 1945 with industrial growth in the north</li><li>Urban-industrialised lifestyles post-1945 and major contribution of youth and public school system to baseball, basketball, football, boxing and track events</li><li>Growing diversity in leisure habits since the 1960s with the rise of a middle class, suburbanisation and the civil rights movement</li></ul>*Source*: Adapted from Andrews (2004)	<ul><li>A rich history of nineteenth-century immigration and urban settlement</li><li>Post-1945 rise of migration, settling on the western seaboard due to an existing Asian population</li><li>Historically low levels of participation in physical recreation, sedentary lifestyles and long hours of work</li><li>Preferences for spectator sports, games for individual and group interaction, especially indoors</li><li>Where visits to the outdoors are made, these tend to be based around large family groups</li><li>Key role of family, kinship and community in leisure activities</li><li>Major cultural activity in leisure time – the consumption of food, which reinforces ethnic identity and the leisure lifestyles</li></ul>*Source*: Adapted from Sasihatian (2004)

● *Individual racism*, where the attitudes of individuals to ethnic groups reproduce discrimination, such as chanting at football matches or a very unwelcome approach to new immigrants or those of different beliefs, country of origin or skin colour.

These issues have become a major concern for the public sector in relation to social inclusion, and research and action to try to address the under-representation of ethnic minorities in many sports has been a major area of work. Discrimination occurs when one group seeks to try to make itself feel superior to another, thereby excluding the other group. Leisure patterns and participation rates do vary with ethnicity, although the situation is complicated by a range of socioeconomic and life-cycle influences (see Floyd *et al.* 2008 for a detailed review). For example, in South Africa during apartheid 63% of whites went on holiday compared to only 10% of urban blacks, which highlights the limited access and the exclusion of the non-white population. Much of the research on race and leisure has been undertaken in North America (e.g. see Floyd 1998 for a review) and it tends to suggest that there are differences between non-white and white Americans in their leisure and recreation habits and distinctive leisure lifestyles (see Table 3.3), although there is also a distinction between middle and lower social class ethnic groups.

Existing research also points to the ever-changing nature of immigration flows, as the principal research concerns in the 1960s were with black–white differences in leisure, especially in the USA. More recently these have been supplanted by concerns of white–Hispanic and white–Asian issues in leisure research in the USA (see Table 3.3), given the changing ethnic composition of the US population and population forecasts. While variations do exist in leisure participation on the basis of race, numerous factors do constrain ethnic groups from participating in leisure activities.

Summary

This chapter has shown that in understanding leisure and its social dimensions, it is clear that some forms of leisure bind people together, as Roberts (1999) argues. This is because people often share common leisure interests and hobbies which help them to socialise and interact communally in their leisure time. It is also clear that leisure has an important role to play in one's satisfaction with life, a feature which will be investigated in more detail in Chapter 4. The scope of the issues which have been examined in this chapter illustrate the important function which leisure performs for both the individual and groups, as well as some of the specific nuances which are related to participation in leisure by different social groups such as the elderly, women and young adolescents. Among sociologists, there are also concerns about the way in which the social aspects of leisure interact with notions of consumption to create specific experiences of leisure. In fact, historical reviews of leisure and consumption (e.g. Cross 1993, 2002) suggest that it is now a central feature of leisure.

As Roberts (1999: 49) suggests, one of the key dimensions of the experience of leisure is quality. Roberts highlights four central issues which we need to be aware of in relation to leisure and the quality of the experience:

- The amount which people now spend on holidays, as a proportion of their household budget, in many developed countries has increased to make it a major element of their annual spending (see Chapter 4 for more detail). The issue here is whether this additional spending creates any better form of leisure experience compared to whether they had spent less money.

- Many former self-organised and non-commercial activities within the domain of leisure now require investment in the electronic infrastructure to enjoy them within our leisure time.

- Increased spending on leisure by individuals is also being shaped by desire, not necessarily in terms of the desire for the product, but by the ability to exclude others from the same leisure experience. For example, this is expressed as being able to purchase the most recent and expensive brand labels in fashion clothing or the ability to travel first and business class on an aircraft to have a personalised experience where others are excluded. This highlights an increased dissatisfaction amongst many middle-class leisure consumers about sharing their social space in terms of leisure.

- The issue of time pressure and the emergence of the harried class, as discussed in Chapter 2, has meant that many social experiences of leisure within the family, particularly out of the home, are based on fitting activities into compressed periods of time.

It is clear that we are now living in a contemporary society where leisure is a key element of our lives. This is reflected in the notion of leisure lifestyles, and the incredible complexity surrounding individual and family-based experiences of leisure. Some of the factors examined in this chapter, such as social class, ageing, gender, ethnicity and the social basis of human interaction as a form of leisure, demonstrate that we are now entering a postmodern society in which our lives are being subject to major changes. For example, the issue of globalisation highlights how widespread this process is in relation to the forces shaping the types of leisure that we now consume both in the home and out of the home in Western societies. Other societies in Southeast Asia, China and South America are also being subjected to very similar processes of globalisation in relation to leisure, albeit perhaps not with the same intensity and degree to which it is now embedded in the everyday lives of citizens in Western society. What has changed, and continues to change, is the way in which leisure is consumed by different social groups. The simple analogy of non-work and work time is no longer a means by which we can explain how leisure now features in our everyday lives. For example, technologies such as the MP3 player now give much greater flexibility in how and when we listen to music. This is just one example of how the consumption of leisure has become much more flexible and individualised in how it fits into our daily lives, where leisure is not necessarily something which is formally scheduled into a daily routine as it would have been 50 years ago.

Just as goods and services can now be produced in a more flexible way, our consumption of leisure is also much more flexible in terms of what, where and how we consume, as technology, such as social networking and Facebook, provides much greater flexibility and accessibility. There are still examples where leisure is programmed into the daily and weekly lives of individuals, particularly the continued existence of a weekend in some shape or form, even though the 24-hour society has certainly challenged the routinised notion of a weekend as non-work time. Changing trends in society associated with globalisation not only affect the macro processes of change within society, but also the micro level of the individual and family. This has had a profound effect on the *demand* for leisure, particularly the timing, location and provision. For this reason, the next chapter examines the demand for leisure, focusing on how we begin to understand and explain individuals and groups participation in leisure.

Discussion questions

1. What are the social benefits of leisure?

2. How would you go about addressing issues of gender and race in the provision of leisure by the state?

3. How important is the home as a site for leisure consumption?

4. Why is music such an important leisure pursuit for young people?

References

Aitchison, C. (2000) 'Poststructural feminist theories of representing others: a response to the crisis in leisure studies discourse', *Leisure Studies* 19 (3): 127–44.

Andrews, V. (2004) 'African-American leisure', in G. Cross (ed.) *Encyclopaedia of Recreation and Leisure in America*, Volume 1, Thomson-Gale: Woodbridge, CT, pp. 8–12.

Argyle, M. (1996) *The Social Psychology of Leisure*, Penguin: London.

Bouthoul, G. (1924) La durée du travail et l'utilisation des loisir (The hours of work and leisure use). Thèse pour le doctorate sciences politiques et economiques, Faculté de Droit de l'université de Paris: Paris.

Braham, P. and Janes, L. (2002) 'Social differences and divisions: introduction', in P. Braham and L. Janes (eds) *Social Differences and Divisions*, Blackwell: Cambridge, MA.

Bull, C., Hoose, J. and Weed, M. (2003) *An Introduction to Leisure Studies*, Prentice Hall: Harlow.

Critcher, C. (2006) 'A touch of class', in C. Rojek, S. Shaw and A. Veal (eds) *A Handbook of Leisure Studies*, Palgrave: Basingstoke, pp. 271–87.

Cross, G. (1986) 'The political economy of leisure in retrospect: Britain, France and the origin of the eight-hour day', *Leisure Studies* 5(1): 56–90.

Cross, G. (1990) *A Social History of Leisure since 1600*, Venture Publishing: State College, PA.

Cross, G. (1993) *Time and Money: The Making of Consumer Culture*, Routledge: New York.

Cross, G. (2002) *An All Consuming Century: Why Commercialism Won in Modern America*, Columbia University Press: New York.

de Botton, A. (2009) *The Pleasures and Sorrows of Work*, Hamilton Hamish: London.

Deem, R. (1986) *All Work and No Play: The Sociology of Women and Leisure*, Open University Press: Milton Keynes.

Evans, A. (1969) 'Work and leisure 1919–1969', *International Labour Review* 91 (1): 45–69.

Floyd, D. (1998) 'Getting beyond marginality and ethnicity: the challenge for race and ethnic studies in leisure research', *Journal of Leisure Research* 30 (3): 3–22.

Floyd, R., Bocarro, J. and Thompson, T. (2008) 'Research on race and ethnicity: A review of five major journals', *Journal of Leisure Research* 40 (1): 1–22.

Freysinger, V. and Harris, O. (2006) 'Race and leisure', in C. Rojek, S. Shaw and A. Veal (eds) *A Handbook of Leisure Studies*, Palgrave: Basingstoke, pp. 250–70.

Fuess, S. (2006) *Leisure Time in Japan: How much and for Whom?*, IZA Discussion Paper No. 2002, Institute for the Study of Labour, Bonn.

Gershuny, J. and Fisher, K. (1999) 'Leisure in the UK across the 20th century', in A. Halsey (eds) *British Social Trends: Across the 20th century*, Macmillan: Basingstoke.

Glover, T. and Hemingway, J. (2005) 'Locating leisure in the social capital literature', *Journal of Leisure Research* 37 (4): 387–401.

Glyptis, S. (1981) 'Leisure lifestyles', *Regional Studies* 15 (5): 311–26.

Glyptis, S. (1985) 'Business as usual? Leisure provision for the unemployed', *Leisure Studies* 2(3): 287–300.

Glyptis, S. (1989) *Leisure and Unemployment*, Open University Press: Milton Keynes.

Glyptis, S. and Chambers, D. (1982) 'No place like home', *Leisure Studies* 1(3): 247–62.

Hall, P.A. (1999) 'Social capital in Britain', *British Journal of Politics* 29 (4): 417–61.

Harahouson, Y. (2006) 'Leisure and ageing', in C. Rojek, S. Shaw and A. Veal (eds) *A Handbook of Leisure Studies*, Palgrave: Basingstoke, pp. 231–49.

Harper, R. and Kelly, M. (2003) 'Measuring social capital in the United Kingdom', National Statistics, London, www.statistics.gov/socialcapital accessed 3 February 2009-02-04

Harrington, M. (2006) 'Family leisure', in C. Rojek, S. Shaw and A. Veal (eds) *A Handbook of Leisure Studies*, Palgrave: Basingstoke, pp. 417–32.

Hauser, H. (1928) *Ouvriers du temps passé* (Workers of the past), 5th edn, Felix Alcan: Paris.

Haworth, J. and Lewis, S. (2005) 'Work, leisure and well-being', *British Journal of Guidance and Counselling* 33 (1): 67–79.

Haywood, L., Kew, F., Bramham, P., Spink, J., Capenhurst, J. and Henry, I. (1989) *Understanding Leisure*, Stanley Thornes: Cheltenham.

Henderson, K. and Shaw, S. (2006) 'Leisure and gender: challenges and opportunities for feminist research', in C. Rojek, S. Shaw and A. Veal (eds) *A Handbook of Leisure Studies*, Palgrave: Basingstoke, pp. 216–30.

Herbert, D. (1988) 'Work and leisure: exploring a relationship', *Area* 20 (3): 241–52.

Holland, J. (2002) *Black Recreation: A Historical Perspective*, Burnham Inc. Publishers: Chicago.

Hutton, W. (1995) *The State We're In: Why Britain is in Crisis and How to Overcome it*, Jonathan Cape Limited: London.

Iso-Ahola, S. (1980) *The Social Psychology of Leisure and Recreation*, William Brown Company Publishers: Dubuque, IA.

Jenkins, J. (2009) 'Non-resident fathers: Leisure with their children', *Leisure Sciences* 31 (3): 255–71.

Khan, A. (1997) 'Leisure and recreation among women of selected hill farming families in Bangladesh', *Journal of Leisure Research* 29 (1): 5–20.

Kleiber, D., McGuire, F., Aybar-Damali, B. and Norman, W. (2008) 'Having more by doing less: The paradox of leisure constraints in later life', *Journal of Leisure Research* 40 (3): 343–59.

Kraus, R. (1994) *Leisure in a Changing America: Multicultural Perspectives*, Macmillan: New York.

Kynaston, D. (2007a) *Austerity Britain 1945–1948: Smoke in the Valley*, Bloomsbury: London.

Kynaston, D. (2007b) *Austerity Britain 1945–1948: A World to Build*, Bloomsbury: London.

Li, C., Chick, G., Zinn, H., Absher, J. and Graefe, A. (2007) 'Ethnicity as a variable in leisure research', *Journal of Leisure Research* 39 (3): 514–45.

Lincoln, S. (2005) 'Feeling of noise: Teenagers, bedrooms and music', *Leisure Studies* 24 (4): 399–440.

Mannell, R., Kleiber, A. and Staempfli, M. (2006) 'Psychology and social psychology and the study of leisure', in C. Rojek, S. Shaw and A. Veal (eds) *A Handbook of Leisure Studies*, Palgrave: Basingstoke, pp. 109–24.

Ministry of Social Development (2008) *The Social Report*, Ministry of Social Development: Wellington.

Mumford, L. (1961) *The City in History*, Harcourt, Brace & World, Inc.: New York.

Neulinger, J. (1974) *The Psychology of Leisure*, 2nd edn, Charles C. Thomas: Springfield, IL.

Northcote, J. (2006) 'Night clubbing and the search for identity: making the transition from childhood to adulthood in an urban milieu', *Journal of Youth Studies* 9 (1): 1–16.

Page, S. J. (2009) *Tourism Management: Managing for Change*, 3rd edn, Elsevier: Oxford.

Parker, S. (1971) *The Future of Work and Leisure*, Praeger: New York.

Parker, S. (1976) *The Sociology of Leisure*, Allen & Unwin: London.

Parker, S. (1983) *Leisure and Work*, Allen & Unwin: London

Parliamentary Office of Science and Technology (2005) 'The 24 hour society', *Postnote*, November, number 250, www.parliament.UK/parliamentary_offices.

Pine, B. and Gilmore, J. (1999) *The Experience Economy*, Harvard University Business School Press: Boston.

Putnam, R. (1993) *Making Democracy Work*, Princeton University Press: Princeton, NJ.

Rapoport, R. and Rapoport, R.N. (1975) *Leisure and the Family Lifecycle*, Routledge: London.

Riesman, D. (1950) *The Lonely Crowd*, Doubleday Anchor Books: New York.

Roberts, K. (1997) 'Same activities, different meanings', *Leisure Studies* 16 (1): 1–15.

Roberts, K. (1999) *Leisure in Contemporary Society*, CABI: Wallingford.

Rojek, C. (1985) *Leisure and Capitalism*, Tavistock: London.

Rojek, C. (1995) *Decentring Leisure: Rethinking Leisure Theory*, Sage: London.

Rowntree, S. and Lavers, G. (1951) *English Life and Leisure: A Social Study*, Longmans Green & Co.: London.

Rowntree, S. (1901) *Poverty: A Study of Town Life*, Longm6an Green & Co.: London.

Rybczynski, W. (1991) *Waiting for the Weekend*, Viking: London.

Sasihatian, V. (2004) 'Asian-American leisure', in G. Cross (ed.) *Encyclopaedia of Recreation and Leisure in America*, Volume 1, Thomson-Gale: Woodbridge, CT, pp. 4–8.

Schor, J. (2006) 'Overturning the modernist predictions: Recent trends in work and leisure in the OECD', in C. Rojek, S. Shaw and A. Veal (eds) *A Handbook of Leisure Studies*, Palgrave: Basingstoke, pp. 203–15.

Tönnies, F. (1964) *Community and Society* (Gemeinschaft and Gesellschaft). Michigan State University: East Lansing, M I.

Torkildsen, G. (1999) *Leisure Management*, 3rd edn, Routledge: London.

Van der Poel, H. (2006) 'Sociology and cultural studies', in C. Rojek, S. Shaw and A. Veal (eds) *A Handbook of Leisure Studies*, Palgrave: Basingstoke, pp. 93–108.

Veal, A. (2000) *Leisure Lifestyles: A Review and Annotated Bibliography*, Online Bibliography No. 8, School of Leisure, Sport and Tourism, University of Technology Sydney, Sydney, business, www.UTS.edu.au.

Warde, A., Tampubolon, G. and Savage, M. (2005) 'Recreation, informal social networks and social capital', *Journal of Leisure Research* 37 (4): 402–425.

Washburne, R. (1978) 'Black under-representation in wildland recreation: alternative explanations', *Leisure Sciences* 1 (2): 175–89.

Zuzanek, J. and Mannell, R. (1983) 'Work–leisure relationships from a sociological and social psychological perspective', *Leisure Studies* 2(3): 327–44.

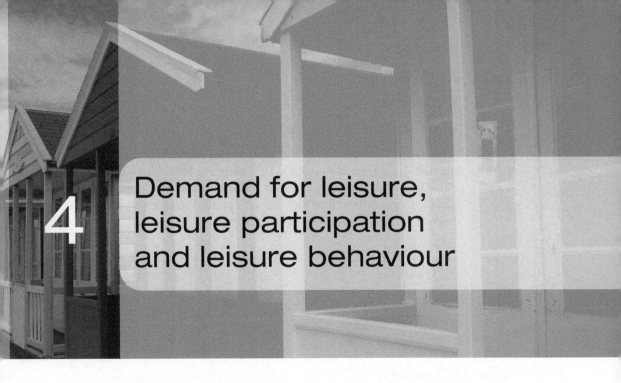

4 Demand for leisure, leisure participation and leisure behaviour

Learning outcomes

After reading this chapter, you should be able to:

- Explain the concept of demand and participation in leisure
- Outline some of the main explanations of leisure motivation
- Identify the problems associated with social exclusion and leisure

Introduction

The term demand is used to describe the aggregate patterns and volume of leisure activity which individuals and groups undertake, which is the outcome of individual and group motivation to engage in leisure, as well a deliberate decision to engage in certain forms of leisure behaviour. As Lipscombe (2003: 107) argues, national studies of demand have highlighted a number of key factors that shape demand:

- Population.
- Economic growth.

- Car ownership.

- Education.

- The amount of leisure time.

However, demand does not equate exactly with participation because demand is an aggregate measure of numerous individuals' participation rates. Participation is largely based on the individual and family, and Lipscombe (2003) suggests that the following explanatory factors typically shape participation rates in different forms of leisure:

- Education.

- Age and sex.

- Race.

- Place of residence.

- Leisure time.

- Personality.

- Preferences and tastes of individuals and other family members.

- Price and price of competing goods or leisure opportunities.

- Disposable income.

- Experience in childhood.

- Lifestyle.

What this illustrates is that:

- The social context and social factors identified in Chapter 3 are critical in shaping our predisposition to certain forms of leisure.

- A wide range of factors affect leisure demand and leisure participation.

- Different factors will facilitate and constrain leisure at the individual level.

Leisure demand is not just an abstract concept, because our understanding of how many people require a specific service or will participate in a specific activity is critical when planning for leisure services. For example, in 2007, Southwark Council in inner London commissioned a review of leisure demand to assess the future investment needs in its urban leisure centres, prior to making an investment of £12.3 million in upgrading the facilities. This review sought to understand who used each centre, the distance users travelled and the existing and potential use of these facilities, which illustrates how important it is to understand leisure demand and the levels of participation that exist.

Much of the interest in demand by leisure researchers focuses on the actual demand that exists, which is often measured through different surveys and studies of participation. This chapter examines the notion of demand and the factors which help to determine and shape demand, as well as the explanations which have been advanced to explain the motivation to engage in specific forms of leisure behaviour by individuals. This has to be understood in relation to the apparent paradox of leisure, where those with low incomes often have large amounts of time, so that the young have abundant leisure time but limited income. This time diminishes as you pass through the family life cycle until older age, as income notionally increases through time but then diminishes in older age once you stop working.

As Argyle (1996) argues, leisure is about 'those activities which people do in their free time, because they want to for their own sake, for fun, entertainment, self-improvement, or for goals of their own choosing, but not for material gain' (Argyle 1996: 3). This is an important starting point in seeking to understand leisure demand because this quotation highlights that there are a wide range of motives which shape the individual patterns of leisure participation: these patterns are then aggregated to depict patterns of leisure across the population and different social groups. Argyle focused on the distinction between out-of-home and at-home leisure, highlighting 10 types of typical leisure activities which arise in most studies of leisure participation. As Figure 4.1 shows, these 10 types of leisure tend to dominate any analysis of demand in most Western countries. This forms a useful overview of the reality of leisure participation, and raises one very important question: why do people engage in different forms of leisure activity? In other words, how do we explain what shapes the demand for leisure and, more specifically, what motivates individuals to engage in leisure? This enters the realms of social psychology, since leisure has a

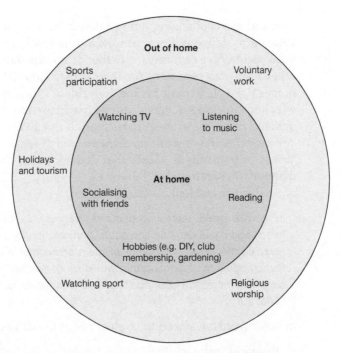

Figure 4.1 Ten types of leisure – in home and out of home

Source: Adapted from Argyle (1996: 4–5)

wide range of roles and meanings for individuals, as we discussed in Chapter 3. For example, leisure can have a significant effect on the personality of an individual and has an important socialisation role too. But above all, motivation 'is an important aspect of the study of leisure because it can provide part of the explanation of why people engage in leisure activities, or particular leisure activities' (Argyle 1996: 152) and so will be examined in detail in this chapter.

Yet demand cannot be viewed in isolation from other aspects of leisure, because as Coppock and Duffield (1975: 2) argued: 'the success of any study of outdoor recreation depends on the synthesis of two contrasting elements: the sociological phenomenon of leisure or . . . that part of leisure time which an individual spends on outdoor recreation and . . . the physical resources that are necessary for the particular recreational activities'. This means that we need to understand how demand (expressed as participation or a desire to engage in leisure) and supply of opportunities allow demand to be fulfilled, the latter which will be examined in Chapter 5. Patmore (1983: 54) recognised that 'leisure is far more easily recognised than objectively analysed . . . the difficulties are only in part conceptual: equally important are the nature and limitations of available data', which illustrates the challenge of measuring demand statistically. But what do we mean by the term demand?

Leisure demand

Demand is a challenging term to define because of the multiple meanings developed to define it. For example, at one level, demand refers to an 'individual's preferences or desires, whether or not the individual has the economic or other resources necessary for their satisfaction' (Pigram 1983: 16). At a more practical level, it may be the individual's preference for specific activities which are measured statistically as participation. But as researchers indicate, demand is *not* the same as participation due to one important concept – *latent demand* (i.e. the amount of demand which remains unsatisfied because of a lack of opportunity to satisfy that demand), and the different forms of leisure demand are illustrated in Table 4.1.

As Pigram and Jenkins (2006) argued,

In the real world, recreation demand rarely equals participation. The difference between aggregate demand and actual participation (or expressed, effective, observed, revealed demand) is referred to as latent demand or latent participation – the unsatisfied component of demand that would be converted to participation if conditions of supply of recreation opportunities were brought to ideal levels. *(Pigram and Jenkins 2006: 26)*

In other words, we need to be clear about the distinction between:

- Demand and participation.
- The different measures of, and forms of, demand.

Table 4.1   Forms of leisure demand

1. *Effective demand* is that demand which exists and is sometimes referred to as participation

2. *Latent demand*, which is demand than has been constrained for various reasons and could be realised if the variables that restrict participation are removed

3. *Future demand*, which is demand that may occur if further provision of resources becomes available in future

4. *Induced demand*, which may occur when latent demand is converted into effective demand because of the provision of new facilities or the promotion of the existing facilities that the population remained unaware of

5. *Diverted demand*, which is demand that can be supplanted or displaced by the provision of a new facility whereby the participants move to a new resource or form of provision

6. *Substitute demand*, where people may relocate their demand to alternative provision, such as shifting from attending a public swimming pool to a private sector swimming pool which is located nearer to their home.

Source: Adapted from Lipscombe (2003: 106–7)

Other forms of demand which are important to the study of leisure include deferred demand, which is demand that remains unfulfilled due to a lack of opportunities, along with potential demand, which is where demand is constrained by issues such as income or mobility but may potentially be realised in the future if barriers are removed. In the case of participation, Veal and Collins (2003: 356–357) argue that trying to measure both non-participation and participation is very problematic within leisure studies. One of the principal challenges is recognising that individuals may participate in a single activity or multiple activities and they may participate at different frequencies and with different levels of commitment. In other words, Veal and Collins (2003) point to the importance of understanding the type of participation which people engage in as well as key variables shaping participation, such as social grouping, age, gender, income and stage in the family life cycle. Even so, constraints on demand as well as tastes and preferences will combine with other factors to produce this multiplicity of reasons which affect how and where people participate in specific activities. Therefore, while we may attempt to find measures of demand, measuring participation is never going to be perfect because of the different factors which may restrict or promote participation. In fact, Lipscombe (2003) argues that demand is impossible to measure directly since it is also dependent upon the supply of leisure opportunities.

What we do need to recognise, as Pigram (2003a: 100) argued, is that the individual's freedom to choose to engage in leisure is a significant element of leisure behaviour. This is not a purely random process, as a number of factors influence the choices which individuals exercise because leisure is a

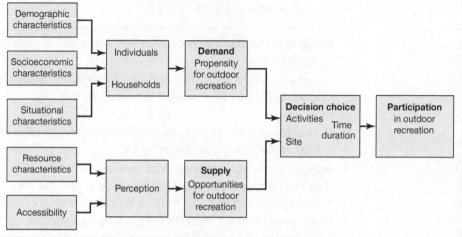

Figure 4.2 The decision process in outdoor recreation
Source: Pigram (1983). Copyright © Routledge, 1983

discretionary activity and different variables will coalesce and group together to influence the interaction between demand and supply and the decisions and choices made to then participate in leisure and recreation. In other words, leisure is not dependent upon the daily regime of working, because there is a much greater degree of choice involved in the decision-making process. To synthesise these factors into a model of recreation choice behaviour, Pigram (1983) constructed Figure 4.2, which highlights a process that individuals and groups go through in deciding to participate in leisure and recreation. Figure 4.2 shows that a range of variables can be grouped together which will facilitate or constrain leisure behaviour and the decision on whether to undertake a specific type of activity in an outdoor setting. Of course, this does not apply to more in-formal forms of leisure which occur within the home, but this does illustrate the importance of different factors, such as situational characteristics, which in-clude the place of residence, the time available to the householder and their mo-bility (i.e. access to transport). A considerable amount of research has been undertaken on leisure choice behaviour, especially by economists, and much of the focus is on the range of opportunities available in different environments that can appeal to different tastes and preferences, as illustrated by the Clark and Stankey (1979) Recreation Opportunities Spectrum (ROS).

Most research on leisure has examined effective demand (i.e. actual partici-pation) as opposed to latent demand, and distinctions are normally made be-tween passive recreation and active recreation, as observed by Coppock and Duffield (1975). This builds upon the research by Rowntree (1941) which ident-ified a five-fold classification for leisure (building on earlier classifications by Davis (1915) that divided it into three classes of spontaneous, communally or-ganised and commercially organised):

- Active leisure
  - Taking place indoors (e.g. visits to social clubs)
  - Taking place outdoors

- Passive leisure
  - Taking place indoors
  - Taking place outdoors
- Religion (although since the 1930s, this aspect of leisure has been subsumed into passive forms of leisure)

Source: Rowntree (1941)

Rowntree's seminal study of leisure in York in the United Kingdom in the 1930s highlighted that passive recreation was by far the most important type of leisure numerically, and this has remained the case for many of the subsequent studies of leisure which have looked at the individual as well as leisure in specific cities and in entire countries. The Rowntree study is useful because it provides the in-depth overview of demand for leisure amongst the population of one city and provides many interesting insights into participation in leisure, largely pre-dating most of the government-sponsored social surveys of leisure demand that emerged in many countries in the 1960s and 1970s. For example, in the case of visits to public houses, Rowntree found that the extent of growth in provision dropped from one for every 330 people in 1901 to one for every 576 people in 1938 in York, where 175 public houses existed (excluding 15 redundant premises). Rowntree's survey found that over 12,000 visits were made to 10 public houses in 1938 over a one-week period. This equated to around 180,000 visits a week for the whole city of York; and about two visits a week for every man, woman and child in York. Rowntree calculated that for the working classes of York, alcohol consumed about 10% of the household income, which illustrates the importance of this informal social activity in the leisure lifestyles of the town's population. Citing a decline in the number of arrests due to drunkenness, Rowntree pointed to a growing diversity of attractions which had altered leisure participation in the 1930s, with a growing focus on indoor and outdoor leisure. What this short example illustrates is that the analysis of demand and its measurement requires an understanding of the factors which determine leisure demand and individuals' leisure needs. This is important so that we can understand the population's leisure habits and the factors which determine aggregate patterns of demand.

Determinants of demand

There are three principal determinants of demand:

- Economic determinants.

- Geographical determinants.

- Social-psychological determinants.

The *economic determinants* of demand have a long history of study within the field of leisure, which Veal (2006) traced back to Veblen's (1899) *The Theory of the Leisure Class*. Much of the focus on the economic determinants, within leisure research is the issue of *price*. Classic economic theory suggests that the higher the price, the less willing people are to consume a particular product or experience. In market economies, it is the price that is the key determinant of an individual's decision to purchase leisure where an economic transaction is required. Even so, many forms of leisure are not associated with commercial transactions, but where a transaction is involved price is a key determinant. A further complicating factor in the demand for leisure is that many of the resources that consumers may use, such as the countryside, do not require a direct payment but are managed and in the stewardship of the public sector, which is funded indirectly via taxation. In this respect, the users of leisure resources are not necessarily charged for the real cost of use. Economic studies of leisure, such as Gratton and Taylor (1985), suggest that the issue of price affects demand in two ways:

- Through the *average cost of participation*, which may include the direct costs such as travel and any fixed costs such as equipment or the purchase price of the car.

- The *marginal cost*, which is what affects the frequency with which individuals participate in leisure. For example, the marginal cost is often associated with small additional charges, such as the cost of petrol when the major cost of owning a car has already been paid for.

One other key concept which needs to be considered in relation to the demand for leisure is what economists call the *price inelasticity of demand*. This refers to the effect of price changes on the volume of demand. For example, changes in different aspects of demand are described through the elasticity concept where, traditionally, leisure has been perceived as a non-essential item in household budgets. Therefore it was argued that leisure has relatively low elasticity, because small changes in price lead to major changes in demand. Yet in a postmodern society, where leisure is no longer viewed as luxury expenditure and is associated with the daily consumption of goods and experiences, it is seen to be more inelastic because it is now seen as an essential component of our lives. Even so, the price of leisure goods has to be viewed in the context of household budgets and expenditure, so that as the prices of other goods and services rise, the disposable income available for leisure may decrease. Conversely, where there is a surplus of household income, this may be spent on additional leisure goods and services or in the upgrading of leisure expenditure on more luxury items. In this respect, income has a critical effect on the purchasing power of individuals and households, and, as discussed in Chapter 2, was a key factor associated with the rise of mass leisure.

Economists have also examined the opportunity cost of leisure. The term opportunity cost refers to the trade-off between, for example, earning additional income from work and spending the same amount of time on leisure which is not remunerated. In other words, should an individual spend more time working and less time on leisure or vice versa? Gratton and Taylor (1985) highlight an optimum point where the trade-off between leisure and income is reached, so that people have adequate income to enjoy leisure. Yet as Chapter 3 indicated, hours of work in many countries have risen, despite enjoying successive declines until the 1990s.

Geographical determinants

Geographers have a long tradition of studying the demand for leisure (see Hall and Page 2006 for more detail) which is often focused on the resources and locations in which people choose to undertake leisure and recreation and the interactions between demand and supply. What the geographer has been able to illustrate is that the demand for leisure occurs in both time and space (i.e. geographical space), which affects when and where leisure occurs. While individual trends, shaped by fashions and tastes, may influence the shape of demand, geographers have identified how individuals and groups spend their leisure time in different geographical settings, ranging from the home and near to home through to out-of-home locations. For example, Patmore (1983) examined the patterns of participation in leisure and identified many of the seminal contributions in understanding the geographical determinants of demand, especially seasonality.

One of the key features in terms of leisure out of the home is the accessibility of resources such as the countryside, the coast, National Parks and wilderness areas. As Chapter 2 highlighted, the major impact on accessibility for many populations has been the increase in car ownership, leading to improved access to many of the resources for leisure activities that hitherto remained largely visited on an annual basis for holidays. What the car has done is make those resources more accessible in terms of day trips, no longer requiring a high degree of pre-planning. Access and travel distance have been two of the key aspects which early studies by geographers focused on, building on many of the models and concepts used by economists to understand the interaction between price, distance, accessibility and participation. Many of the geographical determinants of demand will be returned to in later chapters where we will explore how participation is shaped by these factors in different settings. In contrast, the socio-psychological aspects of leisure demand, as introduced in Chapter 3, provide the basis for much of the research which has been undertaken on why individuals are motivated to participate in specific activities. For this reason, the next section focuses on this issue as it is the substantive element shaping the individual's demand.

The social-psychological determinants of leisure demand: the role of motivation

According to Pigram (2003b: 310–311), 'as with other aspects of human decision-making, the explanation of leisure behaviours is complex. An underlying dimension common both to leisure and recreation is discretion – freedom to choose and the exercise of choice'. Pigram argues that choice is not a random process because it is subject to a range of influences that are not particularly unique to any one individual. Even so, Dumazedir (1967) suggested that we needed to recognise that there were three interdependent functions to leisure: relaxation, entertainment and development of the personality, and these will underpin leisure behaviour which is a condition of daily experience.

As Iso-Ahola (1980) indicated, human actions in leisure are motivated by subjective goals and rewards that can be intrinsic or extrinsic. The point is developed a stage further by Pigram (2003b: 311), who suggested 'when an activity is engaged in for its own sake, rather than as a means to an end, it is said to be intrinsically rewarding. This implies the enhancement of self and progressive satisfaction from that pursuit'. As Argyle (1996) shows, part of the reason why people undertake leisure and recreational activities can be found in the process of socialisation and personality traits, where childhood influences such as parents and peers are forms of social influence and learning that affect future activity choice. In fact, nearly half of adult leisure interests are acquired after childhood, and personality factors influence preferences towards specific forms of recreation. However, understanding the broader psychological factors which motivate individuals to undertake forms of recreation is largely the remit of psychologists, because much of our leisure activities are based on intrinsic forms of motivation (i.e. something one is not paid to undertake). As Dumazedir (1967: 16) indicated in relation to leisure and its contribution to personality, 'leisure serves to liberate the individual from the daily automatism of thought and action. It permits a broader . . . social participation on the one hand, and on the other, a willing cultivation of the physical and mental self over and above utilitarian considerations of job'. What this suggests is that leisure is a positive factor in personality development that offers a liberating experience for some people.

Yet the challenge for leisure researchers is how you access individuals' views and attitudes, because even when you ask people questions as part of a social survey, there is no guarantee that they are going always tell you what is motivating them. What is clear is that the motivation for any form of leisure is a purely subjective phenomenon that we need to understand, as well as how people then make choices about the types of leisure activities they engage in. This is based on the freedom to choose and the constraints that exist, such as restrictions of time and obligations such as work and family. Argyle (1996) outlined the early attempts to try to understand leisure motivation, citing the influential study by Crandall (1980) which asked people what actually motivates them. Crandall (1980) outlined 17 factors from leisure motivation research (Figure 4.3), derived from previous studies in this field, which was also followed by a later study by Kabanoff (1982). Figure 4.3 shows that relaxation, the need for excitement and self-satisfaction are apparent, though Argyle (1996) argues that specific motivations are evident in particular forms of recreation.

The motivation for leisure

Torkildsen (1999) argued that homeostasis is a fundamental concept associated with human motivation where people have an underlying desire to maintain a state of internal stability. At a rudimentary level, human needs have to be met, where physiological theory maintained that all human behaviour is motivated.

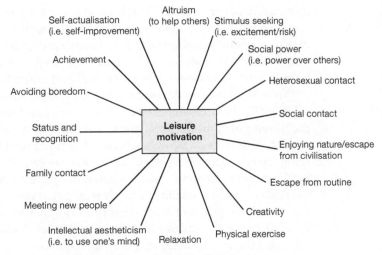

Figure 4.3 Crandall's (1980) motivations for leisure

Source: Crandall (1980). Copyright © National Recreation and Park Association

This leads to one of the most commonly cited studies in relation to recreation and tourism motivation – Maslow's hierarchy of human needs.

Maslow's hierarchy model of human needs and leisure motivation

Maslow's (1954) needs hierarchy follows the principle of a ranking or hierarchy of individual needs (Figure 4.4), based on the premise that self-actualisation is a level to which people should aspire. Maslow argued that if the lower needs in the hierarchy were not fulfilled, these would dominate human behaviour. Once these were satisfied, the individual would be motivated by the needs of the next level of the hierarchy. In the motivation sequence, Maslow identified 'deficiency or tension-reducing motives' and 'inductive or arousal-seeking

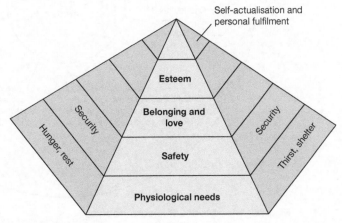

Figure 4.4 Maslow's hierarchy of human needs

Source: Maslow (1954)

motives' (Cooper *et al.* 1993: 21), arguing that the model could be applied to work and non-work contexts. Maslow's research has had a universal application in leisure to understand how human action is related to understandable and predictable aspects of behaviour compared to research which argues that human behaviour is essentially irrational and unpredictable.

While Maslow's model is not necessarily ideal, since needs are not hierarchical in reality because some needs may occur simultaneously, it does emphasise the development needs of humans, with individuals striving towards personal growth. Therefore, Maslow assists in a leisure context in identifying and classifying the types of needs people have. This has generated a great deal of interest in the notion of *leisure needs*, as shown in Figure 4.5. What Figure 4.5 shows is the wide range of possible approaches to understanding an individual's leisure needs and the different ways of approaching various aspects of leisure need. As Hall and Page (2006) illustrate, a variety of studies have been developed that contribute to this classification of leisure needs, which help to explain the diversity of leisure needs which these studies identified.

Other researchers (e.g. Iso-Ahola 1980; Neulinger 1981) prefer to emphasise the importance of perceived freedom from constraints as a major source of

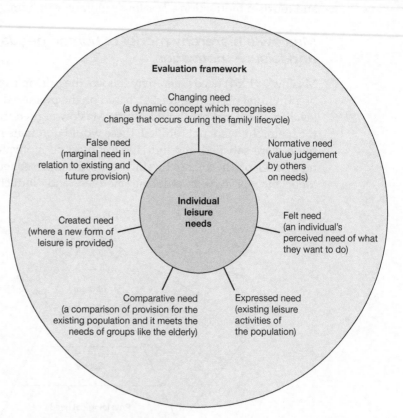

Figure 4.5   Model of leisure needs

Source: Based on Hall and Page (2006)

motivation. Argyle (1996) synthesises such studies to argue that intrinsic motivation in leisure relates to three underlying principles:

1. Social motivation.

2. Basic bodily pleasures (e.g. eating, drinking, sex and sport).

3. Social learning (how past learning explains a predisposition towards certain activities) – see Figure 4.6.

One useful concept which Csikszentmihalyi (1975) introduced to the explanation of motivation was that of flow. Individuals tend to find a sense of intense absorption in recreational activities, when self-awareness declines, and it is their peak experience – a sense of flow – which is the main internal motivation. The flow is explained as a balance resulting from being challenged and skill, which can occur in four combinations:

1. Where challenge and skill are high and flow results.

2. Where the challenge is too great, anxiety results.

3. If the challenge is too easy, boredom may occur.

4. Where the challenge and skill level are too low, apathy may result.

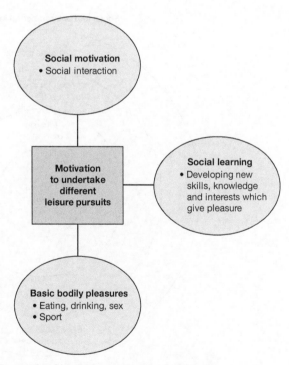

Figure 4.6 Sources of intrinsic motivation in leisure

Source: Based on Argyle (1996: 164–165)

In spite of the significance of motivation, it is apparent that no consensus exists in relation to leisure. Instead, 'in theories of motivation need is seen as a force within the individual to gain satisfactions and completeness. There appear to be many levels and types of need, including the important needs of self-actualisation and psychological growth' (Torkildsen 1992: 86). One model of leisure behaviour suggested by Iso-Ahola (1980), shown in Figure 4.7, suggests that leisure needs are caused by the interplay of a wide range of factors conditioning human behaviour and that intrinsic motivation remains a powerful process shaping leisure needs. This model is a result of the different elements of theories suggested as explanations of leisure behaviour (Table 4.2), each of which focuses on a specific aspect of human behaviour which illustrates the wide range of issues to consider. Different approaches have been adopted towards the study of leisure needs, as Table 4.3 shows, focusing on specific aspects of how leisure needs illustrate the types of motivations that may arise. To provide a model of how all these facets of leisure behaviour were interconnected, as layers which contributed to specific leisure outcomes, Iso-Ahola developed a model of leisure behaviour (Figure 4.7) which synthesises all these different aspects of leisure needs, intrinsic motivation and other factors that contribute to leisure behaviour. One way to begin to understand the outcome of this behaviour is to focus on the aggregate patterns of demand which emerge from studies of leisure.

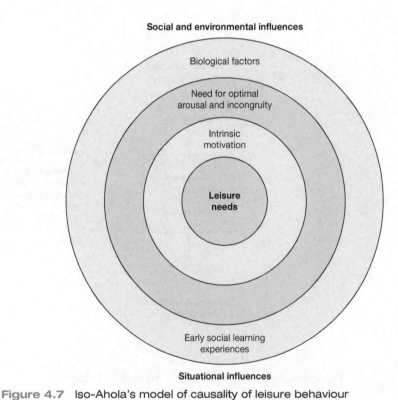

Figure 4.7   Iso-Ahola's model of causality of leisure behaviour

Source: Simplified and developed from Iso-Ahola (1980). Copyright © Professor Seppo Iso-Ahola, Ph.D

Table 4.2   A range of theories of leisure behaviour

Theory	Implications for leisure behaviour
Surplus energy theory	• Key motivation for play is to use surplus energy, especially among children, and wider relevance to adult leisure (e.g. physical activity)
Recreation theory	• To re-create energy and to engage in physical activity
Relaxation theory	• To relax after work or stressful situations; applies to many physical and sedentary leisure activities
Compensation theory	• Leisure occurs to meet needs not met in work settings (see Chapter 3 and the work–leisure relationship)
Generalisation theory	• Acquiring skills in one's leisure time which are relevant to work settings
Instinct-practice theory	• Based on the notion that play is motivated by a desire to practise inherited traits necessary for human survival
Learning theory	• Assumes all skills are learned (in contrast to instinct-practice theory) and leisure is a form of learning
Catharsis theory	• Leisure is a means of release, of built-up emotion, especially negative feelings
Self-expression theory	• Leisure as a form of developing self-expression
Optimal arousal	• Leisure behaviour is motivated by arousal, but this varies by individual, in different situations and by activity. This theory is illustrated by Iso-Ahola's (1980) model. This model integrates many of the existing features of the prevailing theories of leisure behaviour, highlighting the needs, satisfaction and benefits derived from leisure. Figure 4.7 illustrates four different types of factors where biological factors are based on self-expression theory, arousal and incongruity from other theories of leisure and freedom (based on being free from constraints and work) and motivation based on Maslow and other explanations of leisure behaviour

Source: Adapted from Leitner (2004: 84–109)

Table 4.3   Leisure needs

Tillman (1974)	Bradshaw (1972)	Mercer (1973)

Leisure needs include the pursuit of:
• new experiences
• relaxation, escape and fantasy
• fantasy identity
• security
• dominance (over one's environment)
• social interaction
• mental activity
• creativity
• need to be needed
• physical activity and fitness
	• need
	  • normative* need
	  • felt need
	  • expressed need
	  • comparative need
		• need
		  • normative
		  • felt
		  • expressed
		  • comparative
		  • created
		  • changing
		  • false

*Based on value judgements

Plate 4.1 How would you explain the different leisure motivations which these visitors to a small Devon fishing village are displaying? What models and explanations might help to explain the interest in this leisure-time activity?

The reality of leisure demand: country studies of leisure participation

When seeking to understand the outcome of leisure motivation for individuals and groups, researchers tend to adopt different research methods and approaches to try to gather information on how people spend their leisure time. But we need to recognise that a diversity of research methods are needed to understand that 'leisure is still experienced in fragments in diverse activities . . . analysing their interdependencies and arranging them in balance to form a style of life is difficult' (Dumazedir 1967: 233). This fragmented nature of leisure in our daily lives also has to be set against the wider social setting, such as the family, work, responsibilities and our daily time–space routines. As discussed earlier in the chapter, different studies have been conducted in the past, such as Rowntree (1941) and Rowntree and Lavers (1951), to construct patterns of participation in leisure and recreation in inter- and post-war Britain. Even so, researchers recognise that precision is needed to identify participation, non-participation and the frequency of each. But the development of systematic studies of leisure is comparatively recent within the wider field of social science, as highlighted by Patmore (1983: 55), who argued that:

> Prior to the 1960s sources were scattered and fragmentary, and lacked any coherent basis. The studies undertaken for the American Outdoor Recreation Resources Review Commission and published in 1962 gave the impetus for work in Britain. Two wide-ranging national surveys were carried out later in the latter part of that decade: the Pilot National Recreation Survey . . . and the Government social survey Planning for Leisure. . . . These surveys remain unique at national level.

These national surveys were 'one-off' studies, but were a starting point for analysing demand. These types of survey typically ask individuals questions about their leisure habits. Patmore (1983: 57) pointed to the example of the General Household Survey in the UK which asked respondents: 'What . . . things have you done in your leisure time . . . in the four weeks ending last Sunday?'

Yet here we have to consider whether social surveys really gather all the information we would like on the leisure habits of individuals. There are inherent problems with using social survey techniques which ask people to recall what they have done in the previous period of time, as their recall may not be very accurate and tends to decline the further back in time you go. For this reason, in seeking to understand leisure demand, particularly leisure motivation, we try to use a wide range of techniques that may complement each other and give us different insights on individual and household leisure habits.

As Hall and Page (2006) observed, three techniques are normally used:

1. A continuous record of activities of a sample population for a given time period which involves respondents keeping a diary of activities (the time budget approach).

2. Questionnaire surveys, which require respondents to recall activities with qualitative and quantitative questions, and are small scale owing to the cost of administering them.

3. Questionnaire surveys which are large scale, enabling subsamples to be drawn which are statistically significant.

One of the most popular techniques is the time budget method.

Leisure time budgets

Time budgets provide a record of a person's use of time. They describe the duration, sequence and timing of a person's activities for a given period, usually of between a day and a week. When combined with the recording of the location at which activities occur, the record is referred to as a space–time budget. Time budget studies provide for the understanding of spatial and temporal (i.e. through time) behaviour patterns which may not be directly observable by other research techniques, either because of their practicality or because of their intrusion into individual privacy. Such studies are often undertaken through the use of detailed diaries which are filled in by participants. This technique is widely used in audience research by organisations such as the BBC to understand viewing or listening habits. Respondents are usually asked to keep a record of their listening and viewing habits as a diary, where they fill in their activities for a full week with half-hour entries. But even these research methods have inherent problems because people sometimes forget to fill in part of the diary, or they may be preoccupied with other things or may fill in the diary inaccurately.

Thrift (1977) provides an assessment of three principal constraints on our daily activity patterns which emerge in time budget studies:

- *Comparability constraints* (e.g. the biologically based need for food and sleep).

- *Coupling constraints* (e.g. people need to interact and undertake activities with other people).

- *Authority constraints* (e.g. where activities are controlled, not allowed or permitted at a certain point in time).

Thus, choice and constraints will influence the specific activities and the context of daily activities, which will be discussed in the next section of the chapter in relation to leisure constraints. Chapin (1974) found that time budget studies may choose to use three main survey techniques:

- *A check list technique*, where respondents select the list of activities they engage in from a pre-categorised list.

- *The yesterday technique*, where subjects are asked to list things they did the previous day.

- *The tomorrow technique*, where the participant keeps a diary on what they do.

Probably the most significant study of leisure using diaries was by Glyptis (1981), which examined a sample of 595 visitors to the countryside. Respondents were asked to keep a diary record spanning three days and five evenings, recording activities in half-hour periods. Glyptis was able to group the results of individuals statistically to identify the leisure lifestyles of respondents. A large number of countries have developed this technique to look at the time use of the population (see Dumazedir 1967 for studies of France in the 1950s). There are over 50 countries which now undertake time use studies. For example, The UK 2000 Time Use Survey (ONS 2002) measured how people spent their time. It comprised a representative sample of households and individuals within households, based on a household questionnaire survey and diaries. For all adults, at 8.00 a.m., 7% were engaged in leisure, which increased to 14% at 12 noon, which increased to 23% at 4.00 p.m. and to 57% at 8.00 p.m., dropping to 13% at midnight, when 79% were sleeping. At weekends, rest and recuperation were principal leisure activities.

At an EU level, the July 2003 *Time Use at Different Stages of Life* survey of time use in 13 different EU countries provides some comparable transnational data (http://www.europa.eu.int). It is useful because it highlights some of the specific points raised in Chapter 3 in relation to gender and stage in the life cycle as important determinants of leisure demand. In the case of Belgium, for example, just over 10,000 people were interviewed, whereas in France this was 15,541 people and just over 10,000 in the UK. In Romania, almost 18,000 were interviewed, whereas in Denmark 2739 people were interviewed. There was no harmonised method of selecting the population who were measured, as this varied from those aged 10 through to those aged over 20. The survey found that within Europe, the amount of free time which the population had available ranged from 4.5 to 6 hours a day, with 40% of that free time occupied by watching television. Hours spent viewing television were greater in Hungary, rising to 50% of the use of leisure time, but dropped to below 40% in Norway and Sweden. Time spent socialising accounts for around 20–25% of free time in most countries. In each country, men had more free time than women, typically up to one hour per day.

Some countries have a long history of conducting time use surveys, as discussed in Chapter 2, with evidence in the United States of small studies of specific groups such as farm workers undertaken in the 1920s and 1930s. Since 2003, the United States Department of Labor has undertaken the *American Time Use Survey*, which examines a sample of the population aged 15 or over. The following results are taken from the 2007 survey which is based on a Computer Assisted Telephone Interview method (CATI) where people are telephoned and asked about their time use (as opposed to a self-completion diary method):

- For those people aged 25 to 54 with children, the survey found that they spent 8.7 hours working on related activities; 7.6 hours sleeping; 2.6 hours on leisure and sports; 1.2 hours caring for others; 1.1 hours eating and drinking; 1.1 hours on household activities; and 1.7 hours on other things.

- For the total population aged 15 and over, their total leisure time was 4.9 hours a day, spent in the following way: 2.6 hours watching television; 38 minutes spent socialising and communicating; 21 minutes reading; 19 minutes participating in sports, exercise and recreation; 20 minutes spent playing games using the computer for leisure; 17 minutes for relaxing and thinking; and 20 minutes on other leisure activities.

- The amount of time spent per day on leisure and sports activities also varied significantly by age group. For example, those aged 15 to 19 years of age spent 2.1 hours a day watching television, whereas those aged 75 years and over spent 4.3 hours a day watching television. Conversely, those aged 75 and over spent 1.1 hours a day reading compared to those aged 15 to 19 years of age who spent 0.1 hours a day reading.

In the UK, *Social Trends* remains one of the best sources documenting the leisure habits of the population, drawing together many of the different surveys undertaken by government departments which shed light on different aspects of leisure demand. A snapshot of the leisure habits of the UK population in 2008 is highlighted in Table 4.4. The findings are not dissimilar to those in the USA or the EU Time Use survey and illustrate a broad consensus on the amount of time spent on leisure by the population in different countries.

Table 4.4   A snapshot of the leisure habits of the UK population in 2008

- Based on the 2005/2006 *Taking Part Survey* from the National Survey of Culture, Leisure and Sport, those activities undertaken in the population's free time were dominated by watching television (82%), spending time with friends and family (75%), solo activities such as listening to music (69%) and reading (64%), shopping (60%), eating out at restaurants (59%) and days out (55%).

- Those households owning digital television had increased from 65% in 2000 to 81% in 2007.

- The average amount of time spent watching television ranged from two to three hours a day, with the most popular programmes being the news, watching films, comedy and live sports performances. In contrast, the average amount of time spent listening to radio was 19 hours. In 2007, around 99% of homes had at least one radio and 20% were using digital audio broadcasting (DAB).

- Some 51% of households had broadband connections and the most common usage was for looking up information on goods and services (86%), sending and receiving emails (85%), and booking and planning travel and accommodation services (63%) as well as entertainment, particularly amongst the 16-to 24-year-old age group.

- Around 48% of adults visit the library each year, with 34% visiting once a month and 28% three to four times a year. The main reasons to visit the library were to borrow and renew books, to accompany children, to browse and read books and to use the Internet.

- In the previous year, 67% of those aged 16 years or over had attended an arts event, which included theatre performances, the carnival and live music.

- The 2007 *British Gambling Prevalence Survey* found that the National Lottery was the most popular gambling activity, undertaken by 57% of the population who had purchased a ticket in the last 12 months. The survey also highlighted the rise of remote gambling (i.e. online, mobile or using interactive television) as a new trend for 9% of those who gambled and was particularly concentrated in the18–44 age group.

- The number of people taking overseas holidays had increased from 6.7 million in 1971 to 45.3 million in 2006. The majority of trips were taken in the period July to September. Spain was the most popular destination for 28% of holidays followed by France with 16%. Some 80% of overseas holiday destinations were within the European Union, and 6% of trips were made to North America, 3% to Turkey, 4% to Africa and 3% to Asia.

Source: Adapted from ONS (2008)

Yet motivation itself is not the only area that shapes demand and participation in leisure by individuals, as Chapter 3 and Torkildsen's influences on leisure participation observed (Figure 3.1) in terms of three categories: personal, social and circumstantial, and opportunity factors. It is widely recognised that barriers to leisure participation exist, to which attention now turns.

Barriers to leisure participation

According to Scott (2003), leisure constraints are factors which affect an individual's ability to participate in leisure, and thereby affect their satisfaction, enjoyment and perception of their own ability to lead a fulfilling life. In other words, leisure constraints may contribute towards issues such as the marginalisation of different population groups, and the result, as Scott (2003) argued, was significant differences in the ability of various population groups to participate in leisure, with common constraints cited as time, cost, access, perception of opportunities and social conditioning. Scott (2003) also identifies the significant relationship between leisure and constraints: that is, that these constraints may be compounded by other factors, such as the lack of a companion with whom to engage in leisure, which is then compounded by limited financial resources. From the diverse range of studies published, two forms of constraint have been identified:

- *Intervening constraints*, which intervene between a preference and participation.

- *Antecedent constraints*, which influence a person's decision not to undertake an activity.

Although the constraints on leisure research emerged in the 1960s, the 1980s and 1990s saw a range of studies published (e.g. Crawford and Godbey 1987; Crawford *et al.* 1991; Shaw *et al.* 1991) which were particularly influential in discussing the issue of leisure constraints. Initially, Crawford and Godbey (1987) suggested that leisure constraints were associated with intrapersonal, interpersonal and structural constraints. Subsequently, Crawford *et al.* (1991) proposed a hierarchical process model, with their three types of constraint integrated. As a consequence of their model, they proposed that:

- Participation in leisure is a negotiation process, where a series of factors became aligned in a sequence.

- The order in which constraints occur leads to a 'hierarchy of importance', where intrapersonal constraints are the most powerful in sequence, ending with no structural constraints.

- That social class has a strong influence on participation and non-participation, leading to a hierarchy of social privilege (i.e. social stratification is a powerful conditioning factor and may act as a constraint) (Hall and Page 2006).

Jackson *et al.* (1993) suggested that the real key to understanding leisure constraints was the negotiation process. This means that we need to understand how an individual will proceed with experiencing an activity even when constraints are apparent, since Shaw *et al.* (1991) found in a study in Alberta, Canada that only ill-health and a lack of energy impacted on lower rates of participation. Yet they did observe that constraints tended to be ordered, with the interpersonal ones being the most important (e.g. lack of time or money). Patmore (1983) focused on the main physical barriers to recreation which needed to be overcome, which included four main categories: seasonality; biological and social constraints; money and mobility; and resources and fashions as well as time.

Argyle (1996) highlights that one of the main reasons for examining constraining and facilitating factors is to understand 'how many people engage in different kinds of leisure, how much time they spend on it, and how this varies between men and women, young and old, and other groups' (Argyle 1996: 33). This is because some groups such as 'women, the elderly and unemployed face particular constraints which may affect their ability to engage in leisure and recreational activities which people do because they want to' (Argyle 1996: 33). But as Scott (2003) argued, overcoming constraints to leisure really depends upon the individual and the level of commitment towards the issue.

Seasonality

Patmore (1983: 70) argued that 'one of the most unyielding of constraints is that imposed by climate, most obviously where outdoor activities are concerned. The rhythms of the seasons affect both the hours of daylight available and the extent to which temperatures are conducive to participant comport outdoors'. This is reflected in the seasonality of outdoor recreation activity, which inevitably leads to peaks in popular seasons and a lull in less favourable conditions. According to Butler (2003), seasonality will affect participation in

Plates 4.2 and 4.3 Seasonality plays a major role in visits to outdoor attractions such as Alnwick Castle (*left*) and the newly created Alnwick Gardens visitor attraction, in North East England (*right*).

Figure 4.8 The relationship between seasonality and leisure participation

Source: Palmore (1983). Copyright © Wiley Blackwell

the number of ways, from annual climatic variations through to temperature, precipitation, the amount of daylight and other factors such as wind speed. Consequently, these factors combine so that leisure participation may peak in favourable climatic periods and drop in less popular periods. The result is that in peak seasons, leisure participation may cause congestion at facilities and major resources, which is compounded by cultural factors such as the impact of holidays. Other institutional influences, such as school holidays, which tend to bunch holiday-taking into a very condensed season, will compound the effects of seasonality on leisure participation.

Patmore (1983) identified a continuum in recreational activities, from those which exhibit a high degree of seasonality to those with a limited degree of variation in participation by season, as shown in Figure 4.8. As Figure 4.8 shows, the first type, which is the most seasonal, includes outdoor activities, often of an informal nature, which are weather dependent. The second, an intermediate group, is transitional in the sense that temperature is not necessarily a deterrent since a degree of discomfort may be experienced by the more hardened participants (e.g. when walking and playing sport). The final group is indoor activities which can be formal or informal, and have virtually no seasonality. Although Patmore (1983) argued that resource substitution (e.g. using an artificial resource rather than natural one) may assist in overcoming seasonality in some cases, it may not offer the same degree of excitement or enjoyment from participating in leisure activities in the outdoors.

The impact of financial resources on leisure demand

Argyle (1996) observed that while many studies emphasised lack of money as a barrier to engaging in leisure, Kay and Jackson (1991) suggested that money or disposable income was only a barrier to undertaking activities which were major consumers of money. Patmore (1983: 78) highlighted the effect of financial resources on leisure demand where 'those with more skilled and responsive occupations, with higher incomes, with ready access to private transport and with a longer period spent in full-time education tend to lead a more active and varied leisure life, with less emphasis on passive recreations both within and beyond the home'. However, a complete absence of financial resources and the existence of poverty is an extreme condition that requires discussion since it will have a major impact on leisure participation.

Leisure and poverty

According to Dawson (1988), leisure has a key role to play in the way in which poverty has been conceptualised in capitalist society. In many of the late Victorian social surveys, the primary focus was on establishing a poverty line based on the minimum household budgets required to sustain food, shelter and clothing (i.e. basic needs in Maslow's hierarchy of needs), which comprised an absolute standard of poverty. Even so, Rowntree (1941) was aware of the importance of leisure pursuits as they were becoming part of the list of necessities to achieve a full and meaningful life as a citizen. Much of the post-war research on poverty did not adequately focus on the importance of leisure in maintaining the social life of the population and its quality of life, and only slowly did the concept of deprivation become a successor to the standardised absolute measures of poverty and use of a poverty line.

As new measures such as the quality of life, lifestyles and notions of relative deprivation became more fully integrated into social science research on poverty (e.g. Townsend 1979), the concept of leisure became integrated into the lifestyles of the population as a necessity to enjoy a rewarding and healthy lifestyle. Indeed, Townsend's (1979: 60) landmark study, *Poverty,* defined the poverty line as 'a point in the scale of the distribution of resources below which, as resources diminish, families find it particularly difficult to share in the customs, activities and diets comprising their society's style of living'. In other words, style of living embodied leisure which also constituted part of the customs and activities of that society and so was the defining element of the lifestyle of the population. This was the beginning of the social inclusion and exclusion debate, because once a household drops below the poverty line, individuals and their families are unable to participate in their community's style of living and so are deemed to be poor. As Dawson (1988: 226) argued,

> this is a relative deprivation standard which implies that, up to a point, people experience increasing deprivation in proportion to their decreasing resources, but at some critical level of resources deprivation accelerates disproportionately . . . [and] . . . Townsend established a list of objective indicators of 'style of living' which includes diet, clothing, fuel, housing, conditions of work, family support, recreation, education, health and social relations. In short, all major areas of personal, household and social life are represented. These many indicators are then employed as subjective measures of relative deprivation. Those lacking certain amenities, or not participating in certain activities (for example, has not had an afternoon or evening out for entertainment in the last two weeks) were determined to be deprived with respect to certain areas of national style of life.

This quotation illustrates a number of important points about the relationship between leisure and poverty:

- Leisure and recreation are an important part of the social life of the population, at a national and community level.
- The development of new poverty-related measures such as relative deprivation begins to embody the subjective nature of poverty, where social exclusion highlights what it means to be deprived.
- In Townsend's notion of 'style of life', we see that leisure emerges as one of the indicators of deprivation, suggesting that society and the way it views basic needs has developed so that leisure and holidays are now part of the lifestyle of the population.

Therefore, leisure activities become a key element in the way in which households' lifestyles are measured and evaluated in relation to poverty, and those who are leisure poor tend also to be income poor. In the very influential study by Gordon *et al.* (2000), *Poverty and Social Exclusion in Britain*, leisure was seen as a key element influencing the way in which individuals perceive themselves to be deprived, because leisure was seen by 88% of the respondents as one of the necessities of life: this is a mark of how society has changed from the initial studies of poverty in the late Victorian period (e.g. Rowntree 1901).

Interestingly, Gordon *et al.* (2000) found that poverty affected 25% of British households (similar to the proportions evident in the late Victorian city with around 30% living in poverty). What was worrying in the Gordon *et al.* (2000) study was the proportion (i.e. 4%) deemed to be long-term poor. One of the key concerns amongst policy-makers has been the continued existence of poverty and the implications for the leisure lifestyles of these families and their children. Burns (1932: 168) noted this intractable problem where 'poverty or narrow circumstances are far more cramping to children than adults', particularly in terms of leisure, a feature also highlighted in oral histories such as those discussed in Chapter 2. In other words, the evolution of society and the way in which leisure is now a defining feature of the lifestyles and position in society of the masses suggest 'that leisure consumption [has] crystallized a new poverty, that is, one with an aspiration for goods and other lifestyles that was not only expressed in words, and traumatized and embellished in [the mass-media]' (Kaplan 1975: 233, cited in Dawson 1988), which reinforces the importance of understanding the social context of leisure.

Social constraints on leisure demand: the case of disability

The term *disabled* refers to an individual or group with specific needs. The term has very negative connotations and has traditionally been associated with other negative words such as handicapped, which relates to inequalities which an individual faces in their life. Much of the interest in disability is motivated by the pursuit of a more egalitarian society and a desire to ensure that the diversity of the population is accommodated through accessible forms of leisure. In the UK alone, over six million people have some form of disability and in the USA around 20% of non-institutionalised Americans have some form of disability which affects their ability to participate in leisure, employment and other forms of life. According to Darcy (2003), the term disabled is a social construction, one created by society and its attitudes which exclude marginalised people with different impairments who are seen as *different*. Sometimes these groups are labelled as *special needs,* but this term is increasingly being viewed as one which is derogatory, and labelling groups marginalises them as opposed to recognising the diversity of community experiences of leisure. One of the hallmarks of developing a more inclusive approach to disability and leisure hinges upon the term access and accessibility. The theoretical arguments associated with developing a more inclusive approach to leisure for those groups deemed to be disabled are that removing barriers to participation will enable them to live a full life and become citizens who do not suffer any forms of discrimination or exclusion.

As McLachlin and Claflin (2004) argue, we need to look at the disabling conditions which led to the disability at the time it occurred, because individuals with the same disability can vary considerably in their abilities. They examine the different categories of disability that we need to be aware of when looking at leisure, including specific impairments classified as:

- *Developmental disabilities*, which may include very chronic disability related to a mental or physical impairment or even a combination of both.

- *Physical disabilities*, where the condition may be associated with physical degeneration due to chronic health conditions, congenital malformations, muscular skeletal disorders, and impairments in the nervous system.

- *Hearing impairments*, which are the most common disability, and in the USA around 22 to 28 million people are in this category. In addition, there will be many people who do not wish to be identified as suffering from a hearing impairment and so are not counted in official statistics.

- *Visual impairments*, which may involve partial sight, limited vision, blindness and other forms of impairment.

- *Emotional disabilities*, where the individual suffers from different psychological conditions such as schizophrenia or personality disorders, making it difficult for them to form relationships and enjoy leisure in the same way as those without emotional disabilities.

The importance of this classification is that it identifies a population with specific needs who are entitled to the same access to leisure as the rest of society, often enshrined in legislation. The difficulty is that many forms of leisure provision are not sufficiently adapted to accommodate these disabilities, despite legislation such as the 1990 Americans with Disabilities Act and subsequent legislation in many other countries. Aitchison (2003: 956) high-lighted the role of leisure among young people with disabilities where

> Leisure is recognised as:
>
> • playing an important role in increasing self-esteem, confidence and psychological well-being;
> • enhancing physical health and fitness;
> • reducing the risk of illness;
> • contributing towards positive social interaction and relationships.
>
> Paid employment, too, has been found to contribute positively towards these indi-cators of well-being, but for many disabled people, particularly those with severe impairment, non-work rather than paid employment is the norm and therefore leisure takes on a greater significance as a potential vehicle through which to en-hance well-being.

In other words, leisure has an even greater importance for those with disabilities, although there is still a stigma within society about those people suffering from disabilities. As Darcy (2003) argues, throughout history the treatment of dis-ability and leisure has been based upon misunderstandings and mistreatment, including many groups having segregated leisure. Since the 1960s, there has been a trend towards deinstitutionalising those who are disabled and main-streaming provision in the community. The important point about disabled groups is that they are given the choice of how and where to participate in leisure, even though there are cases where the disabled choose to be segregated so that they can enjoy leisure with friends and other people with similar con-ditions. For example, sporting events such as the Paralympics allow the disabled to compete with people of equal ability on a level playing field and, in these cir-cumstances, the disabled will choose this form of segregation. What also needs to be stressed is that the disabled have less freedom of choice because of a lack of basic skills, opportunity, knowledge and independent mobility in many cases. This means that leisure may not be rated as highly, even though it has a greater significance for their daily lives. As Aitchison (2003: 961) argued, disability has been significantly neglected within leisure studies, and within the study of dis-ability leisure is also being overlooked (in the UK), as it is seen as

> marginal to what is otherwise a well-established discourse addressing issues of social exclusion. In the early 1980s, and following social policy developed by national agencies such as the Sports Council and local authority leisure services departments, 'target groups', 'priority groups' and, now, 'special populations' and 'hard to reach groups' were identified to focus both resources and research on those deemed to be under-represented in leisure and sport . . . Since the 1980s, an expansive literature has developed in relation to some of these 'special popu-lations', where research on women and gender, for example, has been at the fore-front of academic initiatives exploring relationships between leisure and social exclusion . . . The same cannot be said of research examining disability and leisure where the literature remains limited, and is focused towards sport and active physi-cal activity, rather than leisure per se.

In many countries legislation has now ensured that there is a statutory obligation for the public sector and businesses to provide proper facilities for disabled people, although there is still a difference between providing access on equal terms with able-bodied people. The key challenge for many leisure organisations is in redesigning and adapting existing facilities to meet those needs for the disabled, such as toilets, ramps, lifts, parking spaces, handrails, automatic doors and vending machines. The reality is that it is very difficult to plan for virtually every possible eventuality owing to the sheer cost of making these adaptations. Linked to this are issues of perception amongst disabled users, who may not be aware of the facilities, or of their own capabilities and ability to use the facilities which can be associated with a lack of experience and potentially a fear of failure. These situations are often compounded by the fact that the disabled are often on low incomes compared to the average population and so a number of organisations often exist which promote the leisure needs of disabled people. Aitchison (2003) found that the most common activities pursued by young disabled people in their leisure time were watching television, listening to music and playing computer games.

In recent years there has been a significant sea-change in the way that organisations and the public sector view the disabled, focusing more on the abilities as opposed to the disability of individuals, and looking more closely at issues of integration rather than segregation by building bridges between the needs of the disabled and the wider population. Even so, many of the reasons given by disabled people who did not take holidays were related to problems of travel and appropriate facilities in the destination. As Burns and Graefe (2007) suggest, we need to understand the constraints faced by the disabled based on the leisure constraints literature. One way in which policy-makers have sought to address issues such as disability, gender, ethnicity and general exclusion from participation in leisure is through policy measures such as social inclusion and social exclusion.

Social exclusion, inclusion and leisure participation

In the previous section the constraints on participation due to disability highlighted how barriers to leisure may exist for some groups. Many factors influence our participation in leisure, and the barriers which exist at the individual level may also be compounded by structural factors that occur within society. In recent years, social science researchers have explained societal constraints on participation by developing new concepts such as social inclusion and exclusion. Social exclusion emerged as a term to understand the problems in the structure of society, which determines the lives of certain groups. This has superseded earlier arguments and explanations of simpler notions such as poverty. Poverty has been viewed as a relative or absolute absence of resources, notably income as a factor that affects participation. Exclusion, in contrast, is a more dynamic concept which implies that people are shut out (fully or partially) from the systems in society that allow full integration and participation in society. In political terms, exclusion may also be seen as denying the rights of individuals as citizens. In contrast, inclusion is about how we overcome the issues of exclusion. According to Pegg (2003), inclusion is about optimising the opportunities for citizens within a community, allowing them to make choices about what they want to do and then supporting them to do so. Underpinning the arguments on social inclusion are theoretical arguments which suggest that if we remove the restrictions and barriers to individuals, then society will be able to function better as individuals develop to their full potential. This means that inclusion should enable individuals to avoid being socially disconnected (and can develop social networks which they utilise and enrich through leisure), feeling lonely, leading sedentary lifestyles, and, above all, addressing issues associated with deprivation and a low quality of life (Bullock and Mahon 2001). Theoretical explanations of exclusion are attributed to the changing nature of work in society, increased insecurity in employment, a growing service sector and reconstructed welfare state systems to reduce public expenditure.

Social exclusion is a multifaceted process, like poverty, but embodies exclusion from participation in decision making that allows access to the means of being a citizen, employment, and engagement in the social and cultural processes to which the majority of citizens have access. Therefore, when governments intervene in society to try to address social exclusion through measures of inclusion, they are seeking to improve educational achievement, employment prospects and health, to reduce crime and to improve the physical environment. In terms of leisure this may also involve intervening to adopt a more inclusive approach whereby governments aim to influence the opportunities available and reduce barriers through personal and social influences such as age, gender, income and occupational group to positively encourage participation. This builds upon the discussion in Chapter 3 in relation to leisure and unemployment because if leisure activities are beneficial to health, then being excluded from participating owing to unemployment can lead to a negative deterioration in one's health. While we are not arguing that leisure is a panacea to solve all of society's ills, involvement in leisure is one way of improving the life chances of individuals because exclusion for the unemployed can often lead to a vicious circle compounded by frustration, boredom, depression, financial problems, tensions and ultimately the situation where individuals may turn to drink in extreme situations, as discussed by Glyptis (1989).

One way in which local governments have intervened to provide opportunities for unemployed persons is through price concessions, concession cards and packaging of leisure opportunities, although there has often been a very poor take-up of these opportunities. In the case of the disabled, reducing barriers to leisure participation as a means of social inclusion has seen initiatives such as *Easy Going Dartmoor*, in South West England's Dartmoor National Park, to encourage access by people with mobility problems, those who use a wheelchair, parents with pushchairs and young children as well as those who are visually impaired. The production of a user guide, *Easy Going Dartmoor: Access for All*, highlighted the suitability of roads, paths, bridges, their gradients and camber for wheelchair users as well as the provision of specially adapted toilets, facilities and walks. This is part of the sea-change in provision for the disabled through legislation, to address accessibility and the provision of suitable adaptations to remove physical barriers that create inaccessibility. Another useful example is the North York Moors National Park in Yorkshire, Northern England, which set out to encourage wider social groups of visitors as part of a more socially inclusive approach, providing a Moorbus to encourage skilled manual workers, retired couples, single parents and students to visit. The underlying philosophy was to try to encourage those people without cars to visit because they had a greater opportunity to travel independently by bus. For the visually impaired, Forest Enterprise in Scotland has provided sensory trails, while other organisations such as the British Sports Association for the Disabled, the UK Sports Association for People with Mental Handicap and Riding for the Disabled all seek to increase participation in leisure in a positive way.

At a government level, those agencies responsible for different aspects of leisure (e.g. the Department of Media, Culture and Sport in the UK) have developed strategies to target groups at risk of social exclusion in terms of leisure and sport. Many of these initiatives have been targeted at increasing participation in, for example, the arts and sport. In Scotland, funding from Sports Scotland for social inclusion projects has focused on those excluded groups who do not normally participate in leisure, such as the Glasgow City Council Castlemilk social inclusion project which has sought to improve community-based fitness for older people, those with disabilities and very young children (also see Chapter 6 for a more detailed discussion).

Leisure, fashions and tastes: shaping leisure preferences

Models of participation and obstacles to recreation have attempted to predict the probability of people participating in activities, using variables such as age, sex, marital status and social variables. We saw earlier in this chapter that the role of choice and preference gives individuals a range of options. Such choices are shaped by fashions, culture, societal changes, economic transformations and the rise of new technology (e.g. the multimedia home-based entertainment systems associated with television). Yet one important area which is often overlooked is the focus on the negative aspects of leisure (see Case Study 4.1).

| Case Study 4.1 | Dark leisure experiences – a different side to leisure participation |

Much of the discussion in this chapter has focused on the benefits of leisure and the reasons why people undertake leisure activities. The focus in much of the research on leisure participation has been on the positive aspects of leisure in terms of the contribution to individuals' life-satisfaction, the ability to deal with stressful events, and use in enriching family relationships and friendships. There is also growing interest in the negative aspects of leisure or what some commentators have described as *purple or dark leisure* (i.e. activities that are harmful to society). There is a long history of interest in dark leisure which can be traced to the Victorian period and the rapid growth in prostitution. For example, in London it has been estimated that there was one prostitute for every 10 men in the late Victorian period, which highlighted a double standard in Victorian morals: that is, that respectable society publicly frowned upon the activities of fallen women who met the leisure needs of men. Yet privately, some of the participants in this form of dark leisure, the so-called respectable elements of Victorian society, were participating in prostitution. Indeed, Sizer (1917) commented that commercialised leisure had promoted vice. Therefore, dark leisure is not a new phenomenon but its analysis in leisure studies has been largely neglected because of the risk of offending the sensibilities of those studying the positive aspects of leisure. Much of the research on dark leisure has been undertaken in sociology within the field of criminology and focused on the analysis of deviant behaviour. While these aspects of leisure may not be particularly mainstream, they exist and highlight the diversity of leisure experiences that exist in society.

Some researchers use other terms such as deviant leisure and taboo leisure. In essence, these terms focus on forms of leisure which run contrary to the norms, laws and prevailing beliefs in society and so may be deemed marginal or more deviant activities that are not socially acceptable. Irrespective of the terms used to describe this form of leisure, the underlying arguments are that these forms of leisure bring with them costs. This is in direct contrast to many of the arguments put forward in this book so far, which focus on the positive aspects of leisure. Cantwell (2003: 114) argued that deviant behaviour could be conceptualised in one of two ways:

- A *tolerable deviancy* where there is a relatively low threat to the community, with only a small number of people participating in this form of activity and so the prevailing social order is not threatened in any way, and it is broadly tolerated and in some cases overlooked.
- An *intolerable deviancy* which involves social behaviour that could threaten the existing structure of the community and so it is not tolerated.

As Cantwell (2003) suggested, deviant leisure is, broadly speaking, within the domain of tolerable deviancy.

A recent review of deviant leisure by Williams (2009) highlighted that existing explanations of motivations for engaging in these forms of deviant leisure are not fully understood by researchers. Much of the interest in deviant leisure arises from Stebbins' (1997) notion of casual leisure. At a conceptual level, dark leisure is based on the argument that it is constructed by each society, since it is determined by the social context which creates a definition of deviant. As Rojek (1999) has argued, many of these deviant leisure activities are illegal and span a wide spectrum of leisure forms, including:

- underage drinking;
- graffiti;
- prostitution;
- pornography;
- trespassing;
- swinging and group sex;
- drug taking;
- stealing cars for leisure.

These activities are generally motivated by a pursuit of pleasure and Cantwell (2003: 114) argues that the principal motivation is to try to control the outcome, as in the case of gambling, but primarily to enjoy leisure and deviancy as pleasure. Research on deviant leisure has identified that:

- the notion of deviant leisure comprises an interactive element and a participative element;
- it requires both participants and an audience for the activity.

As Stebbins (1997: 18) observed, it is a form of casual leisure because it has an immediate intrinsic reward, based on short-term leisure, and often requires no training to enjoy it. Ultimately, deviant leisure is about challenging authority while also creating a fulfilling leisure experience. A study by Shinew and Parry (2003) examined two leisure pursuits of American college students, namely drinking and illegal drug use. This focused on the leisure choices of this population and the delinquent activities among those students aged 18 and 24 years of age. With a growing interest in binge drinking, drug abuse and associated lifestyles, Pope *et al.* (2001) cited the results of a 30-year longitudinal study on drug use among US college students which found marijuana and ecstasy as the two most commonly used illicit drugs. The research also found that those who were drug users comprised a distinct group on campus. This fits with Stebbins' arguments on casual leisure, since the sensory stimulation and thrill of deviant activity comprised hedonistic activities and created pleasure for the participants. In fact, Stebbins rightly acknowledged that activities such as drinking and drug taking were deviant leisure pursuits, although they were broadly socially tolerated. While there is considerable debate over the notion of deviance, within this context we are largely concerned with the negative elements of deviance. This is because it creates a set of behaviours which are often associated with risk-taking behaviour, as highlighted by Galloway (2006), drawing upon research from adventure recreation and the excitement created by encountering unknown risks. Similarly, Drozda (2006) examined the vehicle theft habits of juveniles as part of their leisure lifestyles, where the principal pleasure derived was from the thrill of stealing the vehicle and 'getting away with it': part of the motivation was as a form of casual leisure to overcome boredom.

Summary

This chapter has shown that many of the traditional approaches to try to understand the demand for leisure have focused on the very explicit benefits of leisure participation, particularly factors which enable and constrain people in terms of their leisure behaviour. There is also growing interest in the negative aspects of leisure, particularly extreme forms such as deviant leisure, given concerns in many countries over the phenomenon known as binge drinking, to cite one example. This is in direct contrast to Cutten (1926), *The Threat of Leisure*: this adopted a very traditional notion of leisure in society, where individuals and society needed to be controlled and their free time channelled in positive ways as

> . . . the problem of leisure is no longer a theoretical one but is an exceedingly practical one. The threat which unorganized, unled, and uncontrolled leisure makes is most apparent; notwithstanding this, little has yet been done to control surplus time. Up to the present, leisure has been organized principally around the playground, the social settlement, and the community theatre . . . It is evident that we shall solve our problem by means of two complementary methods. In the first place it shall be through communities organizing to bring about desirable means for occupying leisure time, and, in the second place, the individual will be trained to spend his own leisure in a satisfying manner. *(Cutten 1926: 113)*

As Cutten (1926: 114) continued to argue, 'leisure should not be spent in a purely negative way, but in doing something pleasant or diverting, cultural or useful. We should remember that many wholesome uses of spare time have come down to us from the past'. This was a clear indication of the Puritan work ethic, avoiding any leisure behaviour that was socially unacceptable, to the point that 'the somewhat sudden acquisition of leisure has found some unprepared for the growing use of so much spare time. This condition has been recognized, and as a result in England, in 1919, there was held the first conference on the leisure of the people' (Cutten 1926: 66) as something that needed to be socially managed, almost reminiscent of the claims of social engineering and social control raised in Chapter 2.

What this chapter argues is that the motivation to engage in some forms of leisure needs to be freely chosen and not shaped or influenced explicitly by the state or its agencies: understanding leisure motivation and individuals' leisure behaviour is a highly complex process which is largely in the realm of social psychology. Here the focus is normally on the individual as the basis for explaining the different motives they have towards leisure. In contrast, the sociologist has looked at group behaviour and the role of the family and has a long history of exploring the interrelationships within families and some of the social motives associated with leisure behaviour. Other notable contributions have been made from subjects such as economics and geography, which also help to explain the complexity of demand and how factors shape individuals' participation (e.g. price and accessibility). There is no universal framework with which we can easily assess the motivation of individuals in relation to leisure. As Durant (1938: 4) poignantly argued, 'enjoyment of leisure is dependent on positive conditions, above all on social status and the position of the means to participate in the activities and pursuits which are available'. This illustrates the enabling factors, including the importance of financial means, where leisure participation is based on consumption of a commercial experience. Yet a key element of understanding patterns of leisure participation relates to the issue of supply, which is now examined in Chapter 5.

Discussion questions

1. How has the social psychologist approached the study of leisure motivation?

2. What is the difference between demand for leisure and motivation for leisure?

3. Is leisure simply about positive experiences and well-being?

4. What is the significance of the study of social inclusion and exclusion in relation to the demand for leisure?

References

Aitchison, C. (2003) 'From leisure and disability to disability leisure: developing data, definitions and discourses', *Disability and Society* 18 (7): 955–69.

American Time Use Survey (2007) Bureau of Labor Statistics, US Department of Labor; American Time Use Survey (ATUS), www.bls.gov/tus.

Argyle, M. (1996) *The Social Psychology of Leisure*, Penguin: London.

Bullock, C.C. and Mahon, M.J. (2001) *Introduction to Recreation Services for People with Disabilities: A Person-Centred Approach*, Sagamore: Champaign, IL.

Butler, R. (2003) 'Seasonality', in J. Jenkins and J. Pigram (eds) *Encyclopedia of Leisure and Outdoor Recreation*, Routledge: London, pp. 447–8.

Burns, D. (1932) *Leisure in the Modern World*, The Century Company: New York.

Burns, R. and Graefe, A. (2007) 'Constraints to outdoor recreation: Exploring the effects of disabilities on perceptions and participation', *Journal of Leisure Research* 39(1): 156–81.

Cantwell, A. (2003) 'Deviant behaviour', in J. Jenkins and J. Pigram (eds) *Encyclopedia of Leisure and Outdoor Recreation*, Routledge: London, p. 114.

Chapin, F. (1974) *Human Activity Patterns in the City*, Wiley: New York.

Clark, R.N. and Stankey, G.H. (1979) *The Recreation Opportunity Spectrum: A Framework for Planning, Management and Research*, USDA Forest Service, General Technical Report PNW-98.

Cooper, C.P., Fletcher, J., Gilbert, D.G. and Wanhill, S. (1993) *Tourism: Principles and Practice*, Pitman: London.

Coppock, J.T. and Duffield, B. (1975) *Outdoor Recreation in the Countryside: A Spatial Analysis*, Macmillan: London.

Crandall, R. (1980) 'Motivations for leisure', *Journal of Leisure Research* 12: 45–54.

Crawford, D. and Godbey, G. (1987) 'Reconceptualising barriers to family leisure', *Leisure Sciences* 9: 119–27.

Crawford, D., Jackson, E. and Godbey, G. (1991) 'A hierarchical model of leisure constraints', *Leisure Sciences*, 13: 309–20.

Csikszentmihalyi, M. (1975) *Beyond Boredom and Anxiety*, Jossey Bass: San Francisco, CA.

Cutten, G. (1926) *The Threat of Leisure*, Yale University Press: New Haven.

Darcy, S. (2003) 'Disability', in J. Jenkins and J. Pigram (eds) *Encyclopedia of Leisure and Outdoor Recreation*, Routledge: London, pp. 114–18.

Davis, M. (1915) *The Exploitation of Pleasure*, Russell Sage Foundation: New York.

Dawson, D. (1988) 'Leisure and the definition of poverty', *Leisure Studies* 7(3): 221–31.

Drozda, C. (2006) 'Juveniles performing auto theft: an exploratory study into a deviant leisure lifestyle', *Leisure/Loisir* 30: 111–32.

Dumazedir, J. (1967) *Towards a Society of Leisure*, Free Press: New York.

Durant, H. (1938) *The Problem of Leisure*, George Routledge & Sons: London.

EU (2003) *Time Use at Different Stages of Life*, Europa: Brussels, http://www.europa.eu.int.

Galloway, S. (2006) 'Adventure recreation reconceived: positive forms of deviant behaviour', *Leisure/Loisir* 30(1): 219–23.

Glyptis, S. (1981) 'Leisure life-styles', *Regional Studies* 15: 311–26.

Glyptis, S. (1989) *Leisure and Unemployment*, Open University Press: Milton Keynes.

Gordon, D., Levitas, R., Pantazis, C., Patsios, D., Payne, S., Townsend, P., Adelaman, L., Ashworth, K., Middleton, S., Bradshaw, J. and Williams, J. (2000) *Poverty and Social Exclusion in Britain*, Joseph Rowntree Trust: York.

Gratton, C. and Taylor, P. (1985) *Sport and Recreation: An Economic Analysis*, Spon: London.

Hall, C.M. and Page, S.J. (2006) *The Geography of Tourism and Recreation: Environment, Place and Space*, 3rd edn, Routledge: London.

Iso-Ahola, S. (1980) *The Social Psychology of Leisure and Recreation*, W.C. Brown & Co.: Dubuque, IO.

Jackson, E., Crawford, D. and Godbey, G. (1991) 'Negotiation of leisure constraints', *Leisure Sciences* 15(1): 1–11.

Kabanoff, B. (1982) 'Occupational and sex differences in leisure needs and leisure satisfaction', *Journal of Occupational Behaviour* 3: 233–45.

Kaplan, M. (1975) *Leisure: Theory and Policy*, John Wiley and Sons: New York.

Kay, T. and Jackson, G. (1991) 'Leisure despite constraint: the impact of leisure constraints on leisure participation', *Journal of Leisure Research* 23: 301–13.

Leitner, M.J. (2004) *Leisure Enhancement*, Haworth Press: Binghampton, NY.

Lipscombe, N. (2003) 'Demand', in J. Jenkins and J. Pigram (eds) *Encyclopedia of Leisure and Outdoor Recreation*, Routledge: London, pp. 106–9.

Maslow, A. (1954) *Motivation and Personality*, New York: Harper & Row.

McLachlin, L. and Claflin, T. (2004) 'Recreation for special populations: an overview', in M. Leitner and S. Leitner (eds) *Leisure Enhancement*, 3rd edn, Haworth Press: Binghampton, NJ, pp. 341–62.

Neulinger, J. (1981) *The Psychology of Leisure*, C. Thomas: Springfield, IL.

Office for National Statistics (ONS) (2002) *Time Use Survey*, ONS: London.

Office for National Statistics (ONS) (2008) *Social Trends*, ONS: London.

Patmore, J.A. (1983) *Recreation and Resources: Leisure Patterns and Leisure Places*, Blackwell: Oxford.

Pegg, S. (2003) 'Inclusion', in J. Jenkins and J. Pigram (eds) *Encyclopedia of Leisure and Outdoor Recreation*, Routledge: London, pp. 250–1.

Pigram, J. (1983) *Outdoor Recreation Management*, Croom Helm: London.

Pigram, J. (2003a) 'Decision-making', in J. Jenkins and J. Pigram (eds) *Encyclopedia of Leisure and Outdoor Recreation*, Routledge: London, pp. 100–2.

Pigram, J. (2003b) 'Motivation', in J. Jenkins and J. Pigram (eds) *Encyclopedia of Leisure and Outdoor Recreation*, Routledge: London, pp. 310–13.

Pigram, J. and Jenkins, J. (2006) *Outdoor Recreation Management*, 2nd edn, Routledge: London.

Pope, H., Ionescu-Pioggia, M. and Pope, K. (2001) 'Drug use and lifestyle among college undergraduates: a 30 year longitudinal study', *The American Journal of Psychiatry* 158: 1519–21.

Rojek, C. (1999) 'Deviant leisure: The dark side of free-time activity', in L. Jackson and T. Burton (eds) *Leisure Studies: Prospects for the Twenty-First Century*, Venture: State College, PA, pp. 81–94.

Rowntree, S. (1901) *Poverty: A Study of Town Life*, Macmillan: London.

Rowntree, S. (1941) *Poverty and Progress: A Second Social Survey of York*. Longmans, Green & Co: London.

Rowntree, S. and Lavers, G. (1951) *English Life and Leisure: A Social Study*, Longmans, Green & Co: London.

Scott, D. (2003) 'Constraints', in J. Jenkins and J. Pigram (eds) *Encyclopedia of Leisure and Outdoor Recreation*, Routledge: London, pp. 75–8.

Shaw, S., Bonen, A. and McCabe, J. (1991) 'Do more constraints mean less leisure? Examining the relationship between constraints and participation', *Journal of Leisure Research* 23: 286–300.

Shinew, K. and Parry, D. (2003) 'Examining college students' participation in the leisure pursuits of drinking and illegal drug use', *Journal of Leisure Research* 37 (3): 364–86.

Sizer, J. (1917) *Commercialization of Leisure*, Four Seas Company: Boston.

Stebbins, R. (1997) 'Casual leisure: a conceptual statement', *Leisure Studies* 16 (1): 17–26.

Thrift, N. (1977) *An Introduction to Time Geography*, Catmog 13: Norwich.

Torkildsen, G. (1992) *Leisure and Recreation Management*, 3rd edn, E & FN Spon: London.

Torkildsen, G. (1999) *Leisure and Recreation Management*, 4th edn, E & FN Spon: London.

Townsend, P. (1979) *Poverty*, Penguin: Harmondsworth.

Veal, A. (2006) 'Economics of leisure', in C. Rojek, S. Shaw and A. Veal (eds) *A Handbook of Leisure Studies*, Palgrave: Basingstoke, pp. 140–61.

Veal, A. and Collins, M. (2003) 'Participation', in J. Jenkins and J. Pigram (eds) *Encyclopedia of Leisure and Outdoor Recreation*, Routledge: London, pp. 356–8.

Veblen, T. (1899) *The Theory of the Leisure Class*, Allen & Unwin: London.

Williams, D. (2009) 'Deviant leisure: rethinking "the good, the bad, and the ugly"', *Leisure Sciences* 31 (2): 207–13.

5 Supply for leisure: leisure places, spaces and environments

Learning outcomes

After reading this chapter, you should be able to:

- Explain the different resource types which exist in terms of leisure supply and the various sectors which are responsible for their provision

- Identify how leisure supply has been conceptualised as a resource

- Outline the relationship between mobility, transport and leisure supply

Introduction

In the last chapter, we found that a wide range of factors affect how and why people choose to participate in leisure. Yet simply looking at demand alone will not explain the reasons why people participate in forms of leisure in different places and at various times, because participation is a function of both demand and supply. Leisure supply is the technical term used to describe the different forms of provision that are available to individuals and groups within society. The supply of leisure is broadly associated with all of the resources, settings and environments that are created or exist to meet different leisure needs. As Kreutzwiser (1989: 21) suggests, 'supply refers to the recreational resources, both natural and man-made, which provide opportunities for recreation. In other words, it is a complex concept influenced by numerous factors and subject to changing interpretations'. Therefore, we need to understand the interaction between the demand by the individual and how they perceive and value the resource or setting in which they consume the supply of leisure opportunities. Consequently, trying to understand the concept of supply requires an analysis of the different leisure resources, facilities and opportunities which individuals and groups engage in, and many of the very early studies of leisure (see Table 5.1) examined supply as a very descriptive element associated with

Table 5.1 Selected examples of early studies of leisure (in date order)

Newell, H. (1890) *The Conquest of Idleness: A Study of Leisure from the Christian Point of View*, Publications Committee of the St Johns Young Mens Bible Class: Wellington.

Veblen, T. (1899) *The Theory of the Leisure Class*, Doves Publications Inc.: New York.

Davis, M. (1915) *The Exploitation of Pleasure*, Russell Sage Foundation: New York.

Cutten, G. (1926) *The Threat of Leisure*, Yale University Press: New Haven, CT.

Bowen, W. and Mitchell, E. (1927) *Theory of Organised Play: Its Nature and Significance*, A. S. Barnes: New York.

Burns, C. (1932) *Leisure in the Modern World*, Allen & Unwin: London.

Landberg, G., Komarovsky, M. and McIllnevy, M. (1934) *Leisure: A Suburban Study*, Columbia University Press: Columbia, NY.

Castle, E. (1935) *The Coming of Leisure: The Problem of England*, New Education Fellowship: London.

Durant, H. (1938) *The Problem of Leisure*, George Routledge & Sons: London.

Meyer, H. and Brightbill, C. (1948) *Community Recreation*, Heath: Boston.

Neumeyer, M. and Neumeyer, E. (1949) *Leisure and Recreation*, Ronald: New York.

Nash, J. (1953) *The Philosophy of Leisure and Recreation*, W. C. Brown: Dubuque, IA.

Robbins, F. (1955) *The Sociology of Play, Recreation and Leisure*, W C Brown: Dubuque, IA.

Hunzinga, J. (1955) *Homo Ludens: A Study of the Play Element in Culture*, The Beacon Press: Boston.

Brockman, F. and Merriam, I. (1959) *Recreational Use of Wildlands*, McGraw Hill: New York.

Brightbill, C. (1961) *Man and Leisure: A Philosophy of Recreation*, Prentice Hall: Englewood Cliffs, NJ.

Dulles, F. (1965) *A History of Recreation: America Learns to Play*, Prentice Hall: Englewood Cliffs, NJ.

participation, highlighting many of the changes which had occurred in the twentieth century.

The resulting participation is derived from the relationship between leisure needs, wants and desires and the resources as well as the opportunities available. Desires are based on how the individual values different elements in relation to motivation and an important component of this is the experience of leisure by the individual. Therefore, while motivation has become very important in terms of how different forms of leisure supply are constructed and provided to individuals, we also need to understand how individuals perceive and derive value from the resources they use to construct their experiences of leisure. A major component of individuals' consumption of different forms of leisure supply, as McIntyre (2003) argues, is how the value of leisure becomes an important element of desire. In other words, leisure in a postmodern society is not just about providing different forms of supply to meet individual needs and wants: it is about how that supply fulfils many of the underlying motivations associated with leisure, as discussed in Chapter 4, and the way in which the supply of leisure is produced (as both a commercial and non-commercial entity) in relation to these desires. This chapter provides a broad overview of the supply of leisure, focusing on how to understand the concept of supply, the importance of different leisure spaces and places, and how we classify leisure resources, and a more in-depth discussion of some of the principal forms of leisure supply such as home-based leisure, out-of-home leisure and the different ways in which we can analyse the provision of leisure.

What is leisure supply?

According to Mihaliĉ (2003), the supply of leisure is rather unusual because:

● It is associated with a variety of goods and services, which may be connected to specific places or environments that determine the characteristics and forms of leisure that may be undertaken. For example, in coastal environments, the natural environment determines the type of leisure activities and uses which are largely resource dependent.

● The supply of leisure is a complex amalgam of different suppliers (i.e. the commercial sector, public sector and voluntary bodies) who have a variety of objectives in relation to the resources, facilities or opportunities they provide. As Chapter 6 will show, the private sector is primarily motivated by profit and so the types of leisure they provide are very carefully targeted to the demand for the product or service. They do not provide the service free of charge, seeking to derive a profit from the product or service they provide as a justification for the return on their initial investment.

Some of the main factors shaping the scope of the supply of leisure are shown in Figure 5.1; these factors are important in shaping its provision and its ability to fulfil individuals' leisure desires through a spectrum of leisure opportunities.

Much of the analysis of the supply of leisure, as the term supply implies, emerged from economics, where supply is defined as the total amount of output which is produced and sold or delivered to consumers. In the public sector, non-profit approaches to provision have often been adopted to try to generate maximum participation, to enable all citizens to enjoy public leisure facilities and activities. However, many of the resources which are consumed for leisure purposes, particularly those outside of urban areas, are managed and funded indirectly through taxation, by organisations on behalf of the government, and so price is not an issue where access to the resource is free at the point of consumption. As Pigram and Jenkins (2006: 76) summarise:

> In a perfect world, demand for outdoor recreation activities would be matched by an ample supply of attractive and accessible recreation resources . . . In reality, interaction between demand and supply factors is qualified by spatial, social/institutional/political, psychological, economic and personal impediments . . . Thus, the supply of recreation resources in quantity and quality and in space and time, is a fundamental element in creating and structuring . . . recreation opportunities. *(Pigram and Jenkins 2006: 76)*

What this quotation illustrates is that we need to understand the interaction between demand and supply, particularly factors which will influence the supply and resulting leisure and recreation opportunities within a given society. Explanations associated with the forms of supply provided in different societies will be highlighted in Chapter 6 in relation to the role of the public,

Figure 5.1 Factors shaping the supply of leisure provision

private and voluntary sectors in relation to leisure provision. What this chapter will highlight is the need to link together and view leisure participation and supply in a holistic manner. Consequently, readers should consider Chapters 4, 5 and 6 as interconnected to help explain the reality of leisure participation based on supply. Even so, it is worth briefly highlighting the scale and scope of leisure provision and some of the ways we can study it.

Conceptualising leisure provision

The study of leisure supply and the resultant provision for the population remains a poorly understood area of research and highlights one of the inherent problems of studying leisure: this is what Roberts (2004) describes as the blurred edges of leisure as a subject which has no clear boundaries. The difficulty is associated with what one considers to be leisure and its scope. What this means is that the breadth and depth of leisure provision are so vast that drawing boundaries around the scope of provision is almost an arbitrary exercise. In other words, the provision of leisure is constantly in a state of flux and evolving as multiple organisations and agencies are involved in provision. What Figure 5.2 shows is that a continuum of leisure provision exists in most societies in relation to home-based and out-of-home leisure, resulting from a combination and interaction of commercial, voluntary association and public sector provision which results in a range of different forms of leisure provision. As Table 5.2 shows, this provision has a wide range of forms and so trying to delineate provision and classifying it is a difficult task. Table 5.2 and Figure 5.2 are based on Roberts'

	LEISURE PROVISION CONTINUUM		
	Commercial leisure	Voluntary associations and leisure	The public sector and leisure
Sport	➤➤	➤➤	➤➤
The Arts/cultural studies	➤➤	➤➤	➤➤
Tourism	➤➤	➤➤	
Hospitality	➤➤		
Events	➤➤	➤➤	➤➤
The media and popular culture	➤➤		
Shopping	➤➤		
Gambling	➤➤		

Figure 5.2 The scope of leisure provision

Source: Roberts (2004). Reproduced by permission of Palgrave Macmillan

Table 5.2 Examples of leisure provision by the commercial, voluntary and public sectors

Area of provision	Commercial sector	Voluntary sector	Public sector
Tourism	• Package holidays • Holiday camps • Eden Project, Cornwall (visitor attraction)	• Co-operative Holiday Association (est. 1891)	• Visitor attractions such as the Guggenheim Museum, Bilbao
Sport	• Football Association and FA Cup	• Working men's clubs • Bowling clubs • Hobbies	• Olympic Games • Swimming pools
The arts/cultural industries	• Fee-paying commercially run art galleries		• Museums
Events	• Glastonbury Music Festival	• Highland Games	• Hogmanay celebration of New Year • Public concerts
Media/popular culture	• Cinema • BSkyB digital broadcasting		• BBC (television and radio broadcasting) • Public service broadcasting
Hospitality	• McDonald's and fast food retailing • All forms of eating out	• Meals for the aged and social meetings • Church outings/picnics	
Shopping	• Shopping malls	• No provision	• No provision
Gambling	• Las Vegas and Macau as gambling destinations for tourists and leisure use • Bookmakers and online gambling	• No provision	• State usually regulates the activity but also licenses National Lotteries with the proceeds to charitable/good causes

Source: Adapted from Roberts (2004). Reproduced by permission of Palgrave Macmillan

notion of leisure as a series of interconnected leisure industries (and organisations within each industry sector) which influence both home-based and non-home-based leisure. But what is perhaps a better approach to adopt is to think of leisure supply and its provision in terms of the different *spheres of influence* which these interrelated sectors (i.e. the commercial, not-for-profit and public sectors) have on leisure. It is the interplay of these three sectors which then lead to the final supply of leisure in any specific context.

One approach which Haywood *et al.* (1989) explored was related to the major factors which shaped the provision of leisure services, which produced a typology of six major leisure activities (recreation; hobbies, crafts and education; tourism and holidays; entertainment; commodities and shopping; gaming and gambling). This typology of six major leisure activities was shaped by the following overarching elements which affected supply:

- *A formal dimension,* which described the characteristics or form of the activity, which may involve a continuum from active involvement through to more passive consumption of leisure time. A related aspect of the formal dimension was that of control of the production of the *leisure experience* (which is discussed below).

- *A contextual dimension,* which is a description of the physical location as well as the way in which the site or location is provided and managed by the public or private sector.

In other words, these two considerations will affect the nature of leisure supply.

As Table 5.3 shows, there are five broad reasons for studying provision of leisure (i.e. economic, social, psychological, political and environmental) and as Figure 5.3 suggests, a continuum exists which comprises interconnected areas of leisure provision. Therefore, it is the setting within which the leisure takes place that is important in terms of supply, as one setting may be the site for multiple forms of leisure supply (as the discussion of the home later in the chapter will show) rather than the form of provision itself. Yet what this brief discussion of the importance of studying leisure supply suggests is that these

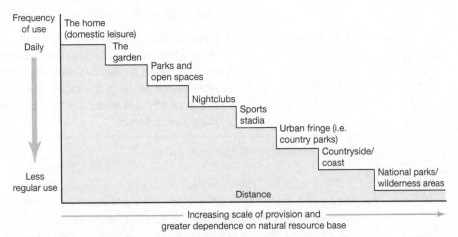

Figure 5.3 A continuum of leisure resources

Table 5.3 Importance of studying leisure provision

Broad area of importance	Explanation
1. Economic	• Leisure provision makes a major contribution to Gross Domestic Product (GDP) in most countries (e.g. sport may contribute up to 3% and tourism around 5% in the UK). • Leisure provision has a varying impact on national, regional and local economies and may have important costs and benefits for communities and residents. • For governments, the economic significance of leisure provision will be related to tax revenue generated by leisure spending and the financial resources needed to provide services.
2. Social and psychological	• Understanding the leisure needs and preferences of existing and prospective users will influence the future shape and level of provision. • Changing tastes and short-term trends (e.g. an interest in skateboarding) may lead to different investment needs to meet community aspirations.
3. Political	• Governments study leisure provision to ensure that issues of social equity and equality are implicit in their policies and plans for public sector leisure provision. • Governments may choose to consider how different forms of provision may meet their political philosophy towards the role of state involvement in leisure (e.g. major involvement through to limited involvement). • Governments may also choose to use different elements of leisure provision (e.g. sport) as a tool to achieve other objectives such as improving the health of the nation.
4. Environmental	• The provision of leisure services and experiences will require the use of natural and artificial resources. The environmental dimension, especially the growing significance of the green lobby, climate change and sustainability, will affect the type of provision and the impacts it creates.

Sources: Developed from Roberts (2004); Authors

types of organising framework are important to understand the influence of provision and its significance in the decision to engage in leisure. One key construct in seeking to understand how supply is delivered to the user or consumer is the organisation.

Leisure supply and organisations

According to Fine (1989), leisure organisations' main purpose is to ensure that the user derives satisfaction and fun, which requires management. Management is concerned with the ability of individuals to conduct, control, take charge of or manipulate the world to achieve a desired outcome. In a practical business setting, management occurs in the context of a formal environment – the organisation. Within organisations (small businesses through to multinational enterprises), people are among the elements that are managed. To achieve their objectives, organisations are often ordered into specialised groupings to achieve particular functions (e.g. sales, human resources management, accounts and finance departments). The goals of managers within organisations are usually seen as profit driven (in contrast to the public sector which is not necessarily profit driven) but, as the following list suggests, they are more diverse:

- *Profitability,* which can be achieved through higher output, better service, attracting new customers and cost minimisation.

- *In the public sector,* other goals (e.g. coordination, liaison, raising public awareness and undertaking activities for the wider public good) dominate the agenda in organisations. Yet in many government departments in developed countries, private-sector, profit-driven motives and greater accountability for the spending of public funds now feature high on the agenda.

- *Efficiency,* to reduce expenditure and inputs to a minimum to achieve more cost-effective outputs.

- *Effectiveness,* achieving the desired outcome; this is not necessarily a profit-driven motive.

There are also four commonly agreed sets of tasks. McLennan *et al.* (1987) describe these tasks as:

- *Planning,* so that goals are set out and the means of achieving the goals are recognised.

- *Organising,* whereby the work functions are broken down into a series of tasks and linked to some form of structure. These tasks then have to be assigned to individuals.

- *Leading,* which is the method of motivating and influencing staff so that they perform their tasks effectively. This is essential if organisational goals are to be achieved. Leadership is a critical role in the success of any enterprise.

- *Controlling,* which is the method by which information is gathered about what has to be done.

More specific factors can also influence the organisational environment (i.e. this is the environment within which the business or organisation operates on a day-to-day basis) and the ability to deliver a service to a specific group of customers or users:

- *Socio-cultural factors,* which include the behaviour, beliefs and norms of the population in a specific area.

- *Demographic factors,* which are related to the changing composition of the population (e.g. birth rates, mortality rates and the growing burden of dependency, where the increasing size of the ageing population will have to be supported by a declining number of economically active people in the workforce).

- *Economic factors,* which include the type of capitalism at work in a given country and the degree of state control of business. The economic system is also important since it may have a bearing on the level of prosperity and factors that influence the system's ability to produce, distribute and consume wealth.

- *Political and legal factors,* which are the framework in which organisations must work (e.g. laws and practices).

- *Technological factors,* where advances in technology can be used to create products more efficiently, such as the use of information technology.

- *Competitive factors,* which illustrate that businesses operate in markets and other producers may seek to offer superior services or products at a lower price. Businesses also compete for finance, sources of labour and other resources.

- *International factors,* where businesses operate in a global environment and factors that obtain in other countries may impact on the local business environment.

In addition, *change and uncertainty* are factors which organisations need to plan for so that they can adapt to ensure continued survival and prosperity. Change continually challenges all organisations and change in any one factor within an organisation can impact upon how it functions. In the case of leisure, irrespective of the type of organisation (i.e. private, public or voluntary sector), they need to be able to align their provision to the prevailing tastes and demands of the population. Where their provision is not in line with leisure needs, the organisation may fail in an extreme case, or at the very least, lose much of its patronage when it is no longer in vogue.

According to Fine (1989), it is only because organisations exist to provide opportunities for leisure that leisure choices exist. In contrast, where there is a lack of organisational structure, the opportunities for leisure will be limited. This was very much the case in the nineteenth-century Victorian city where public sector intervention to create a form of supply led to new opportunities for leisure that did not exist previously, such as public parks and gardens (see Chapter 2). While organisations may help in the provision of more communal leisure forms, in the private sector (and increasingly in the public sector) organisations also help to publicise and promote leisure opportunities. Therefore, organisations are increasingly important to the supply of leisure opportunities, which will affect the degree of participation in leisure by the population. In a free market economy, we also see that private sector organisations compete with each other to attract consumers and participants, with the more successful organisations also using modern business techniques such as advertising and promotion, as we will see later in Chapter 7.

As Fine (1989: 323) argues, the success of leisure organisations hinges upon 'Three elements [which] seem crucial: (a) distribution of knowledge about the leisure activity, (b) opportunities for sociability, and (c) access to identity symbols'. This is because 'All leisure worlds are material worlds. In order to engage in virtually any leisure activity (day dreams are perhaps the exception that proves the rule), a wide array of resources must be managed. This includes spatial, temporal, affective, and material concerns' (Fine 1989: 332). Therefore, the organisation not only has to make the source of provision available, but engage with the population to make them aware of and recognise the latent opportunities that exist for leisure. This is one of the functions of marketing and communication in organisations, as Chapter 7 will discuss. And one function of this communication process is to understand the type of leisure experience being provided and how to evaluate its role in leisure supply.

The leisure experience

A great deal of research exists on the concept of the human experiences of leisure, much of which has been derived from social psychology. In theoretical terms, a leisure experience may be defined as any response to a leisure or recreational engagement: this is based on the different types of responses which a leisure experience will generate for the individual. We know that leisure experiences are intrinsically motivated, based on a voluntary engagement in unobligated time, so our decision to choose to engage in leisure is a response to the different forms of supply provided. In other words, many types of leisure products, services or experiences which organisations seek to provide need to be able to create an enjoyable and meaningful experience. What the concept of the leisure experience tries to examine is one's total experience and the components of that experience which then creates satisfaction and enjoyment from the engagement in a specific form of leisure. Researchers tend to focus on three specific approaches to evaluating leisure experiences:

● The form of the leisure experience, particularly the activity undertaken or where it is undertaken (the setting).

● The immediate experience of leisure at the place of consumption, which is evaluated at the time of experience and during the actual participation in leisure.

● The experience of leisure after the event, to ask people to reflect on the experience.

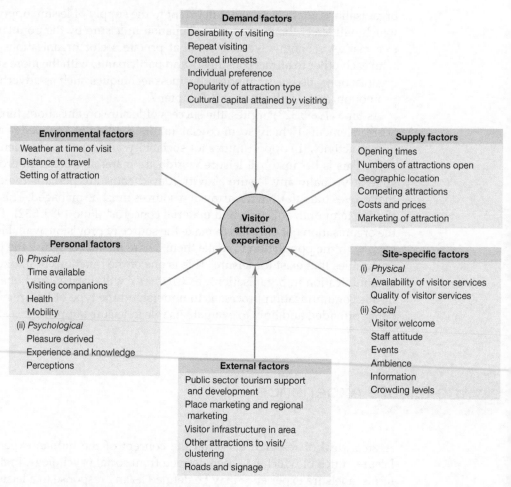

Figure 5.4 Experience of leisure at a visitor attraction

Source: Page and Connell (2009)

Figure 5.4 illustrates the type of supply-led factors which need to be considered in relation to the experience of leisure at a visitor attraction to depict the wide range of factors which affect the total leisure experience, particularly those which are responsible for influencing the supply.

But as Driver (2003: 170) argues,

> more recently there is a growing interest by leisure scientists in understanding the total-leisure experience, a concept explained by Clawson and Knetsch's (1966) five-phase model of outdoor recreation experiences – anticipation, travel to the recreation site, on-site experiences, travel back, and recollection . . . The total experience approach is oriented to what people experience during their entire recreational engagement and is sometimes called the 'lived experience'. Such research relies upon qualitative methods and the use of storytelling by respondents.

Figure 5.5 highlights the principal attributes of the Clawson five-stage model of the recreation experience which situates the leisure experience in a dynamic

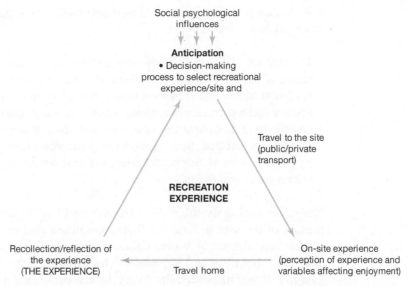

Social psychological
influences

↓ ↓ ↓

Anticipation
• Decision-making
process to select recreational
experience/site and

Travel to the site
(public/private
transport)

**RECREATION
EXPERIENCE**

Recollection/reflection of
the experience
(THE EXPERIENCE)

Travel home

On-site experience
(perception of experience and
variables affecting enjoyment)

Figure 5.5   The Clawson five-phase model of the recreational experience

Sources: Adapted and developed from Pigram (1983); Authors. Copyright © Routledge, 1983

context. It shows that the experience is inherently a social psychological construct, involving anticipation and the experience on site as well as the value derived from reflection and memory relating to the experience.

So we need to understand not only the experience at specific places and sites
but the wider experience (the total experience), and a number of research
papers were published in a special issue of the *Journal of Leisure Research* in
1998 (volume 30, issue 4) on how to evaluate the experience of leisure supply.
What this suggests is that we need to understand the interaction between demand and supply: this interaction results in different types of leisure experiences, mediated by organisations in providing these experiences and
influenced by the types of resources which are provided or exist to create the
resulting experiences. For this reason, attention now focuses on the concept of
leisure resources as a component of leisure supply. As Driver (2003) highlighted, influential studies such as Clawson and Knetsch (1966) had an important bearing on the way in which leisure supply has been studied since the
1960s, particularly in relation to the concept of resources.

The concept of leisure supply and resources

According to Coppock and Duffield (1975: 151), in a geographical setting it is
the 'spatial interaction between the homes of recreationalists and the resources
they use [which] has emerged as a key factor in the demand/supply model' of
leisure provision and so the supply perspective is reliant upon the concept of

how leisure resources are recognised and used by the population. As Hall and Page (2006: 93) argue,

> The concept of a resource may often be taken to include those tangible objects in nature which are of economic value and used for productive purposes. But when looking at leisure and recreation natural resources have an important bearing, particularly those such as water bodies, countryside and open space. The fact that resources have a physical form (i.e. coal and iron ore) does not actually mean they constitute a resource. Such elements only become a resource when society's subjective evaluation of their potential leads to their recognition as a resource to satisfy human wants and needs.

Resources are highly subjective elements and largely dependent upon the perception of the user in terms of their recognition and use. Multiple use of a resource may also occur where different groups wish to use the same resource and their objectives and approach to the resource may not be compatible (see Chapter 11 for more detail). To try to accommodate multiple uses, research techniques have been developed, such as the Recreation Opportunity Spectrum (ROS), to acknowledge the need for multiple uses. This highlights one of the underlying themes in the management of resources, which is to achieve sustainable use for as many people as possible while conserving the long-term value and quality of the resource. Many governments have multiple uses enshrined in their legislative frameworks for leisure resources to try to accommodate a variety of different interest groups. In other words, the underlying principle is how do you accommodate a variety of uses for a specific area or place which are relatively compatible, do not directly compete with each other and do not exclude certain people.

Leisure resources are 'an element of the natural or man-modified environment which provides an opportunity to satisfy recreational wants. Implicit is a continuum ranging from biophysical resources to man-made facilities' (Kreutzwiser 1989: 22), as shown in Figure 5.3. These resources are complex to conceptualise and it is difficult to provide a simple overview of their totality and impact on leisure participation. As Pigram and Jenkins (2006: 80) argued, 'identification and valuation of elements of the environment as recreation resources will depend upon a number of factors (e.g. economics, social attitudes and perceptions, political perspectives and technology' and some of these factors are shown in Figure 5.5, which illustrates that a wide range of individual social psychological factors shape how a resource is recognised, understood and then a decision is made to consume and enjoy the experience in leisure time. As a result, Pigram and Jenkins (2006) recognised that outdoor recreational resources may encompass a wide range of settings associated with space, topography and climatic characteristics. This expands upon Hart's (1966) early notion of the *recreation resource base,* which examined the natural values of the countryside or respective landscape. The recreation resource base, according to Clawson and Knetsch (1966), is totally dependent upon the individual perception of its existence and its potential use as

> There is nothing in the physical landscape or features of any particular piece of land or body of water that makes it a recreation resource; it is the combination of the natural qualities and the ability and desire of man to use them that makes a resource out of what might otherwise be a more or less meaningless combination of rocks, soil and trees. *(Clawson and Knetsch 1966: 7)*

But even when resources have been identified, we need to find some way of understanding the complexity of the real world and almost endless range of options for leisure. To do this, we can devise different schemes for classifying leisure resources which reduce the real-world complexity to a more meaningful framework to understand the scope and scale of leisure supply.

Classifying leisure resources: leisure resource typologies

Clawson *et al.* (1960) examined ways of classifying outdoor recreation and resources based on the principle of distance and zones of influence in terms of whether the resource base had a national, regional, sub-regional, intermediate or local zone of influence. This research helped to explain the 'pull' of the resource (and its potential use), which led to their construction of a model in which three zones existed:

- A 0–16 km zone, where many resource needs for recreation can be met in terms of golf, urban parks and the urban fringe, called a *user-oriented zone*.

- A 16–32 km zone, where the range of activities is greater, though particular types of resource tend to dominate activity patterns (e.g. horse riding, hiking and field sports), called an *intermediate zone*.

- A 32 km or greater zone, where sports and physical pursuits with specific resource requirements (e.g. orienteering, canoeing, skiing and rock-climbing) exist in a *resource-based zone*.

What Clawson *et al.* (1960) highlighted is that the majority of recreational activities are undertaken near to home. Clawson *et al.'s* (1960) classification is still the basis for many attempts to classify leisure resources since it identified a number of important criteria underpinning any classification scheme:

- The importance of location for access to the resource.

- The major types of activity undertaken in specific resource environments, from urban to rural and more inaccessible non-urban environments.

- The timing of the uses undertaken in each location, ranging from near-to-home activities after work through to the role of day trips and vacations for other less accessible resources involving travel.

- The scale and scope of the resource area used, which ranged from one to a hundred acres or more for near-to-home sites through to thousands of acres for the more distant wilderness areas.

- The type of agencies responsible for the different leisure resources, such as local government in the city through to national government bodies and private organisations outside of the city.

For leisure users it suggests that different resources are utilised depending upon their accessibility, appeal and attraction base. This has led to research which describes the features and attractions of specific resource environments; for example, inventories of the resource base in different countries such as Canada, which undertook the Canada Land Inventory to assess the land capability for different uses, including leisure. In the former USSR, Venedin and Miroschnichenko (1971) developed a resource-based classification of the recreational potential of the USSR (cited in Jenkins and Pigram 2003) which resulted in a classification of broad zones for winter-based and summer-based recreation shaped by climatic and other factors. Many other studies have been developed to try to classify the ways in which the supply of leisure resources is analysed. For example, Figure 5.6 examines two of the different taxonomies of leisure supply developed by researchers.

In the case of the Chubb and Chubb (1981) classification, the ownership and management of the resource is seen as a major determinant in the scheme developed, ranging from common pool resources (those which are not owned by individuals or organisations but transcend country boundaries and affect everyone) to privately owned resources and those which are publicly owned as well as those in public and private ownership. In contrast, the typology developed by Ravenscroft (1992) focuses on built facilities and natural resources, distinguishing between those which were primarily designed for leisure and those which have been adapted to leisure uses. In the case of urban recreation, Patmore (1983) identified the importance of focusing on these built and non-built resources as well as parks and gardens, while Williams (1995) added a number of additional resource settings that included:

- The home.

- The street.

- The garden and allotment.

- Playgrounds.

- Other sporting contexts.

What these differing approaches to classifying leisure resources reflect is the complexity of accommodating a variety of variables in relation to ownership, the nature of the resource and the type of use made of the resource (from passive through to very active uses), as well as the way in which non-leisure resources have been modified to accommodate leisure use. An example of a

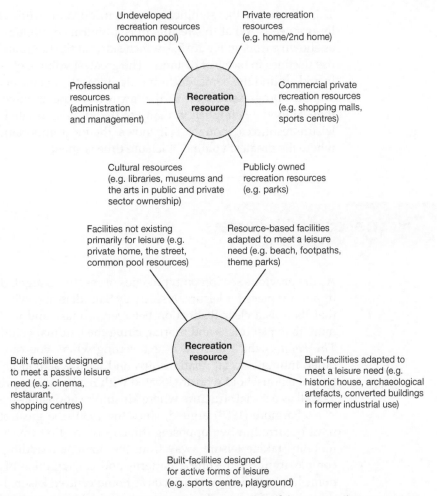

Figure 5.6 Two examples of approaches to classifying recreation resources

Sources: Based on Chubb and Chubb (1981); Ravenscroft 1992; Pigram and Jenkins (2006)

non-leisure resource which exemplifies this modification is the conversion of former railway lines to walkways, cycle paths and trails. What is evident is that the significance of natural resources has led many governments around the world to control and publicly fund the management of these leisure resources (also see Chapter 11). The difficulty of classifying leisure resources is reflected in the following quotation:

the resource base refers to the physical and cultural environment available for the facilitation of recreation, leisure and tourism activities. This encompasses . . . modified natural environments, natural environments modified by humans, and environments that are human-made. The nature of the resource base and its ease of access will in part determine the availability and type of recreation, leisure and tourism activities in each setting. The resource-base therefore underpins a range of leisure experiences for participants in those activities. *(Morgan 2003: 430–1)*

This illustrates the significance of natural and artificial resources to fulfil leisure needs. What this results in is a typical continuum of leisure resources, as shown earlier in Figure 5.3, which starts at the home and then the volume of use declines in terms of distance. The greatest volume of leisure activity occurs in and around the home, declining significantly outside of the urban catchment and then progressively the further away from the resource you live. This hypothetical model is implicit in many of the ideas associated with the analysis of leisure resources, though, as it shows, the most important setting is the home where the greatest volume of leisure time is spent.

Home-based leisure

As the previous section on typologies of resources highlighted, the home is an important place for leisure. A study by Saunders and Williams (1988) observed that there is a clear distinction between a house and the home. The home is more than just bricks and mortar, citing the landmark study by Gilman (1903), *The Home*, which defined it as a setting where you can enjoy a rest, peace, quiet, intimate social relationships and leisure activities. The different members of a household who are located within a home comprise an economic unit as well as a social structure where kinship relationships exist.

As Patmore (1983) argued, since the 1930s the greatest changes in leisure have occurred in two opposing directions: the first was a growth in personal mobility, taking leisure away from the home and adding a greater degree of complexity to the resulting patterns and consumption of leisure; second, the home has become a greater focus as home-centred leisure has assumed a much greater significance. The importance of the home, as Patmore argued, was related to three complementary trends:

- The family as a social unit has become much more self-sufficient, as kinship networks have become weaker. This is reflected in a much greater social independence and use of the home, particularly in the post-war period as suburban communities expanded.

- The relative decline in the demand for communal space for leisure and recreation in and around the home environment.

- The home has become symbolised as a private space for leisure, particularly entertainment. This is not a new trend, but one following on from the Victorian and Edwardian periods, where the home became a focus of leisure activities and conspicuous consumption amongst the middle classes. In the post-war period, in many countries, this development of the home as a social space for leisure has resulted from a process of social levelling where increased private home ownership for the masses has been accompanied by investment in the home as a site for leisure consumption.

Over 20 years since Patmore's seminal work on leisure, his telling comments on the importance of home-based leisure remain as valid today as they did then:

> Despite its self-evident importance, however, home-centred leisure is still . . . [neglected] . . . and there remains major gaps in our understanding of it. Most existing work concentrates on the use of time and not the individual activities; patterns of recreation within and around the home, and their relationship to its physical characteristics, remain largely uncharted territory. *(Patmore 1983: 88)*

This, in part, is explained by Glyptis and Chambers (1982), who suggested it was a result of viewing home-based leisure as so commonplace as not really to warrant attention. Even so, classic studies such as Havighurst and Feigenbaum (1959) observed the importance of the home as a leisure setting and its association with lifestyle and the importance of home-centred leisure, as did a number of other classic studies of leisure (see Table 5.1). This is also apparent in one of the most recent studies of leisure in one city – Quebec in Canada, which observed that home-based leisure was a major growth area of activity in recent years (Thibault 2008).

One ongoing problem with research data on leisure, such as time use surveys, is that they focus on interpretation of time and its use for leisure, treating it as a one-dimensional and relatively passive entity. But the notion of home-based leisure (as something which occurs in or around one's own dwelling) is far from one-dimensional and it remains poorly understood because the interaction between different forms of leisure and the significance of the home has not really progressed since many of the classic studies in the 1980s. Home-centred leisure may have many meanings and is valued in different ways by individuals according to gender/age, illustrating the diversity of psychological attributes associated with the home as a site for leisure (Figure 5.7). Consequently, Figure 5.8 highlights many of the principal attributes of the home as a leisure space which will shape how leisure supply is accommodated and integrated into daily

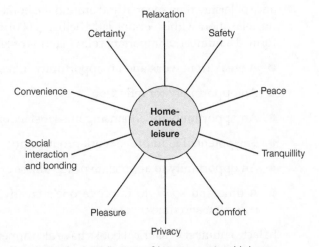

Figure 5.7 Psychological attributes of home-centred leisure

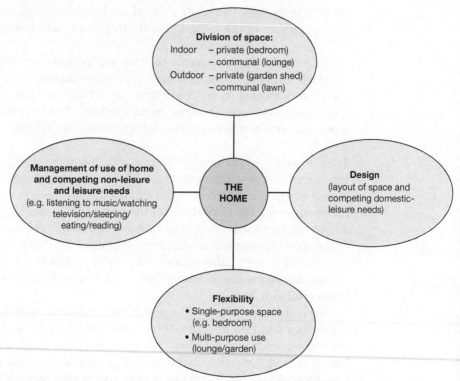

Figure 5.8   The dimensions of the home as a leisure space: key attributes and issues

Source: Adapted from Glyptis and Chambers (1982). Reproduced by permission of the publisher, Taylor & Francis Ltd

life to fulfil many of the psychological attributes of home-based leisure shown in Figure 5.7.

Many existing studies of leisure still refer to Patmore (1983) and the oft-quoted figure of 72% of leisure activities occurring at home. Kleiber (2000) argued that we also need to look at the importance of relaxation and leisure. Given the importance of leisure time spent in and around the home, the current neglect of research on relaxation within leisure led Kleiber (2000) to suggest that relaxation performed a number of important roles in terms of leisure, to provide:

- A break from work and an opportunity to recharge oneself.

- An opportunity for reflection.

- An opportunity for enhancing life-satisfaction.

- The potential to improve work productivity.

- An opportunity to appreciate peacefulness and rest.

- A time and space to improve one's creativity through a combination of reflection and time to focus.

In fact, a number of satirical books have also appeared as a reaction to the excessive work culture and ethic in modern society to expand the role of relaxation and non-activity in leisure time in and around the home, as epitomised in the popular books by Hodgkinson (2007), *How to be Idle*, and Hodgkinson and Kieran's (2008) *Book of Idle Pleasures* (also accompanied by the website idler.co.uk). Much of this satirical debate is about getting people to rethink the Calvinist principles of hard work and less leisure time – and where leisure time is taken, that it has to be put to good use. The idle argument indicates that leisure time can also be used for reflection and non-active pursuits – to literally do nothing. As Kleiber (2000: 83) concluded, relaxation remains a neglected area and worthy of study because of negative associations; but relaxation as non-activity is not necessarily a misuse of one's leisure time.

Nevertheless, our understanding of the home and leisure is still dependent upon a large number of influential studies that were undertaken in the 1980s. For example, Cherry (1984) traced many of the physical changes to housing stock during the twentieth century and the adaptations which occurred to accommodate new trends in home-based leisure, often associated with new forms of technology. This reflects what Patmore described, where many of the changes in housing stock occurred in the 1970s (as well as in the 1990s) with the growth of semi-detached and detached houses, and a decline in the proportion of terraced housing and a compensating growth in the number of flats. In many countries, low-rise compact forms of housing as well as a rise in the amount of space and amenities within the home for leisure were notable trends. In other words, there is a growing pressure within homes to accommodate equipment which is used to support and nurture our leisure interests. Even so, Patmore's comments in relation to the actual use of space for leisure in the home remain largely uncharted research territory.

Veal and Lynch (2001) argue the case for the centrality of home-based leisure, tracing the history of the home and changes in leisure within Australia. They also observed the importance of technology in shaping leisure consumption within the home, as well as the role of the backyard and garden alongside more recent changes in terms of the privatisation and commoditisation of leisure consumption within the home, some of which is associated with the media and mass communication (Rowe 2006). Rowe (2006) has argued that different forms of media, such as watching television and film, reading newspapers and books as well as listening to music and the radio alongside surfing the Internet, constitute mass forms of communication which are essentially consumed within our leisure time, especially in the home. Morley's (1986) study, *Family Television: Cultural Power and Domestic Leisure*, highlighted the important role of television, family life and leisure time. This study questioned some of the negative assessments of the role of television in family life, arguing that we need to look at the family unit rather than the individual viewer and the wider experiences of television watching in relation to leisure time. In this respect, the globalisation trends associated with mass forms of communication such as the media and television have been interpreted as a democratisation of leisure resources within many homes. This means that the television has become a ubiquitous feature in many homes as a leisure resource.

Vilhelmson and Thulin (2008) documented the impact of information technology and its effect on home-centred leisure activity, arguing that it competes with in-home and out-of-home activities such as television, watching videos and DVDs. In Sweden, for example, around 80% of the population have access to a personal computer and around 70% have online access to the Internet. In other words, the use of the Internet in one's leisure time may be displacing other home-based and out-of-home leisure activities. To assess these long-term trends and impact of information technology on leisure, Gershuny (2002) examined the situation in the UK using time diary studies. He observed the twin effects of technology on leisure:

● Indirectly, where the use of computer technology may free up some of our time for leisure.

● Directly, where the technology may create new forms of leisure consumption such as computer games, leading to greater family involvement or solitary participation, shifting the emphasis from public to more private leisure settings.

Vilhelmson and Thulin (2008) also point to the potential impact of the increasing use of the computer in leisure time on the local community and social capital, with the shift towards more solitary leisure activities such as the Internet which impacts upon more communal leisure pursuits. This debate over the impact of new technology is not new. There is also a long history of debates associated with the socially destructive role of television, not only in terms of its influences upon human behaviour and social relationships within the home, but also in terms of its content and potential to generate antisocial behaviour. Yet critics would argue that these concerns have been raised each time different innovations in technology affecting leisure consumption have been adopted on a large scale, such as the introduction of newspapers, computer games and the Internet.

Recent trends in television broadcasting have seen a shift towards *narrowcasting*, which is enabling a greater customisation of media to individual tastes via the availability of satellite, cable and online multichannel subscription-based television content. Most studies of time use and leisure highlight the dominant impact of television and the importance of watching sport, news and popular forms of culture such as soap operas and live reality television. Much of this provision has been based on commercial media, many elements of which have become globalised, such as BSkyB. The Internet is less of a community or social-bonding activity for members of the same household, and some critics have pointed to its impact on leisure, namely a general process of privatisation as people withdraw to home-based forms of social interaction, using technologies such as mobile phones and the Internet instead of face-to-face contact. The Internet may also displace other forms of leisure such as going to the cinema, as it provides a substitute. Therefore, what technology challenges is the traditional balance between the following five forms of leisure consumption and competing opportunities:

● 'In-home versus out of home activities

● Social versus solitary activities

- Local versus regional and global interaction

- Virtual contact versus physical movement; and

- ICT (information communication technologies) use versus media consumption.' (Vilhelmson and Thulin 2008: 606)

What Vilhelmson and Thulin observed in the case of Sweden was a large increase in technology and computer use within the home environment, although interviews with young people indicated that computer use is not rated as a high priority in terms of leisure activities, because socialising and meeting friends are not dramatically displaced by this activity. Even so, Downes (2002) examined the use of computers by children at home as a form of play as well as a form of learning. In the case of children, there is a blurring of leisure and non-leisure use in terms of the computer.

These changing forms of mass leisure consumption within the home highlight the complexity with which we need to view the home as a leisure space, a feature prompted by the important work by Glyptis and Chambers (1982), as illustrated earlier in Figure 5.8. This has shaped our thinking on the importance of the internal spaces within the home for leisure and non-leisure uses, particularly the complexity and dynamic nature of the home and its ability to accommodate different leisure demands in relation to a number of characteristics. We also need to recognise that the home is the setting for communal living. The size of the home is a key determinant of its ability to accommodate different leisure needs, with the physical layout, design and ability to accommodate multiple uses crucial to the management of daily life and integration as well as segregation of different leisure activities. In other words, the flexibility of the resource and its management will determine the ability of the home to meet these different needs and a changing family life cycle. This has been reflected in post-war changes in the design and layout of homes, so that different spaces within the home can be used at different times for leisure and daily life. What has changed over the last 50 years is a growing trend towards individual privacy from families and households, as well as individual members of families who can explore their own leisure needs within private spaces inside the home or adjacent to it (i.e. in a shed or garage). The shed or garage has assumed an important cultural significance in many societies, as a male space separate from the rest of the household and one in which privacy and freedom to explore one's own leisure interests have become dominant, as reflected in popular books in Australia and New Zealand such as *Men and their Sheds*. Therefore, balancing the role of the home as a social environment to accommodate modern lifestyles, so that home-centred living can coexist alongside diverse leisure interests, is a major challenge.

Glyptis and Chambers (1982) also argued that changing meanings attached to the home and family, as extended families have declined, have seen the home become a focal point for social intercourse as opposed to an external family network. Again, this tends to follow the trend from the Victorian and Edwardian middle classes of entertaining friends and relatives in a very formal setting. While this has changed in recent years, with the growth of single-parent households, the importance of gender has remained the dominant theme in relation to home-based leisure because:

● Men undertake far fewer household chores.

● Women's free time is less structured and more opportunistic, fitting in with home-based activities such as rearing children and family leisure.

The role of children's leisure is also important in relation to the home, with an increasing commercial provision, particularly for adolescents. The home also assumes a greater significance for those who are retired, given their interest in hobbies and the popularity of gardening, home-based pursuits and entertaining friends and relatives. One of the principal growth areas for children's leisure within the home has been associated with the Internet and electronic goods. But it is not just the physical space within the home which is important for leisure, as the bricks and mortar and internal structure of the house is only one leisure setting. The external environment, particularly the garden, has a very important leisure function, as discussed in Case Study 5.1.

Case Study 5.1   Leisure and the garden

Bhatti and Church (2000) defined domestic gardens as an area, enclosed within the boundaries of the dwelling, which is cultivated and used for growing plants or other items. They noted the multiple uses to which gardens are put, emphasising the meanings attached to them by their owners. According to Patmore (1983), the garden is an important leisure resource because it can be viewed:

• As an extension to the house, providing space for pets, equipment and other leisure pursuits.
• As a space for outdoor recreation and passive activities such as sunbathing and children's play.
• As a focus for hobbies, particularly where gardening is a popular form of recreation.

As Church (2003: 195) argued:

gardening is a major leisure activity all over the world and provides important insights into the social, economic, environmental and psychological aspects of domestic recreation. Gardening is distinctive as a form of outdoor recreational use as it takes place at home, except for communal allotments and city gardens.

The garden also needs to be seen in a dynamic context, in relation to the family life cycle, so that the changing composition of the household is reflected in its leisure requirements in relation to both the physical space within the house and also in terms of the garden. For single people, with busy working lives, flats may meet their existing needs and therefore gardens may not feature in their leisure decision making in terms of the home. Conversely, those with children often aspire to having a garden which is enclosed and a safe haven for children to play in. Halkett (1978) outlined the scope and significance of gardens as leisure resources, arguing that

> the garden space associated with detached housing is accessible to all members of the household, the garden can be used spontaneously and without incurring travel costs, and it can be used without competition with users other than the members of a single household. In addition the private garden is more flexible than other outdoor facilities: it can be modified to meet the household's requirements and it can be used simultaneously or sequentially for a variety of leisure activities. Given their unique potential for recreational use it is surprising that private gardens have been largely overlooked by leisure researchers and planners. *(Halkett 1978: 14)*

and this neglect has not been dramatically addressed in subsequent years, with a number of exceptions.

The history of research on use of the garden as a leisure setting was examined by Halkett (1978) who reviewed many of the detailed discussions of this leisure resource in post-war studies such as Wilmott (1963). But the significance and history of using gardens for leisure can be traced back much further. As Constantine (1981) observed, the history of gardening can be traced to the sixteenth century when it was a pastime of the wealthy. What we see in the nineteenth century is the adoption of these values and attempts to mimic them amongst the urban middle classes. This reflected the growth of large gardens attached to middle-class houses as a sign of wealth and aspiration to be upwardly mobile. In fact, the middle-class pursuit of gardening may also be interpreted as part of the attempt to develop more rational forms of recreation to diffuse down the social scale to civilise the working classes. Therefore, the middle classes sought to encourage the adoption of gardening habits and their diffusion into working-class life to help cultivate some of the qualities which they themselves aspired to. It was not until the 1930s and state intervention to initiate slum clearance schemes that new housing created gardens on any scale for the working classes as an element of the new housing stock.

As Constantine (1981) indicated, between 1918 and 1939, 2.5 million of the 4 million new houses constructed in the UK were developed by private companies, many of which were for sale to the middle classes. In contrast, working-class home ownership was strictly limited owing to the cost of purchase and access to finance. Therefore, the working classes were largely dependent upon the state or private landlords for new houses with gardens, which were only slowly introduced in many of the larger state housing schemes in the 1930s, such as the Becontree Estate in East London. According to Olechnowicz (1997: 209), during the inter-war period, on the London County Council estate of Becontree in East London, built in the 1920s and 1930s to rehouse people from the overcrowded areas of East London,

> the encouragement of gardening was the most important contribution of the inter-war council estate to modifying working class leisure: nearly four million gardens were created and one-third of men spent their time there. By 1949 the garden was a staple of male conversation in office or factory, and 12.1% of men gardening regularly were in class AB, 18.3% in class C, and 6 to 9.6% in class DE.

This illustrates the significance of the garden and its relationship to the home as a leisure resource. For many of these working-class families, this was their first experience of having access to gardens as a leisure resource. In the UK, both middle-class and increasingly working-class families from the 1930s onwards began to place great value on the garden as a private form of leisure resource which is still a significant element some 70 years later. For example, in the UK almost '84% of homes have a garden, 67% of adults list gardening as one of their hobbies, and although men do more gardening, the most enthusiastic gardeners are often women' (Church 2003: 196).

What Church (2003) also identified was the typical list of activities which were undertaken in the garden:

* cultivating plants;
* growing food;
* mowing the lawn;
* weeding.

Other studies, such as the Mass Observation study (Madge and Harrison 1939) and Willmott's (1963) survey of Becontree found that the typical uses for gardens were growing vegetables, drying clothes, somewhere for the children to play and for sitting in during the summer. In fact, studies such as the Mass Observation suggested that gardening became such an important pastime in many suburban locations because of the absence of public houses. Growing vegetables was also seen as an important household budgetary saving during the 1930s. In addition, Olechnowicz (1997: 212) suggested that the inter-war period and the expansion of suburban council estates such as Becontree provided an opportunity for privatised home life and a leisured home, where entertaining became possible.

While gardening is still a very popular leisure activity, there has been very little analysis of its significance as a leisure activity outside the home, with the exception of a number of leading studies of famous gardens as visitor attractions (see Connell 2004, 2005) which look at gardening on a much larger scale. Bhatti and Church (2000) point to the importance of gardens as a leisure phenomenon that can be conceptualised and analysed in four ways:

- As *an idea*, which helps shape our understanding of nature.
- As a *specific place*, which is often seen as a setting to escape to or use.
- As a *starting point for human action*, which may be the physical activity associated with gardening.
- As *an experience* that helps to give us a clearer link to nature, a feature which Bhatti and Church (2001) examined in a more theoretical manner.

In other words, the garden also has a subjective role in terms of home-based leisure where users derive more complex meaning from that which is conveyed through statistical analyses of leisure, which simply measure participation rates and involvement in different leisure activities in one's garden. These differing meanings of gardens help to explain why the trends and processes affecting the home (i.e. privatism and affluence) have also been transferred to the space around the home defined as the garden. Therefore, the garden may have different social meanings in terms of leisure and while research on homes and houses has examined the internal space of the house, the garden remains a relatively unknown research area despite its importance in daily leisure activities. In recent years, there has been a resurgence of interest in gardening, promoted through the mass media and popular television gardening programmes alongside a growing interest in creating new spaces to model gardens in relation to consumer trends and spending, to enhance property values. What also needs to be emphasised in terms of gardening is the satisfaction it provides as a leisure activity, not least in later life, as Bhatti (2006) outlined. Extending the argument that gardening also helps to expand our understanding of nature, research by Crouch (1989) examined the evolution of allotments as an extension of gardening and a contemporary form of communal leisure (also see Thorpe 1970). What is apparent from the garden as a leisure resource is that it has become an enduring theme since the mid-twentieth century, becoming a highly valued element in home-based leisure, which remains poorly understood in comparison with out-of-home leisure.

Out-of-home leisure

Much of the focus on out-of-home leisure tends to be on active pursuits, especially outdoor recreation, which is in juxtaposition to the more passive analogies associated with home-based leisure (excluding gardening). Recreation is activity focused; it is a voluntary activity undertaken in our leisure time to derive enjoyment, pleasure and satisfaction from the experience. An interesting definition by Mercer (2003: 412) provides an all-encompassing approach to recreation which includes 'activities, either active or passive, enjoyed either outdoors or indoors, which take place during leisure- as opposed to non-work-time'. But herein lies the problem of distinguishing between leisure and recreation: what is leisure and what is recreation? Pigram and Jenkins (2006: 8) suggest that we should view leisure as a *process* and recreation as a *response*. The response can then be examined in terms of an experience, where participation is expected to generate a social psychological response in terms of satisfaction and enjoyment. But providing a definitive classification of recreation is problematic, as Mercer (2003: 413) argues, because

> the range of activities that can be subsumed under the general heading of recreation is almost infinite. One authority catalogued 500 separate recreational activities, but this by no means exhausts the list of possible examples, and new activities are being added all the time, often as a consequence of technological developments.

Thus, the scope of recreation itself is constantly evolving and therefore seeking to provide a simple explanation of what it comprises is complex: we certainly need to focus on the activity being undertaken, as well as the attitude of the person and, from a supply perspective, the intended use and objectives of the organisations that provide the opportunity.

Much of the research literature actually refers to outdoor recreation, which is recreation undertaken in an outdoor setting. In many countries, one of the growth areas in terms of increasing expenditure on leisure is outdoor recreation (also see Chapter 11). This may range from passive forms of recreation, such as walking which is a popular leisure activity in most countries, through to more sport-related activities. Much of the growth in outdoor recreation is, as one would expect, resource based as different organisations seek to promote these activities as well as manage them. As discussed in other chapters, a wide range of factors will explain the resulting participation in different outdoor recreation activities. The discussion of outdoor recreation and leisure away from the home is intentionally short here because the subsequent discussion in Chapters 8, 10 and 11 will examine different resource environments in which out-of-home leisure activities occur. So it is the basic principles behind the supply of these resources which is important to emphasise here rather than the detail on each resource type. A more detailed insight into the organisations and groups which are responsible for the management of these resources will also be discussed in Chapter 6. However, one of the principal factors associated with of the supply of leisure is the extent to which the opportunities provided by organisations and different resource settings are accessible to the users. For this reason, attention now turns to the role of transport in leisure supply to facilitate access to different forms of leisure.

The role of transport in leisure supply

One of the greatest influences upon leisure supply is transport. There are three important concepts we need to understand in relation to transport and leisure:

- *Mobility,* which is the physical ability to move between one or more places.

- *Access,* which refers to the way in which people are given entry to or permission to visit a site for location.

- *Accessibility,* which relates to the extent to which individuals or groups are permitted access to specific leisure resources or opportunities.

As previous chapters have discussed, access and accessibility in relation to opportunities and constraints on leisure provision may affect participation, but the focus here will be on *mobility* in relation to transport and its ability to link the user and resource together. When we think about transport we tend to think about the most obvious motorised forms such as the car. But any form of human movement is based on three distinct forms of transport:

- Self-propelled modes (e.g. walking).

- Augmented modes (using technology or tools to amplify our bodily effort, such as skiing).

- Fuelled modes (especially motorised transport) (Stradling and Anable 2008).

Yet these three forms of transport would not be able to exist without infrastructure which facilitates each form of human movement. These forms of human movement also require energy in some form to propel the individual or vehicle being used to transport passengers. Stradling and Anabele (2008) argue that the three notions of propulsion, combustion and consumption are what characterise modern-day travel, and this can be directly related to leisure as a form of conspicuous consumption. The importance of travel as a leisure and recreational pursuit is reflected in the transport statistics of many developed countries. For example, in the UK around 30–40% of trips are made by car for leisure purposes, and the trips are longer than other daily trips (e.g. commuting).

The significance of transport in relation to leisure and recreation has been a specialised area of research largely examined by geographers, and to a lesser degree by transport. According to Page (1998: 217), 'The relationship between transport, recreation and . . . [leisure] has largely been researched by geographers who have used the concepts developed by spatial scientists to understand the interactions and locational aspects of transport systems as they impact and depend upon recreation . . . [and leisure] activities'. This means that geographers have focused on the different relationships which exist between the place of residence of the leisure user and the resources which they then travel to and through, using very specific techniques to try to understand these relationships. Much of the early research in the area has been based on models of leisure and recreation travel behaviour and the implications for specific places and groups of users.

One of the themes which the geographer has examined is the vital role which transport plays in linking the generating (i.e. home area) and receiving areas (i.e. the destination) for recreational activities at a variety of spatial (i.e. geographical) scales. Such scales range from the world scale for international tourism through the national, regional and local scales for domestic tourism, leisure and recreation. In this respect, transport is a fundamental factor enabling human activity to take place in a recreational context (Page 1998: 218).

But when one attempts to distinguish between the use of transport for leisure and for recreation it becomes increasingly difficult. For example, as Page (1998: 218) argued,

> on a rail journey through a National Park, the train may be carrying local passengers who are enjoying a passive use of their leisure time by sightseeing and it may also be carrying fell walkers who are using the train as a mode of transport into the National Park to reach the starting point for their walk and thereby participate in outdoor recreation. The train may also be carrying non-residents journeying from point A to B. These may be domestic tourists who are staying away from home for more than 24 hours or international tourists who are on holiday. Herein lies the complexity of disentangling the complex relationship between leisure, recreation and tourism and the fact that tourists also undertake recreational activities at their destination area.

Schaeffer and Sclar (1975) identified a three-fold classification of trip purpose and frequency amongst travellers. Their classification included:

- *Extrinsic trips,* where the journey purpose has a precise purpose such as journeys to work.

- *Intrinsic trips,* where recreational or leisure activities were undertaken and which increased as the amount of leisure time increased. For example, motorcycling as a leisure pursuit among many over-50-year-olds at weekends along with hobbies and motorcycle clubs as leisure interests has seen a steady growth in recent years (Plate 5.1).

- *Transport-generated trips* such as to fill the car up with petrol or to have it repaired.

This is a starting point from which we can begin to distinguish between different uses of transport in relation to human activity. For example, we know that recreation and leisure trips are less frequent than commuter trips and the spatial extent and impact of such trips are less prescribed and not necessarily based on a logical choice when compared to the routine of daily trips to work (Page 1998). It is this less predictable component which has continued to prove difficult to

Plate 5.1 The interest in gardening and visiting gardens helps to explain the massive success of the Eden Project in Cornwall, which was developed in a former clay quarry, and is focused on horticultural issues.

model in abstract and behavioural models of travel flows of leisure travellers. This is due to the flexibility which different forms of transport provide in terms of opportunities for activities (the supply of resources) (Page 1998).

Models of leisure and recreation travel

In terms of supply, we might argue that leisure travel is very much determined by the roadways and infrastructure which are provided. Therefore it is very much supply-led, although one of the principal problems of leisure travel since 1945 has been the rapid growth of demand in relation to the supply of infrastructure for leisure travel. Therefore, in any attempt to model leisure travel, much of the emphasis has been on the supply of infrastructure and its influence upon leisure travel. Consequently, many of the attempts to model the relationship between leisure travel, the origin and the destination area have led to various models being constructed. One of the very early models by Mariot (1969; cited in Matley 1976) really typifies much of the research activity which followed. What the Mariot model proposed was that three different routes can link an origin area to a tourist centre (or a recreational site). This is depicted in Figure 5.9, where the main components are:

- an access route;
- a return route; and
- a recreational route.

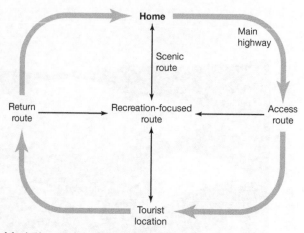

Figure 5.9 Mariot's model of tourist flows

Source: Adapted from Mariot (1969) cited in Matley (1976). Copyright © the Association of American Geographers

Mariot's model may seem very simplistic, but if we can understand these basic principles inherent in the characteristics of leisure travel we can then begin to understand how we manage leisure travel so that the resource base upon which many recreational trips depend is not destroyed for future generations. Conversely, if we understand these basic principles and where constraints may exist, then we can set about removing these obstacles through different forms of intervention which may make leisure resources more accessible to a wider group of people. The Mariot model does highlight one of the difficulties which transport researchers have had to grapple with in terms of developing models of leisure travel: that is, leisure travel does not necessarily conform to many of the basic geographical principles of transport and human movement. What this means is that leisure travel does not necessarily seek to minimise the trip distance as one would do with utility trips such as commuting. In other words, the possible travel options which a leisure user may have at their disposal is particularly complex because they may deviate from the most direct route to a resource; they may double back on themselves to re-look at a feature in the landscape and design their own itinerary, which is not necessarily based on logical principles of selecting the route of fastest journey time and least distance. In the case of motorcycle trips, routes may evolve amongst the sub-culture of these leisure users who seek the challenge and risk of roads and infrastructure which is less than suitable for high-speed and thrill-seeking trips, as evident in the UK with some motorcycle activity in Loch Lomond and Trossachs National Park. For example, in a three-year period, the A530 in Cheshire in the UK, a well-known road for motorcycling, had 10 deaths, 186 casualties and 129 collisions. Many of these accidents were caused by rights of way violations, losing control on bends, issues of manoeuvrability and going too fast. In New Zealand, around 20% of all road accidents occur among motorcyclists, so this leisure activity carries with it significantly higher risks than travelling by other modes of leisure transport, and the increased risk and challenge remain a key motivation for such leisure users.

As Page (1998) suggests, the most important spatial principle inherent in Mariot's model is that of touring: touring is the concept of visiting several places during one trip, rather than travelling directly from A to B. These principles were also incorporated in other models, such as Campbell's (1967) model of travel away from an urban area. As Pearce (1995: 1) argued,

> for the recreationalist the recreational activity itself is the main element whilst for the vacationist the journey as such constitutes the main activity of the trip, with a number of stopovers being made on a round trip away from the city. An intermediate group, the recreational vacationist is shown to make trips from some regional base.

Consequently, the geographical patterns of leisure travel tend to be more diffuse, diverse and less easy to explain than non-leisure trips. For example, Greer and Wall (1979) observed principles of declining traffic volumes from the origin of trips in urban areas as a function of time, money and demand as opposed to just a function of supply. Even so, their resulting model did link demand with supply to identify a series of recreational uses associated with travel distance and blocks of land for leisure available as a series of zones comprising:

- A day trip zone.

- A weekend zone (which may be related to an area of second home ownership).

- A holiday or vacation zone.

The identification of zones or areas of discrete leisure activity has been a dominant feature in relation to the analysis of leisure supply, particularly focused on resources and the way in which these have been accessed and used by different leisure users. Greer and Wall (1979) rejected the simple notion of a simple distance-decay function within each zone, a feature implicit in many transport models in geography, although such models may be a simplification of reality, where multiple use occurs at particular sites.

Elson (1979) examined the responses to solve the spatial problems posed by urban recreationalists in the countryside. These included research on spatial interaction and four types of models were developed to try to explain why people chose and travelled to specific sites or resources. These involved:

- *Trip generation models* (which examine number of trips from the origin area, typically an urban centre).

- *Trip attraction* (which considers the likelihood of each competing or complementary destination to attract people).

- *Models of distribution* (the places to which trips are destined).

- *Assignment models* (which examine how trips are chosen).

Even so, Pigram (1983: 31) highlights the obvious relationship where 'the strength of interaction declines as distance increases . . . this means that recreation sites at a greater distance, or for which the journey is perceived as involving more time, effort or cost, are patronised less'. In most of these models of leisure travel, it is road-based travel which has been a dominant element which the models have tried to reconcile: the major problem these models face is that the car does not follow predictable routes, since the car allows a high degree of flexibility in travel patterns. For this reason, the car deserves special mention given its role in shaping and influencing the supply of leisure travel.

Car-based leisure and recreational travel

Most studies of leisure highlight the importance of the car. Since the 1920s, particularly in the years after the Second World War, the car as a mode of leisure transport has been responsible for a massive expansion in leisure travel. Stradling and Anable (2008) describe the outcome of such travel decisions as a reflection of our obligations, recognitions of opportunities and inclinations, which have made car-based leisure travel a dominant feature in societies with access to motorised transport. It is this access to motorised transport which has posed many planning problems in relation to the supply of leisure resources, where infrastructure not previously designed for leisure use is now being used predominantly for leisure. This has highlighted the following problems in relation to road infrastructure:

● Its suitability to accommodate a large peak of leisure travellers at weekends and during a concentrated summer season.

● The limited capacity of non-leisure road infrastructure, initially designed for traffic to and from non-leisure settings, which has now been adapted to provide access to new leisure environments such as National Parks, which are not of the scale or magnitude to cope with visitor volumes.

But one of the real dampeners upon recent growth in travel as a result of globalisation processes has been the price of oil. Most forms of transport for leisure are dependent upon oil as the basis for energy and this has seen sharp rises in recent years to over US$100 a barrel. Much of the leisure travel growth in the post-war period was been based upon relatively cheap supplies of oil. For example, between 1947 and 2007, the median price of crude oil exceeded US$19.04 per barrel for only half of the time. This has changed dramatically in recent years, with rising petrol prices limiting leisure trips.

A number of seminal studies were undertaken in the late 1960s and 1970s on the impact of the car in terms of leisure and recreation (e.g. Wall's 1972; Coppock and Duffield's (1975). Wall (1972) identified the two principal research methods to analyse recreational activity – namely site studies (of particular facilities or areas) and national studies of travel behaviour. Coppock and Duffield's (1975) survey of recreation and the countryside in Scotland mapped and described patterns of recreational travel, especially those of cara-vanners. It noted the tendency for many recreationalists not to venture far from their car at the destination, also observed by Glyptis' (1981) study of recreationalists using participant observation. A recent study by Connell and Page (2008) updated these seminal studies, mapping the patterns of car usage within Scotland's first National Park and tracing the progress in research on car-based leisure travel since the 1970s. Most of the studies of car-based leisure travel highlighted a range of problems for those locations which attract car-based leisure traffic. Among the problems that occur are congestion, pol-lution, increased risk of accidents and a decline in the quality of the visit experience.

Dickinson *et al.* (2004: 105) point to leisure travel initiatives that have been devised to address problems associated with the car, including:

● Encouraging travel closer to home, to local as opposed to regional facilities.

● Containment/restriction strategies.

● Generation of traffic on uneconomic public transport routes.

● Improving opportunities for cycling and walking, such as the National Cycle Network in the UK and mainland Europe.

● Managing car traffic through the use of parking policy measures such as:

    ● changing the number of available parking spaces;

    ● changes to the location of parking spaces;

    ● parking controls and the fees charged for parking.

But critics such as Stöpher (2004) identified a need for more 'sensible policy di-rections' for transport in the early twenty-first century that encompass the car, rather than deter it, including arguments that consider:

● Encouraging the development and use of less polluting and sustainable engines for cars.

● Accepting that car congestion will never be eliminated and that, as levels rise, policy interventions should be aimed at managing this congestion.

● Recognising that road pricing may be a better option to pursue than conges-tion charging, with a view to supporting fuel-efficient, low-emission car use, varying the pricing of time/day/location of travel.

Ultimately, Stöpher (2004) argues that public transport does not hold the an-swer to congestion, since it is not a new phenomenon (though it is in relation to the car). Instead, policies designed to manage our use of the car more carefully would be more worthwhile than trying to resurrect public transport usage that fitted the needs of previous societies and their economies. Even so, some cities, such as Groningen in Northern Holland, are virtually car-free and cycling

towns to protect the historic city and, in other contexts, the public sector has implemented a range of general actions to manage traffic:

- Promoting alternative travel methods such as rail.
- Limiting private car use by payment parking methods.
- Park and ride schemes to promote private car traffic switching to public transport at key locations outside the city centre.
- Reorganisation of the road network and provision of pedestrian zones.
- The development of cycling and pedestrian tracks to reduce traffic congestion, noise and pollution and to improve the quality of the urban environment for residents and visitors alike.
- Information on websites and in printed form for visitors.
- Tourist coach control systems for managing organised groups.
- Greater integration of local land use and transport planning.
- Enhancement of local and gateway networks, with direct public transport services, including enhanced interchange facilities for people with special needs. (Page 2009)

What these measures highlight is the importance of a growing concern with the environmental impact of leisure travel, which introduces the concept of sustainable travel.

Sustainable leisure transport: an optimistic objective?

There has been a growing interest globally in the effect of transport on the environment, particularly with the effects of climate change and pollution. One response has been to consider the challenges of developing more sustainable options as alternatives to car-based leisure travel to mitigate some of the effects of car-based leisure travel on the environment and places affected by congestion. The basic principles behind sustainability debates are that we need to conserve resources and the environment we have today for future generations to enjoy, which may require restraint or changes to our everyday behaviour in relation to the conspicuous consumption associated with leisure activity, such as car-based travel. According to Lumsdon (2006), leisure destinations have been particularly concerned to seek to reduce car use for travel to and travel within destinations, especially National Parks owing to their sensitive and fragile environmental resource base. As Lumsdon (2006: 749) argues, this has focused on stabilising car use where possible and encouraging bus, rail, cycling and walking as alternative transport strategies. To do this, in the case of bus services, it has required the redesign of services, particularly focused on enhancing the leisure experience so that intrinsic elements of fun and sightseeing are incorporated. But public transport alone is not the only way in which more sustainable forms of leisure travel can be encouraged and developed. According to M. Page (2006: 582),

> Walking and cycling have often been seen as the "Cinderellas" of transport policy, their needs often addressed only after the "main" modes of private and public motorized transport have been considered . . . In the UK, which has more walking and cycling than the USA, but less than much of Europe, walking accounts for 25% of all journeys and 80% of journeys under 1.5 km, with an average of 263 trips made per person per year predominantly on foot. Despite significant falls in usage over recent decades, more trips are made each year using cycle as the main mode (an average of 16 per person) than by surface rail (13) in the UK: However, the average distance travelled per person per year on foot has declined by 20% over the last decade, and the distance cycled by 6%.

Walking is a human necessity for the able-bodied to achieve mobility, to engage in work, social activities and non-work functions. Although the industrial and post-industrial periods have seen a move towards more mechanised forms of transport such as the car, giving people a greater spatial reach and flexibility in travel patterns, walking remains a key activity in everyday life as a leisure activity (Tolley 2003).

M. Page (2006) argues that there are a range of reasons why walking and cycling should be given a greater focus in transport planning and policy for leisure use:

● Walking and cycling are energy-efficient means of mobility, not reliant upon fossil fuels and not contributing to congestion.

● Walking and cycling are more sustainable travel options, contributing much less damage to the environment than motorised forms of travel, with only a limited use of non-renewable resources, and are socially equitable modes of transport because they are more widely available to many sections of the population than motorised forms.

● These modes of transport are less dangerous, with fewer accidents and injuries per distance travelled, and are both healthy forms of transport, since they involve physical activity and a reduction in the risk of cardiovascular disease and other diseases.

But one of the underlying problems in policy terms which M. Page (2006) has identified is the reluctance of many governments to prioritise these two activities if it causes conflict with car users. What this discussion does highlight in relation to transport is the need to find ways to analyse the supply of leisure to understand how to better manage the resources and access to leisure opportunities, particularly the different transport options needed to create more sustainable leisure travel.

Methods of analysing supply: evaluation tools

Analysing the supply of leisure opportunities in any setting or location is an important activity to undertake if you want to understand who is being served by existing provision and who may be served by new forms of provision as well as some of the obstacles to leisure provision. An overriding concern in terms of analysing supply is who is providing the supply and what market conditions are prevailing, which will affect the way in which different organisations make leisure opportunities available. In most societies, the free market economy is the determinant of supply and it exists in the midway point somewhere between no state control and complete state control. The state will often intervene where there is a perceived failure in the market system so that specific forms of provision are not being met. In the case of home-based leisure, much of the provision, as discussed in this chapter and other chapters, is by the private sector which will provide different commercial products and experiences which individuals and households may wish to purchase.

The exception to this is where the state provides television services, such as the BBC, for which a licence fee is levied, requiring consumers to pay for a public broadcasting service they wish to consume. While the next chapter will examine in more detail the role of the public and private sectors, what this section emphasises is some of the techniques used to assess supply and the principles associated with the way in which leisure facilities, products and services are provided out of the home. Many of the principles used to provide leisure resources are based on techniques and tools which have been developed in sociology, geography and planning, with economic concepts used to assess specific themes as highlighted in Table 5.4.

As Chapters 2 and 3 highlighted, the social analysis of leisure by sociologists has a long history. One of the more descriptive techniques used within leisure studies to examine supply was social observation. This was characterised by studies such as Rowntree that involved cataloguing or producing an inventory of supply for a specific location. To illustrate how such inventories were undertaken, a number of brief extracts from a seminal study by Harris (1927), *The Use of Leisure in Bethnal Green: A Survey of Social Conditions in the Borough 1925 to 1926,* is included. This study was based on a one-year investigation where the researcher observed the community in East London to derive what was considered to be an objective picture. While there are some objective features within the study, such as the collation of relevant statistics related to the supply of leisure opportunities and facilities, the study is full of value judgements and commentary reflecting the social status of the observer and their sometimes

Table 5.4   The economist's approach to the analysis of leisure supply

- *Efficiency*: This refers to making the best use of inputs to the supply of leisure, such as ensuring that the maximum number of people benefit from any service (output).
- *Inputs*: This refers to the resources (financial, physical or human) allocated to produce a form of supply.
- *Output*: This will normally refer to the quantity of demand which is served by a specific form of production from inputs allocated. In other words, it is the capacity provided for a service, resource or facility.
- *Capacity at leisure facilities*: This is the capability of the resource being provided to accommodate users, which may be particularly problematic where the resource is a sensitive environment or one that attracts multiple users who do not mix without conflict arising.
- *Productivity*: This is the 'output produced in a given time period per unit of input' (Gratton and Taylor 1988: 112) and may be used to look at labour productivity as well as revenue generation to assess the efficiency of the resource or service being delivered.
- *Costs of production*: this refers to the actual costs involved in terms of inputs (i.e. labour and operating costs as well as income and overall expenditure including the capital used).
- *Pricing of leisure services and goods*: This refers to the ways in which leisure services that are charged for are priced to earn a certain level of profit or return on the investment deployed, reflecting the differing objectives of commercial and public sector supply of leisure resources. For example, Gratton and Taylor (1988) point to the role of price discrimination in the provision of many leisure services, with lower prices for children to encourage leisure use for health reasons. Variable prices may also be charged according to capacity utilisation and a desire to encourage off-peak use, and in the public sector price setting may be undertaken not by operational staff in leisure centres, but by Council committees so that pricing may not always be rational and may be over-simplistic
- *Competition*: This refers to the type of market that exists and the degree of state intervention and regulation as well as the advantages which different suppliers may have in the market. In relation to public sector leisure services, the regulatory environment associated with concepts of Compulsory Competitive Tendering or *Best Value* for money (see Chapter 6) may affect how businesses are permitted to compete and the way limited competition is controlled and managed by a client seeking the service to be provided according to predetermined criteria.
- *Investment decisions for existing and proposed leisure supply and projects*: This is where investment is assessed in relation to the pay-back period over which investment is required and the use of other tools to assess the financing of investment.
- *Cost–benefit analysis of existing and proposed leisure services*: This is a technique designed to try to assess not only the economic costs and direct benefits, but wider benefits that may accrue from a specific investment, such as an improvement to the health of the resident population from additional leisure provision and the indirect benefits to society of reduced health care costs as discussed in Chapter 1.

Source: Based on Gratton and Taylor (1988)

demeaning analysis of working-class leisure in Bethnal Green. For example, Harris (1927: 11) suggested that 'the use that people make of their free time will have a great effect on their character and well-being', which was very much a social deterministic view of how individuals use their free time and its relationship to their perceived character and well-being. Indeed, the study highlighted the notion of undesirable interests, which Harris argued would lead to bad habits amongst the working class, such as a 'love of risk, physical passion, which takes the form of gambling and excessive drinking, tittle tattle, and ennui, which finds an outlet in idling and gossiping in the streets' (Harris 1927: 12). This was seen in juxtaposition to the respectable middle-class values of home-based leisure, which was for many of the residents a virtual impossibility because

This, from all points of view, is the most important of the agencies for the use of leisure, and in a district such as Bethnal Green, it is almost impossible to have satisfactory recreation in the home, owing to housing conditions. (Harris 1927: 14)

This was because the physical structure of the houses and the prevailing social conditions, such as overcrowding, meant that

With practically no privacy, and no private belongings, with the rest of the family using the same room for meals, recreation, and sometimes for sleeping, the [desire] is eventually given up to engage in home-based leisure. (Harris 1927: 14–15)

Yet, as Figure 5.10 suggests, a careful reading of Harris's (1927) survey of leisure supply yields a great many insights on working-class provision in an overcrowded and geographically defined community, with much of the leisure supply focused around the area near to home. In contrast, the occasional days out to recreational sites were described with great gusto, for example going to places such as

Epping forest, the great playground of the East End. It is within easy reach either by train, bus or tram. It is the remains of a vast royal forest, and covers an area of 5,482 acres. (Harris 1927: 64)

These sites were visited on bank holidays and other holidays, with a special social meaning for the users of an area which was saved from deforestation by the Commons Preservation Society in 1871 with support from the Corporation of the City of London. What Figure 5.10 also begins to show is that the setting and scale at which leisure is undertaken within one community highlight the way in which different forms of supply are organised. This also has a salience when it can be supported by oral histories of the period and personal experiences of family life and leisure in this area of the East End of London, with its protracted history of poverty and deprivation.

From this early attempt to analyse supply using participant observation and the production of inventories, other social analytic techniques have been developed and refined, often in conjunction with other disciplines such as geography.

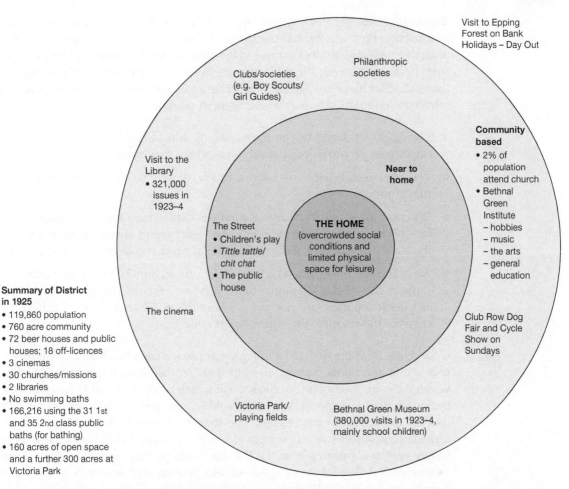

Figure 5.10 Inventory of the supply of leisure in a working-class community: Bethnal Green, East London, 1925–1926

Source: Based on Harris (1927)

For example, research by human geographers in the 1970s on spatial inequalities in service provision within cities and issues of social deprivation also highlighted equivalent issues for the supply of and participation in leisure. Thus, issues such as social inclusion and exclusion have provided the conceptual basis behind the interest in spatially determined research on 'who gets what, where and why', which is based upon the notion of equality.

One of the basic principles used to try to understand the supply of leisure in relation to different social groups and its geographical distribution is associated with how the organisation of leisure supply is delivered (i.e. the provision of resources) based upon *hierarchical principles*. What this means is that the organisation responsible for provision will normally assess the catchment area and potential users and then provide the product or service in relation to that catchment area at different geographical scales. Much of this provision will be based upon access and accessibility to individual sites or facilities. As the previous section on transport highlighted, various constraints will impact upon the use of these different forms of supply, where both time and distance will act as a friction on the potential use of the resource. What this means is that the available time and ability to travel to the resource will decline the further away from home you travel. What is apparent in terms of the supply of resources is that a distinct hierarchy exists, where there are different levels of provision to reflect the population size and catchment in relation to:

- The neighbourhood or community being considered, where a community centre may be provided to meet the needs of that group.

- The local area, where provision at this level may be a recreation ground or playground.

- Different areas within a city or rural districts, where there is a resource or facility provided to meet the needs of a wider group of communities because the facility cannot be viably provided for one individual group or community.

- An entire city or region, where the demand can only be met at that scale because of the specialised nature of the service or facility being provided, such as a central library or art gallery, where the number of users is only sufficient for the resource at a much larger scale.

Underlying this very ordered and logical approach based on hierarchical principles is one additional concept: the *threshold*. A threshold refers to the level at which it becomes economic or the scale at which it becomes viable for an organisation to provide a specific service. In some cases, there is a historical threshold used by organisations who recommend that the supply of different leisure and recreation resources should conform to specific ratios or scale of resource to meet leisure needs. For example, in the UK, the National Playing Fields Association recommended that 2.4 ha of space should be provided for every 1000 of the population during the 1920s. Similarly, the provision of other forms of supply in terms of public open space has been developed in relation to these principles, with access related to the distance from a user's home. According to Patmore (1973), these principles were inherent in the research by the UK Sports Council in the early 1970s where they identified regional differences in provision to advise local government on what strategies to adopt to address weaknesses in the supply of specific sports facilities and infrastructure based on national standards of provision. This type of hierarchical modelling of resources based on population size and thresholds is reflected in Table 5.5. Williams' (1995) hierarchical pattern of public open space provision for urban areas, shown in Table 5.5, is a point we will return to again in Chapter 8 in relation to London. What such hierarchies suggest is that public and private sector organisations can look at the recommended level of provision for specific forms of leisure and then see where there are gaps in provision and where opportunities exist for creating new forms of provision, and the most appropriate scale at which to supply a resource. As Patmore (1973: 479) poignantly argued, 'the effective matching of demand and supply is not merely a matter of academic interest but of great practical importance if the limited finance for recreation is to be spent to yield the greatest benefit', illustrating the continued significance of leisure supply.

Table 5.5   Hierarchical pattern of public open space

Type and main function	Approximate size and distance from home	Characteristics
Regional park Weekend and occasional visits by car or public transport	400 hectares 3.2–8 km	Large areas of natural heathland, common, woodland and parkland. Primarily providing for informal recreation with some non-intensive active recreations. Car-parking at strategic locations.
Metropolitan park Weekend and occasional visits by car or public transport	60 hectares 3.2 km but more when park is larger than 60 hectares	Either natural heath, common, woods or formal parks providing for active and passive recreation. May contain playing fields, provided at least 40 hectares remain for other pursuits. Adequate car-parking.
District parks Weekend and occasional visits on foot, by cycle, car or short bus trip	20 hectares 1.2 km	Landscaped settings with a variety of natural features providing for a range of activities, including outdoor sports, children's play and informal pursuits. Some car-parking.
Local parks For pedestrian visitors	2 hectares 0.4 km	Providing for court games, children's play, sitting out, etc. in a landscaped environment. Playing fields if the park is large enough.
Small local parks Pedestrian visits especially by old people and children, particularly valuable in high-density areas	2 hectares 0.4 km	Gardens, sitting-out areas and children's playgrounds.
Linear open space Pedestrian visits	Variable Where feasible	Canal towpaths, footpaths, disused rail lines, etc., providing opportunities for informal recreation.

Source: Williams (1995)

There are many other techniques which are used to analyse supply and these are developed by the public sector and planners as well as individual organisations that are looking at the profitability of different forms of leisure provision. Some of these techniques and tools will be examined in subsequent chapters. One of the specific tools which both the public and private sector used to analyse supply is forecasting to try to understand and predict future patterns of participation which will then highlight the types of supply which may need to be provided.

Forecasting leisure provision

According to Archer (1987: 77),

> no manager can avoid the need for some form of forecasting: a manager must plan for the future in order to minimise the risk of failure or, more optimistically, to maximise the possibilities of success. In order to plan, he must use forecasts. Forecasts will always be made, whether by guesswork, teamwork or the use of complex models, and the accuracy of the forecasts will affect the quality of the management decision.

Reliable forecasts are essential for managers and decision-makers involved in leisure service provision to try to ensure that adequate supply is available to meet demand, while avoiding oversupply, since this can erode the profitability of their operation. As Veal (2003) suggests, forecasting leisure uses different techniques from across the social sciences and we shall examine these in more detail in Chapter 12.

What is certain about the future of leisure supply is that nothing is certain, and so the variety of methods which are used to try to assess the future for leisure provision have had very limited success, because to understand future changes we need to be able to make certain assumptions about what will change in the future and what will stay the same. This illustrates the difficulty of aligning supply to demand, although the private sector is probably the best suited because their viability as commercial enterprises is determined by their success in meeting consumer needs and so they are more able to align their business activities to consumers in the short term. In contrast, the public sector tends to adopt much longer time horizons in terms of supply because of the way in which local and national government work and the availability of financial resources to make investments in leisure, which are often not prioritised to the same degree as other competing, more pressing needs such as social services.

Summary

What this chapter has highlighted is the comparative absence of research on leisure supply within the existing academic literature. Much of the state-of-the-art research in this area exists within the public and private sectors which are involved in the day-to-day operational issues associated with leisure supply as well as the longer-term strategic planning of supply. This research is normally commercially sensitive and kept confidential. As a result, this is very much a practitioner-focused area of research which is not directly impacted upon by academic research. This is in sharp contrast to what Patmore (1973, 1983) described, where almost 15 years of academic endeavour helped to shape leisure policy and practice. Thus, much of the research in leisure studies during the 1960s and early 1970s, by a limited number of academics, did affect the thinking behind some aspects of supply, particularly issues related to transport and hierarchies. The public sector funded the research and embraced the results. However, as the professionalisation of public and private sector leisure managers has developed, they have assumed more of the long-term responsibility for developing their own approaches and methods of analysing leisure supply, only using academic expertise on an *ad hoc* basis in many cases where specific advice or techniques of analysis are required. They have used many of the tools and techniques which are discussed in this chapter and examined in different parts of the book, with the only notable exception being the impact of Geographical Information Systems (GIS) research, recognised for its potential to build in many of the elements of supply and demand within a geographical setting as illustrated by the research by Connell and Page (2008) in relation to Loch Lomond and the Trossachs National Park. What this chapter shows is that an understanding of leisure supply is critical in terms of understanding what is happening now in relation to the use of resources and what may happen in the future. It is also clear that organisations play a crucial role in the provision and management of different leisure opportunities, and a critical concept in the understanding of leisure supply is the notion of a leisure resource. The analysis of leisure resources has a long history and the field of outdoor recreation (see Chapter 11 for a more extended discussion and also Pigram and Jenkins 2006) uses many techniques and tools to analyse the effects and impacts of leisure activity. In the case of these impacts, both the public and private sectors have a crucial role to play in managing places and spaces as well as the environmental resources which often underpin the use of leisure. For this reason, the next chapter will examine the role of the public and private sectors in relation to leisure.

Discussion questions

1. What is a leisure resource?

2. How do we approach the notion of supply in relation to leisure?

3. What is the role of the twin concepts of hierarchical provision and threshold in relation to leisure supply?

4. How would you go about classifying different leisure resources?

References

Archer, B.H. (1987) 'Demand forecasting and estimation', in J.R.B. Ritchie and C.R. Goeldner (eds) *Travel, Tourism and Hospitality Research,* Wiley: New York, pp. 77–85.

Bhatti, M. (2006) '"When I'm in the garden I can create my own paradise": Homes and gardens in later life', *Sociological Review* 54 (2): 318–41.

Bhatti, M. and Church, A. (2000) 'I never promised you a rose garden: gender, leisure and home-making', *Leisure Studies* 19 (3): 183–97.

Bhatti, M. and Church, A. (2001) 'Cultivating natures: homes and gardens in late modernity', *Sociology* 35 (2): 365–83.

Campbell, C. (1967) 'An approach to research in recreation geography', Occasional Paper 7, Department of Geography, University of British Columbia, Vancouver, pp. 85–90.

Cherry, G. (1984) 'Leisure and the home: a review of changing relationships, *Leisure Studies* 3 (1): 35–52.

Chubb, M. and Chubb, H. (1981) *One Third of Our Time? An Introduction to Recreation Behaviour and Resources,* Wiley: New York.

Church, A. (2003) 'Gardening', in J. Jenkins and J. Pigram (eds) *Encyclopedia of Leisure and Outdoor Recreation,* Routledge: London, pp. 195–6.

Clawson, M. and Knetsch, J. (1966) *The Economics of Outdoor Recreation,* Johns Hopkins University Press: Baltimore, MD.

Clawson, M., Held, R. and Stoddart, C. (1960) *Land for the Future,* Johns Hopkins University Press: Baltimore, MD.

Connell, J. (2004) 'The purest of human pleasures: the characteristics and motivations of garden visitors in Great Britain', *Tourism Management* 25 (3): 229–47.

Connell, J. (2005) 'Managing gardens for visitors in Great Britain: a story of continuity and change', *Tourism Management* 26 (2): 185–201.

Connell, J. and Page, S.J. (2008) 'Exploring the spatial patterns of car-based tourist travel in Loch Lomond and Trossachs National Park, Scotland', *Tourism Management* 29 (3): 561–80.

Constantine, S. (1981) 'Amateur gardening and popular recreation in the 19th and 20th centuries', *Journal of Social History* 14: 389–403.

Coppock, J.T. and Duffield, B. (1975) *Outdoor Recreation in the Countryside: A Spatial Analysis,* Macmillan: London.

Crouch, D. (1989) 'Patterns of cooperation in the cultures of outdoor leisure – the case of allotments', *Leisure Studies* 8(2): 189–99.

Dickinson, J., Calver, S., Watters, K. and Wilks, K. (2004) 'Journeys to heritage attractions in the UK: a case study of National Trust visitors in the south west', *Journal of Transport Geography* 12: 103–13.

Downes, T. (2002) 'Blending play, practices and performance: children's use of the computer at home', *Journal of Educational Enquiry* 3 (2): 21–34.

Driver, B. (2003) 'Experiences', in J. Jenkins and J. Pigram (eds) *Encyclopedia of Leisure and Outdoor Recreation,* Routledge: London, pp. 168–71.

Elson, M. (1979) *State of the Art Review 12: Countryside Trip-making,* Sports Council/ Social Science Research Council: London.

Fine, G. (1989) 'Mobilising fun: provisioning resources in leisure worlds', *Sociology of Sport Journal* 6 (4): 319–44.

Gershuny, J. (2002) 'Social leisure and home IT: a panel time-diary approach', *IT and Society* 1 (1): 54–72.

Gilman, C. (1972) *The Home,* University of Illinois Press: Chicago (reprinted 1903 edition).

Glyptis, S. (1981) 'People at play in the countryside', *Geography* 66 (4): 277–85.

Glyptis, S. and Chambers, D. (1982) 'No place like home', *Leisure Studies* 1 (3): 247–62.

Gratton, C. and Taylor, P. (1988) *Economics of Leisure Services Management,* Longman: Harlow.

Greer, T. and Wall, G. (1979) 'Recreational hinterlands: a theoretical and empirical analysis', in G. Wall (ed.) *Recreational Land Use in Southern Ontario,* Department of Geography Publication Series No. 14, University of Waterloo.

Halkett, I. (1978) 'The recreational use of private gardens', *Journal of Leisure Research* 10 (1): 13–20.

Hall, C.M. and Page, S.J. (2006) *The Geography of Tourism and Recreation: Environment, Place and Space,* 3rd edn, Routledge: London.

Harris, C. (1927) *The Use of Leisure in Bethnal Green: A Survey of Social Conditions in the Borough 1925 to 1926,* The Lindsey Press: London.

Hart, W. (1966) *A Systems Approach to Park Planning,* International Union for the Conservation of Nature: Morges, Switzerland.

Havighurst, R. and Feigenbaum, K. (1959) 'Leisure and lifestyle', *The American Journal of Sociology* 64 (4): 396–484.

Haywood, L., Kew, F., Bramham, P., Spink, J., Capenhurst, J. and Henry, I. (1989) *Understanding Leisure,* Stanley Thornes: Cheltenham.

Hodgkinson, T. (2007) *How to be Idle,* Penguin: London.

Hodgkinson, T. and Kieran, D. (2008) *Book of Idle Pleasure,* Ebury: London

Jenkins, J. and Pigram, J. (2003) 'Introduction', in J. Jenkins and J. Pigram (eds) *Encyclopedia of Leisure and Outdoor Recreation,* Routledge: London, pp. vii–xiii.

Kleiber, D. (2000) 'The neglect of relaxation', *Journal of Leisure Research* 32 (1): 82–8.

Kreutzwiser, R. (1989) 'Supply', in G. Wall (ed.) *Outdoor Recreation in Canada,* Wiley: Toronto, pp. 21–41.

Lumsdon, L. (2006) 'Factors affecting the design of tourism bus services', *Annals of Tourism Research* 33 (3): 748–66.

Madge, C. and Harrison, T. (1939) *Britain by Mass Observation,* Penguin: Harmonsworth.

Matley, I. (1976) *The Geography of International Tourism,* Resource Paper No. 76-1, Association of American Geographers, Washington, DC.

Mcintyre, N. (2003) 'Desire', in J. Jenkins and J. Pigram (eds) *Encyclopedia of Leisure and Outdoor Recreation,* Routledge: London, p. 113.

McLennan, R., Inkson, K., Dakin, S., Dewe, P. and Elkin, G. (1987) *People and Enterprises: Human Behaviour in New Zealand Organisations,* Rinehart Winston: Auckland.

Mercer, D. (2003) 'Recreation', in J. Jenkins and J. Pigram (eds) *Encyclopedia of Leisure and Outdoor Recreation,* Routledge: London, pp. 412–15.

Mihaliĉ, T. (2003) 'Supply', in J. Jenkins and J. Pigram (eds) *Encyclopedia of Leisure and Outdoor Recreation,* Routledge: London, pp. 489–92.

Morgan, D. (2003) 'Resource base', in J. Jenkins and J. Pigram (eds) *Encyclopedia of Leisure and Outdoor Recreation,* Routledge: London, pp. 430–2.

Morley, D. (1986) *Family Television: Cultural Power and Domestic Leisure,* Verso: London.

Olechnowicz, A. (1997) *Working-class Housing in England between the Wars: The Becontree Estate,* Clarendon Press: Oxford.

Page, M. (2006) 'Non-motorised transportation policy', in K. Button and D. Hensher (eds) *Handbook of Transport Strategy, Policy and Institutions,* Elsevier: Oxford, pp. 581–96.

Page, S. J. (1998) 'Transport for recreation and tourism', in B. Hoyle and R. Knowles (eds) *Modern Transport Geography,* 2nd edn, Wiley: Chichester, pp. 217–40.

Page, S. J. (2009) *Transport and Tourism,* 3rd edn, Pearson: Harlow.

Patmore, J.A. (1973) 'Patterns of supply', *The Geographical Journal* 139 (October): 473–82.

Patmore, J.A. (1983) *Recreation and Resources: Leisure Patterns and Leisure Places,* Blackwell: Oxford.

Pearce, D. (1995) *Tourism Today: A Geographical Analysis,* Longman: London.

Pigram, J. (1983) *Outdoor Recreation Management,* Croom Helm: London.

Pigram, J.J. and Jenkins, J. (2006) *Outdoor Recreation Management,* 2nd edn, Routledge: London.

Ravenscroft, N. (1992) *Recreation Planning and Development,* Macmillan: Basingstoke.

Roberts, K. (2004) *The Leisure Industries,* Palgrave: Basingstoke.

Rowe, D. (2006) 'Leisure, media and mass communication', in C. Rojek, S. Shaw and A. Veal (eds) *A Handbook of Leisure Studies,* Palgrave: Basingstoke, pp. 317–34.

Saunders, P. and Williams, P. (1988) 'The constitution of the home: towards a research agenda', *Housing Studies* 3 (2): 81–93.

Schaeffer, K. and Sclar, E. (1975) *Access for All: Transportation and Urban Growth,* Penguin: London.

Stöpher, P. (2004) 'Reducing road congestion', *Transport Policy* 11: 117–31.

Stradling, S. and Anable, J. (2008) 'Individual transport patterns', in R. Knowles, J. Shaw and I. Docherty (eds) *Transport Geographies: Mobilities, Flows and Spaces,* Blackwell: Oxford, pp. 179–95.

Thibault, A. (2008) *Public and Civic Leisure in Quebec: Dynamic, Democratic, Passion-Driven and Fragile,* Presses de l'Université du Québec: Québec.

Thorpe, H. (1970) 'A new deal for allotments: solutions to a pressing land use problem', *Area* 2 (3): 1–8.

Tolley, R. (ed.) (2003) *Creating Sustainable Transport: Planning for Walking and Cycling,* Woodhead: Cambridge.

Veal, A. (2003) 'Forecasting', in J. Jenkins and J. Pigram (eds) *Encyclopedia of Leisure and Outdoor Recreation,* Routledge: London, pp. 184–5.

Veal, A. and Lynch, R. (2001) *Australian Leisure,* 2nd edn, Longman: Sydney.

Vedenin, Y. and Miroschnichenko, N. (1971) 'Evaluation of the national environment for recreation purposes', *Ekistics* 184: 223–36.

Vilhelmson, B. and Thulin, E. (2008) 'Virtual mobility, time use and the place of the home', *Tijdschrift voor Economische en Sociale Geografie* 99 (5): 602–18.

Wall, G. (1972) 'Socioeconomic variations in pleasure trip patterns: the case of Hull car owners', *Transactions of the Institute of British Geographers* 57, 45–58.

Williams, S. (1995) *Recreation in the Urban Environment,* Routledge: London.

Willmott, P. (1963) *The Evolution of a Community: A Study of Dagenham after 40 Years,* Routledge and Kegan Paul: London.

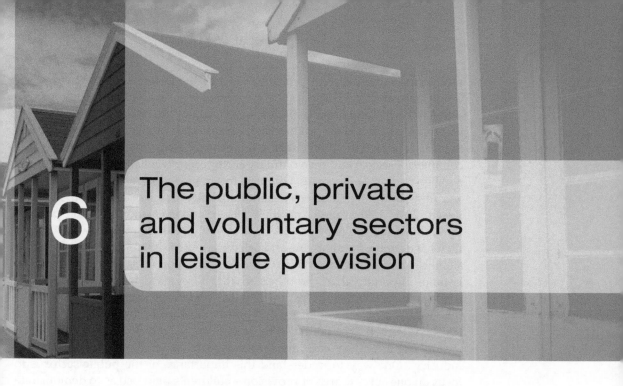

6 The public, private and voluntary sectors in leisure provision

Learning outcomes

After reading this chapter, you should be able to:

- Identify the role of the public sector in policy making to guide the development of leisure activities

- Describe the functions and activities of the public, private and voluntary sectors in leisure provision

- Understand the current debates associated with how these different organisations collectively meet different leisure needs

Introduction

In Chapter 5, the important role of organisations in the supply of leisure was briefly introduced. In this chapter we will explore the involvement of these organisations in considerably more detail, focusing on the political context in which leisure provision occurs and the characteristics of the public, commercial and voluntary sectors. The political context is largely conditioned through the policy frameworks which are determined by governments, their political philosophies and different priorities towards the leisure sector. What is clear from Chapters 2 and 5 is that the provision of leisure is a complex amalgam of different bodies and organisations that collectively are responsible for the form of supply which is then produced and consumed. In this chapter, we explore the way in which the public sector, the private sector (often referred to as the commercial sector) and the voluntary sector coexist, collaborate, work in partnership and in some cases compete to provide different forms of leisure according to the stated objectives and rationale of each organisation. As Torkildsen (2005: 129) argued, 'people's leisure and recreation is made possible through a wide range of providers' and many of these roles now overlap as they have evolved and organisations have adopted different roles and responsibilities towards leisure. While no one organisation or category of provision is more important than the other, what is recognised in many countries is that a political framework for leisure policy and provision exists. As a result of this, we need a clear understanding of the public sector because, as Robinson (2004: xi) argued, 'the public sector is both the largest provider of sport and leisure opportunities and the largest source of employment within this industry'. One way to understand this importance of the public sector is to focus on one specific area of provision – children's play – so as to demonstrate why the public sector often takes a lead role.

Understanding the role of the public, commercial and voluntary sectors in leisure: the case of children's play

The importance of the public, commercial and voluntary sectors in leisure provision is well illustrated in the case of provision for children to play. As Collins (1995) observed, children's play was the *little orphan Annie* in the British leisure system in the 1990s, with provision being divided between different organisations within the voluntary, public and private sectors. While this situation has changed somewhat since Collins' research, it does illustrate a key theme which this chapter will address: the relative importance of the public, commercial and voluntary sectors in fulfilling the need for leisure in society through provision. Responsibility for provision of children's play within local authorities in the UK was divided between a multitude of departments, with no unifying body responsible in each authority. Collins (1995) observed that children's play was provided by a whole host of organisations, starting with district and parish councils in the UK, with provision in housing areas, adventure playgrounds, play centres, after-school clubs, holiday play schemes and the youth service. It may also be provided by social service departments, education authorities and hospital management (i.e. provision for sick children), as well as by voluntary organisations such as in after-school playgroups, out-of-school clubs and youth clubs. In addition, commercial operators are involved, ranging from individual child minders through to operators providing play schemes, indoor play centres and nurseries. These all feature in the overall provision for children's play.

Play is important in children's everyday lives as a form of leisure, as it provides opportunities for children to explore their own independence and interact with others while also contributing to their health, growth and development, according to Torkildsen (2005). Conversely, children deprived of play opportunities will have lower levels of physical activity and be less able to develop social skills, which will potentially impact upon their emotional intelligence and its development as well as their self-confidence and overall personal development. This is an important area of leisure provision because play provides children with opportunities to exercise and explore and freedom, as discussed in Chapter 1. The entire area of children's play has also been surrounded with controversy because of increased bureaucracy associated with the care of children, security screening of people who work with children and legislation which has increased concerns about organisations' duty of care for children. Yet, as Collins has shown, the National Playing Fields Association in the UK has been campaigning for government support for children's play since the late 1930s, supported by many voluntary agencies. While different organisations have taken an interest in this area of provision, Collins illustrates the fundamental importance of ensuring that children have a place to play so that their leisure needs are met. What this example illustrates is the need for an overarching understanding of how the public sector can fulfil an important coordinating role to draw together the different stakeholders involved in children's play so that its strategic development is integrated in line with clear policies that ensure children's needs are met in a cohesive and rational way. For this reason, it is useful to understand what we mean by the term *public sector*.

The public sector

As Page and Connell (2009: 309) argue, 'the public sector is a somewhat nebulous grouping of organisations which comprise a range of government and government based organisations. The unifying focus is to deliver government policy and they have power to make decisions of strategic importance'. Public sector bodies with an interest in leisure are linked together in a complex set of working relationships, with their principal purpose to work towards objectives that improve the public good. To achieve these objectives, the public sector uses revenue which it generates through taxation to develop and then implement policies and initiatives which will benefit the resident population, particularly the communities which it serves. In the UK, the Audit Commission acknowledged that over £200 billion was spent each year by 11,000 public sector bodies, illustrating their fundamental importance to the society and economy, not least in leisure where intervention to address social problems may utilise sport and leisure, as Case Study 6.1 shows.

Case Study 6.1	Public sector intervention to address deviant leisure – antisocial behaviour and leisure

An Audit Commission (2009) report entitled *Tired of Hanging Around: Using Sport and Leisure Activities to Prevent Anti-Social Behaviour by Young People* illustrated how leisure and recreation activities could be used as a tool to positively engage with young people at risk of entering the criminal justice system. The purpose of such engagement was to use leisure and sport to divert attention away from antisocial behaviour and deviant activity as a leisure time-filler. This is because antisocial behaviour is a criminal offence in the UK. Such behaviour has been managed through Antisocial Behaviour Orders that cost around £2,500 for each order. In 2005, for example, over 1500 such orders were served on young people. Antisocial behaviour in youth leisure time (as a deviant form of leisure) may take many forms but among the most commonly observed amongst youth were:

- vehicle vandalism;
- littering;
- graffiti-tagging;
- false alarm calls to the emergency services;
- harassing local community members;
- excessive noise;
- behaviour that generates neighbour complaints (e.g. rowdiness and being a nuisance);
- drunken behaviour in a public place, such as a park or street corner (which in Scotland is associated with the cult of drinking a tonic wine from a religious establishment in Devon – Buckfast Abbey's, as it is a fortified wine which causes the participant to get drunk very quickly and relatively cheaply);
- drug taking or dealing.

Source: Based on Audit Commission (2009: 10)

The reasons cited by young people for engaging in such deviant behaviour in their leisure time, according to the Audit Commission, were: bullying experienced by the individual, poor environmental surroundings and feelings of dejection, as well as a perception that there was nothing to do. By using sport and leisure, projects targeted at first-time offenders or at-risk individuals are run by government-funded groups who seek to divert youth attention to schemes which will build their self-esteem. These schemes seek to develop the very qualities highlighted earlier in the chapter in relation to the positive benefits of children's play so they can become active citizens and participants in society rather than being isolated and deviant.

As the Audit Commission report noted, it cost £200,000 to care for a young person during their time in the criminal justice system by the age of 16, so targeted initiatives by the public sector costing up to £50,000 may be money well spent. Coalter (1996) identified the value of using sport and leisure to address antisocial behaviour, which is a well-documented relationship, with the Audit Commission (2009) report suggesting that if only 1 in 10 of young offenders were diverted from such behaviour, it would save the criminal justice system £113 million a year. Even so, the Audit Commission criticised the short-run term of many such initiatives by the public sector which would inevitably have a limited impact on antisocial behaviour as projects are constantly looking for additional funding. This is one example of where public sector support may seek to use sport and leisure with specific political objectives and outcomes, which in this case was the reduction of antisocial behaviour.

In many countries, the organisations which make up the public sector are not particularly commercially oriented but they do have to work with commercial objectives in mind to justify the efficiency with which they deliver their services. National policy is normally formulated by national government organisations (see Siehl 2000 for an example of post-war national recreation policies in the USA) with economic and social factors in mind, and they often fund other government agencies which operate at arm's length from government as quasi-autonomous non-governmental organisations (QUANGOs). For example, in the UK, the pattern of funding and structure of sports policy is illustrated in Figure 6.1 which

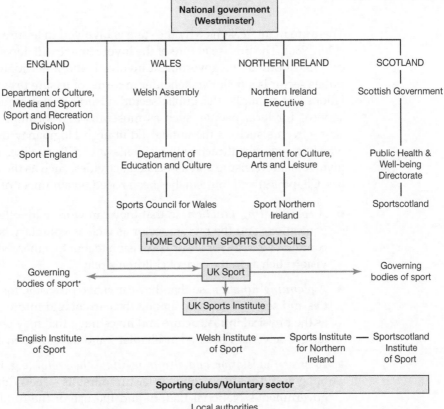

*These now have links with Sport Councils to help increase participation.

Figure 6.1 The structure of UK sports policy

highlights the central government funding for Sport England which then funds the body UK Sport.

Funding then cascades down the system to voluntary bodies. This is complemented at the local level by local authorities who are responsible for a defined area, where there is a democratic system of electing representatives from the local community and a full-time staff within a local council. This system is similar in many countries, as illustrated by Robinson (2004):

> The structures for delivering sport and leisure within the UK are complex falling into four broad sectors: local government, education (schools, further education and higher education establishments), the voluntary sector made up of clubs and national governing bodies and the private sector. *(Robinson 2004: 3)*

Therefore, from the initial discussion of the public sector it is apparent that there is a clear rationale for state involvement in leisure provision in view of its wide-ranging role, to which attention now turns.

Rationale for state involvement in leisure provision

There are many reasons why the state is involved in leisure provision (Coalter *et al.* 1986). The precise nature of the involvement will depend upon the political philosophy of the government involved, and it is widely accepted that the public sector is a major stakeholder in forms of leisure provided for the population. For example, the public sector subsidises and manages facilities and services for local people, such as museums and swimming pools, and also stages events such as the annual Edinburgh Hogmanay on New Year's Eve which are equally attractive to residents and visitors alike. The nature of state involvement in leisure and associated activities, such as the cultural industries (see Chapter 9) and tourism, has been based on a number of principles:

- *A coordinating function*, so that they can work with other government organisations and the private sector as well as voluntary bodies to develop a common strategy for leisure provision to join together the multitude of provision such as in the case of children's play.

- *A planning function*, so that they can make provision for the types of facilities and services required among the current and future population as well as the physical infrastructure and investment that may be needed for future leisure needs as discussed in Chapter 5 and developed in detail in Chapter 7.

- *To create legislation and also to regulate the sector* (e.g. in relation to gambling and drinking alcohol as leisure pursuits – see White 1999 on the UK government's National Lottery and the use of the funds for leisure projects), so that growth and development issues are managed in a way which is tailored to government objectives as well as community needs.

- *To stimulate the sector*, by providing incentives to achieve development and other social objectives, such as employment generation.

- *Marketing and promotion*, to raise public awareness of government strategies and programmes such as healthy living and the importance of leisure activities to achieve these objectives.

- *Intervention* in the free market system where there is a perceived market failure, where different leisure facilities may not be provided without public sector assistance or where there is a demonstrable benefit from intervention such as in the case of antisocial behaviour.

- *To protect the public interest* and to mediate between competing interests so that the immediate short-term economic gains are balanced with longer-term needs. This may seem an acceptable goal within a democratic society, but in some countries where there is not a tradition of democracy, the public interest may not always be served by the public sector.

In other words, we need to recognise that leisure provision is part of the political system and that a number of key concepts affect the way provision is managed and provided in the public sector: first is the notion of accountability in relation to the spending and provision which results; second is the diverse role of stakeholders whose interests and activities need to be recognised and accommodated. Much of what the public sector provides at a national and local level in relation to leisure is determined through leisure policy, to which attention now turns.

Policy making and the state: the case of leisure policy

According to Coalter (2006: 162),

> The history of public leisure policy in the United Kingdom (but also elsewhere) has been characterized by an essential duality. Government involvement and investment has a dual purpose of extending the social rights of individuals' citizenship while recognizing the potential wider social benefits associated with leisure provision.

and so we need to understand what the term leisure policy means. Coalter (2006) talks about the duality of policy and this refers to the sometimes conflicting objectives which leisure professionals face: on the one hand they have to focus on operational issues, such as ensuring value for money; and on the other, they have to focus on social priorities which may not necessarily be profitable. Even so, there are debates on the level of policy intervention that is needed in any given society in relation to leisure because 'many find the idea of leisure policy a contradiction in terms. How can one promote government intervention in an area of life which, almost by definition, is self-governed by the autonomous citizen?' (Bramham *et al.* 1993: 1). But without a degree of intervention, many of us would not be able to enjoy the range of services and experiences we consume without the level of support, coordination or policy frameworks developed by the public sector.

The term *policy* is frequently used to denote the direction and objectives an organisation wishes to pursue over a set period of time. According to Turner (1997), the policy process is a function of three interrelated issues:

- The intentions of political and other key actors.

- The way in which decisions and non-decisions are made.

- The implications of these decisions.

There are various factors which shape policy making, such as the political environment, different values and ideas prevailing within society, where power and decision making are based as well as the different types of organisations and institutions which exist within a country. At a theoretical level, policy making helps to understand how people make decisions that affect others. Therefore, policy making is important within leisure because it helps us to understand the political nature of provision, resulting from policies which have been developed along with the sources of power which exist in terms of the policy making that shapes the approach to leisure. It is also useful to understand the different choices made by governments in terms of the approaches they adopt towards leisure and the way in which they assess the effectiveness of the policies they implement. Policy making is a continuous process and Figure 6.2 outlines a

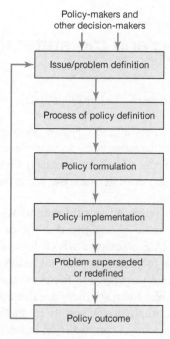

Figure 6.2 The policy-making process

Source: Adapted from Turner (1997)

simplified model of the process that is applicable to the way leisure issues are considered by government bodies.

According to Henry (2001), public policy (i.e. policy developed in the public sector) includes the actions of governments, both their stated intentions as well as the unintended consequences of the policies they had considered and rejected and options they had not considered. As a result, Lowi (1972) (cited in Henry 2001) identified four types of public policy which focus on:

- *Distributive policies*, which are likely to benefit all of the population without any particular targeting, such as the funding of sport (see Figure 6.1 as an example).

- *Redistributive policies*, which are designed to focus on one particular group or section of the population, such as the unemployed and leisure provision and those with particular needs such as the disabled.

- *Constituent policies*, which set out the procedures to be followed within society.

- *Regulative policies*, which are associated with the management of the behaviour of the population, such as no smoking in public buildings or public places.

What this means for leisure is that there is a whole mix of policies which can be targeted directly at leisure or may have an unintended effect on leisure. Much of the state intervention implies a level of activity to develop the rights of citizens (who also have obligations as was highlighted in Case Study 6.1) in relation to leisure (see Coalter 2006 for a more detailed discussion of this concept). For example, education policy may have specific objectives that impact upon leisure provision, such as encouraging sport and active participation by children, which then require the provision of specific facilities or the out-of-hours use of school leisure facilities by the public (i.e. mixed use). In addition, the issue of the power of the professionals in the public sector who set and implement policy decisions needs to be recognised, as emphasised in Chapter 5.

History of state involvement in leisure policy and provision

According to Bull *et al.* (2003: 168), 'the historical development of policy for leisure is obviously closely linked to the historical development of leisure itself' and this chapter should be read in conjunction with Chapter 2. National leisure policies have been characterised by a range of approaches that span a spectrum from a free market orientation to those based on planned resource allocation. The market-oriented view has been pursued on the premise that centralised state control of leisure produces an unwieldy and often unresponsive service requiring unnecessarily high subsidies from state taxation. By introducing a greater degree of private sector involvement and competition it is argued that improved services should result and the need for public subsidies should diminish. In contrast, supporters of the regulated planned response towards state involvement in leisure have pointed to classical economic theory which recognises that, in a free market economy, supply imperfections result. State intervention in the market economy is justified to rectify supply imperfections on social efficiency and environmental grounds to avoid inequalities. Consequently, we can identify a wide range of areas in which the public sector is involved in leisure, especially at the local level, a feature highlighted earlier in relation to Figure 6.1 on sport policy in the UK. What Figure 6.3 shows is that the scope and scale of local government provision are diverse and vary between council areas but a distinguishable series of spheres of involvement are evident. This has both a historic and a contemporary element as long-standing areas of involvement are sometimes reviewed and supplanted by new initiatives and trends which can add to the leisure portfolio managed by the public sector.

Thus, government intervention is sometimes characterised in terms of two simple positions: to *facilitate* or *regulate* a particular activity and, in some cases, to bring order to the different components of the leisure system so that the public sector and other agencies can operate in harmony for the wider public good. This is because it is often acknowledged by researchers that within the wider policy universe (which comprises the organisations, groups, associations and businesses as well as the stakeholders involved in leisure), these diverse interests coexist in a fragmented manner. Bull *et al.* (2003) refer to the existence of policy communities among these fragmented groupings who have a common interest focused on a particular area of policy. As Weed (2001) suggests, these policy communities may have a wide range of relationships, from a very tightly organised identity through to a very loosely structured format. Among the defining features of these policy communities are their membership, interdependencies, relationships with the communities they interact with and their dependence upon resources to function. It is also important to recognise that the policy community may also suffer from interference from external bodies, where its objectives may be either supplanted or enhanced. These policy communities have to be engaged by the public sector through a process of consultation and partnership working as part of the normal policy development process. The consultation process is usually used to consider the varying views and needs from across other public sector organisations and the commercial and voluntary sectors.

Henry (2001) argues that we can trace the evolution of leisure policy in many countries, although the specific history will vary by country as the study by Bramham *et al.* (1993) suggests. Table 6.1 shows how political ideology (i.e. the different political views and philosophies that shape political groups and parties) will change with governments and influence policy making through time. This means that policy will always be in a state of flux and evolving through time, thereby influencing the shape and direction of leisure policies within different governments. Indeed, Henry has suggested that the past 30 years in the UK have seen the delivery of leisure services by local governments subject to major ideological shifts and greater financial and political pressure in terms of its

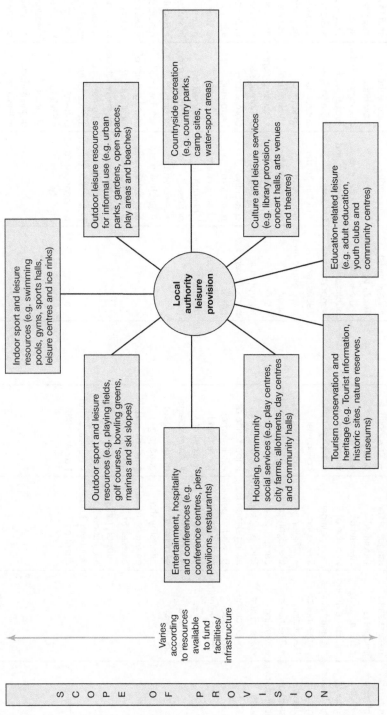

Figure 6.3 Scope of local authority leisure provision

Sources: Based on Torkildsen (2005: 132); Authors

Table 6.1 Eras in the evolution of leisure policy in the UK – a summary of key characteristics

Pre-1780	1780–1840	1841–1900	1901–1939	1939–1945	1945–1976	1976–1984	1985–1997	1998–
• *Ad hoc* state intervention permits certain forms of leisure in the cities • The country-side and leisure are largely unregulated and based on ancient customs and habits	• The state develops measures to suppress popular forms of leisure during the early stages of the Industrial Revolution • The rise of a working-class leisure consciousness organised around voluntary bodies (i.e. clubs and societies)	• The evolution of the later stages of the Industrial Revolution and rise of new political ideologies • Challenge to the eighteenth-century laissez faire philosophies as legislation is passed to permit local authority provision • Growing role of philanthropic efforts by the emerging middle classes to support rational recreation via voluntary bodies/charities	• Growing state involvement • New political philosophies such as the labour movement and collectivist movement (e.g. 1917 Inquiry into the Munitions Workers and importance of leisure time) for rest and relaxation • Antecedents of the welfare state (e.g. gardens and council houses in the 1920s and 1930s) • Holidays with Pay Act 1938	• Second World War	• The founding of the welfare state • Collectivist ideals to support the case for public sector support in the 1950s for the arts, leisure and sport • Leisure accepted as part of everyday needs • Maturity of the public sector model	• Rise of 'new right' political philosophy based on reducing state involvement and funding • Return to the eighteenth-century ideology of the minimal state role to create the maximum freedom for the individual to choose • Labelled the 'Thatcher Years' with a dogmatic adherence to political ideology to implement policy direction in the economy and society	• A gradual easing of the most extreme 'new right' ideology with the evolution of a more flexible approach to state involvement • Development of Compulsory Competitive Tendering to create competition and outsourcing of leisure activities and management of local authority leisure resources • Formation of the National Lottery • Shift to voluntary organisations in leisure provision	• New Labour philosophy and a shift towards a more responsible 'market system' in leisure provision by the state • Greater focus on partnerships (especially the voluntary sector and the 'Third Way') • Emphasis on social inclusion, with leisure, sport and culture as tools to address deficiencies in social exclusion • Regulation of global media companies • Development of Trusts in the voluntary sector with funding rooted via the National Lottery as one source to supplement state resources for leisure • Growing role of the commercial sector in health and fitness provision

Sources: Based on Henry (2001); Coalter (2006); Borsay (2006); Authors

direction and what is provided for the population. The politics of leisure service provision examined by Henry (2001) highlights that policy analysis has acquired an important role in seeking to understand the changing balance and role of the public, private and voluntary sectors in terms of leisure provision.

These arguments have been taken a stage further by Coalter (2006: 163), who indicated that

> the politics of leisure policy have been characterised by another duality – a frequently strong political and ideological rhetoric about the importance of various aspects of leisure provision has been combined with government reluctance to be involved directly . . . Much leisure provision was a non-statutory responsibility of local government and the voluntary sector.

So public sector involvement in leisure policy is not as clear cut as we may initially think. It is not just a simple cause-and-effect relationship: policy does not necessarily lead to provision. Coalter argues that central government interest in the changing role of policy for leisure can largely be dated to the 1960s in the UK, and at other points in time as the review of leisure policies for individual European countries contained in Bramham *et al.* (1993) and summarised in Table 6.2 suggests. While the UK has been through various phases, as Table 6.1

Table 6.2 Schematic outline of the evolution of leisure policies in France, Spain and Germany

FRANCE

1945–1959:	Post-war reconstruction and rebuilding of national/civic pride and popular leisure culture
1959–1980:	Centralised planning in an era of economic prosperity
1981–1991:	New policy development amid economic uncertainty

SPAIN

1939–1975:	Franco dictatorship with the state controlling all aspects of social and economic life. Modernisation period in 1950s and 1960s with festivals for local people and the growth of international tourism
1976–1982:	Transition to a liberalised politics
1982–1992:	Leisure policy under socialism

GERMANY

1848–1918:	Rise of the workers' movement and rational recreation movement
1918–1932:	Weimar Republic and new leisure markets based on social democracy
1933–1945:	National Socialism and the cult of the strong leader
1945–1969:	Reconstruction of leisure markets in Federal Republic of Germany
1969–1982:	Politics of coalition and state socialism with quality of life issues/social inclusivity in leisure and recreation
1982–1989:	Shift towards tourism in leisure policy
1989–:	Reunification and refocusing on work-based policies

Source: Based on Bramham *et al.* (1993)

suggests, with a golden age of social-democratic leisure policy ending in the 1970s, Table 6.2 shows a degree of similarity in a number of other countries and differences in others, depending on the ideological shifts in the politics of the respective governments.

Henry (2001) traced different phases of state involvement in leisure service provision and this helps to explain why there has been a constantly evolving pattern during the twentieth century to create different structures in various countries to deliver local government services. In the UK, for example, in 1974 local authority reorganisation created larger areas and in some cases these new areas created large leisure service departments to provide local provision. This was also accompanied by a policy focus on leisure as 'one of the community's everyday needs' (DOE 1975) which set out the planning roles for local government with respect to leisure (White 1992) in relation to coordinating and leading the planning function to manage the use of resources for leisure, which will be returned to in the next chapter. Central government devolved much of the policy making for leisure to agencies such as the former Countryside Commission and Sports Council (also see Travis 1978). Yet this situation, as with most countries, is in a constant state of flux, with local government in England, for example, being reorganised again in 2009 to try to derive greater economies of scale from the larger authorities and to reduce administrative costs. In 2009, some 55 county and district councils were absorbed into nine unitary authorities, with forecast savings of £100 million through streamlining administrative and delivery costs. Despite this changing political landscape, Hollis *et al.* (1992; cited in Henry 2001) indicated that there were four types of service provision which local authorities undertook to provide in relation to service delivery:

- *Need-based services*, which are provided free of charge to all citizens, such as education and social services, and as discussed earlier, these may also have the leisure dimension.

- *Protective services*, which include policing and other security-related services such as the fire brigade.

- *Amenity services*, often based on the needs of the local community, such as open space provision.

- *Facility services*, such as leisure centres where there may be a direct charge, or provided free of charge such as in the case of libraries.

As Bull *et al.* (2003: 197) suggest, 'leisure provision would normally fall under amenity and facility services; however some amenity provision will assist the provision of leisure opportunities as, for example, in the opening up of premises provided primarily for educational services to the local community for leisure participation'.

The scope and scale of provision are particularly complex, with no two local authorities in any country having an identical level of provision. Much of this is a result of the historical policy decisions made by local authorities, often dating back to the nineteenth century in relation to the local resource base and needs of the local population. We also need to recognise, as discussed earlier in this chapter and in Chapter 2, that much of this provision is not a result of statutory legislation requiring local authorities to provide each category of leisure resource or service. Consequently, the changing role of local government, and its variable political philosophies and the directives received from national government during the 1970s and 1980s in particular, has led to a changing landscape for the local state in relation to leisure provision. This is in contrast to the 1960s and 1970s which saw considerable changes in many countries, with the local authorities making investments in purpose-built facilities.

Since the 1970s, the leisure sector has seen a growing professionalisation in many countries in relation to the development of policy and management. This is part of what has been described as a *new managerialism* with a concern for the development of supply to align more closely with demand as opposed to a supply-led philosophy (i.e. a greater focus on the management of the need and resource using private sector management tools). Robinson (2004) explains the processes behind the development of this new managerialism that has pervaded many areas of the public sector, as a result of:

- A growing trend towards consumerism (i.e. a greater focus on users as consumers seeking value for money and greater accountability in line with government policy measures such as the Citizen's Charter).

- A greater focus in central government policy and legislation on competition in the public sector and attempts to try to introduce measures associated with the free market.

- A greater use of commercial management techniques to shift the focus towards a professional approach to leisure delivery.

For example, the UK government White Paper *Modernising Government* (DETR 1998) outlined three basic principles for improving policy performance which have shaped the direction of leisure policy within the UK (and are not dissimilar to how other countries are constantly reviewing best practice in relation to policy and delivery frameworks for public services):

- 'Policy-making should be joined up and strategic
- The primary focus of public services should be consumer rather than producer interests: and
- Efficiency and high levels of quality in the provision of public services should be demonstrable'. *(Henry 2001: 140)*

What this meant for leisure service provision was:

- The greater focus on consultation in the provision of leisure services.

- A focus on joined-up government, with policy making and delivery harmonised rather than separated out.

● The greater use of partnerships involving the commercial, voluntary and public sectors to deliver leisure services.

● The greater focus on integration in terms of the planning of leisure through strategies and cooperation between different public sector agencies.

● The replacement of the former Compulsory Competitive Tendering (CCT) model in local government services (which required the tendering out of many public services such as leisure provision to the most competitive provider, with many councils' own Direct Service Organisations winning the contracts based on a competitively priced bid – see Page *et al.* 1994 for a detailed discussion of this concept and its application in the UK in relation to the 1985 Local Government Act) with a new concept entitled *Best Value*.

Best Value, introduced in April 2000, set out a series of new concepts to drive local leisure provision (as well as the wider provision of local government services) focused on two specific principles:

● *Fundamental service reviews*, where local authorities have to examine their service provision in considerable detail in relation to four key concepts: to challenge, compare, consult and compete – the four 'Cs' (Henry 2001: 141). The four Cs' meant:

1. *Challenge* the existing rationale of existing provision and the way it is delivered.

2. *Consult* with the diverse range of stakeholders to ensure provision meets local needs (see Page *et al.* 1994 on how such consultation can be undertaken and fed into the review process for policy and strategy development).

3. *Compare* the performance within a local authority with national and local performance standards to ensure that provision is of the highest possible standard, with a focus on best practice from elsewhere.

4. Review the *Competitiveness* of service delivery so that it represents the best value for money available from the potential options available for de-livery so that efficiency and effectiveness are embodied in delivery. These principles follow the current government thinking that aspire to high standards of transparency and accountability in public service delivery.

Source: DETR (1998); Robinson (2004)

These four principles would then be audited by the Audit Commission in terms of the regular reviews they undertake of local authority service pro-vision, one of which is illustrated in Case Study 6.2 for one council's leisure services – the City of Oxford.

● The development of the *Best Value Performance Plans*, which needed to build in national and local standards of provision and set specific targets for

Case Study 6.2   **The role of the Audit Commission in the UK:**
Best Value in public sector leisure provision

In February 2008, the Audit Commission completed its report into Oxford City Council's Cultural Services (also see Chapter 7 on why many English local authorities re-designated leisure services to cultural services), which encompasses many of the Council's leisure services. This case study examines the outcome of the review in relation to the concept of _Best Value_. While the Oxford report is used as an illustration, many other reports exist which can be accessed at www.audit-commission.gov.uk. The report observes the cross-cutting (i.e. it cuts across many of the activities and objectives of the Council's work and so is not just confined to one department or theme) importance of leisure to the Council's overall mission, where it makes a key contribution to social inclusion and the quality of life of the population, mirroring the central government national policy priorities in this field. The scope of the Council's leisure provision was outlined as:

- Operating three leisure centres, four swimming pools, a seasonally operated outdoor pool plus an ice rink.
- A network of seven urban parks, neighbourhood parks, open spaces, cemeteries, allotments and some 97 play areas as well as the Museum of Oxford.
- Operating Tourist Information Centres and supporting heritage and conservation work, art and sport development with a grants programme, an event programme and a range of activities hosted at 23 community centres.
- Employing 200 staff with additional casual staff.
- Consuming around one-third of the Council's budget (excluding housing), which is spent on Cultural Services with a budget in 2007/2008 amounting to £10 million, of which 40% is spent on leisure facilities, 30% on parks and 20% on other services.

The Audit Commission assessed the Council's spending in relation to whether it offered value for money. The services reviewed under the category received an average rating from its users and its high level of spending equated to £36.97 per head of population, the highest for any district council in England. It has a high usage rate for its dry leisure facilities but usage of the swimming pools is low, with five indoor pools receiving 215,600 visits in 2005/2006 for a population of 149,000. Swimming pool visits are heavily subsidised, as there is over-provision according to the Audit Commission. In contrast, 'tourism, arts, and parks and open spaces provide good value for money, with low costs and good quality of service. The Council is targeting its spending in these areas on its priorities of social inclusion' (Audit Commission 2008: 24) even though its spending is in the lower 25% of Councils for this service. In the wider domain of cultural services, the Audit Commission (2008: 26) observed that

> Cultural services are contributing effectively to reducing many aspects of in-equality. This includes the enhanced enabling of partners and the voluntary sector . . . It is also helping meet the needs of new residents, for example by training . . . community champions and using school facilities to teach the new Afghan community. Afghan children are being taught their home language, while the women are being taught English which has enabled them to run their own wellbeing classes for their community.

The report also notes the Council's capacity to improve its overall perform-ance by changing its internal structures and processes as well as through its working relationships with stakeholders. It has good working relationships with other public and voluntary sector organisations.

the performance of service delivery as well as ensure wide consultation amongst the community being served. In the *Best Value* approach, leisure service delivery needs to contribute towards the wider social priorities of the specific local authority in question, often set out in its corporate objectives. These corporate objectives are normally aligned with central government policies, such as seeking to improve the lifestyles of the population. The con-sequence for local authorities is that the former focus in the previous decade of Conservative government administration at a national level, with its 'em-phasis on the three Es (economy, efficiency and effectiveness)' (Henry 2001: 143), was replaced with the four Cs approach. Local service provision in England and Wales is now evaluated by the Audit Commission in relation to specific indicators set by local authorities and their performance is measured against them in relation to national and local targets.

According to Robinson (2004), *Best Value* involves consideration of four poten-tial delivery mechanisms:

- Continuation of in-house provision.

- The pursuit of external partnerships, such as with the private sector.

- The establishment of trusts as a non-profit or charitable undertaking (which are discussed later as a recent development in service provision using a model from the voluntary and not-for-profit sector).

- The development of a public–private sector partnership.

Much of this policy provision and practice is based upon what Coalter (2006) identifies as evidence-based policy making, where policy is designed to increase participation and then develop a series of specific outcomes from policies, as shown in Figure 6.4. What Figure 6.4 shows is that social and economic

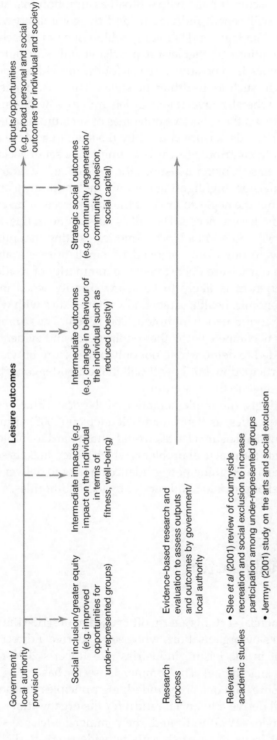

Figure 6.4 The impacts of leisure through intervention policy by public sector agencies

Source: Based on Coalter (2006: 171–172). Reproduced by permission of Palgrave Macmillan

objectives underpin much of the policy direction which local authorities and the public sector pursue, with a broad assumption that state intervention and provision will benefit individuals and the community via a series of leisure outcomes. The logic and thinking behind such approaches to policy making and interventions are that leisure provision will contribute to increased participation that leads to positive impacts for the individual and may lead to behaviour change such as healthier lifestyles. This then feeds into more strategic outcomes whereby investment in leisure has a wide-ranging benefit for the community via the collective outcomes of such provision.

In other words, leisure is used by the state to achieve not only leisure outcomes but to contribute towards a cumulative set of social and economic outcomes. Even so, Coalter questions the logic of such a large public sector role in leisure provision, highlighting not only the importance of the mixed economy of leisure but the neglected role of the commercial or private sector, which targets specific leisure needs. The UK is not unique in this context, as Crompton (2000: 65–66) argued in a North American setting that publicly funded leisure services were often only enjoyed by small numbers and so 'providing resources to our leisure departments so a minority of residents can have enjoyable experiences is likely to be a low priority when measured against the critical economic, health, safety and welfare issues with which most legislative bodies are confronted' (Crompton 2000: 65–66). Thus, public sector leisure provision has to compete with other public needs and evidence-based policy making is needed to demonstrate not only how leisure provision seeks to increase leisure participation, but how it will make a wider contribution from the individual through to the community.

Interestingly, the implementation of the *Best Value* approach has not been without its critics, as Benson and Henderson (2005) argued that many of the Council-owned leisure centres would find it hard to implement this approach. It highlights the practical problems which policy-makers sometimes cannot anticipate when designing new guidance on how to deliver and assess measures of the level of provision and service by local authorities.

The commercial sector

The commercial sector is a term often used to describe the provision of services or activities by organisations who seek to derive a direct profit from their involvement in the leisure industries (see Roberts 2004 for an extended discussion of this theme). The commercial sector has a long history of provision within leisure, and one of its underlying principles is to seek out opportunities which will derive a financial return for the organisations involved. Nevertheless, as Taylor (1993) indicated, the commercial leisure sector has not been a traditional focus of research activity aside from market intelligence reports

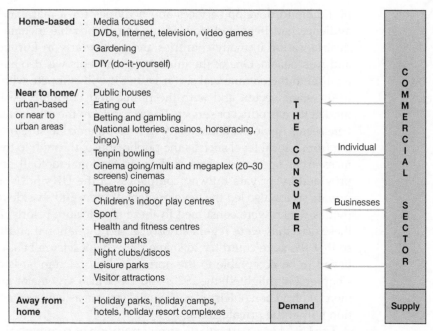

Figure 6.5   The scope of the commercial sector in leisure provision

Sources: Torkildsen (2005); Authors

from various consultancy firms. Figure 6.5 illustrates the scope and scale of the private sector provision of leisure services and products in most countries. What Figure 6.5 shows is that there are five main areas in which the private sector provides commercial leisure services and products:

● In and around the home.

● As a form of social recreation.

● As a form of entertainment, and in providing different forms of art and culture.

● Through different forms of sport and physical recreation.

● In the provision of tourism, holidays and other informal forms of recreation (after Bull *et al.* 2003: 218).

Figure 6.5 also indicates the importance of the marketing process associated with how companies communicate with their customers to entice them to purchase leisure goods and services, as Chapter 7 will discuss. Many of these forms of commercial provision have been discussed in earlier chapters and need not be reiterated here. What is important to emphasise is the changing competitive environment in which many of these businesses operate within countries, as they compete for customers to purchase their wares.

As Chapter 2 indicated, historians such as Cross (2004) talk about the late nineteenth century as a period which saw a growing commercialisation of leisure as a result of the development of a rational recreation era when it became profitable to develop services and activities for a mass audience. This mass audience had benefited from increasing disposable income as a result of industrialisation in many countries and particularly in Europe, North America and Australasia. One of the underlying concepts we also need to recognise in relation to the commercial sector is that it will compete with other businesses in the same sector, and with the public and voluntary sectors, to derive its market for a product or service. For example, in the nineteenth century the private sector made available many new commercial leisure opportunities, ranging from a local level such as the public house, through to the development of mass urban spectator sports, such as professional football, and excursion trips provided by private railway companies in the UK and North America. The private sector also led the development of piers and seaside resorts and the activities which were consumed in these new leisure resorts. Even so, many of these activities were regulated or licensed by national and local government so that the state could try to shape the type of leisure behaviour which it believed to be acceptable to the norms and moral standards of the society. As Chapter 2 highlighted, the 1920s and 1930s also saw major growth in the commercial provision of leisure such as the cinema as well as a growing specialisation within the private sector.

The USA has a particularly strong tradition of commercial leisure provision, as Cook (2004: 220) suggests that

> the ongoing commercialisation of leisure in American culture continues to inform the character and reach of American culture . . . the notion of commercialisation indicates a process whereby market-oriented business interests, practices, and institutions come to direct, rather than respond to, the character, trajectory, and shape of leisure pursuits.

What Cook illustrates is the market leadership role that the private sector played in leisure provision in the USA. Bull *et al.* (2003) observed that two categories of private sector leisure businesses exist: first, there are those involved in providing specific *leisure services* such as travel, entertainment or attractions; second, there is the growing category of companies supplying *leisure products* such as radios, magazines, books and other forms of commodity to meet the demand for leisure consumption, especially in the home in response to hobbies and activities (see Table 6.3).

Kline (2004) traces the evolution of the commercialisation of one specific type of leisure provision – children's play in the USA with the development of toy and game marketing, as children were recognised as an important market. This can be dated to the formation of the American Toy Manufacturers Association in 1916, with major global companies such as Fisher-Price founded in this period. One of the early mass market toys was the simple yo-yo in the 1920s together with the growing mass production of toys such as the electric train set. Television gave toy manufacturers an added impetus in terms of advertising, with advertising spend of around $1 million in 1954 rising to US$7 billion by 2000. Toy-makers adopted all of the commercial practices of successful business, including marketing and advertising, epitomised in the 1960s by Mattel's launch

Table 6.3   Home-based leisure pursuits and hobbies

Amateur radio	Dinner parties
Playing pool/snooker	DIY
Birthday celebrations	Entertaining family and friends
Board games	Home brewing
Book reading	Internet use
Card games	Pet ownership
Children's play	Radio and CB listening
Coin collecting	Smoking
Comic book reading	Stamp collecting
Computer/video games	Television watching
Cooking for pleasure	

of the Barbie doll which has become an iconic toy with around 90–95% of American girls owning at least one Barbie doll. The globalisation of such toys illustrated one of the later stages of the toy industry in the USA by the 1990s.

One other important area of children's leisure which the commercial sector developed was the comic book. As McIntosh (2004) observed, these developed during the 1930s as inexpensive serials and by the 1940s around 84% of those aged 12 to 17 years of age were reading such material in the USA, with 35% of those aged 18–30 also reading the comics. Critics opposed the comic book as affecting one's ability to think, while others pointed to such comics as a cause of juvenile delinquency. Despite such criticisms, they are still in existence today as a popular leisure pursuit as new markets were nurtured by the commercial sector alongside the rise of men's and women's mass circulation magazines. In fact, the USA's major women's magazines were founded in the late nineteenth century (*Ladies' Home Journal, Woman's Home Companion, Good Housekeeping, Delineator, Pictorial Review* and *McCall's*) (Scanlon 2004). These have been replaced in subsequent years by seven major women's magazines (*Family Circle, Woman's Day, Good Housekeeping, Ladies' Home Journal, Better Homes and Gardens, McCall's* and *Redbook*). These are important leisure-time reading for American women, with the top seven magazines having a circulation of around 34 million (Scanlon 2004). They are an important element of the consumer culture, appealing to the leisure interests and aspirations of its readership, and are a major source of consumer advertising to reach the growing consumer audience of women.

Therefore the private sector has a long history of profitable provision of leisure services and products for the population and, as Irvine and Taylor (1998) indicated, the value of the commercial sector within the UK's leisure industries was equivalent to around 17.5% of GDP. This illustrates its significance, with over 6000 companies operating within the sector. As Rojek *et al.* (2006: 16) argued, accompanying this commercialisation of leisure has been a significant impact from the Americanisation of leisure at a global scale, where 'American television, film, music, literature, social science, computer systems, sport, restaurant chains, systems of education, beer, clothing, sports equipment, automobiles and countless other commodities' have led to a major impact upon leisure and its provision by commercial organisations. Marling (2004) traces the globalisation of American leisure starting with the export of tobacco as a leisure product dating to 1775, ranging through to the export of film from the 1930s onwards, television programmes, the fast food system and the franchise model developed to export it, and leisure travel overseas by Americans, alongside theme parks and American sport. Concerns over this Americanisation of global culture were raised as long ago as the 1930s by Adorno in relation to the USA's popular culture industry (also see Chapter 8 for a more extended discussion and Bernstein 1991). This has been followed by concerns over the ways in which global organisations have produced these commodities and services. For example, the impact of large leisure multinationals using labour from the less developed world, such as sport shoe manufacturers, has raised serious questions about the way in which the profitability of these companies has been developed.

While the private sector has very specific goals associated with a commercial orientation (i.e. a focus on the buyer–seller relationship, an exclusive relationship with consumers and a focus on higher levels of service provision), there is a significant degree of competition between businesses within the commercial sector. Therefore, we can say that many commercial organisations are not concerned with the leisure sector *per se*, but with the sector as a source of profit for their businesses. As Torkildsen (2005: 195) argued, 'the most significant change over the past two decades has been the increase in the size of the multinational companies through mergers, takeovers and diversification of interests. Multinational companies have power and influence on people's leisure, supply and what we want and are willing to pay for'. One notable area of significant growth since the 1990s has been in the Internet and the provision of these services by commercial organisations in many countries, as discussed in Chapter 5.

As discussed in other chapters, the commercial sector has benefited in many countries from continued household expenditure on commercial forms of leisure both inside the home and outside it, including the growth of holidays, eating out and the purchase of leisure commodities. Even so, commercial leisure businesses will only provide services where they can make a profit and so this leaves opportunities for both the public and voluntary sectors to fill in many of the gaps where the private sector businesses do not wish to make provision. In the UK, one of the areas where there has been significant change in terms of the competitive environment for leisure businesses has been the public house. In 1989, based on a report by the Monopolies Commission, they found that six breweries controlled the whole market. These breweries had over 2000 public houses and many of them were tied to each brewery. The outcome of the Monopolies Commission report was that many breweries sold off their smaller and unprofitable businesses, with other non-brewing business interests purchasing public houses. This combined with other trends such as the growth of food provision in public houses and the entry into the market of new companies to develop public houses as eating establishments. This marks a further change in the evolution of the public house from its historic origins which were examined in Case Study 2.1. New investment in these premises alongside new trends such as the rise of the *gastropub* (i.e. premises specialising in serving high-quality food as opposed to the basic concept of pub grub that was associated with the public house) meant that public houses embraced food provision both to diversify the products and to appeal to different consumer groups which these premises now compete for. As Torkildsen (2005) argued, the provision of food within these establishments now expands their appeal and there are increased profit margins on food in comparison to alcoholic and non-alcoholic drinks. One notable development has been a rise of the family public house, with indoor and outdoor play areas for children so that families can be attracted to the premises. In many cases, these public houses have adopted many of the commercial practices apparent from other sectors of the hospitality industry through the use of branding and marketing, which will be examined in Chapter 7.

Coalter (2000) argued that the commercial sector has largely been neglected in leisure studies, particularly the new forms of consumerism which have arisen in recent years. 'One has to recognise the distinction that two types of leisure exist: consumerist and participatory' (Parker 1997: 149). Coalter (2000) discusses Parker's two types of leisure, distinguishing between *participant-led* which is often active and spontaneous, and *consumerist* which is characterised as being more passive, packaged and supply-led. While there is a theoretical debate over the merits of this distinction, it is apparent that consumerist-led leisure has an important role to play in the wider domain of leisure studies, as apparent from our discussion so far. Coalter argues that part of the neglect of this consumer perspective within leisure studies has arisen as a result of opposition to the new right in Europe and a focus on the free market and profit motives. What this debate shows is that a mixed economy of leisure exists, where there is a changing balance between public and private sector depending upon the political philosophies evident in Tables 6.1 and Table 6.2. While this focuses only on the UK, similar patterns can be discerned in New Zealand and Australia, while the culture of leisure provision in North America has been heavily influenced by the private sector in the post-war period.

In the UK, for example, the private sector benefited from leisure contracts during the 1980s when Compulsory Competitive Tendering was introduced for leisure services. During the 1990s, new models of public–private sector partnerships were developed, setting up a new role for the private sector. As Ravenscroft (1996) observed, the emphasis upon markets and the private sector has emerged as a dominant element in many societies, not least of all the UK, as a central feature of capitalism as 'the ability of consumer-orientated capitalism to deliver leisure goods . . . equates the public interest with the pursuit of private gain by both seller and buyer. Leisure is a perfect model of the free play of market forces' (Clarke and Critcher 1985: 223).

The private sector is a significant, if not under-recognised sector of the leisure industries which makes significant investments in the services and products it provides to the population, in return for a profit on its investment. It is a major employer in many countries and a source of tax revenue for the public sector. Yet with private sector leisure being based upon consumer spending, leisure markets are extremely volatile, as is evident during the credit crunch which commenced in 2008. If demand for leisure products drops dramatically, as it has done in recent years, then private sector businesses may face significant challenges in terms of cash flow and demand for their products. Even so, there is evidence within some leisure markets that there is a process of market concentration occurring, which means that the ownership of leisure businesses has become concentrated in a few large companies. Where such activity occurs, then the public sector may intervene if the control of the market becomes anti-competitive and the consumer does not have access to competitively priced products, as a business may use its monopoly position to control the market and prices. The public sector would intervene in such situations to regulate any excessive profit, potentially requiring the break-up of large conglomerates as in the case of the UK brewing industry and its public houses. This is also the case in the UK with the impending break-up of the British Airport Authority's monopoly position in airport provision, forcing the sale of certain airports to other private sector businesses to provide greater competition. Consequently, within the private sector, the market and business environment are constantly changing and so the composition of businesses and competition between them are in a constant state of flux. Ultimately the commercial sector is focused on profitability, because unprofitable activity will mean that it could have to cease operating. But one area where the private sector has a long history of involvement in leisure provision is with the notion of eating out, as shown in Case Study 6.3.

| Case Study 6.3 | Consuming food as a leisure pursuit – eating out as a commercial form of leisure |

According to Finkelstein and Lynch (2006: 406), 'dining out is not a new social convention, however, its character has changed dramatically from being a necessity for those who travelled and had no choice of meals . . . to now being the source of entertainment and a valuable part of the economy of the leisure industries'. This illustrates that eating out emerged as an important leisure pursuit in the twentieth century, reinforcing trends which developed in the late nineteenth century as increased consumer spending was directed towards this form of leisure activity (see Jacobs and Scholliers 2003 for European examples). This case study will briefly trace the evolution of eating out from a Western European perspective and then focus on its significance as a contemporary form of commercial leisure. Many of the contemporary forms of eating out have their origins in the nineteenth century and so an understanding of their development illustrates how significant eating out was in the past as well as in contemporary society.

Burnett (2004) traced the evolution of eating out in the UK as a commercial activity from the Norman conquest through to the modern day. Table 6.4 outlines some of the commercial forms of eating out which developed up to 1914 when many of the forms of mass catering had been established. What Table 6.4 shows is that the evolution of eating out in the UK has a long history, initially focused around providing hospitality for travellers (e.g. provision made by monasteries in the medieval period) through to the evolution of a

Table 6.4 The evolution of commercial eating out establishments in England 1066–1914

Era	Typical forms of commercial eating out establishment
Norman Conquest	Medieval cookshops (restaurant eating in and takeaway)
Tudor period	Inns, taverns and alehouses (see Case Study 2.1 for more detail) Pleasure or tea gardens and coffee houses
Mid-1700s	Rise of coaching inns to serve travellers and rise of the gastronomy movement among the social elites Early stages of the development of inns into hotels Spa development and the formation of hotels to serve the privileged few travelling to resorts such as Bath and Scarborough Development of the restaurant concept in Paris with 100 operating in 1789; 500–600 in 1804 and 1000 by 1830 and dissemination thereafter to other parts of the world
1830s	Hierarchy of eating establishments operating (e.g. from the humble cookshops to the ordinaries, chop-houses, dining rooms and taverns and hotels)
1840s	Early establishment of canteens in industrial premises (e.g. factories)
1860s	Rise of the fish and chip shop with between 10–12,000 in existence by 1888 and 25,000 in 1910 Development of temperance coffee houses and palaces as a counterweight to the public house and mid-Victorian drunkenness among the working classes
1880s	Growth of gastronomy era with the development of haute cuisine by George Escoffier and expansion of the concept of 'Grand Hotels' at many resorts Diffusion of French cuisine as a trend in restaurants and among social elites The rise of the gentlemen's club with a growing middle-class patronage and dining as a major element of the provision for members
1880s–1914	The development of the first major catering chains (e.g. 1878, the People's Café Company) Rise of J Lyons and Co. and the Lyons Teashop in the 1880s, with 37 operating in London by 1900 and 180 in 1914, becoming the largest chain in the UK by 1914

Source: Adapted from Burnett (2004)

network of inns as discussed in Case Study 2.1. In other words, what we see is the evolution of eating out to fulfil economic (i.e. for profit), military (i.e. to serve the needs of travelling troops and military personnel) and social needs (i.e. for social interaction and entertainment). In the fifteenth and sixteenth centuries, commercial provision within England was reflected in its international reputation for entertainment and banquets available to the traveller. By the eighteenth century, pleasure was increasingly being built into the provision of eating establishments, with the evolution of the gentleman's club and its private membership. In the nineteenth century, hotels evolved, providing meals for the residents, and by the late nineteenth century many of the grand hotels were established, with public dining rooms offering opportunities for dining out for non-residents for pleasure. For example, in 1889, in London the Savoy Hotel opened its dining room. Yet as Table 6.4 suggests, the restaurant as a concept can be traced back to Paris in the 1770s and subsequent years, when this novel form of eating establishment gradually spread to other countries.

By the early part the twentieth century, eating places were also associated with holidays while eating out had become well established as a leisure pursuit. Similar patterns of development can also be observed in the USA, with the evolution of eating-out establishments to meet the needs of a growing urban population, new settlements and the expanding transport network. By the late twentieth century eating out was an important form of entertainment in its own right and part of the social life of many citizens within Western societies.

According to Finkelstein and Lynch (2006), we can observe three contemporary types of eating-out establishment:

- The chain restaurant.
- The bistro or café.
- The special occasion or spectacular restaurant.

Each of these types of eating-out establishment provides food and drink for paying customers and the type of service and provision will vary according to the price charged and the characteristics of each business. Indeed, one of the defining features of restaurants (aside from the chain restaurant) is a focus on being different and unique in terms of what is provided to distinguish themselves from the competition. Yet it is not just the restaurant which has become an important social setting for eating out and its significance as a leisure activity. We also need to focus on what characterises eating out. Eating out as a leisure activity has a number of distinct characteristics which can be summarised as follows:

- There is a social and geographical separation from the domestic setting and routine of everyday life.
- There is no work involved for the participants, with the food being prepared and served by others; the food can range from the humble takeaway

through to the more exclusive and niche form of provision such as catering in your own home by a chef.

- Eating out inevitably involves a payment. This is the commercial transaction which has evolved from the notion of hospitality in many societies where there is a reciprocity (i.e. you will host and entertain someone with an expectation that the guest may well host you at a future point in time). This reciprocity has now assumed a commercial dimension where the consumer pays a fee in return for the reciprocal relationship of being hosted and receiving hospitality and an experience.
- The experience of eating out has many special properties, so that it is an *experience* associated with what is eaten, the frequency with which one eats out and the location chosen, as well as the reason for eating out (i.e. many special occasions are often celebrated with a meal).
- Eating out will normally involve a full meal, where there is a choice of menu, service, a structured experience, and different forms of social etiquette such as being shown to your table, being seated and waited upon.

One of the exceptions to these general conventions is the rise of the chain restaurant in America in the 1920s and 1930s as an eating-out experience while in transit on a long-distance highway journey. These were established along major routeways and, by 1945, there were about 7000 in existence (Hurley 2004). Many of these diners reached their heyday in the 1950s, with very flamboyant architecture and décor, and pre-dated the fast food chain restaurants such as McDonald's which emerged during the 1950s. The mass-market fast food chains which developed during the 1950s had an underlying philosophy based on the principle of Keep It Simple Stupid (KISS) (Finkelstein and Lynch 2006), using mass produced methods of industrial catering to keep prices low and to provide a standardised product range where portion size and menu choice were carefully costed and controlled. Other chains such as Kentucky Fried Chicken (KFC) evolved and also embraced the concept of franchising to gain national and later international reach.

The USA is an important setting in which to examine the rise of commercial eating-out establishment because, as Schlosser (2002: 3) argued, Americans 'spend more money on fast food than on higher education, personal computers, . . . New cars . . . On movies, books, magazines'. This illustrates how important eating out has become in American culture, not least in their leisure time. This is reflected in the commonplace practice of eating out within the USA, particularly the consumption of fast food as part of everyday life. Yet it is not just the USA which has a highly developed eating-out culture. According to Warde and Martens (2000), in the UK around 21% of the population eat out at least once a week and national surveys such as the National Food Survey (DETR 2000) illustrate that there are distinct variations in participation in eating out according to the region in which you live, the income group you belong to, family composition, gender and age.

For example, between 1990 and 2000, the National Food survey found that those in London had a higher propensity to consume ethnic meals when eating out compared to those with the lowest propensity in southwest England. Similarly, those in higher income groups ate out more often than those in low-income groups or old age pensioners. Those families without children also had a higher propensity to eat out than those with children. Males were much more likely to eat out than females, while those aged 35 to 44 years of age were more likely to eat out than those aged 15 to 24 years of age. Other data sources such as the UK Day Visits survey also illustrate that food and drink are an important component of such leisure trips, particularly when travellers stop at cafés and tea shops. Tourism organisations, such as Tourism New Zealand, found that tourists tend to eat out more than residents. For example, certain nationalities like the British and Germans spent significant sums of money on visiting restaurants during their trip to New Zealand, this being a high-ranking activity for many visitors. There is also evidence, such as in the UK Family Expenditure Survey, which shows that between 1960 and 1993, the percentage of household budgets expended on eating out rose from 9.8% in 1960 to 20.8% in 1993. More recently, this has risen to over 30%.

Some of the explanations given for eating out as a leisure activity were cited by Warde and Martens (2000) in terms of:

- *Providing a change from the norm*, such as a break from cooking, and opportunity for relaxing, trying different types of foods as well as a novelty factor.
- *Providing an opportunity for socialising*, with friends or as a romantic experience.
- *An opportunity to celebrate a special occasion*, particularly for those people who are short of money who may think of eating out as a special treat akin to a luxury.
- *Fulfilling an interest and liking for good food.*
- *Fulfilling a physical need*, such as the desire to be away from the home environment.
- *A social obligation*, where there is peer pressure from friends and relatives to join them in a social occasion (e.g. an office Christmas Party) even though you may dislike the food, the price being charged or even the company as it mixes work with your leisure time.

The 1980s saw the evolution of new food trends and a growth of café-restaurants, with the rise of urban café culture in many countries. Some of these cafés developed new forms of cuisine, from nouvelle cuisine through to a more recent trend towards fusion cooking where elements of eastern and western cuisine are blended together, becoming highly developed in Australasia in the 1990s. The significance of food and eating out to the hospitality sector as a major employer and contributor to tax revenue is reflected in the growing clustering of food areas within some American cities. These have developed into restaurant or eating quarters. Yet above all, one trend is clear in the post-war period: the democratisation and popularisation of the restaurant and eating-out experience, as more people have been able to enjoy such experiences as the supply of eating-out options has grown exponentially in many countries since the 1980s.

There have been many sociological investigations into the meaning of eating out (see, for example, Wood 1995 and his seminal study on the *Sociology of the Meal*) but there is growing evidence of a blurring of what we eat at home and what we eat out of home. In other words, the two areas of home and out-of-home eating show a remarkable degree of consistency, with many consumers favouring familiarity over the unknown in food, particularly with the media focus on food scares and food safety in terms of the source of ingredients. In addition, the definitions of eating out have changed since 1945 with the rise of fast food and a growth of takeaway food (i.e. the ubiquitous Chinese, Indian or pizza takeaway) diversifying the range of takeaway options. This challenges many of the conventional notions of eating out since the food is eaten at home or in a non-restaurant location but prepared out of home. Irrespective of the mode of consuming the meal, the meal has a significant component within any eating-out experience, where the ambience, sociability and style of food has different meanings which people attach to the experience.

There is also a growing debate among sociologists associated with a decline in family cohesion within the home where family members do not sit down to a meal together. This has been attributed to the impact of two-parent working, the flexibility provided for irregular eating habits associated with ready-prepared meals, and the busy social schedules of parent and children, thereby creating a transitory and fluid social setting around meal times. The consequence is that the meal is no longer the focus of the family in everyday life. Therefore, eating out may be seen as a symbol of family cohesion where the family unit is gathered and consumes the food experience communally, enhancing family bonding and relationships in much the same way as holidays are seen as a mechanism for family cohesion. As Table 3.1 demonstrated, some ethnic groups such as Asian Americans put a high value on family meals and the dining experience for entertaining family and friends in their leisure time.

Eating out is rich in symbolism because it has many meanings to individuals and groups which can be shared, such as at special occasions, while there will be a sensory awareness (i.e. it will appeal to your sight, hearing, smell, taste buds and feelings) of the experience while the meal is being consumed. This sensory stimulation will occur in the restaurant setting dependent upon the ambience, occasion, aesthetic appeal of the venue, quality and type of food being consumed and levels of service. These sociological interpretations suggest that, as Pilsbury (1990: 10) argued, eating out is a cultural barometer where 'the restaurant has unwittingly become a symbol of contemporary life' and so from a leisure perspective, it is not just the food and drink being consumed: it is the experience which is important in terms of the individual, the setting, level of socialisation and interaction which occurs. This also has a significant trend element to it, as eating out has seen a significant renaissance in recent years as people seek out *the place to be seen*.

Eating out also has a significant postmodern element to it, with evolution of food landscapes in many large cities. For example, the ubiquitous fast food restaurant chain is in existence in many urban settings, such as McDonald's which has over 18,000 outlets in 90 countries. Eating out will also be an important element in how individuals acquire cultural capital, particularly through the knowledge and experience they gain from consuming food, a feature accentuated by the rise of celebrity chefs and television programmes focused on food trends and restaurant food. For those seeking cultural capital, the ritual pursuit of restaurant food and the latest trend is often interpreted as a spectacle, with some restaurants placing the food cooking area in the middle of the premises to accentuate that spectacle and atmosphere. Within a tourism setting, eating out and the use of food has been associated with regional identity and the promotion of distinct food experiences as a consumable experience. Therefore what this case study illustrates is that eating out has become a major and expanding sector in the leisure field, particularly where it is combined with activities such as going to an event, a day trip or simply to celebrate a special occasion. Above all, it has created a significant commercial opportunity for the private sector throughout the ages, although it is a sector very sensitive to consumer spending and trends. The sector also experiences high levels of turnover among the businesses operating, due to the challenge of developing and retaining a profitable clientele as well as competition between businesses. Eating-out establishments operate in a market based on selling a culinary experience where the competition is constantly changing along with consumer tastes and demands.

The voluntary sector

The voluntary sector performs an essential role within leisure even though it is often overlooked in terms of its significance. Roberts (2004) illustrates the diversity of the leisure interests and activities which the voluntary sector provides, as the 'types of leisure where the voluntary sector is pivotal are sport, artistic production and performances and hobbies'. In fact many sports were invented and are still managed by voluntary bodies, with the exception of those commercial sports with large spectator audiences. The study by Newton (1976) of voluntary sector activity in Birmingham highlighted the scale of such organisations, which amounted to around 3000 in the city in the 1970s, of which around half had a leisure function as their primary or secondary goal. This confirmed that the voluntary sector has an important role in both formal and informal types of leisure, ranging from hobbies through to sports organisations, often focused on a specific type of leisure interest or which seek to provide leisure for people other than their membership. Tomlinson's (1979) review of the field of clubs and associations in leisure found that in the UK there were around 4000 working men's clubs and around 7000 clubs for the elderly in England and Wales. As Haywood *et al.* (1989) observed, there are five principal categories of voluntary organisation:

- *Recreation and sport organisations*, which they described as the archetypal leisure organisations based around common interest with a membership.

- *Community service groups*, which have a client-focused membership which provides a service, such as the Women's Volunteer Service which looks after the leisure needs of the housebound.

- *Community development groups*, which focus on self-help, which means that they wish to enable people to meet their own leisure needs.

- *Community action groups*, which may often be a pressure group that has a focus on a particular issue, such as a group of people wishing to establish a children's play facility in an area. They are focused on a specific issue or an organisation which has a more general interest in leisure.

- *Social groups*, which seek to promote a specific range of leisure opportunities to meet social and emotional goals amongst the population, such as working men's clubs, in the absence of public sector provision for these groups.

Hutton (1992) added an additional category to consider with each of these groups, depending on how they were *organised* and *managed*:

- Those with a small organising committee and large audience, such as a sports club.

- Those with a large committee, such as charitable trusts.

- Those with no formal organising committee, such as mothers and toddlers groups.

As Figure 6.6 shows, the scope and range of voluntary organisations within any society are very wide, but unlike the public sector, where there may be a focus on the collective needs of society, voluntary organisations may sometimes focus on the notion of social exclusivity to promote the interests of their members or target audience. Early studies of voluntary organisations, such as Komarovsky (1946) and Gordon and Babchuk (1959) in the USA, highlighted their significance for leisure, and there are now over 23,000 non-profit membership organisations. These organisations are an important element of the social fabric of communities and their leisure economies.

Unlike the public sector, the voluntary sector cannot raise income from tax revenue and so looks to the public and sometimes the commercial sector for donations and other forms of income such as grants. As Bull *et al.* (2003) argued, voluntary groups are not focused on profit maximisation like commercial operators: they will often seek to make a small profit or to just break even

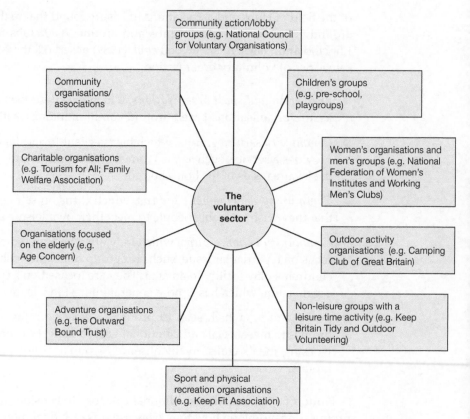

Figure 6.6   Scope of the voluntary sector involvement in leisure – a UK perspective

Sources: Based on Torkildsen (2005); Authors

as their focus is on their members as opposed to their trading activities. Hence the associated term used to describe these organisations – *not for profit*. This does not mean a voluntary organisation will not adopt commercial principles, as some leisure-based voluntary organisations such as the National Trust in the UK have multi-million-pound operations and different revenue sources. As a contemporary study of the countryside in 1926 observed of these voluntary bodies (which pre-dated state intervention on a large scale in landscape conservation in the UK such as National Parks), 'The National Trust . . . has been very active during recent years, in acquiring and preserving all manner of beauty spots in England, including various sites in the mountains of the Lake District, strategical points on the North and South Downs, river banks, hilltops and cliff-tops' (Briggs 1926: 65). However, voluntary organisations seek to derive their income from a wide range of sources, including membership subscriptions, fund-raising appeals and commercial trading as well as grants. As Bull *et al.* (2003: 236) suggest, there are many categories of voluntary organisations within the field.

The significance of these organisations is that they play an important role in filling in the gaps in the mixed economy of leisure provision, enabling different elements of the population to participate in leisure pursuits which the public and private sectors are unable to provide. For example, a voluntary organisation provided a major stimulus to the development of playgrounds in the USA. The development of playgrounds in the USA can be traced to the playground movement in Germany in the nineteenth century. The first outdoor gymnasium was provided in Massachusetts in 1821 and later influenced the design and development of outside play equipment. In the early twentieth century, the playground movement gathered momentum with the formation of a voluntary organisation – the *Playground Association of America* – in 1906 (later called the Playground and Recreation Association of America). This contributed to the diffusion of the idea from just over 20 cities with playgrounds in 1906 to 342 cities by 1913, with regular paid workers to supervise them. This was accompanied by the evolution of the play equipment industry providing merry-go-rounds, swings and slides. The early motivation for park provision was to protect children from the rapidly expanding and industrialising cities and to separate them from the delinquency of older children (Frost 2004).

As Torkildsen (2005) suggests, we can look at the voluntary sector from two perspectives:

● It constitutes a body of volunteers who undertake unpaid work in their leisure time because it gives satisfaction and may help others. In other words, people may engage in volunteer forms of leisure for altruistic reasons (i.e. a desire to help others with no expectation of reward or payment).

● The voluntary sector (also referred to as the not-for-profit sector) comprises a myriad of societies, associations, organisations, clubs and charitable bodies focused on leisure or providing leisure opportunities.

In each of these categories, it is apparent that the voluntary sector contributes to the notion of social capital which was introduced in Chapter 3, because it seeks to enhance community spirit and cohesion, as well as developing the concept of citizenship, trust, shared values and involvement within one's community, as outlined by Torkildsen (2005: 165).

The evolution of voluntary organisations

As Table 6.1 suggested, voluntary organisations have a long history and can be dated to the early eighteenth century, according to Haywood *et al.* (1989). In fact Haywood *et al.* (1989) argue that such societies also existed in ancient Greece and that the voluntary sector principles are based on similar ideals of the extended family or local community, where mutual support and common interests combine in shared leisure activities. However, many authors point to the emergence of coffee houses in cities such as London and Bath which then transformed into clubs with limited membership as the basis of voluntary organisations that we see today. One study of voluntary organisations by Gordon and Doughan (2006) pointed to the exclusion of women from many such clubs and associations historically, a feature in part rectified by such organisations adopting more transparent processes on membership and admission. What is important within a historical context is that clubs and organisations in the voluntary sector were important to the social life and leisure activities of local communities (Plate 6.1). One of the most important worldwide organisations in terms of leisure is the Scout and Girl Guide movements. It is estimated that there are over 28,000,000 Scouts in 213 countries, with 400,000 Scouts in the UK alone. Over two-thirds of Scouts are located in developing countries, illustrating the global reach of the movement initially started by Baden-Powell in 1908. It is not just the members but also the volunteers who give of their time to assist the Scouting movement. Indeed, from a policy perspective, voluntary organisations are growing in significance within many countries to fill the void left when the public sector has withdrawn from certain activities. The voluntary sector has also partnered with the public sector to enhance provision.

Whatever explanations one adopts to identify the growth of the voluntary sector, it is clear that the transition from a rural and agrarian society to an urban industrial one had a significant impact on the evolution of voluntary groups to fill the void left by this community transition. It may also be the case that such organisations met very specific needs which the public sector would never be able to fulfil, particularly where there are very niche interests being served. In the nineteenth century, much of the involvement in charitable bodies that were formed to promote different forms of leisure

Plate 6.1 The Birnam Institute in Dunkeld, Scotland, was established initially in the nineteenth century as a community leisure facility and is run with voluntary support today.

were based on different motives and principles of philanthropic founders. In the case of volunteers, we also need to understand the underlying motivation of those who volunteer to pursue specific agendas (see Stebbins and Graham 2004 for a detailed discussion). For example, the efforts of individual philanthropists benefited youth groups through the provision of sports clubs or facilities in deprived inner city environments. This was evident in Chapter 5 in relation to the 1920s study of Bethnal Green where a range of philanthropic organisations existed in the East End of London to try to improve the lot of the poor, often impacting upon their leisure, to provide opportunities that did not exist.

According to Bull *et al.* (2003), voluntary groups provide a number of important roles within leisure, including the following:

- The provision of leisure resources, such as the National Trust in Britain which owns around 1% of the land area and manages many important coastal resources.

- Meeting the needs of private individuals and the community.

- The engagement of voluntary labour.

- Lobbying and campaigning to meet specific leisure needs.

- Organising leisure activities.

- Collaborating and working with local and national government.

- Providing social and psychological benefits from increased leisure provision.

The importance of voluntary organisations also raises the issue of volunteers and the motivation for volunteering, which illustrates the diverse range of factors and stimuli that encourage people to give their time to help others. According to Stebbins (2006: 449), volunteers are people who are not coerced and who offer their time/help either formally or informally with no expected benefit, which is incorporated in his concept of *serious leisure* which we discussed in Chapter 1. What Stebbins highlights is that volunteering within a leisure context provides a fulfilling and enjoyable experience, characterised as a form of serious leisure because of six identifiable qualities:

- The need to persevere.

- Finding a career in the endeavour of volunteering.

- It involves personal effort based on acquired knowledge, training or skill.

- It provides a number of durable benefits or outcomes for the individual, such as self-gratification.

- The volunteer will identify strongly with their chosen area.

- It will often lead to a specific social world or social circle.

As volunteering in a leisure context will involve the free provision of time, be entered into freely and not attract any form of payment, Parker (1997) observed that there are four types of volunteer:

- The altruistic volunteer who will give time and effort willingly to others.

- Market volunteering, where there is less altruism even though the time is given freely, and there may be an expectation of a payback at a later time.

- The volunteer motivated by a specific cause in which they believe.

- The volunteer seeking a leisure experience as the main motivation.

For some people, volunteering may offer the opportunity to develop their leadership skills, or simply to undertake mundane roles of providing labour because of a desire to be involved with a cause or organisation which they believe in. Volunteering may also provide some people with a chance to gain social interaction on a group basis at regular intervals.

The wide range of voluntary organisations operating within the sphere of leisure may work independently or in partnership with other voluntary groups in the public and private sectors. As Table 6.1 illustrated, the most recent trend within the UK has been for an enhanced role for the voluntary sector in terms of leisure provision. One explanation of this growing role is that voluntary bodies may have a better understanding of groups' and individuals' leisure needs and how leisure organisations can interact more meaningfully with the community. This is a departure from the traditional approaches, which were outlined in Chapter 6 in terms of the analysis of leisure provision by the public sector. One area of considerable growth has been in terms of volunteer working on conservation projects in both the urban and rural environments, such as those sponsored by Natural England. Many National Parks have volunteer schemes which work on landscape improvements and issues such as litter picking. In some cases, organisations like the National Trust and the British Trust for Conservation Volunteers even organise working holidays for volunteers. Haywood *et al.* (1989) observed that voluntary sector organisations operating in leisure have expanded considerably since the mid-1970s, although the geographical and social coverage has been uneven. It is more likely that motivated middle-class professionals who live in suburban areas or within gentrified neighbourhoods and cities will be active in voluntary organisations to promote their own leisure needs within their home environments.

As Curson (1995) found, charitable trusts as one category of voluntary organisation have had a relatively short history within leisure in the UK. One of the most notable was the National Trust, founded in 1895. They have seen considerable expansion in recent years and the concept of trusts has been incorporated within local authority leisure provision because they may offer greater control of the decision-making process for leisure provision and the opportunity to experiment with provision and to foster community development and involvement (Simmons 2004). They are also an important method of distancing the management of the resource from direct political control. This often involves transferring the assets to charities which are then managed by a trust.

A report by the Audit Commission (2006) summarised the local authority management of leisure services via a trust, with over 90 operating in the UK and accounting for 21% of leisure facilities in England. The key features of such trusts are:

- They provide an arm's-length and independent way to manage the leisure resource(s).

- They do not offer councils as much direct day-to-day control over the management of the resource but councils can control this via grants and subsidies to ensure their aims are met, as well as having elected council members comprising 20% of board membership.

- Local authorities can enter into this process by setting up a new trust, joining an existing trust or creating a hybrid trust that is set up by a private sector company which is then managed by a contract awarded to that company.

- The leisure assets of the trust are normally leased from the local authority for between 15 and 25 years.

- The 1976 Local Government Act in the UK permits the setting up of such trusts for managing leisure and sport facilities, which means the facilities are exempt from non-domestic rates and may be exempt from value added tax (VAT).

Such trusts also allow the local authorities to access development funds from charitable sources such as the UK National Lottery (White 1999). Therefore, this evolving model of leisure provision by the public sector has been used in many countries due to the greater flexibility it offers over the development and financial management of leisure resources, by removing taxation charges through using a voluntary sector model – a charitable trust.

Summary

From the discussion of the public, commercial and voluntary sectors it would be easy to separate out the activities of each and to isolate them as specific agencies affecting leisure provision. However, we need to understand how all these organisations contribute to leisure by considering two key themes from this chapter:

- First, the notion of continuity and change developed in Chapter 2 needs to be reconsidered in the light of the discussion of these agencies because of the relative importance of each which has increased or declined through time.

● Second, the roles of these sectors need to be viewed almost like a spider's web, where different forms of leisure provision are made available as the web expands, with each sector collaborating and competing to fill niches or gaps in the web where opportunities exist.

These ideas are best illustrated with a summary review of the effect of the Great Depression in the USA on leisure, which has particular salience in view of the recent credit crunch. Hunnicutt (2004) argues that during the inter-war period, the voluntary sector in the USA saw a massive expansion, with many organisations we see today being founded, such as Rotary International and Lions. The public sector also enabled the development of municipal community centres using schools out of hours. Women's clubs and voluntary groups were founded, such as the Farm Bureau Federation (1920) that was serving over 210,000 groups by 1922 in rural areas (Hunnicutt 2004). But the most profound change which occurred in the early 1930s was a sudden retraction of the commodification and commercialisation of leisure that had occurred in the private sector in the 1920s. A sudden contraction of consumer spending led to an abrupt end to the 1920s consumer age for a number of years. For example, attendance at baseball games dropped (which led to heavy discounting to attract crowds) and there was a 40% drop in takings at cinemas in the early 1930s, while a third of all American theatres closed. This in itself was notable, but what is interesting is the way the public and voluntary sectors intervened to fill a void in American leisure needs. As Hunnicutt (2004) observed, where private leisure failed, public leisure emerged as the not-for-profit sector grew and community activities (e.g. visits to libraries, public spaces and parks) grew alongside the development of community organisations. Similarly, the federal government intervened to support the leisure sector with large capital projects such as the National Youth Administration to support the nation's leisure needs. This, however, was relatively short-lived, according to Hunnicutt (2004), as Roosevelt's New Deal chose between expanding leisure through a six-hour day and public investment to grow full-time employment, with the latter being the long-term strategy that saw a reflation of the economy and move towards economic growth.

What this shows, and what is particularly relevant in view of the global credit crunch, is that economic circumstances alongside public policy will create a policy arena where the relative involvement of the public–commercial–voluntary sectors will constantly change and develop in response to the prevailing situation facing policy-makers. Therefore, what this chapter has demonstrated is that the relative importance of the public, commercial and voluntary sectors in leisure provision in any given country or area will change through time and be affected by national and local policy setting as well as the interests and motivation of stakeholders that seek to provide leisure services and products. The policy context is a complex area for analysis and, as Henry (2001) indicates, it has not attracted a great deal of detailed research aside from useful summaries such as Bramham *et al.* (1993). These different sectors and the organisations operating within each create a very complex mixed economy of leisure which is not always appreciated by the public and users. This chapter has shown that the scope and wide-ranging significance of leisure as an activity and focus in people's everyday lives are shaped by a wide range of organisations, policies and structures as well as the resources which were examined in Chapter 5. Understanding leisure provision as an interconnected web of different interests that is politically determined and shaped by a multitude of agencies illustrates the overall significance of overarching bodies such as the public sector to try to plan, coordinate and manage leisure provision. For this reason, the next chapter examines this theme to illustrate how policies are put into practice, and the way provision is communicated to consumers.

Discussion questions

1. What is public policy making and how do different organisations and stakeholders contribute to the policy-making process?

2. How can leisure be used as a tool for addressing antisocial behaviour?

3. In what ways can the private sector complement the role of the public sector in leisure provision?

4. Compare and contrast the roles of the private and voluntary sector in leisure provision.

References

Audit Commission (2006) *Public Sports and Recreation Services: Making them Fit for the Future, Local Government National Report*, Audit Commission: London.

Audit Commission (2008) *Cultural Services: Oxford City Council, Service Inspection Report*, February, Audit Commission: London.

Audit Commission (2009) *Tired of Hanging Around: Using Sport and Leisure Activities to Prevent Anti-Social Behaviour by Young People*, Audit Commission: London.

Benson, A. and Henderson, S. (2005) 'UK leisure centres under best value: a strategic analysis', *International Journal of Public Sector Management* 18 (3): 196–215.

Bernstein, J. (ed.) (1991) *Adorno: The Culture Industry: Selected Essays on Mass Culture*, Routledge: London.

Borsay, P. (2006) *A History of Leisure: The British Experience since 1500*, Palgrave: Basingstoke.

Bramham, P., Henry, I., Mommas, H. and van der Poel, H. (eds) (1993) *Leisure Policies in Europe*, CABI: Wallingford.

Briggs, M. (1926) *Rusticus or the Future of the Countryside*, Kegan Paul, Trench, Trabner and Co Ltd: London.

Bull, C., Hoose, J. and Weed, M. (2003) *An Introduction to Leisure Studies*, Prentice Hall: Harlow.

Burnett, J. (2004) *England Eats Out: 1830 to Present*, Pearson: Harlow.

Clarke, J. and Critcher, C. (1985) *The Devil Makes Work: Leisure in Capitalist Society*, Macmillan: London.

Coalter, F. (1996) *Sport and Anti-Social Behaviour*, Sport Scotland: Edinburgh.

Coalter, F. (2000) 'Public and commercial leisure provision: active citizens and passive consumers?', *Leisure Studies* 19 (3): 163–81.

Coalter, F. (2006) 'The duality of leisure policy', in C. Rojek, S. Shaw and A. Veal (eds) *A Handbook of Leisure Studies*, Palgrave: Basingstoke, pp. 162–84.

Coalter, F., Long, J. and Duffield, B. (1986) *The Rationale for Public Sector Leisure*, Social Science Research Council: London.

Collins, M. (1995) 'Children's play – little orphan Annie in the British leisure system', in D. Leslie (ed.) *Tourism and Leisure: Perspectives on Provision*, Leisure Studies Association: Brighton, pp. 175–86.

Cook, D. (2004) 'Commercialisation of leisure', in G. Cross (ed.) *Encyclopaedia of Recreation and Leisure in America, Volume 1*, Thomson-Gale: Woodbridge, CT, pp. 220–6.

Crompton, J. (2000) 'Repositioning leisure services', *Managing Leisure* 5 (2): 65–75.

Cross, G. (ed.) (2004) *Encyclopaedia of Recreation and Leisure in America, Volume 1 and Volume 2*, Thomson-Gale: Woodbridge, CT.

Curson, A. (1995) 'Can you place your trust in them? The role of charitable trusts in leisure management', in D. Leslie (ed.) *Tourism and Leisure: Perspectives on Provision*, Leisure Studies Association: Brighton, pp. 63–80.

DETR (1998) *Modernising Local Government: Improving Local Services through Better Value*, The Stationery Office: London.

DETR (2000) *National Food Survey*, The Stationery Office: London.

DOE (1975) *Sport and Recreation*, Cmmd 6200, HMSO: London.

Finkelstein, J. and Lynch, R. (2006) 'Eating out and the appetite for leisure', in C. Rojek, S. Shaw and A. Veal (eds) *A Handbook of Leisure Studies*, Palgrave: Basingstoke, pp. 404–16.

Frost, J. (2004) 'Playgrounds', in G. Cross (ed.) *Encyclopaedia of Recreation and Leisure in America, Volume 2*, Thomson-Gale: Woodbridge, CT, pp. 117–21.

Gordon, C. and Babchuk, N. (1959) 'A typology of voluntary associations', *American Sociological Review* 24 (1): 22–9.

Gordon, P. and Doughan, D. (2006) *Women, Clubs and Associations in Britain*, Routledge: London.

Haywood, L., Kew, F., Bramham, P., Spink, J., Capenhurst, J. and Henry, I. (1989) *Understanding Leisure*, Stanley Thornes: Cheltenham.

Henry, I. (2001) *The Politics of Leisure Policy*, 2nd edn, Macmillan: Basingstoke.

Hunnicutt, B. (2004) 'Inter-war leisure', in G. Cross (ed.) *Encyclopaedia of Recreation and Leisure in America, Volume 1*, Thomson-Gale: Woodbridge, CT, pp. 476–84.

Hurley, A. (2004) 'Diners', in G. Cross (ed.) *Encyclopaedia of Recreation and Leisure in America, Volume 1*, Thomson-Gale: Woodbridge, CT, pp. 273–5.

Hutton, S. (1992) *A Review of the Role of Clubs and Voluntary Associations based on a Study of Two areas in Swansea*, Social Science Research Council: London.

Irvine, D. and Taylor, P. (1998) 'The value of commercial leisure', in M. Collins and I. Cooper (eds) *Leisure Management: Issues and Applications*, CABI: Wallingford, pp. 157–79.

Jacobs, M. and Scholliers, P. (eds) (2003) *Eating Out in Europe: Picnics, Gourmet Dining and Snacks since the late Eighteenth Century*, Berg: Oxford.

Kline, S. (2004) 'Commercialisation of children's play', in G. Cross (ed.) *Encyclopaedia of Recreation and Leisure in America, Volume 1*, Thomson-Gale: Woodbridge, CT, pp. 213–19.

Komarovsky, M. (1946) 'The voluntary associations of urban dwellers', *American Sociological Review* 11 (6): 686–98.

Lowi, T. (1972) 'Four systems of policy, politics and choice', *Public Administration Review* 32: 298–310.

Marling, W. (2004) 'Globalisation of American leisure', in G. Cross (ed.) *Encyclopaedia of Recreation and Leisure in America, Volume 1*, Thomson-Gale: Woodbridge, CT, pp. 402–10.

McIntosh, W. (2004) 'Comic magazines', in G. Cross (ed.) *Encyclopaedia of Recreation and Leisure in America, Volume 1*, Thomson-Gale: Woodbridge, CT, pp. 210–13.

Newton, K. (1976) *Second City Politics: Democratic Processes and Decision-Making in Birmingham*, Clarendon Press: Oxford.

Page, S. J. and Connell, J. (2009) *Tourism: A Modern Synthesis*, 3rd edn, Cengage Learning: London.

Page, S. J., Nielsen, K. and Goodenough, R. (1994) 'Managing urban parks: user perspectives and local leisure needs in the 1990s', *Service Industries Journal*, 14 (2): 216–37.

Parker, S. (1997) 'Leisure and culture: consumers or participants?', A paper presented at Leisure, Culture and Commerce, the Leisure Studies Association Conference, Roehampton Institute, London.

Pilsbury, R. (1990) *From Boarding House to Bistro*, Unwin Hyman: Boston.

Ravenscroft, N. (1996) 'Leisure, consumerism and active citizenship in the UK', *Managing Leisure* 1 (2): 163–74.

Roberts, K. (2004) *The Leisure Industries*, Palgrave: Basingstoke.

Robinson, L. (2004) *Managing Public Sport and Leisure Services*, Routledge: London.

Rojek, C., Shaw, S. and Veal, A. (eds) (2006) 'Introduction: Process and context', in C. Rojek, S. Shaw and A. Veal (eds) *A Handbook of Leisure Studies*, Palgrave: Basingstoke, pp. 1–24.

Scanlon, J. (2004) 'Women's magazines', in G. Cross (ed.) *Encyclopaedia of Recreation and Leisure in America, Volume 2*, Thomson-Gale: Woodbridge, CT, pp. 4–8.

Schlosser, E. (2002) *Fast Food Nation*, Penguin: London.

Siehl, G. (2000) 'U.S. recreation policies since World War Two', in W. Gartner and D. Lime (eds) *Trends in Outdoor Recreation, Leisure and Tourism*, CABI: Wallingford.

Simmons, R. (2004) 'A trend to trust? The rise of new leisure trusts in the UK', *Managing Leisure* 9 (3): 159–77.

Stebbins, R. and Graham, M. (eds) (2004) *Volunteering as Leisure: An International Assessment*, CABI: Wallingford.

Stebbins, R. (2006) 'Serious leisure', in C. Rojek, S. Shaw and A. Veal (eds) *A Handbook of Leisure Studies*, Palgrave: Basingstoke, pp. 448–58.

Taylor, P. (1993) 'Commercial leisure: exploiting consumer preferences', in J. Sugden and C. Knox (eds) *Leisure in the 1990s: Rolling back the Welfare State*, Leisure Studies Association: Brighton, pp. 137–43.

Tomlinson, A. (1979) *Leisure and the Role of Clubs and Voluntary Groups*, Social Science Research Council: London.

Torkildsen, G. (2005) *Leisure Management*, 5th edn, Routledge: London.

Travis, A. (1978) *The Role of Central Government in Relation to Local Authority Leisure Services in England and Wales*, Centre for Urban and Regional Studies, Birmingham University.

Turner, J. (1997) 'The policy process', in B. Axford, G. Browning, R. Huggins, B. Rosamond and J. Turner, *Politics: An Introduction*, London: Routledge, pp. 409–39.

Warde, A. and Martens, L. (2000) *Eating Out: Social Differentiation, Consumption and Pleasure*, Cambridge University Press: Cambridge.

Weed, M. (2001) 'Towards a model of cross-sectoral policy development in leisure: The case of sport and tourism', *Leisure Studies* 20 (2): 125–42.

White, J. (1992) *Leisure – the cornerstone of local government: a discussion paper*, University of Birmingham, Centre for Urban and Regional Studies, West Midlands Chief Leisure Officers' Association: Birmingham.

White, J. (1999) 'Managing the Lottery: evaluation of the first four years and lessons for local authorities', *Managing Leisure* 4 (1): 78–93.

Wood, R. (1995) *The Sociology of the Meal*, Edinburgh University Press: Edinburgh.

7 Planning, managing and marketing leisure

Learning outcomes

After reading this chapter, you should be able to:

- Explain the significance of leisure planning as a concept, its relationship to management and why it is used in leisure organisations

- Outline the different scales at which leisure planning occurs and how it is used to control and direct leisure activity

- Describe the role of marketing in leisure as a communication tool

Introduction

In Chapter 6 we examined the roles of the public, commercial and voluntary sectors in terms of leisure and it is apparent that 'leisure . . . facilities and services are not just there – they arise as a result of interaction between the public, as users and as political/social groups, and organizations and their activities' (Veal 2002: 6). This means that we need to understand how these interactions are shaped, planned, managed and communicated to leisure participants and the wider population. In the UK, the commercial development of leisure in the nineteenth century was preceded by the development of the voluntary and public sectors which laid the foundations for leisure provision. As Roberts (2004) suggests, the public, private and voluntary sectors each have specific objectives and capabilities in terms of leisure provision and differing ways of making their provision available to the population. Therefore, when we try to understand the way in which leisure is provided and consumed, it is apparent from Chapter 6 that the public policy framework is an important context which conditions the type and nature of provision made available by each of these sectors. But the public policy framework is only one part of a more complex jigsaw puzzle, associated with the planning and management of leisure provision and activities in different societies. As the previous quotation by Veal (2002: 6) implies, we need to understand the process by which the planning, management and marketing occur so that leisure provision and consumption can occur. In Chapter 5, we discussed the concept of management, highlighting its critical role in implementing plans within organisations. Within the leisure sector, managers often face numerous tasks in relation to this diverse area, related to internal processes such as the management of physical resources, human resources, finance and risk within the organisation (see more generic leisure management texts such as Torkildsen 2005 for more detail on the practice of leisure management within organisations). This is complemented by a focus on the external management of issues associated with the business environment, including communicating with customers. One way the private sector does this is through the process of marketing, which we will discuss in the second part of the chapter. However, in the first section, we will focus on the issues of leisure planning as used by the public sector to plan, manage, control and facilitate leisure.

Leisure planning

Henry and Spink (1990) suggest that planning is a tool used by organisations to help them achieve their objectives to strive towards success. In the private sector this success is normally measured in terms of profit, whereas in the public sector more overarching social and economic goals with a longer-term time horizon are often the focus. In the commercial sector planning will help a company achieve its operational objectives through a rational process of thinking and intended action. We will return to this in more detail later in the chapter in relation to marketing because the commercial sector is customer focused and targets the individual more than the public sector. The private sector will use very different tools and approaches to the public sector, undertaking planning with a narrow and exclusive focus on individuals/groups/market segments and the potential to generate profits. This is in stark contrast to the public sector focus on inclusivity, social groups and communities and more basic levels of service provision, with no direct profit motive. This also affects and shapes their approach towards planning.

An important starting point for a discussion of leisure planning is to try to understand what we mean by the term *planning*. According to Chadwick

(1971: 24), 'planning is the process, a process of human thought and action based upon that thought – in point of fact for the future – nothing more or less and this is planning, which is general human activity'. What this means is that planning as a process tries to anticipate, monitor and sometimes regulate change so that the leisure needs of the population can be better understood and managed by those organisations charged with this function. While much of the ensuing discussion will focus on how the public sector plans and manages leisure, this is also a function which many private sector (and voluntary sector) organisations undertake to ensure that their corporate objectives are met in relation to their involvement in leisure. As Veal (2002) suggested, we need to consider five elements in terms of leisure planning and policy making:

- *The leisure participants* (i.e. the people who engage in leisure at an individual, household or community level).

- *The organisations* which interact to create the different forms of leisure provision which were discussed in the previous chapter.

- *The services and facilities provided* in different locations and managed by leisure-related staff.

- *The resource environments* in which leisure occurs, ranging from the natural through to the built environment.

- The different *processes* which link together the participants, organisations, services and resources which are provided and consumed through the process of planning, management marketing and policy making.

What these five elements of leisure planning and policy making suggest is that there are two critical components that this chapter needs to examine:

- The way in which organisations manage the planning process in the public sector.

- The process of marketing, predominantly used by the private sector (although the growing use of social marketing in the public sector is expanding the remit of marketing's application to non-profit-making activities).

Clearly, policy making and planning cannot be easily separated but for the purposes of clarity in understanding, we need to recognise that the policy-making framework is an important determinant of what decisions are made in terms of how leisure is planned, managed and marketed. So while the political processes associated with leisure provision have been dealt with elsewhere, we should not forget the interconnections of policy making and planning. As Veal (2002: 6) suggested, while planning may in practice overlap with policy making, there is a fundamental difference between these two activities:

- *Policy making* is concerned with the process by which decisions are arrived at.

- *Planning* is about the management of operational issues (i.e. day-to-day issues) as well as more strategic matters relating to leisure provision.

A wide range of different policy-making and public policy paradigms (i.e. ways of thinking that prevail at a point in time) have evolved through time according to changing political ideologies (Figure 7.1), which shape the way in which leisure has been planned.

At a national government level, Veal (2002) points out that Western democracies use their government structures to develop and administer the law,

---

1970s: State-led planning for facilities and social groups: plan-led provision

1980s: Retrenchment, new managerialism and a greater role of the private sector focused on projects associated with:

- The heritage industry (e.g. see Hewison's 1987[1] polemical review of the challenges to authenticity with redevelopments such as Wigan Pier and the expansion of heritage centres as tourist attractions such as Jorvik in York)
- Urban regeneration and tourism (e.g. Urban Development Corporations and major projects such as Liverpool and London Docklands) where the commercial sector set the agenda in relation to specific projects

1990s: (NEW LABOUR)

- Evolution of a mixed development model for social and economic regeneration and inclusion with leisure, sports, tourism, retailing and housing projects combined in the thinking behind land use planning
- Public-Private sector Partnership ethos to utilise private sector investment with a degree of public-sector pump priming to ensure state objectives are considered

2000s:

- Cultural industries/cultural economy focus with a revitalised and holistic view of leisure as a strand of culture in city-wide planning frameworks to harness social and economic regeneration and inclusion
- Continued role for the private sector in neighbourhood revitalisation, including expanding focus on privatisation of public space and shift towards private management and development
- Leisure becoming subsumed under other state agendas for well-being (e.g. to address social and health issue such as obesity) and a loss of national guidance on public-led leisure provision in favour of more overarching social, economic and cultural strategies alongside an enhanced role for sport (especially in the lead up to the 2012 London Olympics)

2012

---

[1]Hewison, R. (1987) *The Heritage Industry*, Methuen: London.

Figure 7.1   Public sector paradigms for leisure planning in the UK

which will control and sometimes place limits on individual and collective behaviour as well as the economic activity associated with delivering goods and services. Yet the process through which they do this in leisure is not straightforward, as the last chapter suggests with the interaction of the private, voluntary and public sectors. In addition, in the public sector, there may be a multiplicity of organisations involved. For example, Figure 7.2 shows that the responsibility for leisure planning in the public sector may be split between those with a primary function and those with a secondary or peripheral function. This may lead to duplication of effort, overlaps in responsibility and gaps in policy and provision where no one organisation takes overall charge. Therefore, leisure will often be a cross-cutting function across numerous government departments.

Despite the significance of leisure planning as a prerequisite to create the infrastructure and opportunities for leisure, Henry and Spink (1990: 33) pointed to the dearth of academic research on leisure planning as,

> the treatment of leisure planning in the literature can be described as unsystematic and fragmented. At the outset it is important to make the distinction between the organisational planning which commercial bodies in leisure and recreation conduct, and statutory planning which the public sector undertake, where the public good is normally the underlying rationale . . . The public sector is often charged with the management and maintenance of facilities, locational issues and wider strategic goals for the population.

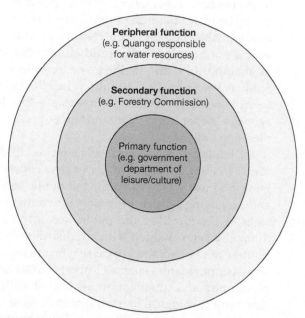

Figure 7.2 Responsibility for leisure planning in the public sector at a national/state level

Sources: Based on Mercer (ed.) (1981); Authors

This was subsequently reiterated and reinforced by Ravenscroft (1992: 135), who concluded that

> the whole framework upon which planning has been predicated has, for the most part, tended to neglect recreation. By largely basing development plans on land use zoning, it has tended to subjugate multiple uses in favour of primary ones. . . . This means that in areas where provision for recreation is seen as important, such as National Parks, primary uses such as agriculture and forestry still dominate . . . [and] the reactive nature of the planning process means that opportunities to secure recreation provision are not taken up.

Therefore it is not surprising to find Veal (1993: 85) arguing that

> planning for leisure in a comprehensive, systematic way is a relatively new form of human endeavour. In many countries, during the latter half of the 20th century, attempts have been made to determine appropriate roles for planning in relation to leisure and to devise suitable planning techniques and approaches.

While these three quotations illustrate a range of issues associated with the neglect of leisure planning as a practitioner and academic endeavour, since these studies in the 1990s there has been a noticeable decline in academic research on leisure planning. In the 1970s and 1980s, the subject was still in its ascendancy, reflected in the books and publications on the subject (see Patmore 1983; Henry and Spink 1990; Hall and Page 2006 for a review), but there have been comparatively few syntheses of the subject subsequently. One of the possible explanations of this neglect is that there is an assumption that the mainstream planning professions have adopted leisure as a theme and it has been absorbed into their research agendas. But this is not the whole story as it is not a high priority amid all the competing demands for resources in local authorities, despite the evidence of leisure spending illustrated in Case Study 6.2 of Oxford's cultural services. If anything, the adoption of a cultural services remit in planning terms means that leisure is subsumed in broader agendas rather than more resource-specific people-focused and land-use planning issues.

Yet while the names or labels attached to different aspects of leisure provision in local government circles may constantly change, there is an underlying premise which remains: the public sector is responsible for planning and managing leisure provision for communities. We should also not lose sight of the fact that the public sector, philosophically speaking, has traditionally been charged with a redistributive function so that leisure opportunities can be extended to those who are socioeconomically deprived. While some commentators such as Roberts (2004) are sceptical of the public sector philosophy and intervention associated with these motives, this remains a dominant ideological starting point in most countries for the planning and management of leisure. There are different philosophical debates on the merits and changing role of the state and how it intervenes in terms of leisure: these range from arguments related to encouraging citizenship through to rectifying perceived social and economic inequalities, as discussed in Chapter 6. However, the fact remains that the public sector is involved in leisure provision and planning and so we need to understand the evolution of the concept of leisure planning.

The evolution of leisure planning

In the context of the UK, Veal (1993) describes a number of phases in the evolution of leisure planning, which mirrors the evolution of policy positions discussed in Chapter 6 and paradigms of leisure planning as shown in Figure 7.1 which typify how many Westernised countries approached leisure planning. These phases can be summarised as follows:

- A *demand phase* which characterises the period from the 1960s to 1972 where leisure became a public planning issue focused on the notion of leisure demand. Much of the interest was a result of increasing affluence, rising car ownership and the growing impact of participants on leisure resources epitomised by Dower (1965) and the fourth wave as discussed in Chapter 3. As Veal (1993) indicated, the demand focus led to the creation of many public sector leisure facilities such as indoor leisure centres, swimming pools, arts centres, Country Parks, long-distance footpaths and the creation of different public sector organisations to manage specific leisure resources as reflected in Table 7.1, which outlines many of the countryside resources which the local authorities are responsible for planning.

- A *need phase* ranging from 1973 to 1985 where the previous focus on demand was questioned by many academic and government studies. New ideas emerged which suggested that planning needed to understand leisure

Table 7.1 A range of countryside recreational resources which require consideration in leisure plans in the UK

- Village greens
- Commons
- Country Parks (167 designated in England and Wales by the 1968 Countryside Act)
- Picnic places (also formalised for local authority planning requirements by the 1968 Countryside Act)
- National Parks
- Areas of Outstanding Natural Beauty, RAMSAR sites and other sites of special significance
- Archaeological sites
- Coastlines
- Canals, waterways and reservoirs

needs in more detail (we also consider this issue again later in the chapter in relation to marketing and its focus on consumer needs as commercial opportunities). As Chapter 4 highlighted, such a needs-focus led to the recognition that leisure was an important aspect of the population's daily needs and so leisure was to be considered in much the same way as other basic services such as housing, health and infrastructure provision.

● *An enterprise phase* ranging from 1983 through to 1993 based on many of the policy ideas of the Conservative government led by the British Prime Minister Margaret Thatcher. This saw a shift towards a greater private sector focus in leisure provision, with a re-focusing on competition to create private sector involvement in leisure provision.

As Table 6.1 suggested, other policy shifts since 1993 have led to a new generation of policy making and resulting approaches to leisure planning, for example a growing focus on social issues such as inclusivity, as discussed in Chapter 6.

These different phases of leisure policy created different approaches to leisure planning and principles used in planning. Veal (1993) argued that during the 1960s the only policy guidance available to leisure planners was the National Playing Fields Association standard that for every 1000 people, there should be six acres of open space provision. This standard dates from 1925, and while it has been regularly reviewed, it also stipulated that for every 1000 of the population, about 200 would be involved in some form of active sport, setting a threshold for sports facility provision. Consequently, much of the focus for public sector leisure planning in the 1960s was on understanding the volume of demand and then trying to provide facilities to meet that demand. During the needs phase, a range of more geographically focused techniques were developed and applied to leisure and recreation, epitomised by many of the studies reviewed in Patmore (1983). Many of these studies will be highlighted in future chapters, particularly in relation to urban recreation where they are still in evidence. Yet Patmore argued that the resources available for leisure provision are fragmented and the

> vagaries of the [planning] systems are a response not only to the variety of resources they control, or even to the variety of the providers themselves, with the differing philosophies of the public and private, commercial and voluntary sectors: rather, priorities and even philosophies still need to be articulated, and provision becomes haphazard in an at times alarming way. *(Patmore 1983: 237–8)*

This quotation illustrates just how important the lead role of the public sector is in coordinating these different priorities and philosophies towards leisure. Consequently, leisure planning offers a rational and organised approach to the way leisure is planned, managed and provided for the wider public good. For this reason, the public sector planning profession adopt different tools and techniques to plan for leisure and this is now the focus of the next section.

The purpose, process of, and techniques used in leisure planning

According to Veal (2002), leisure planning is something which an organisation undertakes based on its values, goals or policies, which can be viewed in two ways:

- First, planning is a *technical process* undertaken in the public sector, normally within the auspices of a planning department, or in specialist leisure departments or their equivalent.

- Second, we have to recognise that planning is also a political process associated with public policy, as discussed in Chapter 6. What the public policy framework should do is provide a context within which planning activity may be undertaken, so that the process becomes a technical one because the political aspects have already been identified and agreed.

Henry and Spink (1990) outlined three specific planning approaches used in leisure:

- *Profession-based*, which uses objective and rational tools such as a standards approach (as discussed in other chapters, such as the National Playing Fields Association space standards) to examine demand and impacts where established tools from the planning profession can be harnessed. There is also the recent introduction of Geographical Information Systems technology to create a more holistic view of the spatial aspects (i.e. geographical dimensions) of planning and how different facets are related and correlated.

- *Public-based approaches*, which are seeking to be participatory.

- *Private-sector focused*, which is a market-led approach seeking to bring commercial techniques to the process of planning or which favour the private sector. For example, the notion of *planning gain* (i.e. if a developer can be encouraged to develop a site, they must provide community facilities or make a social contribution elsewhere as a *quid pro quo*). In other words, the developer has to provide a social or community benefit back to the area rather than simply take an enhanced profit from the development opportunity. This principle is widely used in housing developments, so that developers have to provide play areas in return for the opportunity to develop a site, reducing the cost to the local authority to provide a leisure spaces. One additional example in the UK context is that local authorities approving new housing developments will often insist on mixed patterns of leisure so that luxury homes are built alongside a quota of social housing for rent or part ownership to help address local housing needs, providing a planning gain for the local authority.

However, what has been a dominant paradigm (i.e. a dominant way of thinking or philosophy/approach) in leisure planning is the *pluralist approach*: this suggests that society has competing interests and acknowledges that the public sector's role is to mediate between these interests to resolve conflict between them, often within communities and between the public and commercial sectors. This resolution of conflicting and competing demands is mediated through the planning process, which tries to embrace all the ideas and wishes of different stakeholders where possible. These interests are consulted and incorporated through the leisure planning process.

The leisure planning process

We can identify a number of distinct stages which the public sector leisure planner will follow in developing a plan. This process will be run alongside the planning process and illustrates the type of activities which a leisure officer may be expected to perform within a planning context. This will involve desk research and in some cases primary research as well as the development of a leisure strategy which will set out the guiding principles and objectives for the organisation in relation to the leisure plan. Leisure plans typically run for a period of three to five years and are periodically reviewed.

As Figure 7.3 shows, there are a number of steps involved in the leisure planning process and this should be seen as an ongoing activity which is constantly evolving and being monitored and evaluated. There are an important number of distinctions between leisure planning and the statutory planning functions which many local authority planners undertake. For example, leisure is a complex and wide-ranging phenomenon and so no two local authorities will provide the same range of services, facilities or resources because it is not a statutory requirement for local government to meet all of the needs of the population. In contrast, local government departments concerned with housing or social work need to meet its local obligations because there are statutory requirements and legislation setting out what it must do. Therefore, while leisure receives planning guidance from national government (devolved governments operate in Scotland, Wales and Northern Ireland with their own planning frameworks), it is only guidance, because local authorities will choose which aspects of leisure they wish to favour and invest in. A further complication is that leisure behaviour is not predictable and so even the provision of out-of-home leisure by the public sector may not match actual behaviour and needs of the population. This is because such behaviour is constantly evolving as new trends and fashions develop.

What this highlights is the difficulty and resourcing dilemmas the public sector faces in leisure provision: at the local authority level, they often have a historical legacy of resources which have developed in response to previous needs and demands and require resources for their maintenance and ongoing development. One notable example is the development of urban parks and open spaces which will be discussed in more detail in Chapter 8. In juxtaposition to these historical resources is a growing demand for capital-intensive

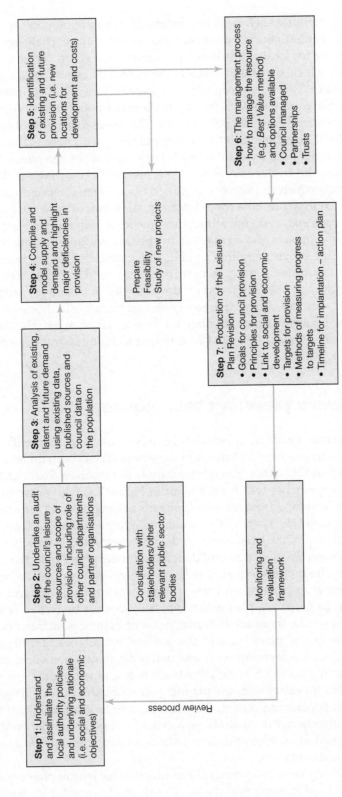

Figure 7.3 The leisure planning process at a local authority level – a step by step guide

Sources: Developed from Torkildsen (2005); Authors

sports facilities such as leisure centres and swimming pools which will require multi-million-pound investment and pose significant challenges in terms of resourcing for local authorities. For example, if a sports centre is constructed because of local demand, we need to recognise that many local authority budgets are finite. This may mean reducing expenditure on other areas of leisure provision to fund the sports facility, so there is an opportunity cost to any form of leisure spending in the public sector. This poses many ethical and equity issues for local government officers. For example, we know that urban parks and open spaces are used by a much larger section of the population than sport centres. But in the case of sport centres, politicians may see them as flagship projects which characterise their success as elected representatives for a local area, so they promote these large capital-intensive projects. In contrast, parks and open spaces do not attract the same level of interest among politicians and decision makers and so may fall by the wayside and become the poor cousins of leisure provision within a public sector context. This has been highlighted in many countries as a legacy of maintenance and investment needs has built up as parks and open spaces move down the list of leisure priorities drawn up by politicians. We also need to recognise that planning for leisure is not a static activity, because as public policy for leisure has changed, the nature of leisure planning has also changed as different techniques and principles have been adopted and developed.

Leisure planning techniques

Numerous technical approaches have been developed over the years in terms of leisure planning and much of the emphasis has been on how demand is assessed and then met through the supply of resources. Veal (2002) identified 11 such approaches which are set out in Figure 7.4, with an additional category added resulting from the developments in Geographical Information Systems. Some methods, such as the standards approach, have a long history of use which Veal (2008) reviewed to discuss alternative techniques, although the specific techniques used will depend upon the policy objectives. In theoretical terms, the process of planning has typically been plan-led, where public bodies draw up plans, then consult with local communities and other organisations to prepare a plan which typically lasts for up to five years. Within the public sector, there are different types of planning framework which reflect the history of planning and the political boundaries and organisations that exist in different countries. A selection of different frameworks for planning are shown in Figure 7.5, which illustrates how a range of different administrative boundaries exist for leisure planning reflecting the various geographical scales at which planning occurs. For example, Mercer (1981) highlighted the role of the public sector in Australia as a major focal point for planning as well as the divergent ideologies in different states on how they approached leisure planning and provision.

In many countries, much of the attention for leisure planning is directed towards local authorities at the local level who have statutory responsibilities for

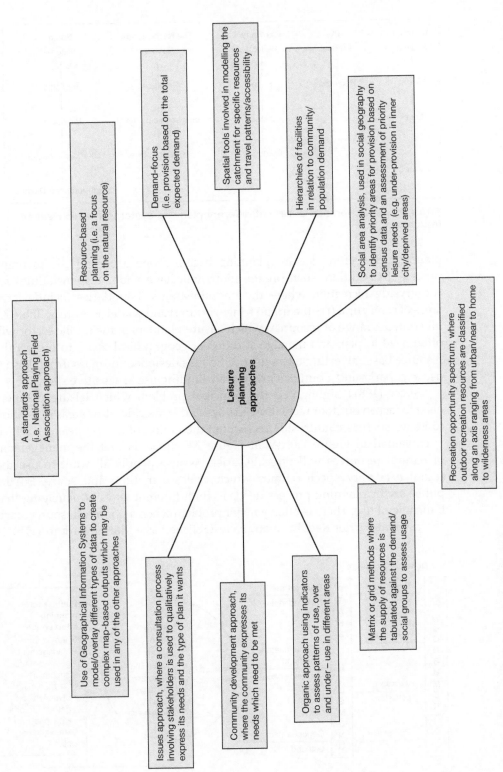

Figure 7.4   Technical planning approaches used in leisure

Sources: Adapted from Veal (2002, 2006); Authors

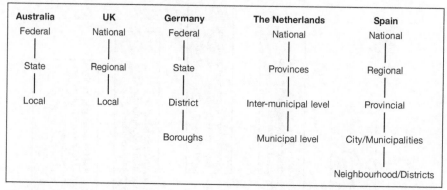

Figure 7.5 Schematic outline of different planning systems in which leisure features

planning. Therefore, leisure planning becomes one aspect of the planning process. In addition, such organisations will have wider responsibilities for countryside recreation where their administrative boundaries include large areas of semi-rural (i.e. the urban fringe) or rural and wilderness areas. Table 7.1 illustrated a range of resources which leisure planners in the public sector will often need to plan and manage at different geographical scales to protect the resource base, diverting users to specific sites designed for mass urban leisure use (e.g. parks and Country Parks) while limiting use at sensitive sites.

Mercer (1981) highlighted the principal problem which leisure planners need to face in outdoor recreation settings and at specific sites/areas in relation to issues such as countryside recreation: the notion of *leisure peaking* which is explained in Figure 7.6. What Figure 7.6 shows is that the management of natural resources will typically arise because people all want to use the resource at very specific times which coalesce in time and space. So the public sector planning process needs to find different ways of managing that bunching of use. There is often a major problem when a popular resource, such as the Great Barrier Reef in Australia (established as a Marine Park in 1975), is

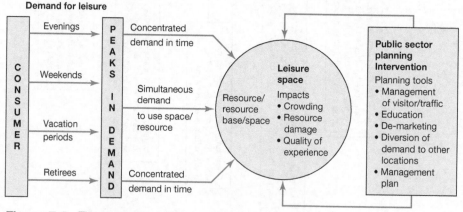

Figure 7.6 The concept of leisure peaking and planning

Sources: Adapted from Mercer (ed.) (1981); Authors

designated as a specific area for management and conservation. This popularises its use among leisure and tourist users, since it assumes a higher profile in how areas are marketed and then incorporated into visitors' activity patterns. It then almost always leads to a rise in visitation and pressure on the resource: this is the catch 22 for the public sector – it needs to designate the area as special to attract the resources to manage and protect it which then attracts more visitors, requiring more resources to manage it. In fact, while National Parks have been established since the late nineteenth century with the best of intentions, they have assumed a major attraction for visitors, owing to their designation, definition and creation as destinations for leisure and tourists trips. This intensified in the post-war period with the increasing levels of car ownership, making these resources more accessible to larger numbers of mobile leisure travellers. This is why the issue of leisure peaking needs careful planning and management. When such peaked demand occurs in wilderness and sensitive natural environments, planning and management may need to be very interventionist so that the whole arsenal of planning tools is harnessed to constrain or even ration use, as Figure 7.7 suggests. Figure 7.7 indicates that the planner is seeking to manipulate the leisure user's behaviour, as Grandage and Rodd's (1981) overview of planning constraints illustrates.

This highlights the delicate role of planning in any leisure context, which can best be described as trying to provide a framework where individuals and groups can exercise choice of what they do balanced with the ability of the resource to support such usage in time and space. This is so that leisure peaking does not lead to irreversible damage, and a decline of the quality and existence of the resource in an outdoor recreation context. In these very sensitive environments, which are sometimes under the management of National Park organisations, they will be responsible for the resource and typically produce a management plan which they implement as part of the planning process. This planning process will try to ensure that they balance use, enjoyment and

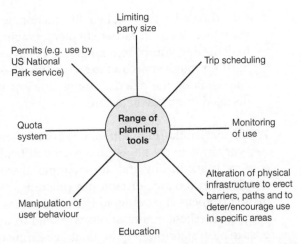

Figure 7.7 Planning techniques to constrain/ration access to wilderness areas

Sources: Adapted from Grandage and Rodd (1981); Authors

conservation needs. In stark contrast, leisure planning in urban areas will need also to address contemporary issues and barriers which exist in usage, as we will explore in the next chapter.

Green and Singleton (2007) highlighted some of the barriers which existed among young Asian Muslim women in Northern England, who felt unsafe in many public spaces in terms of leisure. They felt at risk in these public spaces and developed diverse strategies to address these concerns. The result was that young Asian women tried to walk in groups, used male chaperones, accepted lifts from family and friends to get to leisure venues and were less likely to participate in sport. They preferred to use indoor community venues that were comfortable and tension free. This also reflected a major leisure activity of young Asian women, namely socialising in groups. Consequently, leisure plans need to recognise these inherent barriers to out-of-home leisure for such groups, due to perceived risks. Therefore, measures need to be adopted in the planning process to adapt existing provision to fit these needs.

As planning in most countries has a statutory aspect, which means that it is established in legislation, this legislation will set out the nature and scope of the planning process. Typically, this involves the control of land use, the conservation of resources and the way in which leisure is integrated into these processes. This often means a focus on how resources are provided and managed in relation to land use and the needs and demands of the population.

According to White (1992), the focus of local authority planning is to coordinate and lead the planning function. White summarised the strengths of the planning system in England as it impacted upon leisure as:

- Being very community responsive.

- Enabling and encouraging people to engage in leisure.

- Providing value for money and quality leisure services.

- Caring for the environment.

- Providing a large social benefit function, which is associated with many of the issues raised in earlier chapters, ranging from crime reduction through to deflecting youth from antisocial behaviour, improving the community's health through sport and exercise as well as improving their quality of life, and assisting the elderly, young single parents, ethnic minorities and the disabled to engage in leisure.

Within local authorities, different types of planning framework exist and these will vary by country, although it is very difficult to generalise on a country-by-country basis. In England, for example, there over 400 planning authorities which cover the area of land use planning, ranging from county councils to district councils and National Park authorities through to the urban planning authorities. These organisations will tend to produce plans for a specific purpose to meet statutory requirement. As an illustration of what these plans do, it is useful to focus on one country – England – to illustrate their significance and role. While this is not necessarily replicated in the planning systems for leisure in other countries, it highlights common planning principles and what different plans seek to achieve.

There are three broad types of plan developed by the local authorities in England:

- Structure plans.

- Local plans.

- Development plans.

These also exist in many countries in different shapes and forms. *Structure plans* are often produced around national targets typically associated with aiming to match demand with current and future supply of leisure resources. Structure plans tend to look at land use policies as one way of geographically identifying patterns of demand and supply. The second type of plan produced by the public sector, normally within local authorities, is the *district or local plan* which looks at specific areas at a local level. This is often the level at which leisure and recreation are examined and analysed within communities so that issues of demand and supply are examined in relation to the existing resource base in an area. As the ODPM (2001) report outlined, within a planning context, some of the issues which planners address in relation to leisure are:

- Locational policies and strategies to identify the preferred location for new leisure development.

- Traffic and transport issues related to leisure.

- General policies for leisure use as well as specialist use such as building multiplexes.

- The development control process, managed via planning applications for new leisure development.

- The application of national planning guidance and its local implementation.

To which we can add:

- The sustainability of development (to which attention turns later).

Within England and Wales (a separate planning system exists in Scotland), local authorities also have to prepare *leisure development plans* to understand what the local development needs will be in the next five to ten years.

Overlaying these local authority organisations is the planning policy guidance provided by national government in relation to specific themes. For example, in the UK national government provides Planning Policy Guidance (PPG) 17: Planning for Open Space, Sport and Recreation. This was first produced in 1991 and set out the national government's main planning objectives which defined a range of strategic issues for local authorities in terms of developing new facilities and planning for leisure. PPG 17 is important because it suggests that standards of open space provision should be set at a local level rather than national level. It also suggested that local authorities should look at the standards of provision in relation to the quantity, quality and accessibility of these resources and that provision should be built into development plans.

As the review of leisure development plans by the ODPM (2001) report found, this was a weakly developed area in planning because:

- Under 33% of local authorities responding had undertaken audits of their existing leisure facilities.

- 60% of London Boroughs had problems identifying suitable sites for leisure development, especially for commercial projects.

- Only 25% of authorities had carried out market demand/need studies.

- 33% of local authorities had carried out liaison and consultation on the development plans while only 17% had undertaken research on planning effects of leisure uses. This is not surprising given the competing demands within planning departments.

Yet existing planning guidance requires local authorities to assess local needs, highlighting where there are deficiencies in provision, to develop suitable sites for further provision and to coordinate provision in relation to these land use planning functions. In addition, the guidance also highlights the importance of preserving open space, which has an immediate value for the local population. Yet as Torkildsen (2005) argued, it does not specifically refer to the principles of the NPFA and its six-acre standard. The guidance also views leisure as a flexible area for provision, where open space and sports facilities should be protected. PPG 17 also provides guidance on other issues such as allotments, indoor sports facilities and developing commercial partnerships, along with other issues. What is important here is that local authorities are given guidance from national government and so the development of a public policy framework is set at a national level and has to be adapted and tailored to local needs within specific settings. All of these activities in relation to planning also have to fit within the current planning legislation such as the UK's Town and Country Planning Acts. In any planning context, the local authority also has to recognise the interests of different stakeholders and so the development of leisure plans will tend to follow a logical development process within most countries, so that the strategic development of leisure needs is built into the ongoing process of planning for the social and economic activities of specific areas.

This national system of planning in England is also changing as government planning guidance is moving from PPGs to a new style of Planning Policy Statements (PPS) where

Planning Policy Guidance Notes (PPGs) and their replacements Planning Policy Statements (PPSs) are prepared by the government after public consultation to explain statutory provisions and provide guidance to local authorities and others on planning policy and the operation of the planning system. They also explain the relationship between planning policies and other policies which have an important bearing on issues of development and land use. Local authorities must take their contents into account in preparing their development plan documents. The guidance may also be relevant to decisions on individual planning applications and appeals. (http://www.communities.gov.uk)

This provides a greater focus on the holistic nature of planning and the cross-cutting issues which affect it, including the concept of sustainability.

Towards sustainable leisure planning and provision: a challenge for the twenty-first century?

Sustainability and the associated concept of sustainable development, as discussed in Chapter 5 in relation to mobility, have become dominant features of how the public and private sectors now approach the development of many aspects of human activity, especially the planning system. Sustainability is now a commonly used term in everyday use and arose from a growing consensus during the 1980s over concern with environmental issues and the impact of different forms of economic development, particularly its link to climate change and global warming. This international growth in *environmentalism* has meant that there is a greater emphasis on the protection, conservation and management of the environment as a natural and finite resource (i.e. it is a renewable resource such as water that can replenish itself). Within the planning profession and public sector, this concern has emerged in the form of the concept of *sustainable development* which highlights the vulnerability of the environment to human impacts and the need to consider its long-term maintenance. Much of the initial stimulus to a global awareness of sustainable development can be traced to the influential 1987 World Commission on Environment and Development (WCED) report *Our Common Future* (WCED 1987), which asserts that 'we have not inherited the earth from our parents but borrowed it from our children'. In other words, sustainable development is based on the principle of 'meeting the needs of the present without compromising the ability of future generations to meet their own needs' (WCED 1987). In 1992, the World Earth Summit held in Rio de Janeiro highlighted many of these global environmental problems and the issues of global warming and climate change. In 1997, the Kyoto Protocol was signed by over 100 countries to pledge to cut greenhouse gases such as CO_2 that contribute to global warming. A Rio plus 10 summit held in Johannesburg revisited many of the issues raised in 1992. In the UK this led to a revision of national planning guidance, such as Planning Policy Statement 1: Delivering Sustainable Development (ODPM 2005) which replaced a 1997 PPG.

What this means is that all forms of local authority planning in England must consider this issue across all of its planning activity. In terms of leisure, it also means that leisure opportunities need to be accessible, while the quality of the environment is protected along with the amenity value of the countryside and urban areas. It places an onus on planners to consider their stewardship of resources which they manage for future generations, as well as new concepts of reusing brownfield sites (i.e. derelict sites and those polluted) for new uses as opposed to developing greenfield sites. It also re-emphasised the role of development plans to accommodate future leisure developments, with a greater emphasis on development that promotes mixed uses to reduce the need for additional travel by communities for leisure and recreation alongside employment. This has been complemented in England by the need for regions to produce Regional Transport Strategies and Plans for a 15–20 year period to inform local authority planning for issues such as leisure, after an extensive process of consultation with stakeholders as it will affect long-term land use.

Yet from a leisure user perspective, the main challenge for planners to grasp is a problem highlighted many years ago by Blackie *et al.* (1979) – how far are the patterns of participation represented in periodic surveys of the population more than just a snapshot? – as such surveys tend to view leisure in a type of vacuum. Indeed, what the concept of leisure planning does not necessarily find easy is to link the understanding of demand as measured through participation surveys with the notion of individual and group leisure activity across all areas of their life. One key dimension to this is the level of personal mobility which people have and how this will determine where and when they consume leisure resources, as a dynamic series of continuous time–space actions that are not necessarily planned and ordered. Leisure activity may be ordered, random or a combination of both. For the planner, understanding the time and space dimensions of leisure behaviour and how they impact on resources and create specific needs is a principal challenge for any planner or planning process. It requires the planner to translate the dimensions of leisure supply and demand into a land use (i.e. a spatial) framework for planning purposes, where out-of-home leisure is allocated to different spaces and places. This is also complicated by needing to be able to think about current and future needs and planning requirements. So while the immediate challenge of leisure planning may be about accommodating peak use at the more popular sites, we also need to find ways of understanding the nature of leisure as a process.

Leisure has many multidimensional components made up of each individual in a community and their potential to consume resources. Even so, the practicalities of embracing the principles of sustainability in leisure planning are that many people are very aspirational about sustainability. This means, as a DEFRA study (Dresner *et al.* 2007) found, that leisure users have very good intentions about wanting to be more environmentally sensitive and sustainable in their daily lives, but they do not follow it through with action (i.e. they may think it is a good idea to help save the planet by thinking green but are unwilling to adapt their lives or behaviour such as using public transport, as that is for other people). This is why the state sometimes has to intervene at different levels through the planning and legislative processes to change behaviour, particularly in the case of leisure. Figure 7.8 illustrates the levels of public intervention which may occur in relation to leisure and sustainability, such as seeking to reduce car use for leisure trips. It also shows how effective certain measures are and the different policy choices available as well as how a spectrum ranging from no intervention through to regulation exists. It also shows the difficulty of developing policy at a national level and then asking local authorities to implement it at a local level.

Research for the Department for Communities and Local Government (2006) also identified the need for local government to adopt a more strategic role to shift their planning focus from a preoccupation with capacity planning and facilitation to focus more attention on leisure needs, such as target groups and connections with other agendas such as healthier communities, and of course, the sustainability agenda. While this is in evidence in some of the *Best Value* audits by the Audit Commission, the sustainability agenda poses many planning challenges. One illustration of the types of conflicting challenges which local authorities face from a sustainability perspective are reflected in the case of second homes as places for leisure. As the concept of sustainability has economic, socio-cultural and environmental dimensions, the example of second homes examined in Case Study 7.1 illustrates the issues that planners need to weigh up in forming a judgement on how to plan and manage this aspect of leisure provision.

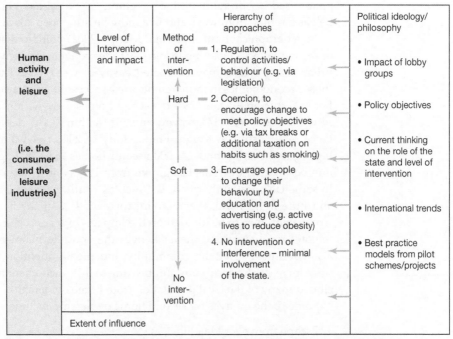

Figure 7.8 Levels of public sector intervention to regulate individual/group behaviour in society: implications for leisure planning and sustainability

Case Study 7.1   Second homes – curse or blessing

Second homes are one of the more contentious areas of tourism and leisure accommodation, especially in rural/coastal areas where incoming tourist purchases push local property prices up above the reach of local residents. The term second home can have a wide range of meanings, including recreational homes, summer homes, cottages and weekend homes (Hall and Müller 2004). Second homes are defined as 'a permanent building which is the occasional residence of a household that usually lives elsewhere and which is primarily used for recreation purposes. This definition excludes caravans, boats, holiday cottages (rented for a holiday) and properties in major cities and industrial towns' (Shucksmith 1983: 74). The definition provides a basis for understanding the nature of holiday cottages and seasonal use, a feature found in many countries, but it excludes the growing volume of mobile second homes and alternative forms of accommodation.

Seminal studies of this phenomenon (e.g. Coppock 1977) and recent studies (Hall and Müller 2004) identify three groups of second homes: stationary, semi-mobile and mobile second homes. Historically, the second home was an exclusive home for nobility and the wealthy classes in ancient and pre-industrial times, and the practice continued during the industrial revolution, as the new middle classes emulated the upper classes, purchasing land and building properties in locations accessed by new forms of transportation. In the twentieth century this idea permeated down to the working classes, epitomised in London with the development of holiday homes in the green belt as a refuge from work and in a more healthy open space.

In geographical terms, Hall and Müller (2004) point to distinctive patterns of second homes clustering in journey times convenient from origins in major urban areas, which may be visited easily at weekends. They also identify those second homes in more remote areas, accessed only once or twice a year. For example, in Sweden 25% of second homes were within 14 km of a main residence, 50% were 37 km away and 75% within 98 km, depicting a clear distance relationship. A Knight Frank study in 2008 (www.knightfrank.co.uk) highlighted that around 241,000 second homes exist in England, while the number located overseas has grown from 115,000 in 1996 to 248,000 in 2007. In some UK local authority areas, such as South Hams in Devon and Argyll and Bute in Scotland, they account for over 11% of the housing stock. Research continues to be divided on the impacts of second homes, especially in remoter rural areas and the challenges they pose to planners. The issue has also continued to attract community and media attention where property price increases for local communities due to this phenomenon has socially excluded many of the local population from home ownership.

Some of the motives for second home ownership include:

- Escape from everyday life.
- Getting back to nature.

- A clear relationship with personal identity, with family connections to a location/area.
- The ownership of global travel options, where global time-shares or apartments are purchased, which has become a major trend for UK holiday-makers.
- A life-cycle component, with people buying property for the later stage of life (i.e. retirement).

While such trends may contribute to economic impacts in the destination area, there is an ongoing debate on whether these are a blessing or curse (Coppock 1977). The impact on property prices may be cited as negative for local residents, but the reuse of redundant buildings and generation of new tourism income are cited as beneficial for localities. But the controversy of absentee owners paying only partial domestic rates has remained highly controversial, along with the social blight on localities in community terms outside of the tourist season. Not only are local people squeezed from the local housing market, but the area lacks the social vitality and community spirit of day-to-day life with all-year residents. This also creates a social gradient between residents and more affluent incoming tourists. Indeed, the seasonal impact of incoming tourists poses many strains on local services. For example, in the Spanish municipality of Torrevieja, a local population of 35,000 also had 70,000 second home owners who were perceived as tourists by residents. Yet the problems of managing second homes at the local government level remains a perennial problem, as many local authorities have inadequate records.

Scotland was examined in a study published by Communities Scotland (Bevan and Rhodes 2005). It identified the scale of second home ownership using the 2001 Census, estimating that there are 29,299 second and holiday homes in Scotland with 47% located in very remote rural areas. The geographical concentration illustrated that second homes were predominantly in rural areas with high scenic qualities. The Communities Scotland report identifies the geographical clustering of second homes in remoter rural locations where certain districts (e.g. in West Argyll) have a strong dominance of second homes. The continued growth in this market has placed additional inflationary pressures on house prices and poses a number of risks for the sector, not least in terms of alienating local communities if the issue is not managed. The effect on rural service provision is particularly marked where owners are not resident all year round and able to support the viability of vital services (e.g. shops and post offices).

In a Western context, with the ageing population and rising affluence, increasing second home ownership seems set to grow further, posing ongoing challenges for planners. As Müller and Hall (2004) acknowledge, in 2000 11% of the world's population was aged 60 years or more; by 2050, this will rise to 20%. Many parts of the world with highly developed tourism economies already have a large clustering of second homes (e.g. the Mediterranean, Iberian Peninsula, Australia's Gold and Sunshine Coasts, the South-West

USA, California and Florida). The second home remains a feature of many national cultures, including the 'Cottage' in Canada, 'Stuga' in Sweden, 'Hytte' in Norway, and 'bach' in New Zealand and the various elite forms in the former Soviet Union (dacha). However, the extent to which second home development is 'more of a blessing than a curse for many regions' (Müller and Hall 2004: 278) remains debatable and dependent upon the local context, the impacts tourism generates and local acceptance of the phenomenon along with the political context.

Source: Page and Connell (2009)

What Case Study 7.1 illustrates is the competing demands for planners between those favouring tourism, because of the economic vitality such spending provides for rural areas, versus the social and cultural problems this poses for destination communities as well as the environmental impacts of new development (where second home development is not based upon reuse of redundant or vacant buildings). Therefore, public sector planning has to address many leisure challenges, and understanding its significance is a major theme to consider in the analysis of leisure policy and how it is interpreted and then implemented. In contrast, the private sector adopts different approaches to planning and managing business activities to interact with leisure consumers and, for this reason, attention now turns to how non-public-sector organisations use marketing as the principal way of communicating with consumers. Marketing also embodies a range of planning techniques to develop a profitable customer-focused business model and for this reason the discussion commences with a focus on the leisure consumer and leisure organisations because the consumer is the central feature of leisure consumption.

The leisure consumer and leisure organisations

According to Horner and Swarbrooke (2005), there are a wide range of commercial organisations which provide leisure opportunities for consumers, including those associated with:

- Food.
- Accommodation.
- Shopping.
- In-home leisure.
- Spectator organisations.
- Recreation organisations.

- Organisations concerned with learning.

- Transport organisations.

Each of these will seek to communicate with the consumer, as Winlow and Hall (2006: 75) indicated, in relation to urban leisure, 'now that leisure no longer fulfils the mere function of periodic refreshment but has become a crucial profit-making cog in consumer capitalism's machine'. The significance of commercial leisure is that it is now a dominant feature of our lives as it is 'woven into the fabric of everyday life and imbued with crucial meanings, hopes and fantasies, as it becomes so central to their sense of self and self-belonging it also becomes diffuse with a complex range of anxieties, tensions and pressures that direct the increasingly fragmented, unpredictable and isolating nature of the society' (Winlow and Hall 2006: 91) we live in. One area of major growth has been sport and the application of marketing principles, where supporters have become leisure consumers, purchasing merchandise which in turn has been deemed fashion items. This is a feature examined by Mason (1999) in relation to two key questions marketers ask:

- What is the sports product?

- Who buys it?

But it is not just the physical consumption of leisure products that interests marketers. We also need to recognise the growth of the Internet as a virtual meeting place, where communities of consumers gather – known as *e-tribes* (Kozinets 1999). These comprise the virtual communities of consumers, with different defining characteristics for each e-tribe, which researchers examine using an anthropological research technique – ethnography, adapted to Internet research and called netnography. Such research seeks to understand how these online communities of consumers use the Internet in their leisure time and the marketing opportunities, as highlighted by Cova and Cova (2002).

One of the other notable aspects of leisure consumption is that it comprises an *experience* (see Chapter 5 and the concept of the experience economy – see Lonsway 2009) which results from the consumers' decision to purchase a specific product, experience for service. Some of the defining characteristics of the leisure experience which organisations have to be aware of when communicating with consumers are as follows:

- The consumption of leisure products and services is intrinsically linked to the concept of individual lifestyle and consumer trends.

- The way in which leisure products and services are supplied to the consumer results from complex commercial and non-commercial distribution networks.

- The way in which leisure is priced as a product or service does not necessarily take into account the true cost of provision as publicly owned resources are sometimes included in the leisure experience, such as National Parks which do not charge for their use.

- Many leisure purchases involve high levels of expenditure on infrequently purchased products which are consumed alongside freely available experiences that are consumed on a daily basis, such as visiting a museum or art gallery or walking in a park.

- Leisure may be a service, a product or a complex interaction of both service and product elements which the consumer has a high expectation of in any purchase.

Source: after Horner and Swarbroke (2005); author

Organisations need to recognise that the leisure experience for consumers will be affected by a number of important elements in relation to their behaviour and decision-making processes associated with consumption, including:

- Their motivation, where their personality, lifestyle, experiences and image of the leisure experience will shape their overall motivation for different types of leisure products and services.

- Following on from the motivations are a range of determinants that affect the decision-making process because the consumer will look at their own personal circumstances (i.e. do they have enough income available?), their knowledge of the product or service, their attitudes and perceptions towards the product or service as well as their prior experience.

On the basis of the motivations and determinants, the consumer will then go through a set process in terms of deciding whether they wish to purchase a product or service, which follows the typical format:

- This will start with the *pre-purchase stage*, where the consumer will look at the choices available, consider their perceptions of leisure as well as other important factors such as the services available and importance of significant issues such as brands (discussed later in the chapter).

- The consumer then goes through an *information search stage* which is where the marketing communication process from the leisure organisation becomes important, because it can then influence the consumer through the types of products, services and brands they offer.

- The consumer then goes through a *purchase stage*, where the organisation may sell directly to the consumer, through a third party or increasingly may sell to the consumer through the Internet.

- This is followed by a *post-purchase stage* where the organisation will continue to engage with the consumer through after-sales support or through types of initiative which build a relationship between the consumer and the organisation.

- Lastly, there is the *re-purchase stage* where the ongoing relationship between the consumer and the organisation, through specific incentives such as loyalty schemes, may encourage the consumer to re-purchase a product, service or experience from the organisation in question.

It is widely recognised within leisure that the major cost in marketing is in recruiting the consumer initially and so efforts to maintain the consumer's loyalty and interest in the organisation illustrates the importance of the post-purchase and re-purchase stage. This is very much an iterative process from the initial pre-purchase stage through to the post-purchase stage, because consumers are constantly purchasing different forms of leisure product or experience and evaluating what they wish to purchase.

Source: Developed and modified from Horner and Swarbrooke (2005)

The way in which leisure organisations communicate and interact with consumers to influence the consumer purchase process is through the practice of marketing. This reflects the fact that many organisations offering products to the leisure consumer will need to follow a market-led approach so that they align their products with what the consumer needs and wants. For this reason it is now pertinent to examine the relationship between leisure and marketing.

Leisure and marketing

Marketing has an important role to play in the analysis of leisure because the fundamental concepts with which it deals are human needs and wants for services or products which it will then fulfil. As Kotler *et al.* (2005: 9) argued,

> companies address needs by putting forth a value proposition, which is a set of benefits that they promise to consumers to satisfy their needs. The value proposition is fulfilled through a marketing offer – some combination of products, services, information, or experiences offered to a market to satisfy a need or want. Marketing offers are not limited to physical products. In addition to tangible products, marketing offers include services, activities or benefits offered for sale that are essentially intangible and do not result in the ownership of anything.

This illustrates, as Kotler *et al.* (2005) suggest, that marketing is a process whereby individuals and groups obtain the type of products or goods they value – a process of satisfying needs, which is particularly significant for leisure in relation to the concept of leisure needs. These goods are created and exchanged through a social and managerial process which requires a detailed understanding of consumers and their wants and desires so that the product or service is delivered effectively to the client or purchaser. This is summarised in Table 7.2 which outlines the nature, objective and way in which marketing is achieved.

One way in which consumers make choices through the consumer decision-making process is the concept of *customer value*. This is one way in which consumers will compare different products and services and then make a judgement in relation to which service or product gives them the best value. In

Table 7.2   A summary of marketing

What is marketing? A managerial process deployed by an organisation (individual or group).

What is its objective? To fulfil the needs and wants of the deploying organisation. These could be anything. They could be to maximise profits, although the objective of commercial marketers is usually to achieve sales targets or market share objectives. More generally, the objective for a profit or non-profit organisation could be to change the needs and wants of other individuals or groups.

How is this achieved? A social process whereby other individuals or groups obtain needs and wants by creating an exchange of products and value. This limits how the deploying organisation behaves. It has to understand the needs and wants of other individuals or groups and change itself so that it can create products and value that it can exchange.

Source: Kotler *et al.* (2005: 8). Copyright © Pearson Education Ltd

the case of leisure, it is evident that products and services may be tangible or intangible and consumers may judge them very objectively or very subjectively, particularly in terms of their perceived value. This is where the process of marketing becomes important, because this is where organisations will decide to offer products and experiences which satisfy needs and wants through this exchange process, helping the consumer to make a decision on what to purchase. The exchange process is where people can obtain the service, experience of product they desire in return for payment, donation or through participation where there is no charge involved for a leisure experience. This usually involves a transaction between two parties which may bring a response to a specific offer being made by an organisation. As leisure is a wholly discretionary element of consumer spending (i.e. people do not have to spend money on this to survive), the notion of relationship marketing becomes important. *Relationship marketing* is about the way in which organisations build and maintain strong relationships with their consumers or other stakeholders. This all hinges upon the concept of exchange, and the relationship between consumer and producer which then creates a market for a product, service or experience. As Figure 7.9 shows, the combination of these different components leads to the creation of the marketing system in leisure where the leisure industries will supply the different goods and services which the consumer requires.

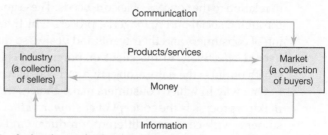

Figure 7.9   A simple marketing system

What Figure 7.9 suggests is that the buyers and sellers in the marketing system are connected together through four types of flow:

- The leisure organisation will produce products and services and communicate with the market.

- The consumer will supply money in return for the products and services as well as information which helps the organisation to make decisions about what to produce now and in the future.

- The exchange process between the buyer and seller is based upon an exchange of money for goods.

- The outer loop involves an exchange of information.

Therefore, leisure organisations will be focused on the concept of selling goods and services, which will require sales and promotion activities focused on the market and customers' needs. Therefore, the process of marketing will have an ultimate goal of achieving profit for an organisation supplying commercial goods and services through enhanced customer satisfaction.

In the case of leisure, there are also a number of other concepts which we need to think about in terms of marketing. There is the notion of *social marketing*, which focuses on the use of marketing to increase the acceptability or involvement of the target group in a leisure activity or form of leisure consumption that is not based on purchasing a product or experience. It may involve the promotion of government social targets through public health campaigns with a leisure dimension to reduce smoking, drug abuse and obesity. But social marketing is more complex than advertising which is applied to these issues. It reflects the application of marketing concepts which replace the focus on profits with human welfare and well-being. Social marketing has been widely used within the leisure domain by non-governmental organisations (NGOs) to promote their activities and to communicate to target audiences. As Bright (2000) argued, social marketing has a valuable role to play in social ideas and the use of commercial marketing techniques to influence voluntary behaviours of the target audience. Part of this process is to convince people to participate as well as communicating with people to highlight the personal benefits of leisure, especially active recreation and the contribution to personal well-being.

Irrespective of the motives for marketing, it is clear that for leisure organisations which seek to attract the leisure consumer they will need to be customer focused and aware of the competition and the need for added value to the experiences they offer (i.e. the additional benefits derived from a purchase or experience that the consumer perceives as offering them a better experience). This requires a sophisticated understanding of consumer markets, particularly the focus on the individual as a consumer which has been discussed in detail in earlier chapters in relation to needs, wants and motivations of leisure consumers. To understand consumers, organisations will need to engage in market research and surveys to understand these markets and the behaviour of individual and aggregate groups of consumers. While readers should examine seminal texts such as Kotler *et al.* (2005) for an in-depth evaluation of marketing, there are three specific issues which we should examine in relation to leisure marketing to understand how an organisation aligns itself with specific customers to develop a range of leisure products and experiences targeted at specific markets:

● Strategic planning.

● Marketing research as a way of understanding leisure consumers.

● The marketing mix, which allows the organisation to produce a response in relation to how to target specific markets.

Strategic planning

Within any business or company, there is a need to provide some degree of order or structure to its activities and to think ahead. This is essential if companies are to be able to respond to the competitive business environment in which they operate. For this reason a formal planning process, known as *strategic planning,* is necessary. According to Kotler and Armstrong (1991: 29), strategic planning can be defined as 'the process of developing and maintaining a strategic fit between the organisation's goals and capabilities and its changing marketing opportunities'.

Businesses need to be aware of their position in the wider business environment and how they will respond to competition and new business opportunities within an organised framework. To illustrate how strategic planning operates and its significance to leisure, it is useful to focus on the structured approach devised by Kotler and Armstrong (1991). The first stage is the definition of an organisation's purpose, which requires a company to consider:

● What business is it in?

● Who are its customers?

● What services do its customers require?

The stage following the setting of objectives and goals is termed the *business portfolio.* Here the company analyses its own products or services in terms of its own business expertise and how competitors' products and services may affect them. This is frequently undertaken as a SWOT analysis, which considers:

● the **S**trengths;

● the **W**eaknesses;

● the **O**pportunities;

● the **T**hreats;

● its products and services in the business environment.

Part of the wider strategic analysis of the business environment will also involve environmental scanning to try to understand what will be driving future change in a company's marketing activity (i.e. driver analysis). This involves a wide-ranging analysis of informal and formal sources of information to understand key uncertainties which will shape the future. One key element of the information-gathering process for strategic planning is marketing research.

Marketing research

This process is often seen as synonymous with market research but as the following definition by Seibert (1973) implies, in reality it is a much broader concept as 'marketing research is an organised process associated with the gathering, processing, analysis, storage and dissemination of information to facilitate and improve decision-making'. It incorporates various forms of research undertaken by organisations to understand their customers, markets and business efficiency. The actual research methods used to investigate different aspects of a company's business ultimately determine the type of research undertaken. The main types of research can be summarised into the following categories:

● Market analysis and forecasting, used to measure the volume, value and likely changes in markets.

● Consumer research, to examine specific market segments or the ability to position oneself at a specific point in the marketplace.

● Product/price-based studies to assess the price sensitivity consumers have for specific products.

● Distribution research, which examines distributor awareness of products.

● Evaluation studies, which can include customer satisfaction studies.

Clearly marketing research allows the company to keep in touch with its customers to monitor needs and tastes that are constantly changing in time and space. However, the actual implementation of marketing for leisure ultimately depends on the 'marketing mix'.

The marketing mix

The marketing mix is 'the mixture of controllable marketing variables that the firm [or company] uses to pursue the sought level of sales in the target market' (Kotler, cited in Holloway and Plant 1988: 48). This means that for a given leisure organisation seeking to attract leisure consumers, such as an airline, there are four main marketing variables which it needs to harness to achieve the goals identified in the marketing strategy formulated through the strategic planning process. As Kotler *et al.* (2005: 34) suggest, the marketing mix is a 'set of controllable tactical marketing tools – product, price, place and promotion – that the firm blends to produce the response it wants in the target market'. These variables (as set out in Figure 7.10) are:

● *Product formulation* – the ability of a company to adapt to the needs of its customers in terms of the services it provides. These are constantly being adapted to changes in consumer markets.

● *Price* – the economic concept used to adjust the supply of a service to meet the demand, taking account of sales targets and turnover.

● *Promotion* – the manner in which a company seeks to improve customers' knowledge of the services it sells so that those people who are made aware may be turned into actual purchasers. To achieve promotional aims, advertising, public relations, sales and brochure production activities are undertaken. Not surprisingly, promotion often consumes the largest proportion of marketing budgets. For transport operators, the timetable is widely used as a communication tool, while brochures and information leaflets are produced to publicise products. Some of the other promotional tools used to increase sales include promotional fares, frequent flyer programmes and 'piggy-back promotions where purchasing one type of product gives consumers an opportunity to enjoy a special deal in relation to another product' (Horner and Swarbrooke 1996: 322).

● *Place* – the location at which *prospective* customers may be induced to purchase a service – the point of sale (e.g. a travel agent).

As marketing variables, production, price, promotion and place are normally called the four Ps. These are incorporated into the marketing process in relation to the known competition and the impact of market conditions. Thus the

Marketing mix

Product	Promotion	Price	Place
Variety	Advertising	List price	Channels
Quality	Promotions	Discounts	Coverage
Design	Personal selling	Allowances	Assortments
Features	Publicity	Payment period	Locations
Brand name		Credit terms	Inventory
Packaging			Transport
Services			
Warranties			

Target market

Figure 7.10   The four Ps: the marketing mix

Source: Adapted from Kotler *et al.* (2005). Copyright © Pearson Education Ltd

marketing process involves the continuous evaluation of how a business operates internally and externally and can be summarised as 'the management process which identifies, anticipates and supplies customers' requirements efficiently and profitably' (UK Institute of Marketing, cited in Cannon 1989).

In fact, Kotler *et al.* (2005) suggest that companies might also wish to look at the four Ps as the customer four Cs:

- Customer needs and wants (product).

- Cost to the customer (price).

- Convenience (place).

- Communication (promotion).

Source: Developed from Kotler *et al.* (2005: 35)

As leisure is widely seen as an experience, product or service, rising consumer expectations mean that it is important to understand what we mean by the term service as it has distinct characteristics in how it is marketed, understood by the consumer and the way in which quality is assessed in relation to leisure experiences.

Leisure consumers, leisure services and marketing

Defining the term 'service' is difficult owing to the intangibility, perishability and inseparability of services. Kotler and Armstrong (1991: 620) define these three terms as follows:

- *Service intangibility* – a service is something that cannot be seen, tasted, felt, heard or smelt before it is purchased.

- *Service perishability* – a service cannot be stored for sale or use at a later date.

- *Service inseparability* – a service is usually produced and consumed at the same time and cannot be separated from providers.

Van Dierdonck (1992) argues that the intangible nature of a service is determined by the fact that, unlike manufactured goods, a service is provided and consumed at the same time and same place, making it difficult to define and communicate its form to customers. Even so, it is possible to identify six core elements in a service if it is defined as a product, where each element affects customer perception of the service:

- The image of the service.

- The image of personnel with whom customers interact.

- Image differences within the same sector as the service *provider* (e.g. how a service compares with those offered by its competitors).

- The customer group targeted.
- The influence of the physical environment in which the service is delivered (e.g. the building).
- The working atmosphere in which the service is formulated, designed and delivered (modified from Flipo 1988, cited in Van Dierdonck 1992).

For example, if we look at leisure travel and how this is construed as a leisure service, Middleton and Clarke (2001) point to the specific services offered to leisure travellers as transport combining:

- Service availability.
- Cost in comparison to competitors on the same route.
- Comfort and speed.
- Ambience.
- Convenience and ticketing arrangements.
- Contact with staff.
- Image and positioning of each operator.

An alternative view of a service is that it constitutes a process rather than an end product, which actually disappears once it has been made. In this respect, a service can be conceptualised as a process that responds to the diverse needs of consumers. Since consumers are not homogeneous, it is difficult to standardise a product to meet every need. The process of providing a service that tailors something to meet precise and varied needs is integral to the concept of responsive service provision.

From the consumer's perspective, critical incidents (Bitner *et al.* 1990) in the service process (e.g. where the leisure service delivery breaks down) have been used to analyse the consumer's service encounter and how they view it under adverse conditions. If we accept that there is a consensus amongst marketing researchers that service provision needs to be seen as an ongoing process, how does this process operate? Cowell (1986) examined this process as a four-stage system (see Figure 7.11), with the provider trying to offer a service in response to actual or perceived customer demand. The process is based on the following concepts: consumer benefit, the service concept, the service offer and the leisure service delivery system.

The consumer benefit

At the outset, the supplier of a leisure service tries to understand what the consumer wants and how they may benefit from the service. At this stage a detailed understanding of consumer behaviour is required that recognises the relative importance of the factors influencing the leisure purchase decision.

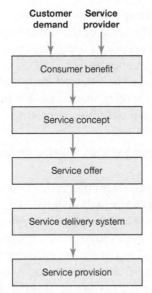

Figure 7.11 The service process

Source: Adapted from Cowell (1986). Copyright © Elsevier, 1986

Following the consumer benefit stage, the service provider translates the assessment of consumer demands into a service concept.

The service concept

At this point the leisure supplier examines the means of producing a service and how it will be distributed to consumers. Marketing research at both the consumer benefit and service concept stage is essential to assist in identifying the specific leisure market segment to target and the nature of the consumer/producer relationship (e.g. is the service to be sold direct to the public or via a different distribution channel such as a travel agent?). Lastly, the producer identifies and develops the image that is to be associated with the leisure service. Having established what the service will comprise in concept form, it is developed further into the service offer.

The service offer

At this point the service concept is given more shape and developed within precise terms set by managerial decisions, which specify:

- *The elements* – the ingredients.

- *The form* – how it will be offered to consumers.

- *The levels of service* – what the consumer will expect to receive in terms of the quality and quantity of the service.

The composition of the service elements is discussed in detail by Gronroos (1980). The form of the service concept also needs to be considered in terms of how the corporate image will be communicated to the public. Furthermore, the service levels, the technical aspects of service quality and how it is rendered also need to be assessed as part of the service offer. Despite the significance of the service offer, there is little evidence to suggest that consumers judge service quality in a definitive way.

The service delivery system

This is the system that is developed to deliver the leisure service to the customer and will comprise both the people responsible for different aspects of the service experience and the physical evidence such as the place or environment in which it is delivered (Bitner 1992). The leisure user's experience of these components is embodied in the *service encounter* (Laws 1991). It is in the service delivery system that barriers may occur in the provision of a satisfactory encounter and a great deal of marketing research has been directed to identifying deficiencies, critical incidents and ways of overcoming dissatisfaction in this area (Bitner *et al.* 1990). The pursuit of excellence in service delivery has meant companies monitoring what the consumer wants and then providing it. In this context marketing assumes a critical role in terms of both research and communication with customers. By providing quality in service provision, it may help to develop customer loyalty in the patronage of the service. As the competitive market for the leisure service intensifies, the demand for service delivery systems that are customer-centred is likely to be an important factor in the purchase of these leisure services. The consumer is a key player in the service process, being an active participant and important judge of quality (Zeithmal and Berry 1985). It is therefore essential to consider how leisure businesses can integrate many of the perspectives discussed in the chapter so far to meet customers' needs and to run their leisure business successfully, as shown in the study by Mackay and Crompton (1988) which proposed a model of how consumers evaluate recreation service quality. Their study highlighted how the consumer evaluates the issue of service quality, being a combination of how the consumer's purchase led them to compare their expectations and what they received, and how they evaluated this as part of the recreation experience. Yet there have also been debates on the wider application of leisure marketing as a tool being harnessed by the public sector (aside from the use of social marketing), to which attention now turns.

The role of marketing in public leisure services

Crompton (2008) traced the evolution of leisure services marketing in the USA and identified different stages in its evolution since the early 1970s. What Crompton highlights is that many of the business concepts associated with marketing did not easily translate across into public leisure. Crompton's critique of the application of marketing principles to public leisure high-lights the direction in which public policy making has shifted in many countries such as the UK, where public leisure service departments develop community-based strategies to address social and economic goals other than leisure. Crompton's main argument is that the weakness of public leisure lies in the discretionary, non-essential role of leisure in public sector budgets. Through the application of marketing principles to communicate with consumers and political decision makers, Crompton argued that public leisure may play a more significant role if it can harness wider goals that have social merit. In other words, through the use of marketing techniques, public leisure that seeks to alleviate problems associated with the concerns of politicians and policy-makers may have a higher priority in local authority budgets. This is reflected in many of the policy statements which local authorities produce to illustrate the wider role of leisure and the community. In this respect, communicating the wider benefits of leisure to the public and other decision makers through the process of marketing will certainly raise the status of leisure in the public sector and indicate how to leverage a greater role for leisure.

Communicating with leisure consumers: the role of advertising and the media

The media assumes an important role in leisure, as discussed by Rowe (2006: 318), where 'the process of mass communication and the services provided by the media have been central to the development of contemporary leisure . . . mass communication has become increasingly central . . . [as] . . . Mass communications enabled the media (first in print form, then electronic) to bring the world to increasingly large audiences without ever having to leave home'. The media has played a major role, not only through the digital age, providing personalised communications, but in the way the media has been used by organisations to communicate to large audiences and to market and promote different products and experiences. This highlights the way in which organisations have developed strategies to communicate with their target audiences, particularly through advertising and the diverse forms of media available.

Communicating value to the leisure consumer: the role of branding

One of the important developments in the late twentieth century in relation to leisure consumers has been the development of strategies by commercial leisure organisations to differentiate their products and experiences from their competitors. One way in which they have done this is through the marketing tool known as *branding*. According to Kotler *et al.* (2005: 549), a brand is 'a name, term, sign, symbol or design, or a combination of these, intended to identify the goods or services of one seller or group of sellers and to differentiate them from those of competitors'. The reasons why branding has become such a powerful tool within marketing is that it is one way organisations have sought to associate product quality with brand names, so the consumer can be assured of a guaranteed level of quality each time they purchase the branded product, service or experience. It also helps the consumer to make decisions from a wide range of choices they have. Branding also has the added value element in terms of the perceived benefits it may confer on the consumer. This may offer the organisation which is the brand developer a competitive advantage because of the amount of power or value they have in the marketplace. As Kotler *et al.* (2005) suggest, the brand will represent different aspects of the consumers' perceptions and feelings about the product, service or experience and so a successful brand which has a very powerful position is described as one which has a high level of brand equity. As Kotler *et al.* (2005: 556) argue, brand equity is 'the value of a brand, based on the extent to which it has a high brand loyalty, name awareness, perceived quality, strong brand associations, and other assets such as patents, trademarks and channel relationships'. A successful brand will often have a higher price and so its ability to command a premium in a leisure setting reflects a successful marketing strategy for the organisation in question. The extent to which the brand is successful will depend upon these attributes, benefits for the consumer, the values it conveys to the buyer, its personality and how these combine to give different meanings to the consumer. Communicating these brand values to the consumer will often depend upon five specific promotion tools which are used in marketing:

- *Advertising*, which may be the way in which ideas are presented to the target audience using different media such as print, radio, television, and other forms of advertising, as shown in Table 7.3.

- *Personal selling*, which is the way a company's sales force will build customer relationships' to sell their products.

- Through *sales promotions*, which are short-term incentives to encourage people to buy a specific product, service or experience.

- *Direct marketing*, which involves targeted communication directly with consumers using different media such as the telephone, mail and e-mail.

- *Public relations*, which is how an organisation will build beneficial publicity to enhance its image.

Source: Based on Kotler *et al.* (2005)

One of the most visible forms of communicating with leisure consumers is through advertising.

Table 7.3 Profile of major media forms

Medium	Advantages	Limitations
Newspapers	Flexibility; timeliness; local market coverage; broad acceptance; high believability	Short life; for reproduction quality; small pass-along audience
Television	Good mass-market coverage; low cost per exposure; combines sight, sound and motion; appealing to the senses	Higher absolute costs; high clutter; fleeting exposure; less audience selectivity
Radio	Good local acceptance; high geographic and demographic selectivity; low cost	Audio presentation only; low attention (the half-heard medium); fleeting exposure; fragmented audience
Magazines	High geographic and demographic selectivity; credibility and prestige; high-quality reproduction; long life; good pass-along readership	Long ad[†] purchase lead time; high cost; some waste circulation; no guarantee of position
Direct mail	High audience selectivity; flexibility; no ad[†] competition within the same medium; allows personalisation	Relatively high cost per exposure; 'junk mail' image
Outdoor	Flexibility; high repeat exposure; low cost; low message competition; good positional selectivity	No audience selectivity; creative limitations
Internet	High selectivity; low cost; immediacy; interactive capabilities	Small, demographically skewed audience; relatively low impact; audience controls exposure

Source: Kotler *et al*. (2005: 773). Copyright © Pearson Education Ltd
[†]advertising

Leisure organisations will need to make a number of decisions when deciding to advertise, ranging from the objectives they are pursuing through their communication strategy, how much they have to spend, what they seek to achieve in terms of sales and other outcomes, the type of message they want to put across and what type of media they wish to use in relation to reaching their audience, along with how they plan to evaluate the success of the campaign.

As Table 7.3 shows, there are advantages and limitations in relation to the different types of media which are available to advertise to the leisure consumer. The commercial sector has a wide-ranging use of these different advertising techniques, some of which have now been more closely regulated so that they meet the agreed codes of conduct in terms of their content and ethical behaviour. Large multinational organisations involved in leisure will also seek to advertise at a global scale, targeting different consumer groups in other countries in relation to their product and service benefits.

Table 7.4 Marketing and distribution channels used by selected leisure travel operators in the UK

							Form of media		
Operator	Print/ magazines	Billboards	TV	Radio	Direct mail	Website	Online agency	Customer loyalty scheme
National Express	✓	X	✓	X	X	✓	✓Trainline.com	✓
Virgin Trains	✓	✓	X	✓	✓	✓	✓Trainline.com	✓
easyJet	✓	✓	✓	X	X	✓	X	X
BA	✓	✓	✓	✓	✓	✓	✓Opodo	✓

Source: Page (2009)

Advertising is one mechanism through which leisure organisations seek to influence consumer behaviour to purchase their product(s), services or experiences. For example, with low-cost airlines, large-scale billboard advertising, newspaper advertising and promotions combine with many other forms of distribution and promotion, including the Internet. A number of examples are shown in Table 7.4, which shows the complex array of distribution channels that transport operators use to communicate with leisure travellers as well as the diverse use of advertising and communication tools.

Summary

It is evident from this chapter that leisure services and experiences do not just exist: they have to be planned, developed and communicated to potential users or consumers. This requires a complex process of planning by the public sector (and private sector companies) and the coordination of different agencies and organisations where the services and provision are based upon the interaction of different organisations. The responsibility for the planning of leisure at a national and local level is often the responsibility of the lead public sector organisation. Even so, criticisms have been levelled at such organisations about their ability to fulfil this role in relation to leisure as they sometimes fail to adopt a strategic view of planning and development. Running alongside the planning functions which the public sector undertake are those which private sector companies engage in through the process of marketing. In each sector of leisure provision, the consumer or leisure user is the target audience with whom the organisation wishes to communicate and develop a lasting relationship. As discussed in this chapter, this is far from an easy process because of the unpredictability and changeable nature of leisure behaviour, which is not as stable and predictable as weekly shopping habits or daily commuting behaviour. This is inherent in the private sector, with competition between companies to attract the leisure spending of consumers through their adoption of sophisticated marketing techniques to lure the consumer.

As leisure spending and behaviour are discretionary and variable, planning for current and future activity hinges upon understanding two concepts: leisure behaviour and mobility, which illustrates the dynamic nature of what leisure planning has to address. Clearly, one of the current agendas for leisure consumers and their behaviour is the sustainability paradigm that is now embracing all aspects of our lives, not least leisure. Planning for more sustainable leisure behaviour at a community level (see Reid 2001) illustrates how more holistic assessments of human behaviour are needed, where our future leisure lifestyles need to be more aligned with the resource base and ability of the environment to support our very consumptive lifestyles. Sustainability is about striking a balance in our lives between enjoyment and resource use and we are likely to see more government intervention in this area of our lives in the future if we are not weaned off our overdependence on very consumptive carbon-oriented leisure (e.g. long-haul travel) and carborne travel. This may lead to a future refocusing on more localised leisure, which has implications for the future urbanisation of the world's population that will create a rediscovery of the urban environment for leisure. Therefore, the next chapter commences the section of the book that focuses on leisure in different resource environments and the importance of the urban environment.

Discussion questions

1. Why does the government need to intervene in the lives of the population to develop more sustainable forms of leisure activity?

2. Why does the public sector engage in the process of planning?

3. How would you go about developing a community-based plan for local leisure needs in your area? What type of consultation would you undertake?

4. How can we use marketing as a tool to develop leisure products and experiences that are market focused?

References

Bevan, M. and Rhodes, D. (2005) *The Impact of Second and Holiday Homes in Rural Scotland*, Communities Scotland: Edinburgh.

Bitner, M.J. (1992) 'Servicescapes: The impact of physical surroundings on customers and employees', *Journal of Marketing* 56 (2): 57–71.

Bitner, M.J., Booms, B.H. and Tetreanit, M.S. (1990) 'The service encounter: diagnosing favourable and unfavourable incidents', *Journal of Marketing* 1: 71–84.

Blackie, J., Coppock, J.T. and Duffield, B. (1979) *Leisure Planning Process*, Social Science Research Council: London.

Bright, A. (2000) 'The role of marketing in leisure and recreation management', *Journal of Leisure Research* 32 (1): 12–17.

Cannon, T. (1989) *Basic Marketing Principles and Practice*, 3rd edn, Holt, Rinehart & Winston: London.

Chadwick, G. (1971) *A Systems View of Planning*, Pergamon Press: Oxford.

Coppock, J.T. (ed.) (1977) *Second Homes; Curse or Blessing?* Pergamon: Oxford.

Cova, B. and Cova, V. (2002) 'Tribal marketing: the tribalisation of society and its impact on the conduct of marketing', *European Journal of Marketing* 36 (5/6): 595–620.

Cowell, D.W. (1986) *The Marketing of Services*, Heinemann: London.

Crompton, J. (2008) 'Evolution and implications of a paradigm shift in the marketing of leisure services in the USA', *Leisure Studies* 27 (2): 181–205.

Department for Communities and Local Government (2006) *Developing the Local Government Services Market to Support a Long-Term Strategy for Local Government.* Department for Communities and Local Government: London.

Dower, M. (1965) *The Challenge of Leisure*, Civic Trust: London.

Dresner *et al.* (2007) *Public Understanding of Sustainable Leisure*. DEFRA: London.

Flipo, J. (1988) 'On the intangibility of services', *Service Industries Journal* 8 (3): 286–98.

Grandage, J. and Rodd, R. (1981) 'The rationing of recreational land use', in D. Mercer (ed.) *Outdoor Recreation – Australian Perspectives,* Sorrett Publishing, Malvern, pp. 76–89.

Green, E. and Singleton, C. (2007) 'Safe and risky spaces: gender, ethnicity and culture in the leisure lives of young south Asian women', in C. Aitchison, P. Hopkins and M. Kwan (eds) *Geographies of Muslim Identities: Diaspora, Gender and Belonging,* Ashgate: Alderhsot, pp. 109–24.

Gronroos, C. (1980) *An Applied Service Marketing Theory,* Helsinki: Working Paper No. 57, Swedish School of Economics and Business Administration.

Hall, C.M. and Page, S. J. (2006) *The Geography of Tourism and Recreation: Environment, Place and Space,* 3rd edn, Routledge: London.

Hall, C. M. and Müller, D. (eds) (2004) *Second Homes,* Channel View: Clevedon.

Henry, I. and Spink, J. (1990) 'Planning for leisure: the commercial and public sectors', in I. Henry (ed.) *Management and Planning in the Leisure Industries*, Macmillan: Basingstoke, pp. 33–69.

Holloway, J.C. and Plant, R. (1988) *Marketing for Tourism*, Pitman: London.

Horner, S. and Swarbrooke, J. (2005) *Leisure Marketing: A Global Perspective,* Butterworth-Heinemann: Oxford.

Horner, S. and Swarbrooke, J. (1996) *Marketing Tourism, Hospitality and Leisure in Europe*, International Thomson Business Press: London.

Kotler, P. and Armstrong, G. (1991) *Principles of Marketing*, 5th edn, Prentice-Hall: Englewood Cliffs, NJ.

Kotler, P., Wong, V., Saunders, P. and Armstrong, G. (2005) *Principles of Marketing*, 4th European edn, Pearson: Harlow.

Kozinets, R. (1999) 'E-tribalised marketing? The strategic implications of virtual communities of consumption', *European Management Journal* 17 (3): 252–64.

Laws, E. (1991) *Tourism Marketing: Service Quality and Management Perspectives*, Stanley Thornes: Cheltenham.

Lonsway, B. (2009) *Making Leisure Work: Architecture and the Experience Economy*, Routledge: London.

Mackay, K. and Crompton, J. (1988) 'A conceptual model of consumer evaluation of recreation service quality', *Leisure Studies* 7 (1): 41–9.

Mason, D. (1999) 'What is the sports product and who buys it? The marketing of professional sports leagues', *European Journal of Marketing* 33 (3/4): 402–10.

Mercer, D. (ed.) (1981) *Outdoor Recreation: Australian Perspectives*, Sorrett Publishing: Melbourne.

Middleton, V. and Clarke, J. (2001) *Marketing in Travel and Tourism*, Butterworth-Heinemann: Oxford.

Office of the Deputy Prime Minister (ODPM) (2001) *Planning for Leisure and Tourism*, The Stationery Office: London.

Office of the Deputy Prime Minister (ODPM) (2005) *Planning Policy Statement 1: Delivering Sustainable Development*, Office of the Deputy Prime Minister: London.

Page, S. J. (2009) *Transport and Tourism: Global Perspectives*, 3rd edn, Pearson: Harlow.

Page, S. J. and Connell, J. (2009) *Tourism: A Modern Synthesis*, 3rd edn, Cengage Learning: London.

Patmore, J.A. (1983) *Recreation and Resources: Leisure Patterns and Leisure Places*, Blackwell: Oxford.

Ravenscroft, N. (1992) *Recreation Planning and Development*, Macmillan: Basingstoke.

Reid, D. (2001) 'Theory and practice in community leisure planning: a focus on public participation', *Leisure/Loisir* 26 (3/4): 191–212.

Roberts, K. (2004) *The Leisure Industries*, Palgrave: Basingstoke.

Rowe, D. (2006) 'Leisure and mass communications', in C. Rojek, S. Shaw and A. Veal (eds) *A Handbook of Leisure Studies*, Palgrave: Basingstoke.

Seibert, J.C. (1973) *Concepts of Marketing Management*, Harper & Row: New York.

Shucksmith, M. (1983) 'Second homes: a framework for policy', *Town Planning Review* 54 (2): 174–93.

Torkildsen, G. (2005) *Leisure Management*, 4th edn, Routledge: London.

Van Dierdonck, R. (1992) 'Success strategies in a service economy', *European Marketing Journal* 10(3): 365–73.

Veal, A. (1993) 'Planning for leisure: past, present and future', in S. Glyptis (ed.) *Leisure and the Environment: Essays in Honour of J. A. Patmore*, Belhaven: London.

Veal, A. (2002) *Leisure and Tourism Policy and Planning*, CABI: Wallingford.

Veal, A. (2006) 'Economics of leisure', in C. Rojek, S. Shaw and A. Veal (eds) *A Handbook of Leisure Studies*, Palgrave: Basingstoke.

Veal, A. (2008) *Alternatives to Standards: A Review of Leisure Planning Guidelines,* Sport and Tourism Working Paper 6. University of Technology, Sydney.

White, J. (1992) *Leisure: The Cornerstone of Local Government: A Discussion Paper.* University of Birmingham: Birmingham.

Winlow, S. and Hall, S. (2006) *Violent Night: Urban Leisure and Contemporary Culture,* Berg: Oxford.

World Commission on the Environment and Development (WCED) (1987) *Our Common Future* (Brundtland Commission's Report), Oxford University Press: Oxford.

Zeithmal, A. and Berry, L.L. (1985) 'A conceptual model of service quality and its implications for future research', *Journal of Marketing,* Fall: 41–50.

8 Urban leisure

Learning outcomes

After reading this chapter, you should be able to:

- Explain why urban places are significant localities for leisure and outdoor recreation

- Identify a range of planning issues associated with urban leisure, particularly issues of equity and access

- Outline a number of contemporary issues associated with urban leisure associated with challenges of developing different leisure settings such as the street, the urban fringe and children's play areas

Introduction

This chapter commences a new section of the book in which many of the issues and themes developed in the earlier chapters will be illustrated in more detail through the analysis of different resource environments and forms of leisure (i.e. the cultural industries and outdoor recreation). This develops the earlier notion of the continuum of resources that extends from the individual or family and home-based leisure through a series of resources that decline in usage and popularity using simple distance-decay principles (i.e. usage diminishes when mapped against distance and time required to travel to a leisure site – see Wu and Cai 2006 and the example of suburban leisure in Shanghai). This chapter commences this discussion with a focus on the urban setting – the town and city as a containing context for leisure. This is greatly overlooked in many aspects of leisure research because it suffers from many of the same problems that Glyptis and Chambers (1982) observed in relation to research on leisure and the home: we are so familiar with cities as places we live, work and undertake leisure in, that they have not been attractive research environments in the same way that non-urban environments are. There may also be many negative connations with urban research, as it is often associated with socio-economic problems (e.g. crime, poverty, safety, pollution and deprivation), thereby overlooking the obvious positive issues of leisure and its urban setting. Patmore (1983: 87) observed a strange paradox in relation to urban leisure where the shift was from outdoors in the urban setting to indoors and private space as well as a growth in mobility to non-urban sites owing to increased mobility related to car ownership, alongside growing suburbanisation.

Each of the issues discussed by Patmore in relation to post-war changes in leisure habits and patterns has an urban focus, given the growing urbanisation of the population in many countries (including the rise of rural re-population by urbanites commuting or through second home ownership). This has also been compounded by the geographical reach of the urbanisation process and the culture of urban places that now permeates many aspects and different areas of leisure. For example, many of the problems facing non-urban leisure reources, such as National Parks, result from the peak use by urban dwellers with their large-volume impact on fragile environments. While critics might argue that Patmore's (1983) comments on the changes affecting leisure are now dated and have been overtaken by developments in urban leisure research, this is certainly not the case if one looks at some of the recent texts on leisure studies and how they treat the subject:

- Rojek *et al.*'s (2006) *A Handbook of Leisure Studies* epitomises the wider dilution of urban leisure as a separate area for analysis with only two references in the Index to *urban precincts* in relation to leisure and the creative city (i.e. the cultural industries which will be examined in Chapter 9). This affirms the way urban issues have been subsumed in wider theoretical debates on postmodernism and leisure with the city as a backdrop, where social theory constructs such as agency, structure and globalisation are the reference points for the analysis rather than the urban setting *per se*. This assumes a detailed knowledge of sociological theory, where all human action and outcomes are determined by macro political processes at work in society. While we should not decry these important theoretical debates, they do not help to explain the major issues to the unitiated at an introductory level.

- In contrast, the more empirical text by Bull *et al.* (2003), *An Introduction to Leisure Studies*, which covers many of the familiar debates from the 1970s to the 1990s on leisure, has only 12 pages on urban themes scattered across different chapters rather than consolidated in one place.

In each case the urban recreation perspective, which was firmly signposted in seminal texts such as Patmore (1983), has not been given the full treatment it deserves in subsequent analyses, with the notable exception of Hall and Page (2006). Urban leisure has yet to take its rightful place as the most significant setting for leisure in which home-based and out-of-home leisure occurs among the world's urbanising population. This case for a more rigorous assessment of urban leisure is reinforced by Williams (1995a: 8), who argues that 'urban populations engage in most of their leisure activities within the same urban area in which they live. The geographical patterns of residence are translated very readily into a pattern of recreation that is focused upon the urban environment, purely by the fact that most people spend the majority of their leisure time in, or close to the home', a feature also observed by Hendricks (1971). In fact, a number of the contemporary themes examined in this chapter will highlight the proximity issues of leisure and urban living in relation to leisure, such as in our analysis of the street and children's play areas. What is being suggested is that the patterns of residence and leisure are closely intertwined, and to ignore or downplay the importance of urban places as a predominant focus for leisure analysis is to misunderstand or misconstrue the city's fundamental role in modern-day leisure.

While there is a tradition of urban leisure research within the wider domain of leisure studies, other subject areas have virtually usurped these research agendas since the 1980s, with a growing interest in leisure issues framed in terms of debates on production and consumption in human geography, sociology, marketing, cultural studies, housing studies and the built environment, planning and architecture alongside specialist areas of research in urban studies on themes such as the postmodern city. Inevitably, mainstream leisure studies has been subsumed in many of these debates and research agendas, diverting attention from generic reviews of urban leisure and recreation. For example, Godbey *et al.* (2005) point to one such debate associated with leisure and active living among the population, many of whom are urbanites, where leisure is the vehicle to enable wellness and quality of life issues to be addressed. Here the leisure and urban focus is secondary to the wellness and quality of life issues. This chapter seeks to rectify these weaknesses which divert attention from leisure *per se*, in part by examining the scope and scale of urban leisure to develop a more holistic view of the subject area and the contemporary issues associated with urban leisure.

Urban areas as a setting for leisure

Towns and cities are complex environments in which people live, which are sometimes described as a mosaic of interconnected land uses including residential, commercial, administrative and leisure uses which have developed through time. According to Page and Connell (2009: 471), urbanisation is a major force contributing to the development of towns and cities, where people live, work and shop (see Johnston 1981 for a definition of the term 'urbanisation'). Towns and cities function as places where the population is concentrated in a defined area, and economic activities locate in the same area or nearby, to provide the opportunity for the production and consumption of goods and services in capitalist societies. Consequently, towns and cities provide the context for a diverse range of social, cultural and economic activities which the population engage in, and where tourism, leisure and entertainment form major service activities.

Urban places are potentially the most significant environments in which to examine modern-day leisure given the increasing urbanisation of the world's population. One visible sign of this urbanisation is the rise of world cities and megacities (i.e. there will be 30 cities with over 10 million population by 2015 worldwide). The United Nations has suggested that by 2020 the number of world cities with over 20 million people will have risen to 16, of which 10 will be in Asia-Pacific, illustrating the growing significance which leisure will play in these urban settings in the next decade.

Urban settings for leisure also help us to understand the holistic nature of many of the issues which we have examined in Chapters 1 through to 7, where the different dimensions of demand, supply, planning, the social setting and the resulting patterns of leisure are increasingly focused on urban issues. The difficulty for many observers of leisure is the complexity of trying to disentangle all of these elements and then make sense of them. These elements of urban leisure are normally divided into component parts, then examined by different social science subjects. The result is that few syntheses of urban leisure exist, the most notable being the excellent reviews by Seeley (1973) and Williams (1995a). The latter identifies many of the different dimensions of urban leisure, including the conceptualisation of urban leisure resources, the role of outdoor recreation and leisure lifestyles, leisure provision, the importance of home-based leisure and domestic gardens, the role of the street as a leisure space, children's play space, parks and open spaces and the role of outdoor sport. This excellent empirically grounded overview of urban leisure and recreation by Williams (1995a) provides an important starting point to understand the scope and range of issues which we can examine in terms of urban leisure. We have already looked at some of the different elements of urban leisure earlier in the book (e.g. see the Case studies on the home and the garden in Chapters 3 and 5). What this chapter sets out to do is to provide an overview of many of the principal issues and a selection of contemporary themes associated with urban leisure.

Understanding the urbanisation of leisure

Historically, the evolution of urban leisure, as Chapter 2 highlighted, followed a process of development which closely mirrored the way in which society evolved from a pre-industrial to an industrial and urban lifestyle (e.g. Abrams 1992 provides a review of the evolution of urban leisure in Imperial Germany during the nineteenth and early twentieth centuries). As cities became the focus of industrial capital and economic development, the population migrated to these growing centres, particularly in the nineteenth century, which continued to develop into many of the cities we live in today. Since classical times, towns and cities have performed tourism and leisure functions (Page 2009) and therefore such places have a long history as places where tourism and leisure experiences have been produced and consumed. In recreational terms, town and city dwellers traditionally consumed their leisure time in the areas where they lived, with the exception of the wealthy elites who were able to afford properties in the country. Up to the mid-nineteenth century, mass forms of urban leisure and recreation were undertaken in close proximity to the home, often involving local family and kinship networks where local pastimes and holidays were undertaken.

In many parts of the non-Western world, the development of newly industrialising countries in Asia and developing countries in Africa have seen rapid rates of urbanisation in the past decade which have created new patterns of urban development and new forms of leisure associated with these developments. For example, in Kenya the concerns over deviant adult behaviour associated with the consumption of illicit palm wine and other distilled spirits such as chang'aa (Mutisaya and Willis 2009) highlight one of the contemporary debates in common with adult leisure habits in Western cities: the role of alcohol consumption, drug taking and other forms of deviant behaviour in leisure time which have negative connotations among policy makers.

Why cities are an important context in which to examine leisure is that they have become widely recognised as the source of leisure demand, particularly since the nineteenth century with the development of coastal resorts in close proximity to major centres of population. For example, in North America the cities of Boston, Massachusetts and New York were responsible for creating a demand for coastal leisure in the latter part of the nineteenth century as well as localised demand within the city. According to Souther (2006), in North American cities the expansion of the built environment made possible the separation of work and leisure, radically altering the patterns of activity, typically along the lines of social class. Historically, this manifested itself in terms of a number of distinct forms of urban leisure in American cities comprising: the development of urban parks, the rise of the department store and leisure shopping, ballparks, vaudeville houses with their risqué theatre and variety shows, urban amusement parks, and night-time leisure economy created through the use of electric lighting and amusements and attractions along with the growth of urban tourism (see Page and Hall 2003 for more detail). However, as Souther (2006) argued, these forms of urban leisure which emerged in the nineteenth century suffered a period of decline in the 1930s as new forms of urban leisure emerged, illustrating patterns of continuity and change. For example, the growth of Las Vegas and urban tourism based on gambling and entertainment as well as the rise of other forms of urban leisure entertainment such as Walt Disney's Anaheim complex, which opened in 1955 as Disneyland, created a new form of leisure. Similarly, in the post-war period new sport stadiums were created to house major forms of spectator sports while whole areas of cities emerged as entertainment districts through a process of redevelopment and the clustering of leisure activities in distinct areas.

This urbanisation of leisure has to be viewed against a series of distinct processes of change in urban areas which have affected the growth and development of urban leisure:

1. *Consistent growth and changes resulting from the process of urbanisation,* as urban areas have passed through a process of industrialisation, through to a post-industrial phase set out in detail in Chapter 2. What Chapter 2 did not examine in detail was the fact that many cities have seen a complex series of processes of change in the way their land use is organised, which led to the creation of leisure landscapes: but these landscapes have not been static, going through a series of stages of evolution, growth and change through time. For example, from the 1930s onwards the process of suburbanisation led to rapid expansion of the built environment of many cities, a different form of urban living as well as new forms of leisure. One consequence was that home-based leisure developed in new suburban environments, often facilitated by the rise of car ownership. Since the 1980s, the process of suburbanisation has also been accompanied by the rise of what has been described as edge city. Edge city is a term developed by Garreau (1992) which was developed to explain how the central areas of cities have lost much of their rationale and services, as suburban areas on the edge of cities have developed shopping malls and out-of-town developments which now attract consumers and workers who travel there by car (see Case Study 8.2 later in the chapter). This posed many planning problems in terms of leisure, as many inner city environments were neglected and starved of investment, while edge city has been a popular focal point for new space-extensive leisure developments such as multiplexes, regional shopping centres and large-scale leisure infrastructure such as football grounds and other stadia (see Page and Hall 2003 for a theoretical explanation of the edge city).

2. *Many cities have been characterised by a growing social segregation of the population* since the nineteenth century, where the residential patterns have evolved into distinct social areas with common characteristics. As cities grew through a process of in-migration and natural population growth, new migrants tended to congregate within inner city environments in the lower-status neighbourhoods vacated by those who moved to the suburbs. Although there has been some evidence of some middle-class families relocating back to inner city environments since the mid-1970s through the process of gentrification, the inner city has traditionally been associated with overcrowded and poor standards of living, limited access to facilities and a social stigma (i.e. the prevalence of a cycle of poverty and deprivation). These patterns have persisted and intensified through time in many cities across the world, as urban areas have neighbourhoods characterised by socially divided environments, often reflecting the mobility and status of those who chose to live in specific residential areas. Those less fortunate have no choice of where

they can live and have occupied the least desirable locations. As a result, the level and standard of leisure provision in different social areas of cities will reflect the ability of residents to access and lobby decision makers to ensure that leisure provision meets local aspirations.

3. *A range of responses by the planning profession who have sought to try to control and regulate the geographical growth and nature of urban development through time.* These responses have been focused on the three stages which Williams (1995a) identified:

   (1) foundation in the nineteenth century;
   (2) consolidation in the early twentieth century up to 1939; and
   (3) expansion after the Second World War.

   During the post-war period several key trends emerged, including 'greater levels and diversity of provision in which traditional resources established in earlier phases have been augmented by new forms of provision designed to reflect the diversity and flexibility of contemporary recreational tastes' (Williams 1995a: 20). We might also add a new stage to Williams' (1995a) three-fold classification reflecting the reconfiguration of the postmodern city and leisure – *diversification and growing cultural complexity*, where the notion of leisure has been fragmented further and included as part of the wider cultural industries (Myerscough 1988; Pratt 1997), which we shall address in the next chapter. This has required many new leisure planning tools and strategies where leisure and tourism are often blurred in the concept of place consumption around the concept of culture. In some cases, during the expansion stage, planners have also created new urban environments on greenfield sites such as new towns, which led to the design of leisure and recreation in new model towns (e.g. Milton Keynes in the UK and Almere in the Netherlands – see Wezenaar 1999), sometimes with initial success. But the success has been short-lived as the planning concepts have been overtaken by new trends and demands for leisure services. Planners have also sought to control the expansion of existing towns using containment strategies such as green belts to protect the rural hinterland of cities (see later in the chapter). In other cases, cities have been confronted by a lack of urban space and consequently have chosen higher-density solutions to urban growth and leisure as in the case of Singapore and Hong Kong (Wong 2009). In other words, we need to look at each individual town or city to understand their locational characteristics, resources and historical legacy of leisure provision before assessing how they develop and plan for the population's leisure time and activities.

4. *Within city environments, planners have also sought to use leisure and the public spaces to enhance the built environment as well as meeting a need for passive leisure and outdoor recreation.* For example, recent trends in the use of public areas in cities have led to urban leisure spaces promoted by planners and politicians as a way of enriching the urban environment as well as promoting areas to a wider audience through public art, new urban precincts and the visual identity of places.

5. *The dynamic nature of urban areas, particularly in the post-war period with the demand for growth and expansion has seen the emergence of one powerful process affecting built environments: the urban redevelopment process.* This process recognises that areas develop through a series of stages of economic growth, development and expansion which then matures and in some cases will decline or stagnate as the economic rationale of an area ceases. This is very much the case in many post-war cities in relation to their waterfront areas as these industrial areas lost their rationale because containerisation required more space-extensive locations and deeper draughts for ships, usually outside of major urban areas. Many inner cities saw large tracts of land previously used as dockland laid waste in the 1970s. Notable examples where these changes occurred are London, Rotterdam in the Netherlands, New York and Sydney along with many other cities that had developed their economic rationale based on trade and importing and exporting goods. This ocurred alongside a shift to a service-based economy, as these inner city environments became seen as *problem areas* for planners. In recent years, planners have redefined how leisure fits into such redevelopment schemes, as it is now just one part of a wider portfolio of redevelopment based on residential, commercial, tourism, leisure and other public uses of the environment known as the mixed development model. This illustrates that urban areas are in a constant state of flux, as the development process is forever changing alongside the evolving social and economic fabric of cities. For example, Evans and Shaw (2001) highlighted the critical role which transport can play in leveraging leisure-related economic development in relation to urban regeneration, a theme also highlighted by Page (1995) and Page and Hall (2003).

Source: Williams (1995a); Authors; Page and Hall (2003)

With these processes of change in mind, it is now pertinent to examine the latter stage of change in many urban environments – the rise of the postmodern city.

Understanding the postmodern city and leisure

The postmodern city is a complex amalgam of different productive and consumptive economic activities of which leisure is just one component. For example, Page and Hall (2003) provide a taxonomy of how different people use cities for tourism and leisure alongside the uses made by residents and workers, as shown in Figure 8.1. What Figure 8.1 suggests is that these different uses all coexist alongside each other and that the consumption of leisure within any city will depend upon the nature of the resources available and the pursuit of

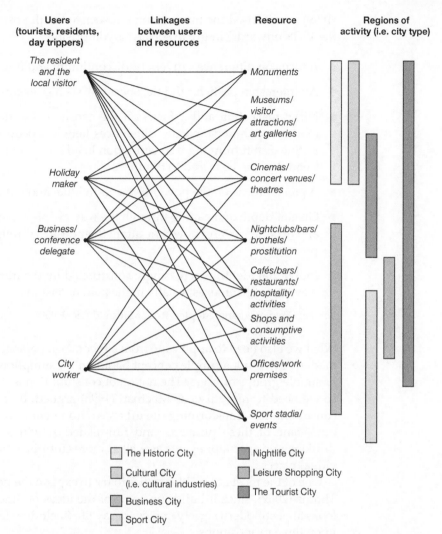

Figure 8.1 Areas in the Tourist City, modified and developed from Burtenshaw *et al.* (1991); Page and Hall (2003)

home-based and out-of-home leisure as well as the needs of other users of the urban environment.

What is most striking from Figure 8.1 is that rather than being able to demarcate leisure, tourism and other uses of the built environment for pleasure and fun, the line between tourism and recreation blurs so that, at times, one is indistinguishable from the other, with tourists and recreationalists using the same facilities, resources and environments: they intermingle alongside other users of the city to create a wider visitor or user population. It highlights the need for a more profound theoretical explanation of the postmodern city (sometimes referred to as the post-industrial, post-Fordist city as discussed by Byrne 2001) to try to unravel some of the complexity. For example, Mansfeld

(1999) summarised the main changes associated with postmodernity (i.e. from the 1970s onwards) in urban society as comprising:

- A focus on differences, diversity, discontinuity and fragmentation.

- An interest in pastiche and the spectacle, such as events and carnivals.

- Niche marketing and a focus on the consumer to identify differentiated markets to understand the differences between people and groups, illustrating a shift from mass consumption in all areas of life for some groups, a trend that can be traced to the 1970s.

- A greater focus on the power of the individual and enterprise.

- Greater depth of meaning through the way people consume goods, services and experiences and how they attain their desires through the consumption process.

- Individual identity increasingly constructed by the individual through the way they consume, especially in the field of leisure.

Source: Developed and adapted from Mansfeld (1999: 330)

What we also need to appreciate from a theoretical perspective is that the postmodern city is not a simple concept based on consumption of individual users or simple groups of users. The notion of consumption is very generalised and so we need to recognise, as Meethan (1996) argued, that the very process of consumption is transforming the urban environment into one of pleasure and fun. Some of these pleasure- and fun-related activities include eating out, drinking and spectator events as well as more cultural activities linked to individual places.

One of the most accessible studies to try to explain the postmodern city is by Thorns (2002), since it builds on some of the ideas outlined by Mansfeld and looks at postmodern society and everyday life (including leisure) which hinges upon three propositions:

- Consumption.

- Changes in the visual form of the city.

- A revival in heritage, culture and its use to emphasise the uniqueness of urban places related to the notion of place or city image and brands (which we discussed in Chapter 7).

Thorns also explains that one of the defining features of the postmodern city is the persistence of inequalities between the *haves* and *have nots*, as the *haves* embellish themselves via increased consumption power through affluence and changes in their lives. For example, sociologists such as Bordieu (1984) are cited by Thorns as demonstrating how the notion of culture and cultural capital (associated with the capacity to take part in elaborated speech and to understand different codes through education), especially among the growing middle classes, is used to differentiate themselves from others in the population. The search for markers of style associated with culture and consumption is reflected in the pursuit of social mobility through membership of clubs and organisations in people's leisure time, as well as seeking to purchase the right objects that denote status through the search for difference and individuality in their leisure lives. In other words, the middle classes and aspiring groups now see symbols and consumer goods as important cultural collateral. For the social theorist, we need to understand how these groups and individuals read and engage with the symbols and different meanings of what urban leisure experiences and places can offer. These experiences are increasingly complex and layered, so the educated can explore deeper into them and derive added value from the experiences. Among other notable elements of the postmodern city are what Thorns refers to as the *new cathedrals of the city* – the shopping mall. In fact, studies such as Hannigan's (1998) *Fantasy City* illustrate one attempt to explain how urban places have been transformed for leisure consumption, from an industrial to postmodern state where their very rationale is pleasure and fun (see Case Study 8.1). Other aspects of these changes to leisure in the city include the rise of urban precints and specialised areas of consumption targeted at specific groups such as the gay districts in Manchester and San Francisco.

Case Study 8.1   Hannigan's 'Fantasy City'

Plate 8.1 An example of Hannigan's entertainment city – Universal Studio Citywalk, with cinemas, food and an entertainment area adjacent to the theme park.

One of the most interesting and balanced analyses of the postmodern city and the role of tourism and leisure is associated with Hannigan's (1995) initial survey and subsequent publication of Fantasy City (Hannigan 1998). What Hannigan (1998) observed was that at the end of the nineteenth century in America, a new commercial culture, based on leisure and entertainment, emerged in urban areas. Of particular importance was the emergence of new sources of capital, the new entertainment entrepreneurs – the 'merchants of leisure' to lure a wide cross-section of society in the industrialised city. Such forms of recreational entertainment, including the theatre and theme parks, were enshrined in popular culture. What is interesting in Hannigan's analysis, in a tourism and leisure context, was that aside from the major urban centres such as New York, Chicago and San Francisco, the downtown area had little to attract the day visitor or tourist. What Hannigan observed was that the cultural industries of many downtown areas reported lower sales and revenue in 1958 compared with 1945, and the post-war period saw the demise of North American downtown areas as sites of leisure consumption. What this signified was the demise of the urban entertainment district, with a focus on the suburbs and recreation and tourism opportunities outside of urban areas (e.g. the drive-in).

It was mainly during the 1980s that the public and private sectors in many downtown areas embarked on urban revitalisation projects, with investment and capital attracted to flagship destination projects. Although some of the origins of tourism and leisure projects can be found in the 1970s when festival markets were developed to attract consumer activity in downtown areas, in tourism terms there were insufficient to expand the visitor base to the downtown areas in North American cities. They were supplemented by a range of 'special activity generators' (i.e. sport arenas, stadia, casinos, entertainment complexes) which were able to attract tourists and day-trippers (Robertson 1995) and to compete with the suburbs. Alongside these strategies for urban revitalisation, shopping and dining out underpinned the consumption experiences while culture and entertainment complemented urban regeneration, especially in the formation of cultural and entertainment districts. During the 1990s, entertainment re-established itself as a dominant theme in the burgeoning entertainment economy of many cities. What Hannigan (1998) focused on was consumption in the contemporary American city, which was not a new phenomenon, but its cultural significance and its construction into entertainment experiences in themed environments were new. This led to the development of fantasy experiences packaged in safe, reassuring and predictable environments such as theme parks.

Hannigan (1998) identified six defining characteristics for Fantasy City:

- *A focus on themocentricity*, namely that it is based on a scripted theme.
- *The city is aggressively branded*, reflected in the place-marketing strategies and product range.

- *Day and night operation is a common feature*, unlike shopping malls which are largely day-time operations.
- *Modularisation of products*, where a diverse array of components are assembled to produce a wide range of experiences.
- *Solipsisicity*, where the city is economically, culturally and physically detached and isolated from surrounding neighbourhoods in a City of Illusion.
- *Postmodernity*, where the city is constructed around the technologies of simulation, virtual reality and the thrill of the spectacle. The city draws a major source of inspiration from the Disney model which is widely imitated. The Disney model merges the concept of the motion picture and amusement park into a fantasy world using technologies which create conditions of hyperreality. Soja (1989) has termed such creations 'postmodern agglomerations', with their attendant concerns for globalisation.

From the leisure and tourism perspective, many powerful business interests have recognised these trends as part of the growth sector for the future. Critics of the entertainment value of formerly dry and uninspiring museum exhibits in the commodified 'heritage industry' (see Hewison 1987) have voiced concern at urban attractions that are seen as lacking authenticity, accuracy and integrity being transformed into living heritage. Instead they were seen as part of the crass commercialisation of the Fantasy City concept. Goldberger (1996) criticised Fantasy City for its creation of new landscapes of leisure based on urbanoid environments, where cloning and reality were distorted by the eradication of the former living city in downtown areas.

City authorities have seized upon the urban regenerative effects of Fantasy City for inner cities which had lost many former productive functions, as conspicuous consumption creates a controlled, organised and measured urban experience. However, theme parks, which are part of the Fantasy City experience, have been criticised as the high-technology playgrounds of the middle classes, of little benefit to local communities.

An interesting perspective proffered by the French sociologist Bordieu (1984) interprets the patronage of theme parks as part of the acquisition of cultural capital: 'been there, done that', which confers status in the postmodern society. In fact Christiansen and Brinkerhoff-Jacobs (1995) progress this argument a stage further, suggesting that the architects of Fantasy City are creating a new kind of experience for the consumer. In the context of theme parks, the consumer is requiring a constant and technologically dazzling level of amusement to be incorporated into their repertoire of cultural capital. Yet Rojek (1993) observes that an important element in the packaging of the fantasy experience is the provision of a safe, reassuring and predictable environment, termed the 'recurrence of reassurance'. This is part of what Ritzer (1993) has termed the *McDonaldization of Society*, based on the principles of efficiency, calcability, predictability and control epitomised in the theme park environment. A further element is the easy-to-decipher signs, the standardised behaviours and limited human interactive experiences. Although critics may be concerned that in the postmodern city we may be amusing ourselves to death (Postman 1985), these developments are not confined to Europe and North America. The development of theme parks in Asia-Pacific is emerging as a hybrid form globalisation of Fantasy City (see Teo *et al.* 2001).

Although Ritzer (1993: 32) argued that theme parks such as Disneyland are 'a world of predictable, almost surreal orderliness', Hannigan (1998) pointed to the organisational model adopted by globalised brands and sites of consumption based on new modes of thematic representation. The globalised themed consumption of the entertainment city also mutually converges with four major consumer activity systems: shopping, dining, entertainment and education, which are interconnected by transport. Hannigan (1998: 89) describes these in terms of 'three new hybrids which in the lexicon of the retail industry are known as shopertainment, eatertainment and edutainment'. Shopertainment is part of the interaction of leisure shopping, fantasy fun and the pleasure of consumption. Eatertainment is where the interaction of play and eating combine and are both a pleasure and source of gratification, with themed restaurants such as the Hard Rock Café. Lastly, edutainment is where educational and cultural activities are joined with technology and entertainment.

Garreau (1992) described 'Edge City' on the urban fringe which has challenged the notion of the urban core as the location of the city's cultural industries. In the post-war American city, many entertainment functions are located in suburbs, but what Garreau (1992) pointed to was the move to the urban fringe, socially and spatially excluding inner city users without the means of transport to access suburban developments. This contributed to a geographical isolation and social exclusion from the new leisure consumptive activities in the urban fringe.

In Hannigan's (1998) review, it highlights some of the dynamics of urban change in the development of tourism and leisure in the postmodern metropolis, with a focus on entertainment. What it is useful in explaining is the evolution of the tourism and leisure elements of the industrial and post-industrial American city, highlighting geographical changes in the use of leisure and tourism spaces in the city over a 100-year period. Yet consumption *per se* is not just a postmodern phenomenon in the city. What is different in the postmodern context is the cultural embodiment of consumption in the everyday lives of residents and visitors to the city.

Source: Page and Hall (2003: 44–47)

While the analysis of the postmodern city has many different interpretations from various areas of social science, most notably urban studies and sociology, it is evident that individual cities have begun to compete with each other to attract mobile forms of capital via place-marketing as well as inward investment to redevelop localities and areas within cities so that they can become globally competitive. One consequence of this is that investment in leisure is now seen as an important aspect of the quality of life for residents and workers in these cities, which is why it has become a higher priority for governments and decision makers who seek to use marketing techniques to promote the attributes of individual cities as places to live, work and invest in. This competitiveness is most marked between world cities such as London, New York, Paris and Tokyo, as reflected in recent attempts to stage international events to raise the profile of these localities and to enhance their cultural infrastructure. Therefore, when we look at the urban environment and leisure, we need to be aware of some of the theoretical debates associated with urban areas as places to live, work and enjoy our leisure. These debates are often focused on the contemporary themes associated with the provision and consumption of different urban leisure resources and the scale at which we can analyse leisure participation in urban areas, as shown in Figure 8.2.

What Figure Figure 8.2 shows is that there are different scales at which we need to understand urban leisure, as it reflects the way in which planning and provision is accommodated in public planning, as discussed in Chapter 7, which is best understood in relation to the scope, scale and planning for urban leisure.

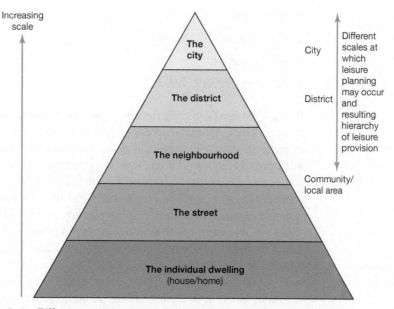

Figure 8.2 Different geographical scales for the analysis of urban leisure

The scope of urban leisure provision

As we have discussed in other chapters, such as Chapter 5, the supply of leisure resources has utilised the concept of a *hierarchy of facilities*, which is the catchment relating to the users' willingness, ability and knowledge of the facility or resource (Hall and Page 2006). What the hierarchy concept does is allow one to ascertain what type of catchment a recreational resource has at different geographical scales, taking into account users' willingness to travel to use them. Constraints of time and distance act as a friction (i.e. as a counterweight) to the potential use of resources. The outcome is an ordered pattern of resources which serve specific catchments and geographical scales.

Patmore (1983) outlined the range of urban leisure resources and facilities within the UK, which is typical of many other countries in terms of:

● Capital-intensive facilities (those with modest land requirements but a high capital cost – and those with a high capital cost where the land requirement is extensive) such as leisure centres;

● Parks and open spaces;

● Golf courses;

while Williams (1995a) expands upon this list in terms of:

● The home;

● The street;

● Gardens and allotments;

● Playgrounds;

● Other sporting contexts.

But as Patmore (1983: 98) rightly argues, patterns of facility use are not related to location alone: effective access is not synonymous with convenience of location, as barriers may also exist. Using the key variables, which reflect basic resource attributes, Williams (1995a) devised a practical typology of urban recreational resources as illustrated in Table 8.1, which highlights the different scale at which various types of provision may occur and the planning challenge – that certain types of resource or facility may be placed at different scales in an urban setting. Table 8.1 also suggests that two basic types of urban leisure resource exist in relation to outdoor recreation: those which are linear, such as footpaths, and those which are space extensive and based on areas such as parks and woodlands where both passive and active recreational uses occur. The challenge for recreational provision in any urban context is the planning and management undertaken for indoor and outdoor provision (excluding private spaces like the home and garden) to ensure that principles of equity and equal access are permitted where possible.

Table 8.1 Basic typology of outdoor recreation facilities in urban areas

	Public facilities		Private/voluntary facilities		Facilities that may be 'annexed' for recreational use by particular groups
	Formal	Informal	Formal	Informal	
Large scale; city-wide catchment	Major parks Major sports fields/stadia Municipal golf courses	Major commons Major urban woodland Major water space Urban country parks	Private golf courses		Major shopping centres Major transport centres e.g. airports, stations
Medium scale; district catchment	Recreation grounds Small parks	Urban greenways Minor urban woodland Minor water space Cycleways	Sports clubs e.g. bowls or cricket	Natural areas or reserves	Roadways Towpaths
Small scale; local catchment	Children's play areas Allotments	Local footpaths		Domestic gardens	Local streets/ pavements Waste ground Grass verges

Source: Williams (1995a)

Urban leisure planning

According to Patmore (1983: 117–118):

> It may be possible to view [urban leisure] provision in a rational, hierarchical frame, to develop models for that precision that equate access and opportunity in a spatial pattern with mathematical precision, but reality rarely gives an empty canvas where such a model can be developed in an unfettered form. Rather, reality is conditioned by the accident of historic legacy, by the fashions of spending from the public purse and by the commercial dictates of the public sector.

From a planning perspective, this quotation suggests that urban leisure grew in a very random and *ad hoc* manner until planners began to grasp the issue in the 1960s, as highlighted in Chapter 7. Urban leisure and recreation provision in towns and cities grew in an *ad hoc* fashion in many Western European contexts, with some communities better served than others. What planners had to address was decades of provision, where incremental growth had created a diverse range of resources, sometimes based on rational and agreed principles, and sometimes on irrational and political grounds. The 1970s saw what was described by some commentators as a consolidation of this incremental growth by public sector leisure departments. As Burtenshaw *et al.* (1991) argued, this led to debates on the extent to which such activities should be a commercial or municipal enterprise, as highlighted in Chapters 6 and 7. The result is that despite government planning and policy advice, the use of mixed planning principles in leisure provision through time has left this legacy of resources, facilities and environments. As Veal (1993: 185) recognised in relation to urban leisure planning, 'urban outdoor recreation takes places primarily in parks, playing fields and playgrounds. The provision of such facilities constitutes the largest single public leisure sector, in terms of expenditure, land allocation and staff and is the longest established'. What this suggests is that within cities, open space can provide a focal point for community interaction, conservation, visual amenity and an important backdrop to enhance many residential areas and their desirability.

A review of regional planning policy towards open spaces in cities from Europe and the USA (van der Valk and van Dijk 2009) provides an up-to-date review of the subject and progress towards trying to meet the ideals of open space as a community resource in an expanding metropolis. Van Herzele *et al.*'s (2005) study of creating new urban woodlands on the periphery of Antwerp as a form of open space raised many of the distributional issues already discussed in other chapters on equity, social inclusion and proximity to the home, and the value of hierarchical planning principles also arises. Through the use of GIS, they were able to identify seven alternative locations for new forests on the urban fringe of Antwerp to expand the provision of recreational greenspace. As their study highlighted, the planners faced the perennial challenge for land use and spatial planning: who gets what, where and why, implying that some communities and groups would be major beneficiaries and others would be less able to benefit.

As this research suggests, within leisure plans for urban environments, we need to understand some of the tools and techniques that planners employ in terms of land use planning, which may involve corridors of green or open space; these are called small buffer zones or wedges which separate dense development and may stop a continuous zone of uninteresting and homogenous development from occurring (see van Rij *et al.* 2008 on the preservation of open space as nature). Land use planning often has to work from an established base of provision, reflecting the historical legacy of provision. This also has to be balanced with the type of methods used to allocate the types of space required for different leisure uses in the urban environment. For example, in the Netherlands, Wezenaar (1999) discussed how the reclamation of a polder area (land reclaimed from the sea) in Almere was used as a blank canvas for planners to develop the notion of leisure locales (see Chapter 11 for a more detailed discussion of this concept) where leisure is planned at a community level in a new town. What this example suggests is that planners have to be cognisant of the need to balance efficiency in the method of provision, equity in terms of access and transparency throughout the planning process which meet local needs as well as wider strategic planning objectives to fit with current leisure consumption trends. Planning also has to make provision for more formalised services which the public and private sectors locate in urban areas such as leisure centres.

Leisure centres and leisure provision in the urban environment

There is a comparative neglect of this theme within many academic critiques of leisure, even though it poses an interesting philosophical issue: these are places which provide a formal setting for the practice and pursuit of leisure. Leisure centres have a much shorter history of evolution than open spaces and other outdoor leisure resources, as Chapter 7 highlighted, mainly dating from their growth in the late 1960s and early 1970s. In the UK, public sector assistance from the Sports Council provided grants to develop these leisure facilities, in common with the practice in some other countries. According to Torkildsen (2005), a leisure centre, broadly defined, will have a multi-purpose sport hall, be open to the public and be run by either the public, private or voluntary sector (or may be a combination of these where different management models are used, as discussed in Chapter 6). While their initial growth was promoted by the public sector, the period since the 1970s has seen a significant growth in their formation and development by the private sector, to the point where around 2500 exist in the UK. Sometimes private sector centres have a specialised function, such as private membership for a squash or tennis club, and in some cases they have a more general range of services epitomised by the growth in independent sport and fitness clubs, offering personal training and fitness activities. Around 100 private health and fitness clubs have been opening in the UK each year and these are now worth about £600 million a year, with approximately 6 million private members (Roberts 2004). In the UK, in common with other countries, a number of large private sector operators have taken control of the private leisure and fitness centres, with their focus on the more affluent ABC1s as consumers, with five major businesses controlling this sector. Some of these organisations have also undertaken management contracts for local authority providers; Bull *et al.* (2003) estimated that around 200 leisure centres were affected by such contracts in 2001, dating back to the 1990s process of Compulsory Competitive Tendering. A number of these clubs evolved in response to trends and short-term booms in specific media-driven fashions such as disco dancing and keep-fit in the late 1970s as a response to the hit movie *Saturday Night Fever* and subsequent trends such as step and other keep-fit trends (see Oakley and Rhys 2008). Participation in sports activities at such centres is viewed as entering the domain of sport studies, so much of the research activity has been undertaken within the growing field of sport studies. Even though participation rates in activities provided at leisure centres may not represent the majority of the population, we do need to recognise that 'sport is such a pervasive feature of contemporary life that, while not everyone participates in it actively or can be considered a fan, no one is unaffected by its presence' (Birrell 2006: 335). Psychologists have analysed the meaning of these trends, where many individuals regularly attend leisure centres and fitness centres in pursuit of the body ideal as almost a fantasy, so that exercise will help them achieve and maintain this image, while others recognise the growing fcous on healthy living, of which exercise is a part.

In both the public and private sectors, these purpose-built facilities are extremely costly to build and maintain, requiring a constant programme of capital investment to stay ahead of the trends in the market so they remain used and popular with those targeted for their use. Part of this targeting can occur through the use of the *programming* management tool, which is how activities and resources are scheduled, planned and timetabled to maximise the use of the facilities to meet a wide range of demands (e.g. how a swimming pool may be used for diverse needs such as swimming, school swimming lessons, water polo, aquarobics and other activities). Part of the technique of programming may be combined with wider social objectives, such as seeking to encourage under-represented groups to engage with leisure activities. To encourage a wide community use of such facilities, public sector owned and managed leisure centres may use different tools such as financial incentives (e.g. reduced entrance fees), marketing techniques to promote their use among groups unaware of the opportunities and outreach schemes to encourage groups with perceived obstacles, such as the provision of crèches. This is because it is widely accepted that these centres have very limited appeal when no action is taken to broaden their use compared to other leisure resources. So leisure centre managers are constantly seeking to widen their appeal and visibility. But a well-known fact is that many people sign up to membership schemes in leisure centres after the Christmas period, with the best of intentions, but many fall by the wayside through a drop in interest or regular programming of time to pursue regular exercise. Even so, different leisure users can be identified, from the avid and devoted user through to school groups (where swimming pool facilities exist), the unemployed and off-peak users who are less time-restricted. These resources pose many economic issues for local authorities, in terms of pricing and accessibility as well as difficult decisions on ongoing investment plans in view of the cost and benefits associated with their development. An Audit Commission (2003) inspection report for one local authority leisure centre service in Preston, North West England illustrates these issues, including what to provide, whom to target and the costs and challenge of making leisure centres accessible to all.

Preston has a population of around 135,000 of whom around 10% are from ethnic minorities. It operates two leisure centres which were rated highly by the users, and seeks to attract a wide range of users through concessionary options and long opening hours, albeit at a relatively high cost compared to operating costs for other centres in different local authorities. Both of the Council's leisure centres have 25m swimming pools, a wide range of health and fitness services and sports provision. This is complemented by a range of smaller community recreation centres at three other locations. In 2002/2003 the sport development budget for Preston was £3.8 million with revenue of £1.4 million, with net expenditure of £1.8 million on the two leisure centres. In contrast, the expenditure on community centres was £249,000. These costs for the two main centres reflect the concessions offered, which included free access to the two leisure centres for those on no or low incomes, disabled people and pensioners over 60 years of age. Those under 18 years of age received half-price admission along with full-time students residing in the city, while swimming for under-fives was free, with no charges for the use of crèche facilities. What this illustrates is the difficulty of balancing the encouraging of local use and meeting leisure needs and the cost of providing this service. Although the Audit Commission (2003) judged this to be one of the highest-cost services compared to similar local authorities, they also acknowledged that it was almost impossible to identify true costs. In contrast, parks and open spaces appeal to a much wider section of the population than leisure centres on a daily or weekly basis, to which attention now turns.

Urban parks and open space provision in urban areas

Urban parks and open space are by far the most important outdoor leisure resources which urban dwellers will use on a daily, weekly or less regular basis. In England and Wales, they represent 13.5% of the land area, illustrating their extent and significance. There has been a surprisingly long history of research on parks and open spaces as leisure resources, in part reflecting their historical origins. They have been described as the lungs of growing industrial cities, places where people could enjoy clean air, open space free from the dense development of city environments, and a tranquil social setting for formal and informal forms of leisure. The depth of research on this subject is, in part, reflected in some of the studies listed in Table 8.2, where many of the themes are associated with international examples of urban park research.

Previous studies of urban park use indicated that their catchments were localised and informal, fulfilling short-distance and short-stay leisure needs (Patmore 1983). Table 8.2 shows that since the early 1980s, research on urban parks has focused on:

● Historical reconstructions of urban park development.

● User-based research (including behavioural and perception-type studies).

● Park planning.

● Access-related studies.

● The application of management principles to parks.

Table 8.2 The evolution of selected studies on leisure and urban parks: International perspectives

1960s

Greater London Council (1968) *Surveys of the Use of Open Space*, Volume 1, Greater London Council Research Paper 3, Greater London Council: London.

1970s

Balmer, K. (1971) 'Urban open space and outdoor recreation', in P. Lavery (ed.) *Recreation Geography*, David and Charles: Newton Abbot, pp. 112–26.

Balmer, K. (1973) *Open Space in Liverpool*, Liverpool Corporation: Liverpool.

Bowler, I. and Strachan, A. (1976) *Parks and Gardens in Leicester*, Recreation and Cultural Services Department, Leicester City Council: Leicester.

Godbey, G. (1976) *Recreation and Park Planning: The Exercise of Values*, University of Waterloo: Ontario.

Haley, A. (1979) 'Municipal recreation and park standards in the United States: central cities and suburbs', *Leisure Sciences*, 2: 277–91.

Strachan, A. and Bowler, I. (1976) 'The development of public parks in the City of Leicester', *East Midland Geographer*, 6: 275–83.

1980s

Burgess, J., Harrison, C. and Limb, M. (1988a) 'People, parks and the urban green: a study of popular meanings and values for open spaces in the city', *Urban Studies*, 26: 455–73.

Burgess, J., Harrison, C. and Limb, M. (1988b) 'Exploring environmental values through the medium of small groups. Part one: Theory and practice', *Environmental and Planning A*, 20: 309–26.

Burgess, J., Harrison, C. and Limb, M. (1988c) 'Exploring environmental values through the medium of small groups. Part two: Illustrations of a group at work', *Environment and Planning A*, 20: 457–76.

Duffield, B. and Walker, S. (1983) *Urban Parks and Open Spaces: A Review*, Tourism and Recreation Research Unit: Edinburgh.

Milton Keynes Development Corporation (1988) *Study of the Use and Perception of Parks in Milton Keynes*, Milton Keynes Recreation Unit Study 18: Milton Keynes.

Milton Keynes Development Corporation (1989) *Parks Visitor Survey*, Milton Keynes Recreation Unit Study 18: Milton Keynes.

Seeley, I. (1983) *Outdoor Recreation and the Urban Environment*, Macmillan: Basingstoke.

1990s

Barber, A. (1991) *Guide to Management Plans for Parks and Open Spaces*, Institute of Leisure and Amenity Management: Reading.

Conway, H. (1991) *People's Parks: The Design and Development of Victorian Parks in Britain*, Cambridge University Press: Cambridge.

Grocott, A. (1990) 'Parks for people', *Leisure Management*, 8: 31–2.

Madge, C. (1997) 'Public parks and the geography of fear', *Tijdschrift Voor Economische en Sociale Geografie*, 88, 237–50.

Page, S.J., Nielsen, K. and Goodenough, R. (1994) 'Managing urban parks: user perspectives and local leisure needs in the 1990s', *Service Industries Journal*, 14(2): 216–37.

Taylor, D. (1999) 'Central Park as a model for social control: urban parks, social class and leisure behaviour in nineteenth century America', *Journal of Leisure Research*, 31(4): 426–77.

Welch, D. (1991) *The Management of Urban Parks*, Longman: Harlow.

Wooley, H. and Ul-Amin, N. (1999) 'Pakistani teenagers' use of public open space in Sheffield', *Managing Leisure*, 4(3): 156–67.

2000s

Floyd, M. and Johnson, C. (2002) 'Coming to terms with environmental justice in outdoor recreation: a conceptual discussion with research implications', *Leisure Sciences*, 24(1): 59–77.

Gobster, P. (2002) 'Managing urban parks for a racially and ethnically diverse clientele', *Leisure Sciences*, 24(2): 143–59.

Ravenscroft, N. and Markless, S. (2000) 'Ethnicity and the integration and exclusion of young people through urban park and recreation provision', *Managing Leisure*, 5(3): 135–50.

Wong, K. (2009) 'Urban park visiting habits and leisure activities of residents in Hong Kong, China', *Managing Leisure* 14 (2): 125–40.

As Hall and Page (2006) suggest, the largest single area of research on urban parks has focused on accessibility issues for certain social groups. In the UK, public-sector-managed green space has experienced many budget cuts over the past 30 years, leaving these resources very neglected in some areas, despite their significance as part of the built environment.

A study by Page *et al.* (1994) examined the user groups within the hierarchy of open spaces in the London Borough of Newham and confirmed many of the assumptions on park use cited in earlier studies, namely:

● The overwhelming pattern of use was local in relation to the catchment area and focused on passive leisure uses.

● Parks perform an important social role, being an accessible leisure resource regardless of gender, race, age or disability.

● New management practices such as Compulsory Competitive Tendering procedures in the early 1990s had reduced the quality of perceived maintenance of parks.

● There were concerns related to conflicts between dog owners and those who did not own dogs.

● Local park plans were seen as an innovative way of matching user needs to the management of parks and open spaces.

Therefore, as Hall and Page (2006) argued, while parks and open spaces may not be as fashionable as capital-intensive leisure facilities, they are operated on a non-commercial basis and offer access to the entire population, being an important aesthetic element of the built environment. What this suggests is that we need to start thinking more about their inherent qualities and value in the urban environment. Parks and open spaces are probably the ultimate sustainable urban leisure resource, because they can accommodate multiple uses, engage with the local communities (despite concerns on certain ethnic groups being excluded as studies in Table 8.2 suggest) and enhance the built environment. We sometimes forget that these leisure resources are an integral feature of the urban landscape and how important they are in the daily lives of local communities. Even so, the report *Improving Urban Parks, Play Areas and Green Spaces* by the Department for Transport, Local Government and Regions

(DTLR) (2002) highlighted a number of persistent barriers to the use of green spaces by urban dwellers, which are also apparent in other countries, given the findings in numerous research studies (Table 8.2). These barriers are structured around five principal issues:

- The lack of provision of play facilities for children.

- The undesirable nature of other users within these leisure spaces.

- Concerns about the control of dogs and dog faeces.

- Psychological concerns associated with fear and safety.

- Environmental detractors such as litter, graffiti and vandalism.

What the report also highlighted was a positive link to urban regeneration and renewal where urban green spaces can make a positive contribution to enhancing an area in terms of making it more attractive and pleasant, often as a flagship project to kick-start the process. Other tangible benefits of using parks and open space in neighbourhood regeneration include strengthening the local community and, of course, stimulating the local economy. This is because parks may be a flagship project and focal point for neighbourhood renewal (i.e. rebuilding local pride in their environment), bridging the objectives of public-sector-led regeneration for sustainability that incorporates economic, social and environmental dimensions.

One of the difficulties which the DLTR report highlighted relates to the persistent theme of social exclusion, particularly for the disabled, the elderly and different ethnic groups, along with the evolving and changing needs of children and family lifestyles. One of the key principles highlighted, in parallel with our discussion of the street which follows, is the importance of design features. Design is seen to be a central feature in tackling many of the existing barriers, in terms of engaging with people to use urban green spaces. At one level, encouraging community involvement in design has been seen as one way of engaging with the local community to bridge these barriers. The DLTR report highlights successful examples where local authority park service providers have changed their own culture so that they can engage more with the local community in order to understand their needs and how these needs can be built into local parklands (see Page *et al.* 1994 for a very detailed example of the process of research to inform such an engagement exercise).

A study of urban park visiting habits by Wong (2009) examining the leisure activities of residents in Hong Kong illustrated the central role that these spaces play in such a highly urbanised setting. The Hong Kong government is responsible for 1491 parks, gardens, playgrounds and other recreational facilities in a setting where high-density residential living is complemented by these green spaces for leisure and recreation. These help to punctuate the highly urbanised environment, where the typical dwell time for Hong Kong visitors to urban parks was between half an hour and two hours, in common with other studies of park usage. Among some of the barriers to use reported in the study were a lack of time, a lack of interest, distance from home, a lack of attractive facilities and activities, overcrowding and no one else to go to the park with. As these research studies suggest, there is continuity in the issues facing parks and open spaces across the world in relation to their use and under-use. The development of sustainability agendas in many countries has seen a refocusing of attention back to these resources, often with a rich history which can be revitalised to meet modern-day uses (see articles in the journal *Urban Forestry and Urban Greening* for many detailed aspects of open space and leisure in different countries and how they are being planned and developed for future use). One way of understanding how these resources can be developed and managed is to consider one setting – a large city such as London.

Understanding urban park and open space provision in London: principles and practice

London is an interesting city to focus on in the case of open space, because it has a wide diversity of resource types, some dating back to their royal origins such as the Royal Parks and others associated with specific initiatives by local government over the past 150 years to create a green oasis amid rapid urban industrial development of this world city. Interestingly, one of the most often cited studies is the 1968 study by the then Greater London Council (GLC) which set out a planning framework for these spaces in the city. But the planning of these spaces has passed through several organisations since the abolition of the GLC in 1986, and is now in the remit of the London Assembly and local authorities. Since 1986 each London Borough has had to develop a Unitary Development Plan (UDP) to formulate policies to guide the provision of parks and open spaces. This planning aproach is now shifting over to Local Development Frameworks (LDFs) which will cover a 20-year timeframe. If we consider the current spatial development strategy for London (http://www.london.gov.uk), which sits above the UDP (and new LDFs), it sets out what the strategic objectives should be for open space in the city, covering the 33 London Boroughs and their UDPs/LDFs. What is apparent from the London-wide strategy is that a distinct hierarchical set of principles used by the GLC have been maintained and enhanced, as Figure 8.3 suggests. Figure 8.3 shows a range of open space and park designations that fulfil various functions according to their size and distance from the user's home. But such a hierachy is far from ideal when we begin to look at the issues and problems facing individual people. For example, Burgess *et al.* (1988) questioned whether such a hierarchical model of provision met local needs, as most people in their survey felt that open spaces closest to their home failed to meet their leisure needs. So how does this situation fare in one of London's inner city boroughs – the London Borough of Newham?

Newham is an east London borough (http://www.newham.gov.uk) with a population of over 260,000. It is very ethnically diverse, with ethnic groups

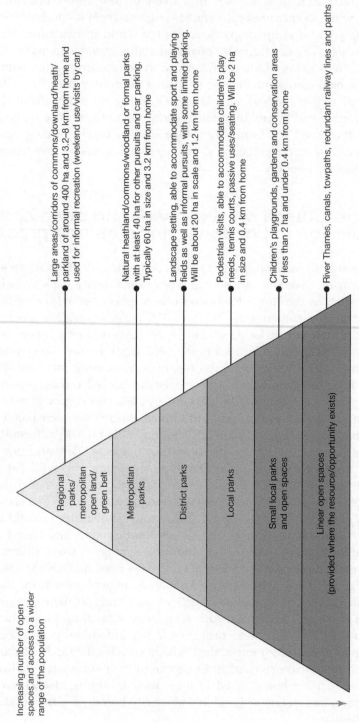

Increasing number of open spaces and access to a wider range of the population

Regional parks/ metropolitan open land/ green belt

Metropolitan parks

District parks

Local parks

Small local parks and open spaces

Linear open spaces (provided where the resource/opportunity exists)

Large areas/corridors of commons/downland/heath/ parkland of around 400 ha and 3.2–8 km from home and used for informal recreation (weekend use/visits by car)

Natural heathland/commons/woodland or formal parks with at least 40 ha for other pursuits and car parking. Typically 60 ha in size and 3.2 km from home

Landscape setting, able to accommodate sport and playing fields as well as informal pursuits, with some limited parking. Will be about 20 ha in scale and 1.2 km from home

Pedestrian visits, able to accommodate children's play needs, tennis courts, passive uses/seating. Will be 2 ha in size and 0.4 km from home

Children's playgrounds, gardens and conservation areas of less than 2 ha and under 0.4 km from home

River Thames, canals, towpaths, redundant railway lines and paths

Figure 8.3 Hierarchy of public open space in London – key characteristics

Source: Developed from London Planning Advisory Committee (1994). Copyright © Greater London Authority

now accounting for 60% of the total, an increase from 43% in 2001. Despite being classified as an outer London borough, Newham has many inner city characteristics and many of its open spaces and parks were created in the Victorian and Edwardian periods. Only 6.95% of the Borough is designated as open space or parks, considerably lower than the national average.

According to the London Borough of Newham, their leisure plan sets out their vision for the Borough based on five objectives:

- To prevent the loss of existing leisure facilities and to seek a wide range of new and improved leisure facilities which would tackle the current leisure, sports and recreation deficiencies, and meet the increasing demand for leisure activity.

- To promote arts, culture and entertainment developments/activities in town centre locations and appropriate areas with good public transport access.

- To encourage the development of new museums to attract interest and visitors to the Borough.

- To promote Newham's town centres as the preferred locations for new leisure/entertainment developments, through the application of the sequential test (i.e. allocating land uses to this function as a priority over and above other uses); and

- To promote accessibility to and the efficient use of all leisure facilities.

Source: Based on London Borough of Newham UDP (http://www.newham.gov.uk)

The Council emphasises the protection of existing leisure and recreation facilities, and will allow them to be lost from the current stock only if alternative provision is made. The Council also seeks continually to expand its new leisure facilities in conjunction with the private and voluntary sectors to address existing deficiencies in terms of the need for new sites and buildings for leisure.

Using the National Playing Fields Association Standard of 2.43 ha of playing space per 1000 population, the Borough had only 1.1 ha per 1000 population, with many areas also inaccessible because they were well short of the 0.4 km from any park area over 2 ha set out in Figure 8.3 (see Hall and Page 2006 for more detail). In addition to the issues of open space provision, allotments are one neglected area which planners are beginning to think about and devise planning responses for, given a shortfall in provision for allotments which also comprise a form of open space and a leisure resource. The National Society of Allotments and Leisure Gardeners in the UK consider that there are over 330,000 plot holders and around 100,000 on waiting lists. The subject of allotments has become very controversial because of their loss through local authority land sales to developers in some areas and failure to find alternative locations. This is a very contemporary theme in urban leisure and provides a natural lead-in to the next section.

Contemporary issues in urban leisure: the street as an urban leisure space

According to Williams (1995b: 23), because 'little is known . . . In the realm of public space, it is arguably the street that has been overlooked as the location for popular leisure'. This abject neglect of the street as a leisure setting is somewhat surprising, because the street has traditionally been viewed by leisure historians as a focal point for celebrations, retail activity (e.g. shops and markets) and children's play as well as for social gatherings (Abrams 1992), a feature observed in Chapter 5 in relation to Bethnal Green in the 1920s. The street has also been the setting for popular television soap operas such as *Coronation Street* and *Eastenders* set in the UK, where social interaction takes place on a daily basis as a form of leisure. One possible explanation for this neglect may be the retreat away from the street by many urbanites because of concerns over safety, the pursuit of safety strategies such as cocooning children within the home (see Chapter 12 for a discussion of this concept), and a lack of private or supervised spaces (e.g. play areas) where risk is potentially minimised. What is clear is that the use of the street as a leisure resource has evolved through time, and has undergone a process of change. This change has potentially reconfigured the street as a cultural landscape in some instances, where local culture and spectacles have been popularised and marketed as leisure activities. For example, street markets in London, as discussed by Page (2009), represent one category of the street popularised as a leisure setting because they are a colourful element of the leisure landscape in different parts of the city and attract residents and tourists alike. In other words, the use of the street in the postmodern city has seen a distinct change in terms of its rationale and use not only for leisure, but also other uses that impact upon and compete with leisure such as increased car use.

Social changes have also shifted leisure consumption indoors both in a home and commercial setting, to the detriment of the street. Nevertheless, as Williams (1995b: 23) argues, 'people at leisure may use streets in a number of ways. Streets are, of course, a means of access to other recreational resources in the built-up area but they are also recreational resources in themselves'. In the main, streets have a linear configuration and are used in a number of ways as a backdrop or setting for leisure:

- By pedestrians to get from A to B as part of the leisure or to go shopping or to start a commuter journey.

- To commence a journey on a bicycle or in a motorised vehicle.

- As the setting for leisure activity, such as in the case of children's play.

- As a containing context for other leisure-related activities such as socialising or, in the case of young people, as a place to hang out (which may also be interpreted in a negative context where antisocial behaviour occurs).

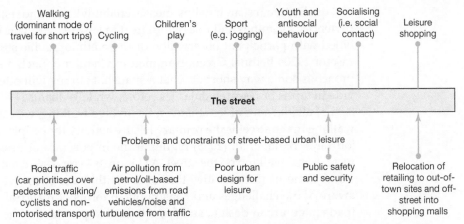

Figure 8.4 Leisure and recreational uses of the street and constraints on its development in urban areas, based on Williams (1995b)

These issues are outlined in Figure 8.4, which also documents some of the problems associated with the street as a leisure domain, where there are a number of potential constraints that may limit its leisure and recreational potential from being realised. Gehl (1980, cited in Williams 1995b) outlined six distinct activities that occurred within the street, based on research undertaken in Canada and Australia:

● People sitting down or standing around.

● People engaged in domestic chores such as washing the car.

● Walking (particularly where it can be used as a recreational activity to address the ongoing national epidemic of obesity in many developed countries, as discussed by Huston *et al.* 2003).

● Social interaction.

● Children's play.

● Movement of traffic within the street.

To this classification we can add a number of other leisure-related activities as observed by Jansen-Verbeke (1989) based on research in the Netherlands, which identified shopping, sightseeing, eating and drinking as street-related.

Williams rightly identifies the problem we have in seeking to understand leisure activities within the setting of the street. This is because they do not feature within official government statistics or surveys. What we find is that many government surveys identify the activities which people undertake in their leisure time, such as walking, shopping or socialising, but fail to understand the setting in which these activities occur. In other words, we not only need to understand how leisure fits into the time budgets of individuals, but simultaneously recognise how those time budgets coalesce in time and space and relate to the resource being consumed or activity being undertaken. This often requires a variety of integrated research methods that can combine quantitative and qualitative research to link measurement with an understanding of the experiences, meanings and role of the street in leisure lives. This may also be combined with participant observation or more ethnographic studies, such as the case of 1920s Bethnal Green examined in Chapter 5. Such a sophisticated approach is some way short of what a snapshot survey will often be able to provide in terms of research data. Therefore, while Williams (1995b) suggests that 80% of all journeys of less than a mile involve walking, we cannot deduce that walking in the street is the primary leisure activity for people undertaking such journeys. Baran *et al*. (2008) highlight the importance of design in facilitating recreational walking on the street. As Figure 8.4 suggests, even when we understand some of the activities that occur within the street we also need to be aware of the challenges and constraints in terms of road traffic, pollution and inadequate urban design, such as a failure to provide public seating, lighting and environmental enhancement such as trees and vegetation to make the street a more attractive environment. We also need to recognise that the street is not simply a residential phenomenon in terms of leisure.

In the case of leisure shopping, the street was a dominant element of daily life in many cities right up until the 1960s when their traditional role as shopping areas began to be challenged by the development of out-of-town sites for retailing in different countries. One consequence is that many town centres and their retailers have seen increased competition from out-of-town developments as well as the rise of shopping malls within town centres which have shifted leisure shopping into private spaces. This has been described as the privatisation of shopping, a trend which has accelerated in many countries since the 1980s following many of the trends in the USA. The rise of department stores in the USA and Europe created an invigorated role for the street as a shopping cavalcade and experience, although in the USA a number of notable stores closed their doors in the 1980s and 1990s as new forms of leisure shopping and retailing evolved. In one respect, their competitor – the out-of-town shopping mall – evolved in the USA from the 1930s concept of a pedestrian mall or street in a town to replace the American notion of 'Main Street' or the UK concept of the High Street, a concentration of shops and retail outlets often dating to the late Victorian and Edwardian years. Yet it was not until the 1950s that the first US shopping mall was created, an enclosed area within a private space with about 50 shops – Southdale in Minnesota. By the 1960s, these malls were becoming commonplace in the USA, including out-of-town retail developments. During the 1970s, the scale of malls expanded to include multiple levels, developing as a social setting for meeting family and friends and replacing the street as a social setting in some cases. These trends in leisure epitomise the rise of a consumption culture, where people can spend their leisure time evaluating the goods and products they want to consume in the private spaces of their home or to parade in in their leisure time. These themes and issues are discussed in Case Study 8.2.

However, one of the major challenges which planners have faced within areas outside of shopping malls in town centres is the issue of safety and the perception of crime alongside other social problems which exist on public streets. For example, in the night-time economy of some cities red light districts have developed where a downward spiral of prostitution, homelessness,

| Case Study 8.2 | Leisure shopping and the shopping mall in the postmodern city |

The global standardisation of consumer products has meant that the search for the unique shopping experience continues to remain important. The growth of the North American shopping malls and the development in the UK of out-of-town complexes (e.g. the Metro Centre in Gateshead and Lakeside at Thurrock, adjacent to the M25) have extended this trend. For example, in the case of Edmonton Mall (Canada), Jansen-Verbeke (1991) estimated that 10% of the total floor space is used for leisure facilities with its 800 shops and parking for 27,000 cars. Finn and Erdem (1995) describe West Edmonton Mall (WEM) as a mega-multimall (MMM) given its scale, since the developer of WEM claimed that such a development attracted nine million visitors a year. The difficulty with most existing studies of leisure shopping is that they fail to disentangle the relationships between the actual activity tourists undertake and their perception of the environment. For this reason, Jansen-Verbeke (1991) distinguished between intentional shopping and intentional leisure shopping in a preliminary attempt to explain how and why people engage in this activity; she also suggested that several criteria need to be considered to distinguish between intentional shopping and intentional leisure and tourism in relation to the:

- Behaviour pattern of visitors
  - trip length – short, possibly longer;
  - length of stay – limited or rather unplanned;
  - time of stay – a few hours during the day, an evening, a full day;
  - kinds of activity – window shopping, intentional buying, drinking, eating, various leisure activities, cultural activities, sightseeing;
  - expenditure – goods, possibly some souvenirs, drinks, meals, entrance fees to leisure facilities.
- Functional characteristics of the environment
  - wide range of retail shops, department store, catering, leisure and other facilities, tourist attractions, spatial clustering of facilities;
  - parking space and easy access;
  - street retailing, pedestrian priority in open spaces.
- Quality of the environment
  - image of the place, leisure setting, display of goods on the street, street musicians and artists;
  - accessibility during leisure time, including weekends and evenings;
  - aesthetic value, image of maintenance and safety;
  - architectural design of buildings, streets, shops, windows, sign boards, lighting;
  - social effective value, liveliness of the open space;
  - animation, entertainment, amusement and surprise.

- Hospitableness of the environment
  - social, visual, physical;
  - orientation, information, symbolism, identification.

Source: Jansen-Verbeke (1991: 9–10)

According to Mansfeld (1999), shopping as a consumption activity has assumed a new significance in urban areas, especially now that globalisation and capital investment in shopping malls are becoming commonplace in the retail landscape. The evolution of shopping malls as commercial entities in pursuit of profit is now commonplace in towns, cities and the urban fringe (Edge City) where the threshold of population (residents and visitors) is sufficient to support such a development. Mansfeld's (1999) cultural analysis of the mall as a cultural form of production is useful in explaining how contemporary capitalism is now responding to tastes and fashion, just as the café culture is a complex reflection of new leisure practices. A great deal of interest has been shown in the development of West Edmonton Mall in Canada as a reflection of postmodernity. It represents a landscape of spectacle, fantasy, pastiche and artificial creations of new shopping environments. To encourage the throughput and circulation of shoppers, malls often have an anchor tenant at each end of the development, interspersed with precincts, lifts and escalators to encourage the flow of shoppers. Much of the shoppers' activity is subject to surveillance by cameras to assist in the exclusion of undesirable elements. Many malls have distinct gender appeal, with retailers targeting women as primary purchasers of goods, making leisure shopping in these locales a significant form of consumption.

Source: Page and Hall (2003)

poverty, and drink and drug problems combine to create a black economy of illegal and illicit leisure activities which are deemed to be deviant. It is interesting to find that the introduction of surveillance techniques such as closed circuit television (CCTV) creates a sense of public ease and perceptions of safety through the creation of enhanced surveillance of the street.

Since Williams' (1995b) research on the street as a leisure setting, other studies have emerged which have expanded our understanding of the street. For example, Soja (1996) developed the concept of the *third space* which has been examined in relation to the street as a safe space and social venue for leisure and other activities. This focus on the street as a third space has been examined by Matthews *et al.* (2000) in an interesting paper entitled 'The street as third space', which examined how those aged 9 to 16 years of age used a street in terms of their leisure time. For example, 74% of those interviewed hung out with friends at least once a week, illustrating its important role as a social venue, despite the progressive retreat from the street by many urban children as a result of parental control. Conversely, MacDonald and Shildrick

(2007) examined some of the negative connotations associated with young people and the street as the setting for youth culture and some of the dimensions of social exclusion. In addition, Defilippis (2008) provided an interesting analysis of how a public space such as South Street Seaport on the east side of lower Manhattan was transformed from an open air public museum to a privately controlled and commercialised space. What this study is important in tracking, over a 20-year period, is the shift from a public leisure industry to more commercialised and privatised leisure spaces.

What these debates highlight is the potential challenge for public policy makers in finding ways of revitalising the street as a leisure setting, given the perceived retreat to the home and indoor leisure facilities according to social theorists. As Figure 8.5 suggests, there are a range of potential public policy solutions which may be pursued. These range from taming the car and rethinking urban design (Girling and Helphand 1996) through to more enlightened planning responses which adopt a more holistic view of the street in relation to the sustainability agenda which we discussed in Chapter 7. What is required, from a planning perspective, is an integrated policy and planning response which draws together these different elements identified in Figure 8.5 to help breathe life back into streets and reconfigure them to accommodate many of the current-day leisure pursuits in which people now want to engage. For example, the rise of a cappuccino society as some commentators would suggest, with the rise of cafés and restaurants on urban streets, may often breathe an important source of economic life back into a street, bringing economic vitality, ambience and activity which create a sense of atmosphere and place. This is very much the case in many mainland European streets, most notably in cities such as Paris, Madrid and Amsterdam. However, one of the most protracted issues which policy makers have had to address is the issue of safety and security.

Contemporary constraints on urban leisure: issues of safety and fear in the urban environment

Since the 1980s, there has been a growing interest in the role of fear, personal safety and the spatial implications in the urban environment (Schroeder and Anderson 1984), most notably expressed in a UK setting by the Winlow and Hall (2006) study on the night-time economy of cities. In the USA, Pendleton (2000) pointed to the increase in criminality in non-urban areas, traditionally seen as safe. This also has a very distinct gender dimension as we discussed in Chapter 7, where certain groups are socially excluded from leisure sites such as the street because of fear. The most obvious response by some governments has been to invest in surveillance technology, to the point where the UK is one of the most surveilled urban societies. But Koskela and Pain (2000) suggest that such responses do not address the problems of designing out fear from urban environments such as streets (e.g. well lit and a greater focus on the uses to be made of the street in day and night-time). Interestingly, some social groups, for example young people, address their concerns of victimisation or fear by using

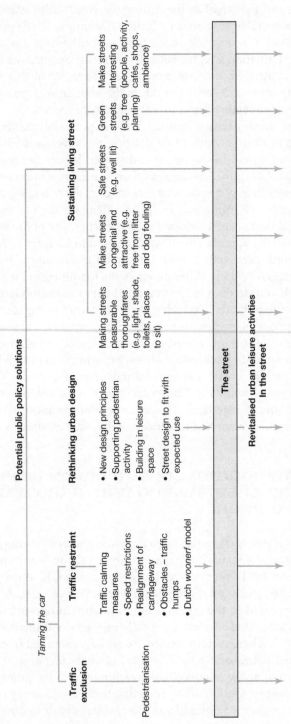

Figure 8.5   Potential solutions to revitalise the street as an urban leisure resource, based on Williams (1995b)

mobile phones as a way to negotiate risk (Pain *et al.* 2005) as they have become an integral part of young people's lifestyles (Wilska 2003). Indeed, the mobile phone is part of a postmodern trend where the phone is a means of self-expression and identity formation and a source of consumption. Even so, Cybriwsky (1999) recognised that the growth in surveillance of public spaces like streets to improve security may result in a shift to private spaces, which may be self-defeating if we are seeking to revitalise streets. Norris (1999) traced the evolution of surveillance and closed circuit television and described its wider use in many urban leisure settings (e.g. football grounds, shopping malls, town centres and other public spaces) and concerns over the rise of Big Brother which was enapsulated in George Orwell's book *1984*.

Critics such as Button (2004: 2) argued that running alongside the monitoring of public behaviour and leisure through CCTV, 'during the post-war period there has been a growth in what has been termed "mass private property" encompassing large shopping malls, leisure facilities, gated communities, airports . . . These facilities, which are usually private but freely open to the public, have created new debates concerning . . . what is termed "quasi-public" or "hybrid" space'. The most obvious example is the gated community, examined by Atkinson *et al.* (2003), which further segregates the *haves* and *have nots*. For example, Atkinson *et al.* (2003) point to the rise of gated communities in the USA where citizens live behind managed and surveilled environments in which entry is controlled. As a new phenomenon, gated communities grew from around 500 such examples in the USA in the 1960s to over nine million people living in three million residential units by 1997, where resident associations exist. Part of this response is against the fear of crime, where social exclusivity is a dominant feature. If we are trying to redevelop a communal culture in the use of the street as a leisure setting, then public spaces need to meet our psychological needs and preferences so that people reconnect with the street. One interesting example that runs contrary to this trend in the Western world was observed by Drummond (2000) in Vietnam. Here the street is a pseudo-public leisure space and is actually expanding as a phenomenon. Yet the retreat from the street in many Western countries owing to fear and crime has been a major feature of the period since the 1960s, although in many Asian cities it is a dominant mode of leisure activity and focus for daily life, including shopping, eating and socialising.

Urban neighbourhood leisure: children's leisure spaces and play

One of the most contentious areas of urban leisure provision linked to the street is the issue of children's play space. We have already highlighted the importance of children's play in other parts of the book, but in an urban context we need to recognise that such provision is an essential activity. For public sector planners, the issue of children's play space is contentious because of the concerns over supervision, potential litigation from accidents and injuries resulting from equipment which the local authority provides, and parental concerns over unsupervised play. There is a consensus within research on open spaces, parks and gardens and their use by children that the past 20 years have seen a decline in the ability of neighbourhoods to support children's outdoor activity. This is not a reflection of gaps in provision, but more an issue of parental preferences and anxieties and their restrictions upon children in terms of limiting what they can and cannot do in their playtime. Even so, Jenkins (2006) points to the way children display their own street wisdom and negotiate risk. As Williams (1995a) argued, these limitations have led to a distinct territoriality in terms of children's play space, a feature highlighted in the case of the London Borough of Newham in Table 8.3 which documents the issues of provision and policy responses of one local authority to levels of under-provision.

For geographers, their interest is focused on the types of space in which children play, along with the implications for the areas they will occupy in their leisure time (Karsten 2003). As Moore (1986) noted, there are three types of leisure space which children use, as depicted in schematic form in Figure 8.6:

● Contiguous space, which, as the word implies, denotes the area in and around the home which was termed the *habitual range*. This immediate environment around the home is used on a regular daily basis, particularly when there are constraints imposed upon play in terms of time, and may certainly include environments such as the street.

Table 8.3 Children's playspace in the London Borough of Newham

---

The issues
- Newham has the greatest proportion of children in the population for any local authority.
- Around 10% of the population is under five years old.
- Play areas need improvement, new equipment, resurfacing and better surfaces for other uses.
- NPFA recommend children play areas for those aged under five should be less than 200m distance from home.
- Newham is deficient in play space according to the NPFA standard, requiring an additional 12ha of space.

Policy response
- 'Policy OS12: Developers of housing sites containing a minimum of 25 dwellings will be required to make appropriate provision for children's playspace', following policy guidance from National Government (PPG3) which suggests 'new family housing developments should include adequate provision of suitable areas for children's play, including informal play space, with safe pedestrian access' while PPG17 permits Local Authorities to require new housing developers to address such issues in their proposed housing schemes.

Source: Adapted from London Borough of Newham (1991) www.newham.gov.uk, accessed 7 May 2009

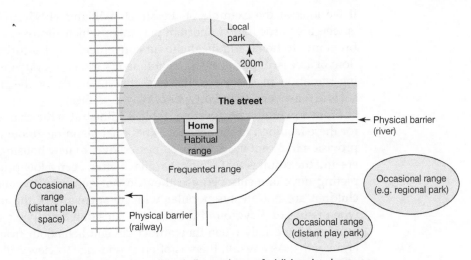

Figure 8.6 The geographical dimensions of children's playspace

- Moving away from the home, second area was termed the *frequented range*, which denotes an area in which the child plays when they are not constrained by time and will certainly involve the child exploring outside of the immediate sight of a parent, and could include areas which have been mutually agreed with parents where there are physical barriers or hazards highlighted as defining the boundary of the play area.

- Lastly, there is the *occasional range*, which is further afield than the other areas, accessed quite infrequently and may comprise a whole series of unconnected destinations or locations. Here, special permission is needed to visit the location or someone to supervise the child when he or she is taken to the location as a special treat.

While we can define the areas in which children play, the important point to stress is that children also have leisure needs which should be built into urban planning exercises, particularly at a neighbourhood level because that is where much of their leisure time is occupied through play. Williams (1995a) also refers to research by Coffin and Williams (1989) which looked at children's evolutionary development in terms of play and segmented children into five categories:

- Toddlers, aged 1 to 3.

- Preschool children.

- Primary school children aged 5 to 10 years of age.

- Older children aged 10 to 13 years of age.

- Adolescents aged 14 to 16 years of age.

What this classification illustrates is that each of these groups of children has very specific play needs reflected in how they use leisure resources, particularly if we look at the example of the street. Williams (1995a: 138) suggests that 'streets are particularly important play areas which affords several advantages: proximity to home and its attendant convenience and security; ease and freedom of access; opportunity for spontaneous and temporary grouping; interesting variation in street activity; and the suitability of the paved or tarmac surface for several popular types of play or games'.

From a planning perspective, Table 8.3 illustrates the challenge of planning for these facilities. In the absence of national planning guidelines, much of the provision in recent years has been passed over to new housing estate developers and the result is that play spaces have often been a low priority when completing developments because they do not generate revenue. Furthermore, children are not always popular with all segments of the local community when issues of playground location are considered as they may be deemed a nuisance, especially when they attract deviant behaviour from older children and youths. As a result, there is often a tendency to view children's play provision as a complex problem with no easy solution, and, in some instances, land use planning tends to allocate space according to a minimum standard approach for an entire community, so that accessing sites may often be difficult or inconvenient for some children. Consequently, where open space provision is seen as a marginal activity it can often be allocated to the least desirable sites within a settlement, further compounding the problem where a lack of visibility means that vandalism can occur if play spaces are incorrectly sited within settlements.

Children's play provision needs to be interesting, and well located at neighbourhood and district levels in terms of playgrounds, playing fields, adventure playgrounds and other open spaces in view of the developmental benefits of play as discussed in Chapter 6. While there are numerous studies setting out hierarchical principles for provision of all sorts of urban leisure facilities, including children's play provision, meeting any target set within plans and strategies will often be contingent upon the availability of public funds as well as land where settlements are expanding. This is one reason why local authorities adopt the principle of planning gain for such facilities when approving new developments, although this may only be a temporary solution because such facilities will need reinvestment and upgrading in due course, from local authority budgets.

Leisure and the urban fringe

With the growth of Edge City, there has been considerable interest in how the urban periphery is used for leisure alongside the development of new out-of-town locations. Elson (1993) recognised that the urban periphery could accommodate urban leisure and recreation in different ways as shown in Figure 8.7, which depicts some of the characteristics of the urban fringe. What Figure 8.7

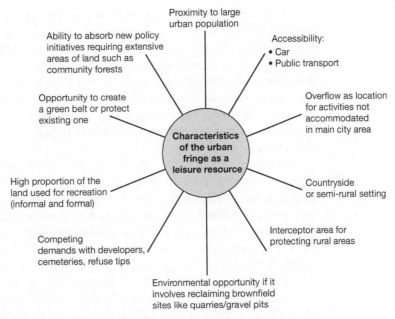

Figure 8.7 Characteristics of the urban fringe

illustrates is that the urban fringe abuts the countryside in many instances and so has the capacity to absorb leisure demand, especially where the urban fringe has a defined green belt. In the 1930s the green-belt concept was developed in London and in many other European cities, based on the influential work of Raymond Unwin and the 1933 Green Belt Act, and applied in many places (see, for example, Lloyd and Peel 2007 on Scotland; Yang and Jinxing 2007 on Beijing).

A green belt is a band of open space on the city's periphery in order to compensate for the lack of open space in the built urban environment, and subsequently used to try to contain the pressure for urban growth through urban sprawl. In Wellington, New Zealand this principle was developed as a concept via a town belt and urban development subsequently developed on the other side of it, but it illustrates the principles of developing an urban containment strategy with a green buffer.

In the case of the UK, green belts were developed as a tool to contain the urban environment (Hall 1974). Yet as the experience of London suggests, the green belt was irreversibly damaged in the 1970s and early 1980s when London's infamous orbital motorway – the M25, sometimes euphemistically called London's biggest car park owing to the constant congestion and high volume of use – was built through stretches of London's green belt. This was a direct function of government policy that favoured road building and personal freedom for mobility as opposed to state-subsidised public transport that was more sustainable. What the M25 example illustrates is a global problem for green belts, where urbanisation and urban development have focused attention on the demand for land for housing and economic development to accommodate suburban growth.

The green belt has also emerged as a tool used in other situations since its original designation in the 1930s, and in many other countries across the world such as Melbourne (Buxton and Goodman 2008), which are reviewed on a country-by-country basis in Amati (2008). In a UK context, the green belt concept potentially got a new lease of life in the UK in the late 1960s (in contrast to some of the examples in other countries in Amati 2008) when the Countryside Commission established Country Parks in the urban fringe, following on from a UK government White Paper on Leisure and the Countryside (1966).

As Hall and Page (2006) discussed, the Countryside Commission viewed Country Parks as an area of '25 acres in extent, with basic facilities, for the public to enjoy informal open air recreation' (Harrison 1991: 95). Their history and evolution have been assessed by Lambert (2006), tracing their relatively short history in the UK compared to urban parks. Between 1969 and 1993 the Countryside Commission spent £16 million developing Country Parks, comprising 206 Country Parks and 239 picnic sites. In 2003, it was estimated that they attracted 57 million visits a year, comprising 0.13% of the land surface of England and Wales but accounting for 4.2% of leisure trips. By 2009 the 400 sites calling themselves Country Parks were receiving 70 million visits a year. There has been an ongoing debate over the value of Country Parks because critics suggest that they divert only a small proportion of potential countryside recreation from rural areas. In fact, Groome and Tarrant (1984) found public transport to Country Parks effective over a 5–8km distance (i.e. short distance) for a local population but less so over longer distances. Even so, a UK Parliamentary House of Commons Select Committee Inquiry in 1999 began to suggest signs of an apparent renaissance in the role of the Country Park in urban leisure (Lambert 2006). The recent interest in redeveloping the resource base of these sites has been accompanied by public concerns over the serious decline in open space provision in the UK that has occurred, especially as many of these Country Parks rely upon local authorities for their funding. This shows that the urban fringe is one additional outdoor leisure environment in which leisure and recreational use occurs that complements the other types of setting we have discussed throughout this chapter.

Summary

As Williams (1995a: 219) rightly argues, 'we should start by reasserting the significance of the urban environment as a venue for outdoor recreations and the special value of locally based policy for provision . . . Fundamentally people shape their recreational habits according to the opportunities they see around them, so the local dimension to development of recreational policy should remain central'. As was discussed at the end of Chapter 7, the emergence of the sustainability agenda within urban areas and the need to absorb leisure demand at a local level are creating a renewed interest in the future role which urban leisure will play in our leisure lives. Yet urban leisure has been neglected in recent years by the growing interest in the cultural sector, of which leisure is now seen as one element. There are certainly many arguments, based on empirical evidence, that urban leisure remains the poor partner of public sector leisure provision. In stark contrast, the cultural industries are the emerging sector, seen as dynamic, interesting, and offering significant economic growth potential. It is this latter point – the economic potential of the cultural industries – that has focused the minds of politicians over and above the sustainable leisure needs of society. Consequently, there is a great danger, as this chapter has argued, that this pursuit of new political agendas such as the cultural sector is detracting from the inherent value and qualities of urban leisure as a focal point for public policy making and planning. We need constantly to stress the importance of urban leisure, even though it may not seem a very exciting area to politicians and planners, where operational issues may be focused on grass cutting, tree maintenance, dog fouling and vandalism, in contrast to grand and ambitious plans within the cultural sector. To take an analogy from critics of the modern-day education sector, we need to go back to basics and recognise the significance and importance of urban leisure to the everyday lives of the population, especially outdoor resources.

As the world's population is continually urbanising, to neglect this important area and to under-resource or overlook how it is interconnected with everything we do is a major oversight. Ordinary people see and experience the resources which comprise urban leisure every day and the difficulty is that because it is so familiar to us, it tends to get neglected and overlooked as routine and uninteresting. These new political agendas that focus on the importance of place, quality of life (Lloyd and Auld 2003) and the importance of attracting inward investment need to recognise that enhancing urban leisure resources also adds value to the lives of the resident population. If we are really committed to the notion of sustainability, rather than the green rhetoric that surrounds this issue, then we need to put sustainability into practice as custodians of the environment for future generations. This will involve investing, developing and maintaining urban leisure resources as a central tenet of any sustainability policy which national and local government promote. We need to re-look at the investment programmes of the Victorian and Edwardian periods and realise that their leisure legacy needs to be embraced in terms of sustainability and reinvigorated, encouraging people to undertake leisure near to home, thus avoiding car-based transport and CO_2 emissions. While this may be desirable, urban leisure is overshadowed by the significant attention which has been directed to the evolving concept of the cultural industries as part of a wider leisure domain. For this reason, the next chapter will examine the cultural industries to see why they have attracted so much attention.

Discussion questions

1. Why are urban areas probably the most important setting for leisure in contemporary society?

2. How would you set about developing improved play spaces for children in a city?

3. Compare and contrast the role of leisure provision for indoor leisure and outdoor leisure and recreation by the public sector.

4. How can different stakeholders begin to work together to further the objectives of a sustainable leisure future for towns and cities?

References

Abrams, L. (1992) *Workers Culture in Imperial Germany: Leisure and Recreation in Rhineland and Westphalia*, Routledge: London.

Amati, M. (2008) 'Introduction', in A. Amati (ed.) *Green Belts: A Twentieth Century Experiment*, Ashgate: Aldershot, pp. 1–18.

Atkinson, R., Flint, J., Blandy, S. and Lister, D. (2003) *The Extent and Neighbourhood Impacts of Gated Communities*, University of Glasgow: Glasgow.

Audit Commission (2003) *Preston City Council: Sport and Recreation,* Audit Commission: London.

Baran, P., Rodriguez, D. and Khattak, A. (2008) 'Space syntax and walking in new urbanist and suburban neighbourhoods', *Journal of Urban Design* 13 (1): 5–28.

Birrell, S. (2006) 'Sport and sport studies', in C. Rojek, S. Shaw and A. Veal (eds) *A Handbook of Leisure Studies*, Palgrave: Basingstoke, pp. 335–53.

Bourdieu, P. (1984) *Distinction: A Social Critique of the Judgment of Taste*, trans. R. Nice, Harvard University Press: Cambridge, MA.

Bull, C., Hoose, J. and Weed, M. (2003) *An Introduction to Leisure Studies*, Pearson: Harlow.

Burgess, J., Harrison, C. and Limb, M. (1988) 'People, parks and the urban green: a study of popular meanings and values for open spaces in the city', *Urban Studies* 26: 455–73.

Burtenshaw, D., Bateman, M. and Ashworth, G.J. (1991) *The City in West Europe*, 2nd edn, Wiley: Chichester.

Button, M. (2004) 'Private security and the policing of quasi-public space', *International Journal of the Sociology of Law* 31: 227–37.

Buxton, M. and Goodman, R. (2008) 'Protecting Melbourne's green wedges – fate of a public policy', in A. Amati (ed.) *Green Belts: A Twentieth Century Experiment*, Ashgate: Aldershot, pp. 61–80.

Byrne, D. (2001) *Understanding the Urban*, Palgrave: Basingstoke.

Christiansen, E. and Brinkerhoff-Jacobs, J. (1995) 'Gaming and entertainment: an imperfect union' *Cornell Hotel and Restaurant Quarterly.*

Coffin, G. and Williams, M. (1989) *Children's Outdoor Play in the Built Environment,* National Children's Play and Recreation Unit: London.

Cybriwsky, R. (1999) 'Changing patterns of urban public space: observations and assessments from the Tokyo and New York metropolitan areas', *Cities: The International Journal of Urban Policy and Planning* 4: 223–31.

Defilippis, J. (2008) 'From a public re-creation to private recreation: the transformation of public space in South Street Seaport', *Journal of Urban Affairs* 19 (4): 405–17.

Department of Transport, Local Government and Regions (DTLR) (2002) *Improving Urban Parks, Play Areas and Green Spaces* DLTR: London.

Drummond, L. (2000) 'Street scenes: practices of public and private space in urban Vietnam', *Urban Studies* 37 (12): 2377–91.

Elson, M. (1993) 'Sport and recreation in the green belt countryside', in S. Glyptis (ed.) *Leisure and the Environment: Essays in Honour of Professor J.A. Patmore,* Belhaven Press: London, pp. 131–7.

Evans, G. and Shaw, S. (2001) 'Urban leisure and transport: regeneration effects', *Journal of Retail and Leisure Property* 1: 350–72.

Finn, A. and Erdem, T. (1995) 'The economic impact of a mega-multi-mall. Estimation issues in the case of West Edmonton Mall', *Tourism Management* 16 (5): 367–73.

Garreau, J. (1992) *Edge City,* Doubleday: New York.

Gehl, J. (1980) 'The residential street environment', *Built Environment* 6 (1): 51–61.

Girling, C. and Helphand, K. (1996) *Yard–Street–Park: The Design of Suburban Open Space,* Wiley: New York.

Glyptis, S. and Chambers, D. (1982) 'No place like home', *Leisure Studies* 1 (3): 247–62.

Godbey, G., Caldwell, L., Floyd, M. and Payne, L. (2005) 'Contributions of leisure studies and recreation and park management research to the active living agenda', *Amercian Journal of Preventive Medicine* 28 (2): Supplement 2: 150–8.

Goldberger, P. (1996) 'The rise of the private city', in J. Vitullo Martin (ed.) *Breaking Away: The Future of Cities,* The Twenty Century Fund: New York.

Groome, D. and Tarrant, C. (1984) 'Countryside recreation: Achieving access for all?', *Countryside Planning Yearbook 1984:* 77–98.

Hall, C.M. and Page, S. J. (2006) *The Geography of Tourism and Recreation: Environment, Place and Space,* 3rd edn, Routledge: London.

Hall, P. (1974) 'The containment of urban England', *The Geographical Journal* 140 (3): 386–408.

Hannigan, J. (1995) 'The postmodern city: A new urbanisation', *Current Sociology* 43 (1): 151–217.

Hannigan, J. (1998) *Fantasy City: Pleasure and Profit in the Postmodern Metropolis,* Routledge: London.

Harrison, C. (1991) *Countryside Recreation in a Changing Society,* TML Partnership: London.

Hendricks, J. (1971) 'Leisure participation as influenced by urban residential patterns', *Sociology and Social Research* 55 (4): 414–28.

van Herzele, A., De Clercq, E. and Wiedmann, T. (2005) 'Strategic planning for new woodlands in the urban periphery: through the lens of social inclusiveness', *Urban Forestry and Greening* 3 (3-4): 177–88.

Hewison, R. (1987) *The Heritage Industry: Britain in a Climate of Decline*, Methuen: London.

Huston, S., Evenson, K., Bors, P. and Gizlice, K. (2003) 'Neighbourhood environment, access to places for activity, and leisure-time physical activity in a diverse North Carolina population', *American Journal of Health Promotion* 18 (1): 58–69.

Jansen-Verbeke, M. (1989) 'Fun shopping as a geographical notion, or the attraction of inner city Amsterdam as a shopping area', *Tijdshcrift voor Economische en Sociale Geografie* 80 (3): 171–83.

Jansen-Verbeke, M. (1991) 'Leisure shopping: A magic concept for the tourism industry?', *Tourism Management* 12 (1): 9–14.

Jenkins, N. (2006) 'You can't wrap them up in cotton wool! Constructing risk in young people's access to outdoor play', *Health, Risk and Society* 8 (4): 379–93.

Johnston, R. (1981) 'Urbanisation', in R. Johnston, D. Gregory, P. Haggett, D. Smith and D. Stoddard (eds) *The Dictionary of Human Geography*, Blackwell: Oxford, pp. 363–4.

Karsten, L. (2002) 'Mapping childhood in Amsterdam: the spatial and social construction of children's domains in the city', *Tijdshcrift voor Economische en Sociale Geografie* 93 (3): 231–41.

Koskela, H. and Pain, R. (2000) 'Revisiting fear and place: women's fear of attack and the built environment', *Geoforum* 31: 269–80.

Lambert, D. (2006) 'The history of the Country Park 1966–2005: towards a renaissance?', *Landscape Research* 31 (4): 43–62.

Lloyd, K. and Auld, C. (2003) 'Leisure, public space and quality of life in the urban environment', *Urban Policy and Research* 21 (4): 339–58.

Lloyd, M. and Peel, D. (2007) 'Green belts in Scotland: towards the modernisation of a traditional concept?', *Journal of Environmental Planning and Management* 50 (5): 639–56.

London Planning Advisory Committee (LPAC) (1994) *Advice on Strategic Planning Guidance for London*, LPAC: London.

MacDonald, R. and Shildrick, T. (2007) 'Street corner society: leisure careers, youth (sub) culture and social exclusion', *Leisure Studies* 26 (3): 339–55.

Mansfeld, J. (1999) 'Consuming spaces', in R. Le Heron, L. Murphy, P. Forer and M. Goldstone (eds) *Explorations in Human Geography: Encountering Place*, Oxford University Press: Auckland, pp. 318–43.

Matthews, H., Limb, M. and Taylor, M. (2000) 'The street as thirdspace', in S. Holloway and G. Valentine (eds) *Children's Geographies: Play, Living, Learning*, Routledge: London, pp. 58–69.

Meethan, K. (1996) 'Consumed (in) in civilised city', *Annals of Tourism Research* 32 (2): 322–40.

Moore, R. (1986) *Childhood's Domain: Play and Space in Child Development*, Croom Helm: London.

Mutisaya, D. and Willis, J. (2009) 'Budget drinking: alcohol consumption in two Kenyan towns', *Journal of Eastern African Studies* 3 (1): 55–73.

Myerscough, J. (1988) *The Economic Importance of the Arts in Britain*, Policy Studies Institute: London.

Norris, C. (ed.) (1999) *Surveillance, Closed Circuit Television and Social Control*, Ashgate: Aldershot.

Oakley, B. and Rhys, M. (eds) (2008) *The Sport and Fitness Sector: An Introduction*, Routledge: London.

Page, S. J. (1995) *Urban Tourism*, Routledge: London.

Page, S. J. (2009) *Tourism Management: Managing for Change*, 3rd edn, Butterworth Heinemann: Oxford.

Page, S. J. and Connell, J. (2009) *Tourism: A Modern Synthesis*, 3rd edn, Cengage Learning: London.

Page, S. J. and Hall, C.M. (2003) *Managing Urban Tourism*, Pearson: Harlow.

Page, S. J., Nielsen, K. and Goodenough, R. (1994) 'Managing urban parks: user perspectives and local leisure needs in the 1990s', *Service Industries Journal*, 14 (2): 216–37.

Pain, R., Grundy, S., Gill, S., Towner, E., Sparks, G. and Hughes, K. (2005) 'So long as I take my mobile: Mobile phones, urban life and geographies of young people's safety', *International Journal of Urban and Regional Research* 29 (4): 814–30.

Patmore, J.A. (1983) *Recreation and Resources: Leisure Patterns and Leisure Places*, Blackwell: Oxford.

Pendleton, M. (2000) 'Leisure, crime and cops: exploring a paradox of our civility', *Journal of Leisure Research* 32 (1): 111–15.

Postman, N. (1985) *Amusing Ourselves to Death*, Viking: New York.

Pratt, A. (1997) 'The cultural industries production system: a case study of employment change in Britain 1984–1991', *Environment and Planning A* 29: 1953–74.

Van Rij, E., Dekkers, J. and Koomen, E. (2008) 'Analysing the success of open space preservation in the Netherlands: The Midden-Delfland case', *Tijdshcrift voor Economische en Sociale Geografie* 99 (1): 115–24.

Ritzer, D. (1993) *The McDonaldisation of Society*, rev. edn, Pine Forge: Thousand Oaks.

Roberts, K. (2004) *The Leisure Industries*, Palgrave: Basingstoke.

Robertson, K. (1995) 'Downtown redevelopment strategies in the United States: an end of century assessment', *Journal of the American Planning Association* 61 (4): 429–37.

Rojek, C. (1993) *Ways of Escape: Modern Transformations in Leisure and Travel*, Macmillan: Basingstoke.

Rojek, C., Shaw, S. and Veal, A. (eds) (2006) *A Handbook of Leisure Studies*, Palgrave: Basingstoke.

Schroeder, H. and Anderson, L. (1984) 'Safety in urban recreation', *Journal of Leisure Research* 16 (1): 178–94.

Seeley, I. (1973) *Outdoor Recreation and the Urban Environment*, Macmillan: Basingstoke.

Soja, E. (1989) *Postmodern Geographies: The Reassertion of Space in Critical Social Theory*, Verso: London.

Soja, E. (1996) *Thirdspace, Journeys to Los Angeles and Other Real and Imagined Places*, Blackwell: Oxford.

Souther, J. (2006) 'Urbanisation and leisure', in G. Cross (ed.) *Encyclopedia of Recreation and Leisure in America, Volume 2*, Thomson-Gale: Woodbridge, CT, pp. 383–91.

Teo, P., Chang, T. and Chong, H. (eds) (2001) *Interconnected Worlds: Tourism in Southeast Asia*, Pergamon: Oxford.

Thorns, D. (2002) *The Transformation of Cities: Urban Theory and Urban Life*, Palgrave: Basingstoke.

Torkildsen, G. (2005) *Leisure Management*, 5th edn, Routledge: London.

UK Government White Paper (1996) 'Leisure in the Countryside', Cmnd 2928, HMSO: London.

Van der Valk, A. and van Dijk, T. (eds) (2009) *Regional Planning for Open Space*, Routledge: London.

Veal, A. (1993) 'Planning for leisure: past, present and future', in S. Glyptis (ed.) *Leisure and the Environment: Essays in Honour of J. A. Patmore*, Belhaven: London.

Wezenaar, H. (1999) 'Leisure land use planning and sustainability in the new town of Almere, The Netherlands', *Tourism Geographies* 1 (4): 460–79.

Williams, S. (1995a) *Recreation and the Urban Environment*, Routledge: London.

Williams, S. (1995b) 'On the street – public space for popular leisure', in D. Leslie (ed.) *Tourism and Leisure – Perspectives on Provision*, Leisure Studies Association: Brighton, pp. 23–56.

Wilska, T. (2003) 'Mobile phone use as part of young people's consumptions styles', *Journal of Consumer Policy* 26: 441–63.

Winlow, S. and Hall, S. (2006) *Violent Night: Urban Leisure and Contemporary Culture*, Berg: Oxford.

Wong, K. (2009) 'Urban park visiting habits and leisure activities of residents in Hong Kong, China', *Managing Leisure* 14 (2): 125–40.

Wu, B. and Cai, L. (2006) 'Spatial modelling suburban leisure in Shanghai', *Annals of Tourism Research* 33 (1): 179–98.

Yang, J. and Jinxing, Z. (2007) 'The failure and success of greenbelt program in Beijing', *Urban Forestry and Greening* 6 (4): 387–96.

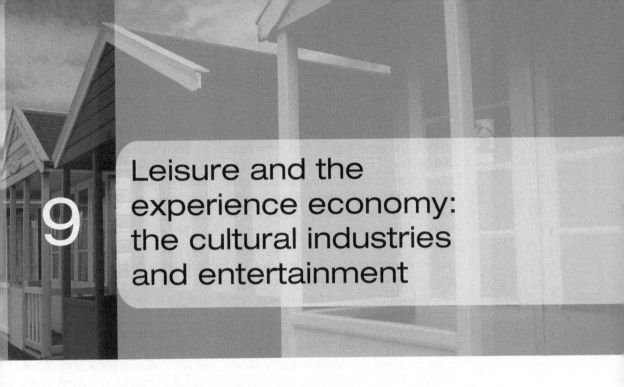

9

Leisure and the experience economy: the cultural industries and entertainment

Learning outcomes

After reading this chapter, you should be able to:

- Identify the difference between the cultural industries and the creative industries

- Explain why leisure has been incorporated into cultural strategies

- Describe the significance of specific forms of leisure entertainment and how they focus on the intangible experiential elements of consumption

Introduction

In Chapter 8 we focused on the urban dimensions of leisure and highlighted the growing interest in the concept of the cultural industries. As Stevenson (2006) argues, the cultural industries are a truly interdisciplinary area of study, although there has been comparatively little research merging leisure studies and culture. Much of the research in this area has emanated from the sociology of culture, media studies and cultural economics, along with contributions from other subjects such as geography. In this chapter, we will explore the concept of the cultural and creative industries and the role of entertainment as a leisure experience, elements of which show a continuity from Chapter 8 owing to the common association with an urban focus for the cultural industries, although rural dimensions have also been examined (e.g. see Cloke 2007). This builds on the earlier concept developed in the book on the *experience economy* (Pine and Gilmore 1999; Sundbo and Darmer 2008) or an *entertainment economy* (Wolf 1999; Moss 2009), in which a considerable element of the leisure experience is the value added or enjoyment derived from the experience as opposed to the tangible elements of the product or service. While there are certainly critics of these theoretical interpretations of leisure as experience, they do offer an interesting starting point for our evaluation of how a series of transformations are occurring in contemporary leisure which have definite experiential elements that are related to wider changes in our society and economy.

Sharpe (2008) discusses how individuals engage in leisure practices and seek experiences which challenge existing ideologies so that leisure becomes a form of resistance to existing ideas and a means of pursuing social or political change. This is highlighted through the example of attending events in one's leisure time, such as Live8, and young people's participation as a desire to be part of an event and a political movement as a wider collective leisure experience. Stevenson (2006) suggests that the shift towards the cultural industries in a leisure context reflects two important trends:

- The highly individualised nature of the leisure experiences being provided by the cultural and creative sectors.

- The dominance of the commercial sector over and above publicly funded culture.

This raises a number of important policy debates since, as Stevenson (2006) argues, the focus on cultural industries challenges the traditional public-good ethos of state-funded leisure. Conversely, the free market and commercial sector become the arbiter of cultural provision, albeit within settings such as public sector regenerated urban precincts as attractive spaces for leisure. What Stevenson's (2006) debate highlights is a trend towards cultural planning by the public sector (see Evans 2001; Stevenson 2005 for more detail) to foster wide-ranging social, economic and cultural objectives where leisure becomes part of culture, as an element of our everyday life. This suggests that leisure is being merged with the arts, entertainment and wider cultural industries as national and local government pursue this agenda with the stated objective of improving the quality of everyday life, especially our leisure experiences. While there are obvious social welfare objectives within these cultural plans, it does raise a significant question: *who benefits?* Some of the principal beneficiaries have been the middle classes, epitomised by Florida's (2002) focus on the emerging *creative classes*. Towns, cities and rural spaces have been regulated and controlled through public sector strategies to manage leisure behaviour in these environments. One consequence is an underlying privatisation and control of leisure space to meet the leisure needs of the middle classes and specific affluent groups such as Florida's (2002) creative classes.

Therefore, our starting point for this chapter is that we have seen a number of new concepts develop and impact upon our conventional understanding of leisure since the 1990s. These changes have led to a series of transformations that are occurring globally in the way leisure is being understood as part of the wider notion of culture. One important element of this transformation, which we will explore throughout this chapter, is embodied in the following quotation from the UK Department for Culture, Media and Sport (DCMS) – the shift from a public leisure focus to one rooted in a wider cultural focus:

According to the DCMS (2000: 2),

> The word culture has been deliberately used in preference to leisure to promote a broad and inclusive view, ranging from arts and sports, from libraries and museums to tourism, parks and recreation. Providing a coherent vision in this area is an important part of improving the quality of life, and enhancing the way in which local communities see themselves and are seen by others. The cultural services themselves provide a wide range of benefits, some of which are not so immediately apparent. They can help tackle the problems of social exclusion, promote a wider social inclusion, and assist with regeneration. They can also make a significant economic contribution through tourism and the creative industries.

This is fairly typical of the policy transformation occurring at a government level, recognising the wider significance of leisure-related activities that can be encompassed under the umbrella of the wider notion of cultural activities. For example, the contrast in scale and significance is shown by a comparison of the leisure and cultural/creative industries in the UK. The leisure industries are estimated to have a £20 million turnover a year, whereas the DCMS (2000) estimated that the creative industries accounted for £60 million turnover and £7.5 billion in exports a year and employed around 1.4 million people. What this illustrates, as Beyers (2008: 375) argued, is that the 'cultural industries are defined . . . [as] . . . a broad collection of economic activities associated with the consumption of culture': this embodies the primary concern of policy makers with the use of culture as a lever to promote economic growth as something consumed in our leisure time.

What this discussion illustrates is that we need understand the significance of three key terms: *culture*, *cultural industries* and the relatively new alternative term being used as a substitute for cultural industries – *creative industries*. The latter two terms have a great appeal to governments, not least because of their economic potential to generate employment and taxation revenue. This is because one of the consequences of this shift towards a postmodern society has seen many mature Western economies lose employment because of deindustrialisation and economic restructuring. Such changes have occurred in tandem with a shift towards a service sector economy, of which the cultural and creative industries are part. In other words, changing patterns of production of goods and services and consumerism have provided new opportunities to transform ailing economies. The result has been that since the 1980s, many governments have discovered the importance of tourism as a tool for regeneration in both urban and rural areas and pursued different development strategies to harness this new growth potential based on leisure consumption. During the 1990s, as was discussed in Chapter 6, this interest in tourism was subsumed in new political debates at a global level focused around the discovery of the potential of the role the cultural and creative industries could play within economic development based upon leisure spending (Paddison and Miles 2006).

One additional transformation we have to recognise is the transition to a knowledge economy, in which our intellectual property[1] is now a traded commodity, expressed in different forms (e.g. printed, digital or other formats), which illustrates that there is an economic role for exploiting that intellectual property however it is produced and then consumed in people's leisure time. As Chapter 8 illustrated, one of the key propositions related to the postmodern city is the focus upon the individual seeking to differentiate themselves from others, which has led to the creation of cultural consumers who engage with the cultural industries and creative sector in their leisure time. The cultural consumer tends to be more affluent and uses their education and knowledge to consume culture which confers status and prestige, enriching their repertoire of cultural capital. In contrast, low or mass forms of culture (also called popular culture, such as pop music) do not confer such status. High culture is primarily designed for the consumption by elites and includes niche activities such as ballet and opera. Interestingly, these activities raise an important paradox: in many countries major state subsidies are provided for these forms of high culture, effectively benefiting those who have the means to experience these leisure interests. As we discussed in earlier chapters, the consumption of high culture raises the notion of cultural capital, which was introduced by Bordieu (1984), highlighting the association between the consumption of high culture (i.e. the visual and performing arts) and taste, etiquette and understanding of the social codes which permit social and economic mobility.

The tourism and leisure industries have pursued different strategies to create uniqueness in order to differentiate places and experiences for consumers, including the development of events and celebrations which highlight local culture and the attributes of the place. It is difficult to adequately explain the overarching importance of the cultural and creative industries in our everyday lives, but the following quotation, albeit somewhat lengthy, starts to

---

[1]Intellectual property refers to the legal rights one has over any creation an individual, group or organisation makes in relation to their thoughts or activities (e.g. artistic pursuits). Typically, this will include the creation of written works such as books, computer software, film, music, photographs and other creations covered by copyright.

encompass many of the issues and dimensions which we will explore in this chapter:

According to Stevenson (2006: 354):

> Among the many products and practices categorised as the arts and entertainment are some of the most popular forms of leisure in contemporary society. Of particular significance are such commodities and activities as the expressive arts, popular music, motion pictures, television and multimedia. Indeed, the leisure experiences and priorities of people living in the West, increasingly, are being satisfied by, and understood in terms of, the cultural industries sector rather than the leisure and recreation industries as they traditionally have been defined. Even tourism is now often included under the remit of culture rather than leisure. The creative industries are also at the centre of a range of city reimaging and city branding exercises which seek to turn former place of work and production into spaces of leisure and consumption.

To try to understand some of the explanations of these transformations which are occurring in the way leisure is now being incorporated into cultural agendas, we need to undertake a critical review of the relationship of leisure, culture and postmodern society, expanding upon the discussion developed in Chapter 8.

Theoretical issues and postmodern society: culture and leisure

The evolution of the cultural industries concept

Hesmondhalgh and Pratt (2005) chart the rise of the cultural industries, pointing to the commercialisation of cultural production in the nineteenth century as the shift to capitalism was followed by the rise of mass culture. The term the culture industry is not new, as it can be dated to the 1930s and the Frankfurt School, which is the name given to a group of critical theorists who worked at the Frankfurt Institute for Social Research in the 1920s. Notable theorists such as Adorno and Horkheimer created the term culture industry because they were highly critical of the commoditisation of art and its reproduction to create repetitive cultural products for mass consumption. Mato (2009) points to the influential study by Adorno and Horkheimer (1947), *Dialectic of Enlightenment*, which examined the cultural industry and cultural consumption. Their arguments were based on the assumption that the culture industry was run by capitalism for profit and so the experiences which the culture industry provided were for popular mass appeal. The Frankfurt School, as Roberts (2004) argued, was highly critical of popular culture because they saw it as a form of social control, where popular entertainment socialised the mass population into passivity to make them compliant citizens.

During the 1950s, the growth of the culture industry accelerated owing to growing prosperity and increasing consumerism. Yet the term did not really enter public policy realms until its use in 1985 by the Greater London Council. This was followed in the 1990s in the UK by the use of the term creative industries, thereby replacing the cultural industries, reflected in the UK Creative Industries Taskforce in 1997 and the subsequent Creative Economy Programme in 2005. In the UK, a *Creative Britain: New Talents for the New Economy* Creative Industry Strategy was launched in 2008 by the DCMS (www.culture.gov.uk) as part of an attempt to position the UK as a world creative hub. This was a reflection of the fact that 33% of the UK's creative economy is located in and around London, employs around 140,000 people and accounts for around 5–7% of the London economy.

Another transformation which has occurred within postmodern society has been a transition from *tangible* elements of culture such as the built heritage, museums and monuments to more *intangible* leisure resources such as image, identity, lifestyle, narratives of the city, creativity and the media. All of these elements enhance the consumer's experience of culture and its consumption in their leisure time. Hughes (2000) draws an important distinction within the cultural industries between the arts and the wider concept of entertainment. The consumption of the arts (especially high culture) as a leisure experience is characterised by adjectives such as expressive, emotional, creative, inspirational and cultured. In contrast, entertainment experiences are characterised by adjectives such as enjoyment, pleasure, delight, amusement, escapism, fun and transitory. Even so, Hughes points to the blurring of arts and entertainment and the same can be said for the distinction between the cultural industries and entertainment. From a policy perspective, some of the early examples of the use of culture in terms of urban development are reflected in the development of cultural quarters or districts within cities which initially based their rationale on the concept of entertainment, festivals and tourism (Tallon 2008).

A further transformation which has occurred is the shift from culture to the concept of creativity, where we see the rise of a symbolic economy emphasising creativity over and above the traditional tangible cultural products. As Richards and Wilson (2007: 5) argue, 'the transformation of the cultural industries to the creative industries arguably stems from the media boom of the 1990s, where emerging sectors of cultural production, such as multimedia and software production, the audio-visual industries, architecture and design became increasingly hard to encompass within traditionally defined sectors of the cultural industries'. What the creative shift has done has seen a move towards increased use of cultural signs and symbols, sometimes embodied through the use of branding in the commercial sector, to enable consumers and places to differentiate themselves from competitors. According to Stevenson (2006: 354), 'The creative industries are acknowledged as being one of the fastest growing sectors of the economy – central pivots of what Sharon Zukin (1995) describes as the symbolic economy'.

The leisure experiences which are consumed need to satisfy the consumer, particularly in how they creatively enchant them in different settings. As Richards and Wilson (2007) suggest, the very experienced experience providers have engaged with consumers to get them involved in designing, performing and distributing the experiences themselves. These consumers have been termed prosumers and are prominent in the creative industries, most notably in terms of film locations which visitors seek out. This was evident in the BBC Children's Television series *Balamory* filmed on the island of Tobermorey (Mull in Scotland) where the visitors wanted to re-live and experience the scenes and sets. This television programme used a sophisticated set of symbols and landmarks to create a narrative and storyline which was translated into people's pursuit of a fantasy experience for their children who wanted to visit the location. What this example illustrates is the shift towards intangible culture and creativity, not least as part of the development of leisure experiences. As Cloke (2007) argues, the element of creativity has led to the creation of many subjective leisure experiences in rural settings which have become central to the acquisition of cultural capital, such as the participation in world-famous bungee-jumping experiences in New Zealand. The process of creativity has also become more significant for businesses in the leisure sector as products, experiences and places suffer from the global process of serial reproduction. This means that competing places and businesses reproduce successful products and experiences (including place-products such as leisure and tourism destinations) so that successes are replicated elsewhere by capitalists, investing in locations where opportunities exist for economic development and profit. A case in point is the development of the globally ubiquitous shopping mall. Therefore, with this transformation from cultural to creativity in mind, it is appropriate to focus on how to define and classify the cultural and creative industries as well as the distinguishing features of each.

Defining the cultural industries

One of the perennial problems of trying to establish the definition of the cultural and creative industries relates to differentiating between culture, the cultural industries and the associated and yet different term the creative industries. How we approach and define any of these terms ultimately depends upon one key proposition – what do we mean by the term culture? Stevenson (2006) describes the term as particularly amorphous, which means it is difficult to delineate because culture is generally interpreted in very broad ways. As Rojek (2006) indicated, a nineteenth-century study by Tylor (1874) probably gives a broad overview of the term as 'that complex whole which includes knowledge, belief, art, morals, law, custom and other capabilities and habits acquired by man as a member of society' (Tylor 1874: 1). Interestingly, Pieper (1952) defined leisure as the basis of culture. What the many studies of culture highlight is the holistic nature of people's ways of life as well as their customs, and so culture becomes an important context in which to situate leisure (see Williams 1989 for more detail on the definition and analysis of culture), creating an ongoing debate amongst critical theorists on the issue. Culture is a very difficult term to define, which is one reason why policy makers tend to focus on the term creative industries. What the term creativity tends to stress is the inventive, innovation and imagination associated with the expansion of creative industries in the 1990s, such as the media, multimedia and audio-visual forms of communication as well as new forms of creativity such as architecture (Edensor *et al.* 2009).

One of the starting points from which to analyse the term culture in relation to leisure is to examine some of the early studies on the link between art and entertainment as a component of leisure. One of the early studies in the UK by Myerscough (1988), *Economic Importance of the Arts in the UK*, set out to identify the scale and scope of the art and entertainment sector. This was the beginning of a considerable research effort designed to assess the scale and impact of the arts in many countries, with arts bodies sponsoring studies (e.g. Travers *et al.* 1996; Reeve 2002) to highlight their economic, social and political significance.

One important distinction to make is that the cultural industries comprise cultural institutions such as libraries and museums which are producers of cultural content. In contrast, the creative industries produce much of the content which the cultural institutions then display or use as an asset which is then consumed by people in their leisure time. Yet even this distinction becomes complex because if you start to include the notion of everyday leisure pursuits as cultural activities, such as indigenous people performing a traditional dance or celebration, then this form of experience is not something which can easily be stored or displayed in a cultural institution. Therefore, simply focusing upon creative products and artefacts may not necessarily encompass the wider role of the creative industries and the way in which they can be consumed within people's leisure time.

Classifying the cultural industries and creative industries

Hesmondhalgh (2007) is one of the most widely cited books on the subject, highlighting that a pivotal issue for defining the cultural or creative industries hinges upon how you define culture. He commences his discussion of the subject by highlighting the characteristics of cultural industries as illustrated in Figure 9.1. This shows that it has a diverse range of possible means of consumption, although the majority of the experiences and products are targeted at our leisure time or the wider leisure economy. Figure 9.1 also indicates that the range of industries or industry sectors involved is very diverse, and even within individual sectors the nature of the businesses involved are also diverse. Some sectors enjoy public sector support directly through grants from agencies like Arts Councils or their equivalent bodies in different countries, sometimes through state-operated gambling proceeds (i.e. Lotteries, where they exist) which have traditionally funded highbrow or high culture. In contrast, some sections of the cultural industries are more private sector oriented, such as the music industry. Yet, as Williamson and Cloonan (2007) show, the music industry, as one sector within the cultural or creative industries, comprises a range of different sub-sectors which contribute to the overall significance and impact of this industry, as shown in Figure 9.2. This suggests we need to think about the wider cultural

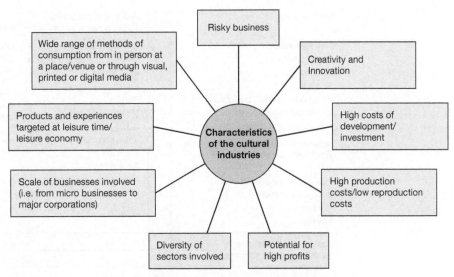

Figure 9.1 The characteristics of the cultural industries

Sources: Hesmondhalgh (2007); Authors

industries domain and how these different sub-sectors are connected to, and interact with the wider economy.

According to Throsby (2008), there are different ways in which we can distinguish between the cultural industries and the creative industries. Throsby identifies six different models which have been used to construct various definitions of the scope and range of the cultural industries in different countries, including criteria which has been used by UNESCO. UNESCO includes certain industries while other categorisations emphasise different criteria. To

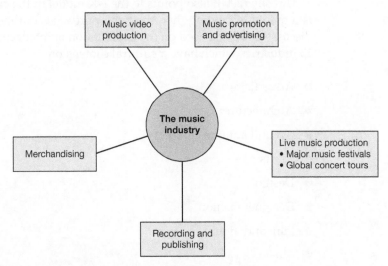

Figure 9.2 The scale and scope of the music industry as a component of the cultural industries

Sources: Adapted from Willams (2007); Anheir and Isar (eds) (2008)

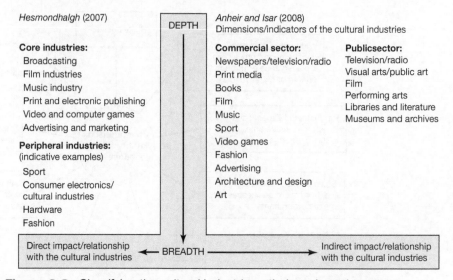

Figure 9.3   Classifying the cultural industries – their scale and scope
Sources: Developed from Hesmondhalgh (2007); Anheir and Isar (eds) (2008); Pratt (2008)

simplify this approach, we are going to draw the distinction between two contrasting approaches by Hesmonhalgh (2007) and Anheir and Isar (2008). Each approach, depicted in Figure 9.3, differentiate between a common range of industry sectors which divided into either public or private sector businesses and the more accepted view of Hesmondhalgh (2007) of core and peripheral cultural industries. Added to this is what Pratt (2008) argues for, which is a much deeper and broader interpretation of the term cultural industries to understand the wider impact of the sector than simply businesses within individual sectors.

Throsby (2008) also points to the UK model of the creative industries which is more wide ranging than the two approaches outlined in Figure 9.3. It is, as discussed earlier, based on the exploitation of intellectual property, comprising 13 industries which have a cultural dimension:

- Advertising
- Architecture
- Art and antiques markets
- Crafts
- Design
- Designer fashion
- Film and video
- Music
- Performing arts
- Publishing

- Software

- Television and radio

- Video and computer games (i.e. interactive leisure).

Other models discussed by Throsby (2008), such as the concentric circles model, extend this simple classification using the notion that there is a core range of creative arts responsible for creative ideas which give the cultural industries their basis, flowing from literature, music, the performing arts and visual arts. These are complemented by other core cultural industries such as film, museums and libraries which then cascade down into settings where the commercial attributes of these core cultural industries are commoditised by publishing, recording, broadcasting and other organisations producing cultural goods. At the periphery of this model are the related industries of advertising, architecture, design and fashion which use creative and cultural content. Such classifications are complemented, for example, by the UNESCO Institute for Statistics model which proposes that cultural industries comprise five cultural domains:

- Cultural and natural heritage

- Performance and celebration

- Visual arts, crafts and design

- Books and press

- Audio-visual and digital media

and a related domain of Tourism, Sport and Leisure.

Whatever model for classification we use, it is clear that a range of industries' or different groups of industries' characteristics can be used to define the cultural or creative industries. Depending on which criteria or classification we use, we can derive different estimates of the size or scale of such industries in various countries. For example, Throsby (2008) examined three different models and their application to Australia. In 1994 the Australian government set out its Creative Nation initiative, looking at the creative industries as a new growth sector and a future source of employment. The number of employees in the cultural industries in Australia ranges from just fewer than 200,000 to almost 500,000 people, depending upon the criteria used to define the sector, which illustrates the importance of developing a working definition which we can accept and use. Throsby (2008) also points to one way to analyse the cultural and creative industries through the use of value chain analysis. This tries to understand how the initial creative idea then passes through a set of stages, where value is added in each stage through, for example, marketing, to the point when it reaches the final consumer. Other techniques of analysis have also been used to assess the scale and impact of cultural industries, using economic techniques such as input–output analysis. But a more recent development is the way in which the creative concept has led to the evolution of the creative city idea.

The creative city

As Richards and Wilson (2007) argue, the concept of cultural industries has gradually given way to a new concept – creativity, which refers to the inventive, imaginative and innovative nature of the creative sector, and this has been applied to a place setting – the creative city. This compares with the more staid image of the cultural sector as less dynamic and socially isolating for the masses and not able to incorporate the needs of diverse audiences such as ethnic groups. The shift towards creativity as a concept based on the creative industries idea, with their exploitable intellectual property (i.e. ideas, creative goods and knowledge), reflects the new emphasis on creative leisure industries and the creativity in leisure experiences provided by innovative organisations. This is part of the shift towards more intangible leisure experiences which have seen elements of the production and consumption in leisure time blurring, especially with the rise of the digital age. Hannigan (2007) suggested that culture and creativity have become the new saviour of cities, where the creative city is a unique form of culture-led regeneration (Paddison and Miles 2006), with the target population, the middle classes, epitomised by Florida's (2002) study of the creative class.

Landry and Bianchini (1995) devised the term creative cities to illustrate how all these processes of change were coalescing to create a number of elements in cities structured around the concepts of creativity. This expanded upon some of the earlier research on how individual areas of cities have fostered and developed cultural quarters and creative districts. As Mommaas (2004) explains, cultural clustering strategies in cities evolved from the simple linkage between culture and the arts in urban regeneration. This is where cultural and leisure functions are grouped together in a greater variety of geographical areas, as illustrated by Berlin's creative industries clusters.

One important stimulus to this process at a global level was the UNESCO creative cities network formed in October 2004. This was launched to promote social, economic and cultural development of cities in developed and developing countries. UNESCO focused on cities as a natural breeding ground for creativity, where public–private partnerships could help to develop the creative potential within cities. To date, a number of categories of creative city have been designated, as shown in Figure 9.4.

According to the London Development Agency (LDA) (2006), Berlin became the first German city to be appointed a UNESCO *City of Design*. The city has a well-developed leisure and tourism industry, as well as being a popular venue for international conferences and trade fairs. The city had gone through a period of protracted industrial decline in the 1990s, so focusing on the creative industries was a natural direction to choose in redeveloping the city's economy. Just under 4% of Germany's GDP is generated by Berlin's creative economy according to the LDA (2006), employing around 80,000 people, equivalent to 8% of the population in the city of whom about a quarter are self-employed.

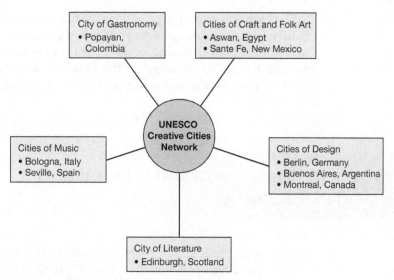

Figure 9.4 UNESCO creative cities network

There are around 20,000 individual companies within the creative industries sector, generating about 8 billion euros in turnover each year. Many of these enterprises are clustered in different areas of the city, such as the media cluster in the former East Berlin.

Vanolo's (2006) study highlights how these cultural clusters, through a process of marketing and creative development in cities, have embraced place-marketing, to promote their attractiveness for inward investment and mobile workers (such as Florida's creative classes) who are high-spending leisure consumers. Vanolo (2006) highlighted how place-marketing in pursuit of these goals encapsulated the following imagery and elements:

● Social interaction among people in the city, with people chatting to portray a buzz and activity with a focus on multi-ethnicity, to imply social inclusivity.

● The local art scene to highlight the diversity of cultural capital available in the locality.

● A focus on public spaces, in which leisure takes place, such as in parks and open spaces and at other key landmarks or icons.

● The importance of nightlife and the leisure infrastructure such as restaurants, and scenes which will appeal to young and trendy consumers.

● The importance of high-quality education in the locality as an attractor to mobile workers.

These features illustrate how important these intangible cultural elements are in terms of leisure consumption, seeking to communicate the vibrancy of the place and atmosphere, as many cities worldwide have engaged in this creative place-marketing process. While the creative city is a relatively new concept being developed around the world to expand the creative industries in cities, the global attraction of the idea is reflected in the growing significance of the cultural industries and creative industries to which attention now turns.

Global dimensions of the cultural and creative economy

For the commercial sector, Lash and Lury (2007) argue that a global culture industry has developed, which is, in part, a function of globalisation. They describe how cultural products have been produced and consumed, thereby contributing to the process of capital accumulation and profit from culture. In a capitalist society, the focus is on capital accumulation so that capitalism can continue to thrive and prosper from different forms of production and consumption. This process is simplified and depicted in Figure 9.5 which illustrates how cultural products, commodities and services are produced, circulated and distributed globally and then contribute to consumer experiences of leisure. One of the notable shifts in the process of capital accumulation in a postmodern society is how cultural products have embraced branding, so that companies can differentiate their consumer offer from their competitors (see Chapter 7 on marketing and branding).

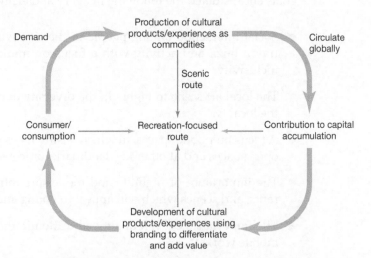

Figure 9.5 Simplified theory of the production and consumption of cultural products and experiences in a capitalist society

Sources: Developed from Hesmondhalgh (2007); Lash and Lury (2007)

According to Anheir and Isar (2008), the cultural economy makes a significant contribution to national economies. For example, Anheir and Isar (2008) suggest that cultural industries contribute 7% to GDP in the United States, 5% in the United Kingdom, 5% in Canada and over 6% in Brazil. What is interesting in terms of the businesses operating in the cultural industries sector can be classified in two ways:

- A significant group of self-employed individuals and micro businesses, where the creative elements often start, at an initial stage in the value chain.

- A small number of large international corporations which have highly developed skills in commercialising intellectual property and creative ideas, such as the music, publishing and film industries.

One of the defining characteristics of this sector, from a public policy perspective, is that government expenditure on cultural items such as leisure and recreation ranges from around 1% on average in terms of government expenditure, although this can increase to over 4% in some countries such as Luxemburg. According to Anheir and Isar (2008), one way of looking at the global dimensions of the cultural industries is to consider the concept of trade in cultural goods which introduces the area known as international business, where cultural products and services are traded between countries. One way of looking at the significance of the cultural industries is to examine different facets of these cultural flows. For example, in terms of visitors to museums as a cultural leisure activity, the Smithsonian in the United States received over 23 million visitors in 2006 as one measure of interest in high culture. Similarly, internationally acclaimed art galleries such as the Louvre in Paris attract almost six million visits a year whereas the Tate Galleries in London attracts over six million visits a year. Anheir and Isar (2008) suggested that almost 20% of the world's trade in cultural goods was based on books. For example, in 2005 they estimated that the market was worth US$25 in the USA, with the market continuing to grow as e-books have been developed. The market for books is controlled by five major publishing houses, which illustrates the international domination exercised by these global companies. In a similar vein, the film and entertainment businesses are also controlled by five major corporations based in the USA (i.e. the Disney/Buena Vista Corporation, Sony Pictures, Universal Studios, Paramount and Warner Brothers). These corporations have diversified into new markets which have been opened up through the Internet and digitalisation so that online movie downloads have become a significant proportion of their business.

Individual countries have also seized upon the growth of the cultural sector as an international trade opportunity for export, as China has seen major growth in this sector. But we also have to recognise the challenges of global trade and globalisation, so that countries are not adversely affected by the mass culture provided by global corporations, to ensure that it does not end up dominating and obliterating local cultures. For these global corporations, one additional concern, which we highlighted earlier in the book, is the issue of piracy which is estimated to cost the American film industry over US$18 million a year. Music is also a significant element of the cultural industries, with major music festivals attracting large audiences, such as the summer fiesta in Milwaukee which attracts almost a million visitors a year. For this reason attention now turns to the issue of festivals and events as a form of leisure entertainment. Events are multifunctional, as the discussion of cultural quarters suggests, because they can be used in regeneration strategies, as a tool to build the cultural industries where they have a cultural element such as the Highland Games (see Case Study 9.1 below) as well as a visitor attraction in their own right to grow their leisure and tourism industries.

Case Study 9.1   The Scottish Highland Games as a cultural event

The Highland Games (HG) are an endearing part of Scottish sporting culture for many people and take place across Scotland throughout the summer months owing to the goodwill of volunteers who organise these annual events on a not-for-profit basis (although a number are organised and sponsored by local authorities). There is considerable debate over the precise origin and evolution of the Games as a sporting event but it is clear that it has developed from its Gaelic origins to become established as a significant modern-day cultural event in the calendar of many communities (see Brewster *et al.* 2009 for more detail on the evolution of the event in Scotland) (Plate 9.1).

Plate 9.1 The cultural industries, based on literature and the arts, have been a major marketing tool for many community facilities such as the Birnam Institute in Dunkeld, Scotland, which has integrated the link with the famous children's author Beatrix Potter who spent some of her summer vacations in the area.

The HG is a complex event with many individual components which together create these spectacles of sport and competition, enjoyed by competitors and spectators alike who are drawn from residents, domestic and international visitors. In Canada and the USA a large number of HG events also take place. Irrespective of the size of the event at a community level, each specific event has a unique place where it is staged and some HGs have a very long history, which originated in rural areas, although a number of urban-based events now exist across Scotland. Others are termed hybrid Games and are held in conjunction with Gala Days or Agricultural Shows or fairs, which hold true to their traditional roots and present a colourful community event.

Core features of the HG

A variety of activities take place within every HG and whether they are a large-scale event which can attract up to 17,000 spectators or a small community event with a crowd of 1500, the core features remain the same in varying degrees of importance and size which are depicted in Figure 9.6. There is no doubt that the HG events are created from Highland tradition and culture, with their roots steeped in authenticity even though they have evolved and adapted over time. But the core features remain unchanged, as highlighted in Figure 9.6. First and foremost it is a competitive event, and although it includes music and dance it is predominately a sporting event through the staging of events such as athletes competing in feats of strength

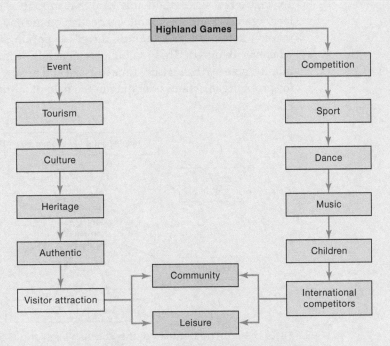

Figure 9.6 The core features of the Scottish Highland Games

and skill (e.g. wrestling and tug o' war). Regardless of the size of the individual HG, it is predominantly a local community festival in view of its audience and annual staging. It also has a range of specific benefits for the local community.

Benefits of the HG for the community

The HG is an opportunity for family and friends to return to their roots where the community comes together to strengthen community ties, and Figure 9.7 highlights a number of these benefits in a leisure setting. Competitive events and attractions are varied and attract a variety of spectators and competitors who help to boost the local economy, albeit over a short duration. Clearly, the HG provide a competitive forum for athletes from many disciplines, such as sprinting, hill running and cycling along with Highland dancers and bagpipe players, often with international competitors from across the world from countries afar afield as Indonesia, New Zealand, Africa and North America. Yet such an event would not occur without a successful Games organisation and structure to plan, stage and manage the event. This means that the Games need the cooperation of and interaction with a variety of stakeholders, which can be described in terms of direct links which exist between the Games, its stakeholders and a range of primary supporters of the event.

Direct links and primary supporters of the HGs

To stage a HG successfully it is vital that support is provided by the volunteer organisers and the volunteers needed on the day of the event to man admission gates, sell programmes, direct car parking and generally help out wherever required. These volunteers generally come from the local community, give up their leisure time to assist and are the backbone of many not-for-profit organisations operating in the field of leisure. Volunteers will help

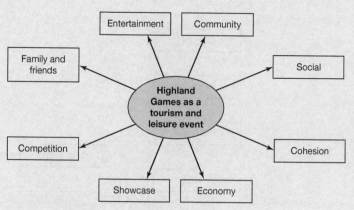

Figure 9.7 The benefits of the Scottish Highland Games for the community

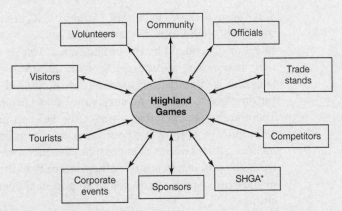

Figure 9.8 The direct links and primary supporters of the Scottish Highland Games

*Scottish Highland Games Association

to organise the officials, who judge events and take note of any records achieved, look after the competitors and provide the setting for the visitors who come to enjoy the Games. One of the principal elements which most Games require is a sponsor or sponsors (Figure 9.8) who support the event in monetary form or in kind, complemented by trade stands which all help to provide a festival atmosphere and also contribute to the financial viability of the HG as an event. Many of the individual HGs are affiliated to the Scottish Highland Games Association (SHGA) on a voluntary membership basis. Some events have also recognised that an opportunity exists with corporate sponsorship to encourage organisations to hold corporate events within the Games' environment. The HG also faces a number of ongoing challenges for community events.

Challenges facing the Scottish Highland Games

It is difficult to identify clearly all the individual challenges that HG organisers may face in sustaining this sporting cultural event. But they do face ongoing issues of financial viability, with some under constant threat, and many reporting a lack of support from public bodies. Some of the challenges include:

- HGs do not feature as a clear category within the funding remit of public sector culture or sports public bodies.
- Declining numbers of new committee members willing to continue the tradition of HG events, reflected in the decline in the number of events staged since the post-war period.
- Adverse weather conditions which can force event organisers to abandon or postpone a specific event, since spectators will not turn out to support an outdoor event in inclement weather.
- Loss of long-term spectator appeal among younger generations.

Yet in spite of these challenges, images of HG often adorn promotional literature for Scotland, but they are not viewed as a central element of the event calendar of Scotland by the public sector, despite the benefits they bring and their historic significance in Scottish culture. Faced with increasing challenges, it is vital that these events are recognised and some form of support put in place to ensure the survival of these iconic cultural sporting events. There are indications that some of the HGs would be in a very precarious situation if there were two poor years, due to inclement weather conditions or incurring losses due to rising costs and reduced spectator numbers. This illustrates the problem of ensuring the continuity of these events, and their ability to showcase a particularly colourful part of Scotland's heritage and sporting culture.

Further reading

Brewster, M., Connell, J. and Page, S. J. (2009) 'The Scottish Highland Games: Evolution, development and role as a community event'. *Current Issues in Tourism* 12 (3): 271–283.

Events and festivals as leisure entertainment

The issue of events and festivals is not something new, as it reflects the way in which society has always found ways to celebrate publicly and privately major life events and other meaningful periods in the year. Folk festivals, celebrations according to the agricultural season and the changing of the seasons as well as traditions associated with religious beliefs such as Christmas and Chinese New Year epitomise the importance of periods of celebration. What is new in a postmodern society is the way in which these events are now used as part of a cultural strategy to develop the economic potential of leisure (and associated activity such as tourism) in urban and rural spaces. For example, the significance of these strategies is reflected in the hosting, staging or creation of events such as the European Union's annual designation of a City of Culture (which was awarded to Liverpool for 2008). This event provides a year-long celebration of the arts and culture as a stimulus to leisure and tourism, developing the cultural infrastructure and cultural industries. In the case of Liverpool, it has harnessed a wide range of visitor markets, from leisure travel to business travel, as well as the lucrative conference and conventions market. European City of Culture status was expected to generate 14,000 jobs, attract an additional 1.7 million visitors and leverage £2 billion of investment from the public and private sector for the city. As the example of Liverpool suggests, there are a range of possible motives among organisations for hosting leisure-related events, as Table 9.1 suggests. As the table indicates, we need to recognise three key issues:

- What type of events can be used and developed as part of this process of regeneration and investment in the cultural industries?

- What are the underlying motives pursued by organisations to develop events around leisure activities?

- What types of impacts will arise from the development of event-led strategies in relation to leisure?

The scope of events has been explained by Getz (2008: 403) in relation to event management as:

> the applied field of study and area of professional practice devoted to the design, production and management of planned events, encompassing festivals and other celebrations, entertainment, recreation, political and state, scientific, sport and arts events, those in the domain of business and corporate affairs (including meetings, conventions, fairs, and exhibitions), and those in the private domain (including rites of passage such as weddings and parties, and social events for affinity groups).

Table 9.1 Primary organisational motives for hosting events

Public sector	Not-for-profit sector	Private sector	Community groups
• To attract tourists • To attract inward investment • To demonstrate ability to mobilise resources • To engender civic pride • To achieve positive imaging • To promote economic development • To celebrate identity • To achieve a range of social, economic and environmental goals	• To attract revenue and raise funds for projects • To stimulate awareness and interest • To promote appreciation of specific features • To educate (through enjoyment) • To achieve social, environmental, economic, cultural, sport, leisure or community goals	• To enhance core business and profitability • To generate revenue off-peak and in shoulder months • To develop products and markets for commercial purposes • To stimulate consumer interest • To encourage repeat visits and increased spending • To encourage good public relations	• To raise funds for specific projects or groups • To assist in community development • To celebrate local traditions • To raise awareness of area's attributes • To enhance an area's reputation • To keep old traditions alive • To generate civic pride • To have fun!

Source: Page and Connell (2009: 607)

Table 9.2 Typology of events

Type of event	Explanation
Hallmark events	May be referred to, or encompass, 'special' or 'mega' events. A hallmark event is described by Ritchie (1984: 2) as being:
	major one-time or recurring events of limited duration, developed primarily to enhance the awareness, appeal and profitability of a tourism destination in the short and/or long-term. Such events rely for their success on their uniqueness, status, or timely significance to create interest and attract attention.
Festivals	Defined by Getz (1997: 8) as a 'public, themed celebration' and they may help to maintain community values through increasing a sense of social identity, with historical continuity in the staging of the event (such as the Scottish Highland Games) as well as celebrating the survival of the local culture.
Fairs, exhibitions, expos and shows	May include commercial shows or exhibitions (e.g. the Ideal Home Exhibition) or a localised event such as an agricultural show. It is estimated that there are around 12,000 expos a year, which generate around 70 million visits a year.
Meetings and conferences	These range in scale and scope from conclaves (those meetings held in private/secret) to seminars and workshops which may have an educational and training function.

Source: Adapted from Page and Connell (2009)

This illustrates the wide-ranging scope and scale of events which is demonstrated further in the typology in Table 9.2, which indicates the range of events from festivals through to mega events.

This area of study has evolved into a specialised research domain as illustrated by Table 9.3, which illustrates how the landmark studies can be traced to the 1960s and the subject's gradual evolution through the 1970s and 1980s. As Table 9.3 suggests, there are examples of early attempts to analyse events but, as Page and Connell (2009) suggest, the initial starting point for serious academic study of events is attributed to Boorstin (1961) in relation to the phenomenon of 'pseudo events'. A second influential study by Greenwood (1972) of a Basque festival highlighted the negative influence of visitors on authentic cultural celebrations. However, Getz attributes the first event tourism study to Ritchie and Beliveau (1974) on how 'hallmark events' could combat seasonality of tourism demand. Within the 1980s, the field expanded rapidly and then almost exponentially in the 1990s as more journal articles and books appeared on the theme. What is becoming increasingly evident from the study

Table 9.3   Key studies on festival and events

Year	Study
1922	Allix, A. 'The geography of fairs: illustrated by old-world examples', *Geographical Review* 12 (4): 532–69.
1972	Greenwood, D. 'Tourism as an agent of change: a Spanish Basque case', *Ethnology* 11 (1): 80–91.
1973	Boorstin, D. *The Image: A Guide to Pseudo-Events in America,* Athaneum: New York.
1973	MacCannell, D. 'Staged authenticity: arrangements of social space in tourist settings', *The American Journal of Sociology* 79 (3): 589–603.
1974	Ritchie, J.R.B. and Beliveau, D. 'Hallmark events: an evaluation of a strategic response to seasonality', *Journal of Travel Research* 3 (1): 14–20.
1978	Jackson, B. 'The Shakespeare Festival: Stratford, Ontario 1953–1977', *Shakespeare Quarterly* 29 (2): 164–91.
1984	Ritchie, J.R.B. 'Assessing the impact of hallmark events: conceptual and research issues' 23 (1): 2–11.
1989	Getz, D. 'Special events: defining the product', *Tourism Management* 10 (2): 125–37.
1990	Goldblatt, J. *Special Events,* Wiley: New York.
	Long, P. and Perdue, R. 'The economic impact of rural festivals and special events: assessing the spatial distribution of expenditures', *Journal of Travel Research* 28 (4): 10–14.
1991	Getz, D. *Special events,* Wiley: New York.
1992	Hall, C.M. *Hallmark Tourist Events: Impacts, Management and Planning,* Belhaven Press: London.
1992	Roche, M. 'Mega-events and micro-modernization: on the sociology of the new urban tourism', *British Journal of Sociology* 43 (4): 563–600.
1993	Saleh, F. and Ryan, C. 'Jazz and knitwear: factors that attract tourists to festivals', *Tourism Management* 14 (4): 289–97.
1993	Getz, D. *Event Management,* Cognizant: New York.
1994	Zelinsky, W. 'Conventionland USA: The geography of a latterday phenomenon', *Annals of the Association of American Geographers* 84 (1): 68–86.
1997	Crompton, J. and MacKay, S. 'Motives of visitors attending festivals', *Annals of Tourism Research* 24 (2): 425–39.
2002	Getz, D. *Event Tourism*, Cognizant: New York.
2003	Rogers, T. *Conferences and Conventions,* Butterworth Heinemann: Oxford.
2007	Getz, D. *Event Studies: Theory, Research and Policy for Planned Events*, Elsevier: Oxford.
2008	Getz, D. 'Event tourism: definition, evolution, and research', *Tourism Management* 29 (3): 403–28.

of events is that in the context of this chapter, they fit in a postmodern society, with the pursuit of the distinctive and uniqueness in place experiences where they are successful staged. As Getz (1997) suggests, successful event development will include:

- A *multiplicity of goals*, where the idea of *diversity* is implicit in the creation of the event.

- A *festive spirit*, so that an ambience of joyfulness, revelry and freedom from constraint is built into the appeal, such as through music.

- *Satisfying basic needs*, so that it appeals to a range of leisure motivations.

- *Uniqueness*, to create a must-see or a once in a lifetime opportunity to experience something as well as featuring as a critical element in the experience of the place.

- *Quality*, so visitor expectations are exceeded.

- *Authenticity*, so that the local community feels that it is engaged and the event is embedded in their local history and traditions and it encourages them to participate alongside visitors.

- *Flexibility*, so that events require minimal infrastructure and investment.

- *Tangibility*, where the event is the conduit and vehicle to encourage the visitor to experience the destination attributes and resources through a range of activities.

- *Theming*, to maximise the value of authenticity and increase interaction with visitors.

- *Symbolism*, where the use of rituals and symbols may give extra significance to the experience.

- *Affordability*, to encourage as wide a range of visitors as possible.

Source: Page and Connell (2009)

For the postmodern leisure environment, events perform a major role in helping to create an experience that can bring a place to life and create an emotional response in relation to fun, pleasure and leisure satisfaction (Table 9.4). Yet the development of events in any location is not without its impacts, some of which are positive and others negative. As Table 9.5 suggests, the impacts which result from staging events will depend upon what the organisers and planners are seeking to achieve, where the economic benefits tend to be prioritised over and above some of the lesser-known social and environmental impacts. It is also evident that some small-scale events that are community based may also help in fostering community cohesion and development in much the same way as the development of open space and urban parks may in community regeneration schemes. One such example was examined earlier in Case Study 9.1 featuring the Scottish Highland Games.

Table 9.4   The role of events in leisure and tourism

Leisure and tourism development	Social and economic development and regeneration	Adding value
A way of increasing the visibility and appeal of a tourism destination, e.g.: • Events can help build destination images and create place, e.g. Korea has used events extensively to shape international image as well as create an international tourism destination since 1988 (1988 Olympic Games, 2002 World Cup) • Increasing the number of visitors • Clustering of events and attractions to create a critical mass of interest for visitors • Lengthening of tourist season beyond the peak season, e.g. a Spring Gardens Festival in Cornwall led to a 9% increase in visitors during spring; Quebec Winter Carnival saw its off-peak season become the peak season • Attracting repeat visits	The event bidding process and associated spin-off benefits guaranteed by major event and partnership organisations can contribute to urban renewal and major redevelopment. Mega-events are most effective in this role, e.g.: • Regenerating post-industrial cities, e.g. the London 2012 Olympic Games bid included the regeneration of a significant swathe of East London, while the Atlanta Olympics created sports facilities, an urban park, low-cost housing and educational facilities • Improving the environment, e.g. the Millennium Dome in London (now O_2 Stadium), built on an ex-industrial site, required major environmental clean-up • Improving transport infrastructure such as airports and roads, e.g. 1984 Los Angeles Olympics	Use in 'animating' a destination (Getz 2008) through bringing specific features to life, which can enhance the visitor experience, e.g.: • Creating additional attractions at existing tourist attractions • Re-enacting scenes through live interpretation of historic sites, such as battlefields, castles and other heritage sites • Hosting living history events at historic sites, e.g. use of actors to perform scripted pieces to visitors • Stimulating interest in the heritage and traditions of a destination, encouraging a better understanding of place and people • Reviving lost traditions, interests and areas, encouraging both tourist and community involvement

Source: Page and Connell (2009: 602)

Yet evaluating the impacts of events is a complex process, with critics sometimes highlighting negative social issues such as increased levels of crime as a function of staging an event. For example, Barker and Page (2002) examined the visitor safety issues associated with hosting a special event such as the America's Cup in Auckland, observing a range of challenges for policing a short-run event. Barker *et al.* (2002) also modelled the impact of crime during the event to illustrate the typical range of victimisation issues faced by visitors to the event, such as theft, assault and minor issues as well as loss of personal

Table 9.5 A comparison of the impact of events

Positive economic impacts	Negative economic impacts	Positive socio-cultural impacts	Negative socio-cultural impacts	Positive environmental impacts	Negative environmental impacts
• Increase in tourist expenditure • Increase in tourist length of stay • Employment created and sustained • New business opportunities • Sponsorship and grants attracted to fund infrastructure projects with long-term benefits • High ratio of revenue to costs • Increase in tax revenues • High local income multipliers – indirect spending • Media profile and increased awareness of a region • Stimulation of tourism demand • Economic legacies	• Financial input through pump-priming: opportunity costs for other projects • Displacement effect on areas outside main event core • Benefits not distributed effectively within a region's tourism economy • Cost of dealing with negative impacts	• Employment • Provision of social services • Community participation • Improved community identity and welfare • Environmental improvements funded • Housing projects e.g. post-use of Olympic villages • Expanded trade opportunities • Increased cultural understanding	• Noise • Increased crime • Loss of community identity • Loss of sense of place • Social dislocation • The effect of vandals and undesirable behaviour • Increase in retail prices • Increase in property prices and rents • Displacement and evictions e.g. to make way for event infrastructure development	• Promote understanding of unique or special environment • Encourage participation in conservation work • Reclamation and detoxification of waste or contaminated land for infrastructure development • Enhancement of derelict areas and removal of eyesores	• Excessive consumption of resources and use of local services e.g. water, electricity and sewage systems • Wear and tear • Litter and waste disposal • Traffic congestion and air pollution • Threat to biodiversity • Water and land pollution • Infrastructure development on greenfield sites • Damage to heritage sites

property from theft from cars. This illustrates that events can also have negative impacts, especially when hosting mega-events such as the Olympic Games which have a short-term duration. These impacts have to be set against the expected cost of £9 billion for the London 2012 Olympic Games. Interestingly, supporters of such events point to the potential legacy of regeneration for the local community (even though such large regeneration schemes will lead to community displacement to develop the Games site) and other intangible benefits. Yet this has to be seen in the context of a financial legacy of hosting and developing the infrastructure for a two-week event, as few Olympic Games have ever made a profit. Consequently, event strategies are very controversial, with conflicting research evidence over the benefits of hosting an event. In theoretical terms, such events may also be part of the wider strategy discussed earlier in relation to nurturing the creativity of a city or place, not only through the cultural industries but also through the creativity of its people. Yet events are one-off leisure spectacles, whereas leisure attractions such as theme parks provide ongoing opportunities for leisure-related entertainment.

Leisure as entertainment: the theme park industry

In contrast to the development of interest in the cultural industries, the expansion of entertainment as a form of leisure has a much longer history, especially given the rise of the global theme park industry (Sorkin 1992; Lukas 2009) as the archetypal form of mass organised leisure, since the 'post modern is associated

Plate 9.2   Theme park rides seek to cause an adrenaline rush and a heightened sense of controlled risk.

with consumer lifestyles and mass consumption' (Lyons 1994: 56). King (2006: 363) defines a theme park as 'a social artwork designed as a four-dimensional symbolic landscape, evoking impressions of places and times, real and imaginary'. As Anton Clavé (2007) illustrates, although the theme parks may be an important element of our postmodern society, their roots can be traced right back to the medieval period and fairs through to the rise of the amusement park in the mid-nineteenth century, epitomised in the USA by the example of Coney Island, Brooklyn, New York. In the case of Coney Island and other examples such as Blackpool Pleasure Beach, the main market stimulus was enabled by the provision of railway network connecting the area to the centres of urban demand. As Anton Clavé (2007) suggested, we can also trace the origins of the theme park in other countries, such as the development of New World in Singapore in 1917 which was rebuilt in 1932 as a full-scale amusement park. The growth of theme parks in North America passed through three important growth phases:

- A major growth phase, between 1950 and 1969, building on the development of the concept and its amusement park origins.

- A second stage of growth during the 1970s and early 1980s, where major players such as the Disney Corporation diversified and developed new park locations such as Florida (see Case Study 9.2).

- A third phase of growth in the 1980s and 1990s as regions such as South Florida expanded.

To these three phases of growth we can add a fourth phase – *maturity*. By the turn of the new millennium many of these parks were entering a stage of consolidation and needed to diversify their markets as competitors were developing a market presence.

Case Study 9.2   The development of Disneyland

In 1955, Walt Disney opened the Disneyland theme park in Anaheim, California. As a visitor attraction it has set the direction of development and standards which many other parks have sought to emulate. Its commitment to quality, epitomised by its Disney model, is widely studied by analysts in terms of the focus on the careful management of the visitor experience. As Page (2009) shows, this model is carefully scripted and focused on the needs of the visitor to create a special and memorable experience, since during a theme park visit visitors will have many encounters with guests and these need to be rewarding and special. Page (2009) suggests that Disney created a positive image by ensuring it creates the right ambience and feeling among visitors by harnessing visual and non-visual details such as design, landscaping, lighting (which can affect visitor moods), colour, signage, texture of surfaces, music and ambient noise as well as sensory elements such as smell, touch and taste. Above all, tidiness and cleanliness in mass visitor attractions are seen as critical to the image created. As Page (2009) argues, the Disney formula for customer service is based on set of values, which come from integrating its commercialism with a quality experience for the visitor. It is based on three elements:

- *A quality staff experience,* since each individual staff member impacts on the customer experience.
- *A quality customer experience,* based on being customer driven and seeking to exceed customer needs and expectations rather than simply meeting them.
- *A quality set of business practices,* where knowledge, marketing, innovation and other elements are blended to ensure commercial success.

In particular, the Disney philosophy is to 'exceed customer expectations and pay attention to detail', with the visitor at the centre of all elements which drive business activities.

Walt Disney's development of Disneyland was influenced by the staging of world fairs during the 1930s with their corporate pavilions (Meebling 2006) and the importance of an internal transport system in a purpose-designed space. This initial theme park was an opportunity for Disney to expand its merchandising in the 160-acre former orange grove site in Anaheim, Los Angeles. This was accompanied by a one-hour television programme on the ABC channel entitled *Disneyland,* which was filmed at the new park, and it received over a million visitors in its first year of operation, rising to three million in 1956. As new stories and films were released by Disney, these fantasy features were embodied in storylines and themes in the park.

As Meebling (2006) suggests, the theme park site was meticulously designed with the visitor experience at the heart of the development, with a Disney railroad running around the edge of the park and acting as a barrier to stop people looking in, creating a cocooned fantasy world, sometimes interpreted as a utopia (Lyons 1994). Following paying for admission, visitors pass under the railroad as they enter the park and arrive at Main Street, which extols the virtues of the American way of life. It is like entering a film set and the park is in a constant state of evolution, with new attractions constantly being added. Subsequent parks developed in Florida adopted the model of Anaheim but on a much larger scale.

Naturally, there are many critics of Disneyland and its subsequent iterations in other sites in the USA and across the world, most notably the European (i.e. EuroDisney) and Asian parks (i.e. in Tokyo and Hong Kong), with their synthetic and staged experiences, to create a spectacle. As a large film set it is often described as the archetypal postmodern leisure experience, based on a created and artificial environment where signs and symbols associated with the Disney culture are consumed, portraying different meanings and messages to the visitor.

Consequently, different cultural interpretations of the Disney experience have been made. Whatever interpretations we look at, it is clear that Disney has created one of the most successful mass leisure visitor attractions, despite underlying tensions about the Disneyification of American culture (Meebling 2006). In fact, King (2006: 367) argues that 'beyond direct recreation, the park's thematic legacy has now converged with every sort of public space, from malls, airports, office buildings, restaurants, and hotels to college campuses, main streets, re-created historic spaces, zoos, and museums' in terms of the design and development via the 'art of thematics . . . [creating] . . . experiential places from a basic collection of perceptual cues (music, motifs, icons, architecture, landscapes and historic touchstones) to become mainstream and metropolitan design for public spaces and reinstated forms of public leisure' (King 2006: 368). In other words, the principles of the Disney approach have been embraced and applied to many other leisure settings and spaces in a postmodern society.

Source: Meebling (2006); King (2006); Page (2009)

As Anton Clavé (2007) suggests, oversupply led North American parks in the 1990s to look at new niche markets and to develop destination parks in Florida and California where a typical seven-hour dwell time was gradually translated into a holiday experience, such as in the case of Euro Disney in Europe. Leisure visits were transformed into a broader tourism experience where families and groups would spend a number of days at the park. According to Anton Clavé (2007), the following characteristics are useful in defining the attributes of a theme park and its contribution to the leisure experience:

● It is a closed space with controlled access.

● It has a capacity to attract families and individuals.

● The typical dwell time will be five to seven hours and will involve rides and other forms of entertainment.

● It will create an entertaining atmosphere for fun and enjoyment.

● It will have a range of services and facilities, including catering and shops selling branded merchandise.

● It will require a high level of initial and ongoing capital investment to stay ahead of the market in terms of the adrenalin rush and pursuit of market leadership in terms of rides and thrill seeking.

● It will require a high standard of cleanliness and hygiene.

● Technology will feature as a dominant component in terms of the experiences provided, such as with the rides or entertainment as well as in the management of the physical infrastructure.

● It needs a highly developed model of visitor management relating to visitor flows and value-added experiences.

Source: Based on Anton Clavé (2007)

Plate 9.3   Universal Studios, Los Angeles, is a working film set and also provides tours of the set to provide visitors with a 'behind the scenes' experience of the making of films, past and present.

Among the appeal of these artificial environments is that they offer a high level of safety because they cocoon visitors and manage out any issues of fear and security through high levels of staffing and technology such as CCTV. These are without doubt highly developed entertainment landscapes which can accommodate large volumes of visitors and are very carefully designed to appeal to different markets and visitor interests. Other parts of the world, such as Dubai in the Middle East, have also focused upon the development of theme parks as an element of the visitor experience. While this development is primarily focused upon tourists, the scale of development in Dubai is huge.

As Robothan (2005) illustrated, the planned development of DubaiLand as an entertainment complex was expected to have a capacity of around 40,000 visitors a day, at a cost of AE\$ 235 billion, and to generate around US\$20 billion a year. It is expected to be about twice the size of Walt Disney world in Florida. Yet while theme parks are large artificial areas for entertainment, there are a number of examples of much larger-scale entertainment settings, such as Las Vegas.

Las Vegas: the ultimate leisure entertainment destination

In Chapter 8, Hannigan (1998) examined *Fantasy City* as an interpretation of the entertainment city, where fantasy and reality blur, with its 24-hour operation and focus on glitz and glamour as well as the underlying funding of its rationale – gambling. The city developed its main rationale in the 1930s as a boom town in a depression when it was a location for the construction workers of the nearby Hoover Dam, which led to an expansion of its tourism and hospitality sector. This was followed by the development of the gambling industry (legalised in 1931), with a further boost provided in the 1940s with a munitions plant and air force base located there. It was during the 1940s that the resort hotel evolved, with the development of Boulevard Strip outside the city limits in Clark County. Las Vegas has always been associated with the entertainment industry, with Hollywood shows and Hollywood glitz. During the 1960s it was one of the USA's leading tourist destinations, only surpassed in visitor volumes in the 1970s by the development of Florida (Gottdiener 2006). Famous casinos developed, such as Caesar's Palace, and the city continued to grow in the desert, one of the most unlikely places to develop a tourist destination. It receives over 38 million visitors a year and has over 140,000 hotel rooms, 55,000 slot machines, 30 casinos and 3200 gaming tables. The city has expanded its accommodation capacity to cater for these huge visitor numbers, pioneering the mega-resort hotels with their associated casinos as shown in Table 9.6. Many of these resort hotels have over 2000 rooms. The gambling revenues from Las

Table 9.6   A selection of Las Vegas' 'mega-hotels' and casinos

	Number of rooms
Venetian/Palazzo	7128
MGM Grant Hotel & Casino	5044
Wynn Las Vegas/Encore	4750
Luxor	4408
Mandalay Bay/The Hotel	4332
Excalibur Hotel Casino	4008
Bellagio	3993
Circus Circus Hotel & Casino	3774
Flamingo	3565
Caesar's Palace	3348
Mirage	3044
The Venetian	3036
Monte Carlo	3002
Las Vegas Hilton	2956
Paris	2916
Treasure Island	2885
Bally's	2814
Imperial Palace	2635
Harrah's	2576
Planet Hollywood (Aladdin)	2567
Sahara Hotel	2000

Source: Page and Connell (2009: 241). Copyright © Cengage Learning, 2009

Vegas, according to Gottiender (2006), exceeded US$6.6 billion a year, supplemented by $20 billion in visitor spending on associated services such as accommodation (though Macao has now exceeded this turnover as a gaming destination). Las Vegas has also re-imaged itself, with one notable development in the 1990s being its pursuit of the family market, with Circus-Circus adding a US$90 million 30-acre theme park. Yet the city still has many negative images associated with the darker side of the entertainment industry, with sex and prostitution alongside the misery caused by gambling losses. Yet despite this, it remains one of the USA's most successful tourist and leisure destinations, where image and fantasy encourage risk taking in terms of gambling as a form of leisure experience. Yet gambling and leisure entertainment are not just confined to urban settings such as Las Vegas. Hart (1998) examined the impact of the 1988 Indian Gaming Regulatory Act which allowed native Indian tribes to operate gambling activities on their reservations. By 1994, there were 143 reservation casinos operating in 24 states, the majority which were small. But Foxwoods Casino, New London in Connecticut had a turnover of US$1 billion a year, reinvesting the proceeds back into the community.

Summary

The cultural industries and the associated term creative industries are an interesting development within the wider domain of leisure studies. Nevertheless, it highlights one essential theme running through this book: leisure is a very amorphous subject, constantly developing, expanding and evolving as new concepts and areas of interest emerge. For example, one recent phenomenon that has developed as a new cultural activity linked to leisure travel is *couchsurfing*, abbreviated to *couching*, enabled by social networking. Couching has developed from the surfing fraternity in 2004 where a community of 227,000 in 218 countries host people with this interest and you stay on the couch, though there is evidence that this may be expanding as a concept. It challenges many of the established conventions of hospitality where the guest is known and invited rather than inviting themselves and are unknown to the host. But such developments in the cultural sphere may dilute the study of leisure *per se* as the emergence of the cultural industries concept has shifted the emphasis to much higher-profile issues for politicians and planners seeking to access the new-found financial resources among governments and private sector investors to pump-prime the culture sector with its economic growth potential. Critically, policy makers may now cherry-pick the elements of the leisure sector they feel will give them a return on their investment. This leads to the commercialisation of the cultural infrastructure for its revenue-generating potential, sometimes with wider social inclusion objectives, but primarily to drive forward employment growth for visitor and resident spending. Winners and losers result from these political objectives and it is certainly part of a wider trend within local and national government seeking to differentiate towns, cities and non-urban areas as attractive locations for leisure spending. It reflects overarching economic development goals that seek to enhance the status of places for leisure, owing to the competitiveness of places seeking to secure the discretionary spending of the middle classes aligned to the cultural industries, and the pursuit of unique and distinctive leisure experiences. Yet in a climate of limited resources for public sector investment, opportunity costs exist for investing in the cultural industries, potentially to the detriment of less high-profile elements of local culture such as the interest in coastal leisure to which attention now turns.

Discussion questions

1. What are the cultural industries? How would you go about developing a classification of this area as a dimension of the leisure industries?

2. How would you differentiate between the cultural and creative industries?

3. Why are events an important tool for developing leisure in the postmodern city?

4. Why are the creative industries being harnessed as a tool for economic and social regeneration?

References

Adorno, T. and Horkheimer, M. (1947) *Dialectic of Enlightenment*, Verso: London.

Anheir, H. and Isar, Y. (eds) (2008) *The Cultural Economy*, Sage: London.

Anton Clavé, S. (2007) *The Global Theme Park Industry*, CABI: Wallingford.

Barker, M. and Page, S.J. (2002) 'Visitor safety in urban environments', *Cities: The International Journal of Urban Policy and Planning* 19 (4): 273–82.

Barker, M., Page, S.J. and Meyer, D. (2002) 'Modelling the tourism-crime nexus', *Annals of Tourism Research* 29 (3): 762–82.

Beyers, W. (2008) 'Cultural and recreational industries in the United States', *Service Industries Journal* 28 (3): 375–91.

Boorstin, D. (1961) *The Image: A Guide to Pseudo-Events in America*, Harper & Row: New York.

Bordieu, P. (1984) *Distinction: A Social Critique of the Judgement of Taste*, Harvard University Press: Cambridge, MA.

Brewster, M., Connell, J. and Page, S.J. (2009) 'The Scottish Highland Games: evolution, development and role as a community event', *Current Issues in Tourism* 12 (3): 271–83.

Cloke, P. (2007) 'Creativity and tourism in rural environments', in G. Richards and J. Wilson (eds) *Tourism, Creativity and Development*, Routledge: London, pp. 37–47.

DCMS (2000) *Progress Report on Local Cultural Strategies*, DCMS: London.

Edensor, T., Leslie, D., Millington, S. and Rantisi, N. (eds) (2009) *Spaces of Vernacular Creativity: Rethinking the Cultural Economy*, Routledge: London.

Evans, G. (2001) *Cultural Planning: An Urban Renaissance?*, Routledge: London.

Florida, R. (2002) *The Rise of the Creative Class: And How it is Transforming Work, Leisure, Community and Everyday Life*, Basic Books: London.

Getz, D. (1997) *Event Management and Event Tourism*, 1st edn, Cognizant Communications Corporation: New York.

Getz, D. (2008) 'Event tourism: definition, evolution, and research', *Tourism Management* 29 (3): 403–28.

Gottdiener, M. (2006) 'Las Vegas', in G. Cross (ed.) *Encyclopaedia of Recreation and Leisure in America, Volume 1*, Thomson-Gale: Woodbridge, CT, pp. 497–500.

Greenwood, D. (1972) 'Tourism as an agent of change: a Spanish Basque case', *Ethnology* 11: 80–91.

Hannigan, J. (1998) *Fantasy City*, Routledge: London.

Hannigan, J. (2007) 'From fantasy city to creative city', in G. Richards and J. Wilson (eds) *Tourism, Creativity and Development*, Routledge: London, pp. 48–56.

Hart, J. (1998) *The Rural Landscape*, The John Hopkins University Press: Baltimore, MA.

Hesmondhalgh, D. (2007) *The Cultural Industries*, 2nd edn, Sage: London.

Hesmondhalgh, D. and Pratt, A. (2005) 'The cultural industries and cultural policy', *International Journal of Cultural Policy* 11 (1): 1–13.

Hughes, H. (2000) *Arts, Entertainment and Tourism*, Butterworth Heinemann: Oxford.

King, M. (2006) 'Theme and amusement parks', in G. Cross (ed.) *Encyclopaedia of Recreation and Leisure in America Volume 2*, Thomson-Gale: Woodbridge, CT, pp. 363–8.

Landry, C. and Bianchini, F. (1995) *The Creative City*, Demos: London.

Lash, S. and Lury, C. (2007) *Global Culture Industry*, Polity: Cambridge.

London Development Agency (2006) *Strategies for Creative Spaces: Lessons Learned*, London Development Agency: London.

Lukas, S. (2009) *Theme Park*, Reaktion Books: London.

Lyons, D. (1994) *Postmodernity*, Open University Press: Buckingham.

Mato, D. (2009) 'All industries are cultural: a critique of the idea of cultural industries and new possibilities for research', *Cultural Studies* 23 (1): 70–87.

Meebling, J. (2006) 'Disneyland', in G. Cross (ed.) *Encyclopaedia of Recreation and Leisure in America, Volume 1*, Thomson-Gale: Woodbridge, CT, pp. 285–9.

Mommaas, H. (2004) 'Cultural clusters and the post-industrial city: towards the remapping of urban cultural policy', *Urban Studies* 41 (3): 502–32.

Moss, S. (2009) *The Entertainment Industry: An Introduction*, CABI: Wallingford.

Myerscough, J. (1988) *The Economic Importance of the Arts in Britain*, Policy Studies Institute: London.

Paddison, R. and Miles, R. (eds) (2006) *Culture-Led Urban Regeneration*, Routledge: London.

Page, S. J. (2009) *Tourism Management: Managing for Change*, 3rd edn, Elsevier: Oxford.

Page, S. J. and Connell, J. (2009) *Tourism: A Modern Synthesis*, 3rd edn, Cengage Learning: London.

Pieper, J. (1952) *Leisure: The Basis of Culture*, Pantheon: New York.

Pine, B. and Gilmore, J. (1999) *The Experience Economy*, Harvard University Business School Press: Boston.

Pratt, A. (2008) 'Locating the cultural economy', in H. Anheir and Y. Isar (eds) *The Cultural Economy*, Sage: London, pp. 42–51.

Reeve, M. (2002) *Measuring the Economic and Social Impacts of the Arts: A Review*, Arts Council: London.

Richards, G. and Wilson, J. (eds) (2007) *Tourism, Creativity and Development*, Routledge: London.

Ritchie, J.R.B. and Beliveau, D. (1974) 'Hallmark events: an evaluation of a strategic response to seasonality in the travel market', *Journal of Travel Research* 14: 14–20.

Roberts, K. (2004) *The Leisure Industries*, Palgrave: Basingstoke.

Robothan, M. (2005) 'Creating DubaiLand', *Leisure Management* 25 (5): 50–4.

Rojek, C. (2006) 'Leisure, culture and civilisation', in C. Rojek, S. Shaw and A. Veal (eds) *A Handbook of Leisure Studies*, Palgrave: Basingstoke, pp. 25–40.

Sharpe, E. (2008) 'Festivals and social change: intersections of pleasure and politics at a community music festival', *Leisure Sciences* 30 (2): 217–34.

Sorkin, M. (ed.) (1992) *Variations on a Theme Park: The New American City and the end of Public Space*, Hill and Wang: New York.

Stevenson, D. (2005) 'Cultural planning in Australia: texts and contexts', *Journal of Arts Management, Law and Society* 35 (1): 36–49.

Stevenson, D. (2006) 'The arts and entertainment: situating leisure in the creative economy ', in C. Rojek, S. Shaw and A. Veal (eds) *A Handbook of Leisure Studies*, Palgrave: Basingstoke, pp. 354–62.

Sundbo, J. and Dormer, P. (eds) (2008) *Creating Experiences in the Experience Economy*, Edward Elgar: Cheltenham.

Tallon, A. (2008) *Urban Regeneration in the UK*, Routledge: London.

Throsby, D. (2008) 'Modelling the cultural industries', *International Journal of Cultural Policy* 14 (3): 217–32.

Travers, A., Stokes, E., Kleinmann, M. and Johnstone, H. (1996) *The Arts and Cultural Industries in the London Economy*, London Arts Board: London.

Tylor, B. (1874) *Primitive Culture*, Estea and Lauriat: Boston.

Vanolo, A. (2006) The Image of the Creative City, Dipartimento Interateneo Territorio, Politecnico e Universita di Torino, http://web.econ.unito.it/vanolo.

Williams, R. (1989) *Keywords: A Vocabulary of Culture and Society*, Fontana: London.

Williamson, J. and Cloonan, M. (2007) 'Rethinking the music industry', *Popular Music* 26 (2): 305–22.

Wolf, M. (1999) *The Entertainment Economy: How Mega-media Forces are Transforming Our Lives*, Penguin: London.

Zukin, S. (1995) *The Culture of Cities*, Blackwell: Oxford.

10 Coastal leisure

Learning outcomes

After reading this chapter, you should be able to:

- Explain the evolution of coastal leisure

- Identify the attractions of the coastal environment and the way in which people use the coast for leisure

- Outline the impacts that arise from leisure use of the coast and how these impacts are managed

Introduction

The coast is a distinctive environment which has evolved in many forms as a unique and special leisure place enjoyed by people throughout the world. Indeed, the coast dominates the supply and demand for tourism products and experiences, and is a core feature of marketing and promotion for many regions. Since the 1950s, the 'three Ss' – that is, Sun, Sand and Sea – have become synonymous with mass tourism. However, as this chapter will show, the use and enjoyment of the beach as a coastal leisure resource is far more important in terms of volume and significance for day trips and local residents' use. In addition, for some communities, the beach is not simply a place for leisure but an important aspect of cultural, regional and national identity, for example in Southern California and most notably Australia, where the beach is a 'national preoccupation' (Booth 2001) and 'the primary national image' (Mercer 1972: 123). The beach also plays an important role in more temperate climates, for example *'England's beaches and coasts have a special place in the nation's consciousness'* (Tunstall and Penning-Rowsell 1998: 319).

The number of visits made to beaches and coastal areas around the world is testament to the popularity of the coastal environment as a leisure place. Data sources, of course, should only be considered as estimates given that it is impossible to record actual numbers of visitors to beaches and the coast; however, available statistics highlight the significance of the beach as a leisure environment. For example:

● The Day Visits Survey for Great Britain (TNS Travel and Tourism 2004) indicates that 80 million trips were made to the seaside, accounting for about 7% of all leisure trips in 2002/3.

● In the USA, studies consistently rank beach recreation as one of the most popular outdoor recreational activities (West 2005), with over 275 million visits to beaches reported in 2008 (United States Lifesaving Association 2009).

● In a study of beaches in Perth, Western Australia, Houghton (1989) states that a number equivalent to 1.4% of the city's population was using the city's beaches on one day (identified through an aerial survey).

● Heatwole and West (1980) estimate that around 1.5 million people cram into New York's Coney Island on a peak summer holiday day.

This popularity is not solely a phenomenon of the modern age, and as Ryan (2002) comments, 'for centuries coastlines have fascinated human beings'. In fact, the evolution of modern beach leisure encompasses a passage of over 300 years, which this chapter later considers in more detail.

In this chapter, the coast as a leisure environment is explored from a number of perspectives. It briefly charts the historical evolution of leisure at the coast, before exploring what it is about the sea that attracts us there to enjoy leisure time. The social dimension of the beach forms a third focus of the chapter, identifying the divisions in society that make the beach a socially constructed place. The chapter then explores the leisure activities and behaviours that typify beach use, along with the meanings and values placed on the coastal environment. Finally, the resulting impacts from human interactions with nature and the commercialisation of the beach as a leisure area are summarised and, as many forms of coastal leisure require some degree of intervention, the scope and nature of management deployed in coastal areas are identified.

Studying coastal leisure

Studying the coast as a leisure environment may appear simple at first glance but this is not the case. Indeed, if you dig below the surface of the subject, a complexity of social, economic, political, moral, cultural and ecological histories, interconnections and interactions emerges, yielding a dynamic, intricate and substantial area of academic and popular cultural study. In effect, studying leisure at the coast is rather like studying the development of society in a microcosm, in that changes in society are constantly reflected in changes in how people enjoy leisure time at the coast. As tastes and preferences changed through time, so did the way in which people understood, appreciated and used the beach as a leisure space. In different parts of the world, the rise and fall of the beach as a leisure destination tells a different story – a story about wider changes in society in a given region. For example, the peak of beach tourism in the UK was reached in the 1960s; after that, foreign beach holidays became increasingly accessible and the traditional seaside resorts declined in terms of popularity and in turn investment. Likewise, as Booth (2001) argues, the beach was one of the few sites that urban Australians could go to for recreation on Sundays but by the 1970s many alternative leisure options had become available, including shopping. However, in other parts of the world beach tourism was only just starting during this period.

While there has been a decline in the popularity of resorts in many Western nations, the wider coastal environment remains a popular recreation space. In the twenty-first century, new forms of leisure and the re-popularisation of the beach as an environment for physical and spiritual escape and a place for short breaks and second homes have emerged, underpinned by new patterns of consumption in the postmodern style which rejects the mass recreation and tourism of modern beach use (see Plate 10.1). People today, it might be argued, have started to see the seaside in a different light, not the old run-down seaside resorts that previous generations frequented in the 1950s and 1960s. Instead, they see places that are starting to become fun and fashionable to a new generation of coast lovers who find a heady interaction of curiosity, beauty and nostalgia in regenerated resorts, along with a new set of recreational activities and interests that define specialised consumption patterns of postmodernism. The uptake of beach pursuits (e.g. surfing) by older generations (so-called 'silver surfers'), continued purchase of second or retirement homes in coastal areas, uptake of the marine theme in interior design and popularity of television programmes and magazines dedicated to the coast all point to a partially continuing and partially renewed interest in all things marine.

In parallel, as social stratification divided (and continues to divide) people in wider society (as Chapter 3 explored), so it did (and still does) in leisure (see Chapter 2 for a more general account of the history of leisure). It would be fair to say that the coast, and in particular the seaside, is a socially constructed

Plate 10.1 A typical beach scene highlighting the three critical elements associated with beach leisure – sun, sea and sand.

environment that has evolved as a site of physical, cultural and conspicuous consumption. This means that the meanings, values and associations attributed to specific coastal places have created and defined distinctive place meanings which denote the status, role and taste of the individuals participating in leisure at specific places. This interpretation is not new and has dominated leisure use of the coast throughout its historical evolution, as this chapter later illustrates. As Chapter 1 outlined, Veblen (1899) first used the term conspicuous consumption to describe the evolving phenomenon of consumerism, which linked the rise of leisure time and the leisure class with the achievement of social status through affluence and the ability to participate in certain kinds of activities. We shall have a look at this concept later in the chapter to see how it relates to coastal leisure.

What is coastal leisure?

So, what precisely do we mean by the term *coastal leisure*? In the coastal arena, perhaps more than in any other type of leisure environment, disaggregating tourism and recreation in terms of the historical evolution of leisure, recreational uses and impacts is highly problematic. If one takes a strict definition of tourism as involving an overnight stay, then in a leisure and recreation context we are less interested in the overnight stay component and more interested in the daily activities pursued (see a similar debate in Chapters 8 and 11 on urban and rural leisure, respectively). However, there are many obstacles in following this line, particularly as it is inherently difficult to disaggregate tourists from local residents and day visitors, given that residents and day visitors use many of the same facilities as staying guests and can display similar behavioural traits when engaging in specific types of activity. A number of authors have noted that it is a significant leisure, rather than strictly tourism, use that places considerable pressure on many coastal environments, for example the urban beaches of Spain, Australia and USA are used heavily by local residents as opposed to tourists (Breton *et al.* 1996). Yet, it is now widely acknowledged that beaches play a significant role in the leisure and tourism economies of many regions and that management and investment are required to improve and maintain quality in order to retain or increase visitors and visitor expenditure in the local area, in addition to conservation and ecological imperatives. As such, a balanced approach to coastal leisure is required that considers the range of issues affecting the coastal environment and contribution of a number of academic perspectives that help us to understand the subject.

Multidisciplinary contributions to coastal leisure

Academic study of the coast as a leisure environment is multidisciplinary, with contributions from a number of different academic subjects, and is not simply a field of interest within leisure studies and tourism studies. The way in which people use beaches has prompted a number of studies within a number of disciplinary and subject contexts, including history, planning, ocean and coastal studies, anthropology, sociology, philosophy, geography, planning, ecology, psychology, cultural studies, transport studies and economics, along with a number of other interests. In particular:

● Geographers have been interested in the spatial use of the coast, and the patterns of recreational demand, activity and impact at coastal sites.

● Philosophers and anthropologists have explored the meaning of the beach and the complexity of interactions between the natural environment, social environment and human interpretations of the environment.

● Historians have taken a particularly prominent role in the understanding of the coast as a leisure place and have assisted us in developing an understanding of how leisure developed at the seaside from its early origins, through to mass explosion of leisure at seaside resorts through to the altered patterns of consumption of the coast that we see today in the twenty-first century.

● Coastal and environmental scientists have also added an interesting perspective to our understanding of the coast as a leisure place, particularly from the point of view of human impacts on the natural environment but, moreover, the dynamic coastal environment itself and the need for a wide range of management tools, techniques and schemes to be implemented around our coastlines to retain recreational and amenity value.

- The more recent tradition of tourism and leisure research as an area of academic study has given further impetus to the coast as an area of interest.

In general terms, the bulk of the academic literature can be split into three broad camps. First, there is a significant body of literature on the historical development of seaside leisure, dominated by the work of Professor John Walton. The second body of work lies within the specific field of tourism studies, and focuses on the coast as a tourism space, including the impacts of tourism and its management. The third field is that of understanding how people use, and interact with, coastal environments in a leisure sense. These various interests will be highlighted further through the chapter.

What is the coastal environment?

Perhaps some definitions of words as they will be used in this chapter are useful at this point:

- *Coast:* an area where land meets the sea, which includes the beach, the region behind the beach, the sea and surrounding area within specified limits. The definition of a coast varies between countries depending on social and economic linkages (e.g. settlement patterns), environmental and political prerogatives, including regional development and local planning objectives, and coastal influences and activities. In some countries, the coast is defined as a fixed width, and often extends to the first point at which the landscape is no longer influenced by maritime processes: beyond this point is known as the coastal hinterland. A coast is subject to both human and natural forces and is a dynamic environment, and coasts are often subject to specific statutory planning regulations, policy guidance and directives as well as the terms of voluntary management initiatives to secure conservation or regeneration of the coastal environment. Globally, coasts offer a wide variety of rich natural habitats which in many cases are protected by international and national conventions. Demand for recreational use of the coast often creates a need to protect significant habitats while promoting access.

- *Seaside:* a subjective term denoting a leisure space by the sea. Often used to define a seaside resort, an urban development created mainly, but not solely, for recreational use.

- *Beach/seashore:* a natural (or human-altered) environment, which includes an intertidal zone and an area above the high tide mark which is composed of unconsolidated beach-type materials (e.g. sand, shingle, dunes, mud and rocks).

In addition, there are several ways of thinking about the coast as an environment, as summarised in Figure 10.1. This illustration identifies the scope of the

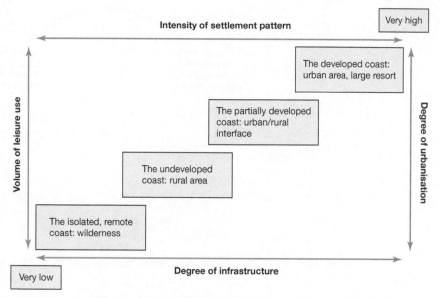

Figure 10.1   The scope of the coastal environment

coastal environment, which encompasses highly developed resort-style towns and cities right through to remote and isolated areas which are devoid of significant human settlement and use. Each of these coastal environments offers distinctive but important leisure uses and possesses quite separate qualities, while the degree of investment, management and marketing for recreational uses are poles apart.

The beach itself is often described as a liminal landscape, as Hall and Page (2006: 293) argue: '. . . the coast represents a liminal landscape in which the juncture of pleasure, recreation and tourism is epitomised in the postmodern consumption of leisure places'. A liminal environment in this case refers to the fact that the beach is neither land nor sea, and it can be experienced in a number of different ways at different times and in different conditions. There is, as such, no one 'beach experience'. For example, there is a significant difference between a beach experience on a hot, sunny day in peak season and the same beach on a cold, windy day in winter; the sea can be calm or turbulent, and the scene can be soothing or frightening. In other words, the beach experience is temporary, personal and dynamic (Preston-Whyte 2001). This particular theme is ever-present if one takes a look through the development of coastal leisure from early antecedents to contemporary times.

The history of coastal leisure

The evolution of coastal leisure is highly complex and intricately bound up with changes in the structure and outlook of society. It is this complexity that means that the multiplicity of events, changes in society's outlook on the coast

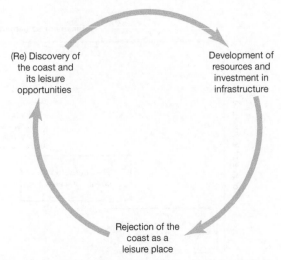

Figure 10.2   The cycle of society's approaches to coastal leisure

and the many interpretations of the history of the coast as a leisure place cannot be covered in great depth in this chapter – sources such as Corbin (1995),
Lenček and Bosker (1999), Walton (1983) and Walton (2000) offer more expan-
sive coverage of the subject. As such, the coast through time has been viewed
through a number of very different perspectives characterised by a cycle of
invention, rejection and rediscovery of the beach as a place for enjoyment
(Figure 10.2) (see Booth 2001; Corbin 1995; Lenček and Bosker 1999).

The early origins of coastal leisure

Lenček and Bosker (1999) evaluate historical perspectives of the coast and the
sea in detail, and argue that for hundreds of years the sea was feared. It was
characterised by terrifying myths, legends, beliefs (such as the Storm Gods)
and biblical references (such as the Great Flood) that made people reject it as a
place for either habitation or contemplation. It was considered to be an unpredictable and dangerous environment and people avoided it, apart from those
who earned a living from it. Even those engaged in the fishing industry tended
to build their homes facing inland and away from the sea.

In classical times, the Greeks discovered the pleasures that the beach could
offer and considered it as a wonder of creation. The Greeks constructed beach
houses to take in scenic coastal views, while physically engaging with the sea
became a favoured activity for the wealthy, including sailing and swimming.
The Romans developed a real passion for the beach, creating many early resorts along the Italian coast, developing summer residences and an infrastructure to support the enjoyment of the coast, including open air theatres, island
excursions and carnivals, the idea of opulence and luxury dominating the experience of the coast. Following the end of the Roman Empire, the onset of the
Dark Ages through to the medieval period saw a remarkable change in the perception and appreciation of the beach. Once again, the beach became both a

physically and socially prohibited place. This change can be explained by two broad factors:

- A period of geological and tectonic instability, resulting in earthquakes, tsunami and a rise in sea levels, affected many coastal environments through flooding and topographical changes which confirmed the dominant view that the sea was an aspect of the physical environment to which humans should turn their back.

- The moral rejection of the days of indulgence of the Roman Empire and a move towards a strict Christianity in the Western world. As Corbin (1995) argues, the spread of Christianity impacted on the beach as biblical images of the sea as an inhospitable place linked to the Devil abounded. This is partly explained by there being no sea in the Garden of Eden, while the Great Flood was associated with the Fall of Man, creating a fear of water linked with sin and the Devil.

Such fears and moral concerns waned gradually through time, although negative perception of the beach continued through the sixteenth century. Sea-bathing was considered to be an extravagance associated with depravity and eroticism. In fact, the practice of sea-bathing to get clean was frowned upon and dirt and odour were viewed as sanctity. Indeed, bath houses were initially viewed as dens of ill repute! It was not until the eighteenth century that a re-evaluation of the beach occurred, which was to mark the very early beginnings of coastal leisure in the way in which we understand it today.

The rebirth of the coast as a leisure space

During the middle part of the seventeenth century, perceptions of the beach and the coastal environment began to change and, as Inglis (2000) points out, people started to return to the sea from the 1650s onwards, influenced by scientific and aesthetic 're-imagining' of the coastal environment. Much of this early reorientation took place in Northern Europe, and particularly in the UK. However, the shift in thinking towards the beach as a recreation place was a gradual transformation and it took many decades for the coast to develop into an accepted place for leisure. As Corbin (1995) argues, it was not until around 1750 that a real shift was noticeable in perception of the coast and new practices in visiting it became established. The process was influenced by a number of factors over the course of a century, including:

- The period of global exploration and the paradisiacal images of beach environments, particularly the Pacific Islands, which exuded the contented way of life of coastal indigenous populations, which were brought to the attention of the aristocracy and learned society and prompted a re-evaluation of the way in which the coast was viewed (Lenček and Bosker 1999).

- The end of the Napoleonic Wars in 1815 removed the hazards of coastal settlement during successive naval conflict and started to make the coast a place that was less dangerous (Gilbert 1939). In addition, a safe passage could be assured for coastal steamers transporting visitors to coastal destinations.

● The intensification of the Grand Tour (see Page and Connell 2009 for more information) and the cultural retraining of the artistic eye to consider beaches as a beautiful environment came to be appreciated as part of a tour of Europe's grandest environments and cultural stopping points (see also Corbin 1995; Lenček and Bosker 1999).

● The development of the picturesque movement and the romantic ideas espoused by writers and artists through sea-inspired poetry and literature and seascape paintings. Like rural and mountainous areas, this shift in thinking revolutionised the history of taste in landscape and seascape and created a whole new set of environments in which it would become fashionable to spend time at leisure.

This paradigm shift in thinking about the coast was focused on the most affluent sections of society, often termed 'polite society'. It was the aristocrats and those wealthy enough to enjoy a lifestyle of leisure that first began to discover the beach as a leisure environment, and gradually this taste for the seaside became more fashionable and began to filter through to others in society.

'Dippers to trippers'

Significantly, it was not the beach *per se* that first attracted people to spend time at the seaside, and Hewitt (1995: 302) neatly summarises the process as transforming recreationists 'from dippers to trippers'. What precisely does this mean? The earliest seaside resorts came into being primarily as health spas, referred to as 'watering places' and frequented by those seeking therapies and cures for all kinds of medical conditions (although these claims were often spurious and appear to have no real basis in modern medicine). In 1660, Dr Robert Wittie wrote about the curative powers of sea-water at Scarborough (on England's North Sea coast) (*The Scarborough Spaw*) for 'melancholic vapours, nightmares, apoplexy, catalepsie, epilepsie, vertigo, nerves, yellow and black jaundice', where the discovery of mineral springs on the beach by a local woman in the 1620s stimulated a growing number of people to seek the healing powers of the water. This discovery, and Dr Wittie's subsequent promotion, prompted the early development of what was to become known as the seaside resort across England and Wales. Scarborough developed initially as a fashionable spa town, and later became Britain's first seaside resort. Brighton, on the south coast of England, was to follow suit after the publication of Dr Richard Russell's successful book on the curative power of the sea at Brighton. The search for better health that immersing in and drinking sea-water might yield was widely understood by 1800, creating demand for new centres and helping to form the basic geography of seaside resorts in many parts of Europe and the USA. Many destinations became popular and fashionable following a visit by a Royal family member, for example Weymouth became popular after the visit of George III who was advised to take a water cure for his condition of insanity. So, the early origins of mass coastal leisure are firmly rooted in health, well-being and medical matters, not fun, enjoyment and relaxation. But at some point, this focus was to change and the seaside as a place for leisure rather than health began to emerge, particularly when opportunities for leisure opened up to the working classes around the middle of the nineteenth century, and the seaside became in reach of the day-tripping public.

Consuming the seaside: the peak, the trough and the new era

The development of the seaside resort is well documented by a number of authors, most notably Walton (see particularly Walton's classic 1983 study *The English Seaside Resort: A Social History 1750–1914* and later work *The British Seaside: Holidays and Resorts in the Twentieth Century* (2000) which chronicle the development of seaside resorts in Britain in detail). According to Gilbert (1939), there are two types of English seaside resorts in relation to development styles:

- Ancient ports and/or fishing villages, which after the decline of their core industry in the seventeenth century took on a new role. Good examples include Brighton, Scarborough, Weymouth and Hastings.

- New towns founded on previously unoccupied land, which rapidly developed as new resorts, such as Bournemouth, Blackpool, Southport and Southend.

In terms of the leisure requirements and desires of an expanding social and economic profile of coastal recreationists, the seaside started to cater for a range of needs, ranging from rest and recuperation for health to more novel ideas of pleasure and the pursuit of recreational activities. In addition, the ability for an individual to confirm or heighten their social status through visiting fashionable or even newly developing coastal locations became an important aspect of visiting the coast, through the idea of visible, or as Veblen (1899) called it, conspicuous consumption. Most recreationists at the coast sought a range of opportunities to help them structure and enjoy their time in a useful way, for example the provision of regulated opportunities for social mixing (Walton 1983) and interesting and even educational pursuits. The rational recreation movement that developed in the mid-Victorian period further developed this idea through regulated excursions, and the development of recreational pursuits for the good of the individual such as walking, sketching and painting, the study of seashore plants and the collecting of shells and fossils. Associated religious groups and the temperance movement were particularly keen on organised excursions to the coast (e.g. Sunday school trips to the beach) to pursue spiritually enlightening activities (see Chapter 2). Sea-bathing was popular from the first half of the eighteenth century (Gilbert 1939) and mixed bathing took place. But later, beaches were often zoned, especially in Northern Europe, Australasia and North America, along gender and/or class lines, so men and women, and/or different social classes, were guided to appropriate beaches. Later, this stratification was to apply to race as well, as in South Africa and North America.

As in society more generally, the pursuit of leisure at the beach was strongly influenced by the changing socioeconomic context. The immense popularity of the beach as a leisure site developed and emerged in a socially stratified way (see Figure 10.3), and the democratisation of the beach, like other forms of leisure, is a notable part of the evolution of coastal leisure. However, it is important to state that prior to the beach developing as a fashionable site of leisure consumption, ordinary working people enjoyed leisure time at the beach and this, as Travis (1997) argues, was well established in folk tradition and practice in many locations, such as Lancashire and Devon, well before the trend-setting aristocracy discovered the delights of the beach. In the 1750s, the upper classes 'discovered' the beach for themselves, followed by middle classes around 1815 with the means to travel, and the time and money to do so. By 1841, Granville's map pinpointed 36 principal sea-bathing places in England and Wales. These were numerous and highly specialised places in terms of function and facilities. A precise infrastructure was developed in most resorts, consisting of a promenade for strolling and socialising, assembly halls for social gatherings and entertainments, a bandstand for outdoor music concerts, pleasure gardens (see Berry 2000), sometimes an aquarium and, from the 1860s, a pier for strolling, viewing scenery, embarking on boat trips, and later, amusements and entertainment. Sporting facilities, notably golf courses, putting greens, bowling greens and tennis courts, also became a feature of resort leisure supply from the mid-nineteenth century (see Durie and Huggins 1998).

From the 1850s, the working classes (and in particular the large urban and mostly inland populations of the industrial towns and cities, especially in the case of the UK) started to find the beach. This new demand was facilitated

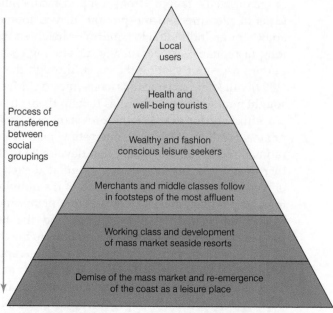

Figure 10.3   Evolution of the coast as a leisure environment

through several factors, as Chapter 2 outlines, including: time off from work (e.g. the Bank Holiday Act 1871 and 'Wakes Weeks' where an entire factory was closed for a given period of days allowing workers to embark on a trip to the seaside); an increasing supply of accommodation and entertainment designed for hedonism and fun; increasing affluence; but perhaps most significantly for the seaside, the advent of the railways and more affordable and convenient travel. As Walton (1983) argues, the seaside became an item of mass consumption in the late Victorian period (the last quarter of the nineteenth century), with a huge range of resort experiences on offer to a range of leisure seekers. Along with the development and commercialisation of previously established and new activities, such as boat excursions, fishing trips, entertainments and amusements (e.g. 'end of the pier' developments where a concert hall was built to accommodate often raucous comedy acts, singing, dancing and other entertainments for a fee-paying audience), the late Victorian seaside started to emerge as a highly complex site of leisure consumption in the form that we recognise today. Walton (1983) argues that by the start of the twentieth century, an increasingly family-oriented and child-centred approach to the seaside began to emerge, and a family visit to the coast was a marker of affluence and stability, again supporting the continuation of conspicuous consumption.

The expansion of what we now think of as traditional beach pursuits and interests, many of which were favoured by children and their parents and through time, developed from the late Victorian period right through the early part of the twentieth century and have become a seaside institution through the generations, such as:

- Punch and Judy shows which, following a long history, were extended to the beach, and adapted primarily for children.

- Donkey rides on the sand, a tradition thought to have started in the East Coast resort of Bridlington in 1895, which became a popular activity although, with concerns about animal welfare, it has declined in recent years.

- Seaside rock, a cane-like boiled sugar confection with writing in the centre, usually with the name of the resort inside, sold by seaside vendors as a cheap gift for low-income visitors to take home.

- Seaside foods, such as oysters, a 'pint of prawns' and other shellfish, while the consumption of fish and chips became a dominant form of meals out in some holiday resorts from the 1920s (Walton 1992).

- Fairgrounds, carousels and amusements: Blackpool Pleasure Beach, now one of the world's top leisure attractions, started life as a helter-skelter in 1905.

- Lidos, dating to around the 1920s and 1930s, are tidal bathing pools on the beach which are suitable for children and safer non-sea bathing. Only a few of these are still in use today, and one or two have been restored to past glories, such as the Tinside Lido on Plymouth Hoe, UK (originally opened in 1935, reopened in 2003 at a cost of over £4m).

Blackpool quickly became the biggest seaside resort in the UK, attracting large volumes of working-class day trippers and holidaymakers from the urban centres of the North of England. Like Blackpool, many resorts became socially stratified too, depending on who used them and the social tone, such as Coney Island, New York's equivalent of Blackpool. The social construction of the coast has had a marked influence on the growth and development of specific coastal towns and regions. In particular, local patterns of land ownership and the ideals of the local government (e.g. by-laws, investments and planning – see Chapter 7) influenced the shape, form and social organisation of resorts, and 'the definition of appropriate social conduct' (Hugill 1975: 216). Hugill (1975) argues that normal social barriers are diminished in holiday resorts, using the example of Southend's Golden Mile, where the physical and social attributes of the location have developed from working-class (particularly East London as that is the biggest catchment for the resort) style, tastes and preferences in catering, activities, material expressions and entertainment. This is a kind of social spectacle, where people have a conception of what being at leisure means to them and how they are viewed by others like them. The theme of continuity and change across Europe and later the rest of the Western world is paramount here, where being seen at a destination or engaging in certain activities is the object of leisure, as well as the intrinsic qualities of the activity to the individual. In other words, leisure as conspicuous form of consumption at the coast is all about 'being seen', as well as 'doing' or 'enjoying', which becomes evident in the public identity of a place, notably in its development, visitors and facilities.

Visiting the beach became a very popular recreational activity in the inter-war years but more markedly following the end of the Second World War, with low-cost activities (apart from the transportation element) such as sea-bathing, sunning and socialising acting as the main attractions for a society on a limited budget. The resort holiday in the UK reached a peak in the 1960s, when the availability of international tourism opportunities began to emerge into the marketplace (see Walton 2000 for more discussion on the decline of the seaside resort). Even holiday camps established in the 1930s became unpopular, with the aspiring middle classes turning to the modern-day holiday camps developed by Center Parcs across Northern Europe in inland forested settings. Has the coast once more been rejected? While the domestic tourism element at the coast has reduced in volume, the leisure day-trip and short-break market has arguably increased, given the increasing mobility of a more affluent population. The simple pursuits of the seaside remain the enduring qualities of the beach, but the attraction of the coastal environment is far deeper than this, and to understand this we need to explore what it is about this special place that we find so alluring in contemporary times.

The attraction of the sea

The interface of the land and the sea creates a complex interaction encompassing the tangible natural and built components of the landscape, along with the less intangible psychological, social and spiritual elements of experiencing the beach as a leisure space. The 'liminal' nature of the beach (e.g. Walton 2000; Hall and Page 2006; Preston-Whyte 2001), i.e. it is neither land nor sea but a place on the margins of both, is significant not just from a physical perspective but from a social psychological angle too. A place on the margins means somewhere where the usual social constraints on behaviour are pushed to one side and where hedonism and fun activities can be pursued.

What features make the coast an attractive leisure environment? These can be summarised as:

- *Natural:* The form and qualities of the natural environment, encompassing beach, sand, sand dunes, shingle, rocks, rock pools, the sea, tidal range, cliffs, landscape views, estuary, sky and flora and fauna.

- *Built:* The form of the associated built environment, including nearest settlement, degree of urbanisation/development, local planning and architecture, walkways, pier, beach facilities, harbour, car parking, and the subsequent effect on use levels, e.g. traffic, and crowding.

- *Social:* The normal level of social engagement associated with a given environment, ranging from isolation through to crowded beach, linking with the idea of social carrying capacity and perceived levels of crowding, which affect user enjoyment. The beach also offers a social environment where individuals can seek the level of social engagement required, from isolation and escape to social or family bonding.

- *Psychological:* The meaning, significance and personal values attached to the natural and structural elements which create a sense of place and a sense of spiritual engagement at an individual user or community level. The beach offers a varied setting for a variety of individual moods and emotions, from solace to escape.

Quite simply, as Walton (2000: 119) argues, the 'simple and uncommodified pleasures play an important part in the hold the sea still has on British consciousness'. These simple pleasures vary, and include gazing at the sea as an object of beauty, listening to the sound of the waves, playing beach games with children, engaging in sea or shore-based activities (e.g. surfing, fishing or swimming), relaxing in the warmth of the summer sun or, on a cold winter's day, battling against the strength of the wind on a beach walk; the list of pleasurable activities is endless. Indeed, as Taussig (2000) debates, the sea and the beach have become sites of fantasy. So, what motivates us to spend leisure time beside the sea?

What motivates visits to the coast?

The question of what motivates people to visit the coast yields a seemingly obvious answer: that is, to use the beach environment in some way. While this is quite true in many cases, studies of leisure use of the coastal environment illustrate the multi-layering of activities, values, meanings and associations that individuals exhibit in their perception and use of the coast. Taking the beach as one facet of the coast, the beach is not simply a leisure environment but one which has a powerful effect on our psyche, which in turn affects the way in which we think about and use the beach as a leisure place. Figure 10.4 outlines the major categories of recreational experiences that the beach environment offers, emphasising that the beach is not simply a space for leisure activity, but one which offers psychological and social qualities, experiences and opportunities for improving individual well-being and enhancing personal relationships. Tunstall and Penning-Rowsell's (1998) classic portrayal of the English beach as a significant and enduring social environment for recreation provides a fascinating review of the motives for visiting the seaside and the types of activities engaged in while there, based on survey work covering a 10-year period and 15 beaches across England. This work emphasises the special qualities of the coastal experience which can be divided into the experiences (Figures 10.4) and the meanings which people attach to the beach as a place and experience (Figure 10.5), which emanate in several ways: *first*, the timeless and enduring nature of the coast, where individuals ascribe meanings and values to the coast that endure over a lifetime; *second*, the special scenic qualities of the coast in its views, peace and quiet, natural scenery and the contrast of inland areas; and *third*, the convenience as a place to go for safety and reassurance, always something to do and kinds of activities available for different kinds of users, e.g. young families playing on the sand, those seeking sport and achievement through the pursuit of adventurous activities like surfing, or ramblers walking on coastal paths. Further to this, Ryan (2002) identifies the 'fun' element of a beach visit, which is carefree, spontaneous and fun, where it is socially tolerated for an adult to behave like a child and engage in what might be considered to be

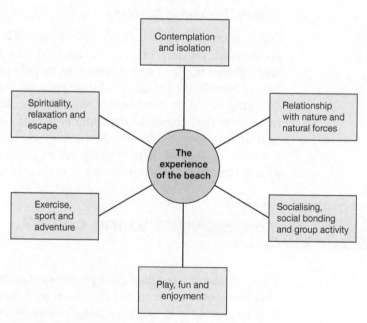

Figure 10.4 Recreational experiences at the beach

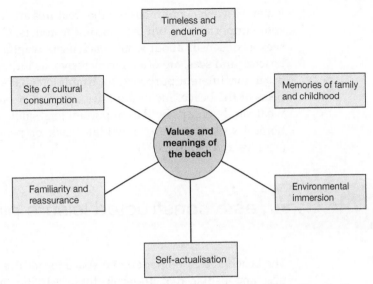

Figure 10.5   Values and meanings of the beach in a recreational context

'silly' pursuits in the context of other environments – eating fun food, playing games like frisbee or volleyball and jumping over the waves with trousers rolled up to the knees! However, as Ryan (2002) also notes, beaches can be a highly organised and commercial environment, focused on specific market segments with clubs, bars, events and organised activities.

In terms of what people are looking for in a choice of coastal environment to visit, Figure 10.6 identifies the main facets, as found in a number of different studies of beach selection. By far the most important element of the beach from a leisure user's viewpoint is the quality of the beach environment, encompassing both clean beaches free from litter and debris, and clean unpolluted sea

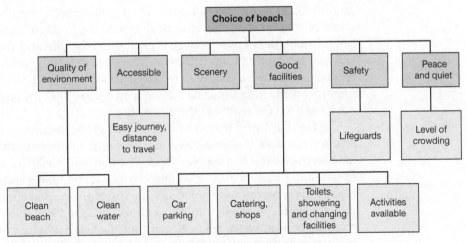

Figure 10.6   Factors influencing choice of beach

Sources: Adapted from Breton *et al.* (1996); Tunstall and Penning-Rowsell (1997); Tudor and Williams (2006); SNH (2007); Phillips and House (2008); Roca and Villares (2008); Roca *et al.* (2009).

water. However, a number of other features are identified by beach users as of some importance, from car parking to toilets. Of course, studies that aim to seek a consensus about what beach users want at any one time, beyond clean beaches and seas, are often inconclusive, as individuals seek different types of beach for different purposes; for example, what surfers want (e.g. physical aspects of the beach, including tides and size of breaking waves) is different to what family groups hold as important (e.g. safety and cleanliness) or conservationists seek (presence of wildlife, lack of people) in a coastal experience (Phillips and House 2009).

The beach as a constructed leisure place

The beach is a combination of a space for leisure activity, the processes, practices and people that underpin these activities and a collection of symbolic values: a physical/socio-cultural/psychological mix that defines use and perception. It is this socially constructed understanding of the beach on which people make decisions about whether a visit to the coast is appealing, and which destinations to go to based on desired leisure type, experience and knowledge. Indeed, as Walton (2000: 94) argues, it is the 'distinctive entertainments and artificial attractions' and the 'natural (but culturally mediated) features of the shoreline and the sea' that act as a magnet for leisure seekers. Shields (1991: 89) argues that 'the beach was not always a pleasure zone but had to be constructed as such'. As such, how we think about the seaside is not simply an objective reaction but a deeply embedded and multi-layered one that reflects a tradition and experience fixed in our cultural and social make-up. For example, Hewitt (1995) outlines the approach taken to designing the LNER railway posters of the 1930s which portrayed the 'joys' of travelling to an East Coast resort. These posters were deliberately colourful and lively, and when posted on the walls of drab streets or the London Underground would provide a stark contrast between 'grey' everyday life and the 'colourful' seaside just a tempting train ride away. The seaside is thus idealised as an escape from the everyday, a chance to recharge the spiritual batteries, although the romanticised and glamorous hedonism which these kinds of posters evoked may not have been the reality at the destinations.

The beach is by no means a homogenous place, frequented by all in a united fashion, nor does it offer a uniform experience. Like most other leisure spaces, the beach is subject to a degree of specialisation and selectivity according not just to taste and preference, but also subject to social conditions and conditioning, including class norms and values. Leisure use of the coastal environment and the public spaces contained within it is clearly reflected in Veblen's notion of conspicuous consumption, where to consume the beach as a leisure experience confers status and leisure activities were undertaken often to be seen doing so, as noted earlier, in both an historic and contemporary context. Thus, rather than simply for the intrinsic pleasure or benefit of the activity, it is the idea of being seen consuming that is the object of pleasure. While we tend to think of the coast as a place of universal fun, freedom and enjoyment, it has not always been that way, nor is it so today. The coast, like rural areas (see Chapter 11), is often a contested leisure environment, beset with a range of recreational, human and biophysical conflicts emanating from access and use. Unlike our associations with the beach as a place for fun and escape, the beach has long existed as a social, cultural and political hierarchy, played out through physical zoning (e.g. segregation according to race, religion or gender) and socioeconomic imperatives (e.g. destination segregation through planning decisions and subsequent development). Within the range of coastal environments, nowhere is this segregation seen more vividly than in the evolution of seaside resorts. As Walton (1993: 52) remarks, a seaside resort is: 'a kind of town and arena for contesting cultures and classes, and as a locus for the continuing struggle for dominance between humanity and nature on the liminal and evocative terrain of the seashore . . .'

Physical beach zoning for leisure

In areas of high use, beaches are frequently zoned to avoid conflicting uses, but zoning has been employed as a more socially divisive tool to segregate different types of people who are seen to clash in some way (see Table 10.1), normally from a political, racial or religious standpoint. Zoning of beaches is not a new mechanism as there is evidence of this practice from the mid-1800s, whereby sections of beach (but not sea) were designated for separate male and female use (Travis 1997).

Social segregation

Racial divisions have highlighted, and continue to play out, some of the most controversial aspects of modern society on the beach. In racially segregated

Table 10.1 Examples of contemporary beach segregation

Country	Segregated groups	Commentary	Year
Iran, Caspian Sea Coast	Women	Fibreglass barriers and water sprays directed out to sea allow women to use beaches more freely and privately while obeying strict Islamic laws on exposure of the female body	2007
Abu Dhabi, UAE	Families and groups of single men	Plans for separate areas on a new beach for each group to allow families to enjoy beach in peace	2008
Italy	Women	Adult female-only beach designed to exclude men and male-oriented activities disliked by women seeking relaxation and 'me time'. Children also excluded on this basis	2009
Egypt	Women	Some female-only beaches to allow Islamic women to bathe and use the beach without men seeing them and without breaking the contraventions of Islamic law	From 2004

societies, beach access was, and is, rigidly defined. From the 1930s, beaches in South Africa were racially segregated spaces where the two major racial groups (black and white) refrained from sharing the same beaches and it was not until 1989 that beach apartheid was eliminated. The USA had similarly segregated beaches up until the civil rights era of the late 1960s, where segregated beach use was strongly enforced, sometimes with the use of violence by local authorities and the Ku Klux Klan. African American community leaders and entrepreneurs made significant efforts to develop beach resorts, such as Val Verde and Atlantic Beach. Despite the lifting of segregation in South Africa, many indigenous African communities still choose specific beaches over others through preference, proximity to residential area, facilities and travel cost, and a degree of territorial attachment is apparent, although as Dixon and Durrheim (2004) note through qualitative research with white beach users, there appears to be some degree of dislocation of the sense of attachment to beaches for them, debatably perhaps demonstrating a resistance to cultural change. Wolch and Zhang (2004) in a study of beach users in Los Angeles County found that there was a lower rate of beach use by African Americans and Latinos which they debate might reflect the history of racism and the inherent perception of the beach as a 'white' domain.

In some cases, segregation has not been purposely designed but has become an unspoken aspect of beach leisure, where certain ethnic groups choose specific beaches over others; for example, Booth (2001) outlines the choice of beach by immigrant Greek and Italian communities in Melbourne being different from those selected by other communities, based on vicinity to residential area and ambience of the beach, where the environment is more akin to a traditional Mediterranean beach with trees and vegetation close to the shoreline.

It is not just race upon which beach segregation has been devised. In several parts of the world, beach designation according to gender is the norm. In Islamic countries, while mixed bathing beaches exist, it is common for women to have access to beaches where they can still obey the Muslim faith but swim freely in swimsuits away from the eyes of men, for example Egypt, Iran and United Arab Emirates. *La Femme*, a beach in Egypt's Maria luxurious resort, is shielded from outside by palm trees which enables women who abide by the Muslim dress code to enjoy the beach without having to wear *sharia* swimsuits (neck to ankle) on mixed beaches. This is liberating for many women, although the use of the beach as a family space often prevents women from using this kind of beach. However, in some countries, e.g. Somalia, Islamic courts have banned women from swimming on mixed beaches. While gender segregation is predicated on the basis of traditional views or religious arguments, and is welcomed by a large number of Islamic women wanting to follow the conduct of their faith, the designation of other beaches does not always follow the same reasoning, highlighting that women simply want space to themselves. For example, on Italy's Adriatic Coast, a private women-only beach has been opened which not only bans men, but also children, in an attempt to allow women the private space they want to relax away from assumed roles and responsibilities. This beach goes further by banning certain types of activity, such as loud music and fried foods. Instead, the facilities provided include fitness activities, beauty treatments and a focus on

Plate 10.2 A major bone of contention in beach use is the conflict caused by resident dog owners versus visitors without dogs, which has led some beach authorities to ban dogs in the peak season.

healthy foods. Incidentally, this example is indicative of what Ryan (2002) terms the industrialisation of the beach, where formal and commercial recreation has supplanted spontaneous use of the beach.

Activity zoning

Many other types of users have become zoned for some reason: nudists, people with dogs (see Plate 10.2) and active recreational pursuits in an attempt for coastal zone management to effect real improvements in the public interest for the majority of users, while making space for those with specialised but conflicting interests, as shown in Table 10.2.

Table 10.2 Conflicting beach activities for multiple leisure users

Hazardous activities	Socially conflicting activities	Other conflicting activities
Horse riding	Smoking	Dog walking and fouling
Sea and shore angling	Beach parties	Diving
Sand yachting	Loud music	Swimming
Boat launching/sailing	Alcohol consumption	Fires and barbecues
Motorised water activities	Naturism	Camping
Surfing	Beach sports	Climbing
Kite surfing/buggies	Motorised water activities	Running
All-terrain vehicles	Group activities	Kite flying
Frisbee and ball games		

The management of recreational conflicts at the coast is highly problematic (see Chapter 11 on the concept of recreational conflict and its management) because the decision as to who should be restricted and when restrictions should be in force are often at the centre of much controversy. The beach offers such a large variety of recreational opportunities that it is difficult to make judgements as to what is a legitimate activity. West (2005) states that recreational zoning on land and in the water has been applied to reduce conflicts between recreational users and activities, and there are hundreds of schemes across the world that physically zone activities in the interests of a range of users (see Table 10.3).

On the water, many authorities have instigated zoning schemes to address conflicts between recreational users, for example swimmers and boat users. One approach is to facilitate multiple uses through management practices which aim to resolve conflict rather than exclude categories of users. A method of managing conflict is for agencies to promote coastal sites where public access is feasible and to identify the facilities available and the types of uses that are most suitable for that area given physical characteristics and infrastructure. Through the appropriate use and dissemination of marketing materials and information, potentially conflicting users may find that certain beaches are more appropriate for certain activities, e.g. boat access and launch facilities, fishing

Table 10.3 Examples of coastal recreation initiatives to reduce user impacts and conflicts between recreational users

Dog exercising	USA: Cape Cod National Seashore, Massachusetts. Some beaches and other areas prohibited for dog exercising. Dogs only allowed on leashes up to six feet (about 1.8 metres) in length.
Motorised water craft	Australia: Sydney. Jet skis banned from Sydney Harbour due to noise disruption to residents and conflicts with other water users.
Swimming	USA: New York City. Swimming is not permitted more than 150 yards away from the shore. No fishing or water sports (e.g. boating, surfing, scuba diving) are allowed in a bathing zone when bathing is permitted. Swimming is not permitted at night or in thunderstorms.
4 × 4 vehicles	Northern Ireland: Benone Beach, Derry. Quads and scrambler bikes banned to protect dune system on one of Ireland's longest beaches.
Kiteboarding	UK: Exmouth, Devon. Voluntary code of conduct to reduce potential hazards for users, other recreationists and wildlife.
Barbecues	Guernsey: Only permitted on specified beaches. A permit must be sought for anything beyond a small family event.

opportunities and surfing beaches. Let us look in more detail at who uses the coast for leisure and what kinds of patterns of use demark the beach as a leisure resource.

Who goes to the coast?

A plethora of research reports aim to gauge the number of beach users in a given area or country each year. Most of these are estimates generated through sample survey techniques and there is no universal model for establishing beach use, but a notable exception to this is the study by Dwight *et al.* (2007), who collected beach attendance and bathing rate data for 75 beaches in Southern California over the period 2000–2004. This study showed that on average some 129 million beach visits took place on an annual basis, with 56 million 'bathing events', i.e. when people make physical contact with the sea. More significantly, the study helps to show the temporal and spatial patterns of beach uses which are replicated in many parts of the world. For example, nearly half of all beach visits occurred at the weekend, over half took place during June, July and August and the majority of beach visits were made to 15 out of the 75 beaches (40% of all visits were to beaches in Los Angeles).

While we tend to link beaches and holidays, many surveys of beach users come to similar conclusions: that the majority of beach users are not in fact tourists but local residents or day visitors, and figures of over 80% of beach users being local residents are not uncommon. It is not just tourism that places pressure on beaches either, and the growing low/middle-class populations in many developing coastal cities use beaches as a cheap and enjoyable place to spend leisure time, particularly on Sundays (Breton *et al.* 1996). Many metropolitan areas are located near the ocean (e.g. Barcelona, New York, Los Angeles, Melbourne, Sydney, Rio de Janeiro, Cape Town), so the resident population has relatively easy access to the coast as a place for recreation.

In terms of the profile of beach visitors, Wall's (1972) study of the Hull region of North-Eastern England identified that coastal locations were more popular with younger age groups and those with children. However, subsequent studies in a wider geographical context show that different people are attracted to different places at different times, and that profiling the coastal recreationist is not a simple exercise. Notwithstanding, the beach is undoubtedly a popular environment for families with young children, and research has identified that around half the visitor groups to the beach in summer contain children under the age of 11 (Tunstall and Penning-Rowsell 1998). The coast, however, is also frequented by lone recreationists, particularly in the case of local residents, wildlife-watchers and dog-walkers, who use the coast in the same style as a local park. It is clear that beaches do take on the role that a park plays in an urban area for many local residents; for example, Breton *et al.* (1996) illustrated that the beach in Barcelona was a place for young mothers with children and young people to socialise, especially during the week.

One aspect of visitor behaviour that appears to be quite marked from an analysis of the UK Day Visits Survey is that the distance people are willing to travel for a leisure visit to the coast is significantly further than for either town or countryside visits. The average distance travelled in the 2002/3 survey was over 60 miles compared with an average of 35 miles for all destinations. In many aspects of leisure and life, a distance-decay model is apparent, where the number of trips made to a specific location will decline with increasing distance (and cost of travel) – as discussed in Chapter 8. In relation to trips to the coast, the distance-decay model does not appear to dominate leisure choices, and studies from many parts of the world since the 1970s show that distance from the beach is not a major detractor in coastal trip decision making (e.g. Mercer 1972; Houghton 1989; SNH 2007), although as Tunstall and Penning-Rowsell (1998) identify, while cost is not so much the issue, journey time can be a detractor given that many groups visit the seaside with young children who tend to not like long car journeys.

Recreational visits to the seaside tend to be longer than visits made to other environments, such as the park or riverside environments, reflecting the longer journey in most cases and the variety of activities in which to engage. Tunstall and Penning-Rowsell (1998) found that because of this time factor, the beach is differentiated from many other leisure environments, where people tend to spend less time. The UK Day Visits Survey showed that the average duration of seaside day trips is 6.5 hours compared with 5.5 hours on average for all destinations.

Like most forms of day visits, the majority of visits to the coast are made by private car. In the UK, the Day Visits Survey 2002/3 identified that some 73% of visits were made by private car, although this is much lower than trips to the countryside at 86%, given that more public transport opportunities exist for trips to the coast than to the countryside (see Chapter 11). As Tunstall and Penning-Rowsell (1998) point out, the car dominates the type of group visiting the coast, as most people arrive in neat car-sized groups rather than in large groups as in former times when coach, bus and train transport dominated the mode of travel. Accordingly, the coast experience is often a small group experience, and often a two-generation one consisting of parent and child (Tunstall and Penning-Rowsell 1998).

In terms of expenditure, in the UK the average spend of visitors on a day trip to the seaside was £18.50 as identified in the Day Visits Survey, the lowest of the three types of destination (coast, urban and countryside). This is interesting given that visitors are more likely to travel further and spend more time at the coast compared with town and countryside destinations, but perhaps denotes that lower-spending visitors go to the coast, that visitors are more likely to be self-sufficient in terms of food and drink and other commodities for a day trip, or simply that visits are made to relax and get away from spending opportunities. As Booth (2001) argues, the idea of beach culture lends itself to one of a relaxed and casual lifestyle, with connotations for clothing, behaviour, leisure activities, and general aspects of style, which perhaps do not lend themselves to high levels of expenditure during the visit (although this does not preclude expenditure in preparation for the visit).

Recreational beach use

The study of recreational use of the coast is now well established. West (2005) states that, traditionally, three forms of activity dominated beach leisure: bathing, shore-based fishing and beachcombing, based on the idea of self-improving rational recreation. In the twenty-first century, the number of beach pursuits has increased dramatically, including more active and adventurous activities as well as more passive, traditional ways of spending time on the beach. For example, the July 2009 edition of the UK-based *Coast* magazine reports on *'100 things to do, from surfing to crazy golf'*, which reflect a new emphasis on coastal leisure, highlighting activities such as coastal running and cycle rides, along with more traditional sea-swims and beach sports. However, the coast is no longer a place just to enjoy the beach – it is a place once more of conspicuous consumption, where specialist shops, seafood restaurants and boutique hotels (see e.g. Padstow (Cornwall, UK), made famous by celebrity chef Rick Stein (see Page 2006)), along with unique and interesting attractions, wildlife reserves, gardens and sailing, mix with lifestyle change, downshifting, retirement and property acquisition to create the new coast of the twenty-first century, for the affluent and aspiring middle-class style of consumption. A visit to the coast is a pluriactive experience (in that it is an experience consisting of many different activities) perhaps more now than ever and this is perhaps more marked than in visits to other leisure environments where there is less of a range of activities in which to engage.

Research shows us that there are different social patterns of beach usage, which conform to the pattern of continuity and change through the evolution of the beach as a leisure entity. Partly, this is explained by the underlying issue of socioeconomic and cultural differences that exist in society, and partly through the idea of liminality, in that an individual may exhibit different beach tastes at different times and in different circumstances. But let us focus on the first of these issues.

Beach activities

Taking part in a variety of activities appears to be the dominant theme of a day trip to the coast. In a Scottish Natural Heritage (SNH) (Land Use Consultants 2007) survey of recreational visitors to the coast in Scotland, the most highly participated-in informal activity was walking (up to 5 miles), accounting for nearly one-third of all activities. A range of other activities show the enduring patterns of beach enjoyment through time and include rock pooling, beach games, picnicking and sea bathing and paddling (see Case Study 10.1). It is these informal activities that appear to dominate both memory and experience of the coast, and as Tunstall and Penning-Rowsell (1998: 329) comment, the beach is a tactile place where individuals can reconnect with nature in a way that is not so easily identifiable in other leisure environments and one of the few places left where children 'are allowed . . . to poke about, pick up, touch, shape and play with its physical material'. These informal activities are important but so are very passive ways of spending time at the sea, such as sunbathing, sitting, thinking or gazing out to sea (sometimes from inside a parked car). The coast is, again, unlike other environments, as people often go there simply to do nothing other than be reflective, physically inactive or simply to 'chill out'. Breton *et al.* (1996) in a study of beach use in Barcelona found that beach use was remarkably passive, with most people simply choosing to lie in

Case Study 10.1   The development of sea bathing as a leisure pursuit

The way in which people have used the beach has changed dramatically since early leisure uses emerged, even in relation to simple aspects such as swimming in the sea. One of the prevailing themes relating to beach use in the Victorian period was modesty. Naked bathing was the norm until the nineteenth century, when costumes became an accepted part of Victorian modesty and in many instances required by law; also, they kept skin white and away from the sun. Bathing machines, a type of beach hut on wheels, were used to conceal bathers until they had reached the water and block views of bathers from the shore to preserve modesty. These machines were first invented in the UK resort of Margate and used from around the early 1700s right up until 1920 in Northern Europe, across America and Australia. Even full-length costumes were considered to be immodest. For many ladies, swimming was not a comfortable pursuit owing to the cumbersome clothing style, by the mid-Victorian period often a two-piece design, with a woollen gown from neck to knee, and trousers with stockings. It was not really until around 1910 that one-piece costumes became acceptable. Daylight bathing was prohibited in many parts of nineteenth-century Australia and New Zealand. For example, it was not until 1903 that bathing in daylight hours was legalised in Sydney, marking the official birth of Australian beach culture (Booth 2001) and the surf life-saving era to rescue inexperienced swimmers.

Today, swimming in the sea is a popular activity but often a contested one, affected by the health and safety agenda (see later in the chapter). The level of E.coli bacteria in some coastal waters resulting from high levels of sewage pollution is a detractor to sea swimming and beach use in certain destinations. Beaches are sometimes temporarily closed to users because of sewage pollution, and high-profile media reporting of such incidents creates damaging perceptions of places as an outcome, which tend to remain even when the problems are dealt with.

However, sea-bathing continues to be a much participated-in activity at the coast. New forms of adventurous activity, such as open sea swimming as a physical sport, appear to be increasing in popularity, while the uptake of the thrill-seeking idea of 'tombstoning' (jumping vertically or diving from a high point or from sea cliffs), despite its real dangers, is increasing.

the sun. Despite this, people do visit the coast in pursuit of specialist active pursuits; walking (over 5 miles) dominates the choice of activity, followed by angling and boating activities, although a very large range of niche pastimes (e.g. fossil hunting, land yachting) are participated in by a small number of people (Land Use Consultants 2007).

Beach behaviour

Why is it important to know about how people use beaches? Simply, so authorities know how best to manage the environment, service provision and any recreational conflict that may exist. A basic method for understanding beach use entails gauging the number of users, which is useful in helping to address the level of service provision required. However, as Breton *et al.* (1996) highlight, it is important for beach managers to understand the characteristics of beach users, their needs and opinions, the activities engaged in, their views of existing management policies and what they would like to see improved. Such information can help to shape the beach as a user-oriented space for leisure and leisure users.

In terms of behavioural patterns on the beach, users tend to display a number of interesting traits, particularly in terms of the amount of space they choose to occupy. Edney and Jordan-Edney (1974) found that through research on American beaches, groups of people tended to distribute themselves evenly, but single men and groups of more than four tended to claim a larger territory. Some of the conclusions of this research were that:

- Females claim less space than males.

- If a beach user is more familiar with the location, they are more likely to adopt a larger territory.

- Family groups and couples were 'inward-looking', creating their own interests and entertainment.

- Same-sex groups were more 'outward looking', using the beach as a social environment to connect with other people (often groups of the other sex).

Smith (1981) contested that there would be a cross-national effect at work in this respect, and when replicating the research in France and Germany, found that French people tended to have little understanding of territory as a concept, and were tolerant of high-density use of the beach. On the other hand, German beach users had a very clear definition of their space on the beach, even to the extent of constructing sand walls around the area occupied, and exhibited a low crowding capacity. Smith found that a French all-male group used 208cm^2 per person, compared with 447cm^2 per person for German equivalents, while Edney and Jordan-Edney found that the same groups in the US took up 377cm^2 per person.

So, the ways in which people use the beach identify the importance of this environment as a place valued by people for all kinds of reasons and leisure activities. Given the importance attached to it for leisure, and the potential for conflicts between users and the environment, the need for management of the coastal environment is clear.

Managing coastal leisure

As this chapter has indicated so far, the coast is a multifaceted environment and is subject to the demands of a multitude of recreational users. Coasts around the world are also a hugely significant ecological resource, while home to a large number of people who live, work and play there. It must also be remembered that the coast is a dynamic physical environment, subject to weather and tides which have the power to alter a coastline almost overnight or at the least gradually through time. These various demands create severe pressures on the coast which must be managed to strike a balance between these competing uses and needs. Chapter 12 examines recreational conflicts in much more detail, but it is worth focusing just briefly on the need for management of coastal leisure.

We tend to think of beaches as a natural environment that requires little input to maintain recreational value. However, it is not as simple as this, bearing in mind the dynamic natural processes affecting the coast and human interventions that have resulted in degradation of some coastal areas. The need for management and investment, usually in the form of public funding of coastal and beach management programmes, has been highlighted by several studies, particularly in the USA. Visitors place importance on clean, wide sandy beaches and it is in the best interests of public authorities, keen to maintain a healthy leisure economy, to invest in the management of these treasured spaces.

In terms of coastal environments, a large number of studies have examined different facets of the impact of leisure. The clash between recreational use and natural resources, and in particular, coastal wildlife and landscape protection, is a dominant theme and outside of developed resorts, there is a clear direction for protection of the natural coastal environment from conflicting leisure uses; in particular, 4 × 4 driving on beaches and dune systems, powerboating and use of personal watercraft, fishing, beach-combing, dog-walking, and cliff scaling, among others, have been shown to adversely affect the ecology of an area and disturb wildlife, particularly nesting coastal birds. In addition, leisure use often necessitates some degree of development and service provision, which has a direct impact on the natural environment.

One of the most significant impacts of leisure at the coast which affects both beach access areas and the hinterland is traffic congestion (see Case Study 10.2 of Cape Cod National Seashore). While coastal access is sometimes constrained by public transport, Heatwole and West (1980) showed that in New York, people visiting the beach used public transport when it provided direct access to the beach but if the journey involved multiple modes or journey legs, with the associated cost, then alternative modes were preferred. Beaches served by the mass transit system were intensively used compared with other beaches. There are knock-on effects for social inclusion as well, where those on low incomes are effectively prevented from access to beaches where transport costs are higher, creating 'rich beaches' and 'poor beaches'. This theme is common in studies of beach use both in cities and in segregated (or formerly segregated) societies.

Coastal leisure in all its different forms creates a significant economic effect for local environments and destinations. Many studies have identified a significant amount of spending through coastal recreation. In California, with its globally renowned sunshine and sandy beaches, the contribution of coastal tourism and recreation to the region's economy was estimated to be around US$22 billion in 2000, generating more than 400,000 jobs (Kildow and Colgan 2005).

For many public authorities charged with the dual aim of protecting natural and cultural resources at the coast while enabling visitor access and enjoyment of these resources, the need to develop sensitive management policies that can deliver on both counts is a key challenge. One example of this is the Heritage Coast scheme which operates in England and Wales (see Table 10.4).

In England, some 32 areas of coastline amounting to over 1000 km (about one-third of England's coastline) are defined as Heritage Coasts by Natural England. These stretches of the country's most beautiful coasts are given special protection and managed for the twin but often conflicting purposes of conservation and recreation. In particular, these areas are managed specifically to improve accessibility. Heritage Coast services work at the local level to protect and improve the coastal landscape and develop visitor management and interpretation while engaging local communities in the process. For some communities, the Heritage Coast badge offers a useful brand on which suitable tourism and leisure opportunities can be developed.

In the USA, the management of National Seashores involves a similar set of objectives, as Case Study 10.2 outlines.

Table 10.4   The purposes of heritage coasts

- To conserve, protect and enhance the natural beauty of the coasts, their marine flora and fauna, and their heritage features.
- To facilitate and enhance their enjoyment, understanding and appreciation by the public.
- To maintain and improve the health of inshore waters affecting Heritage Coasts and their beaches through appropriate environmental management measures.
- To take account of the needs of agriculture, forestry and fishing, and of the economic and social needs of the small communities on these coasts.

Source: Natural England

Case Study 10.2   The National Seashores of the USA

In the USA, the well-developed National Parks system incorporates 10 areas of coast, protected by federal law, named National Seashores, as shown in Table 10.5. These areas are protected for both their natural and recreational significance, and while physical management and conservation objectives are paramount, equally appropriate forms of recreation are encouraged. National Seashores (NS) form an important resource for coastal visiting and in 2008 the total number of visits to the 10 areas combined was nearly 16 million.

Cape Hatteras was the first NS to be designated way back in the 1930s, although formal establishment did not take place until 1953. This NS is famed for its black and white spiral painted lighthouse, the tallest in the USA, relocated from its former position in 1999 because of erosion.

Cape Cod National Seashore, with its iconic lighthouses and 40 miles of beaches, is the most visited of the National Seashores (see Table 10.5), and in 2008 was the tenth most visited protected area in the US National Parks administration. The protected area covers over 44,000 acres and comprises six main beaches managed by the National Park Service. Beaches are serviced with showers, paved parking areas, toilets, changing rooms, drinking water and lifeguards, while two of the beaches are fully accessible for disabled people. The National Park Service operate two visitor centres to help provide visitor orientation and information, as well as playing an educative role.

One of the management issues for Cape Cod NS is the seasonality of visits, as shown in Figure 10.7 which depicts the normal summer season peak.

Table 10.5   National Seashores of the USA

Name	Location	Date established	Visitor numbers (2008)
Assateague Island	Virginia/Maryland	1965	2,011,438
Canaveral	Florida	1975	994,453
Cape Cod	Massachusetts	1961	4,644,235
Cape Hatteras	North Carolina	1953	2,146,392
Cape Lookout	North Carolina	1966	486,899
Cumberland Island	Georgia	1972	82,812
Fire Island	New York	1964	604,577
Gulf Islands	Florida/Mississippi	1971	2,054,201
Padre Island	Texas	1962	635,925
Point Reyes	California	1962	2,248,203

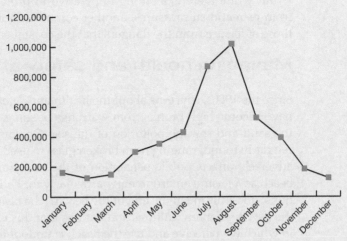

Figure 10.7   Visitor numbers by month at Cape Cod National Seashore

Source: US National Parks Service (www.nature.nps.gov/stats)

In August 2008, one million visits alone were recorded, that is around a quarter of the yearly total. This creates a number of management issues, such as:

- Access and traffic congestion, as most visitors arrive by car.
- Car parking capacity.
- Informal parking, causing damage to roadsides.
- Crowding at key visitor sites.
- Need to continually improve visitor facilities.
- Erosion of natural habitats.
- Incompatible activities and conflicts between users, and between users and the environment.

The National Park Service aims to serve the average summer level of visitation, not the peak level except where safety standards require so. As such, there are days when overcapacity is reached. One of the key challenges is to manage visitors in a more effective way using spatial techniques, such as concentrating high use in the developed managed zone by accommodating large numbers of people, while also orienting visitors to less crowded areas where existing sites can absorb higher recreational demand.

Managing the National Seashore is achieved by regulations and management plans and policies, which are enforced, facilitated and delivered by the National Park Service. Regulations include, for example, beach entrance fees; limited permits for beach fires; strict regulations on pets; no nudity; advice on parking; permits for driving on over-sand routes; and no overnight camping or parking. The National Park Service operates an extensive ranger-led events programme, which helps to not only create enjoyable leisure experiences through interpretation but to increase awareness of resource conservation and the uniqueness of both the ecological and cultural environment.

But while there is a strong imperative to protect the natural environment from recreational pressures, another component of management is protecting those at leisure from the dangers that the coastal environment can present.

Managing health and safety at the coast

Since the 1980s, concerns about the health and safety of the beach environment have become high profile, from warnings of sun exposure, to harmful litter on the sand and sewage pollution of the sea. On some beaches, harmful litter is regularly found, ranging from broken glass to used hypodermic needles, which adversely affects public perception of the safety and desirability of using the beach as a leisure environment, particularly for children. As Booth (2001) questions, does this mean the end of the beach? The beach is so deeply engrained in the psyche of many cultures and nations that this is unlikely, although the way in which we perceive and use the beach is undoubtedly affected.

There has been a significant rise in awareness and activism in relation to the state of the coastal environment and seas since the 1960s (partly driven by popular science books such as Rachel Carson's *The Sea Around Us* (1951), which sold over one million copies and was accompanied by a film version), and the general rise in environmental understanding at a time of increasing pollution and environmental degradation of the coast through industrial development, sewage discharge and poor environmental management. Campaigns and pressure groups representing beach users and conservationists formed and gained widespread attention for the cause of cleaning up beaches and the seas. In the UK, the direct action group *Surfers Against Sewage* (see Ryan 2007; Wheaton 2007; Hassan 2003; http://www.sas.org.uk) has successfully raised the profile of the effects of coastal pollution on human health and enjoyment of the coast, claiming that surfers and other water users were much more likely than the general population to contract viral infections like those found in water contaminated by sewage. Specific objections to contamination of beaches and sea water include:

- Items disposed through waste systems, such as sanitary products, condoms and toilet paper.

- Disposal of medical and drug-use-related products, such as syringes.

- Litter and plastic debris, from a number of sources including shipping, which causes a danger to water users and wildlife.

- Sewage pollution due to raw sewage or poorly treated effluent is discharged close to seashores with high levels of bacteria and viruses, which cause infections in water users, from ear, nose and throat infections and gastroenteritis through to more serious illnesses such as pneumonia, meningitis and hepatitis A.

- Toxic pollution, including chemical wastes from domestic use such as shampoos and cleaning products, as well as serious examples of toxic waste discharge from chemical plants.

- The disposal of radioactive waste. Radioactive particles have been found on some beaches close to nuclear plants, as well as in the water.

These forms of contamination are widespread across the world, and are now acutely felt in parts of the developing world where rapid industrialisation is occurring at the cost of environmental and human health protection. In the UK, investment in a large-scale coastal clean-up was made from the 1990s, while a European Union Directive on clean water has assisted in raising the standards, and now many beaches are significantly cleaner, as demonstrated through regular water quality testing and improved cleanliness of beaches. However, the problem, although reduced where remedial action has taken place, has not gone away, and remains a major issue for many countries, especially the USA, where widespread reporting of beach pollution makes the issue a high-profile one. Despite some concerns levied by environmental groups, the introduction of environmental awards for beaches has contributed to the improvements in the cleanliness and standard of some beaches.

Beach standards

There are a number of independent initiatives around the world, the most renowned being the Blue Flag Award. Blue Flag is an international award given to beach areas that meet strict criteria in relation to water quality, cleanliness, safety, facilities, environmental management and information and education provision. It is a voluntary organisation. Around the world, there are over 3500 accredited beaches and marinas. Outside of Europe, South Africa was the first nation to implement Blue Flag and, since 2001, 37 countries have participated, while the highest concentration of Blue Flag beaches is in Spain, Greece, Turkey and France. Many countries recognise the economic dimension to achieving and promoting Blue Flag status in that clean beaches with good amenities are attractive to leisure visitors. The Blue Flag scheme is operated by a not-for-profit organisation called Foundation for Environmental Education based in Denmark (and by different partner organisations in specific countries, e.g. in the UK, the Keep Britain Tidy Group administer the scheme) and the aim of Blue Flag is to promote sustainable development in the coastal environment. Other award schemes operate too but usually with less strict criteria, and this is one of the criticisms of such awards in that:

- Some awards can be achieved at polluted beaches, where criteria relate simply to facilities at the beach and ease of access, rather than safety of the water.

- There is inevitable confusion about what the awards mean to users.

- There is potential for misleading the public about the level of environmental quality of water, where a beach may achieve only a minimum standard of cleanliness.

- Beaches can, and often do, lose their award status and this can lead to public confusion about the meaning of standards.

While local authority and coastal agencies place a great deal of emphasis on achieving and retaining beach awards, research studies (see e.g. Nelson and Botterill 2002) indicate that leisure users have little awareness and knowledge of such awards and do not place much emphasis on award status when choosing a beach to visit. What does appear to be significant, though, is that beach users do want the results that Blue Flag and similar award schemes produce – i.e. clean litter-free beaches and clean bathing water, so while the award in itself appears to be of little user significance, the adherence to strict management and regulations to keep beaches clean, safe, well managed and user-friendly is important in assuring visitor satisfaction. Indeed, Tudor and Williams (2006) state that the real value of the awards is that they make authorities 'clean up' and that it is not the awards that attract the people but the quality of the beaches. Boevers (2008) criticises the Blue Flag scheme, stating that the criteria omit the protection of sandy beach ecology and local community values in programme design. Boevers (2008) argues that beach managers need to consider the opportunity costs of participation and more particularly the consequences of losing certification through bad press, because although people are perhaps not fully aware of certification schemes, media coverage of beaches that lose their status is likely to have a detrimental effect in at least the short term.

Beach safety

Although we have established that the beach is an important place for relaxation and enjoyment, we are now starting to understand some of the dangers of the beach. Hazards are plentiful, particularly for those who venture into the water, from bites and stings, rip currents, offshore winds, large waves, speed of tidal change, being hit by surfboards or other craft, shark attacks and drowning. Each year, thousands of lives are saved by lifeguards across the globe. Surf life saving started in Australia in 1906, following the increase in sea bathing after the daylight ban (see earlier in the chapter) was lifted, resulting in an increase in drownings. Some key points to note are:

● Surf life-saving organisations operate on a voluntary basis and there are some large organisations dedicated to the task, including Surf Life Saving Australia who performed over 9000 rescues in 2006/7, while attending to thousands more cases.

● The first surf life-saving club in Britain was established at Crooklets Beach (Bude, Cornwall) in 1953.

● The Royal National Lifeboat Institute (RNLI), a charity, is the key organisation in the UK providing patrol and rescue services to 140 beaches, assisting over 10,000 people in 2008.

● Surf life saving is also a competitive sport, and events championing the skills of the life saver are held on a regular basis, especially in the USA and Australia.

● Lifeguards sometimes work on a voluntary basis while others are paid by the local authority.

It is interesting to note the differing perspectives on the provision of lifeguards on beaches. Some categories of beach users view lifeguards as of paramount importance when choosing a beach to visit, particularly so for those engaging in active sea recreation, such as surfing, as well as families concerned generally about beach and water safety (Phillips and House 2009). However, another view, as highlighted by Booth (2001), is that the presence of lifeguards on a beach is a throwback to the old times where beaches were strictly governed and users were told what they could do and where they could do it – for some, this is an infringement of freedom, but for others it is the difference between life and death. Certainly, as active sea leisure pursuits multiply, there is an increasing need to understand risks to users and the deployment of appropriate safety resources (Scott *et al.* 2007).

Summary

On a global scale, coastal leisure is a significant form of outdoor recreation and a focus for tourism. The coastal environment has a long history in terms of leisure use and it continues to act as a powerful magnet for leisure, and one which has universal appeal. This is because the beach can be enjoyed, framed and conceptualised through a multitude of guises, ranging from the remote rural beach to urban resorts.

The evolution of a range of health issues, such as sun safety and water quality, has perhaps impacted on the universal pleasures of the beach, particularly in Australia where Booth (2001) questions whether we are nearing the end of the beach as an icon of pleasure and leisure due to the health and environmental concerns that have become prominent about beaches, water quality and public health.

However, renewed interests in the natural and heritage values of the coast have given a fresh outlook on the way in which we perceive the coast as a place of tradition, cultural icons and memory, as well as a place where we can engage in a variety of informal and specialist activities. The coast offers a variety of attractions, and many resorts have found their own niche in offering certain types of leisure experiences, which have grown from their early origins. For some coastal locations, culture has become a key driver of regeneration and the leisure economy, offering the visitor a unique cultural experience within a coastal environment, for example the internationally acclaimed artist enclave at St Ives (Cornwall, UK) has now become much visited for the Tate Gallery along with its open artists' studios. In Florida and Maine, for example, lighthouses as a form of cultural heritage at the coast are a central part of new tourism promotions. For other locations, the physical environment has become the key driver, with opportunities for active leisure pursuits within dramatic coastal scenery, e.g. New Zealand.

As Brodie and Winter (2007) suggest, it seems difficult to imagine that the seaside in its multiple forms will ever lose its appeal and that it will always remain a special place in our hearts and minds. The same may also be true of the rural environment, to which attention now turns in the next chapter.

Discussion questions

1. Why is the coast described as a liminal landscape?

2. How has the coast developed and changed over the last two hundred years as a leisure landscape?

3. What are the main problems with managing visitor use of the beach and coastal environment? Outline some of the major conflicts and possible solutions which a manager may advocate.

4. How might climate change and global warming affect the future use of the coast as a leisure resource?

References

Berry, S. (2000) 'Pleasure gardens in Georgian and Regency seaside resorts: Brighton 1750-1840', *Garden History* 28 (2): 222–30.

Boevers, J. (2008) 'Assessing the utility of beach ecolabels for use by local management', *Coastal Management* 36 (5): 524–31.

Booth, D. (2001) *Australian Beach Cultures: The History of Sun, Sand and Surf,* Frank Cass: London.

Breton, F., Clapés, J., Marquès, A. and Priestley, G.K. (1996) 'The recreational use of beaches and consequences for the development of new trends in management: The case of the beaches of the Metropolitan Region of Barcelona (Catalonia, Spain)', *Ocean and Caostal Management* 32 (3): 153–80.

Brodie, A. and Winter, G. (2007) *England's Seaside Resorts,* English Heritage: London.

Carson, R. (1951) *The Sea Around Us,* Oxford University Press: Oxford.

Corbin, A. (1995) *The Lure of the Sea. The Discovery of the Seaside 1750–1840,* Penguin: London.

Dixon, J. and Durrheim, K. (2004) 'Dislocating identity: Desegregation and the transformation of place', *Journal of Environmental Psychology* 24: 455–73.

Durie, A.J. and Huggins, M.J. (1998) 'Sport, social tone and the seaside resorts of Great Britain, c.1850-1914', *International Journal of the History of Sport* 15 (1): 173–87.

Dwight, R.H., Brinks, M.V., SharavanaKumar, G. and Semenza, J.C. (2007) 'Beach attendance and bathing rates for Southern Californian beaches', *Ocean and Coastal Management* 50: 847–58.

Edney, J.J. and Jordan-Edney, N.L. (1974) 'Territorial spacing on a beach', *Sociometry* 37 (1): 92–104.

Gilbert, E.W. (1939) 'The growth of inland and seaside health resorts in England', *Scottish Geographical Journal* 55 (1): 16–35.

Hall, C.M. and Page, S.J. (2006) *The Geography of Tourism and Recreation,* 3rd edn, Routledge: London.

Hassan, J. (2003) *The Seaside, Health and the Environment in England and Wales Since 1800*, Ashgate: Aldershot.

Heatwole, C.A. and West, N.C. (1980) 'Mass transit and beach access in New York City', *Geographical Review* 70 (2): 210–17.

Hewitt, J. (1995) 'East Coast joys: Tom Purvis and the LNER', *Journal of Design History* 8 (4): 291–311.

Houghton, D.S. (1989) 'Some aspects of beach use in the Perth metropolitan area', *Australian Geographer* 20 (2): 173–84.

Hugill, P.J. (1975) 'Social conduct on the Golden Mile', *Annals of the Association of American Geographers* 65 (2): 214–28.

Inglis, F. (2000) *The Delicious History of the Holiday*, Routledge: London.

Kildow, J. and Colgan, M. (2005) *California's Ocean Economy*, Report to the Resources Agency, State of California. National Ocean Economics Program, California.

Land Use Consultants (2007) *A Review of Marine and Coastal Recreation in Scotland*, Scottish Natural Heritage Commissioned Report 247 (ROAME No. FO5AA608).

Lenček, L. and Bosker, G. (1999) *The Beach. The History of Paradise on Earth*, Pimlico: London.

Mercer, D. (1972) 'Beach usage in the Melbourne region', *Australian Geographer* 12 (2): 123–39.

Nelson, C. and Botterill, D. (2002) 'Evaluating the contribution of beach quality awards to the local tourism industry in Wales – the Green Coast Award', *Ocean and Coastal Management* 45: 157–70.

Page, S. J. (2006) *Tourism Management: Managing for Change*, 2nd edn, Butterworth-Heinemann: Oxford.

Page, S. J. and Connell, J. (2009) *Tourism: A Modern Synthesis*, 3rd edn, Cengage Learning: London.

Phillips, M.R. and House, C. (2009) 'An evaluation of priorities for beach tourism: Case studies from South Wales, UK', *Tourism Management*, 30: 176–83.

Preston-Whyte, R. (2001) 'Constructed leisure space: the seaside at Durban', *Annals of Tourism Research* 28 (3): 581–96.

Roca, E. and Villares, M. (2008) 'Public perceptions for evaluating beach quality in urban and semi-natural environments', *Ocean and Coastal Management* 51: 314–29.

Ryan, C. (2007) 'Surfing and windsurfing', in G. Jennings (ed.) *Water-based Tourism, Sport, Leisure and recreation Experiences*, Butterworth-Heinemann: Oxford, pp. 95–111.

Ryan, C. (2002) 'Memories of the beach', in C. Ryan (ed.) The *Tourist Experience*, 2nd edn, Continuum: London, pp. 156–71.

Scott, T., Russell, P., Masselin, G., Wooler, A. and Short, A. (2007) 'Beach rescue statistics and their relation to nearshore morphology and hazards: a case study for Southwest England', *Journal of Coastal Research*, Special Issue 50: 1–6.

Shields, R. (1991) *Places on the Margin*, Routledge: London.

Smith, H.W. (1981) 'Territorial spacing on a beach revisited: a cross-national exploration', *Social Psychology Quarterly* 44 (2): 132–7.

Taussig, M. (2000) 'The beach (a fantasy)', *Critical Inquiry* 26 (2): 249–78.

TNS Travel and Tourism (2004) *Report of the 2002-3 GB Day Visits Survey*, TNS: Edinburgh. Sponsored by British Waterways, The Countryside Agency, Countryside Council for Wales, Department for Culture, Media and Sport, Environment Agency,

Forestry Commission, Scottish Natural Heritage, VisitBritain, VisitScotland, Wales Tourist Board.

Travis, J. (1997) 'Continuity and change in English sea-bathing, 1730–1900: a case of swimming with the tide', in S. Fisher (ed.) *Recreation and the Sea*, University of Exeter Press: Exeter, pp. 8–35.

Tudor, D.T. and Williams, A.T. (2006) 'A rationale for beach selection by the public on the coast of Wales, UK', *Area* 38 (2): 153–64.

Tunstall, S.M. and Penning-Rowsell, E.C. (1998) 'The English beach: experiences and values', *The Geographical Journal* 164 (3): 319–32.

Veblen, T. (1899) *The Theory of the Leisure Class: An Economic Study in the Evolution of Institutions*, Macmillan: New York.

Wall, G. (1972) 'Socio-economic variations in pleasure-trip patterns: the case of Hull car-owners', *Transactions of the Institute of British Geographers* 57: 45–58.

Walton, J.K. (1983) *The English Seaside Resort: A Social History 1750–1914*, Leicester University Press: Leicester.

Walton, J. (1992) *Fish and Chips and the British Working Class 1870–1940*, Leicester University Press: Leicester.

Walton, J.K. (2000) *The British Seaside: Holidays and Resorts in the Twentieth Century*, Manchester University Press: Manchester.

West, N. (2005) 'Beach use and behaviors', in M.L. Schwartz (ed.) *Encyclopaedia of Coastal Science*, Springer: Netherlands, pp. 181–3.

Wheaton, B. (2007) 'Identity, politics and the beach: environmental activism in Surfers Against Sewage', *Leisure Studies* 26 (3): 279–302.

Wolch, J. and Zhang, J. (2004) 'Beach recreation, cultural diversity and attitudes toward nature', *Journal of Leisure Research* 36 (3): 414–43.

11 Rural leisure

Learning outcomes

After reading this chapter, you should be able to:

- Identify the characteristics of rural areas as settings for leisure and recreation
- Differentiate between different rural leisure resources and their use by various groups of users
- Outline the main arguments associated with the urbanising of rural leisure and the reasons why this has created conflicts in leisure environments

Introduction

Rural areas and the evolution of leisure

Rural areas have featured prominently in the evolution of leisure, particularly in the pre-industrial period when the majority of the population's leisure activities occurred in the countryside and within a local rural setting. During the pre-industrial period, two distinct types of leisure could be discerned: *first*, leisure occurring in purpose-built leisure landscapes, such as in and around the European country house and American ante-bellum southern mansion in landscaped settings designed for elites and the wealthy for socialising; *second*, the domestic leisure of the working classes, which was aligned to the agricultural seasons and historic events and celebrations undertaken in the rural setting. During the industrialisation of many nations in the nineteenth century, rural areas began to evolve in more diverse ways as settings for passive and active leisure for the social elites, as improved access and transport created fashionable rural leisure pursuits (e.g. sports such as hunting and shooting, sightseeing and the development of rural second homes). In most countries, the nineteenth century marks the creation of the countryside as a leisure resource along with more remote wilderness areas.

These leisure landscapes were then popularised by social elites, creating a demand for leisure and turning many of them into tourism destinations. This was embodied in the creation and popularisation of the image of the Lake District as a recreational landscape by Romantic poets such as Wordsworth, and the Trossachs in Scotland by Sir Walter Scott, reflecting the emergence of a middle-class-led fascination with nature and the environment. This formed the basis of the subsequent national park movement in different countries in the late nineteenth century (and later in other countries such as the UK), with the concerns for the loss of such landscapes in the future. As Wearing (2003) suggests, in the USA there were three main reasons for the concern with protecting natural resources: first, the closing of the American frontier in the late nineteenth century and desire to protect areas as public lands; second, a sea-change occurred in the way people viewed nature, in part reflecting the impact of the Romantic movement and negative effects of urban industrialisation; third, political leadership by notable figures such as John Muir whose ideas influenced politicians such as Theodore Roosevelt who was instrumental in laying the foundations of future legislation to protect natural areas. Much of this then led to the preservation and use of wilderness and other rural landscapes as highly valued environments, in much the same way as the coast was discovered and popularised, as discussed in Chapter 10.

This initial popularisation was gradually expanded to other social groups after 1918 as discussed in Chapter 2, with a growth in outdoor activities in the countryside in many countries in the 1920s and 1930s. This was followed by a substantial post-war boom in demand for leisure trips to rural areas which has been described as the democratisation of rural leisure, as 'universal [rural] leisure is an entirely post-war phenomenon' (Bunce 1994: 98). One consequence is that it created much of the accelerated use, impact and perceived urbanisation of rural leisure, as observed by Bracey (1970).

Leisure activities have certainly transformed many rural landscapes since the industrial period, as an increasingly urbanising population in many developed countries saw the open spaces and qualities of the rural areas (e.g. peace and quiet, traditional ways of life, and a break from the rigours of urban life) as major attractions for leisure (Figure 11.1). In theoretical terms, the changing role of rural areas as a setting for leisure is part of what Perkins (2003: 243) describes as 'capitalism's propensity for constant change means that landscapes

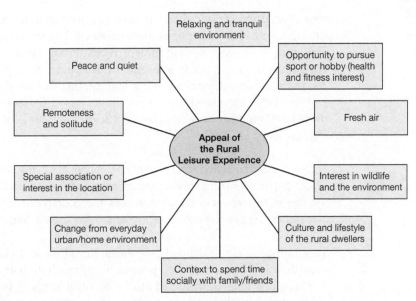

Figure 11.1 Elements of the countryside that contribute to the rural leisure experience

Source: Adapted from Page and Getz (1997)

and the experiences of people who live in them, or who visit them for various purposes, are constantly changing'. It is this process of change which has brought such major transformations to rural areas in the post-war period, not least of which are manifest in leisure. This is compounded by the competing land uses in rural areas, as 'in the countryside, unlike the town, few areas are devoted exclusively to recreation: recreation use must compete with agriculture, forestry, water abstraction, mineral extraction and military training' (Patmore 1983: 124) as illustrated in some of the seminal studies of land use and leisure (e.g. Coppock 1966; Bagnall *et al.* 1978; Carhart 1920; Goodall and Whittow 1975). Therefore, leisure and recreation has:

- created impacts on the rural environment through increased levels of activity since the post-war period;

- generated conflicts between

  - Visitors pursuing leisure and recreation.

  - Residents and recreationists, with the demand for increased access and use of land which often has other immediate uses (e.g. agriculture, water areas and reservoirs).

  - Residents and residents, where rural in-migration creates a new population with different social values and attitudes to rural areas to those of existing residents.

These impacts can best be appreciated by briefly examining the expansion of the scale of demand for use of rural leisure resources in different settings. For example, in the post-war period, the growth in demand for rural recreation rose at an unprecedented rate of 10% per annum in the period 1945 to 1958 in the USA and 10 to 15% per annum up to 1973 in the UK (Hall and Page 2006). This simply shows how significant recreational demand was for rural areas, which has not lessened in subsequent time periods: it persists and continues. As discussed in earlier chapters, it was against this background of growth that Dower (1965) identified the *fourth wave*, based on recreation, which led Patmore (1983) to acknowledge the significance and scale of rural leisure and recreation, as

> countryside recreation is no new phenomenon, but in the last two decades . . . consequent pressure on fragile environments, has fully justified Dower's vision of a great surge in townspeople breaking across the countryside, the fourth wave. By any measure, the phenomenon is of immense significance. *(Patmore 1983: 124)*

This immense significance has continued, albeit at a slower rate of absolute growth, but with a continued geographical reach in many countries.

There is a long tradition of studying rural areas in relation to leisure pursuits, especially the active pursuits embodied in outdoor recreation which we will examine later in the chapter. Yet as Case Study 11.1 shows, our understanding of rural leisure as leisure undertaken among residents of the countryside is greatly neglected, with much of the research attention in the post-war period devoted to countryside users who are not rural dwellers, epitomised in the popular studies of countryside recreation (e.g. Glyptis 1991; Harrison 1991; Robinson 1999).

Case Study 11.1   Rural resident's leisure

There are surprisingly few detailed studies of the leisure habits and activities of rural residents (Ventris 1980 is a notable exception covering a wide range of issues). This makes the analysis of their lives leisure behaviour problematic, especially the role of leisure in community life (see McCormick and McGuire 1996). This is even more surprising, given the rich history of studying rural communities documented in seminal studies such as Bracey (1970), which highlight many of the characteristics of different rural areas and their communities. But few of the studies provide an adequate review of the transformations occurring in rural residents' leisure in spite of the changes occurring in agriculture and the rural economy and society. What the early studies of rural life and leisure chart are the impact of societal changes associated with the transformation in their relative isolation and access in the early twentieth century and the growing mobility of rural residents in the post-war period. For example, Coleman *et al.* (2007) examined the leisure habits of many remoter rural residents in 1920s and 1930s America who drove to their nearest small towns on Saturday nights for a leisure experience which was focused on activities provided on Main Street. This was one way of overcoming the isolation of rural lives and socialising with other people in view of the problems faced by rural residents. The importance of social contact in more remote communities has been widely studied and the introduction of the telephone in North America is widely attributed as helping to give rural women an opportunity for social interaction in the 1920s and 1930s. Even so, other studies (e.g. Melvin *et al.* 1971) indicated that in 1930s America, communities were slow to recognise the needs of youth and their recreational needs (a feature also observed by OECD (2003) as continuing to impact on youth migration from rural areas).

In traditional rural communities, where agriculture dominated, the role of the church and Sunday school played a major role in youth life up to adolescence, and youth leisure was closely linked to family leisure. Innovations in society such as the radio and television had a much greater impact upon rural leisure in relation to breaking down the relative isolation felt in relation to popular culture, adding new activities to traditional ones such as reading (which was also constrained in many rural communities by poor library facilities). This was a feature observed by Rowntree and Lavers' (1951) survey of *English Life and Leisure*, which provides a fascinating snapshot of rural leisure in mid-twentieth-century Britain (and the case studies of other European countries), where four principal social institutions were highlighted in structuring rural leisure: the village hall, the public house, the church and Women's Institutes. What this highlights is an important role for voluntary organisations and commercial leisure (excluding the village hall where it was a public sector managed facility and not linked to the local church).

What these insights on earlier studies of rural residents leisure show is a continuity in the relatively limited access to different leisure resources, in contrast to urban areas (Anderson 1960, 1963). These leisure constraints and the reality of rural residents' leisure are summarised in a comprehensive manner by Sharma (2007: 27) where

> There are often neglected issues of rural residents' leisure and recreation. Other than for access to open countryside, there is a hierarchy of recreational facilities which leaves rural residents at a disadvantage. While villages may possess a football pitch and sometimes, even a swimming pool or a squash court, they will not have cinemas, major spectator arenas or leisure centres. Access to these depend on mobility and distance, and the social filter of accessibility.

What this quotation shows is that it is not economically viable to provide certain types of public or commercial leisure and recreation for residents in these communities, often typified by prevailing government debates over maintaining basic service provision for many remoter communities in relation to banks, schools, Post Offices, village shops and basic services such as petrol stations, bus services, doctors and libraries. Many of these services are provided on a limited basis, reflecting the challenge many rural communities face, where access to a car becomes a necessity to travel to services now located outside of the immediate rural community. As Ventris (1980) highlights, there are also significant differences between rural communities, reflecting the different types of rural areas. The result is that rural residents may have limited access to leisure services and facilities and access will often depend upon affluence and social class.

Different studies of rural communities have highlighted the varied social composition of rural residents, drawing distinctions between those who have been born and who grew up in the community and those perceived as 'outsiders' or 'incomers' (especially urbanites), euphemistically described in some remoter rural areas as 'blow ins', such as in Cornwall. What these labels illustrate is the existence of a social gradient within rural communities, with different groups who have differential access to leisure opportunities. These contrasts are accentuated when the incoming population bring not only urban attitudes, but a greater focus on conspicuous consumption. These social contrasts may be further compounded when a particular village or area has a large visitor population who also display these attributes (e.g. the influx of urban visitors at a weekend with their four-wheel drives and affluence seeking to emulate a pastiche association with their notion of rural life). This questions the perceived image of content and passive rural dwellers, particularly where regulation of the countryside continues to seek to emulate a moral and idealised citizen through the use of Codes of Conduct such as the Country Code in the UK (see Parker 2005). These Codes introduce rules which impact upon daily life and practices in rural environments (e.g. agriculture), especially in relation to growing debates on access to rural land for leisure. Such debates are embodied in the excellent overview by Shoard (1999) and other reviews of the implications of growing demands for access to rural land (see Curry 2001 for a case study of New Zealand and the issues of indigenous people's land rights).

Therefore, what we need to emphasise from this case study is that conflict is also an underlying theme in rural residents' leisure, where conflicts occur with the growing urban influences on the countryside, especially where residents have much less access to the opportunities afforded to urban dwellers. This generates an 'us' and 'them' culture where affluence and urbanised values clash with rural values. Consequently, rural residents' leisure lives face different structural barriers and constraints, ironically, which many urbanites seek to emulate (i.e. escape from the trappings of urban life and conspicuous consumption for the simplicity of the rural environment), excluding, of course, their prized possession and symbol of their status – their car(s). Visitors also have very changeable views of the countryside (see Macnaughten 1995), which illustrates the changing attitudes that urban dwellers have to rural leisure, which are not as stable as many had previously thought, to ensure the long-term preservation of rural environments. The social and economic polarity caused by the in-migration of urban residents to rural areas, with some households possessing three cars in an urban or semi-urban setting, portrays the inequalities that now exist: some rural residents have no access to cars and are dependent upon public transport or are forced to pay inflated prices for petrol, a problem that has been highlighted in the Highlands and Islands of Scotland. Equally, other social groups (e.g. ethnic minorities) are also under-represented in the consumption of rural environments (see Bengston *et al.* 2008) and rural communities. There is certainly a need for us to study and understand rural residents' leisure in more depth to understand some of these apparent inequalities, their effect on the residents' leisure behaviour and the social and cultural impacts of visitors on their residential environment, which suggest we need to consider the analysis of these issues in relation to the associated concepts of leisure, recreation and tourism.

Rural leisure, recreation and tourism: blurred boundaries?

The areas of leisure and tourism in rural areas have been studied largely in isolation as the activities classified as outdoor recreation have been separated from those undertaken by tourists. Yet in recent years, there has also been a growing recognition that to differentiate between leisure, recreation and tourist visitor activities in rural settings may be almost irrelevant (Hall and Page 2006), because in some cases, the attitudes, activities and perceptions of those engaged in leisure pursuits in the countryside are similar (only differentiated by the fact that tourists are staying overnight or longer in the locality and using different travel patterns to reach the area). In this chapter, we are focusing on the wider notion of leisure and so we do not distinguish between leisure and tourism, unless there are specific differences, such as their demand for overnight accommodation which may yield a greater economic impact on rural areas as a result of staying visits (see Page and Connell 2009 for a more detailed analysis of rural tourism). What we wish to stress here, in a rural context, is that the setting, attitudes and behaviour of the individual or group rather than the category of visitor shape the type of activity and effect on the rural environment. However, the subtle difference lies in the distinction between the resident and their leisure versus the non-resident visitor and tourist.

In rural leisure and recreation, one of the defining features of the resulting leisure experiences is the focus on environmentally related resources, meaning that the impacts which occur are more visible and visual in the natural environment than the artificial environments of many urban areas. On this basis, it is not surprising to find rural areas being singled out for special treatment because of their natural environmental resource base. As Patmore (1983: 123) argued, 'outdoor recreation in rural areas rapidly achieves a distinctive character of its own and needs separate consideration for more than convention'. This special treatment, along with the transformations occurring in rural leisure, is sufficient justification for this chapter. Two specific features of rural leisure also mark it out for special treatment:

- In contrast to urban recreation, the variety of rural leisure resources which exist (real and imagined) are much greater in scale, scope and diversity.

- Rural areas have greater amounts of open space, conveying an image of freedom, with an increased potential to accommodate multiple activities.

But before identifying some of the significant issues associated with rural leisure, it is pertinent to examine what we mean by the term *rural*.

What do we mean by rural?

Defining the term *rural* has remained a protracted problem within the social sciences, as there has been little consensus on what attributes to focus on and how to accommodate its changing meaning in a postmodern society (see Woods 2009, for example). Some countries use population criteria to define rural, as in the USA where Flora *et al.* (1992) reviewed the diversity of approaches used by different public sector bodies. For example, one definition took a population of less than 2500 for a settlement or area as a basis for defining a rural area. There are a multitude of problems in adopting definitions based on one type of quantitative variable such as population size or density because we need to appreciate that 'rural can be perceived as a place of safety, with social values, surrounded by open space and natural beauty, where one is treated respectfully and friendly' (Long and Lane 2000: 301). Such subjective evaluations highlight the problem of selecting specific variables to try to and define the term *rural*. In addition, it has been complicated by the use of a similar term, *countryside*, which is often used interchangeably with the word *rural*. As Page and Connell (2009: 495) argue, the term rural has been examined in three ways:

- As anything which is non-urban, particularly land which is beyond the urban fringe, although this means defining rural environments in a negative way as the opposite of urban environments.

- By examining the elements of the countryside or functions of rural space, which describes different elements of rural areas such as their low population density, visual elements and nature of the settlement pattern and land use in rural areas.

- Perception-based and/or user-based definitions, which look at what people think the term *rural* means. For example, Halfacree (1995) suggests that individuals will look at rural environments in different ways depending on

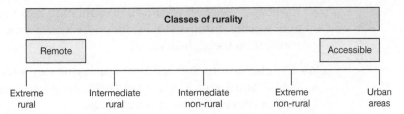

Figure 11.2 Index of rurality

Source: Page and Connell (2009: 496)

what they do within the environment, ranging from living and working there through to consuming the environment for leisure and recreation. Such behavioural approaches mean that the term rural is highly subjective and individualised.

To try to provide a degree of coherence in defining rural areas, Cloke (1977) produced an index of rurality. As Figure 11.2 shows, Cloke identified two distinct types of rural areas:

- The *remote rural area*, which was very distant from urban areas, with a declining, static or modestly increasing population, an ageing population structure and declining employment opportunities as well as high costs per capita of providing basic services (see Bonn *et al.* 2008 for a recent review of remote rural areas).

- The *accessible rural area*, which was defined by its relative proximity to urban areas, with an increasing population due to high levels of commuting, a youthful population structure and high levels of car ownership.

This useful distinction between two types of rural area built on previous studies of rural areas and the differentiation based on accessibility. It reinforces the debate on the significance of rural areas for leisure and accessibility to the urban population, a feature identified by Cracknell (1967) in terms of the short-distance nature of many countryside trips and also observed by Wall (1971) and Glyptis (1981). Such research on accessibility and transport, discussed earlier in the book, underlines the importance of mobility as a critical factor in shaping patterns of use.

Halfacree (1993) provided a synthesis of the specific approaches developed to define rural areas based on the existing research activity within the social sciences, comprising:

- *Descriptive approaches*, which look at the countryside and describe it using empirical data and measures such as the Census and other indicators of rurality such as levels of public service provision.

- *Socio-cultural approaches*, which look at the different attributes of the people that live in the countryside as well as their behaviour and attitudes.

- Rural areas as *localities*, where their defining characteristics and distinctive qualities are what make these specific places rural.

- *Rural as a social representation*, examining how rural areas are perceived and socially constructed by individuals and groups, reflecting developments from social theory.

We can also add to this series of approaches an interesting framework presented by Murdoch and Marsden (1994), based on rural change, which highlights four different types of countryside:

- *The preserved countryside*, which characterises those accessible rural areas with residents who adopt anti-development and preservation attitudes (characterised by self-interest, which is often described as *Nimbyism – Not in My Backyard*).

- *The contested countryside*, which is outside of the influence of the main or urban commuter zones, but has an attraction for farmers and developers who wish to push through plans and projects in relation to economic development, such as leisure.

- *The paternalistic countryside*, characterised by large estates and tenant farms where local landowners adopt a traditional or long-term view of this environment.

- *The clientelist countryside*, which characterises remote rural areas dominated by agriculture and is dependent upon state subsidies for their economic rationale and services.

Yet this classification highlights the complicating factor – the term *countryside*. As Ravenscroft and Parker (2003: 84) suggest, 'there is no universally accepted definition of countryside, often being associated with farmed and rural landscapes'. They suggest that one way the term countryside may be understood is to recognise a continuum of rural spaces, in much the same way that Cloke (1977) devised the index of rurality. In the case of the continuum, Ravenscroft and Parker (2003) identified the categories of countryside shown in Figure 11.3, using the English categorisation of rural spaces. According to Ravenscroft and

Urban area	Peri-urban green spaces	Lowland farmed countryside	Remote rural areas
Types of countryside	←		→
Characteristics of each type of countryside	• Accessibility to urban population • Functionally linked to urban areas, socially, economically and culturally • Dominant leisure and recreation uses from urban population	• Network of regional urban service centres, market towns and other settlement types such as villages • Localised economies with agriculture and other rural business activities • Focus of many forms of postmodern leisure and tourism	• Will include upland areas through to wilderness areas • Limited number of settlements and sparse population • Limited opportunities for income generation • Extensive livestock farming • Dependence on European Union agricultural subsidies and assistance • Small-scale tourism and recreation

Figure 11.3 The countryside continuum in England

Source: Based on Ravenscroft and Parker (2003: 84)

Parker (2003), it is the middle category in Figure 11.3 (lowland farmed country-side) where the countryside is most widely recognised as being located geographically and in social constructions of its existence. Furthermore, this category also attracts the majority of urbanised rural leisure activity. While rural areas are in a constant state of change, a number of transformations are changing rural areas as settings for leisure, compounded by the impacts associated with such changes. For this reason, it is useful to explore some of these transformations a stage further.

Understanding transformations and changes in rural areas as settings for leisure and recreation

What these different perspectives on the term rural (and the associated term countryside) highlight is that there is no one all-embracing definition we can use. The transformations which have occurred in rural areas since 1945 in many countries have impacted upon the traditional definitions and concept of rurality, particularly as the associations we have with rural places have changed. What we need to recognise is that 'a centrally defining feature of the post industrialisation of the countryside of many Western nations, has been the growing significance of recreation, leisure and tourism, as both social practices and as primary uses of land' (Ravenscroft and Parker 2003: 85). Social practices in this context refers to the way in which leisure as a social construction influences what people do, where and why they engage in activities in their leisure time in rural settings. Many of these changes in rural areas have been market driven, and forces of opposition can be discerned between the traditional views and leisure habits of countryside residents and those of urban leisure visitors. These have come into conflict, as illustrated in the UK in the debates over fox hunting which have vehemently polarised the views over the appropriate use of the countryside as a leisure space. For example, in England it is estimated that 370,000 people shoot game and this uses around 8.5 million ha of land, geographically concentrated in Eastern England, Southern England and the West Midlands. It ultimately illustrates the conflict between tradition and a resistance to urban attitudes towards cruelty to animals and debates over the way nature should be idealised and created for the leisure consumption of specific groups. This is interesting, as it fits within the emerging research studies on leisure as a form of resistance, highlighting a political dimension to leisure (see Shaw 2006 for more detail on this evolving area of study).

Macro processes such as globalisation, economic and social change are further shaping rural environments and the leisure needs of different groups, which have assumed different meanings in a postmodern society. As Cloke (1992) suggests, developments in social theory combined with these underlying changes in the postmodern society mean that we need to look at the ways in which the meaning of rural is constructed, negotiated and experienced, as illustrated in Figure 11.4. In fact, Cloke (1992: 55) has suggested that one way to

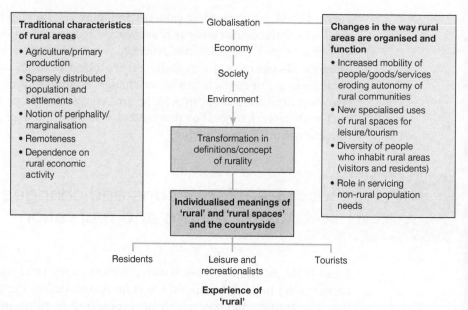

Figure 11.4   Changing dimensions of the concept of rurality

approach the analysis of rural areas and the countryside is to recognise that it has been commodified into products and experiences, which are now the basis for the analysis of activities such as rural leisure and recreation. This has a degree of resonance with the debate in Chapter 9 on the experience economy and experiences of leisure, where rural landscapes are being transformed into leisure experiences, from the simple sightseeing of landscape features to those which have been re-imaged and branded, based on media images and icons, such as *Heartbeat Country* in Yorkshire, following the popular and long-running television drama – *Heartbeat*. Interestingly, Cloke (1992: 55) argues that many of these rural transformations in a postmodern society have led to the following consequences:

> The countryside . . . [is] . . . an exclusive place to be lived in; rural communities [are considered] as a context to be bought and sold; rural lifestyle [is something] which can be colonised; icons of rural culture [are commodities] can be crafted, packaged and marketed; rural landscapes [are imbued] with a new range of potential from 'pay as you enter' national parks, [and] the sites for the theme park explosion.

The implications of Cloke's (1992) quotation are that since the 1990s, there have been many attempts at commodifying rural spaces, although this is not really a new phenomenon: what is new is the speed and scale of development that is unprecedented in rural areas. Above all, these changes are a direct result of the urbanising forces affecting the countryside identified in many of the seminal studies of rural areas (e.g. Bracey 1970; Clout 1972; Davidson and Wibberley 1977). These urban forces have simply gathered momentum and increasing complexity, as Cloke's (1992) insights suggest. For example, new processes of change occurring include a growth in rural re-population in many lowland environments, which is part of a process of reverse migration, in part stimu-lated by middle-class pursuit of the rural idyll and a rejection of the urban. These regenerative effects have changed the social structure and composition of many rural areas, as 'incomers' bring their urban attitudes, seeking to urbanise the countryside to fit their ideals and values of what it should be. Equally, many urbanites moving to rural settlements are shocked that the countryside is not a quiet idyllic setting, but a working landscape where agricultural practices and smells do not meet with their predominantly urban sensibilities.

The rural environment and countryside is not a static entity to be kept in a time warp or vacuum: it has a definite economic rationale, albeit in state of change. The countryside is also actively used by non-rural interests, especially recreationists, reflecting the different stakeholders which need to be recognised in rural recreation (see Long *et al.* 1988 for an example). The result is that the relationship between leisure, rural areas and their landscapes has changed, be-cause leisure activities are now a dominant element in many of these landscapes to a much greater degree than they were in the past. Butler *et al.* (1998: 8) explain the nature of this transformation occurring in rural areas as settings for leisure, recreation and tourism where:

> one of the major elements of change in rural areas has been the changes within rec-reation and tourism. Until the last two decades or so, recreation and tourist activities in rural areas were mostly related closely to the rural character of the setting. They were primarily activities which were different to those engaged in urban centres . . . They could be characterised, at the risk of generalisation, by the following terms: relaxing, or passive, nostalgic, traditional, low technological, and mostly non-competitive.

But as Pigram and Jenkins (2006) suggest,

> whereas the above activities are still common, many other quite different activities are now engaged in, which bring new forms of conflict and impact, requiring differ-ent planning and management responses. These new activities could be charac-terised as: active, competitive, prestigious or fashionable, highly technological, high-risk, modern, individual and fast. *(Pigram and Jenkins 2006: 219)*

In other words, rural areas are being subjected to a much wider range of leisure and recreation activities, each competing for space, creating planning issues and transforming the traditional image of the rural idyll. One dimension of this change in the growth in adventurous activities (as discussed in Case study 11.2 later).

These changes in the growing diversity and increasing fragmentation of leisure have placed greater demands on multiple use of recreational spaces. Accompanying these changes is the shift towards a greater private sector in-volvement in rural leisure, with capital investment in activity centres and other sites for adventure activities and private operators making extensive use of public sites. Consequently, in seeking to try to conceptualise rural leisure based on some of the traditional analyses (e.g. Simmons 1975) and more recent studies (e.g. Page and Getz 1997; Butler *et al.* 1998), we need to recognise that

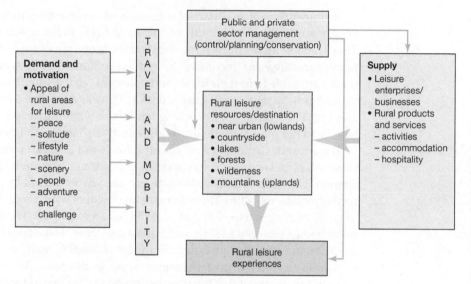

Figure 11.5 Conceptualising rural leisure

there are a number of elements which combine to create rural leisure experiences. As Figure 11.5 shows, there is a demand from consumers, resulting in their mobility in the countryside. This is occurring in parallel with the provision of supply by businesses which are regulated by different public sector agencies which seek to balance conservation goals alongside the leisure use of different rural resources. The issue of transport, as we discussed earlier and elsewhere in the book, is a highly contentious aspect of rural leisure and recreation because of issues of congestion, increased environmental impacts and pollution and an inability of most governments' transport policies to address issues of social exclusion.

Despite the issue of access and transport, 'there is no sharp discontinuity between urban and rural resources for recreation and rather a complete continuum from local park to remote mountain park' (Patmore 1983: 122), which, combined with the discussion of the concept of the countryside, reinforces how conventional distinctions of urban and rural may also be blurring. Such blurring may be compounded by the urban values dominating the supply and consumption of rural leisure, as a commoditised experience. Despite this blurring, as a result of the transformations now affecting rural areas, Patmore (1983) highlighted three distinct elements of rural resources which still remain significant for leisure:

● *The visual character of the resource* provides much of the quality, stimulation and satisfaction with rural leisure. The different ways in which people perceive scenery and its recreational value have led to the development of the concept of landscape evaluation (Wylie 2007). Landscape evaluation emerged in the 1960s, with notable studies (e.g. Penning-Rowsell 1975; Appleton 1974) illustrating how we need to focus on the aesthetic elements of landscape and the ways in which we understand the value and meaning in terms of leisure. Traditional research methods involved an individual assigning a score to a specific visual setting (which is now considerably more sophisticated with the introduction of GIS). But this does not adequately accommodate the multiple meanings people can hold for specific landscapes. What these techniques seek to explore is the value associated with individual landscape elements such as their geological features, land cover, built forms and other artificial elements.

● Rural environments provide the recreational opportunity for outdoor pursuits in different terrains and settings, offering a physical challenge (see Case Study 11.2 later). An illustration of the degree of recreational variety which exists in rural environments is reflected in the existence of resource types for rural leisure and recreation such as forests, national parks and other protected areas, the urban fringe, linear resources (e.g. canals and redundant railway lines), water resources and the coastal fringe where it has a rural dimension.

What this creates is a wide spectrum of resource types and a wide range of settings in which the public sector has progressively intervened in the post-war period to manage the impacts of leisure, especially at pressured locations.

Contemporary issues in rural leisure

Rural areas have gone through a series of dramatic transformations in the post-war period in most countries, and as Figure 11.6 suggests, these transformations have affected rural areas and the way in which they have been constructed and used for leisure. Figure 11.6 illustrates that as a result of these transformations, a number of principal changes have occurred in rural areas that have an important bearing on the nature of rural leisure and recreation.

One of the most profound changes, as discussed already, is the shift from passive to active uses of the countryside so that urban lifestyles and values and leisure pursuits have been transported into the countryside, which we have termed the *urbanisation of rural leisure*. This almost makes the distinction of leisure, recreation and tourism an artificial distinction because of the post-war democratisation of leisure, accelerated by the commoditisation of rural leisure experiences. One notable dimension, Cloke (1992) highlighted, is the way in which rural areas have been re-imaged to appeal to different markets.

At the same time, rural areas have been restructured, which is changing the economic and social basis of many communities, making them more dependent upon new sources of employment such as leisure and tourism. This is because traditional land uses such as agriculture, mineral extraction, forestry and other land-extensive activities have been restructured through increased mechanisation, reducing the demand for rural labour. There have also been significant landscape changes as a result of this mechanisation, such as the removal of

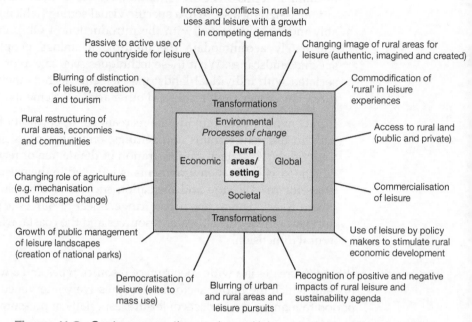

Figure 11.6 Contemporary themes in rural leisure and recreation since 1945

Sources: Developed from Butler, Hall and Jenkins (1998); Author; Pigram and Jenkins (2006)

hedgerows and field boundaries to make mechanised agricultural production easier. These industrialised agricultural landscapes have transformed many rural ecosystems, threatening their biodiversity and removing ancient natural features in the landscape, such as hedgerows which encourage biodiversity, as well as transforming the rural idyllic images of the countryside. The use of artificial materials like polythene and the use of polytunnels have also affected the visual landscape qualities. While some agencies such as the European Union have attempted to address biodiversity loss through schemes such as agricultural land set-aside, so it is not cultivated and allowed to revert to its natural form, this has had a marginal impact in relation to the wider changes affecting the industrialisation of agriculture since 1945 in most Western countries.

There has been a growing commercialisation of leisure in the countryside as business interests seek out new opportunities to provide leisure experiences for urban users. This growing demand for access to rural land for leisure has led to significant conflicts between rural landowners and recreationalists (Pigram and Jenkins 2006), particularly in countries where there is a significant private land ownership in rural areas. This has posed numerous problems for policy makers who, on the one hand, seek to stimulate rural economic development based on leisure, but fail to recognise the impact of such developments on the resident population. As a result, there is a growing recognition among researchers that rural leisure and the conversion of rural landscapes into playgrounds for urbanites may create positive and negative impacts. This has been encapsulated in many of the debates on sustainability, particularly in relation to National Parks which have seen a significant growth in visitor numbers as a result of the continued popularity of rural areas for leisure. Many of these contemporary issues in rural leisure highlight the importance of adopting more theoretically informed research agendas which can try to explain why these changes are occurring and make sense of their impact on rural leisure, and one interesting line of inquiry is the application of social theory to rural leisure.

Rural leisure, social theory and leisure locales

One of the most notable studies derived from theoretical research by geographers using social theory and its application to leisure, as discussed in Hall and Page (2006), is based on the work of Perkins (1993: 116) who argued that a

> social scientist's primary role is to develop theories about society. Theories are sets of logically inter-related statements about phenomena, such as recreation and leisure. The reason for developing such theories is to help us understand the world humans make for themselves. It is on the basis of the understanding reached in the development of these theories that we plan and manage particular social phenomena

such as leisure. In fact, Perkins (1993) embraces social theory, particularly structuration theory (Giddens 1984), to understand locales as a concept for the analysis of human and spatial interaction. Locales comprise a range of settings which are different and yet connected through interactions. The interactions result from:

> the life path of individuals . . . in ways that reflect patterns of production and consumption. These interactions result in a particular pattern of locales which have social and physical forms. Each life path is essentially an allocation of time between these different locales. A particular mode of production will emphasise dominant locales to which time must be allocated. *(Perkins 1993: 126)*

To understand these issues, especially how rural leisure occurs in time and space, we need to look at the theoretical literature on structuration, to show how structure and human interaction are brought together through the concept of the *locale*. According to Perkins (1993), the dominant locales which affect our daily lives are:

- The home
- Work
- School

and they are settings in which consumption occurs. A leisure locale is also a meaningful concept to explore as a setting for interaction whereby 'people pursue leisure within the context of their life commitments and access to resources' (Perkins 1993: 126). The implications of such theoretically informed analysis suggests that we need to consider the role and organisation of leisure in a rural setting, in relation to the dominant locales (i.e. the home, work and school) and other institutional locales such as religion and the arts. This will then help us to understand how, through the use of structuration theory, we can begin to understand what 'both constrains and enables people to take particular life paths, the collective effect of which is to produce and enable new members of society in their life paths . . . [where] geographical behaviour' (Perkins 1993: 117) occurs in a rural environment.

As Perkins (1993) suggests, in a rural setting we would need to consider both structure and human interaction and how it is all brought together in the context of the locale. One interesting research focus which may prove to be useful in this respect is the focus on the home and house to understand the structural constraints on rural leisure. As Perkins *et al.* (2008) examined in an urban setting, this focus will need to use qualitative research to apply social theory to rural leisure. But an underlying problem, as Perkins *et al.* (2008) highlight, is the artificial segmentation of rural people's daily lives into specific narratives associated with the home, family, work, leisure and transport. In reality, these occur on a continuous basis in space and time. What is telling is the absence of a substantial literature on rural leisure and recreation which has emerged from social theory capable of addressing the ongoing weakness which Butler and Clark (1992: 167) observed in terms of rural tourism (but which also has salience for rural leisure and recreation):

> The literature on rural tourism is sparse and . . . conceptual models and theories are lacking. . . . Many of the references in tourism are case studies with little theoretical foundation . . . or they focus on specific problems. . . . Some take a broader perspective focusing on issues and process. . . . There is, therefore, a lack of theory and models placing rural tourism in a conceptual framework.

This highlights the highly empirical and descriptive nature of much tourism (and leisure-related research) in rural areas which has predominantly focused on a number of geographically focused issues associated with the scale, impact and planning issues arising from the impact of leisure visits to the countryside and rural areas. Consequently, we now focus on the nature of supply and demands issues in rural leisure to understand how these pose management challenges in terms of reconciling impacts with access to the resource base for leisure.

Demand and supply issues in rural leisure

Research on rural leisure in relation to demand issues has predominantly had a geographical focus and many of the seminal studies in the late 1960s and early 1970s (see Hall and Page 2006; Patmore 1983 for a review) sought to highlight a number of common themes:

- The nature of travel patterns and destinations which leisure travelers select.
- The scale of visits at a number of geographical scales (i.e. at a national, regional and local level) to understand recreational behaviour and how this is reflected in micro-level examples, such as Glyptis' (1981) participant

observation of leisure behaviour at Beverly, near Hull in the UK, at one specific countryside site.

● Who goes where, why and with what impact on the rural environment and population.

As Robinson (1990: 260) suggested, the focus on these aspects of leisure demand and rural areas have largely remained unchanged since the 1960s and 1970s (despite the aforementioned discussion on social theory and rural leisure) because:

> various studies have shown that, increasingly, people's leisure time is being used in a space-extensive way: a move from passive recreation to participation. Growth has been fastest in informal pursuits taking the form of day or half-day trips to the countryside; with the rise in the ownership of private cars, the urban population has discovered the recreational potential of both the countryside on its doorstep and also more remote and less occupied areas.

This illustrates that accessibility, travel and the destinations chosen by recreationists are key drivers of change. Combined with these drivers are a greater fragmentation and irregularity of the timing and nature of rural leisure visits, occurring alongside a greater shift from planned to unplanned visits. What this means is that visits do not have the same degree of structure and predictability that we have traditionally associated with the timing, seasonality and structure of rural visits. In other words, the geographical fragmentation and more complex ways in which the *rural* is being consumed in leisure has made the search for new and different experiences a feature of leisure behaviour, especially the pursuit of greater depth in the experience. Even so, trying to uncover these trends and patterns of demand are not necessarily easy to piece together without a shift in the style of research employed to understand rural leisure demand. The traditional approach used by government agencies and other organisations has relied upon the social survey method, which either asks people about their previous experiences (i.e. a reflective recall of leisure habits or experiences) or is based upon site-specific surveys which ultimately are data collection exercises to help leisure and recreation policy makers and planners to understand how to balance the perennial problem in leisure management: how to equate demand with supply. The development of participation studies (e.g. The Outdoor Recreation Resources Review Commission in the USA and the General Household Survey in Britain) typified the use of national surveys which seek to uncover some of the following characteristics of rural leisure demand:

● Participation rates for specific resources and usage rates by different social groups (which help partially assess levels of social exclusion).

● The timing and scale of demand.

● The type of travel involved in getting to the destination.

● Specific profiles of leisure uses, including demographic and economic characteristics of different users.

Two typical examples of the outcome of national surveys by different organisations are shown in Table 11.1 for England and Table 11.2 for the USA.

In each case, the data reported in the surveys which are compiled to create Tables 11.1 and 11.2 are snapshots for a particular time period and they do show the scale and breadth of the rural leisure experiences which people seek. It is also apparent that the urban-based demand for and accessibility to sites (often under 30 miles) has a major impact on the propensity to travel, since

Table 11.1 Characteristics of rural leisure in England – summary statistics

- 763.4 million rural leisure visits in England in 2005
- 74.8 million visits to National Parks
- £13.99 average spend on leisure trips to the countryside per person (£25.09 for all leisure visits in England)
- 70% of leisure expenditure was on fuel, admission tickets, food and drink
- At their destination, the most popular activities were:
  - walking (36%)
  - eating out or drinking (16%)
  - pursuing a hobby/special interest (11%)
  - taking part in sports/active pursuits (7%)
- 79% of respondents were concerned about changes to the countryside, especially issues of biodiversity
- 13.5 million visits were made to National Trails in 2006, 13% by walkers, 5% by cyclists, and under 2% by horse riders; 50% of walkers walk for a day or more
- There were 21.6 million visits to open access land in 2005; of which 93% were to the countryside (and 7% to the coast); visits involved walking, rambling, hill walking, with people travelling almost 30 miles to such sites (compared to 21.5 miles for rural leisure trips)
- Rural leisure trips typically last for 2.10 hours compared to 2.38 hours for open land visits
- The Lake District (22 million) and Peak District (22 million) are the most visited National Parks, followed by the North York Moors (9.5 million) and the Yorkshire Dales (7 million)
- 75% of visits to National Parks is by car, typically involving a 35.4 mile trip and a dwell time of 2.57 hours at the destination
- A significant proportion of visitors (e.g. 25%) are repeat visitors who had visited the same park 11 times in the previous year
- 150.6 million visits were made to inland water areas
- 16.7 million visits were made to National Nature Reserves in 2005/2006, a 3.2 million increase on 2000/2001, the most heavily visited in London and the West Midland conurbations (especially Richmond and Sutton in London) with 3 million and 2.5 million visits respectively
- Principal motivations to visit include:
  - accessibility (i.e. ease to reach)
  - ideal location for outdoor recreation
  - safe environment and welcoming to visitors
  - peace and quiet

Sources: Adapted from Spedding (2008); Natural England (2008)

Table 11.2 Characteristics of recreation day visits in the USA in 2007 – summary statistics

- In 2007, 365 of the 391 sites managed by the National Parks Service received over 275.5 million recreation visits
- 23% of all visits were to National Parks, comprising 62 million visits
- The most visited outdoor site was the Blue Ridge Parkway in North Carolina which attracted 17 million visits (this is a scenic highway which is in a landscaped setting)
- The second most visited outdoor recreation site was the Golden Gate National Recreation Area in San Francisco, California with 14.3 million visits. Similarly Lake Mead National Recreation Area in Arizona with 7.6 million visits. A National Recreation Area is a protected area which has a large reservoir or water body at its heart for recreational use
- In terms of National Parks, the most visited was the Great Smoky Mountains in North Carolina with 9.3 million visits; Grand Canyon, Arizona (4.4 million visits); Yosemite, California (3.5 million visits); Yellowstone, Idaho (3.1 million visits); Olympic, Washington (2.9 million visits); Rocky Mountains, Colorado (2.8 million visits)
- The Nationwide Survey on Recreation and the Environment (NSRE) found in 2004 that the most popular outdoor activities undertaken were:
  - viewing/photographing natural scenery (70%)
  - visiting nature centres (63.5%)
  - driving for pleasure (61%)
  - viewing/photographing wildlife (58%)
  - viewing/photographing wild flowers, trees and plants (57%)
  - visiting the beach (56.9%)
  - swimming in lakes and streams (54%)
  - visiting historic sites (53%)
  - picnicking (52%)
  - boating (44%)
  - viewing/photographing birds (39.8%)
  - day hiking (38%)
  - cycling (37.6%)
  - fishing (37.5%)
  - visiting a wilderness or primitive area (33.6%)

Sources: National Park Service (2008); Nationwide Survey on Recreation and the Environment (2004)

many trips to the countryside do not involve large distances or periods of travel. Even so, some organisations in the UK, such as the Henley Centre/ Headlight Vision (2005), suggest that our appetite for rural leisure may be waning as the shift to indoor leisure has replaced some of the demand for rural trips. This is a debatable point, as snapshot surveys may not necessarily track the trends and potential way in which rural leisure is being transformed or occurring in ways not necessarily covered in social surveys. Some researchers have been critical of the inability of demand-related studies to pick up the more subtle changes occurring in rural leisure trips and experiences, and highlight the importance of also understanding individual perceptions and experiences.

As Hall and Page (2006) point out, perception studies have focused on the following range of themes:

- Perception of scenery and evaluation of landscape quality (as discussed earlier).

- Perception of wilderness, wilderness management, and the psychology of wilderness experience (which we will discuss later).

- Social and psychological carrying capacity (discussed in Chapter 4).

- Behaviour at sites and the social meaning of recreation in relation to particular activities.

- Perceived similarities between recreation activities and their substitutability to reduce pressure on crowded sites.

- Recreation activity preferences.

These studies highlight the importance of perception in relation to the supply of leisure resources in rural areas, to which attention now turns.

Rural leisure supply

As Chapter 5 discussed, there are different approaches which have been used to analyse supply, one of which is to focus on the concept of resources. Two specific approaches have also been used to describe rural leisure supply, which has traditionally involved looking at:

- Classifications of different resources, such as the continuum of resource types as discussed earlier in the chapter, or

- Inventories of the resource and its geographical distribution.

As Hall and Page (2006) suggest, the recreational research by Clawson *et al.* (1960) still remains the popular conceptualisation of rural recreational resources and used in seminal studies of rural recreation (e.g. Simmons 1975); it was subsequently modified a stage further by Hockin *et al.* (1978) who classified land-based recreational activities into:

- Overnight activities (e.g. camping and caravanning).

- Activities involving shooting.

- Activities involving a significant element of organised competition (e.g. golf).

- Activities involving little or no organised competition (e.g. angling, cycling, rambling, picnicking and wildlife observation).

Source: Hall and Page (2006)

What classifications of rural leisure resources seek to do is to derive a simplified way of understanding the extent and nature of resource types, as shown in Table 11.3 for the US National Park Service. This illustrates the diversity of the resources for which the organisation now has a responsibility, reflecting the post-war growth in the leisure asset base resulting from a sustained period of development up until the late 1960s.

Siehl (2000) examined the changing nature of public policy towards outdoor recreation in the USA which created this expanding resource base for outdoor recreation, much of which had a rural dimension, identifying the following eras:

● *The post-war context, 1945–1957*, when increased affluence, mobility and the growth in the number of children led to a growth in recreational participation. Important developments included the growth of ski resorts, the white water rafting sector (using military-surplus life rafts), off-roading with the availability of surplus military jeeps, and visits to federal recreation areas such as national parks. The most significant development, however, was the establishment by Congress of the Outdoor Recreation Resources Review Commission (ORRRC).

● *The ORRRC era, 1956–1968*, included the creation of the ORRRC and the compilation of an inventory of outdoor recreation resources in the USA as well as forecast trends in use for 1976 and 2000. The ORRRC generated 27 studies of different recreation subjects compiled as the ORRRC (1962). One consequence of this was the development of subsequent legislation for wilderness areas, forest lands and additional purchases of land to add to existing National Parks. Other developments included the preservation of wild and scenic rivers (river corridor protection) and creating a National Trail System (recreation and scenic trails were established). As Siehl (2000: 95)

Table 11.3 Categories of recreation sites managed by the US National Park Service

Heritage site/artificial resource	Natural environment
● International historic site	● National lakeshore
● National battlefield	● National park
● National battlefield park	● National parkway
● National battlefield site	● National preserve
● National historic site	● National recreation area
● National monument	● National preserve
● National historical park	● National river
● National military park	● National scenic trail
	● National seashore
	● National wild and scenic river
	● Park (other)

suggests, this was the golden era of outdoor recreation in the USA because it expanded the recreation estate (resources).

- *The environmental era, 1969–1979*, saw a stronger national debate on pollution emerge, which led to the National Environmental Policy Act. This started to identify and seek to manage environmental impacts and was the start of environmental legislation including the effects of users of outdoor recreation sites.

- *The era of reinventing recreation, 1980–1992*, where recreational funding was reduced and increased entrance fees were introduced at national parks, and a scenic byways programme was developed.

A similar pattern of growth and development can also be discerned in England, where Figure 11.7 shows that the public and voluntary sectors play a major role in the management and funding of conservation activities in rural areas. It also illustrates that rural leisure and recreation spans different agencies and organisations, from national to local government. To provide a greater degree of coherence in England, a number of bodies with interests in the rural environment were merged to create Natural England, absorbing the former Countryside Agency (formerly Countryside Commission), English Nature and the Nature Conservancy Council to provide a more joined-up approach to rural and environmental issues linked to conservation. Managing rural areas from a public policy perspective therefore involves a major challenge of balancing sustainability and accommodating more visitors, which may sometimes be viewed as an impossible task. Even so, the scope of the resources which government organisations fund in the case of England is illustrated by Figure 11.8, where the diverse range of these resources occur in rural areas, covering large

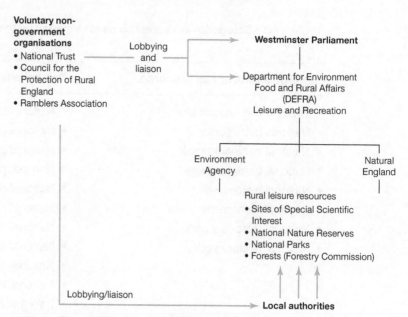

Figure 11.7 Organisations involved in rural leisure

Figure 11.8 Scenic Aras, Community Forests and National Trails

Source: Natural England (2008)

tracts of land. Conserving these diverse landscapes illustrates the importance of state intervention to try to ensure that the transformation of rural areas is not at the expense of the very resource base that leisure depends upon.

Therefore, the two examples of the USA and England's supply of rural leisure resources is an important context for understanding the nature and importance of outdoor recreation as an activity occurring in the rural environment alongside more passive forms of leisure.

Outdoor recreation and the rural environment

Manning (2000) examined the evolution of outdoor recreation which, broadly defined, focuses on recreation that occurs out of doors and in urban and rural settings where opportunities for leisure exist. The evolution of research on outdoor recreation was strongly influenced by North American studies after the Second World War (see Table 11.4 and Wolfe 1964 for a further review) even though earlier studies do exist. Some interpretations of outdoor recreation have stressed the importance of nature in the outdoors as a special characteristic of this form of leisure, illustrating its prevalence in rural settings, and Figure 11.9 summarises three of the interactions which exist where rural recreation occurs in a natural environment or setting. These interactions have to be viewed against the types of activities which occur in the natural environment

Table 11.4   The evolution of outdoor recreation research up to 1970: a North American perspective

Meinecke, E. (1928) *A Report upon the Effects of Tourist Travel on the Californian Redwood Parks,* California State Printing Office: Sacramento.

Bates, G. (1935) 'The vegetation of footpaths, sidewalks, cart-tracks and gateways', *The Journal of Ecology* 23: 470–87.

DeVoto, B. (1953) 'Let's close the National Parks', *Harper* 207: 49–52.

Clawson, M. (1959a) 'The crisis in outdoor recreation', *American Forests* 65: 22–31; 40–41.

Clawson, M. (1959b) *Methods of Measuring the Demand for and Value of Outdoor Recreation,* Resources for the Future: Washington, DC.

Outdoor Recreation Resources Review Commission (ORRRC) (1962) *Outdoor Recreation for America,* US Government Printing Office. Superintendent of Documents. Washington, DC.

Berger, B. (1962) 'The sociology of leisure: some suggestions', *Industrial Relations* 1: 31–45.

Clawson, M. and Knetsch, J. (1963) 'Outdoor recreation research: some concepts and suggested areas of study', *Natural Resources Journal* 3: 250–75.

Lucas, R. (1964) *The Recreational Capacity of the Quetico-Superior Area,* USDA Forest-Service, Research Paper LS-15.

Wagar, J. (1964) 'Quality in outdoor recreation', *Trends in Parks and Recreation* 3 (3): 9–12.

Clawson, M. and Knetsch, J. (1966) *The Economics of Outdoor Recreation,* The John Hopkins University Press: Baltimore, MD.

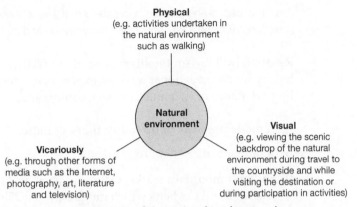

Figure 11.9 Leisure enjoyment of the natural environment

Source: Developed from Spedding (2008)

(Table 11.5), which shows that individual and organised activities are increasingly being supplied by the private sector.

Outdoor recreation appeals to a wide range of social groups and an ageing population in many countries is adding more diversity to the age groups now engaging in outdoor recreation, often typified by one of the most significant activities which has mass appeal – walking. As Hall and Page (2006: 53) suggest,

> walking is a human necessity for the able-bodied to achieve mobility, to engage in work, social activities and non-work functions. Although the industrial and post-industrial period has seen a move towards more mechanised forms of transport such

Table 11.5 Recreational impacts on the natural environment

- Compaction of soil and snow
- Impact on vegetation growth (e.g. trampling of feet)
- Increased run-off from impacts on the soil and vegetation cover
- Alteration of habitats and composition of species
- Decline in water quality from increased erosion and loss of vegetation cover
- Alteration of natural features by building access roads/routeways
- Impact on wildlife through increased human contact (e.g. bears scavenging from humans in American National Parks)
- Loss of agricultural land to recreational buildings
- Impact of man on fragile mountain and upland environments may be the 'tipping point' in environmental change
- Perceived loss of the 'rural' qualities and potential 'wilderness' qualities by increased levels of human activity linked to recreation

as the car, giving people a greater spatial reach and flexibility in travel patterns, walking remains a key activity in everyday life and as a leisure activity.

Research by Tourism Intelligence Scotland (2007), *Walking Tourism*, identified four types of recreational walking experience, which typically involved travelling a distance of two miles or more comprising:

- A moderate walk of up to five miles or more.

- A longer walk of over five miles.

- Hill and mountain walks, including trips up Munros which are over 3000 feet high and Corbetts which range between 2500 and 3000 feet in height. In the UK and Ireland there are over 2600 hills and mountains which are used as recreational sites for hill walking.

- Long distance routes, such as Scotland's West Highland Way.

Using this classification, the majority of walkers preferred a moderate walk of 1–5 miles, with a proportion who will choose to walk and undertake other outdoor recreation activities in protected areas such as national parks and wilderness areas.

Preservation and conservation: national parks and wilderness areas

According to Hall and Page (2006: 253), 'the conservation and commodification of wilderness has become entwined with the growth of recreation and tourism which has seen national parks established not only for outdoor and adventure recreation enthusiasts but also as one of the main sites in which ecotourism occurs'.

But what do we mean by the term national park? Eagles (2003) suggests that these are special sites of cultural and recreational significance, and much of the tradition in establishing such sites can be traced to the USA (see Frost and Hall 2009). The early examples of national parks designated in the USA (e.g. Yellowstone in 1872) provided the precedent which other countries followed (e.g. Banff in Canada) and those in Australia were established at around the same time (see Hall and Page 2006 for more detail), with Canada establishing the first national park management system in 1911. These parks were influenced by the ideas of writers such as George Perkins Marsh (1864), *Man and Nature*, and today there are over 6555 national parks worldwide. National parks, broadly speaking, are large areas of natural environment with important features that permit recreation, where ecological features and other natural elements are protected, with particular conditions for use. While the type and scale of parks will vary by country, they fit into a broader categorisation of areas protected by governments, usually through legislation (i.e. Act of Parliament).

According to the International Union for the Conservation of Nature and National Reserves (IUCN), there are different categories of protected areas, as set out in their *Guidelines for Protected Area Management Categories* (IUCN, 1994), including:

- Nature reserves, which are principally areas set aside for scientific research.

- Wilderness areas, which are generally unmodified natural environments to try and protect their very natural qualities.

- National parks.

- Natural monuments.

- Habitat/species management areas.

- Protected landscape/seascapes.

- Managed resource protected areas.

In the case of the national park category, IUCN designated it as a natural area of land or sea with three specific objectives:

1. To protect the area's ecosystem and ecological integrity for present and future generations (i.e. environmental sustainability).

2. To exclude activities which seek to exploit or are not compatible with objective 1.

3. To provide a 'foundation for spiritual, scientific, educational, recreational, and visitor opportunities, all of which must be environmentally and culturally compatible' (Eagles 2003: 323) (see Eagles and McCool 2002 for more detailed discussion of national parks).

While recreation features in a number of these designations by IUCN, the wilderness and national park categories have attracted the greatest attention for leisure use (see Boyd and Butler 1998 for different country studies of national parks).

Despite this classification of wilderness as a protected area, defining wilderness is highly problematic, as, like the term rural, it is very much a state of mind or in the eye of the beholder. It is culturally determined, being derived from a Northern European notion of nature (see Hall 1992 for an in-depth discussion of the issue). Early attitudes in Judaeo-Christian philosophy shaped European attitudes to wilderness as something to be feared and revered. This began to change in the eighteenth and nineteenth centuries as these landscapes were tamed by man (as discussed in Chapter 10 in relation to the coast). Today, our concept of wilderness has a global meaning and we often associate it with mountain environments due to their characteristics, which include: diversity in type and form, their marginal location in upland environments, their fragility, the difficulty of access and their aesthetic appeal (Nepal and Chipeniuk 2005). These environments have also been a major attraction as wilderness areas and as locations for outdoor recreation. The UK was a relative latecomer in terms of large-scale designation of lands and upland areas as recreational environments protected for posterity, with its 1949 Act establishing national parks. The USA is notable where national parks have the status of national monuments and are public land, unlike England where they are private land. As Hall and Page (2006: 263) suggest, 'broadly defined, the values of wilderness may be classified as being either anthropocentric or biocentric in nature', meaning that the anthropocentric view suggests they are areas for direct human use, such as for leisure, recreation and tourism. In contrast, the biocentric perspective emphasises the value of the natural environment and the importance of stances ranging from preservation to conservation. Where the anthropocentric views are considered and areas permit leisure and recreation, there are many potential experiential benefits, which may include some of the following:

● An aesthetic appreciation of the wild qualities of nature.

● Freedom and escape from the pressures of urban living.

● A challenge which generates satisfaction from the ability to overcome dangerous situations, using highly developed sets of skills.

● An opportunity to experience solitude and tranquillity.

● An opportunity to share the experience through the process of companionship as well as enjoying the delights of discovering and learning about nature and a natural setting.

● The opportunity to experience nature and wilderness close up.

Source: Adapted from Hall and Page (2006: 265)

As Dasmann (1973) suggested, wilderness has a dual role of protecting nature and provision of recreational opportunities. What the designation of such areas for protection illustrates is one of the principal problems of rural leisure – it generates impacts on the physical and built environment, to which attention now turns.

The impact of rural leisure: environmental, economic and social dimensions

There has been a long history of studying the impact of man on the physical environment, with ideas such as Marsh (1864) questioning man's role in the natural environment. This concern gathered pace in the post-war period due to leisure use of the natural environment in rural areas and its associated impacts (Table 11.6). As Hall and Page (2006) suggest, there are various ways of trying to understand the impact of leisure, and one way is to divide the effects into three categories: *economic, social* and *physical/environmental*.

The type of impact can then be summarised into whether it generates positive or negative effects, as shown in Figure 11.10. Yet this is a simplification of the reality of leisure and recreational impacts because, as Hall and Page (2006) indicated, Glyptis (1989) observed that relatively few recreational activities make use of resources that are solely recreational. Leisure and recreation are often a layer of usage that is part of a complex set of primary land uses such as forestry, agriculture, water supply, conservation and other competing uses. This is why managing leisure resources needs to accommodate a diverse range of stakeholders and uses, balancing the environmental needs of the resource base and potential use (i.e. the carrying capacity and sustainability of the resource) which will involve developing a plan to manage the resource where current and future levels of use and the ability of the resource to tolerate usage are assessed. Inevitably this will involve a degree of value judgement in the absence of scientific data and monitoring of visitor behaviour for individual sites.

Such plans for individual sites are necessary given the multiple uses which exist for leisure use of resources designed primarily for other purposes, which can then be adapted for leisure use to coexist alongside the primary function. This is particularly the case in resource settings such as forests and woodlands. Forests have a long history in the provision of outdoor recreation (Bell *et al.* 2008), initially for social elites such as those established in England by William the Conquerer for royal hunting after 1066, and through the ages they have

Table 11.6 Indicative list of outdoor recreation activities

- Picnicking
- Walking
- Cycling
- Sailing
- Snow-related sports
- Horse riding
- Wildlife watching
- High adrenalin activities described as 'adventure activities' (e.g. climbing and mountain biking)
- Commercial adventure activities (e.g. bungee jumping, white water rafting, canyoning)
- Conservation work (e.g. volunteering)
- Hunting
- Camping
- Airborne activities (e.g. hang gliding, gliding, flying)

Sources: Various

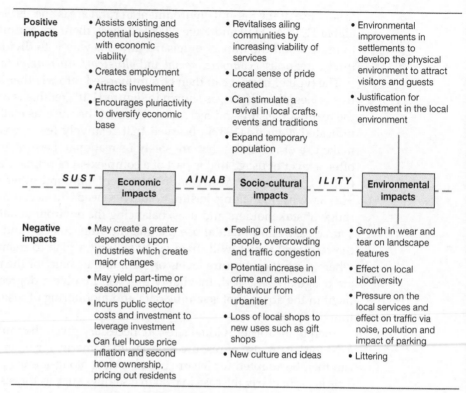

Positive impacts	• Assists existing and potential businesses with economic viability • Creates employment • Attracts investment • Encourages pluriactivity to diversify economic base	• Revitalises ailing communities by increasing viability of services • Local sense of pride created • Can stimulate a revival in local crafts, events and traditions • Expand temporary population	• Environmental improvements in settlements to develop the physical environment to attract visitors and guests • Justification for investment in the local environment
SUST	**Economic impacts** _AINAB_	**Socio-cultural impacts** _ILITY_	**Environmental impacts**
Negative impacts	• May create a greater dependence upon industries which create major changes • May yield part-time or seasonal employment • Incurs public sector costs and investment to leverage investment • Can fuel house price inflation and second home ownership, pricing out residents	• Feeling of invasion of people, overcrowding and traffic congestion • Potential increase in crime and anti-social behaviour from urbaniter • Loss of local shops to new uses such as gift shops • New culture and ideas	• Growth in wear and tear on landscape features • Effect on local biodiversity • Pressure on the local services and effect on traffic via noise, pollution and impact of parking • Littering

Figure 11.10   Indicative impacts of rural leisure

Source: Adapted from Page and Connell (2009: 503)

been transformed to community-oriented recreational resources. Subsequently, Henry VIII purchased land on the periphery of London between 1491 and 1547 to create areas for hunting, including the area now comprising Hyde Park in London (Eagles 2003). As Eagles (2003) explains, some 60 years later, Hyde Park had been opened up to allow access to common people, establishing the future basis of a royal urban park as the city expanded to enclose the area. In North America, forest reserves also form the basis for tourism and leisure, with educational objectives met through trails, visitor centres and facilities for camping and private accommodation such as log cabins. As Figure 11.11 shows, woodlands and forests have a significant role to play in recreation and tourism, which is well developed in North America (Plates 11.1 and 11.2) but only belatedly being recognised in parts of the UK, such as Scotland. Their appeal is related to the diverse range of pursuits they can absorb, in both in public and private ownership. The first forest reserve to be established in the USA was in 1891 – Shoshone National Forest, Wyoming – and soon after the US Forest Service was formed (in 1905). Figure 11.11 illustrates the value of these resources, although turning forests into sites for recreation, through the provision of trails and for activities such as mountain biking, needs investment and careful planning. For example, in southern Scotland, an investment by the public sector of £2 million in the 7Stanes project created a major boost to forest recreation and tourism. What was created was an east–west trail across

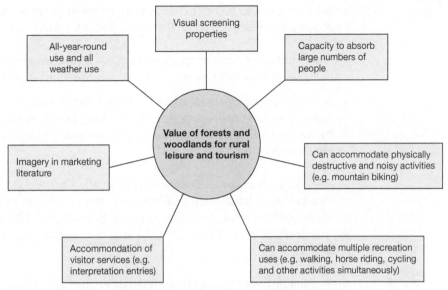

Figure 11.11 The value of forests and woodlands for rural leisure and tourism

Source: Adapted from Martin (2004) with permission from Forest Research, Edinburgh

southern Scotland through Forestry Commission lands, which capitalised on and assisted in the development of the country's reputation as a mountain biking destination. The 7Stanes now attracts around 300,000 visitors a year and is estimated to have generated £9 million a year for the local economy in visitor spending.

Where recreational resources are perceived as highly desirable and attractive, they act as magnets or what are termed *honeypots*, and in extreme cases,

Plates 11.1 and 11.2 Education is a core function of the US National Park Service (*left*). The information board in Yosemite National Park, USA (*right*), illustrates the impact of rural recreation visits on the wildlife and animals who are attracted to the campsites in their natural habitat. (Photos: National Park Service)

access may need to be restricted at peak times or permanently. Such management tools are described as *visitor management,* which can comprise:

- *Hard measures,* such as restricting access, road closures, managing parking, charging for entrance to sites, zoning activities and fencing.

- *Soft measures,* which are more about seeking to modify recreational behaviour rather than restricting it, such as asking people to take home their litter by not providing litter bins, using promotional signs and information provision/education.

Codes of Conduct, as discussed earlier in the chapter, may also be used to change people's behaviour and attitudes where the aim is to balance enjoyment and conservation. In national parks, Suckall *et al.* (2009) identified three approaches which are discernible towards their management to address issues of conflict:

- Regulation, where competing needs are overridden in favour of conservation.

- Allowing parks to evolve over time to reflect user needs.

- Education to develop user awareness.

However, in any rural setting, outdoor recreation inevitably leads to conflicts in the use of the resource base, to which attention now turns.

Managing conflict in rural leisure

Recreational conflict usually occurs in relation to the land uses which exist and the compatibility of the use or multiple uses such as between agriculture and recreation. According to Ravenscroft *et al.* (2003), recreational conflict will tend to be structured around two themes:

- Conflict arises for interpersonal reasons, where another person (or persons) interferes with the goals of another in relation to their recreational experience.

- Conflict arises as a consequence of a clash of social values related to acceptable behaviour in a recreational setting.

These two categories can also be subdivided further according to whether a conflict is actual (i.e. where actual activity is interfered with) or perceived, which is associated with the emotional response to a particular situation or others' behaviours even if it does not directly affect that person's recreation. We need to recognise that individuals have different responses to perceived conflict, which may also be affected by mood, interpersonal differences and experience. As Ravenscroft *et al.* (2003) suggest, the factors affecting perceived conflict responses are multifaceted but can be shaped by:

- Competition for shared resources (e.g. affecting perceived space and solitude).

- Escalating annoyance, as it accumulates.

- Negative experience, where a multitude of factors, including personality and past experience, provoke responses such as intolerance of stressors such as noise, crowding and fear.

- Goal interference.

- Minimisation of expected benefits.

- Clash of goals where there is a multiple use of a resource, which may infringe the norms and codes of acceptable behaviour.

- Manner and purpose of use.

- Lack of control over a situation.

- Prior knowledge and experiences.

- Differences in social values.

The perennial challenge for planners is to accommodate multiple use as well as reconciling conflicting uses, as illustrated in Figure 11.12 in relation to the recreational use of water areas. In terms of recreational conflict, such as that in Figure 11.12, the solution is the use of rational tools, which involves a sound

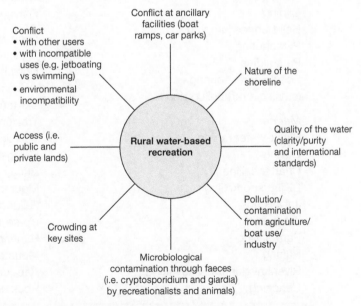

Figure 11.12   Issues in rural water-based recreation

Source: Adapted from Pigram and Jenkins (2006)

knowledge of conflict management and dispute resolution principles, so that all parties reach a mutual understanding and acceptable outcomes for recreational use are the result, which may involve zoning incompatible uses. This suggests that we need techniques to understand and manage conflict so as to understand what interventions are needed. Therefore, two important themes emerge in relation to managing leisure resources in a rural setting (and any other setting: *conflict* and *compatibility* (Bristow *et al.* 1995). These debates have certainly featured in relation to one area of considerable growth in the past decade – adventure recreation, as discussed in Case Study 11.2.

Case Study 11.2   Adventure recreation – a growth area for rural leisure

One of the growth sectors in outdoor recreation over the past decade has been the expansion associated with adventure activities. One of the principal motivations associated with the growth in this area has been the challenge and excitement of participation (Ewert and Hollenhurst 1989) posed by a wide range of activities (see Table 11.7) in rural environments. This list of activities is

Table 11.7 Adventure recreation and tourism activities

Aviation-related	River surfing/river-sledging
Ballooning	Water skiing
Hang gliding	Wind surfing
Gliding	Fishing
Heli-bungee jumping	
Parachuting	***Land-based***
Paragliding	Cross-country skiing
Scenic aerial touring	Downhill skiing
(small aircraft/helicopter)	Heli-skiing
	Ski-touring
Marine	Trekking/tramping
Black-water rafting	Vehicle safaris
Caving	Flying-fox operations
Charter sailing	Bungy jumping
Diving/snorkelling	Mountain biking/cycling
Jet-biking	Guided glacier trekking
Jet-boating	Horse-trekking
Para-sailing	Hunting
Rafting	Mountain-guiding
River kayaking/sea kayaking	Rap-jumping/abseiling
Canoeing	Rock climbing

Source: Page (1997)

constantly developing as innovations create new challenges and experiences (such as sphering, which is rolling down a hill and around the landscape in an inflated ball). There is considerable controversy associated with the classification of such activities, which have been termed adventure recreation, adventure sport and adventure tourism depending upon the focus of the research study. For example, in tourism such events may be a highlight of the holiday experience within destinations, interpreted as an attraction or even a spectacle. Postmodern interpretations of these expanding leisure activities suggest that they are another example of niche products being developed as people look for unique and different experiences, with a wide range of motivations evident in relation to participation. The participants range from the avid sport enthusiast seeking a high degree of risk to those who are occasional or one-off participants, sometimes described as dabblers. As Ewert (1989: 8) suggests, this is focused on 'the deliberate seeking of risk and the uncertainty of outcomes'. The research in this area is largely informed by developments from outdoor recreation, focused on the different elements of the experience and how it generates satisfaction. In New Zealand, this sector evolved in the 1990s as a major visitor attraction and 'must do' set of experiences for many visitors from overseas, such as bungee jumping and jet boating in and around Queenstown on the South Island. New Zealand is relatively unique in the way these experiences have been able to capture international tourist (and domestic tourist) interest, given the reliance on day trips in many other countries to build the markets for these activities.

The natural setting of these physical recreation experiences illustrates how a blurring is occurring with the way these experiences may be defined, ranging from a recreation, tourism or even sport perspective when the essence of the experience is the adrenaline rush associated with the activity, often based on a calculated risk, which is normally controlled by commercial providers who try to identify the main risk factors to minimise the level of injury and accidents (see Bentley and Page 2008 for more detail). The growth potential of the sector has been reflected in different commercial operators and public sector bodies which have invested in the infrastructure and facilities to develop the market. For example, in the UK the development of Go Ape as a novel example of woodland adventure high-wire experiences has proved highly successful. In Aberfoyle, within Loch Lomond and Trossachs National Park, the creation of a Go Ape experience was highly successful with around 30,000 visitors participating in its first year of operation. A further example of the public sector prioritising the growth of adventure activities is also apparent in southern Scotland with the development of the 7Stanes forest mountain biking investment discussed earlier.

Yet even with the broad category of adventure activity, it is evident from Table 11.6 that the level of risk involved with the spectrum of activities that are undertaken ranges from the least risky and 'soft' forms of adventure (e.g. walking) through to the 'hard' or extreme forms of activity such as bungee jumping. In this case, the high risk often associated with adventure activities often has a sustained level of adrenaline rush and perception of risk, where the challenge is high. Different research studies on this area of leisure activity also illustrate that the adventure recreationist is a lucrative market to nurture financially because of the relatively young and affluent, well-educated and high-spending nature of the participants. This is why some tourism organisations have seized upon the marketing opportunities to create clusters of adventure activity providers in specific areas to create a cluster and brand which is marketed to consumers (see Steele *et al.* 2006 for a detailed discussion of the marketing of adventure tourism in Scotland). This is evident in Queenstown, New Zealand which markets itself as the adventure capital, while a similar cluster and marketing opportunity presented itself in North West Scotland in the area around Fort William. Yet the creation of such specialised destinations for leisure and tourism within a largely rural setting, with a town to service the visitor needs, may also raise issues of conflict between the residents, policy makers seeking economic regeneration and the environmental impacts which these activities may pose, especially where the rural landscape is altered by infrastructure to support these activities.

A significant research literature exists in relation to recreational conflict and its resolution (see Pigram and Jenkins 2006 for more detail) and a seminal study in the field by Jacob and Schreyer (1980: 369) observed that 'For an individual, conflict is defined as goal interference attributed to another's behaviour.' As Hall and Page (2006) argued, we need to consider four broad principles in trying to assess the nature and extent of conflict in relation to the interactions with the resource in terms of:

- The nature of the activity and personal meaning attached to it.

- The significance attached to a specific recreation resource.

- The mode of experience, especially how the natural environment is perceived.

- Lifestyle tolerance, namely an individual's willingness to accept or reject lifestyles different from one's own.

Source: Hall and Page (2006: 109)

Recognising the significance of these issues and understanding what causes conflict will enable managers to develop appropriate resolution techniques and plans as well as highlighting future potential uses of the resource base. For this reason, we now focus on the challenges in seeking to assess the future of rural leisure.

The future for rural leisure

Seeking to assess the future for any form of leisure is particularly problematic, as the next chapter will examine. However, given the profound nature of many of the transformations occurring in relation to rural leisure, it is apparent that there are important changes and pressures that will affect rural leisure. Yet to understand these pressures and future transformations, we need to look at the wider changes likely to affect rural society. Numerous studies suggest that the future evolution of rural areas will be influenced by the sustainability agenda, greater pressure on remoter rural areas and wider changes in society. Commins' (2001) analysis of the situation in Ireland is useful because it highlighted three key drivers of change in rural areas which are important for many countries:

● Macroeconomic forces, which will affect the farm and non-farm economy in rural areas.

● The significance of the location of the population within a country and their travel to work patterns in relation to non-farm employment.

● Changes in government policies towards rural areas as well as the impact of the EU rural and agricultural policies which will affect these areas.

One approach, which we will discuss in more detail in Chapter 12, is how potential scenarios of what the rural environment will look like in the future help us to think about change that could occur. Scenario planning is a technique which organisations use to try to recognise that nothing about the future is certain: uncertainty and alternative views of the future need to try to view change as inevitable, and part of that change will involve different drivers and factors. As Chatterjee and Gordon (2006: 255) suggest:

> In scenario planning the aim is to develop distinctive depictions of the future. Alternative scenarios are developed from the present situation for a desired time horizon. In a scenario planning exercise a number of driving forces will be identified. By making different assumptions about these driving forces or key influences, different 'stories' are formulated about how these interact. The scenarios are effectively those issues.

One example of such an exercise was undertaken by Moseley and Owen (2008), who looked at rural services, of which leisure and recreation were one of 10 principal services available in rural areas. They recognised the difference between rural residents and visitors from non-rural areas using rural areas as two distinct components to try to understand. Their research is interesting as it highlights a number of underlying changes occurring in rural society which will directly affect rural residents' leisure, structured around a number of questions:

● How will cultural changes (and increases in the disposable income of rural residents) affect traditional leisure services such as the public house?

- How will Information Communication Technologies (ICTs) such as the mobile phone and internet impact rural leisure? Moseley and Owen (2008) indicated that major challenges will emerge with the growth of additional broadband access in rural areas and home-based leisure (e.g. home-films), with a corresponding decline in the use of local social venues and facilities, accentuated by social networking. This is particularly important, as OECD (2003) highlighted, since leisure provision for youth is poorly served, contributing to out-migration and population loss with inadequate provision of post-18 education.

- What will be the role of the commercial sector in rural service provision? This led Moseley and Owen (2008: 119) to suggest that 'decisions taken . . . by the large superstores, banks and leisure companies will play a big part in fashioning the landscape of rural service delivery', which will further impact upon residents' accessibility to different leisure-related services.

Natural England (2008), discussing the future trends likely to affect rural areas and use of natural resources, pointed to research they had commissioned from the Henley Centre/Headline Vision (2005) study to inform their future strategy towards natural environments. While we will be reviewing the future for leisure more generally in the next chapter, it is useful to highlight some of the main trends they saw as shaping future use in the UK. While this may not be representative of all countries, it does illustrate a number of wider societal trends occurring in some Western countries which are worth highlighting.

As Figure 11.13 suggests, 11 drivers of future change were identified from their scenario planning exercise, which we have grouped into three broad categories (although they are all interconnected):

- Government and public sector drivers.

- Consumer trends driving change.

- Leisure specific trends with an overlapping category of environmental trends.

The Henley Centre/Headline Vision (2005) study provides interesting insights, and these 11 drivers were summarised and prioritised from 38 possible drivers identified through a qualitative research process with different stakeholders. Changes in the public sector related to further centralisation of decision making in England and the growing significance of the sustainability and liveability agendas highlighted the shift in emphasis to the future pressure for housing growth in urban and rural areas and associated land loss. With the expansion of urban areas and infringements of their green belts to accommodate growth, the urbanisation of the countryside is likely to continue. This is compounded when rural land previously used by government (e.g. former airfields and military bases) is deemed to be brownfield sites in countryside settings and viewed as a sustainable solution for future housing growth. This highlights

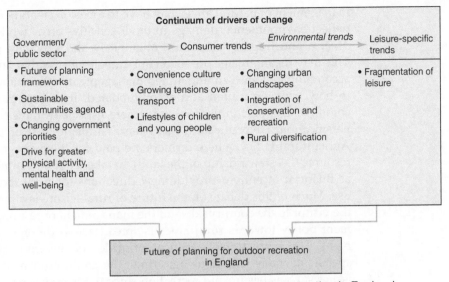

Figure 11.13 The future of planning for outdoor recreation in England

Source: Adapted from Henley Centre (2005)

one underlying tension in the Natural England study: outdoor recreation has to be incorporated into existing planning frameworks which may be traded off against other government priorities for health, housing and economic regeneration (of which reuse of brownfield sites is accepted as a sustainable use even if it places major pressure on rural infrastructure). At the same time, current policy agendas in government, as expressed in Chapter 1, associated with well-being and physical activity will see the active promotion of outdoor recreation in rural areas as a policy objective. Durnin and Passmore (1967) highlighted the importance of physical exercise and its contribution to burning calories through different levels of energy expenditure in leisure and recreation (i.e. sedentary, light, moderate and heavy exercise), which has become a major policy focus.

Yet this seems to be running contrary to some of the consumer drivers such as the growth of a risk-averse society, where people now seek information before they try new experiences, and it reflects the reluctance of parents to allow children to play in natural areas alone near their home. Similarly, schools have reduced the number of trips to the natural environment due to potential litigation issues. In addition, the growth of a convenience culture has permeated recreation. Running alongside these trends are three drivers we have allocated to the category of environmental trends, which suggest that urban landscapes are changing with greater home-based leisure provision and near-to-home consumption.

Travel to natural areas is sometimes associated with congestion, which is likely to intensify and so challenges the way in which leisure and recreation are integrated with conservation ideals. Much of the future planning and management of natural areas may have to focus on creating new honeypots to deflect environmental damage in other sensitive areas while recognising the diverse and fragmented nature of publicly and privately provided leisure. This may mean greater provision at strategic sites so that larger numbers are accommodated with zoning, timed management of visits and careful thought to how trips are routed and accommodated. It may certainly provide new commercial opportunities for landowners, especially in the context of rural diversification. Diversification has been a strategic goal of the EU Common Agricultural Policy, where farmers are paid for the management of the land resource (i.e. stewardship of the land), to take it out of commodity production as financial incentives provide new directions for rural recreation and land use. Much of this debate on the future of rural leisure is almost entirely about the visitor to the countryside and the management of resources, since government policy towards rural areas is spread across different areas of government. The more urgent political priorities of governments will focus on specific agendas (e.g. housing, crime, the credit crunch) rather than single issues such as leisure and recreation since these are not necessarily vote winners or very media worthy.

Summary

Rural leisure is not a homogenous category of leisure provision which we can easily assign to specific social groups and communities. The principal complexities are related to:

- The lack of conceptual clarity over the term *rural* and socially constructed term – *countryside* (see Hoggart 1988, 1990 and the debate over dispensing with the term *rural*). It is far more complex than simply all areas which are not urban (Sharpley and Sharpley 1997) and constitutes land masses affected by human activity, blurring into areas relatively untouched by man such as wilderness areas and designated and protected areas such as national parks.

- The visible difference between relatively hidden rural resident's leisure and the much greater focus on rural visitors not resident in the rural environment.

- The diverse nature of rural leisure resources, many of which have not been created with leisure as the main rationale, and how these are used for recreation given the growing fragmentation of rural leisure activities.

- The diverse range of public, private and voluntary organisations that provide leisure in rural environments, most notably the voluntary sector when the private and public sector are unable to meet leisure needs.

- The constant change occurring in rural environments resulting from a series of transformations that are macroeconomic and societal (i.e. associated with the postmodern society), which have reconfigured rural spaces and led researchers to reconceptualise the nature of rural leisure production and consumption.

The democratisation of rural leisure in the post-war period saw rural leisure ascend into a pivotal position in public sector provision up until the 1970s, then commercialised provision assumed a greater role. The debate in the research literature is currently as to whether rural leisure as a phenomenon is going through one more transformation – its relative demise as urban and home-based leisure are now in the ascendancy. It is notoriously difficult to assess this issue, mainly because many social surveys of leisure and outdoor recreation are snapshots and unable to delve deep into human meanings and behaviour to understand if rural leisure is now less attractive than in the immediate post-war period, when the car opened up more personal freedom to explore non-urban areas. What is more certain is that in many developed countries, the postmodern consumer is seeking more diverse experiences, and rural areas have featured in this process, albeit it with a greater fragmentation of these experiences. The rural landscape is certainly not an idyllic static setting for leisure: it is a living, working landscape in which conflicts occur between different leisure users and residents and also between residents. What rural leisure does show is that we need to look much deeper into the nature of human experiences of rural leisure to understand the basis of conflicts and meanings of leisure in more detail. This is so we can ensure that management of sensitive and highly valued resources is aligned to the needs of users and balanced against sustainability objectives (see Boonstra and Frouws 2005 for the example of Dutch rural policy). To understand these issues in more detail, we need to move on to one final facet of leisure – how we can set about thinking how the future of leisure will unfold.

Discussion questions

1. What is rural leisure?

2. How would you set about trying to understand the impact of leisure in a specific rural setting?

3. Why do people visit rural areas for leisure?

4. How would you go about surveying the leisure habits and behaviour of residents of a rural area?

References

Anderson, N. (1960) 'Aspects of the rural and urban', *Sociologia Ruralis* 3 (1): 8–22.

Anderson, N. (1963) 'Western urban man faces leisure', *International Journal of Comparative Sociology* 1 (1): 3–17.

Appleton, I. (1974) *Leisure Research and Policy*, Scottish Academic Press: Edinburgh.

Bagnall, U., Gillmore, D. and Phipps, J. (1978) 'The recreational use of forest land', *Irish Forestry* 35: 19–34.

Bell, S., Simpson, M., Tyrväinen, L., Sievänen, T. and Pröbsti, U. (eds) (2008) *European Forest Recreation and Tourism*, Routledge: London.

Bengston, D., Schermann, M., Mona, M. and Lee, T. (2008) 'Listening to neglected voices', *Society and Natural Resources* 21 (10): 876–90.

Bentley, T. and Page, S.J. (2008) 'A decade of injury monitoring in the New Zealand adventure tourism sector: a summary risk analysis', *Tourism Management* 29 (5): 859–869.

Bonn, A., Hubacek, K., Stewart, J. and Allot, T. (eds) (2008) *Drivers of Change in Upland Environments*, Routledge: London.

Boonstra, W. and Frouws, J. (2005) 'Conflicts about water: A case study of contest and power in Dutch rural policy', *Journal of Rural Studies* 21 (3): 297–312.

Boyd, S. and Butler, R. (eds) (1998) *Tourism and National Parks*, Wiley: Chichester.

Bracey, H. (1970) *People and the Countryside*, Routledge and Kegan Paul: London.

Bristow, R., Leiber, S. and Fesenmaier, D. (1995) 'The compatibility of recreation activities in Illinois', *Geografiska Annaler B* 77(1): 3–15.

Bunce, M. (1994) *The Countryside Ideal*, Routledge: London.

Butler, R.W. and Clark, G. (1992) 'Tourism in rural areas: Canada and the UK', in I. Bowler, C. Bryant and M. Nellis (eds) *Contemporary Rural Systems in Transition, Volume 2: Economy and Society*, CAB: Wallingford.

Butler, R., Hall, C.M. and Jenkins, J. (eds) (1998) *Tourism and Recreation in Rural Areas*, Wiley: Chichester.

Carhart, A.H. (1920) 'Recreation in the forests', *American Forests* 26: 268–72.

Chatterjee, K. and Gordon, A. (2006) 'Planning for an unpredictable future: Transport in Great Britain to 2030,' *Transport Policy* 13 (3): 254–64.

Clawson, M., Held, R. and Stoddart, C. (1960) *Land for the Future*, Johns Hopkins University Press: Baltimore, MD.

Cloke, P. (1977) 'An index of rurality for England and Wales', *Regional Studies* 11 (1): 31–46.

Cloke, P. (1992) 'The countryside', in P. Cloke (ed.) *Policy and Change in Thatcher's Britain*, Pergamon: Oxford, pp. 269–96.

Clout, H. (1972) *Rural Geography*, Pergamon: Oxford.

Coleman, M., Ganong, L. and Warzinik, K. (2007) *Family Life in 20th Century America*. Greenwood Publishing: Santa Barbara.

Commins, P. (2001) *Future Perspectives on Rural Areas*, Agricultural and Food Development Authority: Carlow, Ireland.

Coppock, J.T. (1966) 'The recreational use of land and water in rural Britain', *Tidschrift voor Economische en Sociale Geografie* 57: 81–96.

Cracknell, B. (1967) 'Accessibility to the countryside as a factor in planning for leisure', *Regional Studies* 1 (2): 147–61.

Curry, N. (2001) 'Right of Access to land for outdoor recreation in New Zealand – dilemmas concerning justice and equity', *Journal of Rural Studies* 17 (4): 409–19.

Dasmann, R.F. (1973) *Classification and Use of Protected Natural and Cultural Areas*, IUCN Occasional Paper No.4, Morges: International Union for Conservation of Nature and Natural Resources.

Davidson, J. and Wibberley, G. (1977) *Planning and the Rural Environment*, Pergamon: Oxford.

Dower, M. (1965) *The Challenge of Leisure*, Civic Trust: London.

Durnin, J. and Passmore, R. (1967) *Energy, Work and Leisure*, Heinemann: London.

Eagles, P. (2003) 'National parks', in J. Jenkins and J. Pigram (eds) *Encyclopaedia of Leisure and Outdoor Recreation*, Routledge: London, pp. 322–5.

Eagles, P. and McCool, S. (2002) *Tourism in National parks and Protected Areas: Planning and Management*, CABI: Wallingford.

Ewert, A. (1989) *Outdoor Adventure Pursuits: Foundation, Models and Theories*, Publishing Horizons: Columbus, OH.

Ewert, A. and Hollenhurst, S. (1989) 'Testing the adventure model: Empirical support for a model of risk recreational participation', *Journal of Leisure Research* 21: 124–9.

Flora, J., Spears, L., Swanson, J., Flora, L. and Weinberg, M. (1992) *Rural Communities: Legacy and Change*, Westview Press: Boulder, CO.

Frost, W. and Hall, C. M. (eds) (2009) *Tourism and National Parks*, Routledge: London.

Giddens, A. (1984) *The Constitution of Society: Outline of the Theory of Structuration*, Polity Press: Cambridge.

Glyptis, S. (1981) 'People at play in the countryside', *Geography* 66 (4): 277–85.

Glyptis, S. (1989) 'Recreational resource management', in C. Cooper (ed.) *Progress in Tourism, Recreation and Hospitality Management*, Volume 1, Belhaven Press: London, pp. 135–53.

Glyptis, S. (1991) *Countryside Recreation*, Longman: Harlow.

Glyptis, S. (1993) 'Leisure and the environment', in S. Glyptis (ed.) *Essays in Honour of Professor J.A. Patmore*, Belhaven Press: London, pp. 3–12.

Goodall, B. and Whittow, J. (1975) 'Recreation requirements and forest opportunities', *Geographical Paper No. 378*, Department of Geography, University of Reading.

Halfacree, K. (1993) 'Locality and social representation: Space, discourse and alternative definitions of rural', *Journal of Rural Studies* 9 (1): 23–37.

Halfacree, K. (1995) 'Talking about rurality: Social representations of the rural as expressed by residents of six English parishes', *Journal of Rural Studies* 11 (1): 1–20.

Hall, C.M. and Page, S. J. (2006) *The Geography of Tourism and Recreation: Environment, Place and Space*, 3rd edn, Routledge: London.

Hall, C.M. (1992) *Wasteland to World Heritage: Preserving Australia's Wilderness*, Melbourne University Press: Carlton.

Harrison, C. (1991) *Countryside Recreation in a Changing Society*, TML Partnership: London.

Henley Centre/Headline Vision (2005) *Paper 5: Planning for Outdoor Recreation. A Report for Natural England's Outdoor Recreation Strategy*. Natural England: Cheltenham.

Hockin, R., Goodall, B. and Whitlow, J. (1978) 'The site requirements and planning of outdoor recreation activities', *Geographical Paper No. 54*, University of Reading: Reading.

Hoggart, K. (1988) 'Not a definition of rural', *Area*, 20: 35–40.

Hoggart, K. (1990) 'Let's do away with rural', *Journal of Rural Studies* 6: 245–57.

International Union for the Conservation of Nature and Natural Resources (IUCN) (1994) *Guidelines for Protected Area Management Categories*. International Union for Conservation of Nature and Natural Resources: Morges.

Jacob, G. and Schreyer, R. (1980) 'Conflict in outdoor recreation: A theoretical perspective', *Journal of Leisure Research* 12 (4): 368–80.

Long, P. and Lane, B. (2000) 'Rural tourism development', in W. Gartner and D. Lime (eds) *Trends in Outdoor Recreation, Leisure and Tourism*, CABI: Wallingford, pp. 299–308.

Long, P., Allen, L., Perdue, R. and Kieslebach, S. (1988) 'Recreation systems development in rural communities: a planning process', *Journal of the American Planning Association* 54 (3): 373–6.

Macnaughten, P. (1995) 'Public attitudes to countryside leisure: a case study in ambivalence', *Journal of Rural Studies* 11 (2): 135–47.

Manning, R. (2000) 'Coming of age: history and trends in outdoor recreation', in W. Gartner and D. Lime (eds) *Trends in Outdoor Recreation, Leisure and Tourism*, CABI: Wallingford, pp. 121–30.

Marsh, G.P. (1864 (1965)) *Man and Nature; Or, Physical Geography as Modified by Human Action*, D. Lowenthal, (ed.) Belknap Press of Harvard University Press: Cambridge, MA.

Martin, S. (2004) 'Leisure landscapes: understanding the role of forests and woodlands in the tourism sector', in *Forest Research Annual Report and Accounts 2003–2004*, pp. 54–6.

McCormick, P. and McGuire, F. (1996) 'Leisure in community life of older residents', *Leisure Sciences* 18 (1): 77–93.

Melvin, B., Webb, J. and Zimmerman, C. (1971) *Rural Poor in the Great Depression: Three Studies*, US Works Progress Administration Research Monographs: Washington DC.

Moseley, M. and Owen, S. (2008) 'The future of rural services: drivers of change and scenarios for 2015', *Progress in Planning* 69 (3): 93–130.

Murdoch, J. and Marsden, T. (1994) *Reconstituting Rurality: Class, Community, and Power in the Development Process*, UCL Press: London.

Natural England (2008) *State of the Environment Report*, Natural England: Cheltenham.

National Park Service (2008) *Statistical Abstract 2007*, US Department of the Interior: Washington, DC.

Nationwide Survey on Recreation and the Environment (NSRE) (2007) *Recreation Statistics Update*, August, US Forest Service: Washington, DC.

Nepal, S. and Chipeniuk, R. (2005) 'Mountain tourism: towards a conceptual framework', *Tourism Geographies* 7 (3): 313–33.

OECD (2003) *The Future of Rural Policy: From Sectoral to Place-based Policies in Rural Areas*, OECD: Paris.

Outdoor Recreation Resources Review Commission (1962) *Outdoor Recreation for America*, Government Printing Office: Washington, DC.

Page, S. J. (1997) *Cost of Adventure Tourism Accidents in New Zealand,* report for Tourism Policy Group, Ministry of Commerce: Wellington.

Page, S. J. and Connell, J. (2009) *Tourism: A Modern Synthesis,* 3rd edn, Cengage Learning: London.

Page, S. J. and Getz, D. (eds) (1997) *The Business of Rural Tourism,* International Thomson Business Press: London.

Parker, G. (2005) 'The Country Code and ordering of countryside citizenship', *Journal of Rural Studies* 22 (1): 1–16.

Patmore, J.A. (1983) *Recreation and Resources,* Blackwell: Oxford.

Penning-Rowsell, E. (1975) 'Constraints on the application of landscape evaluation', *Transactions of the Institute of British Geographer* 66: 49–55.

Perkins, H. (1993) 'Human geography, recreation and leisure', in H. Perkins and G. Cushman (eds) *Leisure, Recreation and Tourism,* Longman Paul: Auckland, pp. 116–29.

Perkins, H. (2003) 'Commodification: re-resourcing rural areas', in P. Cloke, T. Marsden and P. Mooney (eds) *Handbook of Rural Studies,* Sage: London, pp. 243–58.

Perkins, H., Thorns, D. and Winstanley, A. (2008) 'House and home: methodologies and methods for exploring meaning and structure', *Studies in Qualitative Methodology* 10: 35–60.

Pigram, J. and Jenkins, J. (2006) *Outdoor Recreation Management,* Routledge: London.

Ravenscroft, N. and Parker, G. (2003) 'Countryside', in J. Jenkins and J. Pigram (eds) *Encyclopaedia of Leisure and Outdoor Recreation,* Routledge: London, pp. 84–6.

Ravenscroft, N., Groeger, J., Uzzell, D. and Leach, R. (2003) 'Conflict', in J. Jenkins and J. Pigram (eds) *Encyclopaedia of Leisure and Outdoor Recreation,* Routledge: London, pp. 68–70.

Robinson, G.M. (1990) *Conflict and Change in the Countryside,* Belhaven Press: London.

Robinson, G.M. (1999) 'Countryside recreation management', in M. Pacione (ed.) *Applied Geography: Principles and Practice,* Routledge: London, pp. 257–73.

Rowntree, S. and Lavers, G. (1951) *English Life and Leisure: A Social Study,* Longmans Green & Co.: London.

Sharma, K. (2007) *Tourism and Regional Development,* Ivy House Publishing: Sarup, India.

Sharpley, R. and Sharpley, J. (1997) *Rural Tourism: An Introduction,* International Thomson Business Publishing: London.

Shaw, S. (2006) 'Resistance', in C. Rojek, S. Shaw and A. Veal (eds) *A Handbook of Leisure Studies,* Palgrave: Basingstoke, pp. 533–46.

Shoard, M. (1999) *Right to Roam,* Oxford University Press: Oxford.

Siehl, G. (2000) 'US recreation policy since World War II', in W. Gartner and D. Lime (eds) *Trends in Outdoor Recreation, Leisure and Tourism,* CABI: Wallingford, pp. 91–102.

Simmons, I.G. (1975) *Rural Recreation in the Industrial World,* Edward Arnold: London.

Spedding, A. (2008) 'Enjoying the natural environment', Resource: The Rural Information Network, Briefing 704, www.arturrankcentre.org.

Steele, W., Page, S.J. and Connell, J. (2006) 'Analysing the promotion of adventure tourism: A case study of Scotland', *Journal of Sport and Tourism* 11 (1): 51–76.

Suckall, N., Fraser, E. and Cooper, T. (2009) 'Visitor perception of rural landscapes: a case study in the Peak District National Park, England', *Journal of Environmental Management* 90 (2): 1195–203.

Tourism Intelligence Scotland (2007) *Walking Tourism*, Tourism Intelligence Scotland: Edinburgh.

Ventris, N. (ed.) (1980) *Leisure and Rural Society*, Leisure Studies Association: Brighton.

Wall, G. (1971) 'Car-owners and holiday activities', in P. Lavery (ed.) *Recreational Geography*, David and Charles: Newton Abbot, pp. 97–111.

Wearing, S. (2003) 'Conservation', in J. Jenkins and J. Pigram (eds) *Encyclopaedia of Leisure and Outdoor Recreation*, Routledge: London, pp. 72–4.

Wolfe, R.J. (1964) 'Perspectives on outdoor recreation: a bibliographical survey', *The Geographical Review* 54(2): 203–38.

Woods, M. (2009) *Rural*, Routledge: London.

Wylie, J. (2007) *Landscape*, Routledge: London.

12 The future of leisure

Learning outcomes

After reading this chapter, you should be able to:

- Explain what we mean by the term *future*

- Understand how we conceptualise and approach the study of the future of leisure using different research tools

- Outline some of the main *drivers* of future changes in leisure

Introduction

Many conventional textbooks will get to this part of the book, proceed to produce a synthesis and review of what has already been covered in the book and then add a limited number of insights on the future directions they consider that the subject may take. This is a typical approach adopted because most authors are not conversant with undertaking futures research and the tools and techniques used to review the future. In an introductory book such as this, we need to provide a broad overview of how leisure may change, recognising that futures research in leisure is never going to be an exact science,

Plate 12.1   The Badlands National Park, USA: What does the future hold for such leisure resources? (Photo: National Park Service)

and we need to look at how we think and rationally approach the subject. One way to try to make sense of the real world and how it is being transformed is to think about how leisure, leisure time and participation may change in the future.

So let us depart from convention, pick up our crystal ball and try to look ahead and ask one question to structure the chapter: *What does the future hold for leisure?* This is a perennial problem which analysts, managers and policy makers seek to answer when they look at leisure (Veal 1987). But before we try to answer this in a coherent and logical way, we need to try to appreciate what we mean by the term *future* and then enter the world of the futurologist (Plate 12.1).

What do we mean by the term future?

This is one term which, if you look in a dictionary, will typically repeat the principal term in the definition, reflecting the problem of trying to explain it. *What is the future?* The future is something which has not yet happened. The future is an amorphous phenomenon to define, mainly because it is unknown, uncertain, based on individual and wider trends that may exist now or are still to arise and will be affected by a wide range of interrelated and interconnected processes occurring over different timescales. Let us take a simple example of where the concept of the immediate future is examined, which features in our leisure lives on a daily basis. This helps to explain the level of complexity we are talking about, as the case of weather forecasting and leisure (Case Study 12.1) will suggest. This will help to get us thinking about what the future is and why it might be important to leisure.

| Case Study 12.1 | The immediate future and leisure: The role of weather, climate and forecasting as a determinant of leisure behaviour |

Research studies such as Martin (2005) indicate that visits to different environments for recreation and tourism are directly affected by climate and weather, with major determinants being hours of sunshine, snow, wind, precipitation, temperature and the daily temperature range (the diurnal range). However, the highly unpredictable nature of weather means that we set a great deal of store by published and televised weather forecasts, often consulting them the night before planning our recreational activities. This is because climatic factors may make a difference in the way recreation decision making occurs in relation to simple choices – will we undertake indoor or outdoor activities? – which ultimately affects the choice of destination for a day out. As Page and Connell (2009) show, for Michigan in the USA, research studies indicated that a 1 degree increase in temperature contributed to a 1% increase in road traffic. The state has a US$16 billion tourism industry and a large outdoor recreation resource base, so climatic conditions will be an important determinant of demand. Similarly, in the UK in 2007 a wet summer saw the displacement of demand from outdoor to indoor attractions. So we set a great deal of store by the ability of weather forecasters to make predictions, which we either accept or reject according to our experience, before making decisions on which leisure and recreation activities to undertake in the immediate future.

Weather forecasting epitomises all of the difficulties we face with forecasting the future: there are just so many variables to try to understand, and weather is unpredictable, with sudden changes occurring due to alterations in variables such as wind which can change the direction and behaviour of a weather system. The future is no different, where unpredictability is the norm. Like forecasting in general, weather forecasting is not an exact science, despite the scientific research and data available to create highly complex meteorological models. Consequently, weather forecasters are often lambasted and pilloried in the press and by the public when they look at a weather forecast but do not recognise that it is a *forecast*. The tendency is to look at the forecast as something that will definitely happen: but it is a *forecast* of a probable event in the future. So what happens in terms of leisure when forecasts are over-cautious and how do they impact on leisure behaviour?

The late May Bank Holiday is often a period in the UK when the population traditionally head to the coast if the weather is good. On the second May Bank Holiday in May 2009, the UK Weather Forecasting Service forecast a poor weather outlook based on the probability of a weather system affecting the south coast of England. As this is one of the busiest days of the year, the forecast is very influential in shaping recreation decision making. The actual weather was markedly different from the poor forecast: the resort of

Bournemouth had one of the hottest days of the year at 22 degrees celsius, with a dry and warm day as the forecast for a weather system affecting the area did not materialise. Bournemouth Borough Council estimated that the impact of the weather forecast on the local leisure industries was substantial. They calculated that it cost the industries around £1m in lost revenue for that day, based on an estimated drop of 25,000 visitors as a result of the weather forecast (Sturcke 2009). So while we are highly critical of forecasters when they are seen to get it wrong, if we start to look at this example and think critically about it, we can learn a number of things in relation to the immediate future:

- The future, irrespective of the immediate or long term, is uncertain: it is far from predictable.
- Weather forecasters, like any other forecaster, will use their experience, expertise and science (as well as looking at past events) to try to provide a best-case scenario of a weather outlook of what might happen.
- We may think that the future is not something that directly interests us, but as the simple example of the weather forecast shows, we do shape our leisure behaviour according to simple predictions.
- Individuals and the leisure industries need to make assumptions about what the future might hold for them, even if it is just about tomorrow – we all have to plan our behaviour in some way or other, even if that plan involves deciding to be sporadic, making a decision at the last minute.
- The future is affected by a myriad of factors, and as the example of the weather forecast shows, it can be the result of what we know has happened in the past (i.e. *continuity*) or may be something we cannot easily anticipate – *change*. This is why Chapter 2 highlighted the importance of the historical analysis of leisure and the two concepts of continuity and change. As Schwartz (2002: 17) concurred, 'the key judgement anyone wishing to anticipate the future needs to make is whether the future is essentially similar to the past' so we need to understand not only the past but also the present before moving on to the future.

Futurology: the study of the future

From Case Study 12.1, it is evident that the word *future* has now encapsulated many different areas of science and social science research, because planners, decision-makers and businesses would like to know (or at the very least be aware of) what might happen in a specific time period in relation to a phenomenon such as leisure. The study of the future emerged from management science after 1945, growing in scale and significance in the 1960s, assuming a myriad of different names and titles which you might see referred to (e.g. foresight, futures studies, futurology) and using new techniques and a diversity of

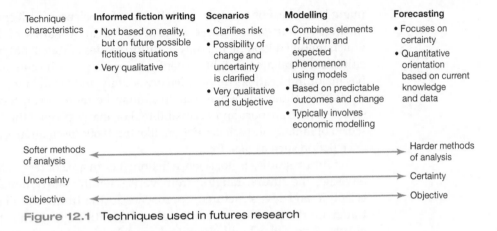

Figure 12.1 Techniques used in futures research

approaches towards the analysis of the future, the most popular of which are shown in Figure 12.1. These approaches have a number of characteristics depending upon the level of certainty the technique wants to embrace, whether a quantitative or qualitative approach is preferred and the research objectives of the task in hand. In particular, the technique(s) selected will seek to explain:

● The elements of complexity associated with how the future will unfold, including the importance of trends and their contribution to future change or continuity in the nature of leisure phenomenon/behaviour.

● How specific aspects of these trends can be summarised into the most important factors affecting the future (e.g. drivers of change).

● How to conceptualise change, its impact and effects as well as the scale and impact on society (i.e. how far will internet access be adopted by sections of the population in the future?).

● The consequences of these potential changes on the specific themes under question, such as leisure.

This means that any analysis of the future requires researchers to be able to take a wide-ranging view of issues, and the starting point for this analysis is the timeframe we need to consider.

Future studies and the time horizon

When we talk of the future, it is always helpful to try to envisage what timeframe we are thinking about, which might be the immediate future (i.e. tomorrow, next week or next month, a year), the medium term (5 to 10 years) or longer term (i.e. 25 years or an even longer horizon, such as the lifespan of an individual). The latter time horizons of 50 years or more are more challenging, particularly as individuals find it hard to visualise such horizons, as one key element making it difficult is anticipating how technology may change. This is apparent in scenario planning exercises which try to visualise what the future might look like. For example, the UK Office for Science and Technology's (2006) *Intelligent Transport Futures Project* looked at scenarios of travel in 2050, which involved looking not only at future modes of travel, but how our towns, cities and rural areas might be configured in a post-oil economy. Clearly, this has major implications for how leisure activity and behaviour might emerge in relation to situations where our lives may be more urban focused and constrained by transport and accessibility. For many people, this is entering the world of fantasy and science fiction, like the 1960s fascination with popular science fiction such as *Star Trek*.

Yet future studies is not science fiction: it is an area of research which tries to envisage the future, ranging from very scientific and rational ways to less scientific and less structured approaches to the future. As Figure 12.1 illustrated, on the one hand, the rational and scientific approach is typified by scientists, who often build simplified models of reality where they can make different assumptions about the future. They then model these assumptions to produce a set of outcomes or effects to explain how change may occur in relation to natural and human-related phenomena, such as the impact of climate change on the erosion of beaches in the next 25 to 50 years. At the other extreme are scenario planning exercises (see Page *et al.* 2006, 2010 for two different examples) where uncertainty is the starting point. As the UK Cabinet Office Performance and Innovation Unit (2001) argues, this reflects the different principles associated with futures research, reflecting the range of techniques we choose to use. Yet irrespective of the technique, there are typically three principal questions we need to ask in relation to leisure futures:

- What may happen? This is described as *possible futures* (e.g. will there be a global convergence in the amount of leisure time available, gradually eroding the wide-ranging differences observed in the amounts of leisure tine available by country? For example, the OECD (2009) report *Society at a Glance* observed that Norway is the most leisurely society, with 25% of their time spent on leisure, whereas Mexicans spend only 16% of their time on such pursuits: will these differences in leisure time converge or diverge in the future?).

- What is the most likely to happen? This is described as *probable futures* (e.g. will the current trend in growing numbers of children in divorced/separated families continue to increase, adversely impacting upon fathers and their limited leisure time with their siblings? See the article by Jenkins 2009 on this issue).

- What would we like to happen? This is known as the *preferable future* (e.g. a study in Sydney, Australia highlighted the existing disparities in children's access to leisure facilities among the poorer families and recommended initiatives and measures to address the inequalities to improve the situation. This is what we would like to happen, but it would depend upon public sector funding and commitment towards reducing barriers to leisure and perceived inequalities; see Brown 2005).

One of the issues which have emerged throughout the book is the different language and terminology that different subjects use when analysing leisure.

The study of the future is no different: it has its own language and method of communicating with other futurologists. The most important term used is *driver(s)*, which refers to the most influential trends which are then subdivided and broken down into components. For example, a study in North East England by Futurematters.org.uk is a comprehensive attempt to look at the future for a region, based on the UK Foresight Programme funded by the Department for Trade and Industry. It examines different themes (the environment, people and place) and the future for these themes is examined in relation to specific drivers which will affect the future. Identifying drivers involves the process of *environmental scanning*, which is a technical term that describes the process of systematically scanning all the trends in a logical and coherent manner. Environmental scanning is undertaken to try to observe what trends to study further and consider which will become *drivers of change*.

The problem is that knowledge and information are held in different forms, in written and verbal forms which need to be understood and synthesised. The complexity of information and the sheer volume available via the World Wide Web is one reason why organisations will purchase market research and reports, where the breadth of knowledge is already distilled down into a format where it can easily be understood and disseminated. But it is not the information itself that is the key: it is the analysis of the information and its assessment to draw out the implications. In other words, what will be the importance of drivers for the future of leisure and how important will uncertainty be in leisure futures?

Drivers and leisure

As Roberts (1999) argues, the theoretical basis for explaining leisure is still relatively weak, and this is especially the case when trying to understand the future. It may explain why future studies do not use any all-embracing theories of the future but prefer to rely upon *drivers*, which reflects the difficulty of predicting human behaviour. This is because there is a wide-ranging debate in social psychology on the extent to which you can predict or model human behaviour, especially in a postmodern society where the focus is on individualism. For this reason, the most attractive explanations of leisure behaviour are those which are described as pluralist. What this means is that there are different influences which affect leisure behaviour, such as age, social and economic status, gender and ethnicity, and the combination of these factors will create different forms of leisure behaviours that occur simultaneously in time and space. Roberts (1999) highlights that we need to try to understand the following issues in relation to future leisure:

- What are the implications of increased working hours for some sections of the population and the knock-on effects for their leisure?

- How are new social trends, such as greater numbers of women entering the workforce, affecting home-based leisure and the domestic sphere? In other words, how does work, family life and leisure get integrated? (See Beach 1989.)

- Are conventional explanations of the family life cycle and leisure still suitable given the way in which leisure occurs amongst males and females, especially with the greater individualisation of people's lives and leisure?

- How will the continued growth of consumption and commercial leisure, combined with a highly developed consumer culture, permeate future aspects of adults' and children's leisure lifestyles?

Manzenreiter and Horne (2006: 412) observed how the commercial sector, in one of the most highly developed consumer cultures – Japan, saw 'companies constantly create new images of social groups in order to assure the continued consumption of goods and services' so as to differentiate their products and services, as a supply-led process of commercial leisure creates different consumer niches for specific segments of society. Yet Japanese leisure has also seen other trends develop, such as low-cost sports, the greater pursuit of self-actualisation (i.e. discovering oneself and one's abilities) and social networking as new forms of leisure. But how do we start to make sense of these different trends and issues to understand what they will mean in the future?

Futuring

One of the main proponents of future studies, Cornish (2004), a founder of the World Future Society in the 1960s, points to the key challenges of understanding the future. As Cornish (2004) argues, an important consideration underpinning the process of looking at the future, *futuring*, is to recognise that we are living in an era of multiple transformations that are shaping our future. These transformations are occurring in technology, the economy and the nature of the social institutions that affect our daily lives. The main challenge we need to address at this juncture is: what transformations are occurring and why are they so important? One of the underlying arguments which Cornish (2004) puts forward is that we are living in a society that is being transformed by supertrends (see Figure 12.2), but it is not just these changes which are important – it is the nature and scale of these changes which we must really grasp.

The concept of change and uncertainty in futures research

One thing that is certain in futures research is that in the next 10 to 20 years, some things will change and other things will stay relatively constant. As indicated by Schwartz (2002) earlier in the chapter, the past is often a good example of understanding what might happen in the future, even if the scale and pace of change may be different. This is because trends tend to have basic elements

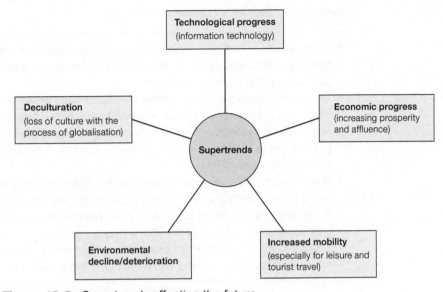

Figure 12.2   Supertrends affecting the future

Source: Adapted from Cornish (2004). Copyright © World Future Society

that can be recognised, where influential drivers will shape the trends. The main debates raised by drivers are often based on an individual's assessment of whether they will induce stability or change. Yet, in most instances, the concept of change is relative, because you need to recognise that in a diverse population, change may affect certain groups and not others. Equally, we need to understand the degree of change that might occur – will it be minor, major or a complete transformation, as with the rise of the Internet and mobile technology? Such technology has transformed how people interact in their leisure time.

Understanding change is an important element of future studies, but alongside change we also need to recognise a further complicating factor that brings in ambiguity – the concept of *uncertainty*. As Cooper and Layard (2002: 3) suggest, 'all predictions are of course uncertain since we could never know all the factors at work nor the exact process through which they have their effects'. In fact, Gordon *et al.* (2005) highlight a number of tools and techniques which researchers can use to help reduce uncertainty in futures research, although uncertainty remains a largely unknown factor in such studies (Helmar 1983).

As Figure 12.1 illustrated, in future studies a wide range of techniques and approaches are used, which are applied dependent upon what you are trying to understand. One of the greatest challenges in any form of futures research is recognising how you build in uncertainty and accommodate ambiguity, if you accept that nothing in the future is predictable or certain. If you accept this proposition, the different futuring techniques which seek to provide a definitive response (e.g. quantitative methods), such as an economic forecast, are based on the notion of certainty in a set time period (Table 12.1), where certain predictable changes will occur in the economy, making assumptions and requiring specific forms of data for observable and measurable factors (Figure 12.3). However, the 2008 credit crunch shows that this throws forecasts and assumptions out of the window, as a sudden unpredictable event leads us into a new era of economic

Table 12.1   Leisure forecasting techniques

- Speculation – often popular assessments of current trends and creative thinking, with some assessment of the likely impact of science, information technology and changes in society.
- Trend extrapolation – more commonly called 'time series' analysis, looking back at previous trends to then extend them into the future (e.g. extrapolation).
- Respondent assessment – what people would like to do in the future, based on social surveys such as the early landmark studies in the UK (e.g. Pilot National Recreation Survey 1967).
- The Delphi technique – comprising a panel of experts who are presented with a range of questions about the likelihood of changes occurring. In the next stage, the answers are collated to suggest possible developments which may occur and subsequent rounds of questions may be built in.
- Scenario writing – to look at potential futures, a series of alternative hypothetical future situations are created, using variables which will affect change.

Source: Adapted from Veal (1987)

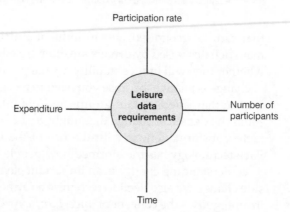

Figure 12.3   Data requirements for leisure forecasting

uncertainty (and uncharted waters) where few historical precedents exist to guide thinking and decision making. It means we need to rethink how we look at issues of uncertainty and change, which is why scenario planning has been widely used to accommodate ambiguity and the uncertainty associated with change.

Scenario planning and uncertainty

While not decrying the role of forecasting (which we discussed briefly in Chapter 4), we do need to recognise that change in society is moving at a fast rate, bringing complexity, stress and shorter product life cycles for goods and services (as will be discussed later in relation to hypercompetition). Bradfield *et al.* (2005) review the evolution of scenario planning as a subject, including the work of large organisations such as Shell which pioneered its commercial use, and the way in which scenario planning is employed, typically crafting a number of diverging stories about the future using uncertain events. As Duinker and Greig (2007: 210) argue, scenario planning performs two important functions: 'risk management, where scenarios enable strategies and decisions to be tested against possible futures, while the other is creativity and sparking new ideas'. A number of innovative applications of scenario planning can be found in Page *et al.* (2006, 2010) together with their use in a public and private sector context, running in parallel with the example discussed in Chapter 11. As these studies suggest, there are a number of clear steps in scenario planning:

1. A review of the literature from existing published sources and scientifically generated research (e.g. peer reviewed academic literature) as well as public and private sector reports.

2. Environmental scanning of trends and issues relevant to the subject.

3. Interviews with industry/subject experts to help clarify and develop a list of potential drivers from the environmental scanning, using proprietary scenario software to incorporate the complexity in the results.

4. Constructing two (or up to four) scenarios based on the drivers and understanding of potential changes that may arise (and in the case of the studies reported by Page *et al.* (2006, 2010), the use of an economic model to identify potential changes which might arise from different assumptions made in the scenarios to create a greater degree of economic reality in the process).

5. Testing of the scenarios in a workshop setting where a selected group of people are asked to read the scenarios and comment on the issues and implications raised.

6. The mapping of the main issues and results of the workshop(s) which are then ranked and rated by respondents to produce an ordered list of changes.

7. Interpretation and identification of potential policy issues by the scenario planning team to analyse the main risks and challenges for the organisation or theme being examined.

Source: Based on Page *et al.* (2006, 2010).

While this process may be varied or designed in a different way, it does highlight how different scenario planning is from forecasting, where a historical time series is used followed by a series of assumptions to form a definite outcome. In contrast, scenario planning can provide a range of alternative futures. The scenario planning process is quite useful if you wish to take a longer horizon and build in significant changes to the way society exists today, to understand more qualitative and contextual issues such as how we might be living in 2025. In fact, Cornish (2004) suggested that the pace of change had

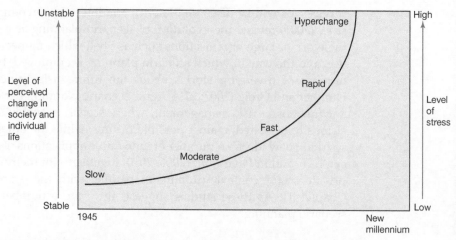

Figure 12.4 Hypothetical model of the pace of change in society

now accelerated to the point that we now live in an age of hyperchange in society (see Figure 12.4), and this hyperchange, combined with the range of supertrends (see Figure 12.2) which affect society, will influence the scale and direction of change in leisure in the future, as shown in Figure 12.4. For this reason, it is interesting to observe how these processes of hyperchange have affected the supply of commercial leisure products, given the impact of an associated process of change – hypercompetition.

Hypercompetition, change and commercial leisure

The past decade has seen major changes in the nature of business and how it operates, not least in the way leisure products and services are delivered. As Kotzab *et al.* (2009) suggest, a power shift has occurred from manufacturers to retailers, and the very successful leisure services that have been able to combine retailing and production (e.g. low-cost airlines) have made major inroads into established markets. One of the most profound changes in the business environment that has induced uncertainty and intense competition is hypercompetition. According to D'Aveni (1998), hypercompetition is typified by:

● Rapid product innovation.

● Aggressive competition.

● Shorter product life cycles.

● Businesses experimenting with meeting customers' needs.

● The rising importance of alliances.

● The destruction of norms and rules of national oligopolies.

D'Aveni (1998) identifies four processes that are fuelling hypercompetition:

- Customers requiring better quality at lower prices.

- Rapid technological change, especially in the use of IT.

- The rise of aggressive large companies willing to enter markets with a loss-leader product for a number of years in the hope of destroying the competition and capturing the market in the long term.

- Government policies towards barriers to competition being progressively removed.

As Kotzab *et al.* (2009) suggest, this is posing many strategic and managerial issues for organisations, with increasing levels of turbulence in the business environment evident. Yet as Koztab *et al.* (2009) argue, there are different meanings of hypercompetition:

- as a description of the intense rivalry between businesses or industries;

- as a conceptual model that examines the strategic behaviour of businesses in this new world of hyperchange.

As Akhter (2003: 20) argues, hypercompetition has meant that:

- Consumers expect and demand more.

- Competitors aggressively introduce new products.

- Businesses change distribution channels (which is the focus of Kotzab *et al.*'s 2009 study).

- Businesses implement cost-cutting programmes.

- Companies imitate each others' innovations.

- The traditional boundaries of markets are redrawn by businesses as they globalise their operations in response to the changing regulatory and competitive climate.

All of these characteristics can be discerned in the intense rivalry posed by the rise of the low-cost airline model in the USA, and its diffusion to Europe and then Asia-Pacific (Page 2009a, 2009b). For leisure passengers, this has slashed the cost of travel, revolutionising supply and distribution, with customers booking via the Internet without the restrictions that previously applied to airline travel. The consequences of creating a new era of low-cost travel, which exhibits the characteristics of hypercompetition, have emerged, where a number of aggressive new entrants have transformed the competitive landscape for air travel:

> Hypercompetition is the extreme rivalry whereby competing firms position themselves aggressively against one and other, and seek to disrupt the competitive advantages of industry leaders . . . while both globalisation and rapid technological change lead to hypercompetition, rising consumer expectations and attacks by competitors also drive this forceful type of business. *(Lahiri et al. 2008: 314)*

The low-cost airline market exhibits many of the characteristics discussed in this quotation, and this has created new expectations amongst travellers (who were predominantly leisure focused in the early stages of low-cost travel but have now been joined by business travellers) in relation to flexibility over booking, pursuit of value for money, the ability to tailor travel to individual needs via personalised booking on the Internet and the creation of new destinations and products that would have been relatively unattractive to travellers a decade ago. It has disrupted the traditional model of business, using a highly streamlined and efficient method of delivery with the use of secondary airports to reduce costs. The outcome for the airline industry has been greater turbulence, with businesses failing where their business model cannot compete with the market leaders, leading to takeovers and mergers to create even stronger market positions. For the consumer, leisure travel by air has ceased to be a luxury product. Hypercompetition has certainly contributed to greater consumption of air travel, as Tourism Intelligence Scotland's (2007) *Scottish Tourism in the Future* observed that 'more than 25% of the world now has a lifestyle that used to belong only to the rich'. This reflects how increased affluence among a proportion of the population has created a demand for leisure consumption. Therefore, the competitive landscape for producing leisure products has become intense and challenging for suppliers.

Microtrends and leisure

Irrespective of whether one accepts or agrees with the selection of supertrends which Cornish (2004) outlined above, hypercompetition and hyperchange have increased the pace and scale of change in many areas of life. It is evident that within these trends, there are many other smaller microtrends occurring. For example, Cooper and Layard (2002) examined a range of macro trends associated with the future, including: population, energy, climate change, work, monetary policy, government and the cybernetic society. Within these broader trends, we can also discern what Penn (2007) refers to as *microtrends*. The criterion used by Penn (2007) to identify a microtrend is that it will affect at least 1% of the population.

Table 12.2 highlights a range of these microtrends based on Penn (2007). For example, one notable shift observed in the USA is called the sleepless society, with people getting less than the 7 to 8 hours' sleep that is deemed to be necessary for a healthy life. This is reflected in the growth of sleeping-pill prescriptions in the USA, a greater consumption of caffeine energy drinks and greater fragmentation of leisure time, with the availability of 24-hour technology. This has seen a proportion of the population spending time on these gadgets and the Internet rather than sleeping.

Remaining on the theme of change and microtrends, Jensen (1999) suggested that we will be moving from an information age to an *imagination*

Table 12.2   Microtrends affecting society and the implications for future leisure

Microtrend	Significance for future leisure
• More single people not in relationships and working	• New types of leisure provision for singles
• Commuter couples and long-distance relationships (3.5 million in the USA)	• Travel and event planning opportunities for businesses and couples
• Internet dating (around 100,000 of the 4.4 million Americans marrying in 2007 will have met online)	• A proportion of the internet users spending their leisure time on virtual interaction
• The growth of working retirees (5 million in the US workforce aged 65 or more in 2007)	• Major growth trend in the future as leisure time is not expanding at age 65, but blurring the work–leisure boundary that was more defined by retirement
• Extreme commuters (i.e. people who spend at least 90 minutes a day to get to work, of whom there are 3.4 million in the USA)	• Less leisure time
• Homeworking (up to 4.2 million in the USA)	• Major growth area and blurring of work and leisure
• Second homes (accounted for 40% of USA home sales in 2005; middle-class trend with 3.3 million purchased in USA in 2005)	• Splitting of leisure and recreation time between different houses
• Growing 'third' sector, non-profit activities emerge as more dominant entities	• Greater proportion of non-profit businesses becoming involved in leisure provision and activities
• Rise in consumer electronic purchases	• At home – leisure expansion
• Rise in risk-seeking outdoor recreation (e.g. skateboarding participation grew 166% 1995–2005; kayaking by 117%, snowboarding 11.4% and mountain biking 37% in the USA)	• A greater 'niching' with more adventurous sports activities while in traditional sports (e.g. baseball, basketball and ice hockey in the USA) interest has been waning as a shift occurs from communal to personalised sport
• Living Apart Together (LAT) couples (1 million couples in the UK or 3:20 of those aged 16–59 years of age) who do not marry	• Running two homes and split leisure lives and challenge to the conventional measure of leisure and a household
• Varying patterns of child rearing (2.1 children per woman in the USA; 1.5 in Europe)	• More no-children households which do not have to combine children in their leisure lives

Source: Adapted from Penn (2007)

age. His arguments were based on the ideas of the experience economy where the emotional fulfilment provided by products and experiences will make us purchase different items to consume in our leisure time. The arguments put forward by Jensen (1999) are interesting from a leisure perspective because he pointed to a number of emerging trends affecting leisure time, such as the rise of adventure activities, togetherness and relationships (i.e. a need for greater intimacy in the fast-changing world we live in), the importance of health and well-being, a greater consumption of heritage and the past which gives us peace of mind, and a greater focus on values and interest groups in product purchasing, such as the development of e-tribes discussed earlier in the book. Shaping these broad changes are a number of specific trends, such as:

- Work will be hard fun and it will rival leisure time.

- Homeworking will not be prevalent (compare this with Penn 2007 and you see why futurologists interpret things in different ways and are often contradictory) because people need social interaction not available from homeworking.

- Work and private life will continue to merge further.

- The development of life stages will emerge, replacing conventional concepts such as the family life cycle, with four distinct stages: childhood/youth, young adulthood, parenthood (starting much later in line with Penn's 2007 microtrends) and a post-family stage with greater health and wealth in later life. What this does not address, however, are the growing microtrends that challenge the parenthood stage, with the expansion of single households, non-children families and even couples living apart.

- The development of cybernations, which are communities of interest (i.e. the e-tribes) linked together by technology.

But among the most widely debated changes which researchers have focused on are the worlds of work and leisure.

Change and the worlds of work and leisure

One of the most influential debates over change, as Jensen (1999) highlights, is how leisure is being transformed by the world of work. Here there are two polarised views on the future of leisure as the antithesis of work, with some commentators arguing for the potential end of leisure due to overwork, with work dominating our lives. Conversely, other researchers have suggested that we will be moving into a more complex leisure age. But Friedman (2002: 170) fervently disputes this position as 'on a world scale, the idea that we have reached a point where a vast majority of people do away with work is lunacy'. Norton (2000) cited results from the British Social Attitudes survey which noted that leisure time had only marginally increased for the population since the 1960s, reflected in the title of the article *Forecasts of the leisure society fail to materialise*. Friedman (2002: 170) suggests that there are a number of underlying trends affecting the world of work (which will have implications for the type and nature of leisure):

- *The feminisation of work,* with more women entering the workplace, in part a consequence of their growing participation in education (where women outnumber males in the annual number of graduating students in the UK).

- *An increasing age and skill structure among the workforce,* with a corresponding shift of the workforce to many less developed countries (LDCs) (epitomised by the rise of the call centre in cities such as Mumbai). Friedman (2002) pointed to the rising proportion of the world's labour force in LDCs, which grew from 69% to 75% between 1965 and 1990 and is set to rise to 85% by 2050.

- *The continued decline in the manufacturing and production of goods in advanced economies,* and a shift to LDCs.

- *Employment growth in health and personal services in developed countries.*

- *The near universal use of computers* and information communication technologies.

There are a range of factors which will affect the work–leisure debate. Friedman (2002) highlighted the following factors which we need to take into account in seeking to understand any future changes and their impact upon leisure:

- The income elasticity of leisure demand (especially the willingness to trade income for leisure time highlighting issues surrounding the work–life balance).

- The impact of technology.

- Future income levels.

- Incentives to work.

- Government policies towards income redistribution in some societies with a strong welfare ethos (e.g. Scandinavian countries) versus the free market economies of the UK and USA, where future inequities in leisure will arise from income distributions, according to Aguiar and Hurst (2007).

One of the major unknown factors which Schwartz (2002) saw as affecting the stability of forecasts was how we treat technology, which we can summarise as three possible scenarios:

- We may know what the future technology is but are uncertain over its future application.

- The science is unknown but the technology is not.

- We do not know about future technology or its application.

The rise of the over-generation?

Whatever the impact of technology will be on the future on work and leisure, we already know that leisure and work have become more fragmented and less routinised, and one consequence for many busy people is the concept of *overclocking* – trying to fit too much into already busy lives. Yet this is not just a trend affecting adults: it affects many children in middle-class and aspiring families (the so-called Y-Generation born after 1982) where the parents also tend to over-schedule their leisure time (also described by some commentators as over-parenting). This overclocking joins a long list of what Touve and Tepper (2007) describe as trends affecting children's leisure:

- *Overconnected* (i.e. too much access and use of the Internet and mobile phones/social networking).

- *Overstimulated* (i.e. too much time spent on computer games and media screens).

No wonder that children growing up in this new millennium may look back on their leisure as part of the *over-generation*, where overloading children and providing them with highly individualised access to consumer goods to fill their leisure time may be eroding the concept of play discussed throughout the book. As the psychologist Levine (2006) argued, the consequences of such over-parenting is to compromise the essential principles necessary for a child's psychological health:

- Independence.

- Competence learning, so that they learn how to do things.

- The cultivation of healthy interpersonal relationships (not forced or stage-managed relationships through over-parenting).

As Levine (2006) found, some of the consequences for teenagers subjected to over-parenting were:

- Teenage depression.

- Anxiety.

- Substance abuse.

Many forced forms of human interaction, through over-parenting and supplanting play by virtual tools as opposed to direct human interaction, are a trend which seems set to continue. But there are significant consequences for the child's leisure time and cocooning by parents so they fail to learn to take risks and use leisure time to build the three important qualities identified by Levine (2006). The pace and scale of change in child and youth leisure is exponential, given the individualisation of their leisure needs. For example, in the USA, iPods/MP3 players amongst the age group over 12 rose from 14% of the population owning them to 30% in 2007. This on-demand and individualised 24-hour access to entertainment is an indication of how technology is shaping and changing leisure.

There is certainly evidence, for some people, that the traditional difference between leisure and work is blurring and that leisure is now more fully integrated within our lives in terms of work and non-work, challenging the more conventional thinking on work and leisure as separate entities. Granter (2008), for example, argues that the world of work is tightening its grip on our lives, and that a world of leisure or the notion of the leisure society which we discussed in Chapter 1 is a quaint and distant notion. This is even more evident in the case of homeworking and the way in which it has invaded the leisure space of the home (see Dart 2006 for a detailed review). Ramey and Frances' (2004) review of a century of leisure and work in the USA found that Americans' actual leisure time was the same in 2004 as it was in 1900. The only major beneficiaries of additional leisure time were children, who were working in 1900 but not in the new millennium. Similarly, the only area where a mass leisure class was discernible in their analysis was in the *third agers*, those aged 50 to 75 years of age who are a growing segment of many developed nations. This is somewhat at odds with Mitton and Wilmott's (2005: 49) assertion that 'the oft-predicted movement towards a more leisure focused society continues at a steady pace'.

Without seeking to adopt a position of whether leisure time is increasing or not in this book, due to the varying evidence and interpretations, or whether work is dominating our lives more, we need to be critical of the interpretations which futures studies develop and question a number of assumptions associated with:

● The data used.

● What themes and issues future studies analyse.

● What arguments and literature they cite to support their position.

● Alternative interpretations of the research data they present.

In addition, we need to recognise the growing fragmentation of leisure and how greater cultural diversity is occurring, so that microtrends and new research evidence may help to explain wider changes that may occur, emerging as future drivers.

Ravenscroft and Gilchrist (2009) provide an interesting attempt to theorise a development they observed from research on creative workers, expanding our focus from Chapter 9. They argue that we are seeing the rise of a *working society of leisure*, blending the arguments on work and leisure merging for one specific group of workers. The study suggests that the conventional division of work as production and leisure as consumption may not be appropriate for creative workers. Their work takes on a creative quality and it fits with their lifestyle choices to combine work and leisure. Creative workers are not motivated by income earning potential, but by quality of life drivers. So we get an inversion of Veblen's leisure class hypothesis: the creative workers are time rich but income poor. Therefore, with these broad principles and arguments in mind, what does this mean for the study of the future of leisure?

How to approach the future of leisure

To return briefly to the starting point of this chapter, we are not going to revisit and provide a synthesis of the main arguments in the book. Instead, our analysis of the future of leisure is to present a simplified model of what the book has highlighted on the key interactions and relationships on how leisure operates (Figure 12.5), its functions and the main themes we need to think about when

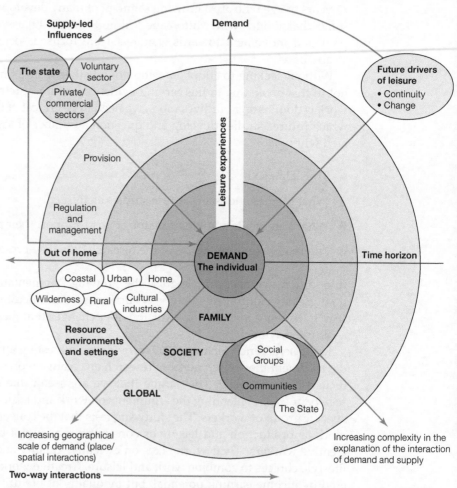

Figure 12.5 Modelling the future of leisure – key interactions and relationships

looking at leisure futures. To summarise the main arguments which the model puts forward, it suggest that the future will need to recognise:

- The scale and different levels at which we need to recognise the demand for leisure.

- The different organisations and bodies providing the supply of leisure.

- The different resource settings where leisure might occur (especially the in-home/out-of-home split).

- The future drivers which might impact upon these different elements, such as globalisation and societal change, the environment, technology and the political context in various time horizons.

Having already examined some of the drivers which different analyses of leisure highlight, we now focus on three contrasting views of the future for leisure to illustrate some of the specific themes that analysts envisage will change leisure in the future.

Three contrasting views of the future of leisure

As discussed earlier, there are no definitive answers when looking at the future of leisure, and to present a range of opinions and outlooks we consider three approaches that have been developed in recent years, focused on North America, to illustrate what trends and drivers are important. The studies have wider applications beyond North America, which is why they are discussed here. The first view, by Godbey, is based on a long period spent studying leisure and future trends, which are discussed in seminal works such as Godbey (1997). Godbey *et al.*'s (2001) study for the US National Park service was interesting as an introduction to the future of leisure given the analysis of one key concept: *time deepening*. Time deepening is described as a process affecting leisure and individuals and families where some of the following characteristics can be discerned:

- A general speeding up of the pace at which people undertake leisure activities, which has some degree of synergy with the earlier discussion of hyper-change by Cornish (2004).

- People seek to save time on their leisure pursuits, by selecting shorter time slots or using time-saving devices to reduce the time commitment needed for a specific activity.

- People multi-task when undertaking their leisure activities, such as watching television and combining it with other tasks.

- The deliberate development of over-scheduling where leisure activities are scheduled too tightly, especially with children as discussed earlier. Here the parallel concepts of over-parenting and over-structuring children's time mean that leisure time is pre-planned and tightly compressed into multiple activities as part of over-parenting.

As Godbey *et al.* (2001) suggest, the outcome is ironic: leisure is supposed to contribute to relaxation and enjoyment. But time deepening among some sections of society leads to growing elements of anxiety and stress in one's leisure time rather than relaxation. This is a sad indictment on the postmodern society where children's leisure and the home have adopted highly consumer-focused attributes that are diminishing the quality of the experience rather than enhancing it. It is no wonder that in the field of tourism, for example, advocates of the slow movement are pointing to the need to slow down and enjoy leisure time more fully.

A further perspective of how Godbey views the future of leisure is evident in Table 12.3, developed from a very useful and perceptive review of the major trends which are influencing, and will continue to influence, the future of leisure (Godbey 2004). One element which comes across very clearly in Godbey's (2004) assessment is the importance of demographic factors, which Foot (2001) in *Boom, Bust and Echo* suggested accounted for two-thirds of all that happens in future changes in society. Godbey *et al.* (2001) suggest that outdoor recreation in the USA will have a slower growth between 1990 and 2050 than the rate of population growth, with an increasingly diverse population and new tastes for leisure. Other major drivers will be climate change and the implications for recreation behaviour, especially holidays, where the main summer season may be supplanted where adverse climatic factors force rescheduling of such activity to the fall (autumn) and spring to avoid hot summer weather.

The second view, by Popcorn and Marigold (1997), *Clicking: 17 Trends that Drive Your Business and Life*, is a more populist view of the future of society and business. They introduce a very interesting concept in relation to leisure – *cocooning*. This term refers to the desire to stay at home and consume leisure time, with the growth in technology and enhancements of home environments as private space. It is evident from other studies of the home that it has become a more complex environment for leisure, where family leisure needs are constantly evaluated and negotiated so that divergent aspirations are met. An interesting set of ironies exist: we know that the time spent cooking meals in the home has been in decline for many years, yet the investment in makeovers for houses and their kitchens reflects a rise of cooking for pleasure. This has been a media-stimulated trend, with celebrity and professional cooking impacting upon social entertaining as high-quality cooking grows in popularity (even if daily food and meals are from the freezer or out of a packet as a prepared meal, expanding upon the original American concept of the television dinner!). The authors also highlighted a growth in what they described as *pleasure revenge*, the pursuit of instant leisure gratification as a result of society not meeting their wider needs. The consequence of this is a greater focus on the leisure

Table 12.3 Trends affecting the future of leisure

- Explosive world population growth, expected to reach in excess of 8 billion by 2025, of which most growth will occur in developing nations.
- Increasing urbanisation and population density, with over half the world's population now living in urban areas and expected to reach 60% by 2030.
- Revolutions in the conventional life-cycle concept, with the process of 'defamilisation' and growth in one-person households, with a decline in marriage and increase in divorce/separation in many developed countries challenging existing concepts such as the family life cycle.
- Ageing of the world population, with 25% of the US and 31% of Europe's population aged 60 years or more by 2025.
- Increasing levels of education leading to greater expectations and complexity in the leisure experiences sought.
- Changes in the roles of men and women, with greater education and economic power attached to women, enhancing their established role as family leisure decision-makers.
- Revolution in work, with more flexibility in the organisation, scheduling and timing/location of work as new work-forms emerge such as hot-desking, homeworking, working on the move (the mobile worker) and a decline in the weekday/weekend distinction of work and leisure. The rise of the 24/7 economy has also led to the shattering and fragmentation of the work–leisure divide.
- The growth and expansion of the experience economy where the entertaining of people occurs through staged, memorable, personalised and sense-stimulating experiences (i.e. those experiences which impact on our sight, hearing, taste, touch, smell and emotions).
- Continued globalisation processes where commercial leisure providers further customise, segment and target consumer leisure purchasing habits.
- A growing diversity of cultures and religions which shape popular culture and leisure, as the dominance of English declines.
- Urbanisation and increased complexity in the form and shape of towns and cities as well as their internal social composition. Continued segregation according to race, income and ethnicity, with a dependence upon the car and continued congestion.
- Environmental change at an unprecedented rate, compounded by the greatest challenges facing humankind: climate change and global warming alongside rapid deterioration in the quality, biodiversity and quantity of the natural environment. These processes of change will be amongst the greatest determinants of leisure behaviour in the future, causing people to change their leisure habits as climate change accentuates the extreme weather patterns that will interfere with recreation and tourist activities.

Source: Adapted from Godbey (2004). Copyright © Taylor and Francis. Permission conveyed through the Copyright Clearance Center

experience and its ability to deliver satisfaction in relation to the immediacy of gratification.

The last view was proffered by Adams (1999) and focused on Canadian society in a provocatively titled book – *Sex in the Snow*. This book points to the growing diversity of society, especially the shift away from traditional values, as the population has less interest in social institutions (e.g. the church) and greater interaction with the rise of the 24-hour society. Interestingly, Penn (2007) questions the growth of a secular society in the USA where the demise of religion is not as widespread as in many other countries. He points to the rise of the mega churches as meeting a new social need for the church as a wider social organisation, moulding leisure time once more for those associated with this microtrend. However, Adams (1999) would acknowledge that the population are seeking a wider spiritual fulfilment but this may not necessarily arise from religion, with the greater focus on the needs of the individual. This means that more recreation and leisure spaces may need to be accessible 24 hours a day, as leisure time is less structured, less planned and sees a greater involvement of women in leisure pursuits, often participating in many activities which were dominated by males. But how should we evaluate the reliability of such research views on leisure futures?

The reliability of leisure futures research and predictions

What these three interesting but different views of the future of leisure inevitably raise are questions about how certain we can be about predictions that we wish to make. One of the principal challenges that anyone faces when we look at the future for leisure is in trying to anticipate what sort of new leisure practices may develop, how they will spread and then how they will affect people's use of leisure time, particularly when focusing on specific recreation activities (Chen et al. 2003). But we also have to recognise what Touve and Tepper (2007) suggest, that leisure is embedded in our everyday routines, including work and our social obligations. In other words, while we argued in Chapter 1 for different approaches to understanding leisure, in reality leisure is:

● Not an isolated element of our lives: it is intertwined, interconnected and central to our lives.

● Part of the current trends affecting society, the economy and wider processes impacting upon leisure.

Even so, when forecasts of changes in leisure have been made, have they been reliable and credible? This is a very difficult task to undertake, mainly because the data used to make forecasts or to examine the future are rarely replicated in longitudinal studies. One exception to this is Mitton and Wilmott (2005), who examined initial forecasts made in 1971 for leisure in the UK and then re-evaluated the same data again in 2001. Their original 1971 forecasts of expected changes in leisure behaviour were remarkably accurate, although they did underestimate the impact of the elderly and ageing on trends as well as overestimating the effects of youth on leisure, as family size declined. Of the 48 leisure activities for which the authors made predictions, 34 achieved their expected increases focused on the four areas of participation (i.e. sport as a participant, sport participation as a spectator, home-based leisure and out-of-home activities).

They also observed the deepening of leisure time as well as the over-scheduling of children. The study was a good example of following societal trends and extrapolating ahead, observing a degree of continuity and change in many areas of leisure behaviour. For this reason, we now turn to a selected range of themes we see at work in terms of leisure and the impact of non-leisure processes of change and how they may reshape certain aspects of leisure.

Current and future changes in leisure

Cultural capital and the leisure travel bug

No discussion of leisure and the future can overlook the significance of tourism, especially international tourism which is a major use of leisure time in a concentrated block of time called the *holiday*. The growth of international tourism since 1950 has been one of the most significant changes that have been associated with the democratisation of leisure, especially in many Western nations as mass holiday travel has become a reality for many sections of society. As Figure 12.6 shows, this growth has been fed by an almost insatiable appetite for overseas travel (as well as domestic tourism which is about three to four times as important in volume terms in many countries). This has been facilitated by a gradual decline in the cost of air travel, fed in part by relatively cheap oil prices and innovations in the holiday industry, especially transport such as the charter aircraft and package holiday as well as the more recent innovation – the low-cost airline. As the case study of hypercompetition illustrates, competition in the tourism sector has been to consumers' benefit, further fuelling the growth in international travel. The UN-World Tourism Organisation forecast that [by 2020] the number of international tourists travelling will have reached 1.6 billion, rising from 924 million arrivals in 2008. These forecasts illustrate the confidence

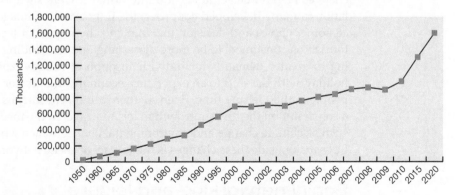

Figure 12.6   Growth of world tourism 1950 to 2020

The data for this figure is derived from the UN-WTO data and the figures for 2009 are based on an estimated drop in the 2008 arrivals of around 3%. The forecasts for 2020 are based on the UN-WTO's own forecasts which pre-date the global recession.

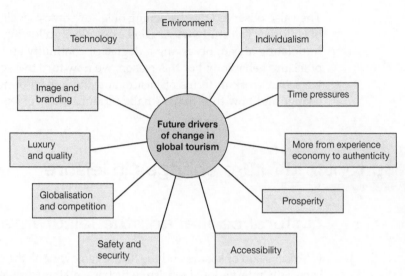

Figure 12.7   Future drivers of change in global tourism
Source: Adapted from Page (2009a)

and expectation that past trends in tourist travel will continue, as new international travel markets grow, especially as China and Asia (i.e. India) develop.

As Figure 12.7 shows, a recent scenario planning exercise undertaken at VisitScotland, the National Tourism Organisation responsible for tourism in Scotland, highlighted the range of drivers and changes which may affect global tourism in the next 5 to 10 years. As Figure 12.7 suggests, holidays are viewed as important elements of household budgets now and will be in the future, as new groups of travellers from Asia enter the tourism system. Travel and the provision of air transport have made most parts of the world accessible to tourists and so gradual drops in the cost of travel per km continue to make travel a necessity rather than a luxury. The international tourism industry also epitomises globalisation, with its impact on different countries and societies. These changes have to be set alongside individual drivers such as an ageing population in many developed countries, the importance of image and branding in customer choice and decision making, and the impact of technology allowing tourists as consumers to be more discerning and demanding. This is also leading to greater demands for individualisation of leisure experiences when on holiday, with the shift to an experience economy and greater time pressures on people in their leisure time. Even so, there are specific factors which may act as a constraint on the further growth in leisure travel in the medium to long term, such as climate change and environmental change which we will discuss later. But set alongside these changes is the impact of social networking.

Social networking and leisure

While it is widely accepted that the Internet has revolutionised how we use and spend our leisure time, new developments, such as the development of

Web 2.0 technology since 2004, have expanded the potential of the net further. Web 2.0 is a term used to describe how the second generation of web-based communities and hosted sites has evolved a stage further to allow interaction, sharing and collaboration among users. This interaction and networking have led to the creation of web-based content. For example, web technologies associated with Web 2.0 have led to the use of Weblogs (commonly called blogs), where entries are displayed in reverse chronological order and where content can be added, including commentary, news, images and links to other blogs, web pages and other forms of media such as music-based blogs (mp3 blogs) and audio-based 'podcasts'. Other variants such as Twitter (140-character text-based blogs called tweets) have become one of the faster-growing forms of social networking. These shorter communications have expanded the ability of individuals and organisations to communicate in a virtual and mobile manner. As Page and Connell (2009) show, since 2004, blogs have become relatively mainstream on the internet and they can be broadcast not only to PCs, but also to other mobile devices such as PDAs and mobile phones (moblogs).

One of the developments related to leisure using Web 2.0 technology is the rise of consumer-to-consumer (c2c) marketing where consumers can post comments and views on products and experiences. A notable development has been the rise of Wikis on collaborative websites. Web 2.0 has allowed consumers to post comments and feedback on impartial websites as virtual communities with common interests emerge. This has also allowed consumers with anxieties or fears to check out websites for feedback to assuage their fears or anxieties. In fact, some analysts have suggested that the majority of Internet content in the future will be created by individuals, rather than being generated by companies and organisations. Developments such as MySpace.com and Facebook allows the user to connect with school and other friends and is based on content which is 'click and trust', impacting upon consumer spending. Yet Web 2.0 is still developing and its long-term potential to revolutionise leisure a stage further may well lead to significant shifts in how businesses and organisations communicate with consumers to help them plan and structure their leisure time. There are also wider trends to consider given the growing urbanisation of the world's population observed by Godbey (2004), with implications for future leisure.

Leisure and the city

When we look at the city and the future of leisure we need to think of two distinct strands of analysis:

- The impact of urban demand (especially its effect on non-urban areas); and

- The future changes and shape of urban areas and how this will shape future leisure.

Forty years ago, Bracey (1970) observed the impact of the growing urbanisation of leisure in the countryside, discussed in Chapter 11, where 'in some respects, in some places, at some times, the town invasion of countryside seems total' (Bracey 1970: 244). What Bracey highlighted is the dominant influence of urbanisation outside the city limits. Bracey's analysis of the management challenges which rural areas needed to embrace to manage urban leisure demand were related to the pressure of a fully motorised society, and the necessity of developing areas on the urban fringe (e.g. country parks) and within cities to absorb demand destined for rural areas, to reduce some of the impacts of urban leisure demand. Some 40 years later these pressures have not waned, reflected in the continued pressure which urban areas place on nearby or adjacent (i.e. coterminous) non-urban land for leisure and recreation. These issues will only intensify with the forecast expansion of the world's urban population. Consequently, Adams' (2003) provocative and insightful book *Future Nature* recognised that in the UK, the leisure industries were worth over £70 billion a year. But as Adams argued, if the population wanted to protect and conserve nature, they would have to set aside land for this purpose and pay for it. Bracey (1970) was also adamant in arguing that the public will need to pay for pleasure and the use of resources such as the countryside via taxes, higher prices on agricultural products, charges for admission and associated charges for services to meet visitor needs such as toilets.

The city and its future development was the subject of a substantial analysis by Burdett and Subjic (2008) in *The Endless City*, reviewing different themes and current issues and future challenges. To take just four of the cities they analysed, they highlight the variations in leisure provision amid constant urbanising changes affecting the built form of the cities:

- *London* has a population of around 7.5 million people and generates 18% of the UK's GDP. It has 500,000 closed circuit television cameras (CCTV) and around 38% of the city's built environment is classified as open space.

- *Mexico City* has seen its urban population grow from 3.1 million in 1950 to over 19 million today and only 7.5% of the land area is available for recreational use.

- *Berlin* has 3.4 million residents, with 50% of the population living in one-person households, and 35.6% of the land area is designated as green open space. It has experienced many of the problems of London and Mexico City, with social polarisation of the population based on wealth, as social segregation creates huge variations inside the urban area.

- *Johannesburg* has 3.2 million residents and issues of safety and security have led to the development of over 600 gated communities (see Atkinson and Blandy 2006 for an international review of gated communities) with 1100 check points to create managed and private areas for those residents able to afford to live in these areas. Health problems dominate the public realm, with over 34% of the 25–29-year-old population infected with HIV and violent crime a major policy issue, as private security businesses have proliferated.

These four contrasting examples illustrate how difficult it is to make any wide-ranging forecasts of how leisure will change in cities at a global scale. The result is that we need to understand many of the wider trends we have discussed earlier in the chapter and how these apply at country and city level. For example, Neuwirth's (2006) *Shadow Cities: A Billion Squatters, A New Urban World* highlighted that a billion of the world's population were living in squatter settlements. This equates to almost a sixth of the world's population being invisible in most analyses of leisure. So drawing up trends that apply to the sections of the world's population able to embrace the consumerist ideals overlooks those people struggling to live on $1 a day. For people in squatter settlements who are socially and economically isolated from society, thinking about leisure is an anathema when every day is a struggle simply to stay alive and feed their family. These trends in homelessness and powerlessness for these sections of the world population are unlikely to diminish: if anything, they will intensify with the growing urbanisation of the world population and the shift from countryside to city in developing countries. Their lives are intricately connected to the informal economies and society of these cities (e.g. Earl 2004), where many developing country cities have to be viewed as organic and evolving forms where any growth in leisure time that may arise from improved living standards will be part of these unplanned areas of expanding cities. One response, as the case of Johannesburg illustrates, is the rise of private space for living and leisure in cities, seeking spatial separation from the poor and dispossessed.

Fear and privatisation of space: Is it the answer for future leisure provision?

Bauman (1998) has described the relationship between urbanism and fear as the *endemic unsafety* of our times. One direct consequence of this is the threat to public space for leisure and recreation, both perceived and real, through the measures and actions of public and private bodies seeking to address this state of unsafety. An example is the creation of private spaces for leisure, such as the development of shopping malls (or the extreme case of gated communities) with the power to exclude people deemed undesirable or displaying undesirable traits. This has been described in Minton's (2006) report, *Privatisation of Public Space,* as the UK sleepwalking into a privatisation of the public realm. One explanation is that this removes public sector responsibility for managing public places, which is part of a global trend (see Banerjee 2001) and a long-term threat to public spaces. The public's perceived acceptance of such moves reflects an overreaction to public fear where

> What is often called urban violence, in reality frequently refers to dis-order, patterns of anti-social behaviour or incivilities (throwing rubbish out of the window, urinating in lifts, spitting on the street, writing graffiti on the walls, making noise during the night . . .). These patterns of behaviour, which are not necessarily illegal . . . are often associated with a youth culture insensitive to order. *(Body-Gerot 2008: 354)*

One consequence in the UK of this privatisation of public space is that there are now over 30,000 CCTVs in operation, making it one of the most surveilled societies in the world as discussed earlier in the book, with some commentators suggesting that we will be photographed up to 300 times a day when going about our normal business. The result is that the creation of private and commercialised leisure spaces which are highly surveilled and controlled is arguably impacting on social cohesion and may contribute to a drop in social citizenship, according to Body-Gerot (2008).

Zukin (1995) has argued that such spaces are the primary sites of public culture and by regulating or removing them from the public realm you remove an important opportunity for leisure. One of the last bastions of the public realm in cities is green open space, especially parks and gardens. Body-Gerot (2008) describes these spaces as *social condensers* in cities, because they can be places of tolerance and civic engagement. This means that social differences are removed and people interact and use the spaces on an equal footing. For example, Body-Gerot (2008) refers to the successful example of Chapeltapec Park in Mexico, part-funded by public subscriptions where a million residents each donated a peso, and it receives 15 million visits a year. Security guards replace CCTV as an unobtrusive and invisible element of the park management. So what this shows is that there are alternatives to CCTV cameras and the marching trend towards the privatisation of public space. The privatisation of space inevitably accentuates social polarisation and divisions in society, although there are no clear signs that this is going to diminish with the increased role of the private sector and commercial leisure provision. For cities this will make leisure experiences more segmented and targeted at certain groups and types of consumer who are able to devote disposable income to this form of consumption. The major challenge for future leisure is that 'There is another broader problem that will plague us all: holding on to privacy and the freedom to proceed without continued surveillance' (Holland 2003: 180). However, two major concerns which will have a global impact on the future of leisure are climate change and the future of oil.

Climate change

Of the different global environmental problems facing the planet, climate change is the number one issue which politicians and policy makers seize upon as likely to constrain the future development of leisure, being intricately linked with sustainability and implying a need for adaptation of human activity and behaviour (Pelling 2009). One of the most visible dimensions which concerns with climate change have focused on is the contribution of air travel to CO_2 emissions and the impact on global warming (Bows *et al.* 2008). What is particularly alarming in this context is the earlier forecast we highlighted from the UN-World Tourism Organisation for future growth in international tourism of around 73% growth in international tourist arrivals 2008–2020. This is because much of this growth will be reliant upon air travel. Given the realisation that all human activity has a carbon footprint and energy cost which contribute to global environmental change, this must be a cause for concern. One response, which is set to continue among many organisations supplying leisure products and experiences, is the quantification of the energy impact of leisure activities, so that people can offset their carbon impact if they wish. A newer development is that some organisations are promoting carbon-neutral leisure activities where the offset has already been addressed, or where alternative modes of mobility (e.g. walking and cycling) are encouraged as alternatives to motorised transport for leisure use. This also begs a much wider issue – how will our future leisure habits be shaped when the oil runs out?

The future of oil and leisure

As Page (2009b) has shown, oil is the basis of what meets many of the energy needs of our society and its exploitation and use have been viewed as a relatively cheap and accessible resource up until recent years. It is only the recent spikes in oil prices that have drawn the attention of governments to the future of a society without oil. This poses immediate problems for leisure if all of the main forms of transport are dependent upon oil as the basis for energy. Some commentators suggest that we have passed the point of peak oil, the term which describes the point at which the peak of oil production has been reached and supplies then begin to dwindle. So while the previous growth in leisure (and especially tourist trips) was based on the assumption of relatively cheap travel, this is certainly not assured for the future. Energy prices seem set to stay relatively high for many countries which are consumers of oil and alternative sources such as gas, but the real challenge for the medium term (i.e. 2030 to 2050) is in developing new energy sources to power transport that will be used for daily and leisure purposes, and which are relatively inexpensive. If the alternative energy sources are expensive, then leisure behaviour will certainly have to change to accommodate these new realities.

Summary

The future is an uncertain place. We have no way of easily forecasting what will happen, how it will affect us and what future shape leisure will take in the medium to long term. Some trends are developing right now that will radically shape our perception of what is possible and feasible in the future. Once the first Virgin Galactic space trips begin, we will see a new dimension in leisure travel emerge that opens up a new domain of leisure. But these new trends will only affect the sections of the population wealthy enough or eager to take a space trip to experience minutes of weightlessness. The reality of many people's future leisure is that it will be a combination of what they do now and new opportunities that present themselves. The most obvious example of a technology that has revolutionised leisure is the internet, democratising leisure further, as a further innovation following the television and then the car in developed countries. This revolution has certainly contributed to a greater interest in home-centred leisure, which is where the technology has traditionally been based. But other developments such as WiFi and mobile technology, despite concerns over the potential health impact of repeated exposure to such technology, may further expand the impact of technology in shaping future leisure.

There are a large number of trends occurring at a macro and micro scale which will shape and determine the future drivers that impact upon leisure for individuals and groups. An interesting insight is offered by O'Keefe's (2006) *The Average American*, which argues that while trends look at averages, few people actually conform to the average or norm, which is an interesting counter-weight to the value of statistical analysis. The individualisation of leisure is set to continue as many of the trends illustrate, but there will come a point in the future where past trends may re-emerge and potentially reorient the way certain uses of leisure time are spent. Despite the complexity of trying to understand the future, this does not mean we should not look ahead to try to understand what is happening to leisure now and where we think it is heading. By understanding the tools and techniques used to try to look ahead, we see that leisure is unlikely to remain unchanged. However, understanding uncertainty and what future role the state will play in leisure, alongside the commercial and voluntary sector and the freedom of the individual to engage in all forms of leisure, remain important questions to ponder. Some commentators suggest that the balance of the state–commercial–voluntary sector has shifted away from the era of public leisure as new policy objectives now dominate and will continue to dominate policy issues in different countries. Leisure is not a high-priority issue unless it is linked with other priorities such as healthy living to address problems such as obesity or deviant behavior. This is likely to continue.

Whatever the future brings, we know that the contents of this book will help you to start to understand: *what leisure is, why it assumes such an important role in our everyday lives* and *how we need to plan and manage it for the wider public good.* Leisure may be under pressure from different directions (e.g. the state, the privatisation of space for leisure, the pressure of work) but it is still an individual (as well as group) phenomenon that has meaning for the individual and other groups. Consequently, it will continue to assume a special place in many people's lives but we also need to recognise that it may only ever be an aspiration for the billion people living in squatter settlements, on the margins of society in the informal world that is almost unknown in developed countries (aside from the growing problem of homelessness in some sections of cities in developed countries). Homelessness is a persistent problem in our postmodern society, influenced by increasing social divisions and a gap between the haves and have-nots, and it is worrying to note that some local authorities have responded in public spaces by introducing leisure-related furniture to stop the homeless from impacting upon middle-class sensibilities by preventing stereo-typed images of the homeless sleeping on park benches. These spaces are also being increasingly surveilled and controlled, so the Victorian codes of conduct and rules introduced for public leisure are returning, where perceived forms of antisocial behaviour are prohibited.

Leisure may be about fun and enjoyment, but to enjoy it our basic needs (i.e. shelter, food, water and employment) have to be met before it can be anything other than a luxury good for those excluded from society. The way governments view leisure and its link to social exclusion is a major step forward in how leisure is acknowledged in many developed countries, though this is only for those within the confines of the norms of society who fit the political agenda of the day. Leisure needs to be viewed as a basic necessity for achieving a fulfilling life. Let us hope that the future will continue to develop the concept of leisure as vital to the well-being of society, so that its enjoyment can be seen as a sign of a civilised society.

Discussion questions

1. Why do we need to examine the future for leisure?

2. What different tools and techniques exist for the analysis of leisure futures?

3. What are the likely changes which will affect the following different groups to 2020: children's leisure, youth leisure and the over-50 age group?

4. Will the city be the future location of all forms of commercial leisure in the year 2050?

References

Adams, M. (1999) *Sex in the Snow,* Penguin: Toronto.

Adams, W. (2003) *Future Nature: A Vision for Conservation,* Earthscan: London.

Aguiar, M. and Hurst, E. (2007) 'Measuring trends in leisure: the allocation of time over five decades', *The Quarterly Journal of Economics* 122 (3): 969–1006.

Akhter, S. (2003) 'Strategic planning, hypercompetition, and knowledge management', *Business Horizons* 36 (1): 19–24.

Atkinson, R. and Blandy, S. (eds) (2006) *Gated Communities: International Perspectives,* Routledge: London.

Banerjee, T. (2001) 'The future of public space: Beyond invented streets and reinvented places', *Journal of the American Planning Association* 67: 9–16.

Bauman, Z. (1998) *Globalisation: The Human Consequences,* Polity Press: Cambridge.

Beach, B. (1989) *Integrating Work and Family Life,* Suny Press: New York.

Body-Gernot, S. (2008) 'Confronting fear', in R. Burdett and D. Sujdic (eds) *The Endless City,* Phaidon: London, pp. 352–63.

Bows, A., Anderson, K. and Upham, P. (2008) *Aviation and Climate Change: Lessons for European Policy,* Routledge: London.

Bracey, H. (1970) *People in the Countryside,* Routledge and Kegan Paul: London.

Bradfield, R., Wright, G., Burt, G., Cairns, G. and van der Heijden, K. (2005) The origins and evolution of scenario techniques in long range business planning, *Futures* 37: 795–812.

Brown, M. (2005) *Better Futures. Inner Eastern Sydney Pre-Teens Research Report,* Waverley Council: Sydney.

Burdett, R. and Sujdic, D. (eds) (2008) *The Endless City,* Phaidon: London.

Chen, R., Bloomfield, P. and Fu, J. (2003) 'An evaluation of alternative forecasting methods to recreation visitation', *Journal of Leisure Research* 35 (4): 441–54.

Cooper, R. and Layard, R. (eds) (2002) 'Introduction', in R. Cooper and R. Layard (eds) *What the Future Holds: Insights from Social Sciences,* MIT Press: Cambridge, MA, pp. 1–16.

Cornish, E. (2004) *Futuring: The Exploration of the Future,* World Future Society: Bethesda, MD.

D'Aveni, R. (1998) 'Hypercompetition closes in', *Financial Times,* 4 February (Global Business Series: Part 2, 12–13).

Dart, J. (2006) 'Home-based work and leisure: Settee or work-station?', *Leisure Studies* 25 (3): 313–28.

Duinker, P. and Greig, L. (2007) 'Scenario analysis in environmental impact assessment: improving explorations of the future', *Environmental Impact Assessment Review* 27 (3): 206–219.

Earl, C. (2004) 'Leisure and social mobility in Ho Chi Minh city', in P. Taylor (ed.) *Social Inequality and the Challenge to Reform,* Institute for South East Asian Studies: Singapore.

Foot, D. (2001) *Boom, Bust and Echo,* Stodart: Toronto.

Friedman, B. (2002) 'The world of work in the new millennium', in R. Cooper and R. Layard (eds) *What the Future Holds: Insights from Social Sciences,* MIT Press: Cambridge, MA, pp. 157–78.

Godbey, G., DeJong, G., Sasidhavan, V. and Yarnal, C. (2001) *N E USA in the Next Two Decades: Implications for the North Region of the National Park Service,* National Park Service: Washington DC.

Godbey, G. (1997) *Leisure and Leisure Services in the 21st Century,* Venture Publishing: State College, PA.

Godbey, G. (2004) 'Introduction: after the anthill was stomped', in K. Weiermair and C. Mathies (eds) *The Tourism and Leisure Industries: Shaping the Future,* The Haworth Hospitality Press: New York, pp. 1–19.

Gordon, T., Glenn, J. and Jakill, A. (2005) 'Frontiers of futures research', *Technological Forecasting and Social Change* 72 (9): 1064–9.

Granter, E. (2008) 'A dream of ease: situating the future of work and leisure', *Futures* 40 (9): 803–11.

Helmar, O. (1983) *Looking Forward: A Guide to Futures Research,* Sage: London.

Holland, J. (2003) 'What is to come and how to predict it', in J. Brockman (ed.) *The Next Fifty Years: Science in the First Half of the 21st Century,* Phoenix: London, pp. 170–82.

Jenkins, J. (2009) 'Non-resident fathers: Leisure with their children', *Leisure Sciences* 31 (3): 255–71.

Jensen, R. (1999) *The Dream Society. How the Coming Shift from Information to Imagination will Transform Your Lives*, McGraw Hill: New York.

Koztab, H., Grant, D., Teller, C. and Halldorsson, A. (2009) 'Supply chain management and hypercompetition', *Logistics Research* 1 (1): 5–13.

Lahiri, S., Pérez-Nordtvedt, L. and Renn, R. (2008) 'Will the new competitive landscape cause your firm's decline? It depends on your mindset', *Business Horizons* 51 (4): 311–20.

Levine, M. (2006) *The Price of Privilege*, HarperCollins: New York.

Manzenreiter, W. and Horne, J. (2006) 'Leisure and consumer culture in Japan', *Leisure Studies* 25 (4): 411–15.

Martin, M. (2005) 'Weather, climate and tourism', *Annals of Tourism Research* 32 (3): 571–91.

Minton, A. (2006) *Privatisation of Public Space*, RICS: London.

Mitton, R. and Wilmott, M. (2005) 'A social forecast revisited', *Futures* 37 (1): 39–50.

Neuwirth, R. (2006) *Shadow Cities: A Billion Squatters, A New Urban World*, Routledge: London.

Norton, C. (2000) 'Forecasts of the leisure society fail to materialise', *The Independent* Monday 27 March.

O'Keefe, K. (2006) *The Average American. The Extraordinary Search for the Nation's Most Ordinary Citizen*, PublicAffairs Publishing: New York.

OECD (2009) *Society at a Glance*, OECD: Paris.

Page, S. J. (2009a) *Tourism Management: Managing for Change*, 3rd edn, Elsevier: Oxford.

Page, S. J. (2009b) *Transport and Tourism: Global Perspectives*, Pearson: Harlow.

Page, S. J. and Connell, J. (2009) *Tourism: A Modern Synthesis*, 3rd edn, Cengage Learning: London.

Page, S. J., Yeoman, I., Greenwood, C. and Connell, J. (2010) 'Scenario planning as a tool to understand uncertainty in tourism: the example of transport and tourism in Scotland in 2025', *Current Issues in Tourism*, in press.

Page, S. J., Yeoman, I., Munro, C., Connell, J. and Walker, L. (2006) 'A case study of best practice – VisitScotland's prepared response to an influenza pandemic', *Tourism Management* 27 (3): 361–93.

Pelling, M. (2009) *Adaptation to Climate Change: A Progressive Vision of Human Society*, Routledge: London.

Penn, M. (2007) *Microtrends: The Small Forces Behind Big Changes*, Allen Lane: London.

Pierson, J. (2009) *Tackling Social Exclusion*, 2nd edn, Routledge: London.

Popcorn, F. and Marigold, L. (1997) *Clicking: 17 Trends that Drive Your Business and Life*, HarperCollins: New York.

Ramey, V. and Frances, N. (2004) *A Century of Work and Leisure*, www.econ.ucsd.edu.

Ravenscroft, N. and Gilchrist, P. (2009) 'The emergent working society of leisure', *Journal of Leisure Research* 41 (1): 23–59.

Roberts, K. (1999) *Leisure in Contemporary Society*, CABI: Wallingford.

Schwartz, P. (2002) 'The river and the billiard ball: history, innovation and the future', in R. Cooper and R. Layard (eds) *What the Future Holds: Insights from Social Sciences*, MIT Press: Cambridge, MA, pp. 17–27.

Sturcke, J. (2009) 'Storms ahead: Bournemouth anger over Met Office's bank holiday forecast', *Guardian* 28 May, www.guardian.co.uk

Tourism Intelligence Scotland (2007) *Scottish Tourism in the Future*, Tourism Intelligence Scotland: Edinburgh.

Touve, D. and Tepper, S. (2007) *Leisure in America: Searching for Forest amongst the Trees*, Paul Getty Trust: Los Angeles.

UK Cabinet Office Performance and Innovation Unit (2001) *A Futurists Toolbox: Methodologies on Futures Work. Strategic Futures Team*, UK Cabinet Office Performance and Innovation Unit: London.

UK Office for Science and Technology (2006) *Intelligent Transport Futures Project*, UK Office for Science and Technology: London.

Veal, A. (1987) *Leisure and the Future*, Allen and Unwin: London.

Zukin, S. (1995) *The Culture of Cities*, Blackwell: Oxford.

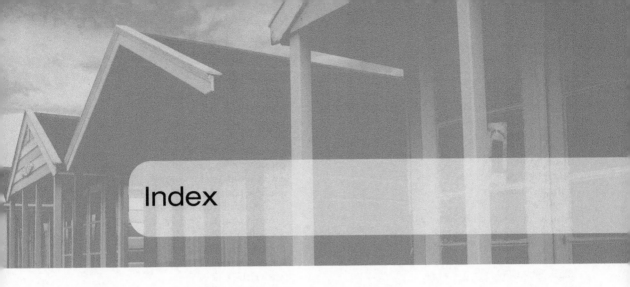

Index